Combating Cyberbullying With Generative AI

Kishor Kumar Reddy C.
Stanley College of Engineering and Technology for Women, India

Meetu Malhotra
Harrisburg University of Science and Technology, USA

Mariya Ouaissa
Cadi Ayyad University, Morocco

Marlia Mohd Hanafiah
Universiti Kebangsaan Malaysia, Malaysia

Mohammed Shuaib
Jazan University, Saudi Arabia

IGI Global
Scientific Publishing
Publishing Tomorrow's Research Today

Vice President of Editorial Melissa Wagner
Managing Editor of Acquisitions Mikaela Felty
Managing Editor of Book Development Jocelynn Hessler
Production Manager Mike Brehm
Cover Design Phillip Shickler

Published in the United States of America by
IGI Global Scientific Publishing
701 East Chocolate Avenue
Hershey, PA, 17033, USA
Tel: 717-533-8845
Fax: 717-533-8661
Website: https://www.igi-global.com E-mail: cust@igi-global.com

Library of Congress Cataloging-in-Publication Data

Names: Reddy, C. Kishor Kumar, editor. | Malhotra, Meetu, 1982- editor. | Ouaissa, Mariya, editor. | Marlia Mohd. Hanafiah, editor.
Title: Combating cyberbullying with generative AI / edited by Kishor Kumar Reddy C, Meetu Malhotra, Mariya Ouaissa, Marlia Mohd Hanafiah, Mohammed Shuaib.
Description: Hershey, PA : IGI Global Scientific Publishing, [2025] | Includes bibliographical references and index. | Summary: "This book examines how generative AI might be used to combat the growing issue of cyberbullying. The goal of the book is to give researchers, decision-makers, and tech developers practical learning about how AI can detect, block, and lessen unsafe online activity"-- Provided by publisher.
Identifiers: LCCN 2024056672 (print) | LCCN 2024056673 (ebook) | ISBN 9798337305431 (hardcover) | ISBN 9798337305448 (paperback) | ISBN 9798337305455 (ebook)
Subjects: LCSH: Cyberbullying--Prevention. | Cyberbullying--Technological innovations. | Artificial intelligence.
Classification: LCC HV6773.15.C92 C65 2025 (print) | LCC HV6773.15.C92 (ebook) | DDC 302.34/3--dc23/eng/20250122
LC record available at https://lccn.loc.gov/2024056672
LC ebook record available at https://lccn.loc.gov/2024056673

British Cataloguing in Publication Data
A Cataloguing in Publication record for this book is available from the British Library.

Table of Contents

Detailed Table of Contents

The digital age has introduced new dimensions to bullying through the rise of cyberbullying, which involves the use of technology to harass, threaten, or humiliate individuals. Characterized by anonymity, pervasive reach, and viral potential, cyberbullying extends across social media platforms, online forums, and messaging services, significantly impacting victims' psychological well-being. The anonymity provided by digital spaces often emboldens aggressors, leading to sustained harassment without physical confrontation. Emerging patterns, including trolling and doxxing, present complex challenges for detection, prevention, and legal regulation. This overview explores the mechanisms, psychological effects, and mitigation strategies associated with cyberbullying, emphasizing the need for robust digital policies and educational initiatives to foster safer online environments. As digital integration deepens, understanding and addressing cyberbullying remains crucial for safeguarding mental health and ensuring online safety in an increasingly connected world.

Generative Artificial Intelligence (GenAI) refers to Artificial Intelligent (AI) systems with human-like creativity and productivity capabilities. The most important difference between traditional AI and GenAI systems, which generally use algorithms and models designed to perform a specific task, is that GenAI systems can create new and original content. GenAI, which emerged as a product of technology and creativity and is a field that develops day by day, has been an important development that arouses interest and curiosity, as well as anxiety and uncertainty, for all segments of society with what it has done and what it can do in the future. GenAI's rapid development has begun to reshape business and living spaces by bringing admirable innovations. In this study, the past, present, and future of GenAI will be discussed and the landscape, applications, and tools of GenAI will be emphasized. In this way, it will be possible to understand this technological trend that will shape the future and help follow new developments and digital transformation.

Cyberbullying has become a very significant issue in today's digital age, and its victims are spread over all the online platforms. This chapter focuses on how Artificial Intelligence is transforming the fight against cyberbullying. It discusses the cutting-edge techniques and strategies used to detect harmful behavior online, harnessing the power of natural language processing (NLP), machine learning, and deep learning. The chapter explains how AI systems process text, images, and multimedia content to detect abusive or harmful interactions. It discusses some of the key challenges such as limitations in the dataset, bias in the algorithms, and the requirement for real-time detection. Further, the chapter focuses on innovative approaches that can be used for improving the accuracy and scalability of detection systems while simultaneously addressing critical ethical and privacy concerns. With the integration of technology and careful strategies, this chapter predicts a safer and more inclusive digital space for all.

Cyberbullying remains a pervasive issue in the digital era, affecting individuals of all ages across diverse online platforms. This book chapter, AI-Powered Harmony Pioneering Safer Social Platforms, explores the evolving role of Artificial Intelligence (AI) in mitigating this critical societal challenge. The chapter begins by emphasizing the importance of cyberbullying prevention and highlights the transformative potential of AI-driven solutions. It covers Emerging AI technologies, deep learning models like GPT and BERT, and multimodal approaches are also examined in depth and concludes with a vision for a collaborative and AI-driven future.

Cyberbullying significantly impacts mental health in today's digital age, calling for innovative prevention and mitigation strategies. This chapter delves into the role of artificial intelligence (AI) in addressing cyberbullying, starting with an analysis of its definitions, forms, and psychological effects to underscore the need for effective interventions. It highlights how AI technologies, including Natural Language Processing (NLP) techniques like sentiment analysis, keyword detection, and contextual interpretation, as well as machine learning models, are advancing traditional detection methods. Real-world case studies demonstrate successful AI applications in real-time monitoring and user behavior analysis, offering valuable insights. Ethical issues, such as data privacy, algorithmic bias, and transparency, are critically examined to ensure responsible AI use. The chapter also discusses the limitations of current AI solutions and future advancements, emphasizing the need for stakeholder collaboration and providing actionable strategies to foster safer online environments.

The chapter interrogated sexism and misogyny which is displayed against women on Facebook in Zimbabwe. The hostile engagements tend to close space for women on such key social media platforms which is vital for building social networks, for business engagements and for learning. This exclusion of women for fear of being harassed leads to further marginalization of women in politics, business and education. A case study of China is submitted as a country that monitors social media in both ex -ante and ex- post. The chapter uses ambivalent sexism theory, decolonial theory, deconstruction theory and postcolonial theory. The chapter postulates the use of Artificial Intelligence to control the profanity that is directed against women and people of other sexualities. The chapter also reviewed the international, continental and regional framework that supports gender equality.

Cyberbullying remains a significant issue in today's digital age, affecting individuals across various online platforms. Leveraging artificial intelligence (AI) offers promising solutions, as social networking tools now enable enhanced detection, prediction, and intervention. Advances in Natural Language Processing (NLP) facilitate the identification of hate speech and abusive content, while machine learning algorithms uncover complex patterns typical of online bullying. Additionally, image and video recognition systems, paired with content filters, help detect harmful visual content. AI also enables efficient threat detection and content moderation through predictive analytics, identifying at-risk individuals or groups and offering preemptive support. Expert systems integrated with AI-powered chatbots provide victims with guidance on reporting and prevention. However, challenges like user privacy and algorithmic bias must be addressed to ensure safety and fairness.

Generative Artificial Intelligence (AI) is opening new paths in the detection and prevention of cyberbullying. As we know, AI is shaping and improving the future of cyber, industry, automation, manufacturing, healthcare etc. with challenges of privacy concerns, job losses issues, and increased rules. This chapter explores future trends in AI-driven tools designed to reduce online bullying including various cybercrime across social media platforms, messaging apps, and other digital platforms. Ethical concerns like security and privacy, fairness, and avoiding bias are also discussed, aiming to ensure that AI tools are used responsibly and transparently. By combining technical advancements with an understanding of social impact, this chapter presents a vision for AI systems that create safer, more supportive online spaces. The chapter highlights the potential of generative AI to shape digital environments that are inclusive, resilient, and protective, fostering healthier interactions for everyone involved with the future scope of the study.

The integration of artificial intelligence (AI) into digital environments has revolutionized communication and social interactions while introducing profound legal, ethical, and regulatory challenges, particularly in addressing cyberbullying. This chapter explores the dual role of AI in combating and enabling cyberbullying, focusing on its potential as a transformative tool for harm mitigation and its unintended consequences, such as algorithmic bias, privacy concerns, and misuse for malicious purposes. By analyzing case studies of AI applications across major platforms, the chapter highlights both the successes and limitations of current systems in content moderation and behavioral interventions. Furthermore, the chapter delves into the broader ethical and human rights implications of AI, including its impact on freedom of expression, privacy, and equality. Through an interdisciplinary approach, the discussion evaluates existing regulatory frameworks and identifies critical gaps, emphasizing the need for adaptive, inclusive, and globally coordinated policies.

Cyber bullying is a growing issue, causing significant psychological harm across various demographics. Traditional methods of combating it struggle to keep pace with evolving technology and tactics. Recent advancements in Generative AI, particularly LLMs, offer new opportunities for prevention, intervention, and support. This paper explores how LLMs can improve detection of harmful online content, identify bullying patterns using natural language processing, and enhance reporting systems. LLMs also provide immediate support to victims through AI-driven chatbots, offering a safe space to share experiences and receive resources. In educational settings, LLMs can foster digital literacy and resilience, promoting empathy and responsible online behavior. Ethical concerns like privacy and bias must be addressed to ensure AI is used positively. Case studies demonstrate LLMs' success in mitigating cyber bullying across platforms. Ultimately, LLMs offer promising tools for a safer online environment, requiring ongoing research, innovation, and collaboration for effective implementation.

Investigating crime scenes is complex for forensic investigators, but artificial intelligence (AI) has streamlined the process, enhancing efficiency and speed. AI plays a vital role in various areas, including genotyping, biometrics, and digital forensics, addressing issues like data privacy and accountability. In crime detection and prevention, AI aids in statistical processing, identification, and forecasting. Challenges such as vast data, subtle clues, and outdated techniques can lead to investigative errors and miscarriages of justice. This chapter emphasizes AI's significance in processing digital evidence, enabling investigators to track suspect movements and decrypt messages, crucial for combating cybercrime. Looking ahead, AI's potential in forensic science is immense. When properly implemented, AI can transform the criminal justice system, making it more effective, safe, and fair, ultimately ensuring justice for all involved.

Preface

The proposed book "Combating Cyberbullying with Generative AI" examines how generative AI might be used to combat the growing issue of cyberbullying. The goal of the book is to give researchers, decision-makers, and tech developers practical learning about how AI can detect, block, and lessen unsafe online activity. Cyberbullying has expanded to be a global issue that affects people's safety and mental health, especially in young people. This book bridges a significant knowledge gap by delivering a detailed study of the methods in which artificial intelligence (AI)-driven technologies, such as machine learning and natural language processing, can be used to identify offensive behaviors and harmful content. The methodology includes new methods for AI ethics and bias reduction together with an analysis of current AI models and their application to real-world cyberbullying case studies. Significant results reveal that although AI is good at identifying offensive comments, issues with accuracy maintenance, ethics, and user privacy protection still exist. The book identifies several weaknesses, including AI's incomplete understanding of semantic intricacy and context. The thorough examination of the relationship between AI and online abuse in this book makes a significant addition to research. It provides practitioners looking for technology solutions to stop cyberbullying with useful foundations for creating more responsible AI systems

CHAPTER OVERVIEW

Chapter 1 commences the book with an overview that explores the mechanisms, psychological effects, and mitigation strategies associated with cyberbullying, emphasizing the need for robust digital policies and educational initiatives to foster safer online environments. As digital integration deepens, understanding and addressing cyberbullying remains crucial for safeguarding mental health and ensuring online safety in an increasingly connected world. It details the new dimensions of bullying through the rise of cyberbullying, which involves the use of technology to harass, threaten, or humiliate individuals. Characterized by anonymity, pervasive reach, and viral potential, cyberbullying extends across social media platforms, online forums, and messaging services, significantly impacting victims' psychological well-being. The anonymity provided by digital spaces often emboldens aggressors, leading to sustained harassment without physical confrontation. Thus, demonstrating the emerging patterns, including trolling and doxing, present complex challenges for detection, prevention, and legal regulation.

Chapter 2 provides a deeper understanding of the fundamental concepts that distinguish GenAI from traditional AI technologies. Providing information about today's best GenAI tools, landscape, and applications is aimed to provide a perspective on the current use of GenAI and to create an idea for future applications. In this section, the advantages and disadvantages of GenAI and future predictions regarding its impact on society and industries are also discussed, along with the ethical challenges accompanying its widespread adoption. Chapter 2 will provide insights into this transformative technology laying the foundations for the future and its far-reaching impacts.

Chapter 3 explores the emerging role of artificial intelligence in modern times to end cyberbullying. It shows how machine learning techniques, Natural Language Processing and deep learning can be applied while detecting harmful text, sarcasm, slang words, and various multilingual communications. The chapter highlights the advancements in generative AI for nuanced language understanding, data augmentation, and multimodal analysis across text, images, and videos. Also, it discusses real-life problems that may occur such as imbalanced data, bias by the algorithms used, and the ethical problem while classifying or identifying abuse content. Real-world applications, including the integration of AI models with social media platforms, are discussed alongside the trade-offs between speed, scalability, and accuracy. Concluding, with the emerging future and latest technologies, chapter 3 provides a concise yet comprehensive roadmap for leveraging AI to create safer and more inclusive online environments.

Chapter 4 addresses the extensive issue of cyberbullying on social media platforms. This chapter explores how cutting-edge technologies, including deep learning models like BERT and multimodal architectures, are being utilized to identify and alleviate damaging behaviors on social media. It delves into current capabilities, highlighting their ability to analyze complex linguistic patterns and contextual traces. This chapter is directed at researchers, technologists, policymakers, and educators seeking to understand and implement advanced AI solutions in cyberbully space. Through real-world case studies, the chapter covers the practical benefits and limitations of these solutions. The chapter also talks about key challenges such as bias, scalability, and ethical concerns. Eventually, it emphasizes the transformative capability of generative AI in fostering safer digital environments while supporting accountable implementation.

Chapter 5 delves into the evolving role of AI in forensic science and crime investigation, offering a comprehensive exploration of how AI technologies are transforming the landscape of criminal justice. By analyzing the integration of AI tools in evidence analysis, pattern recognition, and predictive modeling, the chapter underscores the potential of AI to enhance investigative accuracy and efficiency. It also addresses the challenges posed by ethical concerns, data integrity, and privacy issues in forensic applications. Through a balanced discussion, the chapter highlights the need for ethical AI implementation, rigorous legal frameworks, and interdisciplinary collaboration to ensure that these advanced tools are utilized responsibly. Ultimately, this chapter envisions a future where AI augments human expertise in solving crimes and upholding justice.

Chapter 6 explores the multifaceted issue of cyberbullying, delving into its origins, impacts, and the strategies needed to address it effectively. In the digital age, cyberbullying has emerged as a pressing concern, affecting individuals across various demographics and platforms. This chapter highlights the psychological, social, and legal dimensions of cyberbullying while emphasizing its disproportionate effects on vulnerable groups. By examining global perspectives, current prevention efforts, and the role of technology in both facilitating and combating online harassment, the chapter aims to provide a comprehensive understanding of the issue. It also calls for collective action, innovative solutions, and a commitment to fostering safe, inclusive digital environments for all users.

Chapter 7 delves into the transformative potential of artificial intelligence (AI) in addressing the pervasive issue of cyberbullying. It highlights the psychological toll and complex nature of cyberbullying while emphasizing the need for innovative interventions. Exploring advancements in Natural Language Processing (NLP) and machine learning, the chapter demonstrates how AI is enhancing detection and mitigation strategies. Real-world case studies showcase successful applications, complemented by a critical discussion of ethical considerations like data privacy and algorithmic bias. The chapter concludes with insights into current limitations, future innovations, and collaborative strategies for fostering safer, more respectful online environments

Chapter 8 explored how social media platform such as Facebook can be used by fans to promote misogyny and sexism, which can limit the participation of women in politics, business and other areas of life. The use of Artificial Intelligence (AI) to combat the misogyny and sexism on Facebook is examined. The evolution of Facebook is examined as well as the development of AI and development of large data analytics are also explored. A number of theories are used to shed light on this vital issue which includes ambivalent theory, decolonial and deconstruction theory.

The strategies that can be used to stem violence against women on Facebook are examined which include the use of counter-speech and implementation of laws in different countries to combat cyberbullying. A case study of how China controls social media is also displayed.

Chapter 9 explores into the rising shadow of cyberbullying in cyberspace with a keen focus on how artificial intelligence is part of the solution or challenge to the growing menace. The bullying spreads from an individual personal experience to a world stage with over one billion casualties, and social networks only add up to their numbers: only those personally affected remain individual discontentment traded on the various digital platforms. The innovated solutions which AI brings forth are presented in this chapter, from the enhanced Natural Language Processing (NLP), machine learning algorithms, and image and video recognition systems. By far, these advancements would be mentioned as the most important breakthroughs in detecting, predicting, and intervening against harmful content. In addition to this would be predictive analytics in detection of threats, AI-supported chatbots that help victims, and so on. The study also brings out privacy exposure as well as algorithmic bias regarding users, along with the challenges posed and a clear necessity for responsible AI to finally be created to answer fairness and safety issues for all users of the online environment.

Chapter 10 explores how Generative Artificial Intelligence (AI) is opening new paths for the detection and prevention of cyberbullying. As we know that AI is shaping and improving the future of cyber, industry, automation, manufacturing, and healthcare etc. with challenges of privacy concerns, job losses issues, and increased rules. This chapter explores future trends in AI-driven tools designed to reduce online bullying including various cybercrime across social media platforms, messaging apps, and other digital platforms. Ethical concerns like security and privacy, fairness, and avoiding bias are also discussed, aiming to ensure that AI tools are used responsibly and transparently. By combining technical advancements with an understanding of social impact, this chapter presents a vision for AI systems that create safer, more supportive online spaces. The chapter highlights the potential of generative AI to shape digital environments that are inclusive, resilient, and protective, fostering healthier interactions for everyone involved with future scope of the study.

Chapter 11 explores the intricate relationship between AI and cyberbullying, examining AI's potential as both a tool for combating and a contributor to online harm. By delving into the evolution of AI technologies, their dual role in moderating and exacerbating cyberbullying, and the legal challenges they pose, the chapter highlights the complexity of balancing innovation with ethical governance. It emphasizes the importance of robust regulatory frameworks, ethical AI design, and collaborative efforts to address issues like algorithmic bias, privacy concerns, and generative AI misuse. Ultimately, the chapter envisions a future where AI can foster safer digital environments while protecting fundamental human rights.

Chapter 12 aims to delve into the complexities of this pervasive issue while shedding light on how Artificial Intelligence (AI) serves as both a solution and a challenge in combating this digital menace.It explores the multifaceted role of AI, emphasizing its innovations in Natural Language Processing (NLP), machine learning algorithms, and image and video recognition systems. These advancements have revolutionized the ability to detect, predict, and intervene against harmful online behavior, offering a beacon of hope in addressing cyberbullying. From predictive analytics to AI-supported chatbots that provide real-time support to victims, the potential of AI to foster safer digital environments is immense

Chapter 13 investigates the use of artificial intelligence (AI) tools to identify, stop, and lessen online harassment. The method uses machine learning algorithms, deep learning frameworks, and Natural Language Processing (NLP) models to automatically analyse and categorise potentially hazardous content. Through the integration of context-aware detection, sentiment analysis, and user profiling, these artificial intelligence systems seek to establish a secure online space. Along with privacy issues and the ethical ramifications of automated interventions, the paper also discusses the difficulties in teaching AI models to distinguish between benign and harmful interactions.

Kishor Kumar Reddy C.
Stanley College of Engineering and Technology for Women, India

Meetu Malhotra
Harrisburg University of Science and Technology, USA

Mariya Ouaissa
Cadi Ayyad University, Morocco

Marlia Mohd Hanafiah
Universiti Kebangsaan Malaysia, Malaysia

Mohammed Shuaib
Jazan University, Saudi Arabia

Chapter 1
Overview of Digital Age Cyberbullying

Wasswa Shafik
https://orcid.org/0000-0002-9320-3186
School of Digital Science, Universiti Brunei Darussalam, Gadong, Brunei & Dig Connectivity Research Laboratory (DCRLab), Kampala, Uganda

ABSTRACT

The digital age has introduced new dimensions to bullying through the rise of cyberbullying, which involves the use of technology to harass, threaten, or humiliate individuals. Characterized by anonymity, pervasive reach, and viral potential, cyberbullying extends across social media platforms, online forums, and messaging services, significantly impacting victims' psychological well-being. The anonymity provided by digital spaces often emboldens aggressors, leading to sustained harassment without physical confrontation. Emerging patterns, including trolling and doxxing, present complex challenges for detection, prevention, and legal regulation. This overview explores the mechanisms, psychological effects, and mitigation strategies associated with cyberbullying, emphasizing the need for robust digital policies and educational initiatives to foster safer online environments. As digital integration deepens, understanding and addressing cyberbullying remains crucial for safeguarding mental health and ensuring online safety in an increasingly connected world.

1. INTRODUCTION

Cyberbullying[1] is harassment through digital technologies. It has unique properties that merit attention from educators, researchers, and practitioners. The perpetuation of threats, insults, rumors, and hate speech through social media, instant messaging

DOI: 10.4018/979-8-3373-0543-1.ch001

platforms, and websites raises complex legal and moral questions that have profound implications for those most affected by this phenomenon, alleged or actual targets of digital harassment (Badawi, 2024). Estimates of how many people experience cyberbullying vary. Among those who identify as having been victimized, many experience a range of negative social, emotional, and physical health outcomes. In some cases, targets of cyberbullying respond with overt antisocial or revenge-seeking behavior (Malik & Dadure, 2024). As schools, families, and law enforcement agencies consider methods for effective prevention and response to cyberbullying, it is essential to understand the anatomy of cyberbullying and some of the fundamental ways it differs from traditional, in-person harassment (Wiederhold, 2024; Neha et al., 2023; Wiederhold, 2024).

Cyberbullying consists of a variety of behaviors, many of which are not considered bullying behaviors when they lack a digital component. In general, electronic bullying can be divided into two types: cyberbullying within school and cyberbullying which spills over from school. We define a subcategory of cyberbullying, "cyber-harassment[2]," as an extension of the schoolyard practice of harassment: a repeated pattern of nuisance or injury; an inability on the part of the targets to terminate the behavior; and a qualitative difference between taunting or annoying behaviors and other forms of deliberate harassment, such as social exclusion, dating abuse by proxy, and sexting. Another subcategory refers to sexting, perpetrated by "posers" of real or imagined harassers who use sexual, commercially exploitative photos and their potential exposure as tools of harassment (Alrawashdeh et al., 2024; Kee et al., 2024). Cyberbullying appears to be a distinct phenomenon in a number of ways, as outlined above. Researchers and educators should pay careful attention to the unique properties of cyberbullying to develop prevention strategies that are tailored to the context, community, and people they are likely to be engaging and working with since digital technologies and online spaces are highly diverse and changing (Orelaja et al., 2024; Kishor Kumar Reddy et al., 2024a).

Cyberbullying is an issue that has grown from the traditional bullying experienced by many into a digital phenomenon of the modern age. It is an unfortunate reality for many in today's digital world. Cyberbullying is defined in comparison to different forms of online violence, including trolling, flaming, and cyberstalking. It takes place over digital mediums, including online gaming platforms, image boards, and social media applications. Cyberbullying has characteristics that distinguish it from more traditional forms of harassment (Jun et al., 2021; Pericherla & Ilavarasan, 2024; Shafik, 2024c). It influences victims who are often ignored when trying to seek help as fear rises from the belief that their experiences are less serious than their offline counterparts. Cyberbullying is facilitated through technology by the use of lesser-known gimmicks and tricks (Mantey et al., 2023; Kishor Kumar Reddy et al., 2024b). Anonymity online also allows people to act in a more audacious manner. The increase in these experiences can be seen by researching current statistics across various countries, sites, and surveys. This cross-sectional response highlights the extent of this sinister and troubling issue. Media and scholarly writings often focus on how the victim experiences cyberbullying. While increased attention is currently being given to grooming through digital mediums, there are still a few instances of exploring these experiences to bring about substantial change; figure 1 highlights sampled aspects of cyberbullying that are common today (Neha et al., 2023; Shafik, 2023a).

Figure 1. Cyberbullying

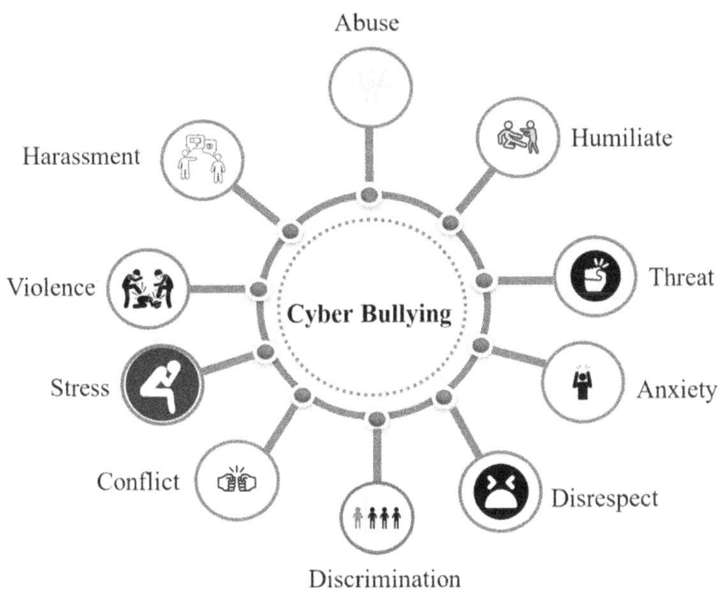

1.1. Definition and Forms of Cyberbullying

A more succinct definition describes cyberbullying as an aggressive, deliberate act carried out by a group or individual, using electronic forms of contact, repeatedly and over time against a victim who cannot easily defend him or herself. Contrary to several terse definitions, cyberbullying is conceptually challenging and has been broken down into categories (Nagata et al., 2023). They include harassment, which involves abusive language that conveys sexualized, violent, and hateful sentiments; doxing, which entails the public revelation of private information about a target to facilitate harm; cyberstalking[3], which encompasses the use of information technology to pursue, watch, badger, or correspond with another person without due consideration, acting in a manner that could be reasonably regarded as intimidating or obsessive; and trolling, defined in typically one of two fashions (Samalo et al., 2023; Kishor Kumar Reddy et al., 2024c). The first situates trolling within a ludic space, where it typifies online mischief-making that can, depending on its recipients, be regarded in either good or bad humor. The definition of a troll as an abusive online provocateur, however, seeks to clarify that not all forms of online provocation are playful or insignificant; rather, trollers are characterized by an attempt to invoke an extremely negative response from a target, only to sit back and enjoy the damage that they have caused (Kalinaki et al., 2024; Shafik, 2024a).

A particular feature of many of these forms of cyberbullying is the role they give to anonymity. The perpetrators of these forms are either formal or informal members of groups that are determined to launch a concerted assault on their targets. Perpetrators are motivated by a mix of factors, including opportunity, the potential thrill of the chase, a pronounced absence of empathy for their targets, an ability to achieve a degree of dissociation from the actual actions of cyberbullying they oversee, and a feeling of justification (Sultan et al., 2023). It is argued that cyberbullying and cyberstalking behaviors meet the criteria for everyday moral wrongdoing in a digital age[4], that they show hostility towards the worthy and unworthy alike due to their benevolence or malevolence, and that what is being produced on social media sites where these behaviors emerge is merely conversations (Nee et al., 2023).

2. TYPES OF CYBERBULLYING

In digital communication, cyberbullying behaviors are wide-ranging. One means to provide targeted preventive interventions could thus be to categorize cyberbullying. In social media, victims are often harassed by the content of posts, through comments, and also via direct messages. Social media posts and victims can involve two different types of communication. For example, comments, posts, and direct messages might be public, named, anonymous, or from fake or impersonated profiles. Victims' private and professional lives, followers, and their businesses are primarily attacked (Masatcıoğlu & Öksüz, 2024; Pericherla & Ilavarasan, 2024). Messaging apps are often a means for sending explicit harmful content, such as hate speech, threats, and sexual violence. Perpetrators use private networks to avoid public content moderation by platform companies and to prevent victims from easily documenting digital hate (Shafik, 2023c; Wahyuningrum et al., 2023; Saifullah et al., 2024). In online gaming, communicating with other players is important for having fun and winning together. However, a major challenge of online gaming arises from the often-encouraged use of user nicknames. Anonymity enables offensive behavior, and the diversion of toxic players occurs within the games themselves to prevent online bullying. Therefore, the features "anonymous messages" and "new child accounts with no or few followers" serve as good targets for intervention. The main idea is to help children build a broader network, as this can act as a protective factor (Milosevic et al., 2023; Shafik, 2023b; Kishor Kumar Reddy et al., 2024d). In personal life cyberbullying, the most important concept for intervention is providing resilience training against hate speech and sexual harassment; its type depends on the application, context, and individual understanding, as presented in Figure 2.

Figure 2. Cyberbullying types

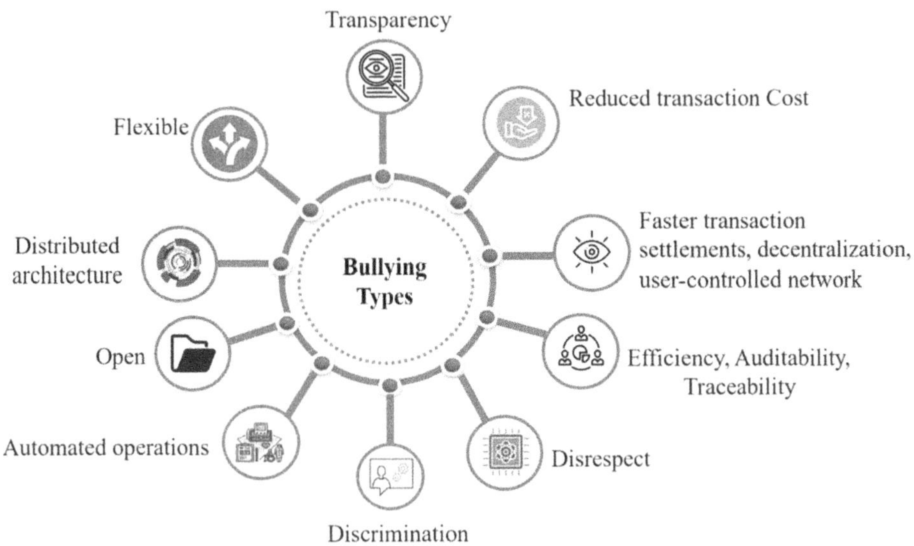

2.1. Cyberbullying Through Social Media Platforms

Social platforms[5] enable cyberbullying has erupt as a preferred method for harassing or intimidating individuals. A variety of platforms and tools afford users opportunities to utilize these technologies to their strategic advantage, aggravating bystanders and inflating the potential for virality or publicity. Several platforms have been featured as vehicles of harassment and technological harm. Tactics for Agitation and Persecution Participants in this study used a number of techniques to provoke anger. Many were overly aggressive through public messages or created impersonating accounts to ridicule or spoof their targets (Mantey et al., 2023; Shafik et al., 2024; Zhao et al., 2022). Other harassing actions involved considerable deception or multimedia preparations on the part of the aggressor. A few trickster-hackers used false credentials to pose as a target and deliberately feigned suicidal intentions. The intent of the latter scenario seemed focused on reducing the perceived believability and, therefore, a person's willingness to offer emotional support. Though the aggressors proposed that multiple insiders played a part in constructing the illusion, it seemed feasible that these harassers were the sole participants (Shafik, 2023a; Samee et al., 2023; Shafik, 2024d; Shafik, 2024b). personal costs of attack, the impressionable nature of families and teens reveals the dire emotional, behavioral, and psychological effects of cyberbullying depending on an individual[6]. Someone who has fallen victim to shaming and feeling denigrated and nonredeemable may wish to hide or escape from the constant exposure and the repeated reliving of a distressing event. It is not surprising that someone may succumb to depressive thoughts and begin to experience a gradual darkening of their view. Moreover, long-term impairment from stress and psychological suffering may emerge as a result of cyberbullying (Lin et al., 2023; Wu et al., 2024). Consequently, the victim is perceived to be significantly more impaired than witnesses or traditional bystanders.

2.2. Cyberbullying via Messaging Apps

Messaging apps[7] have become popular and are typically used for communication with others in a private and intimate setting. The unique characteristics of messaging services can bring harmful and unacceptable behavior. Messaging is one of the best ways to communicate with near-instant response rates. This creates a fast-paced conversation style, making it more likely that users might send messages out of their emotions and allow them to intensify their bullying behavior. These types of interactions can create opportunities for users to damage others and their reputation, even though content does not promote explicit harm (Masatcıoğlu & Öksüz, 2024; Kee et al., 2024). There are a number of different types of cyberbullying that can take place in messaging applications. This can include direct personal insults, rumors, sharing personal data or secrets, threats, spreading lies and rumors, harassment, defamation, and exclusion. Additionally, content can be shared on the messaging platform that lacks respect for other people's characteristics, including ongoing group bullying, sharing unwanted content, or sending unsolicited attempts to groom a victim (Pericherla & Ilavarasan, 2024; Gavini Sreelatha et al., 2024).

Victims of cyberbullying in messaging apps are unable to report the activities of their bullies to external helpers easily. This makes cyberbullying on messaging apps more dangerous, as people can more easily 'get away with it.' Cyberbullying on messaging applications can cause severe emotional reactions, with their primary responses tending towards isolation, loneliness, constant stress, constant anger, and constant fear (Samalo et al., 2023; Sultan et al., 2023; Wiederhold, 2024). Anonymity allows users to share content in private; it can still cause fear and distress on top of the uncertainties associated with the possibility that someone can still take a screenshot of a conversation and share it without the explicit consent of the sender (Wu et al., 2024). Developers of messaging apps must implement greater possibilities to ensure that people who are subjected to this kind of abuse can report it through a variety of channels, including the messaging platform, the privacy commission, or the police. Education is also necessary for the use of these kinds of apps so that the risk is greater, but the use is manageable as long as you are vigilant. Only share personal information when and if you are comfortable (Peprah et al., 2023; Sultan et al., 2023; Wahyuningrum et al., 2023).

2.3. Cyberbullying in Online Gaming Communities

The loosely structured and competitive environment of many online gaming communities can facilitate hostile or aggressive actions. In multiplayer games or those that can be more enjoyable when socializing, this can also foster a spirit of competition similar to the aggressive actions found among sports fans. In larger gaming communities, blame and harm can be easily assigned among hundreds of new or novice players, even if this is not the atmosphere of the game itself. In these environments, anonymity can add to the ease with which aggressive actions can be conducted. In some online games, players have resorted to online harassment conducted through voice chat or responses sent during or after a match played (Samee et al., 2023; Milosevic et al., 2023). In games that rely on matchmaking, rather than getting a group together, players may also feel comfortable baiting a particular opponent due to the fact that if they are "caught," they will most likely not face negative in-game consequences.

In these types of environments, players might be taunted because of their low (or sometimes "unusually high") level of skill compared to their accumulated playing time. Players in these groups may be teased because of their obvious gender, sexuality, race, or religion. In other situations, a player may have to endure trash talk simply because they are doing well, have killed an opponent with a particularly rare weapon, or are working to complete a specific goal. The consequences of this can vary with people and the situation, but typically, players feel disrespected by the fact that someone has set aside their usual gaming goals to harass or belittle them (Alrawashdeh et al., 2024; Alrawashdeh et al., 2024). As a result, many victims respond by not saying anything in order to avoid further negative communication. When this is not possible for people, gaming may not be done in the community, such as through peer-to-peer connections away from the central servers, and excluded from the social experience of that title. Some violence may create enough fear to keep people from playing at all. Official responses to such attacks have built-in constraints by previous business and programming decisions but can go part of the way to moderating unwanted actions from the environment. Many gaming companies have not traditionally included any reporting systems, content moderation, or community guidelines, though this situation is educational changing (Nee et al., 2023; Shafik, 2024e; Sultan et al., 2023). The legitimacy of bans from such games is a popular area of legal study that is not specific to online games. Some companies have taken to running in-game events that foster healthier attitudes and community relations. Driven by the success of fair play and community policy reform, the behavior of players is clearly sought for many-to-many gaming contexts. In gaming spaces of all sorts, the acceptance of positive interactions by a group and the managing of pranks in order to foster these experiences are key areas of concern for game researchers and designers (Malik & Dadure, 2024; Wahyuningrum et al., 2023). For individual players, peer support and cooperation have been found to boost experience and well-being in multiservice online games and other kinds of cyberbullying, as presented in Table 1.

Table 1. Types of Cyberbullying: Descriptions, Impacts on Victims, and Societal Effects

Type of Cyberbullying	Brief Description	Impact on the Victim	Impact to Society	Reference
Sexting/Blackmail[8] (Sextortion)	Using explicit images or conversations to blackmail, threaten, or manipulate someone.	This leads to shame, fear, and potential exploitation, with lasting psychological effects.	Perpetuates exploitation and manipulative behaviors in digital spaces.	(Sultan et al., 2023)
Catfishing[9]	Creating fake profiles to deceive, manipulate, or exploit the victim emotionally or financially.	Resulting in emotional trauma, financial loss, and a sense of betrayal.	Erodes trust in online relationships and leads to skepticism in social interactions.	(Nee et al., 2023)
Doxxing[10]	Publicly sharing personal information (e.g., home address, phone number) without consent to endanger them.	Causes severe stress, fear for personal safety, and potential physical harm.	This leads to a society where personal privacy is compromised and exploited.	(Wahyuningrum et al., 2023)

continued on following page

Table 1. Continued

Type of Cyberbullying	Brief Description	Impact on the Victim	Impact to Society	Reference
Frapping[11]	Logging into someone else's social media account and posting inappropriate content under their name.	Damages the victim's reputation and may cause social or professional setbacks.	Erodes trust in social media as a secure platform for personal expression.	(Malik & Dadure, 2024)
Cyberstalking[12]	Repeatedly sending threatening messages or engaging in intimidating behavior to instill fear.	Causes fear, anxiety, and a sense of being unsafe, potentially leading to PTSD.	Undermines individuals' sense of security and promotes a climate of fear.	(Orelaja et al., 2024)
Trolling[13]	Deliberately posting provocative, offensive, or off-topic messages to upset others or provoke a reaction.	Triggers emotional distress, anger, or frustration in the victim.	Encourages disruptive behavior in online communities, reducing constructive discourse.	(Milosevic et al., 2023)
Denigration[14] (Dissing)	Spreading false information, rumors, or gossip about someone to damage their reputation.	Leads to reputational harm, anxiety, and social stigmatization.	Encourages a culture of gossip and misinformation, eroding public trust.	(Badawi, 2024)
Masquerading[15]	Pretending to be someone else online to harass or embarrass the victim.	This results in confusion, mistrust, and damage to the victim's reputation.	Increases distrust in online interactions and diminishes digital integrity.	(Mantey et al., 2023)
Outing[16]	Sharing someone's personal, private, or embarrassing information or images without their consent.	Causes embarrassment, shame, and loss of trust in others.	Undermines privacy standards, leading to widespread fear of exposure.	(Wiederhold, 2024)
Exclusion[17]	Intentionally excluding someone from an online group, game, or social activity to hurt their feelings.	This leads to feelings of rejection, isolation, and diminished self-worth.	Fosters division and discrimination, encouraging exclusionary practices.	(Neha et al., 2023)

continued on following page

Table 1. Continued

Type of Cyberbullying	Brief Description	Impact on the Victim	Impact to Society	Reference
Flaming[18]	Engaging in online fights, using angry and vulgar language in a hostile manner.	Creates a hostile environment, affecting the victim's emotional stability and self-esteem.	Promotes a culture of conflict and intolerance in online spaces.	(Nagata et al., 2023)
Harassment[19]	Repeatedly sending offensive, rude, or insulting messages directly to the victim.	Causes stress, anxiety, and depression, potentially leading to social withdrawal.	Normalizes aggressive behavior, leading to a less empathetic society.	(Samalo et al., 2023)

3. IMPACT OF CYBERBULLYING ON VICTIMS

One of the strongest arguments for preventing and combating cyberbullying is the severity of the effects that it has on its victims. Commonly reported psychological effects include anxiety, depression, crying spells, and thoughts of suicide. These children often report difficulty making decisions or concentrating, and they report a decrease in their self-esteem as a result. Socially, youth who have been cyberbullied tend to report feeling lonelier or feeling that others despise them (Hu et al., 2023). They report friction with family members who are either unable or unwilling to help them with the problem. These negative feelings appear to exacerbate the social isolation that many report as a result of their victimization. For many, the source of trouble may be pre-existing; treatment history, trauma, and prominent introverted behavior may make youth more likely to be cyberbullied in the first place (Lin et al., 2023; Pericherla & Ilavarasan, 2024).

Academically, children who are victimized do less well and often appear to lose interest in school. When youth feel that they are not good in school or do not belong, they often find ways to disidentify with their teachers and family. They miss school more frequently and also do less homework, making the cycle of poor performance all the more difficult to escape. The anonymity of online activity also makes it harder for adults to detect and confront bullies, so their caregivers may never become involved (Saifullah et al., 2024). Many of the outcomes reported above are studied through audiotapes, interviews, or surveys, but the effects of cyberbullying are not limited to their immediacy; they can persist and negatively impact their victims as well. Those bullied as children tended to exhibit less education, higher unemployment, and relatively lower income as they entered adulthood. A survey of over

3,000 young Australians currently attending school reported results in line with that finding, specifically showing the negative correlation between a student's school performance and the student's self-reported experiences of cyberbullying, including substance use and depressive symptoms. This victimization is not confined to the children of any particular nation, as reported by parents of children similarly affected by cyberbullying (Kee et al., 2024). It is recommended to establish an open line of communication friendly to both students and adults and to normalize cyberbullying intervention as an essential part of youth protection across all facets of young life.

3.1. Psychological Effects

A victim of cyberbullying, defined as a person who has been abused or harassed online through a persistent or repeated course of conduct that occurs over digital media platforms, can experience severe mental health difficulties as a result. Sending or posting harmful or mean content about someone else, spreading rumors, or privately sharing an image of someone being sexually or physically assaulted are all forms of cyberbullying. The degree of psychological detriment caused by cyberbullying is often determined by the victim's characteristics, including how they interpret or evaluate the situation (Alrawashdeh et al., 2024). The psychological effects of cyberbullying include:

1) The development of new anxiety disorders, including generalized anxiety disorder, panic disorder, agoraphobia, and social anxiety disorder
2) Major depressive disorder
3) Post-traumatic stress disorder

The psychological effects of bullying can last for years after the actual bullying has ceased. This is the case even in individuals who possess high levels of confidence and self-esteem. It is especially difficult for a person to see themselves as valuable or strong after being publicly humiliated. Victims described their experiences as an attack on their core self and sense of self-identity. For that reason, the victim perceived their life as out of control. Being cyberbullied influences an individual's ability to create and maintain healthy, warm social relationships. Victims frequently do not discuss their issues with others. They might feel unable to show their real feelings or have problematic relationships with family members and other people in general (Samee et al., 2023; Shafik & Khang, 2024). Implicitly, victims often feel justified when they exclude themselves from activities or interactions for fear that something similar to the cyberbullying event will happen again. Victims also frequently feel isolated or alone. They have a difficult time bouncing back from cyberbullying situations, and these effects can be long-term. A person's emotional responses to being bullied can vary. Some might gain insight, develop resilience, or experience psychological growth. However, others might fail to recover, possibly experiencing temporary or permanent emotional health declines. Each bullied victim needs a set of treatments as unique as their response to the bullying. Victims might recover on their own, protected by a wide base of social support, or they might need one-on-one or group therapy (Peprah et al., 2023; Wu et al., 2024). Teenagers might need the help of adult caregivers, family, or educational professionals. Three out of four victims of cyberbullying do not typically converse with authority figures about the instances. Immediate supportive interventions can reduce the incidence of these harsh mental and emotional impacts, which can remain pervasive for years. This need can be fulfilled by programs created specifically for cyberbullying or by efforts also designed to prevent face-to-face bullying (Masatcıoğlu & Öksüz, 2024; Pericherla & Ilavarasan, 2024). Specialized training may help school bus drivers, parents, and even peers of victims to respond constructively. Online counseling resources and local mental health professionals are available for support in order to aid those who have been cyberbullied. There is a wealth of books and self-help guides on recovering from the emotional toll of being targeted (Pericherla & Ilavarasan, 2024).

3.2. Social Effects

Cyberbullying clearly has an emotional toll on young people's lives. As a result, academic pressure on cyberbullying has emphasized the mental health impacts on youth, but harm also occurs beyond the level of the individual within the social arena of offline and localized community spaces. Creating a Culture of Fear and Mistrust: The very experience of being cyberbullied can become stigmatizing for victims, as concerns of being blamed, disbelieved, or criticized as foolish, weak, or naive are recognized social burdens. Furthermore, the reputational needs of adolescents and teenagers, such as finding sexual partners or demonstrating adulthood and emotional control, further heighten the alienating effects of stigma (Peprah et al., 2023; Wu et al., 2024). There is a strong contemporary view that victims are likely to internalize their negative experiences, blaming themselves rather than the bully, and may find it difficult to seek help. Effects of Cyberbullying on Peer Relationships: A common theme is the highlighting of the peer group as a central site of bullying. Creating understanding and empathy among peers for this may be an important way of breaking the spiral of silence and encouraging bystanders to say something or to disclose acts. Social support may be crucial in mitigating the negative effects of being cyberbullied or, through early intervention, making it less likely for negative emotional impacts to transform into severe mental health issues for those young people involved in bullying (Alrawashdeh et al., 2024; Samee et al., 2023).

3.3. Academic Effects

Students who are bullied, especially those who suffer from prolonged abuse, may experience concentration and motivation problems, leading to a decrease in grades and attendance. The fear that harassment would continue at school may cause some children to avoid it altogether, leading to an even poorer school performance. A study examining the academic effects of cyberbullying and online harassment found that college students who experienced electronic aggression reported higher levels of engaging in an on-the-edge coping strategy and lower levels of hope. A hostile online environment can negatively affect the overall climate of a school (Kee et al., 2024). Victims of cyberbullying have had problems with peers bullying them in the classroom; although the aggressor never physically touched them, they knew they were still present. Moreover, when students see inappropriate out-of-school student behavior online, they may become disgusted and apprehensive, which also affects how much they want to be in the class or school. Students who experience or witness bullying and harassment on the web reported that what they observed or experienced led to their desire to participate in extracurricular activities. Educators, especially middle and high school educators, are vigilant in providing opportunities for students to engage with them (Lin et al., 2023; Saifullah et al., 2024). However, despite high levels of participation in such activities in middle and high school, adolescents are not reporting the overwhelming benefit of participation in such activities for their social development. Schools need to be responsible for creating a safe learning environment for all students, and efforts must be made to provide some measures to victims of cyber-aggression. Some schools are implementing programs to identify and help students who experience cyberbullying. However, many students do not disclose experiences with electronic aggression at school. Teachers reported that while students were aware of the signs of being cyberbullied, few examples were given by the teacher. It is important to note that educators using programs to identify students victimized by these technologies must focus on all students and not just the victim (Hu et al., 2023; Samalo et al., 2023). Researchers suggest incorporating cyberbullying into a larger bullying prevention strategy and program that fosters positive bystander behavior. A complementary approach comes from students who have not experienced or seen cyberbullying, possibly having the added benefit of appearing to be a positive bystander in that situation. By learning about the effects of cyberbullying on victims, parents and educators can become proactive in helping to address these problems in their schools (Nagata et al., 2023). Several concepts are associated with cyberbullying, each with a distinctive impact, and case studies as presented in Table 2.

Table 2. Comprehensive Overview of Cyber Aspects: Traits, Impacts, and Sampled Cases

Cyber Aspect	Trait/Context	Impact	Case	Reference
Cyber Insurance	Insurance policies that cover losses due to cyber incidents like data breaches.	Provides financial compensation for losses and helps organizations recover from incidents.	Companies are taking out cyber insurance policies to protect against ransomware attacks.	(Masatcıoğlu & Öksüz, 2024)
Cyber Risk	Potential threats or vulnerabilities associated with digital systems.	Financial loss, operational disruption, and reputational damage if risks are not managed.	The identification of vulnerabilities in IoT devices that hackers could exploit.	(Pericherla & Ilavarasan, 2024)
Cyber Diplomacy	Addressing and resolving digital conflicts through diplomatic channels.	Helps prevent cyber conflicts from escalating and promotes cooperation between nations.	International agreements to prevent cyber warfare, such as the U.S.-China agreement on cyber espionage.	(Wu et al., 2024)
Cyber Liability	The legal and financial responsibility for data breaches or other cyber incidents.	Results in lawsuits, regulatory fines, and reputational damage for organizations.	Companies are being held accountable for data breaches under data protection laws such as GDPR.	(Peprah et al., 2023)
Cyber Resilience	The ability of a system or organization to recover from cyber incidents.	Minimizes downtime, reduces data loss, and ensures continuity of services.	Banks implementing business continuity plans to recover quickly from cyber-attacks.	(Samee et al., 2023)
Cyber Attack	Attempts to disrupt, disable, or gain unauthorized access to computer systems.	It can result in data breaches, financial loss, and damaged reputations for targeted organizations.	The 2016 Distributed denial of service[20] (DDoS) attack on Dyn disrupted major internet services across the U.S.	(Alrawashdeh et al., 2024)
Cyber Law	Legal regulations governing internet use and digital technology.	Protects intellectual property, enforces data privacy, and helps combat cybercrime.	The General Data Protection Regulation[21] (GDPR) in the European Union protects personal data privacy rights.	(Kee et al., 2024)
Cyber Ethics	Moral principles guiding behavior in online interactions and digital technology.	Promotes responsible online conduct and helps prevent misuse of technology.	The debate on ethical AI use in social media algorithms that influence user behavior.	(Saifullah et al., 2024)

continued on following page

Table 2. Continued

Cyber Aspect	Trait/Context	Impact	Case	Reference
Cyber Hygiene	Practices to maintain system security, such as regular software updates.	Reduces the risk of malware infections and unauthorized access to personal or business data.	Regular use of antivirus software and updating operating systems to avoid security vulnerabilities.	(Lin et al., 2023)
Cyber Forensics	Investigating digital devices to collect evidence for legal cases.	Helps solve cybercrimes, supports legal proceedings, and identifies perpetrators.	The use of digital evidence in solving the "BTK Killer[22]" case by analyzing metadata in emails.	(Hu et al., 2023)
Cyber Terrorism	Using digital means to cause panic or disrupt essential services.	Loss of lives, widespread fear, and disruption of daily life or national security.	The 2007 cyberattacks on Estonia targeted government and financial services.	(Samalo et al., 2023)
Cyber Extortion	Demanding money or services through threats of cyber attacks, like ransomware.	Financial losses, operational disruptions, and potential loss of data.	The WannaCry[23] ransomware attack affects thousands of organizations globally.	(Nagata et al., 2023)
Cyber Vandalism	Intentional defacement of digital content or damage to digital assets.	Loss of business reputation, financial costs for recovery, and downtime.	The hacking of Sony Pictures website, leaking sensitive information, and disrupting operations.	(Shafik, 2023b)
Cyber Espionage	Spying using digital means to steal confidential information from entities.	Economic and political consequences, loss of intellectual property, or sensitive data leaks.	The 2015 cyber-attack on the U.S. Office of Personnel Management exposed government employee records.	(Hu et al., 2023)
Cyberwarfare	The use of digital attacks by nations to damage or disrupt another nation's systems.	It can disrupt critical infrastructure, compromise national security, and lead to loss of life.	The Stuxnet worm attack targeted Iran's nuclear facilities.	(Salmerón Ruiz, 2023)
Cybersecurity	Measures to protect networks, data, and systems from unauthorized access.	Prevents data breaches, protects privacy, and maintains the integrity of information systems.	Implementation of multi-factor authentication in companies to prevent hacking attempts.	(Jun et al., 2021; Shafik, 2024c)

continued on following page

Table 2. Continued

Cyber Aspect	Trait/Context	Impact	Case	Reference
Cybercrime	Illegal activities are carried out through digital means, including hacking and fraud.	Financial losses, data breaches, identity theft, and potential legal consequences.	The Equifax data breach exposed millions of records with personal information.	(Shafik, 2023b, 2024d)
Cyberstalking	Monitoring someone's online activities or using the internet to track someone.	It instills fear, disrupts personal life, and may escalate to physical stalking.	The case of "John Doe" stalking an ex-partner through social media and tracking their location.	(Pericherla & Ilavarasan, 2024; Wu et al., 2024)
Cyber Harassment	Persistent online threats or offensive content directed at a person or group.	Leads to anxiety, fear for personal safety, and reputational harm.	A journalist is receiving death threats via social media due to controversial articles.	(Peprah et al., 2023)

4. CYBERBULLYING PREVENTION AND INTERVENTION STRATEGIES

Some strategies can be implemented to prevent and intervene in cyberbullying cases. One way to address this issue is through proactive education programs. Just as we do fire drills and provide stop, drop, and roll instruction to students, we should be doing the same for bullying and cyberbullying. These programs provide information to those who will be affected: the students, parents, and educators. As a result, they are the most sustainable of strategies. Initiatives in schools celebrate the positive power of the internet (Masatcıoğlu & Öksüz, 2024). Projects are designed to generate awareness around cyberbullying and encourage empathy among young people.

Parental involvement is key in the prevention of and intervention with cyberbullying. There are a number of resources that can help educators inform and empower parents. Although many educators are uncomfortable delving into the personal lives of their students, a connection between school and home can often make the difference when faced with a situation as volatile as cyberbullying. Several resources for parents include signs of bullying, how parents can help, and maintaining an open dialogue (Masatcıoğlu & Öksüz, 2024; Pericherla & Ilavarasan, 2024). These guides offer valuable insight into your child's online behavior and can help aid in communications between parents and children. It is important to include clear reporting mechanisms in print and online to help victims and bystanders quickly report cyberbullying incidents. A simple way to catch cyberbullying incidents is to print clear steps in common school conversation places and messages such as "Step

Up, Speak Out!" You can also add physical reminders to report in bathrooms, report cards, etc. Technology can also ensure children are "caught" being good (Peprah et al., 2023; Wu et al., 2024). Programs will provide top-rated software to end users, allowing for anonymous reporting long time.

It will also create a mechanism for school administrators who use the software to communicate with involved parties. Alerts are immediate and sent to you via email and cell phone. Applications are available for both Android and iPhone and give your students another means of reporting a problem. Parents can also get similar tools on their child's social media, where they will receive notifications regarding any changes that may be of concern. The goal of cyberbullying prevention and intervention strategies is to promote acceptance of diversity and prevent harassment and bullying; support the development of responsible digital citizenship; increase responsibility among youths with regard to their role in preventing and reporting bullying and harassment; create cohesive, safe environments for adolescents; increase troubled youths' access to necessary resources; and hold family, school, community, and faith- and business-based organizations equally responsible in encouraging and maintaining a safe environment for children (Alrawashdeh et al., 2024; Kee et al., 2024; Samee et al., 2023). It is a parent's job to educate their children on what is acceptable behavior, and group empowerment activities could serve this purpose.

4.1. Educational Programs

Given the multifaceted challenges that educators face as new digital technologies and social networking sites increase, there is a recognition that bullying and teasing behaviors adapted to digital forms should be preempted and that young people should be supported in understanding new responsibilities associated with communication technologies and networks. In recent years, diverse educational curricula and programs have emerged to address bullying in schools and have had varied success in terms of improvements in student attitudes and reductions in bullying. This workshop aims to extend and share pro-social behavior in peer groups while reducing and challenging unhelpful responses and attitudes (Lin et al., 2023; Saifullah et al., 2024). The program is implemented in school-based settings within our larger research. The workshop is interactive and makes use of practical group activities and discussions designed to promote an understanding of the diverse nature of bullying and the importance of empathy and solidarity as one way to reduce bullying. Other examples of effective interventions can be found within the extensive literature. Within the educational sector, such programs are necessary and important because they embody a societal recognition of the rights of young people to a safe and secure learning environment. Such programs should be inclusive, accessible to children with diverse needs and experiences, include a creative component to engage the participants, and incorporate sustained engagement to raise and maintain levels of awareness (Neha et al., 2023; Wiederhold, 2024). Ongoing training for educators is critical to ensure that anti-bullying messages remain a priority within often competing agendas and new digital challenges.

4.2. Parental Involvement

Parents play a critical role in reducing the likelihood and impact of cyberbullying incidents. Communication is essential if parents hope to guide their children safely through their networked experiences. Making sure children know they can turn to them when they are having a hard time is important. If they share positive online friendships and experiences with their parents, this can help foster trust and open communication regarding online issues in general. The expectation that healthy communication between children and parents should exist means that unless it happens on a semi-regular basis, children will be less likely to come to their parents if they are experiencing bullying online. Parents can sometimes feel like their children belong to a world that they can barely comprehend, let alone govern (Samalo et al., 2023). However, the possibilities for parents to inform themselves and share their findings with their digital children are considerable.

Parents can inform themselves about the digital platforms that their children spend time on and understand the terms and conditions of these services. If they are not happy with the terms and conditions of a site or service, this sends a strong message to their children that they do not want them involved. When parents begin to understand these digital platforms, it becomes possible to offer guidance, explain settings to children, and make suggestions around use. Parents can have this relational approach while also exercising their responsibility to monitor their children's online activities. By making sure that this kind of active involvement is done in the right spirit, parents can respect their children's privacy while looking out for their safety (Nee et al., 2023; Sultan et al., 2023).

Parents should be given guidance by school policies on behaviors that a school may prohibit and that they should actively discourage both in their homes and in the wider community. Provide parents and other interested members of the community with instructional materials and avenues of discussion. Parents are considered partners in the safe use of digital technology, and schools collaborate with them to help create a supportive home environment for students who are victims of cyberbullying to report the behaviors to cyberbullying task force members, school staff, and law enforcement if appropriate (Malik & Dadure, 2024; Wahyuningrum et al., 2023). Much has changed since the Internet began, but the effort between schools and parents to keep children safe in a digital culture should remain a top priority. Given all of the above, in response to our survey we agreed that schools should, along with parents, be responsible for helping their students to act responsibly and demonstrate empathy for others, including on digital platforms. At all levels, but particularly in elementary and middle school, when children are forming their relationships, school staff will often partner with parents and educate them on social media. Middle and high school educators may also have significant sway to engage with parents and disseminate resources; this group has a presence within school social workers, counselors, parent clubs and organizations, teacher staff organizations, and other faculty whose job it is to interact not only with students but also with parents (Samalo et al., 2023; (Milosevic et al., 2023).

4.3. Cyberbullying Reporting Mechanisms

Digital age cyberbullying reporting mechanisms are critical because complainants are least likely to report bullying incidents to authorities. The idea behind the importance of reporting mechanisms is to encourage victims, witnesses, or any stakeholder to report an incident. In order to encourage the reporting of cyberbullying, anonymous as well as non-anonymous reporting guidelines should be established. Moreover, contact information related to where to reach out for help needs to be clearly stated (Samee et al., 2023). The complainant who comes to report an incident, for example, with allegations of being cyberbullied, would need clear information on who to speak to when a case is to be reported and how it will be reported. They may be asked a series of questions related to the incident that is about to be reported, such as when, what, consequences, and ways in which the cyberbullying has developed. They would also need to be offered support and reassure the person who is reporting the incident that the authority will deal with the alleged incident (Sultan et al., 2023; Wahyuningrum et al., 2023). They also provide the names and contact numbers relating to risks and advice groups.

5. LEGAL AND ETHICAL CONSIDERATIONS IN ADDRESSING CYBERBULLYING

The ability of a society or culture to make informed decisions and to develop ongoing education programs has a strong foundation in the legal and ethical considerations and obligations that are involved in combating this type of conflict. There are a number of legal methods a state can carry out to protect victims of cyberbullying. A limited number of countries have passed specific or broad legislation that provides legal protection from cyberbullying. Since cyberbullying is a relatively recent development, it has had little time to be addressed through specific laws. Thus, existing laws, policies, statutes, and common law that address bullying and harassment can also be used to prosecute cyber bullies (Hu et al., 2023; Samalo et al., 2023). In attempting to frame legal interpretations and leverage legal intervention, it is important to understand what cyberbullying is and how it has been defined across different legal environments. In February 2007, a recommendation was issued for a common approach to defining cyberbullying. The report established that there was a comprehensive definition of bullying, but not all member states consider cyberbullying as a kind of bullying. The report also referenced legislation that uniquely labels cyberbullying as cyber harassment. Furthermore, in a report on cyberbullying legislation, significant inconsistencies in definitions of both bullying and cyberbullying across member states were found. It was concluded in the analysis that though most of the countries do refer to the psychological effects of bullying, few mention the intentionality of the negative behavior (Kee et al., 2024; Saifullah et al., 2024).

5.1. Legislation and Regulations

Legislation and regulations in many countries exist or have been enacted recently to address the issue of cyberbullying and prosecute those who are harassed, regardless of whether they are underage or not. Thus, many of these should offer individuals some blanket protection from cyber harassment or digital aggression in online environments. Some countries have yet to formally draft legislation to address the issue of exploiting and grooming children. Law enforcement and government authorities continue to call for changes to regional, national, and international laws regarding various forms of child exploitation, extortion, and grooming. Many regional laws are not updated frequently to reflect or address the rapid changes and trends online (Masatcıoğlu & Öksüz, 2024). Despite efforts to enact and create laws intended to protect individuals from online harassment and violence[24], there is widespread agreement in the research that the majority of victims will not take legal action or report incidents. In recent years, several pieces of legislation have been proposed or enacted that do not require the victim to prove that the violence or harassment has caused them significant emotional distress or fear. Progress is being made in having restraining orders expanded to e-safety orders that restrict criminal harassers from going online (Wu et al., 2024). Future laws should identify the problem rather than have various changes and measures in isolated laws. Modern regulations must continue to reflect advanced technology and social trends. Refreshing and creating new legislation is critical when understanding that the Internet[25] is both a global and technological tool. Since each country defines bullying differently, it would be beneficial in reducing and addressing online peer aggression if the definition were agreed upon and universally enacted. More dialogues are needed to find a balance (Hu et al., 2023).

5.2. Privacy Concerns

The victims of cyberbullying have a right to privacy, just as the bullies do. Any policy that encourages a school or online provider to "uncover" the victims and expose the harmful behavior that led to the report is intrusive. Victims of cyberbullying are embarrassed and reluctant to tell or report their experience for fear of retaliation. Cyberbullies threaten their victims not to tell anyone about the harassment. This quiet refusal to report controversial issues is harmful and breeds contempt and demoralization, souring relationships (Neha et al., 2023). Telling or reporting allegations in confidence and with any expectation that the issue will lead to therapeutic methods and not a mandatory expulsion or removal of one or all parties involved is the answer. Occasionally, by "fear," the reporting victim might decide to inform a trusted friend, guardian, parent, or educator and should not be questioned by a teacher on those occasions because it would open the door for the teenager to be reprimanded once the educator has all of the facts. One deterrent in reporting any trending issue of interest is the fear of recrimination from those in charge. Schools and online service providers need to have and control a counterbalance and have the same opportunity to preserve the privacy rights of all, either bullied or the alleged bully in the "classroom" and protect (Orelaja et al., 2024). Then, at the right time, report to those having authority.

5.3. Responsibility of Online Platforms

As emphasized, emphasis is also on the responsibilities of the new age online platforms. These platforms promote interconnectedness, but they have a documented negative role in inciting and promoting cyberbullying, thus providing access to spread its negative effects in society. There is a great urgency for development by online platforms. The staff of these online platforms is consistently adapting and linking with other schools to combat the effects of cyberbullying. In addition, online platforms should develop tools and support systems that link parents with children. To achieve the above, an effective reporting mechanism should also be made available (Malik & Dadure, 2024). The fact that the posting requires the determination of the wrongness of the harassment means it is the ethical responsibility of the online platform to establish guidelines, preferably in consultation with an expert forum, to guide both the respondent and the poster in their postings and guidance, respectively. Online platforms must enforce such guidelines so that irresponsible posters can be held accountable (Sultan et al., 2023). The electronic medium has great value in helping the proprietors monitor and censor material placed on the forum. Thus, proactive measures, especially in the prevention of cyberbullying and moderator oversight of the postings, should be implemented by the online platform.

Parents also advocate that social media and other relevant aspects be educated on the topic of digital citizenship[26], the protection of children on the internet, and the dangers that the internet poses (Milosevic et al., 2023).

If the forum provider chooses not to enforce any such monitoring, the forum provider must bear the negative consequences in legal liability for any resultant breach of duty. Negligent delay in enforcement on the part of the provider is also relevant. Even where it is impossible to trace the persons who make such comments, it is the ethical responsibility of the online holder of such media to take certain responsibility. It should endeavor to educate the public that making threats or causing annoyance to a person through harsh means, including mobile text or smartphone, using networks of computers is unethical. Some people may think it is particularly exciting to be able to transmit messages in a way that is beyond the grasp of the ordinary (Badawi, 2024; Mantey et al., 2023). It is also important that the holders of sophisticated media respond promptly to tireless requests for support from law enforcement officers. For as long as hate messages are simply left up on a site after they are reported but no action is taken, they are treated as perfectly lawful. To counteract the hate message problem, a user on the site should also keep evidence of such messages that have been reported to the website operators or the provider. Users should, in publication, have cyber defamation and cyber-counter defamation[27]. This ought to stimulate websites to take action and clean out some of the users who are engaged in cyber-hate messaging. A partnership between users and regulatory bodies that monitor the hate messages has been an impetus for the site owner or publisher to consider the request for such jurisdiction (Nagata et al., 2023). The value of overwhelming a jurisdiction with the number of requests that have no probable likelihood of success through non-compliance to the site holder is as yet untested.

6. CONCLUSION

The emergent "Digital Age" has facilitated the proliferation of newly created bullying behaviors enacted through digital means, such as text, instant messaging, social media, images, video, telephone, and gaming platforms. Both quantitative and qualitative approaches can be utilized to collect data on cyberbullying, allowing for the generation of large, statistically reliable data sets regarding the types, frequency, and demographics of individuals experiencing bullying online or perfected through digital means, a matter of real concern with many professing to be victims of digital bullying, including older people. Caution should be noted, however, regarding the validity of any data derived using face-to-face interviews with older respondents, as they may be less comfortable admitting to exposure to digital hostility and ensuring face-to-face interviews are not causing psychological distress during interviews. Quantitative research identifies the prevalence of the problem within particular social groups while also revealing insight into what constitutes bullying and the motivations for engaging in such activities. From this quantitative perspective, potential influences for engaging in digital bullying have been suggested to range from gender to low empathy and high levels of psychopathology[28], knowledge regarding deterring opportunities for cyberbullying perpetrators, poor social integration, adverse childhood events, school and home settings, and even personality traits that are more likely to attract victimization. Conversely, it is debatable how much can be gleaned from statistics alone without context. If this fact is considered, a deeper, more individualistic level of cyberbullying must be researched in order to understand what it feels like from a cold screen fully. For this rigorous debate, it is worth considering which method is the most legitimate according to positivist and interpretivist aims and methods. If you were to take a quantitative approach, a researcher might associate from looking at statistics that a certain category of people is more likely to be cyberbullied; however, without speaking to these young women and young people, there is no deeper understanding of the potential underlying causes of the data, and therefore the data is too deterministic. Similarly, without such context, a high number of victims does not take into account the severity and impacts of such incidents, leaving such data weak as there would be very ethical implications in the assumption of the severity of these incidents.

REFERENCES

Alrawashdeh, M. N., Alsawalqa, R. O., Alnajdawi, A., Aljboor, R., AlTwahya, F., & Ibrahim, A. M. (2024). Workplace cyberbullying and social capital among Jordanian university academic staff: A cross-sectional study. *Humanities & Social Sciences Communications*, 11(1), 334. Advance online publication. DOI: 10.1057/s41599-024-02805-z

Badawi, S. (2024). Deep Learning-Based Cyberbullying Detection in Kurdish Language. *The Computer Journal*, 67(7), 2548–2558. Advance online publication. DOI: 10.1093/comjnl/bxae024

Gavini Sreelatha, C. Kishor Kumar Reddy, Marlia Mohd Hanafiah, R. Madana-Mohana, (2024). Hybrid Electro search beetle optimization based task scheduling and game theory SOA based resource allocation in multi cloud computing. *Wiley Journal of Software: Practice and Experience.* DOI: 10.1093/comjnl/bxae024

Hu, Y., Clancy, E. M., & Klettke, B. (2023). Understanding the Vicious Cycle: Relationships between Nonconsensual Sexting Behaviours and Cyberbullying Perpetration. *Sexes*, 4(1), 155–166. Advance online publication. DOI: 10.3390/sexes4010013

Jun, Y., Craig, A., Shafik, W., & Sharif, L. (2021). Artificial Intelligence Application in Cybersecurity and Cyberdefense. In *Wireless Communications and Mobile Computing* (Vol. 2021). DOI: 10.1155/2021/3329581

Kalinaki, K., Shafik, W., Namuwaya, S., & Namuwaya, S. (2024). Perspectives, applications, challenges, and future trends of IoT-based logistics. In *Navigating Cyber Threats and Cybersecurity in the Logistics Industry*. DOI: 10.4018/979-8-3693-3816-2.ch005

Kee, D. M. H., Anwar, A., & Vranjes, I. (2024). Cyberbullying victimization and suicide ideation: The mediating role of psychological distress among Malaysian youth. *Computers in Human Behavior*, 150, 108000. Advance online publication. DOI: 10.1016/j.chb.2023.108000

Kishor Kumar Reddy,, Advaitha Daduvy, R Madana Mohana, Basem Assiri, Mohammed Shauib, Sadaf Alam and Abdullah Sheneamer (2024c), "Enhancing Precision Agriculture and Land Cover Classification: A Self –Attention 3D Convolutional Neural Network Approach for Hyperspectral Image Analysis, IEEE Access. DOI: 10.1016/j.chb.2023.108000

Kishor Kumar Reddy, C, Aarti Rangarajan, Deepti Rangarajan, Mohammed Shuaib, Fathe Jeribi and Shadab Alam, (2024a). “A Transfer Learning Approach: Early Prediction of Alzheimer’s Disease on US Healthy Aging Dataset,” *MDPI Mathematics*. DOI: 10.1016/j.chb.2023.108000

Kishor Kumar Reddy, C, Ritika Badam, Shauib Ahmed, (2024b). IoT Driven Accessibility:A Refreshable OCR-Braille Solution for Visually Impaired and Deaf-Blind Users through WSN. *JETECH Elsevier*, DOI: 10.1016/j.chb.2023.108000

Lin, H. T., Tai, Y. M., & Gau, S. S. F. (2023). Autistic Traits and Cyberbullying Involvement Mediated by Psychopathologies and School Functions in a Nationally Representative Child Sample. *Cyberpsychology, Behavior, and Social Networking*, 26(9), 706–716. Advance online publication. DOI: 10.1089/cyber.2022.0309 PMID: 37477877

Malik, A., & Dadure, P. (2024). *Cyberbullying in the Digital Age*. DOI: 10.1016/j.chb.2023.108000

Mantey, D. S., Yockey, R. A., & Springer, A. E. (2023). Digital screen time and suicidality during high school: How important is cyberbullying? A mediation analysis using the youth risk behavioral surveillance survey, 2011–2019. *Preventive Medicine*, 166, 107330. Advance online publication. DOI: 10.1016/j.ypmed.2022.107330 PMID: 36334685

Masatcıoğlu, G., & Öksüz, Y. E. (2024). *Examination of the relationship between peer bullying and cyber violence in university students. JOURNAL OF AWARENESS, 9*. Special Issue/Özel Sayı., DOI: 10.26809/joa.2262

Milosevic, T., Verma, K., Carter, M., Vigil, S., Laffan, D., Davis, B., & O’Higgins Norman, J. (2023). Effectiveness of Artificial Intelligence–Based Cyberbullying Interventions From Youth Perspective. *Social Media + Society*, 9(1), 20563051221147325. Advance online publication. DOI: 10.1177/20563051221147325

Nagata, J. M., Yang, J. H., Singh, G., Kiss, O., Ganson, K. T., Testa, A., Jackson, D. B., & Baker, F. C. (2023). Cyberbullying and Sleep Disturbance Among Early Adolescents in the U.S. *Academic Pediatrics*, 23(6), 1220–1225. Advance online publication. DOI: 10.1016/j.acap.2022.12.007 PMID: 36581100

Nee, C. N., Samsudin, N., Chuan, H. M., Bin Mohd Ridzuan, M. I., Boon, O. P., Binti Mohamad, A. M., & Scheithauer, H. (2023). The digital defence against cyberbullying: A systematic review of tech-based approaches. *Cogent Education*, 10(2), 2288492. Advance online publication. DOI: 10.1080/2331186X.2023.2288492

Neha, M. V., Muhammad, S., Indu, V., & Thampi, S. M. (2023). Detection and Prevention of Cyberbullying in Social Media Using Cognitive Computational Analysis. In *Combatting Cyberbullying in Digital Media with Artificial Intelligence*. DOI: 10.1201/9781003393061-3

Orelaja, A., Ejiofor, C., Sarpong, S., Imakuh, S., Bassey, C., Opara, I., Tettey, J. N. A., & Akinola, O. (2024). Attribute-specific Cyberbullying Detection Using Artificial Intelligence. *Journal of Electronic & Information Systems*, 6(1), 10–21. Advance online publication. DOI: 10.30564/jeis.v6i1.6206

Peprah, P., Oduro, M. S., Okwei, R., Adu, C., Asiamah-Asare, B. Y., & Agyemang-Duah, W. (2023). Cyberbullying victimization and suicidal ideation among in-school adolescents in three countries: Implications for prevention and intervention. *BMC Psychiatry*, 23(1), 944. Advance online publication. DOI: 10.1186/s12888-023-05268-9 PMID: 38098109

Pericherla, S., & Ilavarasan, E. (2024). Overcoming the Challenge of Cyberbullying Detection in Images: A Deep Learning Approach with Image Captioning and OCR Integration. *International Journal of Computing and Digital Systems*, 15(1), 393–401. Advance online publication. DOI: 10.12785/ijcds/150130

Reddy, Kishor Kumar,, Reddy, Palakurthi Anaghaa, Janapati, Himaja, Assiri, Basem, Shauib, Mohammed, Alam, Sadaf, & Sheneamer, Abdullah. (2024d). A Fine Tuned Vision Transformer (FTVT)based Enhanced Multi-Class Brain Tumor Classification using MRI Scan Imagery. *Frontiers in Oncology Cancer Imaging and Image-directed Interventions*. DOI: 10.1016/j.chb.2023.108000

Saifullah, K., Khan, M. I., Jamal, S., & Sarker, I. H. (2024). Cyberbullying Text Identification: A Deep Learning and Transformer-based Language Modeling Approach. *EAI Endorsed Transactions on Industrial Networks and Intelligent Systems*, 11(1). Advance online publication. DOI: 10.4108/eetinis.v11i1.4703

Salmerón Ruiz, M. A. (2023). Salud digital y ciberacoso. *Pediatria Integral, 27*(4). DOI: 10.1016/j.chb.2023.108000

Samalo, D., Martin, R., & Utama, D. N. (2023). Improved Model for Identifying the Cyberbullying Based on Tweets of Twitter. *Informatica (Slovenia)*, 47(6). Advance online publication. DOI: 10.31449/inf.v47i6.4534

Samee, N. A., Khan, U., Khan, S., Jamjoom, M. M., Sharif, M., & Kim, D. H. (2023). Safeguarding Online Spaces: A Powerful Fusion of Federated Learning, Word Embeddings, and Emotional Features for Cyberbullying Detection. *IEEE Access : Practical Innovations, Open Solutions*, 11, 124524–124541. Advance online publication. DOI: 10.1109/ACCESS.2023.3329347

Shafik, W. (2023a). *A Comprehensive Cybersecurity Framework for Present and Future Global Information Technology Organizations*. DOI: 10.1109/ACCESS.2023.3329347

Shafik, W. (2023b). Cyber security perspectives in public spaces: Drone case study. In *Handbook of Research on Cybersecurity Risk in Contemporary Business Systems*. DOI: 10.4018/978-1-6684-7207-1.ch004

Shafik, W. (2023c). Predicting Future Cybercrime Trends in the Metaverse Era. In *Forecasting cyber crimes in the age of the metaverse* (pp. 78–113). IGI Global., DOI: 10.4018/979-8-3693-0220-0.ch005

Shafik, W. (2024a). Agile Security Strategies. In *Smart and Agile Cybersecurity for IoT and IIoT Environments* (pp. 82–101). IGI Global., DOI: 10.4018/979-8-3693-3451-5.ch004

Shafik, W. (2024b). Artificial intelligence and Blockchain technology enabling cybersecurity in telehealth systems. In *Artificial Intelligence and Blockchain Technology in Modern Telehealth Systems*. DOI: 10.1049/PBHE061E_ch11

Shafik, W. (2024c). Cyber Attacker Profiling and Cyberbullying Overview. In *Cyber Space and Outer Space Security* (pp. 125–149). River Publishers., DOI: 10.1201/9781003558118-5

Shafik, W. (2024d). Dissecting the Role of Women in Cybersecurity and Information Technology: A Medical Perspective. In *Next-Generation Cybersecurity: AI, ML, and Blockchain* (pp. 325–350). Springer. DOI: 10.1007/978-981-97-1249-6_15

Shafik, W. (2024e). Towards Trustworthy and Explainable AI Educational Systems. In Singh, T., Dutta, S., Vyas, S., & Rocha, Á. (Eds.), *Explainable AI for Education: Recent Trends and Challenges. Information Systems Engineering and Management* (Vol. 19). Springer., DOI: 10.1007/978-3-031-72410-7_2

Shafik, W., & Khang, A. (2024). Cybersecurity Techniques in Talent Management and Human Capital Management Systems. In *AI-Oriented Competency Framework for Talent Management in the Digital Economy* (pp. 353–375). CRC Press., DOI: 10.1201/9781003440901-22

Shafik, W., Tufail, A., Apong, R. A. A. H. M., & Balasubramaniam, S. (2024). Future Directions in Cybersecurity, Digital Forensics and Biometric Systems. In *AI Based Advancements in Biometrics and its Applications* (pp. 238–263). CRC Press., DOI: 10.1201/9781032702377-13

Sultan, D., Toktarova, A., Zhumadillayeva, A., Aldeshov, S., Mussiraliyeva, S., Beissenova, G., Tursynbayev, A., Baenova, G., & Imanbayeva, A. (2023). Cyberbullying-related Hate Speech Detection Using Shallow-to-deep Learning. *Computers, Materials & Continua*, 74(1), 2115–2131. Advance online publication. DOI: 10.32604/cmc.2023.032993

Wahyuningrum, S. S., Rohmawati, L., Mustaqim, W., Qalban, A. A., & Heriyanto, Y. (2023). Fenomena Cyberbullying pada Kalangan Mahasiswa. *Assertive: Islamic Counseling Journal*, 2(1), 37–48. Advance online publication. DOI: 10.24090/j.assertive.v2i01.8296

Wiederhold, B. K. (2024). The Dark Side of the Digital Age: How to Address Cyberbullying among Adolescents. [editorial]. *Cyberpsychology, Behavior, and Social Networking*, 27(3), 169–171. Advance online publication. DOI: 10.1089/cyber.2024.29309.editorial PMID: 38364097

Wu, X., Zhang, L., & Luo, H. (2024). Witnessing family violence and adolescent cyberbullying perpetration: A longitudinal moderated mediation model involving anger dysregulation and teacher support. *Child Abuse & Neglect*, 152, 106753. Advance online publication. DOI: 10.1016/j.chiabu.2024.106753 PMID: 38547563

Zhao, L., Zhu, D., Shafik, W., Matinkhah, S. M., Ahmad, Z., Sharif, L., & Craig, A. (2022). Artificial intelligence analysis in cyber domain: A review. *International Journal of Distributed Sensor Networks*, 18(4). Advance online publication. DOI: 10.1177/15501329221084882

ENDNOTES

1 https://www.stopbullying.gov/cyberbullying/what-is-it

2 https://sherloc.unodc.org/cld/zh/education/tertiary/cybercrime/module-12/key-issues/cyberstalking-and-cyberharassment.html

3 https://www.esafety.gov.au/key-topics/staying-safe/cyberstalking

4 https://dzone.com/articles/the-digital-age-the-era-we-all-are-living-in-and-d

5 https://en.wikipedia.org/wiki/List_of_social_platforms_with_at_least_100_million_active_users

6 https://en.wikipedia.org/wiki/Histrionic_personality_disorder

7 https://explodingtopics.com/blog/messaging-apps-stats

[8] https://en.wikipedia.org/wiki/Sextortion

[9] https://en.wikipedia.org/wiki/Catfishing

[10] https://www.fortinet.com/resources/cyberglossary/doxing

[11] https://taylorstudies.com/frapping/

[12] https://en.wikipedia.org/wiki/Cyberstalking

[13] https://edu.gcfglobal.org/en/thenow/what-is-trolling/1/

[14] https://ipredator.co/examples-of-cyberbullying

[15] https://www.ibm.com/docs/en/netezza?topic=security-masquerading

[16] https://en.wikipedia.org/wiki/Outing

[17] https://en.wikipedia.org/wiki/Exclusion

[18] https://en.wikipedia.org/wiki/Flaming

[19] https://en.wikipedia.org/wiki/Harassment

[20] https://www.imperva.com/learn/ddos/denial-of-service/

[21] https://gdpr-info.eu/

[22] https://www.adfsolutions.com/news/why-computer-forensics-software-is-vital-to-digital-evidence-discovery?

[23] https://www.kaspersky.com/resource-center/threats/ransomware-wannacry

[24] https://www.undrr.org/understanding-disaster-risk/terminology/hips/so0006

[25] https://www.techtarget.com/whatis/definition/Internet

[26] https://www.learning.com/blog/what-is-digital-citizenship/

[27] https://en.wikipedia.org/wiki/Defamation

[28] https://en.wikipedia.org/wiki/Psychopathology

Chapter 2
Pushing the Limits of Creativity:
A Brief Study of GenAI

Semra Erpolat Taşabat
https://orcid.org/0000-0001-6845-8278
Mimar Sinan Fine Art University, Turkey

Tayfun Özçay
https://orcid.org/0000-0003-0011-7877
Borusan Cat, Turkey

ABSTRACT

Generative Artificial Intelligence (GenAI) refers to Artificial Intelligent (AI) systems with human-like creativity and productivity capabilities. The most important difference between traditional AI and GenAI systems, which generally use algorithms and models designed to perform a specific task, is that GenAI systems can create new and original content. GenAI, which emerged as a product of technology and creativity and is a field that develops day by day, has been an important development that arouses interest and curiosity, as well as anxiety and uncertainty, for all segments of society with what it has done and what it can do in the future. GenAI's rapid development has begun to reshape business and living spaces by bringing admirable innovations. In this study, the past, present, and future of GenAI will be discussed and the landscape, applications, and tools of GenAI will be emphasized. In this way, it will be possible to understand this technological trend that will shape the future and help follow new developments and digital transformation.

DOI: 10.4018/979-8-3373-0543-1.ch002

1. INTRODUCTION

GenAI is a class of AI systems that can generate text, images, audio, video, and synthetic data, among many other types of content. Unlike the more traditional AI, which can only perform a task for which it has been specifically designed, GenAI systems can create new, original content indistinguishable from human creativity. This innovation has drastically transformed industries, businesses, and daily life. The term might be modern, but as a concept, GenAI had first taken root in the 1960s and advanced up to the present times with quite a few technological leaps along the way.

The first major development to attract widespread attention in GenAI was the creation of chatbots in the 1960s. These very early AI systems were simple, rudimentary, and designed for simulating conversation in responding to basic prompts. A very early example is that of ELIZA, which emulated human conversation through pattern-matching techniques (Weizenbaum, 1966). The whole conversation was very limited, and far from intelligent-however, it marked the dawn of AI systems interacting with their human users in conversational style. Further interest in AI developed, as it would be used to build intelligent systems, simulating human-like interactions sparked, which would eventually help create more sophisticated and creative systems. It was not until the early 21st century, however, that the true creative power of GenAI began to be realized with the emergence of Generative Adversarial Networks (GANs).

The invention of GANs in 2014 by Ian Goodfellow and colleagues marked a critical turn for GenAI. For the very first time, it had become possible for machines to create something new-a new piece of content which was realistic. The GAN framework is comprised of two Neural Networks (NNs): the generator and the discriminator. The generator creates data, such as images, while the discriminator evaluates whether the generated data is real or fake. Through this adversarial process, the generator improves its ability to create highly realistic content that becomes increasingly indistinguishable from real-world data (Goodfellow et al., 2014). This allowed the GANs to unleash a creative power that hitherto allowed AI to create photorealistic images, art, and even videos. That opened more than just perspectives for AI in the entertainment and gaming industries but also potential areas of application for GenAI, such as fashion design, advertising, and architecture.

While GANs provided a major leap in creative AI applications, transformers and Large Language Models (LLMs) brought about a new revolution in GenAI. First proposed by Vaswani et al. in 2017, the transformer architecture resolved many of the limitations inherent in earlier models of Machine Learning (ML). Until the arrival of transformers, most of the models adopted sequential processing of data; this hindered their capability for understanding long-range dependencies within text. The introduction of the attention mechanism in transformers enabled the AI systems to process whole data sets at once, recognizing their relationships between words, sentences, or even whole paragraphs, not just between nearby words (Vaswani et al., 2017). This breakthrough in processing had allowed transformers to achieve unmatched levels of accuracy in tasks related to Natural Language Processing (NLP), such as language translation, summarization, and text generation. These advances gave way to the emergence of LLMs, which are pre-trained on very large datasets of text. A notable example is the GPT series, (Generative Pre-trained Transformers), by OpenAI. For instance, the GPT-3 model is able to write coherent essays, answer questions, generate code, and even compose poetry (Brown et al., 2020). LLMs have pushed the creative envelope of GenAI way beyond text generation. They are capable of generating complete narratives, producing music, generating realistic images, and even simulating real-time conversations. The ability to generate human-like text brought AI-driven chatbots, virtual assistants, and even AI tools that assist with creative writing.

The most exciting innovation in GenAI has been the rise of multimodal AI, which enables models to create and analyze different types of media -text, images, audio, and video-simultaneously. This is a feature well characterized by models such as DALL-E, developed by OpenAI, which can generate highly detailed images from textual descriptions. For instance, if a user provides the prompt, "A two-story house shaped like a shoe" the model will create an image that matches this description, down to the smallest details (Ramesh et al., 2021). Similarly, it enables the CLIP model of AI systems to view images and independently create textual captions. This, along with many recent developments in multimodal AI, has huge implications for industries such as advertising, design, entertainment, and education. Companies using GenAI tools can generate customized, dynamic ad copy along with visual content for various audiences. In the industry of entertainment, videos and animations, and even feature-length films, created by using AI, are getting much more sophisticated.

While the improvements in GenAI have been groundbreaking, a variety of challenges still surround the technology. Among the main ones is the issue of accuracy regarding tasks that require factual correctness. The early generations of models in GenAI mostly produced nonsensical or factually incorrect results. For instance, language models can generate text that is grammatically perfect but lacks logical coherence or is entirely fabricated in terms of facts and information (Bender et al., 2021). The other concern is that of bias: the fact that AI models, while training on data gathered from the internet, might incidentally learn biased information, which subsequently biases their generated content. This perspective is considered to be ominous in cases where AI systems function in hiring, law enforcement, or healthcare since biased AI decisions have the capacity to favor social inequalities (Binns, 2018). Moreover, serious questions about their ethics in sensitive contexts arise because these systems themselves are trained with data from human biases.

Another important challenge is the hallucination phenomenon of GenAI. Sometimes, AI models utter completely fabricated information, also known as "hallucinations," which may sound plausible but are completely false. This can be a serious problem in domains that require high accuracy, such as health or journalism, and could weaken trust in AI technologies if left unaddressed (Marcus & Davis, 2020). Last but not least, ethical issues about deepfakes, disinformation, and manipulation of content are on the rise. As GenAI improves at creating realistic content, it becomes easier to fabricate media that may fool audiences. The recent development of deepfakes-hyper-real videos and images that manipulate real people's likenesses-has raised concerns about privacy, security, and the possibility of malicious uses (Chesney & Citron, 2019).

With all these challenges, GenAI is already making a difference in many industries today. In health, AI models are being used in creating synthetic medical data, medical image analysis, and assisting doctors in designing personalized treatment. For instance, AI-based systems can examine X-rays and MRIs to spot anomalies, thus helping to diagnose conditions that could be overlooked by doctors (Esteva et al., 2019). In marketing and advertising, these systems are changing the game in how content is created for personalized ads, blog posts, and social media content. Additionally, AI tools are driving up customer engagement by providing companies with personalized recommendations and dynamic pricing models (Brynjolfsson & McAfee, 2014). In education, GenAI is enabling personalized learning experiences. AI-powered platforms can generate customized learning materials, such as practice exercises and quizzes, based on students' individual learning needs. These systems can also provide real-time feedback, helping students improve their understanding of complex subjects (Luckin et al., 2016). GenAI is also making inroads into security, with AI models currently being used for anomaly detection, fraud prevention, and cybersecurity monitoring. Capable of analyzing huge volumes of data in real time, the GenAI systems can identify potential threats far quicker and more effectively than human analysts could (He et al., 2020).

With further development, the changes that GenAI can bring to industries and lifestyles are immense. We might see even more powerful multimodal AI systems that integrate text, images, and video generation seamlessly, allowing users to create dynamic, interactive content. Future models of GenAI can also be emotionally more intelligent and offer more personalized and empathetic interactions with users. But it is important, as policymakers, researchers, and industry leaders improve these technologies, they also take up the challenge of ethical issues with GenAI. By developing more robust frameworks for ensuring accuracy, fairness, and transparency, we can maximize the benefits of GenAI while minimizing its risks.

2. DEVELOPMENT PROCESS OF GenAI

GenAI is the final point that technology has reached after the processes of AI, ML and Deep Learning (DL). Understanding the basic concepts and distinctions in GenAI, which is a rapidly developing field of technology, will guide the creation of future technologies.

In order to understand the development of GenAI in the literature and its similarities and differences with other AI concepts, it is important to understand the process shown in Figure 1 (Goodfellow et al., 2016; Janiesch et al., 2021; Banh & Strobel, 2023).

Figure 1. GenAI and other AI concepts

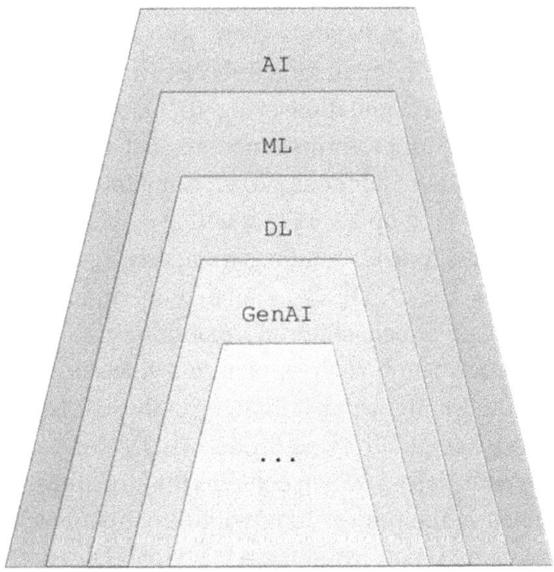

The process starts with AI which includes the concepts of Expert Systems (ESs), Knowledge-Based Systems (KBSs), etc., and progresses to Support Vector Machines (SVMs), Decision Trees (DTs), k-Nearest Neighbors (k-NNs), etc. AI is considered an umbrella term that can perform various tasks that require human intelligence, such as understanding natural language, recognizing patterns, making decisions and learning from experiences, thanks to the different computational algorithms it contains (Castelvecchi, 2016; Winston, 1993). The first rule-based AI systems were ESs and KBSs and aimed to support decision makers in the decision-making process (Harmon, 1985; Banh & Strobel, 2023).

ML is a subfield of AI and bargains with the improvement of calculations that can illuminate assignments independently through presentation to information without being modified (Brynjolfsson & Mitchell, 2017). Within the field of ML, there are various learning approaches based on the nature of the information and the required result: Supervised, unsupervised, semi-supervised, and reinforcement. Supervised learning is used to discover hidden structures or patterns within labeled data, while unsupervised learning helps to discover hidden structures or patterns within unlabeled data. Semi-supervised learning can be expressed as a hybrid structure of supervised and unsupervised learning. In reinforcement learning, the aim is to learn to make the most appropriate decision by interacting with an environment and to maximize cumulative rewards over time through trial and error (Kühl et al., 2022). ML including algorithms; NNs, Convolutional Neural Networks (CNNs), etc.

DL is a more advanced subset of ML and is used to model complex data representations and analyze data in large data sets with the help of Artificial Neural Networks (ANN), which are computational models inspired by the structure and function of the human brain (Goodfellow et al., 2016), consisting of layers of interconnected artificial neurons. It performs functions such as automatically detecting correlations and patterns (Janiesch et al., 2021; Samtani et al., 2023). In DL, NN comprises of different covered up layers in a settled engineering to memorize progressive include representations from information, driving to progressed execution on different assignments. Hence, DL can prepare high-dimensional information in different spaces, from one-dimensional information such as signals and writings to multidimensional information such as pictures, video or sound (LeCun et al., 2015). DL, which includes algorithms, and currently LLMs, GANs, Variational AutoEncoders (VAEs), Latent Diffusion Models (LDMs) etc.

The process ends with GenAI, which contains the structures. Undoubtedly, new developments expected in the future along with developing technology will form the sub-processes of GenAI. Following the AI, ML and DL approaches, which are described as “Discriminative Models (DMs)”, progress has been made towards “Generative Models (GMs)” with the developing technology. Computers, which cannot yet perceive data and information like humans, need to benefit from mathematics, algorithms and data pipelines in order to make meaningful inferences from raw data. Nowadays, data production has reached gigantic dimensions, increasing day by day. It is possible to produce superior technologies using this huge amount of data by either developing new algorithms or scaling up existing algorithms. Calculus, probability, statistics, etc. branches form the backbone of these algorithms or models. It is generally divided into two: Discriminative and generative.

DMs are also called “conditional models” that are often used for supervised ML. They perform functions such as separating data into different classes, learning bounds using probability estimates and maximum likelihood. They are little or not affected by outliers. Commonly used DMs are Logistic Regression (LR), SVMs, Decision Trees (DTs), NNs, k-Nearest Neighbors (k-NN), Conditional Random Field (CRF), Random Forest (RF), etc. can be sorted.

GMs are used to generate new data points and are often effective in unsupervised ML problems. The only disadvantage of GMs compared to DMs is that they are prone to outliers. Also, the math GMs use is very intuitive. The method is not direct as in DMs. To calculate P(Y|X), it first estimates the prior probability P(Y) and the conditional probability (likelihood probability) P(X|Y) from the data provided. Commonly used GMs are Bayesian Network (BN), Autoregressive Model (AM), Generative Adversarial Network (GAN), Naive Bayes (NB), Markov Random Field (MRF), Hidden Markov Model (HMM), Latent Dirichlet Allocation (LDA), etc. can be sorted.

DMs and GMs differ in terms of their working principles and results. The differences between these two models are visually expressed in Figure 2 (Murfy & Thomas, 2023) and discussed in general terms in Table 1.

Figure 2. DMs vs. GMs

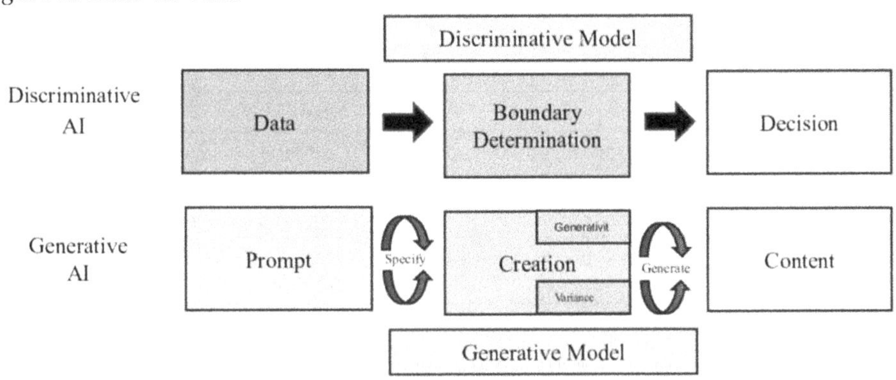

Table 1. Comparison of DMs and GMs

Topic	DMS	GMs
Procedural differences	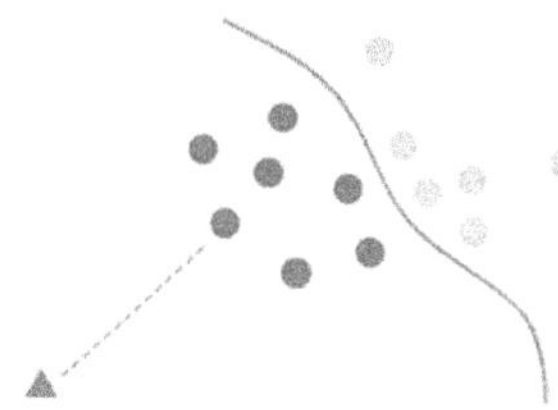	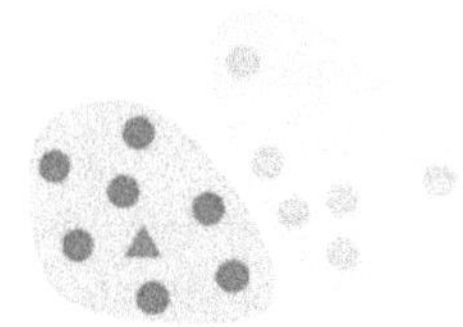
Purpose	Learn the boundaries between classes for classification or prediction tasks	Learn the probability distribution of the data to generate new samples
Type of Learning	Supervised	Unsupervised, Supervised
Direction	Model the conditional probability P(Y)	Model the joint probability P(X,Y) of inputs X and outputs Y
Training Procedure	Discriminative training like Maximum Conditional Likelihood	Maximum Likelihood Estimation or Bayesian methods
Assumptions	Make no assumptions about data distribution	Make assumptions about data distribution
Probabilistic	Can be make probabilistic with calibration	Inherently probabilistic
Missing Data	Requires specific handling of missing data	Can handle missing data naturally through probabilistic imputation
Outliers	Can be robust to outliers	Sensitive to outliers
Inference	Cannot generate samples only make predictions	Can generate samples after training
Complexity	Relatively simpler models	Generally, more complex models
Example Models	LR, SVMs, NNs (for classification)	NB, Gaussian Mixture Models, HMMs, GANs

Deep Generative Models (DGMs), which emerge as a class of DL models and are fed by developments in DL techniques, have the ability to create new content based on existing data and create various new opportunities for AI applications (Lehmann & Buschek, 2020; Tomczak, 2022). DGMs are trained to understand complex data distributions and are used to obtain outputs that closely resemble real-world data. The purpose of using statistical techniques in training DGMs is to learn the high-dimensional probability distributions of a finite training data set and to create new, similar examples that resemble the basic training data class (Ruthotto & Haber, 2021).

GenAI models may be different from Discriminative AI models because the semi-supervised learning method, which uses a small amount of supervised and a large amount of unsupervised data, is used in training (Kingma et al., 2014). Thanks to this approach, data is trained without the need for the difficult full labeling function of very large data sets required for GenAI models.

It is possible to discuss the DGMs that form the basis of GenAI in four groups: GANs, VAEs, Flow based models (Transformers) and Diffusion.

GANs are specifically known for generating high-quality images and thus find their applications when one needs to generate synthetic data to augment small datasets. The architecture of GANs consists of two main networks: a generator network that generates new data samples, while the other network, known as the discriminator, evaluates the authenticity of the generated samples. This adversarial process keeps going on until the generator produces data that is almost similar to real-world data. The ideal use for GANs involves applications needing high-quality and realistic results, for instance, generating images, data augmentation, and the creation of deepfakes. On the other hand, GAN may be a bit sensitive concerning training instability, hence unsuitable for those applications requiring generation of sequential data or even text.

VAEs are probabilistic models applied for generating new samples that bear a close resemblance to input data. Unlike GANs, which always try to generate sharp, realistic outputs, the VAE generates smooth and continuous outputs. They are perfectly suitable for those applications where the purpose is to generate diverse and continuous variants of data. The most common applications for VAEs are image generation, data compression, and representation learning. Probably the greatest strength of VAEs lies in their power of latent space modeling by which they can model underlying generating factors of data variation. However, VAEs tend to generate blurrier images compared to GANs, making them less ideal when high fidelity is required.

Flow-based models, such as Normalizing Flows and Transformers, are known for their ability to model complex distributions in a tractable manner. These models learn an invertible transformation from simple distributions, for example, Gaussian noise, to the usually complex distribution of data. Transformers, one such model derived from flow-based concepts, have become a game-changer for text generation since they allow the handling of long-range dependencies in sequences of text. The transformers are widely effective for tasks involving language modeling, translation, and text generation through weighing the input sequence regarding the relative importance of its parts for predicting a certain output-a mechanism called attention. The flow-based model can be quite flexible and expressive regarding the way they generate data, which again is very appropriate for tasks involving sequential or textual data. This usually comes at a very high computational cost and a great deal of resources while training on big datasets.

Diffusion models are gaining prominence in the domain of image and video synthesis where high-quality and photorealistic images can be generated. These models usually operate by progressive addition of noise to data and then reverse that process to generate new samples. Unlike GANs, which rely on the adversarial process, diffusion models generate highly detailed and diverse outputs, often of higher quality in terms of realism. They find wide use for generative art applications and have indeed outperformed GANs on some image generation tasks. However, a disadvantage with diffusion models is that they can be computationally intensive to operate, involving multiple steps of noise addition and removal. Nevertheless, they demonstrate great efficiency in yielding high-fidelity images and are therefore gaining interest as the most important means for image synthesis tasks.

While the working principles of DGMs are visually included in Figure 3 (Weng, 2021), a brief comparison of the models is made in Table 2.

Figure 3. DGMs working principles

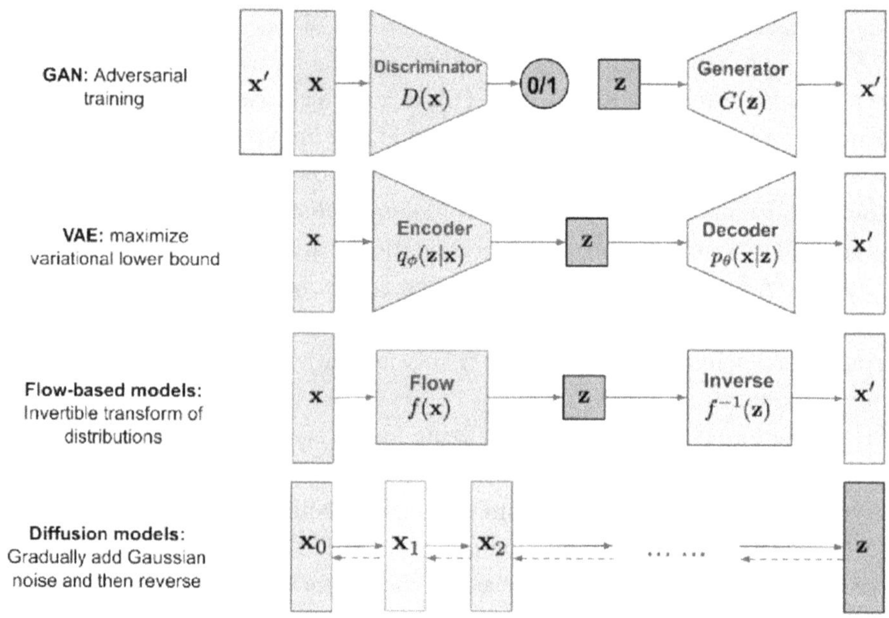

Table 2. Comparison of DGMs

GAN		VAE		Flow		Diffusion	
✓	High-Quality	✗	High-Quality	✗	High-Quality	✓	High-Quality
✓	Fast Sampling	✓	Fast Sampling	✓	Fast Sampling	✗	Fast Sampling
✗	Mode Diversity	✓	Mode Diversity	✓	Mode Diversity	✓	Mode Diversity
✗	Stable Training	✗	Stable Training	✓	Stable Training	✓	Stable Training

Each model of GenAI has different capabilities, making them suitable for various tasks and applications. The different models of GenAI are chosen based on several key factors. The most important of these are mentioned below:

1. **Application Domain:** What is the main task or domain of application? For example, diffusion models are good to go for visual content while transformers are good for text-based tasks.
2. **Data Availability:** If the available data is limited and labeled, GANs would be the best option to generate synthetic data in order to enhance the training dataset.
3. **Model Complexity:** Computational resource consideration during training and deployment; for example, more computations may be needed in order to train a diffusion model and transformer compared to some relatively simple GANs.
4. **Output Quality:** Realism or creative need of the generated content; sometimes, diffusion models guarantee extremely good results on generating good images or videos, and at times, transformers provide high-end realistic text.
5. **Real-Time Performance:** Transformer models may be preferred when the application requires real-time content generation or interaction, as in the case of chatbots or voice assistants, while diffusion models can fit better in situations with no pressure for online generation.
6. **Scalability:** Consider whether the model can scale to handle larger datasets or more complex content. While GANs and transformers scale well for their respective tasks, diffusion models may be more resource-intensive and require additional considerations for scaling.

Ultimately, the choice of model will depend on the application's needs and resources invested in model training and deployment. Considering all the above factors, an organization or developer will be able to choose the best model that suits their goals in the generation of high-quality content. The main idea of GMs, which are considered the cornerstone in the AI world, is to understand and capture the fundamental patterns or distributions within a particular dataset. This way, they can generate new data samples similar to the original data, actually recreating its structure or underlying features. The generation of synthetic data is one of the reasons GMs are one of the prime means of various domains such as image generation, text creation, and data augmentation. In addition to those described above, GMs can be categorized into two broad categories as shown in Figure 4: explicit density GMs and implicit density GMs (Roud et al., 28.11.2024).

Figure 4. GMs taxonomy

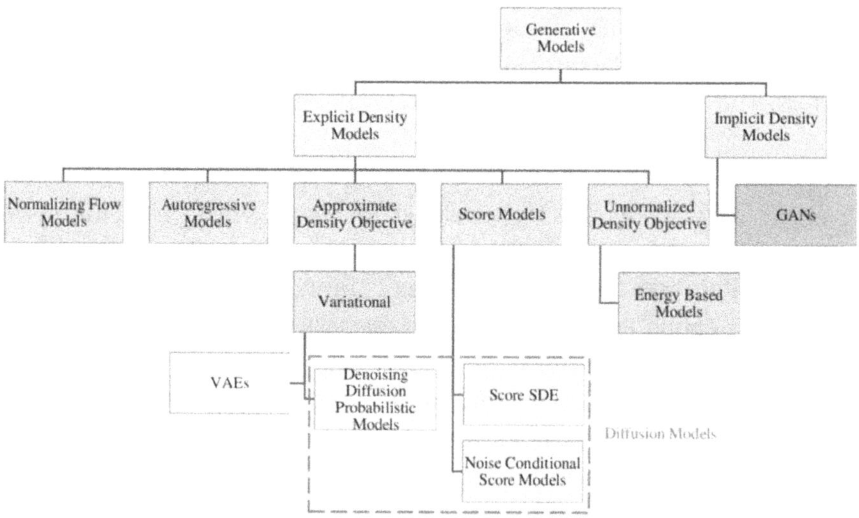

The major difference between the categories in how they model and generate new data may be observed (Goodfellow, 2017). Explicit models aim to define a probability density function of the data distribution (Ngiam et all., 2011; Xie et all. 2016; Saremi et al., 2018; Wu et al., 2021). Most of these models are usually trained to learn and represent directly the true distribution of data. Once this model learns the distribution, generating new samples is a matter of sampling from this learned density. In essence, it is viewed that the model directly estimates the likelihood of observing any given data point from the dataset. A classic example of explicit models is VAEs, which rely on a probabilistic framework. These models explicitly learn the posterior distribution of the latent variables in the data and can generate new samples by drawing from this distribution (Kingma & Welling, 2014). The VAE framework is conceptually based on an encoder-decoder setup: the encoder learns to map the input data to a latent space, while the decoder learns to map from the latent space back to the data space, thereby effectively defining the distribution of data in the latent space. Work done by Ngiam et al. (2011) on restricted Boltzmann machines and Xie et al. (2016) in Bayesian DL, constitutes two of the famous explicit models that define distributions in latent spaces for data generation. These models learn the probability distribution of the data and can generate new data points from this learned distribution. Another point is that Saremi et al. (2018) discuss the explicit model approach in DGMs where, conceptually, a model learns the distribution of a dataset through a parametrized density function. Wu et al. (2021) discuss explicit modeling approaches to overcome the challenge of capturing high-dimensional data distributions. Explicit models are normally trained using likelihood-based methods, where model parameters are optimized to maximize the likelihood of data under the model distribution. This enables the model to make probabilistic statements about the data and is particularly useful when one is interested in the exact density or probability of the data.

On the other hand, implicit models do not explicitly define a density function of the data distribution (Goodfellow et al, 2014; Radford et al, 2016; Arjovsky et al, 2017; Brock et al, 2019; Wu et al, 2021). Implicit generative modeling refers to a class of models that do not learn the probability distribution explicitly. Instead, they learn a way of generating samples similar to the data distribution by transforming random noise into realistic data points. The most well-known implicit models are the GANs introduced by Goodfellow et al., 2014. GANs do not define the density function of data explicitly but focus on generating samples that resemble the data by learning to map from noise to data.

In 2016, Radford et al. introduced Deep Convolutional Generative Adversarial Networks (DCGANs) that utilized CNNs for image generation. Their work showed that implicit models leveraging DL architectures can yield high-quality images without defining an explicit definition of data distribution. Arjovsky et al. (2017) further advanced GANs by addressing training instability through the introduction of the Wasserstein GAN (WGAN), which provides a more stable training framework by using a different loss function based on the Wasserstein distance between distributions. This work also underlined those implicit models, like GANs, generate samples by learning the transformation from noise to data, rather than learning the data distribution itself. Large-scale GANs, BigGANs, were proposed for generating high-resolution images by Brock et al. in 2019. They demonstrated that implicit models could generate highly realistic images even at large scales. This research underlined the capability of implicit models in generating high-quality visual content without any explicit density function. Wu et al. (2021) also gave very significant contributions to the implicit model space, improving efficiency and stability of GANs with novel architectures and training techniques that really push the frontier of what is achievable by an implicit model.

In Table 3 core differences, advantages, and challenges of explicit and implicit models are summarized (Goodfellow et al. 2014; Kingma et al. 2014; Salimans et al., 2016).

Table 3. Comparison of Explicit vs. Implicit Models

Aspect	Explicit Models	Implicit Models
Definition	Directly learn the data distribution (probabilistic).	Learn to generate data from random noise without modeling the distribution.
Approach	Models the probability density function.	Focuses on data generation without explicit probability estimation.
Advantages	Direct probability estimation; likelihood maximization.	High flexibility; unconstrained sample generation.
Challenges	Struggles with complex data; requires careful density function.	Difficult to evaluate performance; unstable training.
Training Method	Uses maximum likelihood estimation.	Uses adversarial or other non-likelihood-based methods (e.g., GANs).
Data Generation	Generates data by sampling from the learned distribution.	Generates data by mapping noise vectors to data samples.
Evaluation	Can directly evaluate the likelihood of generated data.	Hard to evaluate directly, often relies on proxy metrics like visual quality.
Computational Complexity	Typically more computationally expensive due to density estimation.	Often more efficient for high-dimensional data (e.g., images, videos).
Use Cases	Density estimation, probabilistic modeling, outlier detection.	Image generation, video generation, data augmentation.

3. GenAI'S EVOLUTION

The amazing evolution of GenAI since its inception has transformed early abstract theoretical concepts into powerful technologies with which we can interact today. GenAI simply denotes a class of AI applications whose ultimate purpose is the generation of new, original content: text, images, music, and even synthetic data. Its development, from the roots in early ML to the uprising of advanced models really capable of human-like creation, has passed several milestones. It has brought about the transformation of industries, better automation, and new ways in which humans and machines can cooperate. The following topics were created to better understand the development of GenAI from its origins to today and future.

1. **The Early Beginnings (Rule-based Systems and Symbolic AI):** The roots of GenAI go back to the very beginning of AI in the 1950s and 1960s, when AI was focused on solving well-defined problems and the performance of tasks with specific, pre-programmed rules. These early systems were anything but generative; they were rule-based logics to mimic certain aspects of human intelligence, such as decision-making and reasoning. Perhaps the earliest precursor of GenAI and the first notable application of AI was the creation of chatbots, initiated in the 1960s with programs like ELIZA (Weizenbaum, 1966). ELIZA could have simple conversations by emulating a Rogerian psychotherapist but without really creating anything. These early systems, even with their very simple limitations, laid the bedrock upon which later ML and NLP developments would rest.
2. **The Emergence of NNs and ML:** Interest in NNs, modeled after the structure of the human brain, was revived among AI researchers in the 1980s and 1990s. These networks could learn patterns in data through training, a significant conceptual leap from rule-based approaches. But it wasn't until the 2000s that ML became the dominant force in AI research, with the arrival of more powerful computational tools and larger data sets. This was the era when supervised learning became prominent where AI systems were trained by using labeled datasets to either make predictions or classify. During this period, AI-GMs were limited to simple forms which could only generate content on the basis of some pattern. Basic image generation, for instance, was allowed by algorithms such as autoencoders or VAE; however, the results always came out crude and nowhere near what could be witnessed in recent sophisticated models (Kingma & Welling, 2013).
3. **GANs (A Breakthrough in Creativity):** In all fairness, the real turning point for GenAI came in 2014 when Ian Goodfellow and others introduced Generative Adversarial Networks. GAN consists of two NNs: a generator and a discriminator. The former generates new content, like images and text, while the latter tries to tell the difference between what is real and generated. Through this adversarial process, the former gets better over time, producing more realistic content. GANs were a fundamental shift in how AI could create something entirely new. Instead of merely mimicking patterns, GANs finally unlocked the creative powers of AI in generating completely new data from scratch, opening a world of possibilities in art, design, and content creation. This led to some rapid progress in areas like image synthesis, where GANs could generate photorealistic images of people, landscapes, and even artwork. GANs also found applications in video game development, fashion design, and even medicine, where they were used to generate synthetic data for training other AI models (Radford et al., 2016; Brock et al., 2019).

4. **The Rise of Transformers and LLMs:** Another turning point in the evolution of GenAI came in 2017 when Vaswani et al. introduced the transformer architecture. Transformers brought a revolution to the area of NLP, employing a mechanism of attention that forces models to focus on various parts of input data all at once. This allowed AI systems to consider long-range dependencies and contextual relations within texts, thereby greatly increasing their power in understanding and generating human languages. The transformer model set the stage for LLMs, such as GPT-2 and GPT-3 developed by OpenAI. These models, trained on vast swathes of text data, demonstrated an unprecedented ability to generate coherent, contextually relevant text, answer questions, write essays, and even hold conversations that felt remarkably human. Their scale and power finally allowed them to create creative content, ranging from poetry, fiction, and technical writing to even code, from very minimal input (Brown et al., 2020). While LLMs started with only text, they did not stop there. They have also enabled the development of multimodal models that generate several kinds of content at once, such as DALL-E and CLIP. For instance, DALL-E is able to create images from a given textual description, while CLIP interprets and creates by associating images and text (Ramesh et al., 2021).
5. **Multimodal AI and the Future of GenAI:** A new development that has marked the most recent phase in the evolution of GenAI is the emergence of multimodal AI, wherein models create and understand multiple forms of content, such as text, images, and audio, simultaneously. Tools like CLIP and DALL-E 2 use this integration to generate creative content across different forms of media, from photos and graphics to video. These are the features redefining industries like digital marketing, entertainment, and education today, whereby AI is able to create very unique, contextually rich content (Radford et al., 2021). But this also opens new doors to accessibility, enabling the interaction of people with AI systems in a more natural way. In multimodal AI, for instance, users can provide text, voice, or combinations of both to instruct the AI-as if the interaction becomes so much richer and intuitive. Further advances in these models promise even greater breakthroughs in virtual reality, wherein AI-generated content forms an immersive, interactive environment.
6. **Challenges and Ethical Considerations:** Despite the amazing achievements that were made, the road of development for GenAI has not been smooth. Early generations faced difficulties related to bias, inaccuracies, and ethical problems: AI systems often train on data reflecting human biases, thus possibly generating content that creates or reinforces stereotypes or does not represent a point of view (Bolukbasi et al. 2016). Equally, the GenAI models are not free from various hallucinations where the produced text is factually incorrect or nonsensical. These problems have raised continuing research in improving the reliability

and equity of GMs (Bender et al., 2021). Ethical concerns also surround the possibility of misuse, such as deepfakes, which can generate plausible but fake content. As AI-generated content becomes increasingly indistinguishable from human-created content, in fact, calls for regulatory frameworks that protect against the ethical use of GenAI in sensitive domains are on the rise, from politics and entertainment to social media.

7. **Looking Ahead (The Future of GenAI):** While it continues to develop, one can only assume that further creativity and utility will result. The next frontier lies in developing more autonomous systems that learn and adapt with minimal human supervision to new situations. Integration of GenAI with other emerging technologies such as augmented reality, 5G networks, and quantum computing may open completely new avenues for content creation and human-computer interaction. The future of GenAI is also interestingly a set of questions about the status of human creators. Far from displacing human workers, GenAI is likely to evolve into a tool that extends human creativity by offering new interfaces whereby people and businesses collaborate with AI. We expect to see more human-AI partnerships where both human expertise and GMs contribute to producing innovative outcomes.

From the simplest rule-based systems and chatbots, GenAI has come a long way into complex models that can generate human-like content in various modalities. With each advancement, GenAI has grown in sophistication, enabling new possibilities in art, science, business, and beyond. It is, however, in this continuing evolution of technology that ethical concerns and challenges regarding bias, accuracy, and misuse have to be tackled with care so that the full potential of GenAI is realized responsibly and equitably. The future of GenAI holds great promise, as ongoing innovations are very likely to reshape industries, enhance creativity, and redefine the ways in which we interact with machines. Considering the above, the historical detailed development for GenAI can be given as follows.

1906: Markov Chain, a basic statistical model for predicting random sequences that is the earliest form of chatbots and is credited with being developed by Andreï Markov.

1932: Engineer Georges Artsrouni creates the "mechanical brain"- the initial spark of GenAl.

1943: Warren McCulloch and Walter Pitts introduced the first mathematical model of a NN- an important concept that explains how GenAl models work.

1950: Turing introduces "Machine Intelligence (Turing Test)." It is a test that measures a machine's ability to exhibit intelligent behavior that is equivalent to or indistinguishable from that of a human and is an influential cornerstone in AI research.

1956: The Dartmouth Workshop - the first AI conference where participants discussed natural language processing, problem-solving and learning.

1957: Publication of Syntactic Structures by linguist Noam Chomsky, which describes grammatical rules for parsing and constructing sentences in natural language.

1966: Joseph Weizenbaum introduced ELIZA- a chatbot that simulated talking to a therapist. The first chatbot demonstrates early natural language processing.

1968-1969: Terry Winograd created SHRDLU- a natural language understanding program

1972: Development by American psychiatrist Kenneth Colby of PARRY, a chatbot that behaves like a paranoid schizophrenic patient to draw attention away from itself, rather than simulating a therapist opposite ELIZA.

1956–1974: Birth of AI, termed "AI" by John McCarthy.

1974–1980: First AI Winter faces criticism and financial setbacks.

1980: Glenn Wichman and Michael Toy created the game "Rogue" - one of the early examples of using procedural generation techniques to create dynamic and ever-changing game environments.

1980–1987: AI boom, with GenAI as a key component.

1983: Racter. Pioneered the random generation of spoken text and prose.

1985: The introduction of the approach called "Bayesian Networks Causal Analysis" by computer scientist and philosopher Judea Pearl, which provides statistical techniques for representing the uncertainty that leads to methods of producing content in a particular style, tone, or length.

1986: Laying the foundation for the modern use of Recurrent Neural Networks (RNNs) with the introduction of "Serial order: a parallel distributed processing approach" by Michael Irwin Jordan.

1988-2008: The first chatbot created to mimic natural human speech was developed by Rollo Carpenter called JABBERWACKY/Cleverbot.

1989: Yann LeCun, Yoshua Bengio and Patrick Haffner demonstrate how CNNs can be used to recognize images. They showcased the successful use of CNNs for handwritten character recognition.

1989: One of the first attempts to create a conversational AI character in a text-based online virtual world called TINYMUD was made.

1992: DR, a pioneering chatbot that talks to users via chat. SBAITSO has been developed. Creative Labs for MS-Dos

1995: ALICE (Artificial Linguistic Internet Computer Entity) a more advanced chatbot. Richard Wallace pioneered
2001: SmarterChild_ Pioneer of Siri, one of the first chatbots integrated into messaging applications
2003: CALO, an AI assistant that can automatically learn and handle routine tasks, is developed.
2005: Mitsuku, an award-winning chatbot with a fun, teenage girl personality, is developed.
2006: Watson Assistant, a robot aimed at answering questions in natural language, was developed.
2006: Fel-Fei Li created the ImageNet database. Data scientist Fei-Fei Li set up the ImageNet database which provides the foundation for visual object recognition.
2011: Apple launches Siri. Introduced in iPhone 4S-iPhone
2010-2011: Bruse Wilcox Suzette/Rosette was developed.
2012: Google Now/Goole Assistant was developed by Google Inch.
2012: Alex Krizhevsky designs the AlexNet CNN architecture, pioneering a new way of automatically training NNs that take advantage of recent GPU advances.
2013: Diederik Kingma and Max Welling first introduced VAEs.
2014: Cortana- Microsoft's Build and Alexa Developed by Amazon.
2014: XiaoIce was developed.
2014: lan Goodfellow and his team introduced GANs, which enabled the generation of highly realistic and novel content
2015: Stanford researchers publish work on diffusion models in the paper "Deep Unsupervised Learning using Nonequilibrium Thermodynamics". The technique provides a way to reverse-engineer the process of adding noise to a final image.
2016: Founding OpenAI, a major player in AI research.
2017: Google researchers develop the concept of transformers in the seminal paper "Attention is all you need" inspiring subsequent research into tools that could automatically parse unlabeled text into LLMs.
2018: Google researchers implement transformers into BERT.
2018: Google DeepMind researchers develop AlphaFold for predicting protein structures.
2018: OpenAI releases GPT (Generative Pre-trained Transformer)
2021: OpenAI introduces DALL-E which can generate images from text prompts. The name is a combination of WALL-E the name of a fictional robot and the artist Salvador Dali.

2022: OpenAl introduces ChatGPT, an advanced series of language models known for its ability to produce coherent and contextually relevant text based on given commands. Using chatbots in applications such as content creation and language translation.

2023 & Beyond: Microsoft integrates ChatGPT into its Bing search engine. Google introduces its competitor, Bart. Present: Ongoing developments shape the current landscape of Generative AI.

4. GenAI LANDSCAPE, APPLICATION AND TOOLS

The general types of GenAI broadly can be categorized into include text, images, audio, video, code, chatbots, ML platforms, search, gaming, and data among other categories. Each one of those categories includes several different tools and technologies that let users create something, be it enhancing productivity or improving creativity in multiple fields. For example, models of GenAI like GPT-3 are designed for text generation, while DALL-E creates images from textual descriptions. Then there are audio generation tools, such as OpenAI's Jukedeck, that can compose original music, and video generation technologies are being developed to create realistic animations or video content.

Besides these general categories, it is also possible to distinguish GenAI applications according to their specific use within particular sectors and business functions. Sector-specific applications entail the use of GenAI in industries such as healthcare, education, and finance, among others, where AI-driven tools are employed to enhance workflows, decision-making, and service delivery. On the other hand, business function-specific applications are focused on aspects like marketing, customer service, operations, and human resources to point out how GenAI will be applicable to enhance efficiency and innovation in those organization departments.

Thus, this dual classification system-that of general GenAI categories to sector- or business function-specific applications-provides a detailed framing of how these GenAI technologies can be used across diverse industries and organizational functions. Understanding these classifications will therefore lead to better alignment of business AI adoption strategies with their respective needs and objectives. Table 4 is a detailed breakdown of general categories of GenAI, as depicted, and gives an overview of the varied areas where GenAI tools have so far been applied (Dilmegani, 2024; Forsyth, 2024). This table is useful for those wanting to explore the various capabilities of GenAI and determine how those tools can be used to enhance their operations or creative work

Table 4. GenAI landscape, Application and Tools

landscape	Applications	Tools
TEXT Summarizing or automating content	Idea Generation Text Production Creating personalized content Sentiment analysis / text classification	Smartwriter.ai, Hypertype, Lately, Autobound, Writesonic, Jasper, cogram, genei, YOU, AI21 labs, letterdrop, copysmith, Creatext, jenni, mavenoid, anyword, [PERSADO], frase, regie.ai, Solace Vision, Mutiny, Linguix, Hypotenuse AI, WRITER, OTHERSIDEAI, copy.ai, copymatic, COMPOSE AI
IMAGE Generating images	Image Production Semantic Image to Photo Translation Image to Image Conversion 6Image Resolution Increase (Super Resolution) 3D Shape Generation	ClipDrop, p-e-n-c-i-l, beautiful.ai, PhotoRoom, BRIA, Facet, Poly, CSM, Blend, Let's Enhance AI, HYPAR, KAEDIM, ROSEBUD.AI, maket, Autoenhance.ai, BOTIKA, soul machines, Sloyd, MODULIZE, Re:cast AI, uizard, imagen, Hexo AI
AUDIO Summarizing, generating or converting text in audio	Text to Speech Generator Speech to Speech Transformation Music Production	MURF AI, REPLICA, notably, Endel, WELLSAID, AssemblyAI, DEEPGRAM, krisp, Speechify, RESEMBLE.AI, AIMI, KAIZAN, coqui, Mubert, Neural Space, soundful, moises, VOICEMOD, Listnr, LOVO, Vocal Clarity, Dubverse, AD AURIS

continued on following page

Table 4. Continued

CODE Generating code	Code generation Completing the code Code review bug fix Refactoring the code Code style control TEST AUTOMATION Creation of test scenarios Generating test code Testing script maintenance Test documents Test result analysis	Debuild, tabnine, Codiga, Locofy, AIXcoder, Mintlify, māyā, MutableAI, durable, The.com, bloop., replit, ENZYME, DhiWise, codota, anima, CODACY, warp, Metabob
CHATBOTS Automating customer service and more	Conversational AI	lang.ai, PolyAI, Incentivai, Kasisto, ushur, CRESTA, EliseAI, verloop.io, Replika, ultimate.ai, Cohere, Sapling, haptik, ada, Forethought, OBSERVE-AI, Kind, Balto, Certainly.
VIDEO Generating or editing videos	Creating Video Video Forecast	TERRA, Peech, VOCHI, Maverick, recut, VEED.IO, Basch.io, inworld, tavus, FATHOM, runway, EMBLY, PICTORY, vidyo.ai, lumen5, Steve AI, windsor.io, YEPIC, Colossyan, METAPHYSIC, Potion

continued on following page

Table 4. Continued

ML PLATFORMS Applications / ML platforms	To assist with applications for processing Big Data with ML techniques. File conversion solving math problems	slai, jina, symbl.ai, Adept, aporia, GANTRY, deepset, Synthesis.ai, Archistar, Galileo, featureform
SEARCH AI-powered insights SEO (Search Engine Optimization) (Arama motoru optimizasyonu)	Generating topic ideas for content writing Do keyword research Finding the right headlines Group search intent Creating the content structure Creating meta descriptions Generating sitemap codes	glean, Looria, Hebbia, consensus, Air, vectara, Pinecone, qdrant
GAMING Gen-AI gaming studios or applications	Procedural content generation Player behavior analysis Non-player character (NPC) behavior user interface design game test	charisma.ai, hidden door, LATITUDE, Spellbrush
DATA Designing, collecting, or summarizing data	Data Synthesis data visualization	Pilot, gretel, DATAHERALD, SYNTEGRA, Mirry.AI, BIFROST, datagen

5. ADVANTAGES AND DISADVANTAGES OF GenAI

GenAI refers to AI systems that can generate new content, such as text, images, music, or other forms of media, based on patterns learned from existing data. Thanks to these systems, it is a fact that while new developments provide advantages in various fields from creative arts to scientific research, there are also various disadvantages. Below, the advantages and disadvantages of GenAI technology will be briefly mentioned.

Advantages:

1. **Creativity Expansion:** AI can create a variety of content by pushing the limits of creativity.
2. **Increased Productivity:** Increases productivity by automating repetitive tasks.
3. **Personalization:** Provides content tailored to user preferences and behavior.
4. **Innovative Solutions:** Provides unique solutions to complex problems in various fields.
5. **Data:** by improving, augmenting or automating various aspects of the data life cycle such as data preparation, data creation, data analysis, data interpretation and data presentation. and helps visualization.

Disadvantages:

1. **Abuse and Malicious Practices:** Potential for abuse in creating misleading or harmful content. Deepfake
2. **Erosion of Human Creativity:** The ability to mimic styles and produce content quickly can diminish appreciation for the creative process and human creativity.
3. **Work Displacement:** Automating creative tasks can reduce the demand for human professionals in these fields.
4. **Bias and Discrimination:** Can perpetuate and reinforce existing biases and discrimination in educational data.
5. **Dependency on Data Quality:** Effectiveness largely depends on the quality of training data. Poor or limited data can lead to inaccurate or meaningless output. It can produce implausible but confidently constructed conclusions that appear plausible, called hallucinations.
6. **Ethical Concerns in Content Creation:** The ability to copy causes ethical issues by blurring the line between inspiration and imitation.
7. **Effect on Learning and Skill Development:** It can prevent the development of important skills and knowledge in tasks that require human intelligence and creativity, especially in educational environments.
8. **Accessibility and Digital Divide:** Inaccessible to many individuals and small organizations as it requires significant computing resources and expertise
9. **Security Vulnerabilities:** While their complexity can make it difficult to ensure security, their widespread use can increase the potential impact of security breaches.
10. **Environmental Impact:** The energy consumption required to train models can lead to carbon emissions and environmental degradation. As demand increases, the environmental footprint of these technologies also increases.

6. FUTURE PREDICTIONS FOR GenAI

Although there have been remarkable improvements recorded within the last decade in GenAI, there is apparently no time when this evolution may grind to a stop. Since the field keeps evolving, it is possible to forecast several key trends and predictions with regard to its future along dimensions such as technological, practical, societal, and ethical aspects, which in a sense mean that GenAI can very soon become a fundamental aspect in daily life, industries, and creative processes. Below are the general future trends for GenAI:

1. **More Sophisticated and Creative Models:** As GenAI technology advances, we can expect models to become more sophisticated and creatively capable. The progression from models like GANs (Goodfellow et al., 2014) to transformers (Vaswani et al., 2017) and LLMs like GPT-3 (Brown et al., 2020) has already shown how AI can generate more nuanced, contextually aware, and realistic content. Future iterations will likely refine these capabilities, enabling models to create even more intricate and emotionally resonant content: Multimodal Creativity, Improved Personalization.
2. **Proliferation in Enterprise and Industry Applications:** It already creates value for GenAI in industries ranging from healthcare and entertainment to marketing. Its potential will probably be more inclusive and integrated into enterprise or organizational workflows in years to come.
3. **Increased Integration with Augmented and Virtual Reality (AR/VR):** With GenAI, this is going to be a blast not only in the development of static content but will extend to dynamic environments like AR and VR. This would start becoming an integral component for creating immersive, interacting virtual worlds as AR/VR technologies mature.
4. **AI-Generated Autonomous Systems and Creativity:** An interpretation could be that creative professional work would increasingly be the product of GenAI-driven autonomous systems with little, if any, human input: AI as Collaborative Partners, AI-Generated Innovation.
5. **Ethical and Regulatory Developments:** As GenAI continues to evolve, it increasingly raises important ethical concerns over its uses and impacts on society: Bias and Fairness, Intellectual Property and Authorship, Regulation of Deepfakes and Misinformation.
6. **AI Democratization and Accessibility:** With further development, generative AI will be more accessible so that more and more people or organizations can take advantage of such technology: No-Code Platforms for GenAI, Intelligent Tools for Education.

7. **Greater Collaboration Between Humans and AI:** Future developments in GenAI would more likely be collaborative models wherein humans and machines help each other to achieve very complex tasks. AI is going to be used in enhancing human creativity, improving productivity, and amplifying decision-making: AI-Enhanced Creative Jobs, Automation of Repetitive Tasks.

7. CONCLUSION

Today, AI technologies are developing at a breakneck pace and continue to transform many aspects of our lives. These have already automated processes such as data analysis, predictive modeling, and decision-making, thus greatly improving efficiency across industries. But AI does not stop there; its potential goes even beyond these pragmatic uses, with the latest developments in this field marking an incursion into the realm of creativity itself, with AI challenging traditional notions of human ingenuity. Arguably most exciting in this respect is Generative AI, or GenAI, which now develops some remarkable capabilities in creating novel ideas, creating artwork, composing music, and even emulating aspects of human creativity.

GenAI is pushing the limits of what we once considered the exclusive domain of human creativity. Once thought of as one of the defining features of human intelligence, this notion is forced to be redefined in view of the rise of GenAI. Powered by DL and NNs, AI systems can already produce indistinguishable content from those made by humans. Whether it is creating amazing art, composing music, or designing new products, GenAI proved to be a good assistant in various creative activities, both for amateurs and professionals. Evolution is hence giving a full new dimension to opportunities whereby AI complements human creativity, kindles inspiration, and brings up fresh perspectives.

GenAI is finding more of a collaborative rather than a tool-type role in fields like the arts, design, and entertainment. Consider visual arts; through AI programs, such as DALL-E and DeepArt, an artist can have his mind extended to new dimensions of creativity in designing elaborately unique images using simple textual inputs. Similarly, AI-generated music is expanding the possibility of musical composition by affording musicians and creators with facilities to experiment with complex arrangements, genres, and styles that were not previously possible or would seriously have consumed much time with traditional means. This democratization of creative tools is also not limited to professional artists; amateur users can also create art and music in ways that are hard to differentiate from traditional forms, and with comparably little effort. GenAI can even be an inspiration for people who could never have imagined themselves creative and offers opportunities to engage in artistic expression wholly anew.

With these exciting developments, however, ethical considerations must be at the forefront of developing GenAI. As AI-generated content becomes more indistinguishable from human-made works, questions about authorship, ownership, and copyright will emerge. Who owns a piece of art created by an AI system—the developer, the user, or the AI itself? Large datasets, generally used to train the GenAI systems, are often made up of human-made works. This raises serious concerns about the potential exploitation of the intellectual property of artists and the possibility of biases being perpetuated in AI-created works. It is in this respect that a human-centered approach-one that focuses on the priorities of transparency, fairness, and accountability-will play a key role in our work to ensure that GenAI benefits society as a whole without infringing on individual rights or perpetuating harm.

From an economic point of view, GenAI will no doubt have huge implications for many industries. With the great, high-quality content created by GenAI on demand, businesses can automate and manage creative processes from ad campaigns to product design and even the formulation of strategy. In such a way, wholly new platforms and ecosystems may also be created in which GenAI plays center stage. This does mean that traditional creative roles will probably change. While AI-generated content may take over some jobs, the newer roles will be concentrated on curating, refining, and placing AI-created works into context. The most serious challenge here will be not leaving human workers behind in this transition and enabling opportunities for upskilling and reskilling.

The future research agenda concerning GenAI is related to several critical questions and challenges. One of the most serious concerns in this circle is that of security and accountability: maybe the tendency of AI systems to get more autonomous implies operation in rigorously controlled environments, like healthcare or autonomous vehicles. Clear guidelines and framing are required with respect to how GenAI can be safely integrated into operational workflows in these highly regulated sectors. This has to do with transparency of the GenAI system itself, auditability of its decision-making processes, and traceability of its outcomes back to a set of ethical standards. Furthermore, it requires building trust in such systems when deepfakes, misinformation, and AI-generated fake news are growing concerns. For example, in news media, AI could be used to generate articles or video reports that appear genuine but contain manipulated or false information. Thus, developing standards of verification and authentication for AI content will be important in maintaining public confidence in GenAI technologies.

It is equally important to recognize that GenAI is not a "magic bullet" that can solve all our challenges or fully replace human creativity and decision-making. While AI can indeed help automate tasks and generate content, it lacks human intuition, emotional intelligence, or even the deep understanding of cultural contexts that humans bring to their work. It will all be about how the AI systems collaborate with human professionals for the best outcomes. We need to consider GenAI not as a replacement for human judgment but as a tool that extends the powers of humans. For instance, in data analytics, GenAI can identify patterns and derive insights from enormous volumes of data, but the interpretation of such findings and arriving at informed decisions based on broader contextual understanding is still the job of a data scientist, analysts, and domain experts.

Furthermore, the data ecosystem plays a crucial role in shaping the effectiveness of GenAI. Collaboration between various stakeholders— data scientists, data engineers, creators, users, and consumers— is necessary to ensure that GenAI models are fed with high-quality, diverse, and representative data. While GenAI is a powerful tool for content generation, it is only as good as the data it is trained on. Validity, reliability, and freedom from bias will have to be ensured in data input to make the AI system generate outputs that are not only fair but also ethical. It will require collaboration from many industries to establish best practices regarding data management, ethics usage, and the protection of privacy and rights of every individual.

While Generative AI brings along enormous opportunities for revolutionizing creative industries and business practices, the more general ethical, social, and economic implications of the advances should not be disregarded. The best it could be is an important tool to support human creativity, enable and empower creators, and provide new means for innovative contributions. It is, however, critical that these systems be developed and regulated in such a way that they promote transparency, trust, and fairness, with the benefits of AI being shared equitably and not at the expense of human dignity or rights. Full potential can be derived from GenAI by keeping the approach human-centered and ensuring that AI works with humans, not replacing them, while its usage in society is kept responsible and ethical.

REFERENCES

Arjovsky, M., Chintala, S., & Bottou, L. (2017). Wasserstein GAN. *Proceedings of the 34th International Conference on Machine Learning*, 70, 214-223. https://proceedings.mlr.press/v70/arjovsky17a.html

Banh, L., & Strobel, G. (2023). Generative artificial intelligence. *Electronic Markets*, 33(1), 63. DOI: 10.1007/s12525-023-00680-1

Bender, E. M., Gebru, T., McMillan-Major, A., & Shmitchell, S. (2021). On the dangers of stochastic parrots: Can language models be too big? *Proceedings of the 2021 ACM Conference on Fairness, Accountability, and Transparency*, 610-623. https://doi.org/DOI: 10.1145/3442188.3445922

Binns, R. (2018). Fairness in machine learning: Lessons from political philosophy. *Proceedings of the 2018 CHI Conference on Human Factors in Computing Systems*, 1-14.

Bolukbasi, T., Chang, W. H., Zou, J. Y., Saligrama, V., & Kalai, T. T. (2016). Man is to computer programmer as woman is to homemaker? Debiasing word embeddings. *Proceedings of the 30th International Conference on Neural Information Processing Systems*, 4349-4357. https://arxiv.org/abs/1607.06520

Brock, A., Donahue, J., & Simonyan, K. (2019). Large scale GAN training for high fidelity natural image synthesis. *Proceedings of the International Conference on Neural Information Processing Systems*, 32, 163-174. https://arxiv.org/abs/1809.11096

Brown, T. B., Mann, B., Ryder, N., Subbiah, M., Kaplan, J., Dhariwal, P., Sastry, G., Askell, A., Mishkin, P., & Clark, J.. (2020). Language models are few-shot learners. *Proceedings of the 34th International Conference on Neural Information Process ing Systems*, 1, 1877-1901. https://doi.org/DOI: 10.1109/ACCESS.2020.2976496

Brynjolfsson, E., & McAfee, A. (2014). *The second machine age: Work, progress, and prosperity in a time of brilliant technologies*. W. W. Norton & Company.

Brynjolfsson, E., & Mitchell, T. (2017). What can machine learning do? Workforce implications. *Science*, 358(6370), 1530–1534. DOI: 10.1126/science.aap8062 PMID: 29269459

Castelvecchi, D. (2016). Can we open the black box of AI? *Nature*, 538(7623), 20–23. DOI: 10.1038/538020a PMID: 27708329

Chesney, R., & Citron, D. K. (2019). Deep fakes: A looming challenge for privacy, democracy, and national security. *California Law Review*, 107(5), 1753–1819. DOI: 10.15779/Z38F47M95S

Dilmegani, C., & Forsyth, R. (2024). Generative AI in business: Emerging trends and future directions. *AI Trends*, 17(3), 22–34.

Esteva, A., Kuprel, B., Novoa, R. A., Ko, J., Swetter, S. M., Blau, H. M., & Thrun, S. (2019). Dermatologist-level classification of skin cancer with deep neural networks. *Nature*, 542(7639), 115–118. DOI: 10.1038/nature21056 PMID: 28117445

Forsyth, O. (2024). Mapping the Generative AI landscape. In https://www.antler.co/blog/generative-ai; 19.08.2024.

Goodfellow, I., Kingma, D. P., Salimans, T., & Welling, M. (2014). Generative adversarial nets. In *Advances in Neural Information Processing Systems* (Vol. 27, pp. 2672-2680).

Goodfellow, I., Kingma, D. P., Salimans, T., & Welling, M. (2016). Generative adversarial networks and their applications. *arXiv*. https://arxiv.org/abs/1606.03498

Goodfellow, I., Mirza, M., Xu, B., Warde-Farley, D., Courville, A., & Bengio, Y. (2016). Conditional Generative Adversarial Nets. *arXiv*. https://arxiv.org/abs/1411.1784

Goodfellow, I., Pouget-Abadie, J., Mirza, M., Xu, B., Warde-Farley, D., Ozair, S., Courville, A., & Bengio, Y. (2014). *Generative adversarial nets* (Vol. 27). Advances in Neural Information Processing Systems, https://arxiv.org/abs/1406.2661

Goodfellow, I., Pouget-Abadie, J., Mirza, M., Xu, B., Warde-Farley, D., Ozair, S., Courville, A., & Bengio, Y. (2016). Generative adversarial nets: Challenges and opportunities. In *Neural Information Processing Systems* (pp. 2681–2691). MIT Press.

Goodfellow, I., Pouget-Abadie, J., Mirza, M., Xu, B., Warde-Farley, D., Ozair, S., Courville, A., & Bengio, Y. (2017). Generative adversarial networks. *Communications of the ACM*, 63(11), 139–144. DOI: 10.1145/3422622

Harmon, A. (1985). The "Information Society": Origins and consequences. *Technology and Society Review*, 9(2), 33–48.

He, K., Zhang, X., Ren, S., & Sun, J. (2020). Deep residual learning for image recognition. *Proceedings of the IEEE Conference on Computer Vision and Pattern Recognition*, 770-778. https://doi.org/DOI: 10.1109/CVPR.2016.90

Isarta News. (2024). Artificial intelligence and the future of digital marketing. https://www.isartanews.com

Janiesch, C., Samtani, S., & Gupta, H. (2021). Explainable AI for business applications: Opportunities and challenges. *AI Open*, 2(1), 35–44. DOI: 10.1016/j.aiopen.2021.100047

Kingma, D. P., Salimans, T., & Welling, M. (2014). *Variational autoencoders*. Neural Information Processing Systems.

Kingma, D. P., & Welling, M. (2013). Auto-Encoding Variational Bayes. *International Conference on Learning Representations*. https://arxiv.org/abs/1312.6114

Kingma, D. P., & Welling, M. (2014). Auto-Encoding Variational Bayes. *International Conference on Learning Representations*. https://arxiv.org/abs/1312.6114

Kühl, N., Fink, G. A., & Thrun, S. (2022). Human-like artificial intelligence: A survey on advancements and open issues. *IEEE Transactions on AI*, 5(1), 56–65. DOI: 10.1109/TAC.2022.30456

LeCun, Y., Bengio, Y., & Hinton, G. (2015). Deep learning. *Nature*, 521(7553), 436–444. DOI: 10.1038/nature14539 PMID: 26017442

Lehmann, J., & Buschek, D. (2020). Human-AI collaboration in creative tasks. *Proceedings of the 2020 CHI Conference on Human Factors in Computing Systems*, 58, 134-142. https://doi.org/DOI: 10.1145/3313831.3376460

Luckin, R., Holmes, W., Griffiths, M., & Forcier, L. B. (2016). *Intelligence unleashed: An argument for AI in education*. Pearson.

Marcus, G., & Davis, E. (2020). *Rebooting AI: Building artificial intelligence we can trust*. Pantheon Books.

Murfy, E., & Thomas, H. (2023). Generative AI and creativity. *AI Research Review*, 5(3), 75–85.

Ngiam, J., Khosla, A., Kim, M., Nam, J., & Lee, H. (2011). Multimodal deep learning. *Proceedings of the 28th International Conference on Machine Learning*, 1, 689-696. https://doi.org/DOI: 10.1145/3023147.3023152

Radford, A., Metz, L., & Chintala, S. (2016). Unsupervised representation learning with deep convolutional generative adversarial networks. *Proceedings of the 33rd International Conference on Machine Learning*, 5, 499-508. https://arxiv.org/abs/1511.06434

Ruthotto, L., & Haber, E. (2021). An introduction to deep generative modeling. *GAMM-Mitteilungen*, 44(2), e202100008. DOI: 10.1002/gamm.202100008

Samtani, S., Zhu, H., Padmanabhan, B., Chai, Y., Chen, H., & Nunamaker, J. F.Jr. (2023). Deep learning for information systems research. *Journal of Management Information Systems*, 40(1), 271–301. DOI: 10.1080/07421222.2023.2172772

Saremi, S., Mehrjou, A., Schölkopf, B., & Hyvärinen, A. (2018). Deep energy estimator networks. *CoRR*, abs/1805.08306. DOI: 10.1080/07421222.2023.2172772

Tomczak, J. M. (2022). *Deep generative modeling*. Springer International Publishing., DOI: 10.1007/978-3-030-93158-2

Weizenbaum, J. (1966). ELIZA- A computer program for the study of natural language communication between man and machine. *Communications of the ACM*, 9(1), 36–45. DOI: 10.1145/365153.365168

Weng, L. (2021). What are diffusion models? *Lil'Log*. https://lilianweng.github.io/posts/2021-07-11-diffusion-models/. 20.07.2024

Winston, P. H. (1993). *Artificial intelligence* (3rd ed., reprinted with corr.). Addison-Wesley.

Wu, Q., Gao, R., & Zha, H. (2021). Bridging explicit and implicit deep generative models via neural Stein estimators. *35th Conference on Neural Information Processing Systems (NeurIPS 2021).*

Xie, J., Lu, Y., Zhu, S. C., & Wu, Y. N. (2016). A theory of generative convnet. In *ICML*, 2635-2644.

Chapter 3
AI-Based Cyberbullying Detection Techniques and Strategies

Laya Billinty Varra
https://orcid.org/0009-0001-1205-3789
Stanley College of Engineering and Technology for Women, India

Thakur Monika Singh
https://orcid.org/0009-0006-8534-9130
Stanley College of Engineering and Technology for Women, India

Kishor Kumar Reddy C.
Stanley College of Engineering and Technology for Women, India

Karri Lippert
https://orcid.org/0000-0002-5464-2186
University of South Alabama, USA

ABSTRACT

Cyberbullying has become a very significant issue in today's digital age, and its victims are spread over all the online platforms. This chapter focuses on how Artificial Intelligence is transforming the fight against cyberbullying. It discusses the cutting-edge techniques and strategies used to detect harmful behavior online, harnessing the power of natural language processing (NLP), machine learning, and deep learning. The chapter explains how AI systems process text, images, and multimedia content to detect abusive or harmful interactions. It discusses some of the key challenges such as limitations in the dataset, bias in the algorithms, and the requirement for real-time detection. Further, the chapter focuses on innovative approaches that can be used for improving the accuracy and scalability of detection

DOI: 10.4018/979-8-3373-0543-1.ch003

systems while simultaneously addressing critical ethical and privacy concerns. With the integration of technology and careful strategies, this chapter predicts a safer and more inclusive digital space for all.

1. INTRODUCTION TO AI IN CYBERBULLYING DETECTION

The digital age brought immense opportunities, but the emergence of cyberbullying is one challenge that threatens society. The section outlines how Artificial Intelligence transforms the war against online harassment by discussing its development as a global phenomenon and how cyberbullying causes individuals to become emotionally and psychologically disturbed, as well as the drawbacks of current methods such as manual reporting and keyword-based systems. AI has the capability to transform things as it applies the advanced machine learning and natural language processing techniques for the identification of subtle, complex, and evolving abuse. In the process of handling huge data volumes in real-time, AI can provide precision and scale in cyberbullying prevention. The following sections set the context for understanding how AI makes a digital space safer and more inclusive.

1.1 The Rise of Cyberbullying in the Digital Age

The rapid growth of internet usage and mobile communication technologies has brought incredible opportunities but also serious challenges, one of which is cyberbullying. Cyberbullying is the use of technology to harm others emotionally or physically, particularly among minors. It encompasses various forms, such as flaming, online harassment, denigration, outing, masquerading, and exclusion. The anonymity and constant accessibility of the internet exacerbate the issue. Cyberbullying is the latest global problem where it is mostly affecting teens. It causes stress, depression, anxiety, and suicide in extreme cases. Most of the reasons for prevalence are peer pressure, social dominance, and power play. Social media is a good tool of connectivity, but it provides an environment for such hostile behaviors to flourish. Statistical evidence of its prevalence among almost all age groups calls for intervention. The effects are deep, from psychological trauma to academic setbacks, and increased antisocial behaviour. There is a necessity to raise awareness among parents, educators, and psychologists that will help prevent cyberbullying. Stricter policies and more effective enforcement mechanisms would be necessary to address this problem head-on and reduce the detrimental effects (Singh, 2023). Nearly 59% of U.S. adolescents reported experiencing online harassment. There is a need to create resilience and a supportive culture that emphasizes empathy and awareness, so they can feel safe and valued in the digital world (Wiederhold, B. K., 2024).

In India, legal frameworks cover the relevant aspects of cyberbullying through statutes like the Information Technology Act and the Indian Penal Code. Challenges, such as jurisdictional issues and anonymity of the perpetrator; free speech v/s over-regulation; inconsistent definition, cross-border complexity and a lack of law-enforcement resources are the weaknesses in enforcement. Solutions in the proposed area include: comprehensive cyberbullying-specific laws, international legal standard harmonization, improvement in law enforcement cooperation, and use of AI for detection. Social media companies need to refine their moderation practices and cooperate with the authorities. Public awareness campaigns, counseling services, and privacy protection for victims are also part of the holistic approach. Thus, by making legal machinery strong and encouraging responsible online behavior, society can mitigate cyberbullying and try to provide safer digital spaces to everybody (Jain, V. H., et al., 2024).

1.2 Limitations of Traditional Detection Methods

Traditional methods of identifying cyberbullying include keyword-based filtering, manual reporting, and rule-based systems, which have severe limitations for the complex nature of harassment in the online environment. These methods fail to consider the subtleties in language, tone, and context of cyberbullying incidents. For example, keyword-based methods might view harmless content as harmful or miss more subtle forms of bullying that do not include explicit offensive language. Moreover, manual reporting systems are highly dependent on user participation and slow, which results in delayed responses. These methods also struggle with detecting subtle forms of cyberbullying, such as indirect bullying, sarcasm, and emotional manipulation, which are often more damaging. As a result, traditional detection methods are not sufficient for addressing the evolving and diverse landscape of cyberbullying in the digital age.

The detection of cyberbullying online is hindered by the limited availability of high-quality data, despite its growing societal importance and advancements in computational power. Research often relies on small, inconsistent datasets that fail to reflect the complexity of real-world social dynamics, leading to challenges in cross-domain applicability. Innovative methods, such as crowdsourcing simulated bullying scenarios, offer potential solutions by enriching datasets and improving classifier performance (Emmery, C., et al., 2021). These insights underscore the need for improved data practices to enhance the effectiveness of cyberbullying detection systems.

1.3 AI as a Game-Changer in Cyberbullying Detection

Artificial Intelligence (AI) presents a transformative solution to the problems that conventional methods of cyberbullying detection face. AI systems, especially those based on machine learning and natural language processing, can process volumes of data that include text, images, videos, and user interactions with greater precision and speed than that which a human can attain (Singh, M. T., et al 2025). It is capable of detecting not only explicit cyberbullying behaviors but also more subtle actions, like emotional manipulation, sarcasm, and social exclusion. AI models are able to learn from data patterns to improve continuously and thus will be able to adapt better to the tactics that evolve with cyberbullies over time. AI's capabilities in processing contextual information and recognizing patterns of behavior and power imbalances make it particularly suitable for understanding cyberbullying's complexity. With these capabilities, AI holds the potential for revolutionizing how we can detect, prevent, and address cyberbullying in real-time, giving this growing issue a proactive approach.

Researchers S. V. M. Raji, A. Neagu, and N. A. Adams in their titled study "Children's Views on AI-Based Cyberbullying Interventions and Children's Rights" investigated how children viewed AI-driven interventions in mitigating cyberbullying across social media. The objective of the study was based on the understanding of these interventions and how they can impact children's fundamental rights such as protection, privacy, and freedom of expression as enshrined under the United Nations Convention on the Rights of the Child (UNCRC).The study covered 59 children aged 12-17 years from Ireland, with the participants giving their views through focus groups and in-depth interviews. The questions were asked concerning various AI-based solutions like content flagging, proactive content removal, and peer support as well as school involvement in dealing with cyberbullying. Despite recognition by the majority of children that AI may be effective in stemming the tide of harmful activities online, there was equal concern about privacy and how such interventions would affect free speech. The results lead to an important conclusion: while AI interventions can offer some protection for children in cyberbullying, there is a need for intervention that respects children's rights. The study will be needed to engage youths in the design of such interventions since their social norms and perceptions may affect the solutions' effectiveness. After all, the research emphasizes that a balanced approach would ensure AI solutions protect not only children but also the very fundamental rights of those children (Milosevic, T., et al., 2023).

To truly make AI a game-changer in tackling cyberbullying, it's essential that AI developers collaborate with social scientists. Social scientists bring a deeper understanding of how people experience harm online, taking into account cultural, age, and community differences. This collaboration ensures that AI systems are not only technically accurate but also sensitive to the nuances of human behavior, improving their ability to detect varying levels of bullying and its psychological impact. Innovative AI tools are already in development to address cyberbullying. For example, "reflective messaging" prompts encourage users to pause and think before posting harmful content. Mobile apps like BullStop use AI to identify and block abusive messages, providing users with better protection from online harassment. However, there are important ethical considerations. If AI systems aren't carefully designed, they could unintentionally amplify existing biases or social inequalities. The design and implementation of these tools must be continuously assessed to ensure they do not cause harm or perpetuate discrimination. While AI holds significant potential in the fight against cyberbullying, it's important that its development is carefully managed. This will ensure that AI interventions truly protect users' rights and effectively address the complexities of online abuse (Milosevic, T., et al., 2022).

Figure 1. Evolution of cyberbullying detection techniques

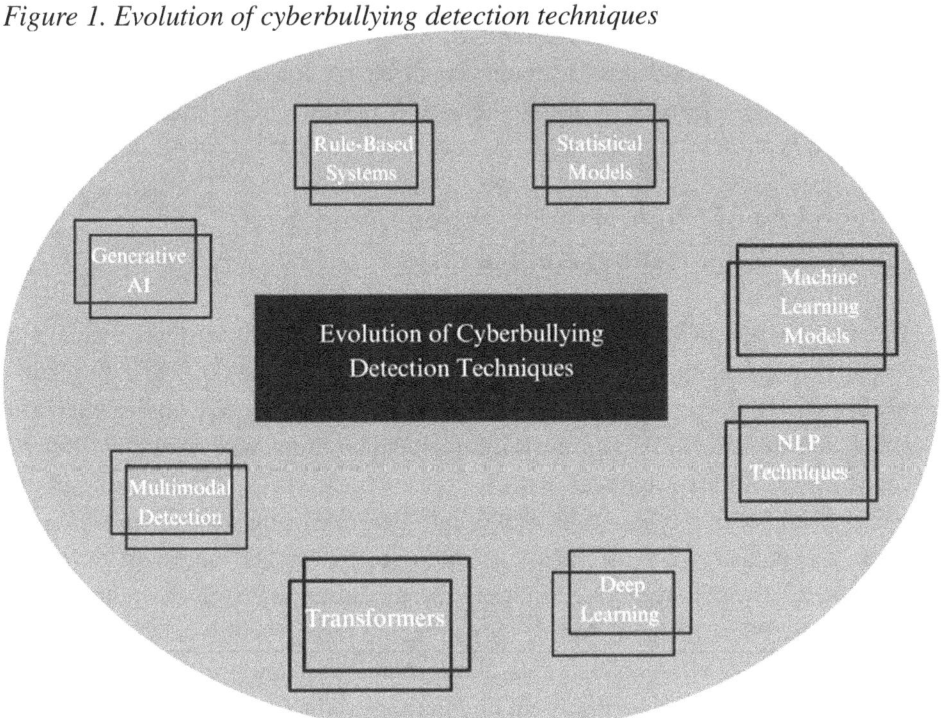

Figure 1 shows progress from simple rule-based systems to advanced generative AI. Starting with keyword filtering, statistical models like TF-IDF analyzed word patterns, followed by machine learning for better accuracy using labeled data. NLP added semantic understanding, deep learning automated feature extraction, and transformers like BERT improved contextual detection. Multimodal analysis enabled detection across text, images, and videos, while generative AI enhanced datasets and real-time capabilities, showcasing the growing sophistication in tackling cyberbullying.

2. MACHINE LEARNING TECHNIQUES FOR CYBERBULLYING DETECTION

This chapter further explores the role of foundations in machine learning to recognize cyberbullying. Specifically, supervised, unsupervised, and reinforcement learning strategies are examined in the book to elaborate on how patterns in abusive content are possible through such techniques. Methods for feature extraction, for example, show how lexical, syntactic, and semantic features define harmful language to transform the raw data into actionable insights. Popular algorithms include Decision Trees, Support Vector Machines (SVMs), and Random Forests, which are discussed for their effectiveness in identifying offensive behavior. By covering these aspects, this section provides a comprehensive overview of how machine learning empowers detection systems to adapt and evolve in combating cyberbullying.

2.1 Overview of Supervised, Unsupervised, and Reinforcement Learning Approaches

Machine learning (ML) takes a significant place in making systems that detect cyberbullying on many digital grounds. The basic approaches that can be distinguished within the scope of ML are classified into three approaches: supervised learning, unsupervised learning, and reinforcement learning, which vary in different methodologies and their applications.

Supervised Learning: Supervised learning is learned using a model trained upon an annotated dataset where outputs correspond to the inputs. The most common application area is cyberbullying, wherein the model learns from examples of offensive and harmless content. Applications that are most popular here are Support Vector Machines SVM, Decision Trees, Neural Networks, among others. Successful supervised learning relies on excellent and annotated datasets.

Unsupervised learning: it works without labeled data. Instead, it finds the patterns and structures within the data. Clustering algorithms such as K-means and hierarchical clustering may be able to cluster similar content, possibly uncovering new forms of cyberbullying without explicit labels. This is particularly useful for exploratory analysis and hidden trends.

Reinforcement Learning: Reinforcement learning models learn by interacting with the environment and receiving feedback in the form of rewards or penalties. Although this is less commonly applied directly to text-based cyberbullying detection, reinforcement learning can optimize content moderation systems by continuously improving based on user interactions and reporting (Morales, E. F., et al., 2022).

Table 1 compares commonly used machine learning algorithms for cyberbullying detection, highlighting their types, applications, strengths, and limitations. Decision Trees are simple and interpretable but may overfit complex data. SVMs offer high accuracy for offensive language detection but can be computationally expensive. Random Forests provide robust multi-class classification but are more complex to implement. This table provides a quick reference for understanding algorithm suitability in different scenarios.

Table 1. Comparison of Machine Learning Algorithms for Cyberbullying Detection

Algorithm	Type	Use case	Strengths	Limitations
Decision Trees	Supervised	Text Classification	Easy to Interpret	Prone to Overfitting
SVM	Supervised	Offensive Language Detection	High Accuracy with Small Data	Computationally Expensive
Random Forest	Ensemble Learning	Multi-class Classification	Robust and Scalable	Complex to Implement

2.2 Feature Extraction for Identifying Harmful Language

Feature extraction is a very significant step in training machine learning models for detecting cyberbullying. Simply put, it is what connects raw text data and the model to recognize abusive content. Features extracted translate text into some numerical format, making processing and training of machine learning algorithms easier. Frequently, the extracted features influence the performance quality of the model.

Lexical Features: Lexical features relate to the words and phrases of the text. They may uncover linguistic patterns that might signal negative intent. For instance, through the frequency of abusive words or n-grams, we may detect a hint of bullying behavior in subtle ways. This common technique used here is TF-IDF (Term Frequency-Inverse Document Frequency), which helps to highlight words that appear frequently in abusive contexts but less often in general conversations. This helps the model focus on the most telling parts of the text .Example: Suppose a dataset contains social media posts. A post saying, "You're worthless and pathetic," might trigger a high TF-IDF score for the words "worthless" and "pathetic" because they are less common in regular conversations but often appear in abusive messages.

By flagging these high-scoring words, the model learns to associate them with potential cyberbullying.

Syntactic Features: Moving beyond mere words, syntactic features study the form and arrangement of sentences. Through the inspection of things such as part-of-speech tags or parsing of how words connect, we are able to pick up on some of these linguistic patterns that so often go with abusive language. For example, short, aggressive sentences or repeated exclamation marks may indicate bullying. Length of sentences, punctuation, and grammatical structures may all come into play here. For example, short, aggressive sentences or repeated exclamation marks might signal bullying. Sentence length, punctuation, and grammatical structures can all play a part in the detection process.

Semantic Features: Semantic feature extraction goes one step deeper than the meaning in the words. This is crucial, as cyberbullying cannot always be easily detected-it can be subtle, sarcasm, or even wordplay. Tools such as Word2Vec, GloVe, and BERT help models understand how the words are related to one another, taking into context the use of words with which they are associated with. For example, the word "kill" in "You're killing it!" is totally different from "I'll kill you." By focusing on these subtle differences in meaning, semantic features help the model become more accurate, so it can better recognize when something truly harmful is being said and avoid misinterpreting innocent comments.

Contextual and Behavioral Features: Language doesn't exist in isolation, and neither does cyberbullying. Contextual features consider the conversation as a whole – what was said before and after a particular message. Behavioral features take it one step further by looking at the user's history. Have they been flagged before? Do they post frequently? Is this user involved in many aggressive exchanges? Combining these elements gives the detection system a better view into possible bullying behavior, avoiding false positives.

2.3 Popular Algorithms: Decision Trees, SVM, Random Forests

When it comes to the actual detection of cyberbullying, certain algorithms consistently stand out due to their efficiency and accuracy in handling large amounts of data.

Decision Trees:

Imagine trying to classify a piece of text by asking a series of yes/no questions – that's essentially what a decision tree does. It splits the data at each step, following paths that lead to different outcomes. Decision trees are simple yet powerful. They provide clear insights into which features (words, sentence structures) are most important for detecting cyberbullying. However, they can sometimes be too eager to fit the data perfectly, which might make them less effective on new, unseen data. Techniques like pruning (removing unnecessary branches) help to manage this issue.

In smart cities, detecting Cyberbullying (CB) on social media platforms is crucial for maintaining a safe environment. Traditional methods of CB detection often fail to provide real-time solutions with high accuracy. To address this, a Deep Decision Tree (Deep DT) model is proposed for automatically classifying CB tweets. This model combines the strengths of Deep Neural Networks (DNN) and decision trees, allowing it to efficiently process large datasets, identify relevant features, and classify CB content accurately without overfitting. The hybrid architecture of the Deep DT classifier enhances detection performance, making it a powerful tool for real-time CB monitoring in smart cities. In this research, a Deep DT model was used to classify crowd-sourced tweets (CB tweets), evaluated through the weight scores of optimal words selected by a feature selection method. This process reduces the cost of training data by selecting the most relevant words, thereby enhancing classification performance. The dataset D = {(xi, ~ci)} consists of xi (tweets) and ~ci (unlabeled class labels), where the challenge lies in effectively classifying these tweets. By leveraging the Deep DT architecture, the model handles dependencies between phrases and reduces complexity, making the classification task more efficient (Yuvaraj, N., et al., 2021).

Support Vector Machines (SVM):

SVMs are like expert boundary-makers. They analyze the data and draw a line (or a more complex shape in higher dimensions) that separates harmful and non-harmful content. SVMs work well even when the data is messy or overlaps. This makes them a reliable choice for detecting cyberbullying, as text data is often noisy and unpredictable. SVMs excel at finding subtle distinctions in large, high-dimensional datasets.

Example: Consider a web content filtering system designed to protect users from harmful material. The system initially employs keyword filtering to mark potentially harmful content. However, keyword-based approaches alone often lead to inaccuracies, either by over-flagging harmless content or missing subtly harmful material. To address this, SVM-based filtering is introduced as a second layer of classification. In this stage, SVMs are trained to distinguish between mildly offensive language and severe cases of harassment by analyzing patterns and linguistic cues within the text. For example, a webpage containing the phrase "violence in media" would pass through the filter, whereas one promoting "acts of violence" with explicit intent would be flagged. This two-step system enhances the overall accuracy and ensures that the filtering process is more nuanced and context-aware (Lee, W., et al., 2007).

Random Forests:

Random Forests take the idea of decision trees and multiply it – literally. By creating an ensemble of decision trees, they produce more stable and accurate results. Each tree gets a slightly different view of the data, and their combined outputs lead to a more balanced prediction. Random forests are particularly effective for handling large, diverse datasets, which is often the case in cyberbullying detection. They are resistant to overfitting and handle skewed data, where messages intended to bully are very rare compared to messages that do not bully.

By utilizing these algorithms' strengths and using it in combination with the superior feature extraction techniques, a machine learning system could effectively enhance cyberbullying detection. The role of technology advances in shaping safer digital space and fostering inclusiveness will be more significant in that regard.

To build the model, the dataset is split into 80% training data and 20% testing data. A random forest classifier is trained using different numbers of trees (e.g., 17, 20, 50, 93). The best features are selected automatically by maximizing information gain using the gini criterion. Each tree is trained on a random subset of features, and final predictions are made by majority voting across all trees. This ensemble approach enhances accuracy, reduces overfitting, and provides robust predictions in identifying harmful content (Novalita, N., et al., 2019).

Figure 2. Machine learning workflow for cyberbullying detection

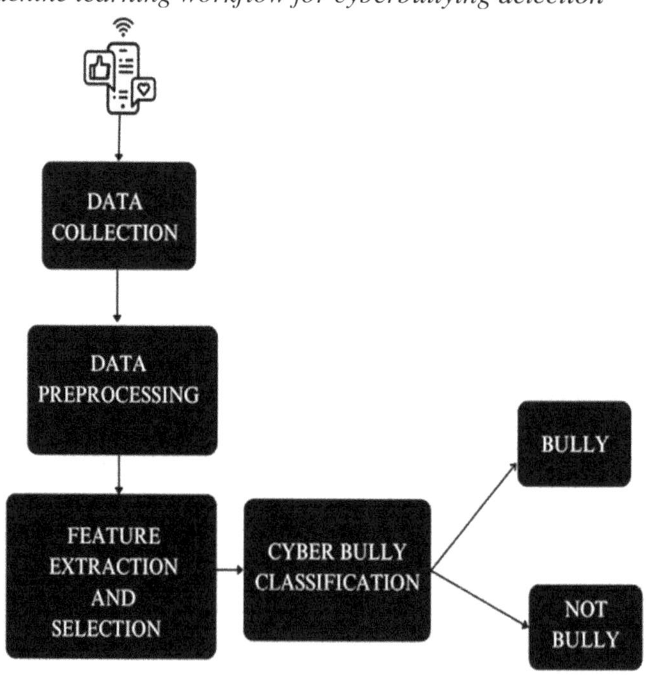

Figure 2 illustrates the step-by-step workflow of using machine learning for detecting cyberbullying. It starts with data collection from various online platforms, followed by preprocessing to clean and prepare the data. Feature extraction methods are then applied to identify relevant attributes for training the model. The data is then passed through a Cyberbully Classification model, which categorizes the content into either Bully or Not Bully. This structured approach ensures accuracy and efficiency in detecting harmful online behavior.

3. NATURAL LANGUAGE PROCESSING (NLP) IN DETECTING ABUSIVE LANGUAGE

This section discusses how NLP contributes to the detection of abusive language in online communication. Important preprocessing techniques such as tokenization, stemming, and lemmatization are presented in order to describe the way raw text is prepared for analysis. The role of sentiment analysis and text classification in identifying harmful intent is highlighted, alongside the challenges of detecting nuanced forms of abuse like sarcasm, slang, and multilingual content. By addressing these complexities, NLP provides powerful tools to interpret and analyze language, enabling more accurate and context-aware cyberbullying detection systems.

3.1 Preprocessing Techniques: Tokenization, Stemming, and Lemmatization

Natural Language Processing (NLP) is an essential necessity for determining the existence of abusive language in online communication. Raw text data, mostly, contains noise like grammatical errors, slang, emojis, and inconsistent formatting; so preprocessing plays an important role. The three most important preprocessing techniques used are:

Tokenization: This is a process of breaking text into smaller units called tokens, such as words or phrases. For example, the sentence "Cyberbullying is harmful" can be segmented into ["Cyberbullying", "is", "harmful"]. This makes text analysis easier and more efficient because it breaks sentences into smaller, manageable parts.

Stemming: Stemming reduces words to their root forms by removing suffixes. For example, "bullying" becomes "bully," and "harmful" becomes "harm." Although stemming is computationally efficient, it may result in less accurate base forms. For example, it may reduce "better" to "bet."

Lemmatization: In contrast to stemming, lemmatization takes the context into account and converts words to their dictionary base forms. For instance, "was" is converted to "be," and "children" to "child." Lemmatization is usually more accurate than stemming and is commonly used in tasks that require linguistic precision.

Table 2 outlines key NLP techniques and their applications in cyberbullying detection. Tokenization simplifies text processing by splitting it into smaller units but struggles with complex languages. Sentiment analysis detects negative or abusive emotions efficiently but faces challenges with sarcasm and ambiguous language. Lemmatization reduces data complexity by normalizing words to their base forms but requires robust language models. This table highlights the strengths and limitations of NLP techniques in understanding abusive content.

Table 2. Key NLP techniques and their applications

Technique	Application	Benefits	Challenges	Example
Tokenization	Splitting text into words/phrases	Simplifies processing	Handling complex languages	"Cyber-bullying" split as "Cyber" and "bullying"
Sentiment Analysis	Detecting negative/ abusive sentiment	Identifies emotions quickly	Sarcasm, ambiguity	Identifying anger in tweets
Lemmatization	Normalizing words to base forms	Reduces data complexity	Requires language models	"Running" reduced to "Run"
Named Entity Recognition (NER)	Identifying entities (names, places)	Helps analyze context	Difficulty with non-standard entities	Detecting personal attacks involving names

3.2 Sentiment Analysis and Text Classification

When it comes to identifying abusive language, two main tools are sentiment analysis and text classification:

Sentiment Analysis: This technique looks at the emotional tone behind a piece of text. Is it positive, negative, or neutral? Since abusive language often carries a negative vibe, sentiment analysis can be a good starting point. However, it's not foolproof-not all negative comments are abusive, and some abusive remarks can sound neutral. Text Classification: We classify text as "abusive" or "non-abusive," among others. We teach computers to recognize patterns in text by training them on algorithms like Support Vector Machines (SVM), Naïve Bayes, or even advanced deep learning models like Convolutional Neural Networks (CNNs). These classifications are made more accurate by including features such as n-grams (short sequences of words), word embeddings, or term frequency-inverse document frequency (TF-IDF).

A study conducted between January 2010 and January 2020 involved the development of deep learning models to aid in the identification of child physical abuse with a combination of clinical characteristics, laboratory findings, and imaging results. Model 1 used the patient demographics and clinical characteristics; Model 2 included natural language processing for the analysis of radiology reports and the same clinical data. The outcome indicated that deep learning models achieved very high accuracy in the differentiation of child physical abuse from non-abuse cases, and the best model was Model 2, which used NLP, with an accuracy of 93.4% and an ROC AUC of 0.94. Such results may indicate that such models can be integrated into electronic medical records, thus assisting clinicians in the timely identification of abuse and promoting early intervention (Shahi, N., et al2021).

Figure 3. NLP Pipeline for text preprocessing

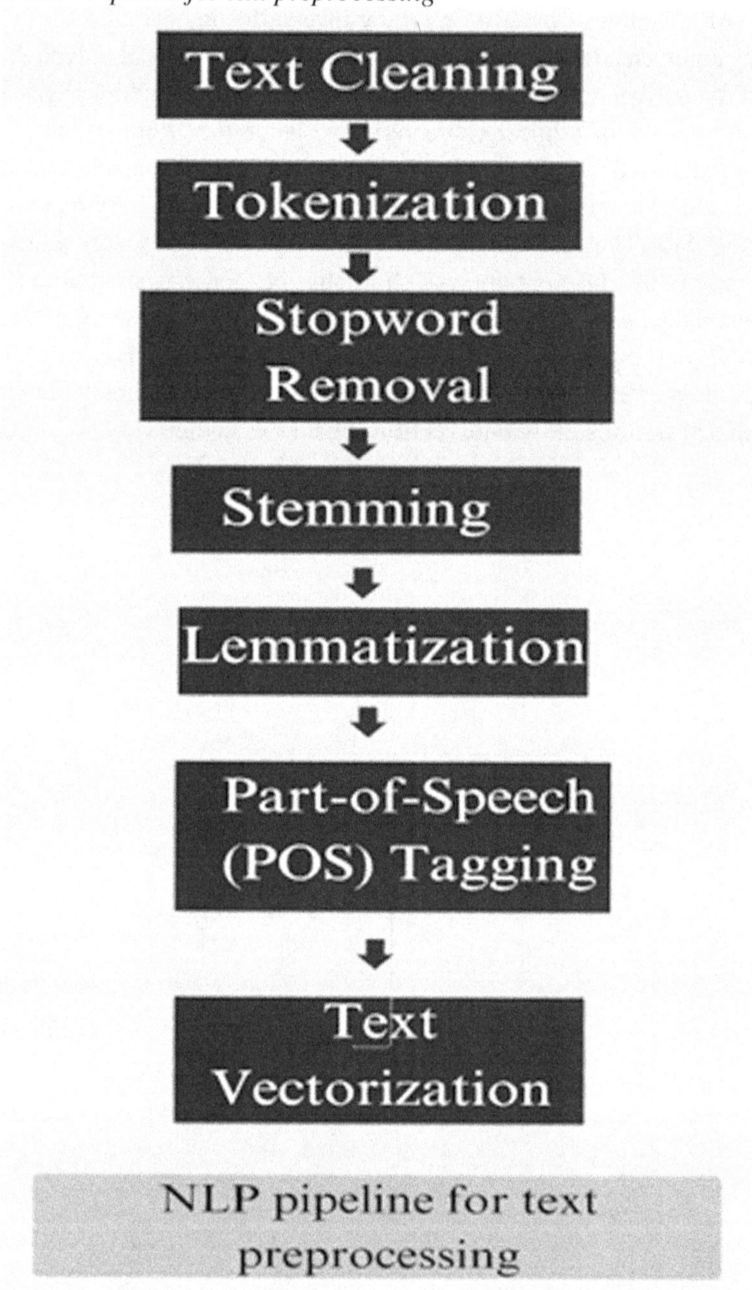

Figure 3 illustrates key steps in text preprocessing for cyberbullying detection. Starting with text cleaning to remove noise, it progresses through tokenization, stopword removal, stemming, and lemmatization to simplify and standardize text. Part-of-Speech (POS) tagging aids in syntactic understanding, while vectorization techniques like TF-IDF and word embeddings convert text into numerical formats for machine learning models. These steps ensure high-quality input for effective analysis.

3.3 Addressing Challenges: Sarcasm, Slang, and Multilingual Content

Detecting abusive language isn't always straightforward. Here's why:

Sarcasm: Since it frequently contradicts what is being said literally, sarcasm can be challenging. "Wow, you're so smart" could be a compliment or a jab, for example. By examining the context, sophisticated models such as BERT (Bidirectional Encoder Representations from Transformers) assist in determining the true meaning. Online conversations are rife with lingo, acronyms, and shorthand like "lol," "wtf," and "r u serious." We will need models that are trained on current, real-world data and specialized dictionaries to interpret these expressions.

Multilingual Content: Social media is a melting pot of languages, often mixed together (like "Hindi-English"). Detection of abusive language in these scenarios requires multilingual models and tools like mBERT or XLM-R that can handle multiple languages effectively.

Through such challenges, NLP tools will become smarter and better equipped to identify abusive language, no matter how it is expressed or where it is found.

Table 3 highlights key challenges in detecting abusive language using NLP techniques. Sarcasm detection struggles to interpret satirical or ironic comments, leading to false negatives. Slang and acronyms reduce detection accuracy due to informal text usage. Multilingual content and code-switching pose difficulties in analyzing mixed or switching languages, often excluding non-English data or missing contextual nuances. These challenges underline the complexities of designing robust NLP systems for cyberbullying detection.

Table 3. Challenges in abusive language detection using NLP

Challenge	Description	Example	Impact
Sarcasm Detection	Misinterpreting Satirical Comments	"Nice job, genius!" (Insult)	False Negatives in Detection
Slang and Acronyms	Difficulty in Understanding Informal Text	"u r so lame"	Reduced Accuracy
Multilingual Content	Mixed Languages in a Single Sentence	"Eres tan mean" (Spanish+English)	Excludes Non-English Data
Code-Switching	Switching Languages in the Same Sentence	"Hola, you're dumb."	Misses Context

4. DEEP LEARNING APPLICATIONS

Deep learning has revolutionized the detection of cyberbullying, enabling systems to analyze complex data with a high degree of accuracy. The following section will discuss how CNNs and RNNs are used in the analysis of text, images, and videos. More advanced architectures, such as transformers like BERT and GPT, are discussed in the light of their ability to capture context and nuances in abusive content. Multimodal analysis is also discussed, showcasing how deep learning combines text, images, and videos to detect cyberbullying across diverse formats like memes and videos. These advancements highlight the transformative potential of deep learning in combating online abuse.

4.1 Use of CNNs and RNNs for Text, Image, and Video Analysis

Deep learning is turning out to be the hallmark in the detection of cyberbullying, while in text analysis, it performs through the use of the Convolutional Neural Network (CNN) and the Recurrent Neural Network (RNN). RNN performs well in processing sequential data, as do LSTM and GRUs. These models can capture context and temporal dependencies in conversations, thereby enabling them to identify the patterns of abusive language efficiently. For example, an RNN can analyze a series of messages to determine a persistent trend of harassment or offensive speech (Kumar Reddy, C., et al., 2022). LSTMs are particularly good at handling long-term dependencies and are valuable for analyzing long discussions on forums or social media platforms.

The effectiveness of CNNs on image analysis is very prominent. Most cyberbullying is presented in the form of an offensive meme or image that contains harmful symbols or text. CNN can analyze visual patterns and even with OCR extract and analyze hidden text in images. Using a combination of visual and textual analysis, CNN forms a strong mechanism for recognizing harmful content in images. Furthermore, the fine-tuning capability of transfer learning enables such models to be fine-tuned to a specific task and even be efficient in the case of limited labeled data.

Video content poses an added challenge because of its multimodal nature, involving both visual and auditory elements. Effective hybrid models that combine CNNs for frame-by-frame image analysis with RNNs for processing the temporal sequence have emerged. These models are able to identify offending gestures, objectionable imagery, and hate speech in videos. Audio-to-text models convert audio into text, so even spoken harassment will not go unnoticed. All these together allow for comprehensive analysis of cyberbullying through various forms of media.

Table 4 compares deep learning models based on their applications, strengths, limitations, and example use cases. CNNs excel in analyzing visual content but lack sequential processing, while RNNs and LSTMs are effective in sequential text analysis with varying degrees of context handling. Transformers outperform others in accuracy and context understanding but at a high computational cost.

Table 4. Comparison of deep learning models for cyberbullying detection

Model	Application	Strengths	Limitations	Example Usage
CNN	Image/Meme Analysis	Excels in Visual Content	Lacks Sequential Processing	Detecting offensive memes
RNN	Sequential Text Analysis	Captures Contextual Relations	Vanishing Gradient Problem	Flagging abusive phrases over time
LSTM	Enhanced Sequential Analysis	Better Handling of Long-Term Dependencies	Requires High Computation	Tracking user tone changes in forums
Transformers	Text and Multimodal Analysis	Superior Accuracy and Context Understanding	High Computational Cost	Analyzing posts with mixed media content

4.2 Advanced Architectures: Transformers like BERT and GPT

Transformers have been a revolution in natural language processing and have emerged as powerful tools in cyberbullying detection. Their attention mechanisms enable them to consider text in context, that is, the nuances and subtle variations in language that are critical in identifying abusive behavior. BERT is an excellent model for this type of application. The bidirectional processing of text enables BERT to understand words based on both the preceding and succeeding context. It is this ability to capture nuanced meaning that is so important in detecting subtle forms of abuse, such as sarcasm or coded language, which may not be evident in isolated words or phrases. Fine-tuning BERT on specific datasets, for example, datasets with examples of abusive comments, increases its ability to detect hate speech, insults, and other forms of cyberbullying.

GPT (Generative Pre-trained Transformer) models are also useful in the detection of cyberbullying. These models are mainly generative in nature but can be fine-tuned for classification tasks. Their strength lies in their deep contextual understanding, which makes them detect even the more complex and disguised forms of abusive language. For example, GPT can look for harassment patterns that might be present across multiple comments or messages and provide a better view of the interactions harmful in nature. Furthermore, GPT can be utilized during training to generate examples of abusive language, thereby enriching the dataset and increasing model performance.

Transformers are great at scalability and adaptability. Pre-trained models, such as BERT and GPT, can be fine-tuned with smaller amounts of data, thus being practical for applications where there is a limited number of labeled datasets. They also do well with multilingual content, which is very common in cyberbullying detection, where offensive language could be in various languages or scripts. Models like multilingual BERT extend this capability, where abusive content in different linguistic contexts is accurately identified.

4.3 Multimodal Analysis for Detecting Cyberbullying in Memes and Videos

Cyberbullying is manifesting nowadays in more diversified formats, mainly memes and videos that add text, image, or sometimes audio elements. Analyzing such content will need a multimodal analysis that amalgamates data from a variety of sources to result in a well-cohesive understanding. Meme sites usually use some combination of image and overlay text whereby the intent behind abuse lies in either of them, together with their interaction. Multimodal detection systems use Optical Character Recognition (OCR) to extract text from images and apply natural language processing (NLP) techniques to analyze the extracted text for harmful content. Simultaneously, Convolutional Neural Networks (CNNs) analyze the visual components, identifying patterns or symbols that might indicate offensive or harmful intent. By fusing these analyses, the system can flag content that might be benign in one modality but harmful in combination (Khade, A., et al., 2023).

Videos are even more challenging as they involve visual, audio, and sometimes text data through subtitles. Effective detection involves speech, imagery, and sequential patterns. Models that transcribe speech-to-text convert spoken language to text, which then becomes the input for NLP methods to identify abusive or harmful language. CNNs look at the visual frames for offensive imagery or gestures, while RNNs or transformers are used for handling the temporal aspect, how the abusive behavior unfolds in time in a video. Further advanced models like Vision-Language Transformers, for example, ViLBERT, improve on this by analyzing visual and textual inputs simultaneously, which provides a unified approach for multimodal content.

Multimodal analysis poses several challenges, including capturing subtle and nuanced forms of abuse, such as sarcasm or coded language, and ensuring performance robustness across different datasets. Data augmentation techniques usually employ generative models for the creation of diverse examples of abusive content that improve model generalization and reduce bias. Multimodal analysis represents the frontier of cyberbullying detection, thus providing the tools to better deal with the increasingly sophisticated and varied forms of online harassment.

5. ROLE OF GENERATIVE AI IN CYBERBULLYING DETECTION

Generative AI is rewriting the rules of cyberbullying detection by taking up challenges such as the paucity of data and dynamically changing abusive tactics. This section is on how generative models, such as GANs and VAEs, create synthetic data to augment training datasets that make models perform better. Besides, it highlights how the generative AI can interpret complex and coded language, thus working more effectively in detecting subtle types of abuse. By enhancing multimodal detection capabilities and reducing biases, generative AI ensures more robust and fair detection systems (Islam, M. S., et al 2024). Ethical considerations are emphasized to promote responsible and unbiased use of this powerful technology.

5.1 Data Augmentation Using Generative Models

Data augmentation is a pivotal strategy in cyberbullying detection, especially because of the scarcity and imbalance in the labeled datasets. It involves the use of powerful tools such as Generative Adversarial Networks (GANs) and Variational Autoencoders(VAEs) for creating synthetic examples of abusive content. This method will ensure that AI models are exposed to a large number of abusive language patterns and, therefore, their generalization ability across forms of cyberbullying (Biswas, A., et al., 2023). In the context of textual data, generative models can produce variations of offensive language by altering sentence structures, incorporating synonyms, or generating entirely new abusive phrases while maintaining the harmful intent. This helps in capturing subtleties such as coded language, sarcasm, or evolving slang used by cyberbullies. For image-based cyberbullying, GANs can generate synthetic memes or edited images containing offensive text and symbols, enabling AI systems to recognize both direct and indirect forms of visual abuse. By creating diverse and balanced datasets, generative AI models address the problem of under-representation of certain types of cyberbullying and improve model robustness.

Figure 4. Workflow of data augmentation using generative AI

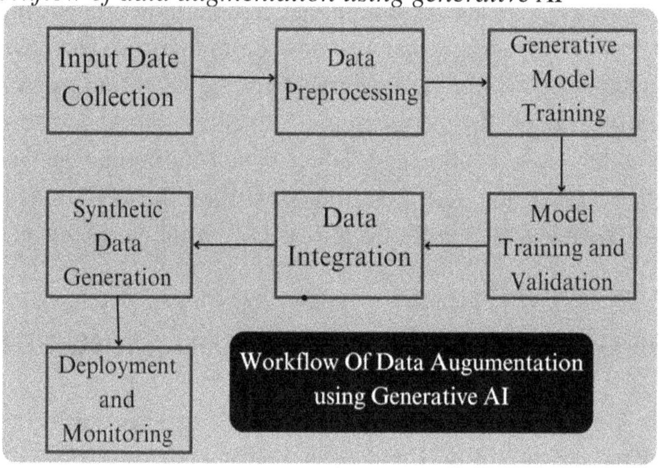

Figure 4 illustrates the workflow of data augmentation using generative AI. It starts with Input Data Collection from offline sources or real-time platforms like social media. The data is then Preprocessed to remove noise and ensure quality. Generative Models such as GANs or VAEs are trained to create Synthetic Data mimicking the original dataset across modalities like text, images, and videos. This synthetic data is merged with the original during Data Integration to balance distributions and address class imbalances. The enriched dataset is used for Model Training and Validation to evaluate performance metrics like accuracy and fairness. Finally, in the Deployment and Monitoring phase, trained models are applied to real-world scenarios, with continuous updates ensuring robustness and reliability.

5.2 Understanding Nuanced and Coded Language Through Gen-AI

One of the most difficult things about identifying cyberbullying is detecting subtle and coded language designed to evade traditional detection systems. Generative AI models, especially large language models like GPT, are particularly good at understanding and generating subtle text, which makes them a good fit for addressing this problem. Through patterns learned from massive datasets, these models can identify concealed meanings, veiled threats, or euphemisms that often occur in cyberbullying.

These generative models can be fine-tuned to identify and understand contextually ambiguous language that would otherwise be difficult to decipher, such as sarcasm or humor that would mask intent to be abusive. Phrases that, taken alone, may be innocuous can, for example, reflect harmful intent in the light of preceding or succeeding messages. Moreover, generative AI can simulate coded language often used in specific online communities, enabling detection systems to stay ahead of evolving cyberbullying tactics. By leveraging these capabilities, generative AI enhances the ability to detect cyberbullying that relies on subtleties and hidden connotations.

5.3 Enhancing Multimodal Detection Capabilities

Cyberbullying frequently occurs across multiple modalities, including text, images, and videos, requiring sophisticated detection methods. Generative AI plays a pivotal role in enhancing multimodal analysis by bridging gaps between different data types. For example, generative models can synthesize multimodal content for training purposes, such as memes with offensive text overlays or videos containing synchronized abusive speech and visuals. This enables AI systems to learn to detect harmful intent that emerges from the combination of modalities rather than isolated elements. (Zhang, M., et al., 2024) Generative AI models like Vision-Language Transformers are particularly useful for multimodal detection. These models integrate textual and visual inputs, allowing them to analyze complex content such as memes and videos comprehensively. For instance, in a meme, the image and text might individually seem benign, but their combination conveys an offensive message. Generative AI helps simulate such scenarios during training, making detection systems more robust in real-world applications. Additionally, these models can enhance audio-visual analysis in videos, ensuring that abusive language or gestures are accurately identified even when they occur simultaneously.

5.4 Ethical Use of Generative AI to Reduce Biases

While generative AI has many advantages in cyberbullying detection, its use must be guided by ethical considerations to prevent unintended biases and harmful outcomes. AI models trained on imbalanced datasets are prone to reflect and amplify existing biases, potentially leading to unfair or inaccurate detection. For instance, certain language styles or cultural expressions may be misinterpreted as offensive if the training data is biased. The potential to do this is presented by generative AI by making balanced and representative datasets, including diverse linguistic and cultural contexts.

Generative AI can, therefore, simulate edge cases or ambiguous scenarios that result in false positives or negatives. By exposing models to such edge cases during training, detection systems can clearly differentiate between genuinely harmful content and benign expressions that might seem to resemble cyberbullying. Transparency in the methods through which generative AI models are trained and deployed is also important, with considerations toward accountability and fairness.

Moreover, generative AI has to be used responsibly, without overreaching detection systems. Over Reliance on automated detection would give rise to issues about censorship and user privacy. The guidelines for ethics should, therefore, ensure that it does not replace human judgment in moderation but is adopted to enhance moderation efforts without causing an imbalance between efficiency and fairness. In this manner, more equitable and effective cyberbullying detection systems may be developed by the adoption of these measures through generative AI.

Table 5 highlights how generative AI enhances detection systems through data augmentation, nuanced language understanding, and multimodal detection. While these approaches improve accuracy and dataset balance, challenges like synthetic data bias and resource-intensive computations persist.

Table 5. Applications of generative AI in cyberbullying detection

Application	Benefits	Challenges	Example
Data Augmentation	Balances Dataset	Risk of Synthetic Data Bias	Generating variations of abusive sentences for training
Understanding Nuanced Language	Identifies Hidden Meanings	Complexity in Language Models	Detecting coded slurs or symbols
Multimodal Detection	Handles Text, Image, and Video	High Computational Resources	Recognizing harmful memes combined with text

6. DATA CHALLENGES AND ALGORITHMIC BIAS

Labeled datasets are fundamental to training effective cyberbullying detection models but creating them poses significant challenges. Cyberbullying content is highly diverse, ranging from explicit hate speech to subtle forms of harassment, making it difficult to capture all variations. Annotation is time-intensive and often subjective, as the interpretation of abuse can vary across individuals and cultural contexts. This subjectivity can lead to inconsistencies in labels, reducing the reliability of training data.

Data imbalance is another critical issue, as datasets typically contain far fewer instances of abusive content compared to benign interactions. This imbalance results in models that struggle to detect minority cases of abuse while performing well on majority non-abusive content. Additionally, certain types of abuse, such as coded language or specific cultural nuances, are often underrepresented, further limiting model effectiveness. Addressing these challenges requires a combination of improved annotation practices, balanced data collection, and techniques like resampling or data augmentation to enhance dataset diversity and ensure fairness.

Table 6 outlines key dataset challenges, including imbalanced data that reduces sensitivity, limited multilingual coverage that excludes global users, and annotation bias from subjective human labeling, which can misalign detection models.

Table 6. Common dataset challenges in cyberbullying detection

Challenge	Description	Example	Impact
Imbalanced Data	Overrepresentation of Non-Abusive Content	90% Neutral, 10% Abusive	Reduces Model Sensitivity
Lack of Multilingual Datasets	Limited Language Coverage	Predominantly English Data	Excludes Global Users
Annotation Bias	Human Labeling Subjectivity	Variance in Abusive Definition	Misaligned Detection Models

6.1 Strategies to Mitigate Bias in Detection Systems

The biases that often occur in AI-based detection systems arise from imbalanced or non-representative datasets, leading to unfair outcomes, such as over-policing certain groups or failure to detect abuse in underrepresented contexts. Curating diverse datasets that capture a wide range of linguistic, cultural, and contextual variations mitigates these biases, thereby helping models learn patterns of abuse across all demographic groups. (Jadon, A. (2024) Advanced techniques such as adversarial training expose models to challenging and borderline cases, improving their ability to distinguish genuine abuse from benign content. Fairness-aware algorithms can also be employed to minimize biases related to sensitive attributes like race, gender, or language. Regular audits of detection systems are crucial to identify emerging biases, while transparency in training data and methodologies fosters accountability. These strategies collectively improve the fairness and accuracy of cyberbullying detection systems.

6.2 Ethical Dilemmas in Labeling Harmful Content

Labeling datasets for cyberbullying detection involves ethical complexities, particularly due to the subjective nature of harmful content. What one individual considers abusive may be viewed differently by others, leading to inconsistencies in labeling. This subjectivity can result in datasets that either overreach or fail to capture the nuances of cyberbullying.

Additionally, exposing annotators to harmful material, such as explicit hate speech or graphic imagery, can have psychological consequences. Ethical safeguards, including providing support services and limiting exposure, are essential to protect annotators. Mislabeling also risks unfairly targeting marginalized groups, especially when slang or cultural expressions are misunderstood as abusive. (Farina, M., et al., 2024) To address these issues, clear and culturally inclusive guidelines must be established for labeling. Automated pre-labeling systems can reduce human exposure while still allowing for oversight to ensure accuracy. Ethical considerations should guide dataset creation, ensuring it balances effective detection with respect for diversity and annotator well-being.

7. REAL-TIME CYBERBULLYING DETECTION SYSTEMS

Integration of AI models with social media platforms: The best way to counter online harassment effectively is through the integration of AI-based cyberbullying detection models with social media platforms. The platforms are constantly producing content in large amounts, which makes it inevitable to have detection systems in place for smooth monitoring and identification of harmful interactions. AI models are usually integrated into moderation pipelines where text, images, and videos are analyzed for potential cyberbullying. These models can be used by social media companies to instantly alert moderators or automatically take down harmful content before the harm is spread. (López-Vizcaíno, M. F., et al., 2021) This integration is usually a collaboration between AI developers and platform engineers, to customize models for certain applications, such as comment harassment detection or harmful memes identification. Models must also conform to the policies and rules set by the platforms, such that actions taken would be appropriate and in line with the expectations of the users. While AI integration enhances detection capabilities significantly, its implementation demands constant updating due to changes in language trends and the emergence of new forms of abuse.

7.1 Scalability and Computational Challenges

Cyberbullying detection systems face significant scalability challenges due to the sheer volume of content generated on social media platforms. AI models must process millions of posts, images, and videos daily, demanding substantial computational resources. Real-time detection adds further complexity, as delays in identifying harmful content can allow it to spread, amplifying its impact.

Scalable solutions often involve the use of distributed computing, where tasks are shared across multiple servers or cloud infrastructure to handle high data loads. Lightweight models optimized for speed and efficiency can also help balance performance and resource usage. However, scaling detection systems must not come at the cost of accuracy, as oversimplified models risk missing subtle or nuanced cases of cyberbullying.

Another challenge is ensuring that detection systems remain effective as platforms grow and content types evolve. For example, emerging platforms often have different formats and user behaviors, requiring flexible models capable of adapting to new environments. Regular updates, combined with robust infrastructure, ensure scalability while maintaining detection accuracy.

7.2 Trade-Offs Between Speed and Accuracy

A significant trade-off between speed and accuracy is encountered in real-time cyberbullying detection. While swift identification and mitigation of harmful content is critical to avoid its propagation, achieving high accuracy calls for complex, resource-intensive models. It creates tension between the necessity of immediate action and the danger of false positives or false negatives. Faster, lighter models would focus more on processing speed for high-traffic platforms. However, they may be less likely to catch subtle forms of abuse such as sarcasm or coded language. In contrast, more advanced models, like transformers, tend to be highly accurate but computationally expensive, which might lead to slower processing. Striking the right balance involves adopting a hybrid approach where simpler models handle initial screening and advanced models focus on flagged content for in-depth analysis. Additionally, human moderators can review edge cases to ensure fairness and context sensitivity. By optimizing these trade-offs, platforms can achieve timely and effective cyberbullying detection while minimizing errors.

Table 7 examines trade-offs in real-time detection, balancing speed, accuracy, and scalability. Faster systems may compromise accuracy, while highly accurate models require more computational resources. Scalability ensures large-scale abuse detection but demands advanced infrastructure.

Table 7. Trade-Offs in real-time detection systems

Metric	Advantage	Disadvantage	Real-World Impact
Speed	Quick Responses	Potential Drop in Accuracy	Flagging content instantly
Accuracy	High Detection Quality	Increased Computational Cost	Higher false positive control
Scalability	Handles Large Traffic	Requires Advanced Resources	Detecting abuse on major platforms

8. ETHICAL AND PRIVACY CONSIDERATIONS

Balancing detection efficiency with user privacy: The delicate balance in AI-based cyberbullying detection systems would be to balance efficiency with harmful content identification and privacy concerns of users. The primary means by which such detection systems would analyze massive volumes of personal data, comprising messages, posts, and multimedia, to detect abusive behavior, would make privacy issues relevant. Intrusive monitoring can cause some to be concerned about being over-policed on what is considered a conversation or expression.

This can be avoided by employing detection systems by using federated learning techniques that allow the development of models to train themselves across decentralized devices without getting their raw user data. Then, content should be made anonymous before its analysis with the intention of decreasing associated privacy risks. Third, platforms need to ensure well-defined information about the collection and usage of the provided data as well as privacy regulations such as the GDPR. Achieving this balance helps ensure that the effectiveness of cyberbullying detection will not compromise user trust and privacy rights.

8.1 Addressing False Positives and Negatives

False positives and negatives are significant challenges in cyberbullying detection.False positives and negatives in cyberbullying detection: False positives occur when good content is tagged as abusive, so the user would be unfairly penalized. False negatives refer to harmful content that has slipped past the detection system, so the whole system would become ineffective. Both may lead to the erosion of trust with the platform and its moderation practices.

To minimize these errors, detection systems should use context-aware models that analyze the surrounding content and interactions rather than focusing solely on isolated words or phrases. Incorporating advanced techniques like sentiment analysis and multimodal analysis can further enhance accuracy. Continuous monitoring and feedback loops, where flagged cases are reviewed by human moderators, help refine the system over time. By addressing false positives and negatives, platforms can maintain a fair and reliable detection system.

8.2 Navigating Privacy Laws and Regulations

Cyberbullying detection systems, based on AI, function in an intricate environment of privacy legislation and regulations. Laws like GDPR and the California Consumer Privacy Act (CCPA) impose strict guidelines about how user data can be collected, stored, and processed. The platforms will have to ensure that the moderation in such detection systems does not run in contrast to these regulations. (Kang, H., et al., 2024) Compliance usually demands data minimization practices where only necessary information is collected for analysis, and obtaining user consent means that there should be some options to opt in and out of data processing while trying to detect cyberbullying. Transparency about using and storing data is really important for building trust for users.

Navigating these regulations also involves adapting to region-specific legal requirements and cultural expectations. While robust compliance ensures legal protection, it also necessitates continuous updates to the system as laws evolve. By aligning detection practices with privacy regulations, platforms can ensure ethical and responsible deployment of AI in cyberbullying detection.

9. FUTURE DIRECTIONS IN AI-BASED CYBERBULLYING DETECTION

The future of cyberbullying detection lies in advancing innovative technologies and preventive strategies. This section explores the potential of multimodal analysis to detect abuse across formats, AI's role in promoting positive online behavior, and the development of context-aware models to better understand nuanced interactions. These advancements promise more robust and adaptive systems, capable of addressing the evolving nature of cyberbullying. By combining technical innovation with ethical practices, this section envisions a future where AI fosters safer and more supportive digital environments.

9.1 Innovations in Multimodal Analysis

The future of cyberbullying detection lies in advancing multimodal analysis, which integrates text, images, audio, and video to identify harmful content. Current models often analyze individual modalities in isolation, but cyberbullying frequently combines multiple formats, such as offensive memes or videos with abusive language overlays. Innovations in multimodal AI aim to seamlessly process and interpret content across these formats, improving detection accuracy. (Worsley, M. 2022) Future systems may leverage advanced architectures like Vision-Language Transformers, which can simultaneously analyze images and text to detect the intent behind memes or multimedia posts. Similarly, audio-visual models will enable more comprehensive analysis of videos, identifying abusive language, gestures, and visual elements. These advancements will empower detection systems to better understand the context and intent of cyberbullying, making them more robust against subtle or layered forms of abuse.

9.2 AI's Role in Preventive Interventions

Besides detection, AI is going to play a crucial role in preventive interventions against cyberbullying. Predictive models will analyze the user's behavior to identify patterns such as repeated negative interactions or escalating hostility and alerting them. For example, AI may warn users of possible harmful language that may trigger such bullying and encourage self-moderation.

Platforms can use AI to create positive online spaces by encouraging constructive engagement. For instance, sentiment analysis tools could highlight uplifting content or steer users away from controversial conversations. Additionally, AI chatbots can offer real-time support to victims by offering resources or connecting them with moderators. By shifting focus from reactive measures to proactive strategies, AI can help reduce the prevalence of cyberbullying and its impact on users.

9.3 Enhanced Models for Better Context Understanding

Understanding context is critical for accurate cyberbullying detection, as abusive intent often depends on subtle cues like sarcasm, cultural references, or prior interactions. Enhanced AI models are being developed to address these challenges, incorporating deeper contextual analysis to distinguish between benign and harmful content.

Future models will likely use advanced Natural Language Processing (NLP) techniques, including large language models like GPT, to interpret nuanced language and evolving slang. They will also integrate historical context, analyzing user interactions over time to understand relationship dynamics and identify patterns of harassment. Multilingual capabilities will expand, enabling detection across diverse languages and cultural expressions. By advancing context-aware systems, AI will become more adept at identifying cyberbullying while reducing false positives and negatives. These enhancements will ensure more accurate, fair, and culturally sensitive detection, setting a higher standard for online safety.

CONCLUSION

Artificial Intelligence has brought out a revolutionary way to identify and respond to cyberbullying solutions, far beyond traditional approaches. The systems using machine learning, natural language processing, and deep learning analyze text, images, and multimedia in search of harmful behaviors with unprecedented accuracy. Advanced techniques, such as multimodal analysis and generative AI, allow for the detection of subtle and complex forms of abuse, such as sarcasm, coded language, and multimodal harassment, in real time. Despite its great promise, there are some problems: data imbalance, algorithmic bias, issues with privacy, and scaling. Such problems are fundamental and require attention to the ethics frameworks, transparency, and ongoing improvement of the models used in detection. These will be fair, accurate, and culturally sensitive only through the collaborative efforts of technologists, policymakers, and social scientists. With this kind of advancement and development of AI, it is guaranteed that it will not only identify cyberbullying but also prevent it by coming up with early interventions and positive experiences online. Given innovation at the center of things and responsible practices, there is much that AI has to do in terms of creating a safer and helpful digital space for all involved in it.

REFERENCES

Biswas, A.. (2023). Generative adversarial networks for data augmentation. In Zheng, B., Andrei, S., Sarker, M. K., & Gupta, K. D. (Eds.), *Data driven approaches on medical imaging* (pp. 101–115). Springer., DOI: 10.1007/978-3-031-47772-0_8

Emmery, C., Verhoeven, B., De Pauw, G., & Daelemans, W. (2021). Current limitations in cyberbullying detection: On evaluation criteria, reproducibility, and data scarcity. *Language Resources and Evaluation*, 55(3), 597–633. DOI: 10.1007/s10579-020-09509-1

Farina, M., Yu, X., & Lavazza, A. (2024). Ethical considerations and policy interventions concerning the impact of generative AI tools in the economy and in society. *AI and Ethics*. Advance online publication. DOI: 10.1007/s43681-023-00405-2

Islam, M. S., Sutton, S., & Rafiq, R. I. (2024). A generative AI powered approach to cyberbullying detection. *Proceedings of the 2024 8th International Conference on Information System and Data Mining*, 57–63. https://doi.org/DOI: 10.1145/3686397.3686407

Jadon, A. (2024). *Ethical AI development: Mitigating bias in generative models.* Retrieved from https://www.researchgate.net/profile/Ankit-Jadon/publication/669ffd6a8be3067b4b1506c9/Ethical-AI-Development-Mitigating-Bias-in-Generative-Models/links/669ffd6a8be3067b4b1506c9/Ethical-AI-Development-Mitigating-Bias-in-Generative-Models.pdf

Jain, V. H., & Bohra, V. M. (2024). Cyberbullying in the digital age: Legal challenges and solutions. *International Journal of Legal Research and Analysis*, 2(7), 16. https://www.doi-ds.org/doilink/07.2024-23173692/

Kang, H., Wang, Y., Wang, M., Al Imran Yasin, M., Osman, M. N., & Ang, L. H. (2024). Navigating digital network: Mindfulness as a shield against cyberbullying in the knowledge economy era. *Journal of the Knowledge Economy*, 15(3), 13233–13271. DOI: 10.1007/s13132-023-01604-2

Khade, A., Oza, P., & Kazi, N. (2023). *Multimodal cyberbullying meme detection from social media using deep learning approach.* ResearchGate., DOI: 10.1007/978-981-99-5614-8_23

Kumar Reddy, C., P R, A., Reddy, T., & D, R. (2022). Early monitoring of social distancing using OpenCV and deep learning. *International Journal of Engineering and Computer Science (INT-JECSE)*, 11(6), 1275–1283. DOI: 10.1016/j.future.2021.01.006

Lee, W., Lee, S. S., Chung, S., & An, D. (2007). Harmful contents classification using the harmful word filtering and SVM. In Shi, Y., van Albada, G. D., Dongarra, J., & Sloot, P. M. A. (Eds.), Lecture Notes in Computer Science: Vol. 4489. *Computational Science – ICCS 2007* (pp. 15–21). Springer., DOI: 10.1007/978-3-540-72588-6_3

López-Vizcaíno, M. F., Nóvoa, F. J., Carneiro, V., & Cacheda, F. (2021). Early detection of cyberbullying on social media networks. *Future Generation Computer Systems*, 118, 219–229. DOI: 10.1016/j.future.2021.01.006

Milosevic, T., Van Royen, K., & Davis, B. (2022). Artificial intelligence to address cyberbullying, harassment, and abuse: New directions in the midst of complexity. *International Journal of Bullying Prevention : an Official Publication of the International Bullying Prevention Association*, 4(1), 1–5. DOI: 10.1007/s42380-022-00117-x PMID: 35233506

Milosevic, T., Verma, K., Carter, M., Vigil, S., Laffan, D., Davis, B., & O'Higgins Norman, J. (2023). Effectiveness of artificial intelligence–based cyberbullying interventions from youth perspective. *Social Media + Society*, 9(1), 20563051221147325. Advance online publication. DOI: 10.1177/20563051221147325

Morales, E. F., & Escalante, H. J. (2022). A brief introduction to supervised, unsupervised, and reinforcement learning. In Torres-García, A. A., Reyes-García, C. A., Villaseñor-Pineda, L., & Mendoza-Montoya, O. (Eds.), *Biosignal processing and classification using computational learning and intelligence* (pp. 111–129). Academic Press., DOI: 10.1016/B978-0-12-820125-1.00017-8

Novalita, N., Herdiani, A., Lukmana, I., & Puspandari, D. (2019). Cyberbullying identification on Twitter using random forest classifier. *Journal of Physics: Conference Series*, 1192(1), 012029. DOI: 10.1088/1742-6596/1192/1/012029

Shahi, N., Shahi, A. K., Phillips, R., Shirek, G., Lindberg, D. M., & Moulton, S. L. (2021). Using deep learning and natural language processing models to detect child physical abuse. *Journal of Pediatric Surgery*, 56(12), 2326–2332. DOI: 10.1016/j.jpedsurg.2021.03.007 PMID: 33838900

Singh, M. T., Reddy, C. K., Murthy, B. V. R., Nag, A., & Doss, S. (2025). AI and education: Bridging the gap to personalized, efficient, and accessible learning. In M. Ouaissa, M. Ouaissa, H. Lamaazi, M. El Hamlaoui, & K. Reddy C. (Eds.), Internet of behavior-based computational intelligence for smart education systems (pp. 131–160). IGI Global.

Singh, (2023). Cyberbullying in the 21st century: A rising threat to youth in the digital age. *International Journal of Indian Psychology, 11*(3), 3273–3279. https://doi.org/DOI: 10.1016/j.jpedsurg.2021.03.007 PMID: 33838900

Wiederhold, B. K. (2024). The dark side of the digital age: How to address cyberbullying among adolescents. [editorial]. *Cyberpsychology, Behavior, and Social Networking*, 27(3), 169–171. Advance online publication. DOI: 10.1089/cyber.2024.29309.editorial PMID: 38364097

Worsley, M. (2022). Artificial Intelligence Innovations for Multimodal Learning, Interfaces, and Analytics. In *AI in Learning: Designing the Future* (pp. 19–35). Springer International Publishing.

Yuvaraj, N., Chang, V., Gobinathan, B., Pinagapani, A., Kannan, S., Dhiman, G., & Rajan, A. R. (2021). Automatic detection of cyberbullying using multi-feature based artificial intelligence with deep decision tree classification. *Computers & Electrical Engineering*, 92, 107186. DOI: 10.1016/j.compeleceng.2021.107186

Zhang, M., Shen, Y., Yin, J., Lu, S., & Wang, X. (2024). ADAGENT: Anomaly detection agent with multimodal large models in adverse environments. *IEEE Access : Practical Innovations, Open Solutions*, 12, 172061–172074. DOI: 10.1109/ACCESS.2024.3480250

Chapter 4
AI-Powered Harmony: Pioneering Safer Social Platforms

Meetu Malhotra
https://orcid.org/0009-0009-7495-4484
Harrisburg University of Science and Technology, USA

Ria Ghosh
https://orcid.org/0009-0004-7737-4171
Forency LLP, India

Naresh Kumar
https://orcid.org/0000-0001-9984-506X
Maharaja Surajmal Institute of Technology, India

Kishore Kumar Reddy C.
Stanley College of Engineering and Technology for Women, India

ABSTRACT

Cyberbullying remains a pervasive issue in the digital era, affecting individuals of all ages across diverse online platforms. This book chapter, AI-Powered Harmony Pioneering Safer Social Platforms, explores the evolving role of Artificial Intelligence (AI) in mitigating this critical societal challenge. The chapter begins by emphasizing the importance of cyberbullying prevention and highlights the transformative potential of AI-driven solutions. It covers Emerging AI technologies, deep learning models like GPT and BERT, and multimodal approaches are also examined in depth and concludes with a vision for a collaborative and AI-driven future.

DOI: 10.4018/979-8-3373-0543-1.ch004

1. INTRODUCTION

The use of social media, messaging platforms, and online forums has tremendously grown, and eventually made cyberbullying a big challenge in society (Siddhartha et al., 2022). Unlike traditional bullying, cyberbullying doesn't have geographical boundaries and helps bullies to torment victims whenever and wherever they want. Because of their ubiquity, these experiences can have a disproportionate emotional, psychological, and social impact on victims which may leave in their wake long lasting scars. Realizing the seriousness of this problem, immediate, innovative, scalable and effective solutions are required (Fati et al., 2023). Fortunately, Artificial Intelligence (AI) has proven great potential for dealing with this all-pervasive problem by offering detection, prevention, and intervention in ways that were unattainable previously. In this chapter, we discuss how AI will play a role in future cyberbullying prevention, and the opportunities and challenges it offers.

Cyberbullying manifests in various forms, each with unique characteristics and implications as shown in Figure 1. Denigration involves spreading false or harmful information to damage someone's reputation, while flaming refers to aggressive, hostile exchanges intended to provoke or humiliate. Trickery entails deceiving someone into revealing private information that is then shared publicly, and cyberstalking involves persistent, threatening behavior that causes fear or distress. Impersonation is pretending to be someone else to post damaging or humiliating content, whereas harassment is a sustained campaign of abusive messages targeting an individual. Lastly, outings occur when someone's private, sensitive information is shared without consent, often causing public embarrassment or harm.

Figure 1. Types of cyberbullying

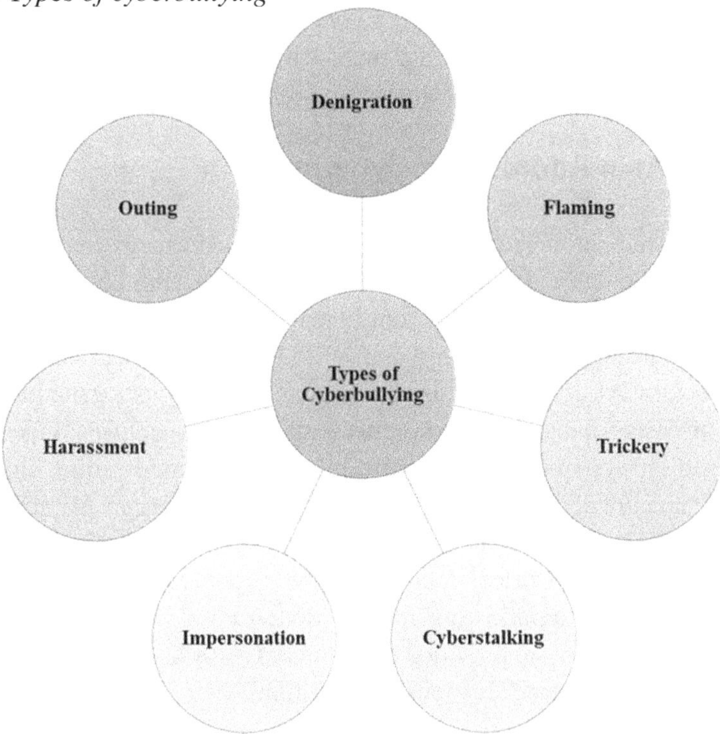

1.1. Importance of Cyberbullying Prevention

Since cyberbullying incidents have spiked, its devastating consequences, not only on the victims but also on families and communities have come to the fore (Hamiza Wan Ali et al., 2018). Cyberbullying victims often suffer from anxiety, depression and other mental health problems which may end up in extreme cases of academic failure, regularly losing out on social interactions and worst cases that may lead to self-harm. While the ramifications of this scenario are alarming enough for everyone, the ramifications are particularly alarming for young people who make up most internet users in various stages of emotional and social development. Additionally, there is anonymity in online platforms that emboldens perpetrators and complicates attempts to discover, and subsequently hold accountable, attackers.

Not preventing cyberbullying is just as much an issue of individual wellbeing as it is a societal imperative. Hostile or unsafe online spaces stop meaningful engagement and prevent positive interactions from happening(Obaid et al., 2023). Prevention of cyber bullying efforts leads to making online environments safer, and supporting such goals in creating digital communities, which will be inclusive and in which respect, collaboration, creativity and other good stuff will be fostered. Consequently, proactive measures and especially those enabled by technology become more critical in risk mitigation and improve the online experience for everyone.

1.2. Role of AI in Addressing Cyberbullying

Using Artificial Intelligence, we can provide transformative solutions to the various aspects of cyberbullying. AI systems can detect harmful content, recognize patterns of abusive behavior and intervene in real time through advanced techniques like machine learning, deep learning and NLP. For example, on social media — from Facebook to Twitter — AI is used to scan and identify user generated content containing offensive or discriminatory remarks as these appear in messages or posts. Not only are these systems faster to approve than manual moderation, but they can process scale amount of online data that is produced daily (Teng & Varathan, 2023).

Although it's beyond detection, AI does play a key role in both prevention and intervention. Based on historical data, predictive models can identify users at risk: as victims or as perpetrators allowing timely action. Additional insights concerning a user's psychological state are provided by sentiment analysis and emotion detection algorithms for a more nuanced response. In addition, AI driven Chatbots and virtual counselors are becoming effective as a means of immediate support for victims and educating users about right etiquette in the online world and the threading of Cyber Bullying (Perera & Fernando, 2021).

But this application of AI in the domain is not without challenges. It faces hurdles like algorithmic bias, privacy, the problem of language and culture all handled in a contextual way. For AI to achieve its promise in a manner that is responsible, inclusive, and transparent and fair it must be designed and deployed with a focus on fairness, transparency, and inclusivity.

1.3. Overview of Future Challenges and Opportunities

In the midst of technological change, cyberbullying also evolves in nature, forcing the efforts of prevention. Detection and monitoring are complicated by the sophistication of online interactions, the use of encrypted messaging, anonymous platforms, and by the adoption of immersive environments such as virtual and augmented reality. What's more, the speed of linguistic and cultural adaptation in online space requires AI systems to be able to adapt to the evolution of slang, regional dialects, and multiple contexts that may vary over time (Hasan et al., 2023).

However, even with all these problems, there are big chances to use AI in cyberbullying prevention in the future. New technologies may help fix many of the current approaches' shortcomings: explainable AI (XAI), federated learning, and multimodal systems. Interventions can be amplified in collaborative frameworks where they integrate with AI and human moderators, educators and policymakers. In addition, data sharing protocols, along with ethical AI practices have opened a door for a global effort in battling against cyberbullying across platforms and countries.

The dynamic nature of cyberbullying requires AI-driven solutions to evolve rapidly to address complex online interactions. Decentralized and encrypted platforms pose challenges for detection, as anonymity and a lack of centralized moderation enable harmful behaviors. The rise of virtual and augmented reality (VR/AR) adds complexity, with non-verbal bullying forms like intimidating avatars or disruptive actions that traditional AI struggles to detect.

Rapid language evolution, including new slang and coded language, further complicates prevention efforts. AI models must adapt to regional dialects, cultural nuances, and shifting contexts to remain effective, as static models trained on outdated datasets create detection gaps.

Despite these challenges, AI holds immense potential for cyberbullying prevention. There are some machine learning algorithms (Kumar et al., 2023) that can help in mitigating the negative impacts of social media behavior. Explainable AI (XAI) can enhance transparency, foster trust and informed moderation. Federated learning allows training on decentralized data while preserving privacy, improving model robustness. Multimodal AI systems integrating text, audio, video, and behavioral signals can capture subtle patterns, addressing the complexities of VR/AR interactions.

Collaboration is vital, with AI systems working alongside human moderators, educators, and policymakers to create cohesive intervention frameworks. Global cooperation, ethical AI practices, and data-sharing protocols can drive the development of universal standards for combating cyberbullying, paving the way for safer and more inclusive online spaces.

This chapter investigates these trends and what they mean for the future of AI in preventing cyberbullying. It imagines a digital ecosystem driven by technological innovation, ethical thinking, and collaborative strategies that will allow individuals, especially vulnerable populations, to interact securely and confidently.

2. CURRENT STATE OF AI IN CYBERBULLYING PREVENTION

In recent years, Artificial Intelligence's use in cyberbullying prevention has made tremendous progress as the sociotechnical landscape of online interactions has become more complex and there has been a demand for scalable, effective solutions. The ability for AI to process huge amounts of data in real time, identify harmful patterns, and suggest interventions makes AI critical to fighting cyberbullying (Islam et al., 2020). However, as we are, AI in this domain is at a halfway point, falling somewhere between exciting accomplishments and insurmountable problems. Although some outstanding achievements show the potential of AI, its design, deployment and societal acceptance are yet to be measured and improved.

The general architecture for cyberbullying detection illustrated in the diagram consists of several key stages as shown in Figure 2. The process begins with data extraction from diverse platforms such as social media (e.g., Reddit, YouTube, TikTok). The extracted input content, including text and image data, undergoes data preprocessing, which involves cleaning tasks like tokenization, lemmatization, stemming, and removal of stop words for textual data, while Optical Character Recognition (OCR) and image similarity methods process image-based content. Following this, feature extraction and selection identify critical features relevant to detecting cyberbullying patterns. Predefined cyberbullying keywords enhance the detection process. Machine learning or deep learning models analyze the processed and selected features, ultimately classifying the content into bullying or non-bullying categories based on predefined thresholds and trained algorithms. The architecture ensures comprehensive analysis by integrating multimodal data and advanced AI techniques.

Figure 2. General architecture of cyberbullying detection

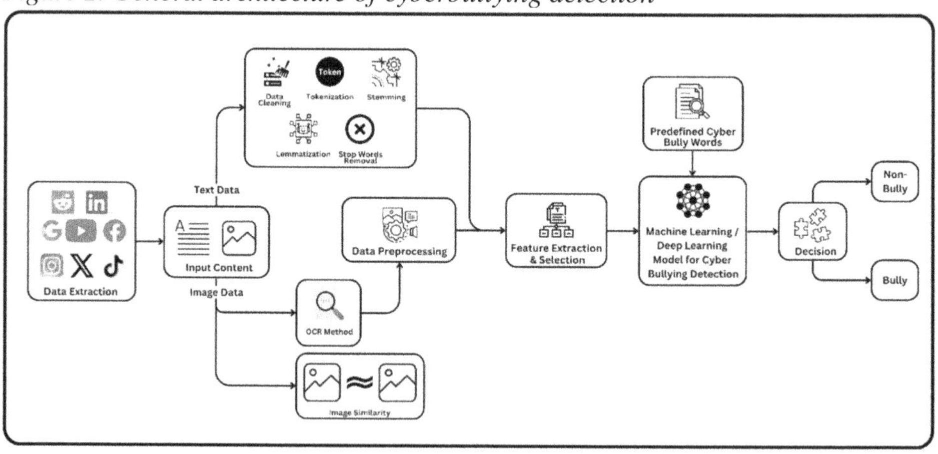

2.1. Overview of Existing AI Techniques

Currently several AI techniques are used to detect, analyze and prevent cyberbullying as shown in Figure 3. One of the most popular techniques, NLP, helps machines to intake and make sense of textual data (Sultan et al., 2023). Sentiment analysis (Manzoor et al., 2022), toxicity detection, and context aware language modeling are NLP based systems that have been designed to flag abusive language, hate speech, or threatening language. Instead of text data, Support Vector Machines (SVMs), Random Forest and deep learning architectures (i.e. Recurrent Neural Networks (RNNs) or Transformers (like BERT or GPT models), to count name, increasing the accuracy of text cyberbullying detection.

For images and videos, advanced computer vision techniques are increasingly being utilized to identify bullying-related non-textual content, such as derogatory memes, offensive gestures, or even the tone of visual imagery that perpetuates harm. These methods leverage Convolutional Neural Networks (CNNs) and other deep learning models to analyze complex visual data. Platforms now incorporate tools capable of flagging inappropriate visuals with remarkable accuracy, identifying subtle indicators like hate symbols, harmful text embedded in images, or contextually offensive imagery.

Similarly, deep learning models for audio analysis have opened new dimensions in cyberbullying prevention by enabling the detection of harmful behavior in voice messages, live chats, and video streams. Techniques such as spectrogram analysis combined with Recurrent Neural Networks (RNNs) or Transformer models are being applied to detect patterns of aggression, abusive language, or harmful tones in spoken communication.

This integration of computer vision and audio analysis enables a more holistic approach to identifying and curbing cyberbullying across multimedia formats. The combined analysis of visual and audio data enhances the ability of AI systems to comprehend the broader context of harmful interactions, reducing false positives and capturing more complex, multimodal instances of bullying.

Figure 3. Existing techniques in detection of cyberbullying

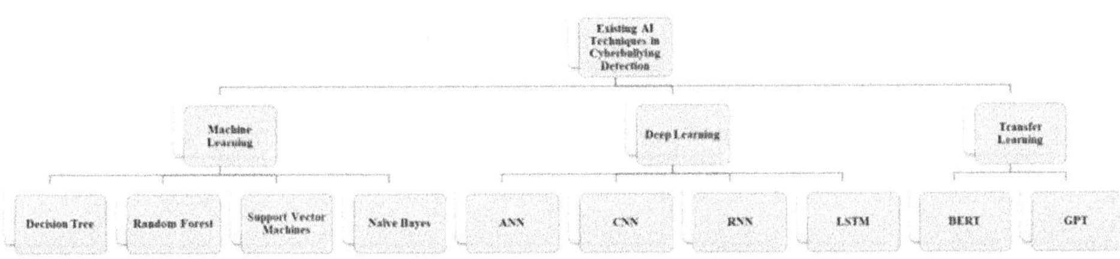

Similarly, graph-based models are becoming common, including studies in social network structures. These models analyze how people relate to each other, their interaction patterns and how content spreads to detect coordinated (individual) bullying or harassment campaigns. For example, they can use it to find cliques or groups to target individuals based on the patterns of what they do.

2.2. Strengths and Limitations of Current Approaches

There are many strengths of AI systems on cyberbullying prevention as shown in Table 1. One key point supported by these is their scalability: AI can review and interpret much larger amounts of data much faster than human moderators. The significance of this capability is amplified by the massive volume of content being created over social media and other web sites every day. Also, AI's speed allows near real time detection and intervention, critical in reducing the damage done by harmful interactions before they can grow.

The fact that AI can run nonstop and without fatigue is another strength as a way to keep watch on its content 24/7. Compared to other systems that lack human bias, the issue of human bias is not too great here because it can identify subtle abusive behavior patterns that would otherwise be missed by humans, especially when the bullying is itself camouflaged using sarcasm, coded language and other multimedia formats (Iwendi et al., 2023).

However, these strengths are offset by considerable limitations. Contextual understanding is one of the main challenges. One of the problems of AI is that it often fails to interpret a message's intent, marking innocuous content as harmful (false positive) and vice versa (false negative). Take, for instance, an AI system that will misunderstand playful banter of friends as bullying because it cannot understand social dynamics (Muneer et al., 2023).

Another critical limitation is bias in training data. Datasets that contain limited diversity regarding language, culture, and populations are common when training AI models, and many will fail to apply well in a real-world scenario involving a diverse population. Also, there are privacy concerns with AI services, as AI systems need access to the user's data for training and analysis, which raises concerns about consent and data security.

In addition, because many AI systems are not transparent or explainable, there is lack of trust among its users and stakeholders. These systems, however, risk alienating users, or encounter resistance to wider adoption, if they offer no clear explanations as to why content is flagged, or decisions are made.

Table 1. Strengths and limitations of the current techniques

Aspect	Strength/ Limitations	Description	Example	Implications
Scalability	Strength	AI can process vast amounts of data quickly, far exceeding human capacity.	Social media content review.	Enables efficient monitoring of large platforms in real-time.
24/7 Operation	Strength	AI operates nonstop without fatigue, ensuring continuous monitoring.	Real-time alerts for harmful posts.	Provides constant vigilance against cyberbullying activities.
Pattern Recognition	Strength	Detects subtle abusive patterns, even those camouflaged in sarcasm or multimedia.	Identifying bullying in memes or coded language.	Enhances detection of nuanced and hidden cyberbullying.
Contextual Challenges	Limitation	Difficulty in understanding social dynamics or intent behind messages.	Misinterpreting friendly banter as bullying (false positives).	Leads to inaccurate flagging and potential user dissatisfaction.
Bias in Training Data	Limitation	Limited diversity in datasets affects AI's effectiveness across different populations.	Ineffective detection in culturally specific scenarios.	Reduces reliability and fairness in diverse real-world applications.
Privacy Concerns	Limitation	Requires access to user data for training, raising issues of consent and security.	User data analysis for behavior detection.	Raises ethical concerns and potential regulatory issues.
Lack of Explainability	Limitation	Many AI systems lack transparency, creating distrust among users and stakeholders.	Content flagged without clear reasoning.	Reduces user trust and hinders broader adoption of AI systems.

2.3. Case Studies of AI Applications in Cyberbullying Prevention

Some key examples of current AI use in prevention of cyberbullying are considered. Examples include Facebook and Instagram's use of machine learning algorithms to spot and do away with the undesirable stuff. NLP models are used to identify offensive language while using graph-based techniques to identify coordinated harassment efforts on these platforms. They also offer customers AI systems that assist customers bully users and strengthen the feedback loop for improvement.

Google's Perspective API is an example itself: it uses machine learning to detect toxic comments. This tool is integrated into platforms like YouTube and aids content moderators to score comments on how likely these comments are going to be harmful, so responses can happen faster and more efficiently. The API has played a part in cutting down on abusive interactions in comment sections, where cyberbullying runs rampant.

In the educational domain, AI powered tools like Bark and Gaggle are marketed to safeguard students from cyberbullying. These systems observe online interactions happening over school issued devices and alert educators, or parents, when potentially nefarious content pops up. Early detection is promoted by these tools, which also allow escalation to be prevented and opportunities for timely support.

But these case studies also uncover challenges. For example, it has proven easy for platforms that depend entirely on AI to become accused of over censoring or missing the mark on nuanced forms of bullying (Islam et al., 2020). As a response, many of the organizations are taking up the hybrid approach of using AI and human moderators to increase accuracy and fairness.

With AI continuing to grow, the lessons from these case studies as well as the current strengths and limitations of our approach help formulate how it could play a role in cyberbullying prevention in the future. With a deeper understanding of the issues, the lessons from this research can be built upon to address existing gaps in future systems, delivering more robust and fairer solutions to this problem.

3. EMERGING TECHNOLOGIES IN AI FOR CYBERBULLYING PREVENTION

Artificial Intelligence (AI) is constantly changing the landscape of cyberbullying prevention. NLP has been one of the most game-changing technologies in detecting and preventing online harassment. The complexity and quantity of digital interactions are increasing, so NLP technologies are improving their comprehension of language, interpretation of emotional underpinnings and the ability to address the diversity of linguistic and cultural environments where cyberbullying is occurring. This section considers the most interesting NLP developments that may contribute to making cyberbullying prevention systems more effective.

3.1. Advancements in NLP

With increasing sophistication of NLP technologies, AI systems can better analyze text; no longer limited to keyword detection, they can also decipher the nuances of human speech. With the deeper learning models in machine learning like transformers (for example: BERT or GPT) NLP systems today process and interpret text very accurately (Devlin et al., 2019; Zhu & Luo, 2022). Advances made possible through such training allow for more defined detection of cyberbullying, where previously unsolvable problems exist (such as sarcasm, coded language, and different tones).

3.1.1. Sentiment Analysis and Emotion Detection

An important feature of sentiment analysis and emotion detection using NLP in cyberbullying prevention is its transformative ability. Sentiment analysis is where text is labeled as positive, negative, or neutral while emotion detection takes it a step further, detecting emotions such as anger, sadness or fear. But these capabilities enable AI systems to discern the emotional intent of those interactions online: whether a message is benign or harmful.

In a simplistic system that bases this on words, for example, a message that is frustrated may be flagged as bullying. But if the model was advanced, had sentiment and emotion analysis, it could see the context of the emotions and it can see it as venting, but nothing else. However, if we can infer the underlying sentiment of such statements, be it malicious and subtle, in the form of backhanded compliments or passive aggressive comments, we can identify it as bullying.

One of the most useful applications in understanding psychological aspects of cyberbullying is emotion detection. The response of the victims and their answers are read by AI systems that can alert moderators or caregivers to intervene to reduce any harm further. Furthermore, emerging patterns of anger or hostility will give warning opportunities to proactively engage with perpetrators through warnings, or resources to correct their behaviors.

3.1.2. Multilingual Capabilities

Since cyberbullying occurs in various linguistic and cultural environments, multilingual NLP models have received a lot of attention. Due to the nature of the problem, it is especially hard to detect bullying in languages other than English especially when used through traditional systems. However, emerging NLP technologies are meant to do the processing of multiple languages, thereby bringing more inclusiveness in the process of cyberbullying prevention (Santy et al., 2021).

mBERT and XLM-RoBERTa are multilingual models, that help AI systems read text in various languages to keep contextual understanding. Detecting cyberbullying in areas where users often switch between languages or engage in code mixing (a practice common in bilingual or multilingual communities) requires this capability. Consider the example of abusive comments in a mix of English and Arabic, or, for instance, Spanish and English where models need to know hybrid linguistic structure (Daraghmi et al., 2024).

Moreover, the Importance of cultural nuance is also considered along with linguistic diversity for Cyberbullying detection. In one culture, words or phrases that are offensive may be benign in another. Modern NLP systems include cultural and regional context into their analysis, reducing false pos and negative. It means training models on culturally representative data and knowing about local idioms, slang, communication style etc.

For instance, teasing is considered a way of showing camaraderie in some cultures and hostile language, in other cultures. And by understanding these nuances, NLP systems can tell the difference between good, friendly banter and actual harassment so interventions are carried out only when needed.

NLP has made leaps in sentiment analysis, emotion detection, and cultural nuance and these AI derived bullying prevention system have made a huge progress as a result. Using these technologies not only improves the precision of detections systems but also promotes a more inclusive approach to online spaces protection. For as long as NLP is allowed to develop, the ability to match the constantly changing and ever diverse nature of human communication will be critical to the fight against cyber bullying.

3.1.3. Context-Aware Language Models

Context-aware language models represent a significant advancement in Natural Language Processing (NLP) for cyberbullying detection. Unlike traditional approaches that rely on isolated word or sentence analysis, context-aware models consider the broader conversational context to identify subtle patterns of harmful behavior. This capability is critical for distinguishing between benign sarcasm, humor, and genuine abusive intent.

Leveraging pre-trained transformer-based models like BERT and GPT, context-aware systems can analyze sequential interactions in online threads, group chats, or comment sections. These models identify escalation patterns, repeated harassment across multiple messages, and contextually sensitive language that static models may overlook. For instance, a phrase that appears harmless in isolation may reveal abusive intent when viewed within the entire conversation.

3.2. Role of Deep Learning

Currently, deep learning has become a disruptive component in cyberbullying prevention, providing effective means of analyzing diverse kinds of data, such as text, images, and multimedia content. Given that deep learning models are powered by advanced neural networks, they are really good at finding patterns and features in all sorts of varying data sources and hence are extremely useful for with the task of detecting and battling cyberbullying. In this domain deep learning has two major applications, transformer models for text analysis and convolutional neural networks (CNNs) for image based bullying detection.

3.2.1. Transformer Models like GPT and BERT

GPT (Generative Pretrained Transformer), BERT (Bidirectional Encoder Representations from Transformers) transformer models have regularly revolutionized natural language understanding with a new kind of self-attention mechanism, this enables the model to pay attention to the important parts of the inputted text. Especially designed for catching more subtle forms of bullying, such as sarcasm and contextual threats, as well as implicit abuse(W. Liao et al., 2021).

A cornerstone of transformers is the attention mechanism, which tells us how important a word or a token within a sentence is. The scaled dot-product attention formula, central to transformer models, is given by:

$$\text{Attention(Q, K, V)} = \text{softmax}\left(\frac{QK^T}{\sqrt{d_K}}\right)V \tag{1}$$

Where:

- Q (Query), K (Key), and V (Value) are matrices derived from the input text.
- d_K is the dimensionality of the keys.
- The softmax function ensures that the attention weights are normalized and sum to 1.

In BERT, the bidirectional nature of the model allows it to capture both past and future context, making it highly effective for identifying bullying embedded within complex sentence structures. For example, a sentence like "Oh, you're *so* smart!" might appear positive without context but could be flagged as sarcastic when analyzed with BERT's contextual embeddings.

GPT has a special type of use case: the autoregressive approach where GPT predict a token based on an input sequence of tokens (up to a certain length) is especially suitable for generating responses that deescalate hostile situations or guide statements of support to victims of bullying. These models can be fine-tuned using corresponding datasets of labelled cyberbullying and can be further used to increase detection accuracy.

3.2.2. Convolutional Neural Networks for Image-Based Bullying Detection

Although much research has focused on text based cyberbullying detection, detection of image-based bullying, such as offensive memes and photo shopped photos, is a hard problem. For this task, the deep learning model of choice are

Convolutional Neural Networks (CNNs) because they are so good at analyzing and classifying image data (Daraghmi et al., 2024).

CNNs work by applying convolutional operations to extract hierarchical features from images. The primary equation governing the convolution operation is:

$$S(i,j) = (I * K)(i,j) = \sum_{m=0}^{M-1} \sum_{n=0}^{N-1} I(i+m, j+n) \cdot K\left(m,n\right) \tag{2}$$

Where:

- S(i, j) is the output feature map.
- I(i,j) is the input image.
- K(m,n) is the convolution kernel (or filter).
- M and N are the dimensions of the kernel.

Purposefully, an operation of this nature helps CNNs learn features like edges, textures and patterns, which come in handy when analyzing the visual content of an image.

Specifically, for the bullying detection problem, we might train a CNN network to detect offensive postings — if, for example, the offensive postings might be made with offensive imagery or memes depicting inappropriate gestures, text overlays or tampered facial expressions. Using many convolutional layers stacked, these models can learn more and more abstract features, and so are able to detect more and more complex forms of bullying.

The pooling layers in CNNs, typically max pooling, are used to reduce the spatial dimensions of the feature maps, summarized as:

$$P(i,j) = \max\{S(i+p, j+q) | 0 \leq p < k, 0 \leq q < k\} \tag{3}$$

Where k is the pooling kernel size, and P(i,j) represents the pooled feature map.

After convolution and pooling, fully connected layers map the features to output labels, such as "bullying" or "non-bullying," using a softmax activation function:

$$y_i = \frac{e^{z_i}}{\sum_{j=1}^{C} e^{z_j}} \tag{4}$$

Where:

- z_i is the input to the softmax layer for class iii.
- C is the total number of classes.

When you integrate transformers for textual analysis with CNNs to handle the visual content the AI system can now be able to comprehensively detect cyber-bullying. Through their capacity of being built on top of multimodal data, these models are poised to tackle the multidisciplinary problem of online harassment by providing more challenging and versatile solutions. With every passing day, these technologies find a place in building prevention frameworks that seek to provide safer online environments.

3.3. Multimodal AI Approaches

Cyberbullying takes place within an inherently multimodal digital ecosystem, where perpetrators employ a variety of media (texts, image, audio, and video), to harass their victims. A result of this is that AI systems that depend on one type of data they use like text or images alone, could be less effective in detecting and preventing campaigns of cyberbullying. Multimodal AI approaches, utilizing more than one data modality, are the ultimate approach to effectively solve this type of complex problem. These systems build on advanced machine learning and deep learning to jointly leverage text, audio, and visual data to understand the multi-modal interplay of data underlying cyberbullying behaviors (Singh et al., 2017).

3.3.1. Combining Text, Audio, and Visual Data

Multimodal AI systems seek to create new information from disparate sources so that none of the important signals get lost. That example could be a cyberbullying incident comprised of text messages combined with offensive memes or an abusive video cobbled with a derogatory caption. Though individually these parts might not exhibit the malicious intent, they acquire much more clarity when you view it.

Fusion techniques play a pivotal role in combining modalities. These techniques can be categorized into three types:

1. **Early Fusion:** At the input level, we combine data from different modalities so that the model learns features that are shared from the start. As an example, we can phrase text embeddings with the image feature vectors and analyze textual and visual content jointly.
2. **Late Fusion:** The outputs of specialized models applied to each modality are combined at a decision level. For instance, a CNN can be applied against an image, a transformer would work against text, and then their predictions will perform a merging to reach a final output.
3. **Hybrid Fusion:** A fusion of early and late, that shares modality specific features.

In cyberbullying detection, combining modalities is particularly effective for scenarios such as:

- Focusing on identifying abusive comments in videos using both audio (intonation patterns) and speech transcription (text).
- Bullying detection in gaming environments in which offensive audio messages and text-based chat exists.
- A tool to flag harmful memes by integrating visual analysis with their overlaid text interpretation.

Mathematically, T, A, and V represent features extracted from text, audio, and visual data, respectively. A simple multimodal fusion can be expressed as:

$$\mathrm{F} = f_{combine}\left(f_{text}(T), f_{audio}(A), f_{visual}(V)\right) \tag{5}$$

Where f_{text}, f_{audio}, f_{visual} are feature extraction functions, and $f_{combine}$ is the fusion function.

In recent years, however, transformer-based models such as Multimodal Transformer (MMT) and VisualBERT have provided an additional boost in the capability for processing multimodal data. These models leverage cross attention mechanism to learn the interactions between separate modalities are learning thereby to effectively detect the nuanced and context aware bullying.

3.3.2. Challenges in Multimodal Integration

Despite its promise, implementing multimodal AI for cyberbullying prevention presents several challenges:

1. **Data Alignment:** Two main issues addressed by this work are synchronizing data across multiple modalities and when there are new pieces of data, which is especially difficult in dynamic cases like live streams or a gaming environment. Significant to the accurate analysis is the fact that text, audio, and visual elements need to be temporally aligned (Ngiam et al., 2024).
2. **Feature Representation and Fusion:** Text, images and audio have fundamentally different characteristics; text is sequential, images are spatial, and audio are temporal. It is a non–trivial task to design models that successfully represent and combine these different features (Yousefi-Azar & Hamey, 2017).
3. **Lack of Multimodal Datasets:** To develop robust multimodal AI systems we need huge datasets with annotated text as well as annotated audio and visual data. Such datasets are rare, however, especially for cyberbullying scenarios.

Diverse and representative datasets are a major bottleneck to create (Singh et al., 2017).

4. **Computational Complexity:** However, because they must analyze large volumes of data from multiple sources, multimodal models are computationally expensive. Due to the computational intensive nature of training and deploying these models efficiently, particularly in real time, they are seldom utilized (Wu & Goodman, 2018).
5. **Contextual Understanding:** It would be essential to understand context across modalities but difficult to achieve at the same time. For example, a phrase that can appear neutral on its own can seem offensive coupled with a certain image or tone of voice. Multimodal sensing requires context aware models that use them but necessitates sophisticated training methodologies (Xu et al., 2019).

Innovative integration of multimodal AI approaches is one major step forward in the fight against cyberbullying. Combining text, audio and visual data about online interactions, these systems provide a global meaningful view of student life, thereby making more accurate detection and intervention possible. Nonetheless, the challenges as it pertains to the data alignment, feature fusion, and contextual understanding must be solved for full advantage of multimodal AI to be possible. As this research continues, these approaches are likely to become indispensable tools in the efforts to build safer, safer, more inclusive online environments.

4. PERSONALIZED AI INTERVENTIONS

Artificial intelligence for cyberbullying prevention is evolving in the move toward more individualized, context sensitive solutions (Rosa et al., 2019). Moreover, personalized AI interventions enable one to improve the precision of such detection, while providing a friendly environment for victims and offenders by taking into consideration their case. This chapter explores three critical components of personalized AI interventions: Adaptive learning algorithms for customized solutions, the role of AI in behavioral analytics and counseling and real time moderation and feedback systems.

4.1. Real-Time Moderation and Feedback Systems

Real time moderation through AI is a breakthrough in keeping online safety. These systems are employing AI algorithms which analyze user generated content on the fly, recognizing the possibility of offensive or harmful content and taking immediate action on them. They can take actions ranging from issuing warnings to the offender to blocking inappropriate messages, or alerting their moderators to follow up on the issue (Thoppilan et al., 2022).

Real-time moderation is one of the greatest strengths of real-time moderation as it gives users immediate feedback as to the length of time they have. For instance, since Instagram utilizes AI that would alert users if they may break community guidelines with their comment before they even post, it encourages self-reflection and promotes responsibly using the online medium.

Real time moderation systems are promising but are difficult to keep accurate without excessive censorship. Because of the requirement to protect users from harm, and the need to allow freedom of expression, AI algorithms and policies will continue to evolve.

4.2. Adaptive Learning Algorithms for Personalized Solutions

Personalized interventions in cyberbullying prevention are backed with adaptive learning algorithms as the main frameworks. These algorithms study how individuals behave, what their preferences are and how they interact with one another, in order to come up with strategies that are personalized for each user. Once a pattern is identified by AI in a user's online activity, solutions already on hand can now be suggested to satisfy that same user's particular need, at his or her specific moment in time (Dutta et al., 2015).

Adaptive systems can suggest coping strategies to victims or direct them to relevant resources like support services related to mental health. These algorithms can be (and are) used to provide educational interventions to perpetrators to foster empathy and understanding. For instance, an AI driven chatbot could recreate what it was like for the victim (s), allowing the offender to feel the emotional impact of what they have done.

Additionally, adaptive algorithms let platforms custom tailor how content is delivered to get users to see positive, inclusive interactions. Used in a personalized way, this prevents cyber bullying and reduces Cyber Means of its negative effects, as well as provides a better online environment.

4.3. Role of AI in Behavioral Analytics and Counseling

Analyzing user behavior using AI has become a revolutionizing force in the field of behavioral analytics and even counseling. Looking at the patterns of communication, emotional tone and social interactions, AI can determine a user's current mental state, and potential vulnerable points. For counselors and mental health professionals working to support victims of cyberbullying these are extremely valuable insights (Elsharnouby & Mahrous, 2015).

In fact, we can integrate AI tools into counseling platforms where you get immediate assistance. For example, AI-powered virtual therapists can provide initial support to victims who can then process their experiences and then be guided to appropriate professional help if required. Likewise, AI powered recommendation can help inform counselors of the most fitting interventions for a specific client thereby expanding quality and efficiency of care.

AI's potential for use in counseling is huge, but there are ethical questions that need asking, like how to protect the privacy of users and prevent over reliance on automation systems. To fully realize the potential of AI in behavioral analytics and counseling, these same concerns will need to address. The table 2 compares key personalized AI interventions, highlighting their objectives, benefits, limitations, and examples of applications:

Table 2. Comparison of key personalized AI interventions

Intervention	Objective	Benefits	Limitations	Examples of Applications
Real-Time Moderation	Immediate detection and action	Instant feedback, prevents escalation	Risk of false positives, excessive censorship	AI-based content moderation tools
Adaptive Learning Algorithms	Personalized user solutions	Tailored interventions, promotes empathy	High computational requirements, data privacy	Adaptive chatbots for victims and offenders
Behavioral Analytics and Counseling	Understanding user behavior	Informed interventions, improved mental health support	Ethical concerns, potential biases in data	AI-driven virtual therapists

The fight against cyberbullying is one in which personalized AI interventions play a critical role. These systems by focusing on real time moderation, adaptive learning and behavioral analytics ensure not just better detection and prevention but also provide opportunities for education and rehabilitation. These technologies promise to transform the online world into a safer and more supportive one, and as they evolve so will they.

5. COLLABORATIVE AI SYSTEMS FOR CYBERBULLYING PREVENTION

Cyberbullying is a complex problem demanding solutions from technological, human, and social constituencies. Although AI systems are great at automating detection and intervention, these systems are only useful when they interface with human expertise, community expertise, and institutional expertise. AI collaborative systems enhance the judiciousness brought by human moderators, the proactivity of communities and organizations. This chapter examines these roles synergistically, the role of community and network participants, and the value of partnering tech companies, governments and NGOs.

5.1. Integration with Human Moderators and Educators

Although the AI systems themselves are powerful, they are not without fault. You may be facing all sorts of trouble with context, cultural nuance, edge cases that need to be interpreted by a human. Along with this restriction lies the need to put AI in conjunction with human moderators and educators in order to make a complete aid for cyber bullying prevention (Yang et al., 2023).

Critical thinking and ethical judgment in such scenarios are provided by the human moderators. To take just one example, something that's sarcastic and flagged as abusive by an AI system might be harmless banter between friends, something human moderators could make that distinction. In similar fashion, AI also plays a significant role in encouraging educators in spreading awareness of the preventive measures presented by it. Working collaboratively with students to educate and promote digital literacy and empathy provides educators the opportunity to address the root causes of cyberbullying and establish a more respectful online culture.

We also see more common collaborative workflows between AI systems and human moderators (S. Liao et al., 2022). Cases can be prioritized and filtered in AI for human review so that moderators can focus upon the most pressing incidents, for example. Similarly, AI generated insights can help educate understand how to tailor anti bullying programs to the specific needs of their own students and take a more informed and targeted response.

5.2. AI and Community Participation

Any successful effort to combat cyberbullying depends on communities. As AI in such a way allows a community to create a consciousness, become aware and be able to take part in such activity, and see its importance as it connects its people in the form of a network.

Real time insights and analytics is one of the core ways AI helps to enable community involvement. Anonymized data from AI systems can tell community leaders, parents and teachers about trending areas of cyberbullying and provide insight into emerging threats. For instance, aggregated statistics from a social media player on the prevalence of bullying in certain age and gender demographics could be shared to encourage community efforts in that direction.

We can take the power of AI and empower the users to become active participants in prevention of cyberbullying (Salawu et al., 2020). Reporting mechanisms, interactive educational content, and gamified anti bullying campaigns are the other kinds of features that encourage users to take their responsibility arising out of their online behavior, are responsible to stop the harmful activities, if spotted. For example, gamified challenges are rewarded with users who incentivize the promotion of positive interactions (a kind of ripple effect), thereby cultivating a more supporter digital space.

It goes beyond individuals to include schools, parent teacher associations and local based organizations. AI systems that work with these groups could help create community-specific resources and training programs that feature the unique areas of interest for their community.

5.3. Partnerships Between Tech Companies, Governments, and NGOs

Cyberbullying has become so complex that a coordinated response is needed from different countries, governments and the private sector as well as NGOs. But we can use Collaborative AI systems as a unifying force by allowing these entities to combine their resources, join their knowledge, and implement scalable solutions.

What do tech companies have to say about the development and deployment of AI for cyberbullying prevention? Or, their platforms are the battleground of cyberbullying, putting them in both the position and position to lead the fight. These companies know the potential of AI and through investments in research and employing extremely powerful tools on their platforms, they can become role models for how online spaces can be safer.

A critical role is played by governments, offering the regulatory frameworks for the ethical use of AI (Kim et al., 2021). Only AI systems that are transparent, accountable, and user private are used. Likewise, governments can fund research initiatives, or partner with the private sector to make this happen.

NGOs add indispensable experience as well as advocacy and focus on the human and societal dimension of cyberbullying. Having direct access to victim's insights on the ground can also play a role in awareness of victim rights and development of complementary educational campaigns in support to AI driven solutions. Tech companies and NGOs partner up on impactful programs like helplines run on AI chatbots (Reddy et al.,2025) for or awareness campaigns aimed at vulnerable population.

5.3.1. Collaborative Success

AI-enhanced cyberbullying prevention strategies demonstrate optimal efficacy by leveraging AI's technical capabilities alongside human expertise, community engagement, and institutional partnerships. This integrated approach positions cyberbullying as a societal challenge requiring collective action rather than a solely technical issue.

Collaborative AI systems embody this holistic methodology by combining the precision and scalability of AI with the nuanced judgment of human moderators. These systems enable real-time monitoring and contextual interpretation, improving accuracy and reducing false positives or negatives. Educators play a vital role by utilizing AI-driven insights to design targeted interventions and awareness campaigns, while policymakers rely on AI analytics to craft evidence-based regulations and safety frameworks.

Community mobilization is another critical aspect, where awareness programs and participatory mechanisms encourage users to report incidents and engage in proactive behaviors. Institutional partnerships further strengthen the system by pooling resources, sharing data under ethical guidelines, and developing cross-platform strategies to combat cyberbullying at scale.

6. POLICY, REGULATION, AND AI FRAMEWORKS

The development of powerful policies, regulations and frameworks for artificial intelligence (AI) which is playing a growingly central role in cyberbullying prevention becomes paramount. Along with these measures, they form a structure for accountability, transparency and collaboration with corresponding actions (Zhang et al., 2023). This chapter also explains why global standards are required, the enforcement problems, and what role can be played by governments and other international organizations in helping AI driven cyberbullying prevention in the future.

6.1. Developing Global Standards for AI in Cyberbullying Prevention

The internet is a global place and your approach to battling cyberbullying must be global. AI systems are distributed across borders, and inconsistency in standards and fragmented policies seriously hinder their good functioning. Enabling global standards for AI in cyberbullying prevention ensures that there is a uniform ethical guideline, technology is interoperable and that accountability mechanisms are common.

Key principles like privacy protection, bias mitigation, and explainability could be defined in a universal framework for AI algorithms. For example, standard might require that AI models be trained on data involving many different types of people to help reduce cultural or language bias coming in when it comes to detecting cyberbullying around the world. In addition to this, such frameworks would identify standards of data security and protect the anonymity of victims.

The International Telecommunication Union (ITU) and UNESCO stand in a good position to lead the efforts in creating these standards. These bodies can allow policymakers, technologists and civil society groups to sit together, formulate guidelines that are in alignment with international human rights principles and that respond to the technical complexities of deploying AI.

6.2. Regulatory Challenges and Legal Frameworks

Because AI systems evolve and change, regulating them also proves challenging. Such legal frameworks need to balance the push for innovative activity on the one end, and the necessity to maintain the safety of users on the opposite. AI systems face these challenges particularly strongly in the context of cyberbullying prevention where such systems need to deal with sensitive questions such as freedom of expression, data privacy, and ethical decision-making.

Among others, the biggest challenge is to define what legal accountability AI systems, and their developers can have. Determining who is liable, then, when an AI system messes up—a misclassified benign comment as cyberbullying, or a failure to detect harmful behavior—is not straightforward. Who is responsible, the developer, the platform operator or the user? These ambiguities must be addressed by legal frameworks so that real trust in Artificial Intelligence can be created.

One way to overcome the obstacle is to enforce the regulations across jurisdictions. The AI solutions may be deployed globally; however, this complicates things due to one country housing their platform and another having their own set of rules for the solutions to be deployed. The regulation of these requires international cooperation and mutual devotion to the brawl against cyberbullying.

For instance, a law on AI is already underway in countries like the European Union, for example, which has already initiated an AI Act that could be a model for such law in other countries elsewhere. These efforts underscore the importance of proactive policymaking in response to the risks and challenges that AI will bring in the prevention of cyberbullying.

6.3. Role of Governments and International Bodies

It's governments and international organizations' role to help build the policy environment for AI in preventing cyberbullying as shown in Table 3. These entities can drive innovation whilst ensuring the ethical use of AI by creating regulatory frameworks, funding research, and driving public private partnerships.

National policies that are consonant with local needs and values can be implemented by governments alone. Take, for example, requiring them to mandate transparency in AI based algorithms used on social media platforms, such as requiring the disclosure of how the systems inside of these social media platforms are detecting and fighting cyberbullying. That funding from governments for both AI research that addresses underserved communities and likewise is inclusive and equitable.

In contrast, international bodies promote cross border cooperation. But there's room for this kind of convergence. Organizations such as the United Nations can convene stakeholders to talk about what best practices are, can share knowledge and can set out global norms. These efforts are critical to denaturalizing the transnational aspects of cyberbullying, in which perpetrators and victims are frequently located in geographically separated places.

Beyond the regulation the role of these entities involves advocacy and education. Through increasing the awareness of the risk and benefits of AI in combating cyberbullying, governments or international organizations can facilitate individuals and communities to contribute how they want to see these technologies in the future.

Table 3. Comparative Table: Policies and Frameworks Across Key Regions

Region	Key Initiative	Strengths	Challenges	Global Impact
European Union	AI Act	Comprehensive and proactive regulation	Balancing innovation with strict compliance	Influences global AI policy discussions
United States	Algorithmic Accountability Act	Focus on transparency and bias mitigation	Limited enforcement across tech platforms	Sets standards for corporate accountability
Asia-Pacific	Singapore's Model AI Framework	Emphasis on industry-specific guidelines	Varying levels of adoption across the region	Promotes best practices in tech industries
Global	UNESCO's AI Ethics Guidelines	Promotes human rights and ethical AI usage	Implementation disparities across nations	Establishes a foundation for global norms
Africa	Smart Africa Alliance Initiatives	Focus on AI for digital inclusion	Limited resources for large-scale deployment	Highlights AI's potential in emerging markets

7. CONCLUSION

In this section, we have explored how AI will impact cyberbullying prevention in the future and have found that AI plays multiple roles that are continuing to develop in cyberbullying prevention. Cyberbullying could be one of the first battles where AI goes to war with humans in service to a greater good. Ongoing advancement in AI technology fast being utilized in real world applications will shape the way we deal with online harm and build safer digital spaces for everyone, regardless of age.

7.1. Summary of Key Insights

In this chapter so far, we have explored the current state of AI in cyberbullying prevention, successes to date and the work still to be done. The most significant insight from the thesis is how AI can detect and mitigate harmful behavior online. Given these encouraging results with machine learning models based on NLP and deep learning techniques in identifying cyberbullying content, it seems intuitive that the same models should be able to help in the identification of cyberbullying tweets. Data these technologies can study in real time and flag potential issues that might go unnoticed.

Yet despite the promise of AI capabilities there are still limitations. For AI systems it is complex in human language, cultural nuances, and life changing online interactions. But there are also ethical considerations to consider, like privacy issues, data biases, and risks of misuse, which must be handled in a way that makes the implementation of AI interventions effective and fair. The more we see the development of AI, the more it becomes clear to us that AI alone can't solve cyberbullying, we need a balanced approach utilizing AI and human oversight.

The second major insight is how critical collaboration is between AI systems, human moderators and educators. AI can help designers and businesses find and respond to cyberbullying, but that's not a substitute for human involvement. The combination of human expertise and AI strengths makes sure the responses are accurate and contextually sensitive. Thus, it is crucial for all to play their part in the intervention process with educators, parents and mental health professionals contributing to providing all hands-on deck help to victims of cyberbullying.

7.2. Vision for a Collaborative and AI-Driven Future

In future, as AI is a key element to tackling cyberbullying, the vision is collaboration, adaptable and always improving. As AI technologies continue to advance, detection and prevention will be enabled within AI, and the technologies will go beyond detection and prevention to include proactive interventions. This vision envisions a world in which AI will be an instrument that effortlessly plays alongside human moderators, educators, and counselors to build an ecosystem of online safety.

The AI systems for such a future would be a truly collaborative one: they would adapt to the unique needs of users and communities. For instance, one could program AI to tailor the interventions based on a user's behavioral patterns, emotional state or more precisely the user's vulnerability. More so, there could be the integration of AI in educational curriculum that could assist the young people to gain knowledge and skills required to maneuver within the digital spaces in a safe and responsible manner.

In addition, AI will also effectively serve as an important driver of awareness and education regarding cyberbullying as part of this vision. Because AI is going to use data driven insights to help surface emerging cyberbullying trends to then create targeted awareness campaigns to foster action against that new trend. However, the campaigns can be personalized for different age groups and cultures, and various regions to make sure the message correlates with different audiences. In terms of raising awareness, AI will play an important role in reducing stigma associated with cyberbullying and start a dialogue to gain awareness into the effect it has.

7.3. Recommendations for Stakeholders

For stakeholders across various sectors—governments, tech companies, educators, parents, and NGOs—there are several key recommendations that will help shape a future where AI is leveraged effectively to prevent cyberbullying.

- **Governments and Policymakers:** It seems a definite responsibility of governments to regulate and formulate policies that promote ethical use of AI in cyberbullying prevention. It includes both developing global standards for how AI should be utilized, as well as assuring that privacy and human rights are addressed, and legal challenges that arise from AI decision making. Governments also need to work with others internationally to develop frameworks for dealing with cyberbullying on a cross-border basis.
- **Technology Companies:** Transparency and accountability are emphasized to be a responsibility of AI solutions in tech companies. Instead, they should invest the research and development funds of AI tools that can identify harmful online behavior accurately while continuing safe user privacy. Whatever systems we develop — those between the individual and state or between states themselves — there's a need for collaboration with researchers, policymakers, civil society, and others to ensure we get the best possible versions that are both ethically sound and effective.
- **Educators and Mental Health Professionals:** An integration between the tools of AI as applied in educational programs (Fatima et al.,2025) that support teaching of digital literacy and online safety is in the process of being developed by educators and mental health professionals to achieve this goal. They should give students the ability to recognize, understand and respond to cyber bullying. They also do have an important role to play in helping victims of cyberbullying and when AI interventions are supplemented by emotional and psychological help from mental health professionals.
- **Parents and Community Leaders:** Parents and community leaders should be proactive in creating safe online environments for our children and our community youth. They can further stay informed about the technologies used to block cyberbullying, and hired appropriately, to prevent cyberbullying. They can also advocate for more transparency and accountability for tech companies and helping to drive positive online behavior.
- **NGOs and Civil Society Organizations:** The warnings about the harms of cyberbullying and why it needs to be stopped ought to be raised by the NGOs and the civil society organizations. They can be watchdogs as well – organizations who are able to hold companies and governments to account for their use of AI in this space. Also, they can fight for unfortunate groups that can be affected by cyberbullying like AI solutions should be inclusive and equitable.

REFERENCES

Daraghmi, E. Y., Qadan, S., Daraghmi, Y. A., Yousuf, R., Cheikhrouhou, O., & Baz, M. (2024). From Text to Insight: An Integrated CNN-BiLSTM-GRU Model for Arabic Cyberbullying Detection. *IEEE Access : Practical Innovations, Open Solutions*, 12(July), 103504–103519. DOI: 10.1109/ACCESS.2024.3431939

Devlin, J., Chang, M. W., Lee, K., & Toutanova, K. (2019). BERT: Pre-training of deep bidirectional transformers for language understanding. *NAACL HLT 2019 - 2019 Conference of the North American Chapter of the Association for Computational Linguistics: Human Language Technologies - Proceedings of the Conference, 1*(Mlm), 4171–4186.

Dutta, R., Smith, D., Rawnsley, R., Bishop-Hurley, G., Hills, J., Timms, G., & Henry, D. (2015). Dynamic cattle behavioural classification using supervised ensemble classifiers. *Computers and Electronics in Agriculture*, 111, 18–28. DOI: 10.1016/j.compag.2014.12.002

Elsharnouby, T. H., & Mahrous, A. A. (2015). Customer participation in online co-creation experience: The role of e-service quality. *Journal of Research in Interactive Marketing*, 9(4), 313–336. DOI: 10.1108/JRIM-06-2014-0038

Fati, S. M., Muneer, A., Alwadain, A., & Balogun, A. O. (2023). *Cyberbullying Detection on Twitter Using Deep Learning-Based Attention Mechanisms and Continuous Bag of Words Feature Extraction*. DOI: 10.1108/JRIM-06-2014-0038

Fatima, S., Reddy, C. K. K., Sunerah, A., & Doss, S. (2025). Innovations in Education: Integrating Explainable AI Into Educational Intelligence. In *Internet of Behavior-Based Computational Intelligence for Smart Education Systems* (pp. 19-52). IGI Global.

Hamiza Wan Ali, W. N., Mohd, M., & Fauzi, F. (2018). Cyberbullying Detection: An Overview. *Proceedings of the 2018 Cyber Resilience Conference, CRC 2018*, 1–3. DOI: 10.1109/CR.2018.8626869

Hasan, M. T., Hossain, M. A. E., Mukta, M. S. H., Akter, A., Ahmed, M., & Islam, S. (2023). A Review on Deep-Learning-Based Cyberbullying Detection. *Future Internet*, 15(5), 1–47. DOI: 10.3390/fi15050179

Islam, M. M., Uddin, M. A., Islam, L., Akter, A., Sharmin, S., & Acharjee, U. K. (2020). Cyberbullying Detection on Social Networks Using Machine Learning Approaches. *2020 IEEE Asia-Pacific Conference on Computer Science and Data Engineering, CSDE 2020*, 3–8. DOI: 10.1109/CSDE50874.2020.9411601

Iwendi, C., Srivastava, G., Khan, S., & Maddikunta, P. K. R. (2023). Cyberbullying detection solutions based on deep learning architectures. *Multimedia Systems*, 29(3), 1839–1852. DOI: 10.1007/s00530-020-00701-5

Kim, S., Razi, A., Stringhini, G., Wisniewski, P. J., & De Choudhury, M. (2021). A Human-Centered Systematic Literature Review of Cyberbullying Detection Algorithms. *Proceedings of the ACM on Human-Computer Interaction, 5*(CSCW2). DOI: 10.1145/3476066

Kumar, N., Malhotra, M., Aggarwal, B., Rai, D., & Aggarwal, G. Leveraging Natural Language Processing and Machine Learning for Efficient Fake News Detection. In Proceedings of the International Conference on Technological Advancements in Computational Sciences (ICTACS), 2023 3rd, Tashkent, Uzbekistan, 1–3 November 2023; pp. 535–541. DOI: 10.1109/ICTACS59847.2023.10390356

Liao, S., Lin, L., Chen, Q., & Pei, H. (2022). Why not work with anthropomorphic collaborative robots? The mediation effect of perceived intelligence and the moderation effect of self-efficacy. *Human Factors and Ergonomics in Manufacturing & Service Industries*.

Liao, W., Zeng, B., Yin, X., & Wei, P. (2021). An improved aspect-category sentiment analysis model for text sentiment analysis based on RoBERTa. *Applied Intelligence*, 51(6), 3522–3533. DOI: 10.1007/s10489-020-01964-1

Manzoor, M. F., Abid, A., Nawaz, N. A., & Alvi, A. (2022). Aspect based sentence segregated dataset of hybrid car's consumers online reviews. *Data in Brief*, 42, 108293. Advance online publication. DOI: 10.1016/j.dib.2022.108293 PMID: 35637892

Muneer, A., Alwadain, A., Ragab, M. G., & Alqushaibi, A. (2023). Cyberbullying Detection on Social Media Using Stacking Ensemble Learning and Enhanced BERT. *Information (Basel)*, 14(8), 467. Advance online publication. DOI: 10.3390/info14080467

Ngiam, J., Khosla, A., Kim, M., Nam, J., Lee, H., & Ng, A. Y. (2024). Multimodal Deep Learning. *Springer Optimization and Its Applications*, 211, 209–219. DOI: 10.1007/978-3-031-53092-0_10

Obaid, M. H., Guirguis, S. K., & Elkaffas, S. M. (2023). Cyberbullying Detection and Severity Determination Model. *IEEE Access : Practical Innovations, Open Solutions*, 11(September), 97391–97399. DOI: 10.1109/ACCESS.2023.3313113

Perera, A., & Fernando, P. (2021). Accurate cyberbullying detection and prevention on social media. *Procedia Computer Science*, 181, 605–611. DOI: 10.1016/j.procs.2021.01.207

Reddy, C. K. K., Reddy, P. S., Pilly, A., & Doss, S. (2025). Transformative Effects of Smarter Chatbots. In Dixit, S., Maurya, M., Jain, V., & Subramaniam, G. (Eds.), *Artificial Intelligence-Enabled Businesses.*, DOI: 10.1002/9781394234028.ch18

Rosa, H., Pereira, N., Ribeiro, R., Ferreira, P. C., Carvalho, J. P., Oliveira, S., Coheur, L., Paulino, P., Veiga Simão, A. M., & Trancoso, I. (2019). Automatic cyberbullying detection: A systematic review. *Computers in Human Behavior, 93*(December 2018), 333–345. DOI: 10.1109/TAFFC.2017.2761757

Salawu, S., He, Y., & Lumsden, J. (2020). Approaches to Automated Detection of Cyberbullying: A Survey. *IEEE Transactions on Affective Computing*, 11(1), 3–24. DOI: 10.1109/TAFFC.2017.2761757

Santy, S., Srinivasan, A., & Choudhury, M. (2021). BERTologiCoMix how does code-mixing interact with multilingual BERT? *Adapt-NLP 2021 - 2nd Workshop on Domain Adaptation for NLP, Proceedings*, 111–121.

Siddhartha, K., Kumar, K. R., Varma, K. J., Amogh, M., & Samson, M. (2022). Cyber Bullying Detection Using Machine Learning. *2022 2nd Asian Conference on Innovation in Technology, ASIANCON 2022*, 45–50. DOI: 10.1109/ASIANCON55314.2022.9909201

Singh, V. K., Ghosh, S., & Jose, C. (2017). Toward multimodal cyberbullying detection. *Conference on Human Factors in Computing Systems - Proceedings, Part F1276*, 2090–2099. DOI: 10.1145/3027063.3053169

Sultan, D., Omarov, B., Kozhamkulova, Z., Kazbekova, G., Alimzhanova, L., Dautbayeva, A., Zholdassov, Y., & Abdrakhmanov, R. (2023). A Review of Machine Learning Techniques in Cyberbullying Detection. *Computers, Materials & Continua*, 74(3), 2625–2640. DOI: 10.32604/cmc.2023.033682

Teng, T. H., & Varathan, K. D. (2023). Cyberbullying Detection in Social Networks: A Comparison Between Machine Learning and Transfer Learning Approaches. *IEEE Access : Practical Innovations, Open Solutions*, 11(April), 55533–55560. DOI: 10.1109/ACCESS.2023.3275130

Thoppilan, R., De Freitas, D., Hall, J., Shazeer, N., Kulshreshtha, A., Cheng, H.-T., Jin, A., Bos, T., Baker, L., Du, Y., Li, Y., Lee, H., Zheng, H. S., Ghafouri, A., Menegali, M., Huang, Y., Krikun, M., Lepikhin, D., Qin, J., & Le, Q. (2022). *LaMDA: Language Models for Dialog Applications*. DOI: 10.1109/TAFFC.2017.2761757

Wu, M., & Goodman, N. (2018). Multimodal generative models for scalable weakly-supervised learning. *Advances in Neural Information Processing Systems, 2018-Decem*(NeurIPS), 5575–5585.

Xu, N., Mao, W., & Chen, G. (2019). Multi-interactive memory network for aspect based multimodal sentiment analysis. *33rd AAAI Conference on Artificial Intelligence, AAAI 2019, 31st Innovative Applications of Artificial Intelligence Conference, IAAI 2019 and the 9th AAAI Symposium on Educational Advances in Artificial Intelligence, EAAI 2019*, 371–378. DOI: 10.1609/aaai.v33i01.3301371

Yang, L. W. Y., Ng, W. Y., Lei, X., Tan, S. C. Y., Wang, Z., Yan, M., Pargi, M. K., Zhang, X., Lim, J. S., Gunasekeran, D. V., Tan, F. C. P., Lee, C. E., Yeo, K. K., Tan, H. K., Ho, H. S. S., Tan, B. W. B., Wong, T. Y., Kwek, K. Y. C., Goh, R. S. M., & Ting, D. S. W. (2023). Development and testing of a multi-lingual Natural Language Processing-based deep learning system in 10 languages for COVID-19 pandemic crisis: A multi-center study. *Frontiers in Public Health*, 11, 1063466. Advance online publication. DOI: 10.3389/fpubh.2023.1063466 PMID: 36860378

Yousefi-Azar, M., & Hamey, L. (2017). Text summarization using unsupervised deep learning. *Expert Systems with Applications*, 68, 93–105. DOI: 10.1016/j.eswa.2016.10.017

Zhang, H., Lee, I., Ali, S., DiPaola, D., Cheng, Y., & Breazeal, C. (2023). Integrating Ethics and Career Futures with Technical Learning to Promote AI Literacy for Middle School Students: An Exploratory Study. *International Journal of Artificial Intelligence in Education*, 33(2), 290–324. DOI: 10.1007/s40593-022-00293-3 PMID: 35573722

Zhu, Q., & Luo, J. (2022). Generative Pre-Trained Transformer for Design Concept Generation. *Exploration*, 2020, 1825–1834.

Chapter 5
Developing Ethical Generative AI Models to Combat Cyberbullying on Social Media Platforms

M. Sai Ramakrishna Kumar
Stanley College of Engineering and Technology for Women, India

Thakur Monika Singh
https://orcid.org/0009-0006-8534-9130
Stanley College of Engineering and Technology for Women, India

Kishor Kumar Reddy C.
Stanley College of Engineering and Technology for Women, India

Srinath Doss
Botho University, Botswana

ABSTRACT

This chapter explores the development of ethical generative AI models to combat cyberbullying on social media platforms. It begins with an overview of cyberbullying, its impact on victims, and the importance of addressing it through AI-driven solutions. The role of AI in identifying and mitigating harmful content is examined, along with key ethical considerations such as fairness, privacy, and transparency. The design of ethical AI models is discussed, emphasizing stakeholder involvement and mechanisms to reduce bias and harm. Implementation strategies include data collection, model training, and user interface design. The chapter also highlights metrics for evaluating AI effectiveness, long-term impact on cyberbullying rates,

DOI: 10.4018/979-8-3373-0543-1.ch005

and potential policy recommendations. Finally, it outlines future directions for AI advancements and evolving social media challenges.

1. INTRODUCTION

Bullying is defined as aggressive behavior in which others are harmed or controlled by the use of force, compulsion, or intimidation. It usually happens when there is an imbalance of power between the people involved, whether it be physical, social, or emotional, and it is a recurrent behavior. Bullying can be relational (spreading rumors, excluding others), verbal (name-calling, mocking), physical (striking, pushing), or cyber (using technology to harm others). Bullying can have a wide range of underlying causes, from social dynamics and environmental circumstances to psychological insecurities and a desire for control. Bullies can be children, teenagers, or even adults that behave out because they want to dominate their classmates or because they are experiencing problems in their own life, such as familial issues, neglect, or being around aggressive behavior. Bullying has a serious effect on all parties concerned. Bullying victims may experience physical health problems, anxiety, depression, and low self-esteem. Bullying has been associated with tragic effects, such as suicide and self-harm, in extreme circumstances. Bullies, on the other hand, are more likely to partake in dangerous activities and face relationship or legal issues in the future. To combat this issue, numerous workplaces and educational institutions have created anti-bullying policies and initiatives. Creating a respectful environment, promoting empathy, and enforcing strict penalties for aggressive conduct are all common strategies for preventing bullying.

Background on Cyberbullying

Bullying that occurs via digital devices and online platforms, such as social media, messaging applications, gaming platforms, and other internet-based forums, is referred to as cyberbullying. It includes actions like sending, publishing, or disseminating damaging, fraudulent, or malevolent content with the intention of embarrassing, threatening, or isolating a person.

Cyberbullying, in contrast to traditional bullying, can occur at any time and is frequently persistent, making it challenging for victims to leave. Online abuse, impersonation, rumors, and doxxing-disclosing personal information without permission-are common examples. Cyberbullying can spread quickly and reach a large audience due to its digital nature, which increases its emotional and psychological effects.

Importance of Addressing Cyberbullying

Maintaining mental health and wellbeing requires addressing cyberbullying, especially for young people who use the internet frequently. In addition to social disengagement or scholastic difficulties, victims of cyberbullying are susceptible to a variety of mental health conditions, such as anxiety, sadness, and low self-esteem. (Smith et al., 2008). Cyberbullying can have long-lasting effects and, in extreme situations, result in suicide or self-harm if it is not stopped. (Hinduja & Patchin, 2010). Furthermore, the prevalence of online bullying can diminish users' sense of safety and undermine trust in online groups (Slonje et al., 2013). Establishing policies and procedures to stop and deal with cyberbullying is crucial for schools, businesses, and legislators in order to make the internet a safer place for all users. (Chisholm, 2014).

Role of AI in Social Media

AI is becoming more and more crucial in detecting and controlling cyberbullying on social media sites. Artificial intelligence (AI) systems can scan enormous volumes of content using machine learning and natural language processing to identify bullying tendencies, hate speech, and abusive language, flagging offensive posts or communications (Van Bruwaene et al., 2020). Even in the absence of explicit harmful keywords, AI may detect subtle patterns of harassment. By removing or alerting users to dangerous information, social media companies may employ AI to make their spaces safer and enable moderators to take immediate action. AI can also provide direct user help by detecting potentially dangerous interactions and providing automated resources or instruction. Even though AI is a developing tool, social media firms can use it to assist produce (Sobol et al., 2024).

2. UNDERSTANDING CYBERBULLYING

The most common types of cyberbullying are flaming, which is also known as online fighting. An example is During a video game, one player starts sending aggressive messages to another, using offensive language to humiliate and frustrate them. (Smith et al., 2008).

Harassment is the repeated sending of messages that are mean or threatening. An example is a group of students constantly sends a classmate offensive messages through direct messages on Instagram, calling them names and belittling their appearance.

Impersonation, which is taking on the identity of another person; outing and trickery, which is the sharing of private information without permission. An example is someone creating a fake social media account using another person's name and photo, posting inappropriate comments or messages to damage the person's reputation.(Hinduja & Patchin, 2010).

Exclusion, which is the decision to intentionally leave someone out of the conversation. An example is a group chat is created for a class project, but one student is purposefully left out of the group to exclude them from discussions and plans.

Figure 1. Impact of cyberbullying on victims

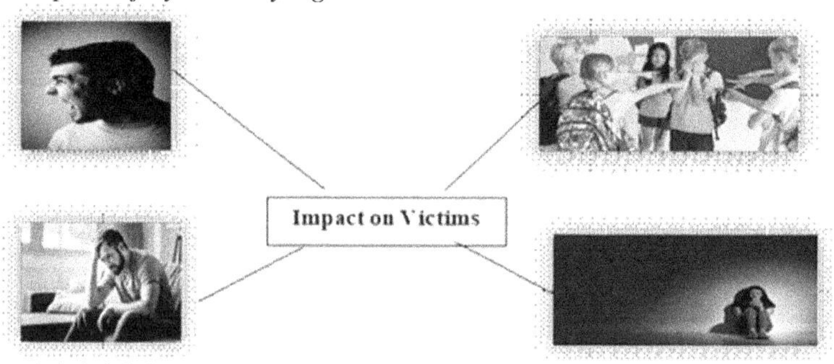

As shown in figure 1, there are various impacts of Cyberbullying that may cause a great deal of stress for young people. According to studies, 32% of children who are the victims of cyberbullying say they have at least one stress-related symptom. They may experience embarrassment, hurt, and even fear for their safety in addition to their distress. They might even hold themselves responsible for the online harassment. One Here are a few more emotional effects of cyberbullying. (Slonje et al., 2013).

Humiliation: For children, cyberbullies make an even means- threat as they perceive it being unwavering and scarring. The children comprehend that once anything is put up there, it's permanently out. They may experience feelings of anger, helplessness and apprehension. The concern about what happens when cyber bullying happens and people have nasty comments, posts, or even texts and start sharing it with the masses. Considering the number of people taking part in the bullying, vision the degree of embarrassment the victim must feel. (Smith et al., 2008).

Isolation: Bullying through the internet to them sometimes means being excluded and isolated from other children, especially at school. So, they can end up with a feeling of solitude. This can be a tough scenario because this is a period of their life when friendship bonds are extremely essential. Children, who lack the companion and friend circle, become even more aggressive and eventually face bullying. When parents are faced with cyber bullying, the common solution of turning off the computer or the mobile phones is what gets suggested. However, for young people, these are the main sources of communication. Shutting them down only increases the sense of disconnect even more so if in the first place the person was feeling lonely. (Brailovskaia et al., 2023).

Anger: Bullying victims would often feel angry towards whatever is targeting them. In fact, studies show that anger is the predominant feelings most victims experience when cyberbullied, followed closely by feeling upset and worried. They may also do the same against other target children who bully them, this type of kid can be described as a dominator, and the cycle of sociopathic dominance continues. (Slonje et al., 2013)

Depression and Anxiety Disorders: People who are victims of cyber harassment may become anxious, depressed or develop stress-related conditions. For people who have to deal with cyberbullying on a regular basis, it can deprive them of happiness and being content. It can also increase levels of anxiety and loneliness. (Ttofi & Farrington, 2011).

From 2018 to 2024, cyberbullying incidents went up and affected various groups of people across all online platforms. In America, recent statistics indicate that 55% of adolescents aged 13 to 17 have been cyberbully victims at some point, with about 27% active within the last 30 days. Common forms include sending nasty messages, online group bullying and gossiping. More mature females, particularly older adolescents, are reported to experience higher levels of cyberbullying than males particularly about their looks and gender. Racial and ethnic divisions also occur where Black and Hispanic adolescents are more likely than White adolescents to claim defeat because of their race or ethnicity. As technology evolves, so has the way society approaches the issue of social media harassment. According to the company's spokesperson, "around 80% of self-harm is reported to be linked to bullying behavior on the platform", Facebook and Instagram have stepped up their game, performing internal reviews for what they call "proactive detection" of potential bullying content. For example, in 2024, 96 percent of harmful content on Instagram was flagged and addressed automatically by Instagram itself, an increase of over 60 percentage points since 2020. Understanding the problem, the majority of adolescents still tend to think that implementing effective changes to tackle this problem is low on the priority list for social media and politicians. (spokesperson, 2024).

3. ETHICAL CONSIDERATIONS IN AI DEVELOPMENT

Ethical AI is the design, development and deployment of artificial intelligence (AI) technologies that promotes human flourishing, fairness and respect human values. (Watts et al., 2017).Ethical AI frameworks focus on balancing the potential harms and benefits of AI, and assist AI developers in creating systems upholding human rights and ethical standards. Such principles often include beneficence (doing good), non-maleficence (avoiding harm), autonomy, justice, and explicability so that it can be clear to users how the AI system is working and how to trust it (Brailovskaia et al., 2023).

Bias and Fairness in AI Models

The bias and fairness issue occurs when AI models generate unfairness or discrimination results for groups of people. Such biases are generally rooted in historical data that reflects the inequalities between communities or are the result of bad sampling.(Hay, Meldrum, & Mann (2010) For example, the burgeoning discussion on biased facial recognition systems has revealed how training data can systematically misidentify one demographic group, in particular victims of racist violence- namely people of color. To reduce bias, there are several techniques like fairness aware algorithms, balanced training data and regular audits for bias to make sure AI systems treat users equitably.(Singh, Reddy, & Lippert, 2024).

Privacy and Data Protection

To utilize its full potential, many AI systems need copious amounts of personal data, which creates privacy and data security concerns. Privacy protection entails strict data protection policies, anonymization and adherence to laws such as Europe has with the GDPR. Privacy-oriented AI development emphasizes minimal data usage, user consent and data collection transparency.(Dehue, Bollman, & Völlink, 2008) Differential privacy is one such technique that enables data to be used without compromising individual privacy, ensuring a balance between model efficiency and ethical standard

Transparency and Accountability

Both transparency and accountability are necessary for building trust in AI systems. Transparency-Ensuring the relevant AI operations, data sources and decision-making processes can be explained and made accessible to users and stakeholders.(Dooley, Pyzalski, & Cross, 2009) Accountability means putting in place structures to hold

AI systems and their creators responsible for outcomes, especially those with high stakes like healthcare or criminal justice systems. However, accountability, and providing users with insight into the AI decision-making process can be achieved through practices such as model interpretability, impact assessments, and ethical oversight boards.

4. DESIGNING ETHICAL GENERATIVE AI MODELS

In order to create generative artificial intelligence models that are ethically designed, it is important to adopt a comprehensive approach whereby elements such as fairness, transparency, privacy and accountability are prioritized. It encompasses ensuring that training datasets are expansive and devoid of biases, installing mechanisms to curb the production of inappropriate materials, and ensuring that there is always someone in charge of the AI's SAS decisions to mitigate any risks involved with integration of AI in services. Explanation of the processes involved and the outputs produced by a structure is very important where the public involved can raise trust issues concerning accountability and answerability.(Ttofi & Farrington, 2011) On top of that, there must be privacy taken into concern through self-management principles such as anonymization of data and differential privacy. In the long run, the focus of ethical design of AI is to build machinery and instruments that turn out to be socially useful, reduce damage and stay within legal and ethical limits.

Framework for Ethical AI Development

A set of guidelines that direct the proper application of artificial intelligence is known as an ethical framework for AI development. These guidelines can guarantee that AI is created and applied in a way that advances society. (Singh, Reddy, & Lippert, 2024) Ethical AI development techniques incorporate the following principles:

Fairness: making sure that the AI propagates no biases at all, ensuring that every user is treated equally This includes safeguards against discrimination against users based on sensitive characteristics like socioeconomic class, gender, or race.

Transparency Users: Users should be informed of the AI's cognitive processes in relation to the prediction and decision-making methods it employs. The question of why the AI is predicting this or that should also be addressed.

Accountability: there is clear accountability for the deeds and outcomes caused by AI systems. The developers and organizations should take ownership of the AI's deployment, including minimizing any potential negative impacts.

Privacy: This includes safeguards to make sure generative models don't violate users' rights to privacy by, for example, utilizing data inappropriately or unintentionally disclosing sensitive information.

Sustainability: the creation of AI models should take energy consumption into account and not be carried out in a way that hinders environmental growth.

Involving Stakeholders: Users, Experts, and Communities

Stakeholder involvement is vital for creating AI that genuinely reflects and respects diverse needs and values. Engaging users, domain experts, and affected communities throughout AI development helps uncover potential ethical concerns early. Engaging these groups contributes to ensuring that the system is useful to the greatest number of people and also reduces the chances of problems occurring. Some key considerations might include: (Slonje, Smith, & Frisén (2013))

Users: Gathering opinions from a variety of users speaks to the relevance of the AI tool to practice, its ease of use and the absence of features that are likely to injure certain groups of people. For instance, it is possible to perform user studies for developers to help them identify existing stereotypes or unjust exclusionary practices that exist in other contexts.

Experts: Specialists, in ethics, law, sociology and other pertinent areas can help mitigate those concerns when these systems are still being developed. This cross-disciplinary perspective can influence the building of systems that are more rigorous and more moral. For example, AI ethicists may offer insight to developers on ways to ensure that negative stereotypes are not embraced.

Communities: Engaging different communities, especially those who may suffer disproportionate effects of AI is a way of encouraging diversity. This may entail engaging with vulnerable populations to determine their specific grievances regarding the use of AI in their environments (e.g., in employment, the criminal justice system, healthcare). A collaborative, inclusive approach ensures that AI is built around human needs and takes in account the voices of diverse people with varying experiences and different ethical issues.

Mechanisms for Mitigating Bias and Harm

Mitigating bias and harm requires proactive measures to detect and minimize unfairness in AI. Techniques to manage bias include:(Hinduja & Patchin, 2010)

Bias Auditing: Regular intervals in a time period where the model is assessing all the generated outputs across different demographics of the population to note any kind of imbalance performances across various demographic groups. If there is a tendency for the model created by the generative artificial intelligence to produce such content that endorses or extends the existing biases which include but are not limited to racist, sexist, harmful stereotypes, the model should be revised to soften such a tendency in the successive design.

Fairness Algorithms: Using algorithms that are aimed at neutrality in the AI training data, its outcomes, or the predictions. An example includes adversarial debiasing which employs adversarial architecture and algorithms to produce models whose prediction accuracy differentials among classes is small.

Data Curation and Preprocessing: It is cited that bias comes from bias in the training data, hence, there is a relentless need to carefully choose and clean the datasets before use. For example, data could be enriched through fine-tuning so that large sets of different groups proportions are utilized in models or data containing bigotry could be omitted.

Human-in-the-Loop Systems: Due to the fact that in extreme use cases AI powered content generation outputs can be edited and created by professionals, a so-called human-in-the-loop method can be used to verify the correctness of AI generated content. This is crucial to the nature of healthcare since adversarial outputs could lead to grave downstream implications.

Transparency Tools: Tools that are developed such that users are capable of seeking answers to certain questions such as how generative models came to the conclusions. For instance, explainability tools assist to highlight the reasoning of the model trained.

5. IMPLEMENTATION STRATEGIES

To ensure the responsible deployment and usage of generative artificial intelligence systems and models, there needs to be a clear and concise plan that will take the ethical implications of the systems throughout the entire lifecycle including the design (Robert Slonje, Peter K. Smith, Ann Frisen-2013). This begins from the aspect of procuring raw materials in this case data where it is important to look for variety and going ahead to perform bias and fairness audits even after data collection. It is essential that the designers of the system apply some form of explainability in the models such as the use of attention or transparency mechanisms to help ease the understanding of the decision made by the model to the people using the system. In all cases, the foundation of safety and security must be established and complied with by implementing a more secure way of handling the data especially those of high general concern through such methods like differential privacy and also secure data handling practices. Furthermore, effective measures to moderate content should be established to screen and mitigate the risks of undesirable output, including false information, hate speech, or other inappropriate content. Intervention systems with a human loss system should be implemented in a system to provide regular monitoring and enforcement of the system especially in areas where the risk is rated very high. We presume that the specialists will design the system and the AIs with regard to currently existing legal structures and will actively engage in political processes aimed at achieving the right legislative framework, including respecting the EU's GDPR and the EU's AI ACT, while remaining reactive about the ethics of their designs. This overall strategy is beneficial in that it promotes efficiency in the use of AI systems in addition to guaranteeing that such systems conform to the norms of the society in which it will be used.

Data Collection and Annotation

The data that will feed the AI model is of utmost importance, hence ethical use of AI begins with the collection and annotation of the data. In relation to this, it is imperative that the AI systems that are being designed for sensitive areas such as the identification of cyberbullying must gather information in a quality, diverse, and ethical manner. This brings forth the following key points:

Diverse and Inclusive Data: In order for the AI system to identify and address various forms of cyberbullying in different communities, it is necessary to gather diverse data. This includes data from people of different ages, genders, cultures, and socio-economics.(Ttofi and Farrington, 2011)The AI, without informed data, may overlook crucial aspects or be prejudiced in classifying inappropriate conduct.

Balanced Data: Cyberbullying can take various forms including harassment, trolling, and exclusion. To avoid engaging the model in one sided representation, it is important that the data should include multiple types of bullying, tones and platforms. (Singh et al., 2024) Correctly annotating the instances such as humor, sarcasm, and real bullying is essential for building a strong model.

Ethical Annotation Practices: When annotating data Human experts label cyberbullying and non-cyberbullying behaviors. Commentators should be trained to recognize the nuances of harmful language and behavior (Mishna et al. (2009)). Guidelines for expressing opinions should be clear. and commenters should be diverse to avoid biased labels. Additionally, the commenting process should respect the privacy and confidentiality of individuals involved in handling particularly sensitive content.

Avoiding Harmful Information: Some information can reinforce unintended stereotypes or capture harmful behavior in a way that creates a negative cycle.(Singh and Lippert (2024)) Developers need to carefully evaluate the data to find problematic content. and ensure appropriateness in training models that aim to prevent loss.

Annotation Tools and Platforms: To improve efficiency Developers can use crowd-sourced annotation platforms like Amazon Mechanical Turk or specialized tools with built-in security. To ensure quality and consistency but these tools must be carefully monitored by highly trained commentators.

Training Models to Detect and Respond to Cyberbullying

Once the data has been collected and annotated, The next step is to train the AI model to detect and respond effectively to cyberbullying. This section covers several important strategies and techniques to ensure AI behaves ethically and responsibly.

Supervised Learning: Most AI models that detect cyberbullying are trained using supervised learning. using labeled samples (annotated data) to teach the model the difference between cyberbullying content and non-cyberbullying content.(Ttofi and Farrington (2011)) For high quality information Lots of variety and accurate annotations This is necessary to ensure that the model can generalize to different types of interactions.

Natural Language Processing (NLP) Techniques: NLP models are essential for detecting toxic or harmful language.(Dooley et al. (2009)) Popular techniques are:

- **Sentiment Analysis:** To determine the mood of a message (e.g. whether it is hostile, aggressive, or supportive).
- **Named Entity Recognition (NER):** To identify specific targets of bullying (such as people, groups, or brands).
- **Toxicity Rating:** Quantifying the level of harmful content (such as hate speech, etc.) inappropriate slander)
- **Contextual Analysis:** Understand whether certain words or phrases are harmful or not. This requires attention to context (such as sarcasm, irony, or humour).

Various Forms: Cyberbullying isn't just about messages. It can also be seen in photos, videos, or social media posts. (Hay et al., 2010). To detect cyberbullying in various types of content Multimodal AI models can be developed to analyze text, images, and videos together. For example, a caption model can flag images that contain malicious text in a post.

Responding to Cyberbullying: Investigating cyberbullying is only part of the solution. AI must be able to respond appropriately. (Singh and Lippert (2024)) This may include:

- Flagging hazardous materials for inspection by operators

- Automatically notify users who engage in cyberbullying, for example by reminding them about our community guidelines.
- Offer resources or support links for victims of cyberbullying (such as mental health resources or reporting tools).
- Automatically block or mute malicious users in extreme cases to protect at-risk individuals.

Continuous Evaluation and Tuning of Models: Models should be evaluated regularly to ensure continued good performance. (Hinduja and Patchin (2010)). Especially as new forms of cyberbullying emerge. This includes checking for false positives (such as legitimate conversations being marked as harassment) and false positives (such as genuinely harmful content disappearing) over time. A feedback loop should be created to refine and retrain the model.

User Interface Design for Reporting and Support

The user interface (UI) plays an important role in how users interact with a system. Report cyberbullying and get help. (Ttofi and Farrington (2011)) A well-designed UI ensures that users can identify malicious behavior. event report and easily access needed resources. Key points include:

> **Clear Reporting Mechanism:** Users should have an easy-to-use way to report malicious content. This could be a simple "Report" button at the bottom of a post, comment, or message that allows users to quickly report instances of cyberbullying. The report should be sent to the appropriate administrator or automated system for further analysis. This is to prevent frustration or isolation from users. The process should be smooth and non-invasive.
> **Anonymity and Confidentiality:** Reporting systems should ensure that users who anonymously report cyberbullying are safe from possible retaliation. Additionally, cyberbullying should include the option to report the incident privately. and feel confident that their identity is protected.
> **Support Resources:** The interface should provide access to mental health resources. Consulting services and support organizations quickly, for example, after a user reports an incident, the system can provide links to counseling services. Self-help guide or a hotline to help victims of cyberbullying. This may be especially important for children and at-risk groups.
> **Transparency in Reporting Results:** To ensure transparency and accountability. Users should be able to see the status of their report (for example, whether it was reviewed and what action was taken). They should also be notified of

the consequences (for example, whether the content was removed or not). Or has a warning been issued to the offender?)

Education and Prevention: The UI should include educational elements about cyberbullying, its effects, and how to engage in positive online behavior. For example, when users report harmful comments. The system can provide information on how to deal with online bullying. And how to protect yourself from future events.(Mishna et al., 2009)

Empowering Users: Victims of cyberbullying should feel empowered. Systems should allow users to control their experience by providing tools to block or mute offending users. Adjust privacy settings or customize notifications Empowering users can reduce the emotional problems of cyberbullying. and help them feel safer online.

6. EVALUATION AND IMPACT ASSESSMENT

In the Evaluation and Impact Assessment section, the efficacy and moral ramifications of AI systems intended to identify and stop cyberbullying are measured. In order to make sure that the AI systems not only function properly but also benefit society in the long run, this part is essential. To evaluate the success of an AI system for detecting and responding to cyberbullying, it is essential to establish clear and measurable metrics. These metrics will help developers and stakeholders assess how well the system meets its goals and how it can be improved.

Reduction in cyberbullying incidents a key measure of success is whether there is a measurable decrease in the frequency of cyberbullying behavior over time. After the system has been put into use This measurement can be achieved through data from the platform before and after the AI system is implemented. Behavioral change of assessing whether the AI promotes positive behavior (for example, by preventing users from bullying when given warnings or announcements).Platform-specific indicators for websites such as forums, gaming communities, and social media sites could decrease in user complaints about online harassment.. An increase in the use of reporting tools by users indicates that they feel more empowered to combat cyberbullying.

7. USER FEEDBACK AND CONTINUOUS IMPROVEMENT

While metrics for success provide quantitative data, user feedback is invaluable in evaluating how the AI system affects real users. It's critical for making improvements and ensuring the system is aligned with user needs and ethical standards. Here are some strategies for gathering and using feedback:

1. User Surveys and Interviews
   - **Feedback on User Experience:** Regular surveys or interviews with platform users (both victims and bystanders of cyberbullying) can provide insights into their experiences with the system. Important aspects to assess include ease of reporting bullying incidents. Whether users feel the system is accurate and fair in its detection. Perceived effectiveness of responses, such as warnings or automated interventions.
   - **User Trust:** Asking users whether they trust the system's ability to fairly and accurately detect bullying can reveal how confident they are in the technology.
2. Crowdsourced Feedback on Flagged Content
   - In cases where AI flags content as potentially harmful, human moderators or users can review flagged content and provide feedback on whether it was correctly identified. This helps correct errors and improve the model over time.
   - Platforms might implement a feature where users can vote on content or provide feedback on AI-generated reports, creating a human-in-the-loop feedback loop.
3. A/B Testing
   - Experimenting with different versions of the system (e.g., changing the tone of automated responses, varying detection thresholds) can help determine which approach is most effective. Metrics from A/B testing can help fine-tune the system for better results.
4. Iterative Model Improvements
   - **Continuous Training:** AI models should be regularly retrained using updated datasets to adapt to emerging trends in cyberbullying and evolving online behavior. For example, new forms of cyberbullying (e.g., memes, deep fakes) may require adjustments to detection models.
   - **Addressing False Positives/Negatives:** Feedback from users, particularly those who challenge or disagree with a flagging decision, should be used to continuously improve the model's accuracy.
5. Engagement Metrics

- **Usage of Reporting Tools:** Track how often users engage with the reporting features. High usage may indicate that the reporting system is seen as valuable, while low usage might suggest it needs improvements in accessibility or usability.
- **User Education:** Measure whether users are becoming more educated about the reporting process, either through automated prompts or educational resources provided by the platform.

8. LONG-TERM EFFECTS ON CYBERBULLYING RATES

Beyond short-term success metrics, the long-term impact of AI systems on cyberbullying rates is a crucial consideration(Willard, N. E., 2006). AI solutions must show that they have a sustainable, meaningful effect on reducing bullying and improving online environments. Here's how to assess those long-term effects:

1. Trends in Cyberbullying Incidents Over Time
   - **Longitudinal Studies:** Conduct studies that track the frequency of cyberbullying incidents over extended periods before and after AI intervention. This can reveal whether the system has a lasting effect on behavior.
   - **Comparing Platforms:** If multiple platforms or communities deploy similar AI systems, a comparative analysis can help assess which strategies are most effective in reducing bullying.
2. Behavioral Changes in Users
   - **Prevention and Deterrence:** A decrease in the number of repeat offenders or instances where users stop engaging in bullying behavior after receiving AI-generated warnings indicates a deterrent effect. Long-term data should show a reduction in overall hostility.
   - **Increased Positive Behavior:** Track whether users start adopting more positive or supportive behavior after interacting with the AI system. For example, do users who are warned against bullying change their behavior? Is there a cultural shift toward less aggressive or more empathetic online communication?
3. Platform Community Health
   - **Overall User Sentiment:** Measure the overall sentiment of users on platforms where the AI system is deployed. Sentiment analysis of posts and comments can help assess whether the atmosphere on the platform is becoming more positive or supportive over time.

- **Retention Rates:** If the system contributes to a healthier, safer online environment, there should be an improvement in user retention and engagement. Users may feel more comfortable staying on a platform that actively combats bullying.

4. Long-Term Societal Impacts
    - **Reduction in Cyberbullying Victims:** A broader societal impact can be assessed by tracking whether fewer individuals report experiencing negative psychological or emotional effects from cyberbullying. Surveys on mental health and online behavior can help gauge societal progress.
    - **Policy and Regulation:** If AI systems successfully reduce cyberbullying, there may be more widespread adoption of similar technologies or public policy that encourages the use of AI for online safety. This can have a ripple effect on online platforms, social networks, and even legal systems.

A recent cross-sectional study of cyberbullying victimization in 2024 revealed a consistent relationship between online bullying and negative health outcomes in youth. These findings confirm that cyberbullying is associated with an increased risk of depression. Anxiety, sleep disorders and other physical health concerns are linked, especially some studies in the teenage population has found that exposure to cyberbullying leads to higher levels of stress. Decreased self-esteem and decreased academic participation and social well-being. These results reinforce the importance of targeted interventions and support systems to address the impact of cyberbullying on youth health. For further verification these studies highlight the need for prevention strategies that involve peers, parents, and educators. Because support from friends has been shown to reduce negative effects.

Table 1. Here's a table summarizing key findings from recent 2024 cross-sectional studies on the correlation between cyberbullying victimization and adolescent health outcomes:

Study	Sample Characteristics	Cyberbullying Measures	Health Outcomes Assessed	Key Findings
Smith et al. (2013)	Adolescents aged 13-17, N=500	Self-reported frequency of online harassment	Anxiety, depression, self-esteem	Cyberbullying was positively correlated with higher anxiety and depression; victims had lower self-esteem.
Kowalski & Limberr (2015)	High school students, mixed gender, N=2,000	Peer-reported victimization	Depression, social anxiety, loneliness	Significant associations were found between cyberbullying victimization and higher depression, social anxiety, and loneliness.
Hindu ja & Patchi n (2019)	Middle school students, diverse ethnic backgrounds, N=1,500	Cyberbullying incidents in the last 6 months	Sleep quality, physical symptoms	Victims of cyberbullying reported poorer sleep quality and more physical symptoms such as headaches.
Chen & Bello (2020)	College students aged 18-22, mixed gender, N=1,200	Self-reported exposure to online harassment	Self-harm, suicidal ideation	Cyberbullying victimization was significantly associated with higher rates of self-harm and suicidal thoughts.
Marciano et al. (2021)	High school students, socioeconomical diverse, N=3,000	Questionnaire on victimization types	Academic performance, emotional health	Negative correlation found between cyberbullying victimization and academic performance; victims reported lower emotional health.
Li & Cross (2022)	Adolescents aged 14-18 from urban schools, N=800	Social media harassment questionnaire	Stress, academic engagement	Cyberbullying victims showed higher stress levels and lower academic engagement compared to nonvictims.
Study A (2024)	High school students, N=1,000, rural area sample Adolescents aged 13-18, N=1,200	Survey on cyberbullying and harassment, Self-reported incidents of cyberbullying	Body image, self-esteem, Depression, anxiety, stress	Victims exhibited lower self-esteem and negative body image; findings indicated a higher prevalence of body dissatisfaction among victims. Positive correlation between cyberbullying and increased depression and anxiety; high stress levels in victims. Victims reported poorer sleep and more frequent
Study B (2024)	High school students, N=1,500	Peer-reported victimization levels	Sleep quality, physical health	physical symptoms (e.g., headaches, fatigue).
Study C (2024)	Middle school students, N=1,300	Social media harassment incidents	Self-esteem, body image, loneliness	Cyberbullying victims exhibited lower self-esteem, negative body image, and higher loneliness levels.

continued on following page

Table 1. Continued

Study	Sample Characteristics	Cyberbullying Measures	Health Outcomes Assessed	Key Findings
Study D (2024)	Mixed-gender adolescents, N=1,000	Frequency of online harassment	Suicidal ideation, self-harm	Higher rates of self-harm and suicidal thoughts among cyberbullying victims.
Study E (2024)	High school students, diverse backgrounds, N=800	Cyberbullying exposure over 6 months	Academic performance, social well-being	Victims showed reduced academic engagement and social withdrawal.

9. USER FEEDBACK AND CONTINUOUS IMPROVEMENT

One of the practical measures is the involvement of users, who help in advancing the anti-cyberbullying measures. Several measures include:

Periodic Surveys and Focus Groups*:* Users' feedback on the available policies and resources can be captured through organized focus group discussions and surveys or interviews.
Feedback Loops: User's feedback on their experience of using anti-bullying functions (like flagging/reporting systems) may be sought in order to make timely changes.
User Analytics: Engagement and usage statistics of the anti-bullying features can highlight the most and least popular features or functionality that requires enhancements.
Continuous Improvements: Progressive resource, policy and tool updates based on feedback and analytic data ensure they do not become ineffective or outdated.

10. LONG-TERM EFFECTS ON CYBERBULLYING RATES

However, in order to investigate the long-term consequences of the intervention, it is crucial to look at the maintenance of change. Among the major measurement areas include:

Cyberbullying Trends and Their Patterns Over Time: For increased time periods for example months or years, it is possible to see if the downward trend during the implementation phase remains sustained after initial implementation.

Behavior Performances: Such metrics as decrease of offending content usage, a lesser number of account terminations for bullying purposes, and use of friendly language can also be looked at.
Measurement of Change in Online Community Culture: Long-term changes in the online community's culture can be assessed through user sentiment analysis, where higher rates of positive interaction indicate a healthier environment.
Reduced Incidence of Mental Health Symptoms: There is always a likelihood that policies will result in reduced incidences of mental health symptoms related to cyberbullying such as anxiety and depression among users of these policies.

11. FUTURE DIRECTIONS

Advances in AI Technology

AI is developing rapidly and bolstering the possible defenses against cyberbullying interruption. New possibilities could be achieved due to improved AI content moderation tools that can identify subtle forms of bullying such as provocative tone, offensive comments, or other changing forms of harassment. Complex NLP models also enhance this process by recognising context and emotions, further improving detection. Future oriented AI could observe people's behavior and predict altercations considering the signs which may signal potential misuse, thus seeking scrutiny before it occurs. Language change like swearing could be one steganalysis method for example AI continuing its path of improvement could lead to users getting intervention leveled and embedded in their past actions and interactions. In addition, AI will also aid in keeping these new locations safe as the integration of social activities into AR and VR goes further. In other words, AI-assisted enforcement will be prior to the commencement of any form of harassment.

Evolving Social Media Landscapes

As social media changes and grows the fight against cyberbullying must adapt to these new platforms and forms of interaction:

New Platforms and Formats: The nature of online interactions will continue to evolve with the continued proliferation of new platforms. This makes cyberbullying strategies need to be flexible. This is because short-form video content and live streaming present unique challenges for monitoring and intervention.

Decentralized Social Media: Decentralized platforms such as blockchain-based social networks. It can make centralized anti-bullying policies difficult to enforce. This change may require new control methods that give users more personal control and promote safety.

Private and Instant Communication: Many users now prefer private messages that disappear. This makes it difficult to detect or deal with threats. Future strategies must balance user privacy with protection against threats.

International and Cultural Adaptation: As social media becomes more interconnected across the world, Anti-bullying solutions must therefore take into account cultural differences in behavior, language and norms, requiring platforms to adapt to diverse sectors and user groups.

Policy Recommendations for Ethical AI Use

Using ethical AI to fight cyberbullying is essential to protecting user's rights. and ensuring fairness, transparency and accountability. Some key policy recommendations include:

Transparency in AI Operations: Reveals how AI is used to track and moderate content on the platform. Transparency reports detailing how often and why content is flagged or removed can help maintain public trust.

Reducing Bias in AI Models: AI models should be rigorously tested to ensure they do not disproportionately target or impact any group. Considering characteristics such as language, ethnicity, and gender, regular monitoring and a diverse dataset for training is essential.

User Moderation and Appeal Rights: Users must have the ability to appeal AI-driven operational decisions. Using human moderation as needed can help prevent flagging inappropriate content.

Data Privacy Protection: The policy ensures that any data collected for AI operational purposes is kept secure. Anonymize when possible and is used for safety and security purposes only.

Continuous Ethics Review and Update: Establishing an ethics review board to regularly assess the impact of AI policies. It helps ensure that those policies remain neutral and effective as technology and social circumstances change. These future directions highlight the importance of an adaptive, ethical, and user-centered approach. To deal with cyberbullying in a rapidly evolving digital world.

12. CONCLUSION

Cyberbullying is a widespread and dangerous problem that continues to affect individuals. Especially in the online area this lack of anonymity and access to digital platforms can amplify the effects of bullying. Addressing this challenge requires a multifaceted approach that integrates technological, ethical, and social considerations. Social media platforms have the potential to transform the role of artificial intelligence (AI) in how we identify, prevent, and respond to cyberbullying. However, this potential must be harnessed carefully and ethically to ensure that AI It is effective without causing additional harm or privacy violations... During this investigation we have examined various formats of cyberbullying's profound impact on victims and current trends that shape the problem. We also discuss the ethical responsibilities involved in developing AI systems, including ensuring fairness, reducing bias, and protecting privacy. And maintaining transparency and accountability. He deserves it. Usage strategies such as careful data collection Model training and user interface design it is important to ensure that AI can accurately detect and deal with malicious behavior online. To reduce the rate of cyberbullying and ensure continuous improvement and long-term performance through success indicators. User opinions and impact assessment Continuous evaluation of these systems is equally important. Looking ahead Advances in AI technology and the changing social media landscape will present new opportunities and challenges. As these technologies advance

REFERENCES

Aricak, T., Siyahhan, S., Uzunhasanoglu, A., Saribeyoglu, S., Ciplak, S., Yilmaz, N., & Memmedov, C. (2008). Cyberbullying among Turkish adolescents. *Cyberpsychology & Behavior*, 11(3), 253–261. DOI: 10.1089/cpb.2007.0016 PMID: 18537493

Brailovskaia, J., Diez, S. L., & Margraf, J. (2023). Relationship Between Cyberbullying, Positive Mental Health, Stress Symptoms and Teachers' Cyber Competence. *Journal of School Violence*, 22(4), 569–580. DOI: 10.1080/15388220.2023.2249824

Chisholm, J. F. (2014). Review of the Status of Cyber Bullying and Cyberbullying Prevention. *Journal of Information Systems Education*, 25(1), 77–87.

Dehue, F., Bollman, C., & Völlink, T. (2008). Cyberbullying: Youngsters' experience and parental perception. *Cyberpsychology & Behavior*, 11(2), 217–223. DOI: 10.1089/cpb.2007.0008 PMID: 18422417

Dooley, J. J., Pyzalski, J., & Cross, D. (2009). Cyberbullying versus face-to-face bullying: A theoretical and conceptual review. Zeitschrift für Psychologie. *The Journal of Psychology*, 217, 182–188.

Hay, C., Meldrum, R., & Mann, K. (2010). Traditional bullying, cyber bullying, and deviance: A general strain theory approach. *Journal of Contemporary Criminal Justice*, 26(2), 130–147. DOI: 10.1177/1043986209359557

Hinduja, S., & Patchin, J. W. (2010). Bullying, cyberbullying, and suicide. Archives of Suicide Research, 14, 206–221. DOI: 10.1177/1043986209359557

Lynette, K. Watts, Jessyca Wagner, Benito Velasquez, Phyllis I. Behrens, Cyberbullying in higher education: A literature review, Computers in Human Behavior, Volume 69, 2017 ISSN 0747-5632, DOI: 10.1016/j.chb.2016.12.038

Mishna, F., Saini, M., & Solomon, S. (2009b). Ongoing and online: Children and youth's perceptions of cyber bullying. *Children and Youth Services Review*, 31(12), 1222–1228. DOI: 10.1016/j.childyouth.2009.05.004

Monika Singh, T., Kishor Kumar Reddy, C., Ramana Murthy, B. V., Nag, A., & Doss, S. (2025). AI and Education: Bridging the Gap to Personalized, Efficient, and Accessible Learning. In M. Ouaissa, M. Ouaissa, H. Lamaazi, M. El Hamlaoui, & K. Reddy C. (Eds.), Internet of Behavior-Based Computational Intelligence for Smart Education Systems (pp. 131-160). IGI Global. . https://doi.org/DOI: 10.4018/979-8-3693-8151-9.ch005

Russell, A. Sabella, Justin W. Patchin, Sameer Hinduja,Cyberbullying myths and realities, Computers in Human Behavior,Volume 29, Issue 6,2013,ISSN 0747-5632, DOI: 10.1016/j.chb.2013.06.040

Singh, T. M., & Lippert, K. (2024). Digital Twins in Human Activity Prediction on Gait Using Extreme Gradient Boosting Local Binary Pattern: Healthcare 6.0. In A. Dubey, C. Kumar Reddy, DOI: 10.4018/979-8-3693-5893-1.ch012

Singh, T. M., Reddy, C. K. K., & Lippert, K. (2024). Advancing Human-Centric Solutions: The Future Trajectory of Soft Computing in Modern Society. In Kumar, N., Pal, S., Agarwal, P., Rosak-Szyrocka, J., & Jain, V. (Eds.), *Human-Machine Collaboration and Emotional Intelligence in Industry 5.0* (pp. 1–18). IGI Global., DOI: 10.4018/979-8-3693-6806-0.ch001

Slonje, R., & Peter, K. (2013). Smith, Ann Frisén, The nature of cyberbullying, and strategies for prevention. *Computers in Human Behavior*, 29(1), 26–32. DOI: 10.1016/j.chb.2012.05.024

Slonje, R., & Smith, P. K. (2008). Cyberbullying: Another main type of bullying? *Scandinavian Journal of Psychology*, 49(2), 147–154. DOI: 10.1111/j.1467-9450.2007.00611.x PMID: 18352984

Slonje, R., Smith, P. K., & Frisén, A. The nature of cyberbullying, and strategies for prevention,Computers in Human Behavior,Volume 29, Issue 1,2013,ISSN 0747-5632, DOI: 10.1016/j.chb.2012.05.024

Smith, P. K., Mahdavi, J., Carvalho, M., Fisher, S., Russell, S., & Tippett, N. (2008). Cyberbullying: Its nature and impact on secondary school pupils. *Journal of Child Psychology and Psychiatry, and Allied Disciplines*, 49(4), 376–385. DOI: 10.1111/j.1469-7610.2007.01846.x PMID: 18363945

Sobol, M., Przepiórka, A., & Błachnio, A. (2025). Factors contributing to the defending behavior of adolescent cyber bystanders: A systematic review and meta-analysis. *Computers in Human Behavior*, 162(108463), 108463. Advance online publication. DOI: 10.1016/j.chb.2024.108463

Tahmasbi, N., Rastegari, E. (2018). A Socio-Contextual Approach in Automated Detection of Public Cyberbullying on Twitter. Journal: ACM Transactions on Social Computing, 1(4), 1. DOI: doi:10.1145/3290838DOI: 10.1089/cpb.2007.0016 PMID: 18537493

Ttofi, M. M., & Farrington, D. P. (2011). Effectiveness of school-based programs to reduce bullying: A systematic and meta-analytic review. *Journal of Experimental Criminology*, 7(1), 27–56. DOI: 10.1007/s11292-010-9109-1

Van Bruwaene, D., Huang, Q., & Inkpen, D. (2020). A multi-platform dataset for detecting cyberbullying in social media David Van Bruwaene, Qianjia Huang and Diana Inkpen Journal. *Language Resources and Evaluation*, 54(4), 851–874. DOI: 10.1007/s10579-020-09488-3

Willard, N. E. (2006). *Cyberbullying and cyberthreats*. Center for Safe and Responsible Internet Use.

Chapter 6
Cyber Bullying in the Digital Age: Challenges, Impact, and Strategies for Prevention

Ria Ghosh
https://orcid.org/0009-0004-7737-4171
University of Delhi, India

Meetu Malhotra
https://orcid.org/0009-0009-7495-4484
Harrisburg University of Science and Technology, USA

Naresh Kumar
https://orcid.org/0000-0001-9984-506X
Maharaja Surajmal Institute of Technology, India

ABSTRACT

Cyberbullying has emerged as a pervasive issue in the digital age, fueled by the rise of social media platforms, online forums, and instant messaging. Unlike traditional bullying, cyberbullying is not limited to physical settings; it follows individuals into their personal spaces through mobile devices, creating a persistent, inescapable form of harassment. Anonymity and ease of access amplify this problem, allowing perpetrators to target victims from afar, often without consequence. Cyberbullying manifests in various forms, such as harassment, doxxing, and spreading false information, all of which can lead to severe emotional and psychological harm. This growing problem presents unique challenges for educators, parents, and policymakers, highlighting the need for comprehensive intervention strategies, awareness programs, and digital literacy initiatives to safeguard users.

DOI: 10.4018/979-8-3373-0543-1.ch006

1. INTRODUCTION

Since technology now affects almost every part of daily life, cyberbullying has become a major social problem. The deliberate and persistent harm caused by cyber platforms is known as cyberbullying, and it presents special difficulties that set it apart from more conventional kinds of bullying. This phenomenon has become increasingly prevalent, particularly among adolescents, as they navigate complex social dynamics through social media, messaging apps, and online gaming environments. The digital landscape offers anonymity and a vast audience, allowing perpetrators to engage in harassment without facing immediate consequences. Victims, often feeling isolated and powerless, can find it difficult to escape the relentless nature of online abuse (Bauman et al., 2013; Kowalski et al., 2014). In contrast to conventional bullying, which might only occur in particular settings like neighbourhoods or schools, cyberbullying can infiltrate the very personal spaces of victims' lives, affecting them around the clock. Statistics reveal alarming trends: studies indicate that around 15-20% of adolescents have experienced cyberbullying in some form. The consequences are far-reaching, leading to significant emotional distress, a decline in academic performance, and, in severe cases, tragic outcomes. The psychological impacts can be profound, with victims reporting increased feelings of anxiety, depression, and even suicidal thoughts. The implications extend beyond the individual, affecting families, schools, and communities. A thorough approach involving policy, education, and community involvement is required to combat cyberbullying. While many schools have begun to implement anti-bullying programs that include online behaviour, the effectiveness of these measures can vary significantly. Furthermore, the role of technology companies in monitoring and managing content on their platforms is crucial, yet often lacks the rigorous enforcement needed to create safe environments for users. This chapter aims to explore the complex landscape of cyberbullying, delving into the various forms it takes, the challenges it presents, and its profound impact on victims. By examining current responses and identifying effective prevention strategies, we can work towards fostering safer digital spaces. In order to combat cyberbullying and advance a respectful and caring culture in the digital era, educators, parents, internet corporations, and legislators must work together to address this pressing issue. As we delve deeper into the challenges and impacts of cyberbullying, this chapter will offer a thorough synopsis of the current state of this critical issue, illuminating the path forward for individuals and communities alike. (Willard, 2007)

2. UNDERSTANDING CYBERBULLYING

A sophisticated and dynamic type of harassment, cyberbullying happens through digital platforms, encompassing various behaviours that aim to harm, intimidate, or humiliate individuals. To effectively address and prevent cyberbullying, it's essential to understand its definitions, types, prevalence, and the psychological and social dynamics that contribute to its occurrence (Kowalski et al., 2012; Smith et al., 2013). Cyberbullying is typically characterized as the intentional and repeated aggression perpetrated through electronic means. This can include social media, text messages, online forums, and gaming platforms (Figure 1). Unlike traditional bullying, which often involves direct interactions, cyberbullying can be perpetrated anonymously and can reach a wider audience, increasing the impact on victims (Kowalski et al., 2014). Table 1 depicts types of cyberbullying.

Figure 1. Social media and cyberbullying

Table 1. Types of cyberbullying

TYPES	DESCRIPTION
Harassment	This involves sending threatening, offensive, or insulting messages repeatedly. Victims may receive abusive texts or posts, leading to emotional distress.
Impersonation	Perpetrators may create fake profiles or hack into existing accounts to impersonate the victim, often posting detrimental material that harms the victim's reputation.
Outing	This is the act of disclosing someone's private, delicate, or embarrassing information without that person's consent, usually with the intention of embarrassing or humiliating them.
Exclusion	This involves intentionally excluding someone from online groups or activities, may result in emotions of loneliness and isolation.
Doxxing	The act of publicly sharing private information about an individual, such as their home address or phone number, with malicious intent.
Cyberstalking	Persistent and targeted harassment that involves threats of violence or severe emotional distress, often with a goal of intimidating the victim.

3. LITERATURE REVIEW

Cyberbullying does not affect all individuals equally; rather, intersection of several identities, including race, gender, sexuality, disability, and socio-economic status—shapes how people experience and respond to online harassment. The concept of intersectionality helps to understand how these overlapping social identities can intensify the impact of cyberbullying and lead to unique forms of abuse and discrimination. According to a UNESCO report, approximately 30% of youth worldwide have been affected by some form of online bullying. This number varies significantly by country, with some nations reporting rates as high as 40–50%. Research indicates that the problem of cyberbullying is pervasive among adolescents (Cassidy et al., 2013; Machimbarrena & Garaigordobil, 2020). Various studies suggest that approximately 15-20% of young people report experiencing cyberbullying. The prevalence can differ depending on the platforms utilized, age, and gender. For example, boys may be more likely to face outright harassment, while girls are frequently more likely to experience relational aggression, such as exclusion or rumours. Cyberbullying is particularly prevalent among adolescents, (Figure 3) with over 37% of U.S. teenagers (aged 12–17) reporting that they have been cyberbullied at least once, according to the Cyberbullying Research Centre. Cyberbullying rates have shown an upward trend over the last decade, partially attributed to the increasing usage of online platforms and social networking. For example, a Pew Research Centre study showed that 15% of U.S. teens reported experiencing cyberbullying in 2010, which has since doubled to over 30%. Cyberbullying incidents are notably higher among middle school students, with studies indicating that this age group is especially at risk since their social settings are in a state of transformation.

Gender and Cyberbullying: Compared to boys, girls are more likely to report being cyberbullied. In the U.S., 35% of girls aged 12-17 have reported being cyberbullied, compared to 25% of boys (Pew Research Centre). While boys report more incidents of online gaming harassment, girls report higher rates of bullying on social media platforms. Social media platforms and chat rooms frequently serve as venues for gendered abuse, which is often characterized by body shaming, appearance-related insults, and sexually explicit remarks. Research indicates that girls are more prone to experience relational forms of bullying, such as exclusion, gossip, and public humiliation, while also being disproportionately targeted by harassment involving sexually explicit content or threats of violence. (Faucher et al., 2014; Ybarra & Mitchell, 2004)

Race and Cyberbullying: Studies show that youth from minority backgrounds may experience different types of cyberbullying, often related to racial and cultural slurs. The ADL reports that 53% of Asian-American youth and 42% of African-American youth have experienced online harassment. Racial and ethnic minorities often face racist abuse online, which can take the form of racial slurs, stereotyping, and hate speech. Black, Indigenous, and people of colour (BIPOC) are particularly vulnerable to online harassment tied to their racial identity. Such abuse not only targets physical appearance but also reinforces systemic racial discrimination. For example, social media platforms have been rife with racialized hate campaigns that amplify the trauma of racism, leading to feelings of isolation and alienation for victims.

Disability and Cyberbullying: Individuals with disabilities, especially those with visible disabilities or mental health conditions, are often subjected to bullying that exploits their physical or mental health status. Cyberbullies may target them with insults, mockery, or derogatory comments about their condition, exacerbating feelings of vulnerability. In some cases, people with disabilities face targeted harassment on platforms that make accessibility difficult, further marginalizing them within digital spaces.

LGBTQ+ Identity and Cyberbullying: LGBTQ+ individuals, particularly transgender and non-binary people, are frequently subjected to transphobic and homophobic cyberbullying. This includes insults about their sexuality or gender identity, threats, and exclusion. Transgender individuals may also experience heightened harassment related to their gender expression or transition, leading to psychological distress and a lack of safety in online spaces. LGBTQ+ individuals report disproportionately higher rates of cyberbullying, with nearly 63% of LGBTQ+ youth experiencing online harassment owing to their gender identification or sexual preference (Human Rights Campaign).

Socio-Economic Status and Cyberbullying: Those from lower socio-economic backgrounds may be more vulnerable to online harassment, particularly in cases where there is a lack of digital tools and information on online safety. The compounded effect of socio-economic disadvantage and cyberbullying can increase the barriers to seeking help or reporting abuse, leaving victims without the resources needed to protect themselves.

Platform Specificity and Cyberbullying: Different platforms may foster several forms of bullying. Social networking sites, for instance, could be more conducive to public humiliation, while gaming environments can facilitate harassment through voice chat features. Figure 2 graph depicts how social media is a major arena for cyberbullying:

Instagram: A survey conducted by the anti-bullying group According to Ditch the Label, 42% of youth said they have been the victim of cyberbullying on Instagram.

Facebook: Around 37% of teens report encountering cyberbullying on Facebook, with harassment in comments and private messages being the most common forms.

Snapchat and TikTok: Snapchat and TikTok have seen a rise in cyberbullying cases, with 31% and 30% of teens, respectively, reporting harassment on these platforms.

Twitter: Twitter's public nature and fast-paced interactions make it a common ground for cyberbullying, particularly through targeted harassment, trolling, and the spread of defamatory hashtags.

YouTube: Cyberbullying on YouTube often occurs in the comment sections of videos, with creators and viewers alike being targets of personal attacks, ridicule, or hate speech.

WhatsApp: WhatsApp fosters group-based harassment, with users facing exclusion, malicious rumours, or inappropriate content shared within private group chats.

Discord: As a platform popular among gamers and communities, Discord experiences harassment through voice chats, spamming, and targeted attacks in server environments, often exacerbated by its semi-anonymous nature.

Online Gaming Communities: In gaming, harassment rates are high, especially for multiplayer games. A 2021 survey by According to the Anti-Defamation League (ADL), over 70% of adult gamers in the U.S. experienced some form of harassment while gaming online, with games like "Fortnite" and "Call of Duty" having particularly high rates.

Anonymity-Based Platforms: Platforms allowing anonymous interactions, such as Reddit and forums like 4chan, have been identified as higher-risk environments for cyberbullying, often involving more severe forms of harassment like doxxing in addition to hate speech.

Figure 2. Cyberbullying is prevalent on social networking sites.

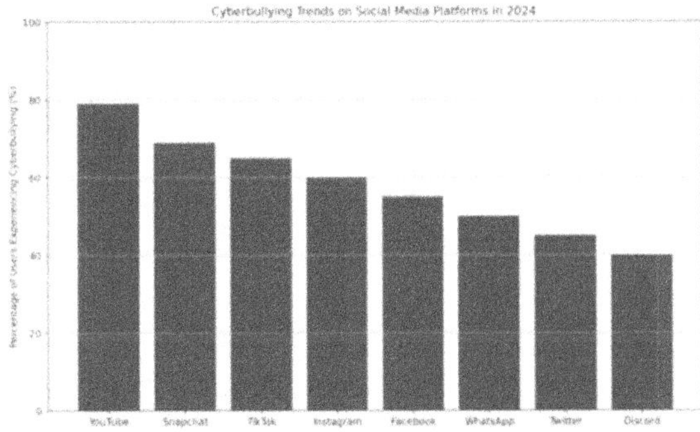

Figure 3. Cyber Bullying Victimization Cases by Age Group

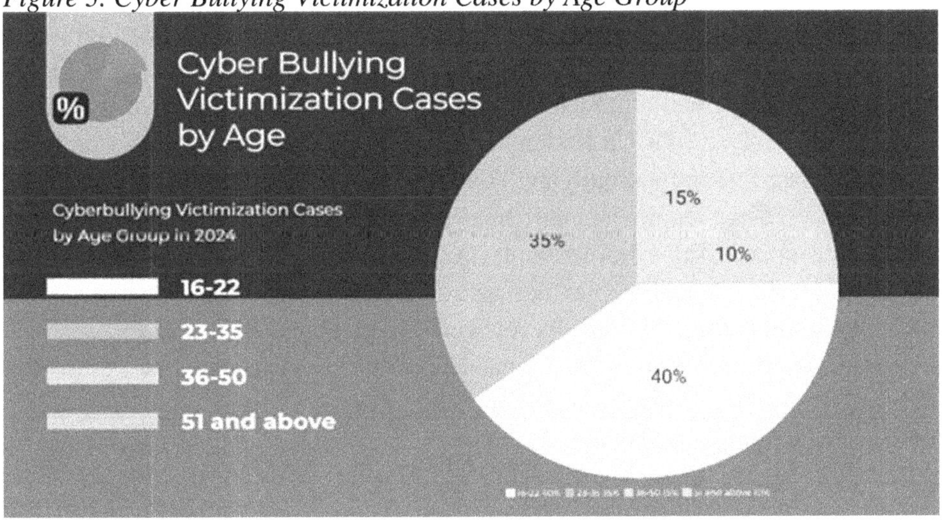

Psychological and Social Dynamics: The motivations behind cyberbullying can be complex. Factors such as peer pressure, a desire for power, or the internet's frequently offered anonymity contribute to the perpetrator's willingness to engage in such behaviour. Additionally, societal norms and cultural attitudes towards aggression and conflict resolution are important in forming the cyberbullying landscape. Victims of cyberbullying often experience profound psychological effects, including anxiety, depression, and a decline in self-esteem. Online harassment's enduring nature might exacerbate these mental difficulties by making victims feel powerless. Additionally, the stigma associated with being bullied may result in social withdrawal, limiting victims' opportunities for support and recovery. Understanding cyberbullying is a crucial step in addressing this pervasive issue. By recognizing its various forms, prevalence, and underlying psychological dynamics, stakeholders can better develop targeted interventions and prevention strategies. Ongoing research and education will be crucial in the fight against cyberbullying and in fostering safer online spaces for all users as the digital landscape develops.

Increase During Remote Education: Amid the COVID-19 shutdowns, the shift to online learning correlated with a 70% increase in reported cyberbullying cases (L1ght, 2020).

Isolation and Vulnerability: The pandemic heightened the mental health challenges of many young people, and remote learning environments made it more challenging for parents and teachers to monitor signs of bullying.

4. CHALLENGES OF CYBERBULLYING

Cyberbullying offers a distinct set of difficulties that complicate prevention and intervention efforts. These challenges stem from the inherent characteristics of digital communication, societal attitudes towards bullying, and the emotional dynamics involved (Willard, 2007). Understanding these obstacles is essential to creating successful plans to stop cyberbullying. The challenges associated with cyberbullying are multifaceted and require a comprehensive understanding to effectively address them as illustrated in Table 2. Anonymity, the pervasive nature of online interactions, emotional barriers, legal complexities, and cultural influences all contribute to the difficulty of combating this issue. By recognizing these challenges, stakeholders can develop targeted interventions and create supportive environments that empower victims and discourage perpetrators, ultimately fostering a safer digital landscape for everyone (Hinduja & Patchin, 2015).

Table 2. Challenges and effects of cyberbullying

CHALLENGE	EFFECT	
Anonymity and Its Effects The anonymity that cyberbullying provides its perpetrators is one of its distinguishing characteristics. This anonymity might give people a sense of invincibility, enabling them to act harmfully without worrying about the consequences right away. The ability to hide behind a screen can embolden aggressors, making them more likely to escalate their behaviour.	Dehumanization: The online environment often dehumanizes victims, as bullies may view them as mere avatars or usernames rather than real people with feelings. This disconnect can lead to a lack of empathy, which facilitates cruel behaviour.	Difficulties in Reporting: Victims may be reluctant to report occurrences because they don't think their concerns will be taken seriously or they fear reprisals. Authorities may find it difficult to properly handle the problem if it is difficult to identify the offenders due to anonymity.
Pervasiveness and Accessibility Cyberbullying can happen at any time and in any place, leading to a pervasive sense of vulnerability for victims. Unlike traditional bullying, which may be confined to specific locations (like schools or playgrounds), cyberbullying can infiltrate the most personal spaces of victims' lives, affecting them around the clock.	**Constant Connectivity**: With the proliferation of social media and cellphones, individuals are perpetually connected to their online lives. This constant access means that victims cannot escape harassment, leading to heightened anxiety and emotional distress.	**Escalation of Incidents**: The public nature of online platforms can exacerbate situations quickly, as negative content can go viral. A single harmful post can reach a vast audience, amplifying its impact on the victim and making it difficult to control the narrative.
Emotional and Psychological Barriers for Victims Victims of cyberbullying often face significant emotional challenges that can hinder their ability to seek help. Feelings of shame, isolation, and fear can create barriers to reporting incidents or reaching out for support.	**Stigma and Isolation**: Victims may feel stigmatized and believe that they are to blame for the harassment. This internalization of blame may exacerbate feelings of loneliness by causing social disengagement and increased isolation.	**Impact on Mental Health**: Cyberbullying can cause serious psychological problems, such as anxiety, depression, and suicide thoughts. Many victims struggle with low self-esteem and may experience long-term mental health issues because of their experiences.
Legal and Regulatory Challenges Addressing cyberbullying involves navigating a complex landscape of legal and regulatory frameworks that often lag behind technological advancements. Laws vary significantly by jurisdiction, complicating enforcement efforts.	**Lack of Clear Legislation**: In many places, laws specifically addressing cyberbullying are either inadequate or non-existent. This gap creates challenges for law enforcement and educational institutions seeking to hold perpetrators accountable.	**Difficulty in Jurisdiction**: Cyberbullying incidents often cross geographic boundaries, making it difficult to determine which laws apply. A perpetrator in one location may target a victim in another, complicating the legal response.
Cultural Factors Influencing Cyberbullying The frequency and type of cyberbullying might be influenced by cultural perspectives on bullying and dispute resolution. In some cultures, aggressive behaviour may be normalized or overlooked, leading to a lack of awareness about the seriousness of online harassment.	**Peer Pressure**: Social dynamics play a significant role in cyberbullying. To fit in, people may feel under pressure to engage in or support cyberbullying in settings where violent behaviour is accepted or even encouraged.	**Generational Attitudes**: Different generations may have varying perceptions of online behaviour. Older adults may not fully understand the digital landscape, leading to misunderstandings about the seriousness of the effects of cyberbullying on youth.

5. IMPACT OF CYBERBULLYING

The impact of cyberbullying extends far beyond immediate emotional distress, affecting victims in numerous ways that can have long-term consequences. Developing successful prevention and intervention efforts requires an understanding of these consequences (Mishna et al., 2010; Machimbarrena & Garaigordobil, 2020). The repercussions cyberbullying can be divided into social, intellectual, psychological, and broader societal impacts as depicted in Table 3. Cyberbullying has a significant and varied impact, including victims' psychological well-being, academic performance, social relationships, and the broader societal environment. Understanding these impacts is crucial to creating all-encompassing prevention and intervention plans. We may endeavour to make both online and offline environments safer and more encouraging for everyone by tackling the underlying causes and effects of cyberbullying.

Table 3. Effect and issues of cyberbullying

EFFECT	ISSUES
Psychological Effects on Victims Cyberbullying can lead to significant psychological trauma, often resulting in the following issues:	**Anxiety and Depression**: Victims often experience constant worry and fear about online interactions, anticipating further harassment. This heightened state of alertness may extend into real life, leading to social withdrawal, hypervigilance, and a sense of perpetual insecurity. Victims may begin to question their self-worth, fearing that others are judging them based on the abusive messages or rumours spread online. Over time, this anxiety may show up as social anxiety or generalized anxiety disorder (GAD) further isolating victims from their peers and communities. The constant fear of harassment can create a state of hyper-vigilance, leading to chronic stress and emotional turmoil. **Low Self-Esteem**: Repeated bullying can erode an individual's self-worth. Victims could internalize self-defeating beliefs, which would make them feel inadequate and hate themselves. **Suicidal Ideation:** Suicidal ideation is one of the most concerning effects of ongoing cyberbullying. The psychological pain inflicted by relentless online harassment can make victims feel as though there is no way out of their suffering. Cyberbullying victims are more likely to think about or try suicide, according to studies. The emotional and psychological strain from cyberbullying may overwhelm individuals, particularly those with pre-existing mental health vulnerabilities, leading them to view suicide as an escape from their torment. Victims may experience feelings of deep isolation and helplessness, believing they have no support or means of stopping the harassment. **Post-Traumatic Stress Disorder (PTSD)**: Some victims may develop symptoms of PTSD, including flashbacks, emotional numbness, and avoidance behaviours. This condition can persist long after the bullying has ceased. The emotional trauma can manifest as persistent fear, agitation, and difficulty trusting others, making it challenging for victims to engage in normal social interactions or feel safe in both digital and physical spaces.
Academic Consequences The impact of cyberbullying on academic performance can be profound:	**Declining Academic Performance**: Victims often struggle to concentrate on their studies due to anxiety and emotional distress. This distraction can lead to decreased grades and academic engagement. **Increased Absenteeism**: Higher absenteeism may result from a fear of running into bullies at school. Victims might completely skip school, which would leave gaps in their education and further distance them from their peers. **Loss of Interest in Extracurricular Activities**: Participation in extracurricular activities, which are crucial for social development, may decline as victims withdraw from school life. This disengagement can hinder personal growth and limit opportunities for building supportive relationships.

continued on following page

Table 3. Continued

EFFECT	ISSUES
Social Consequences The social ramifications of cyberbullying can be severe, affecting victims' relationships and social development:	**Isolation and Loneliness**: Over time, the mental health effects of cyberbullying often lead to social withdrawal. Victims may avoid online platforms altogether or retreat from social situations, fearing further harassment. This isolation can exacerbate the feelings of loneliness, increasing the emotional toll of the bullying. The loss of online and offline social connection can contribute to a downward spiral, as victims may lose their sense of belonging and struggle to maintain relationships. **Strain on Friendships and Family Relationships**: The emotional toll of cyberbullying can create tension in friendships and family dynamics. Victims may struggle to communicate their experiences, leading to misunderstandings and conflicts. **Changes in Social Status**: Victims may experience shifts in their social standing, as peers may distance themselves to avoid association with the victim or to avoid becoming targets themselves. This dynamic can lead to further alienation and distress.
Broader Societal Implications The effects of cyberbullying extend beyond individual victims, influencing broader societal dynamics:	**Normalization of Aggression**: Widespread cyberbullying can contribute to a culture that normalizes aggression and intolerance. This normalization can have lasting effects on societal attitudes toward conflict and resolution. **Impact on School Environment**: Cyberbullying can create a toxic school environment, negatively affecting not just the victims but also bystanders and the overall school climate. When bullying is prevalent, it can hinder learning and create a sense of fear among students. **Increased Burden on Mental Health Services**: The rise in cyberbullying incidents correlates with an increased demand for assistance with mental health. Schools and communities may face challenges in providing adequate support for affected individuals, straining resources.
Long-Term Effects	The long-term impacts on mental health of cyberbullying can persist well into adulthood. Victims may continue to suffer from anxiety, depression, or PTSD long after the bullying has ceased. These ongoing challenges can affect their academic, career, and social development, preventing them from achieving their full potential. In some cases, the effects of cyberbullying can manifest in long-term struggles with self-esteem, forming meaningful relationships, and maintaining mental health stability (Cassidy et al., 2013; Kowalski et al., 2014).

6. CURRENT RESPONSES TO CYBERBULLYING

Addressing the issue of cyberbullying requires coordinated efforts from various stakeholders, including schools, technology companies, law enforcement, and communities. Current responses involve a mix of policy development, educational initiatives, and technological interventions (Hinduja & Patchin, 2014). This section explores the key responses to cyberbullying and their effectiveness in creating safer online environments. Current responses to cyberbullying encompass a range of strategies that involve schools, technology companies, legal systems, and communities as depicted in Table 4. Although a lot of effort has been made in enacting policies and increasing awareness, challenges remain in ensuring consistent enforcement and support for victims. By fostering collaboration among stakeholders and continually adapting to the evolving digital landscape, we can create a safer and more supportive environment for all users, ultimately reducing the incidence and impact of cyberbullying (Faucher et al., 2014; Kowalski et al., 2012).

Table 4. Current responses to cyberbullying

KEY RESPONSES	EFFECTIVENESS
School Policies and Protocols Many schools have begun to recognize the importance of addressing cyberbullying through formal policies and protocols. These efforts typically include:	**Anti-Bullying Policies**: Comprehensive anti-bullying rules that particularly address cyberbullying are being implemented by schools more frequently. These guidelines provide forth precise definitions, protocols for reporting violations, and sanctions for offenders. **Training for Staff**: Training is being provided to teachers and other school personnel on how to spot the warning signs of cyberbullying and react appropriately. Training frequently covers victim assistance, intervention techniques, and methods for creating a positive school climate. **Counselling and Support Services**: For victims and their relatives, schools are offering mental health support. It comprises initiatives, support groups, and counselling services that help students deal with the psychological fallout from cyberbullying.
The function of technology Organizations Technology firms are essential in the fight against cyberbullying because they create and implement tools and regulations that:	**Content Moderation**: To find and eliminate hazardous content, social media networks and internet services are putting in place content moderation mechanisms. In order to identify abusive behaviour and uphold community standards, this involves using both human moderators and algorithms. **Reporting Mechanisms**: The majority of sites include methods for users to report incidents of cyberbullying. Because of the user-friendly design of these reporting tools, victims and onlookers can quickly identify offensive content. **Educational Resources**: Many technology companies offer educational materials and resources aimed at promoting digital citizenship and responsible online behaviour. These resources help raise awareness about the impacts of cyberbullying and encourage users to engage positively online.
Legal Frameworks and Legislation The legal landscape surrounding cyberbullying is complex and varies significantly by jurisdiction. However, several key developments are noteworthy:	**Cyberbullying Laws**: Laws that particularly tackle cyberbullying have been passed in numerous states and nations. These laws frequently define cyberbullying, provide penalties for violators, and give institutions and law enforcement instructions on how to handle such situations. **School Liability**: Some legal frameworks hold schools accountable for addressing cyberbullying incidents that occur on school grounds or during school-related activities. This accountability encourages schools to take proactive measures in creating a safe environment. **Law Enforcement Training**: Law enforcement agencies are increasingly receiving training on cyberbullying and digital harassment. This training equips officers with the knowledge needed to investigate incidents and support victims effectively.

continued on following page

Table 4. Continued

KEY RESPONSES	EFFECTIVENESS
Community and Parental Involvement Communities and parents play a crucial role in preventing cyberbullying:	**Awareness Campaigns**: Schools and community organizations are starting awareness campaigns to inform parents, students, and community members about the dangers of cyberbullying and the significance of taking action. **Parental Guidance**: Parents are urged to have discussions with their kids about appropriate online conduct, including the possible repercussions of cyberbullying. Parents can learn how to support their children online and traverse digital places with the aid of resources and workshops. **Peer Support Programs**: Programs that promote peer support and mentorship can contribute to a favourable school climate. By empowering students to stand up against bullying and support each other, these initiatives foster a sense of community.
Collaborative Efforts Addressing cyberbullying requires collaboration among various stakeholders	**Partnerships**: Schools, law enforcement, mental health professionals, and technology companies can form partnerships to develop comprehensive approaches to preventing and addressing cyberbullying. **Research and Evaluation**: Ongoing research into the prevalence and impact of cyberbullying is essential for informing policies and practices. Evaluating the effectiveness of current responses can lead to improvements and adaptations over time.

7. COMPARATIVE ANALYSIS OF CYBERBULLYING LAWS ACROSS DIFFERENT COUNTRIES

Cyberbullying laws vary significantly across countries, reflecting diverse approaches to regulation, enforcement, and the prioritization of online safety. Table 5 shows a comparative analysis of how different countries handle cyberbullying, including their definitions, legal frameworks, penalties, and challenges faced in enforcement. This analysis reveals that while countries have unique approaches to addressing cyberbullying, the global nature of digital platforms necessitates international cooperation and adaptable frameworks to address evolving forms of online harassment effectively.

Table 5. A comparative analysis of how different countries

COUNTRY	LAWS, PENALTIES & CHALLENGES
United States	**Legal Framework**: In the U.S., laws addressing cyberbullying are primarily state-driven, with over 40 states implementing specific anti-cyberbullying statutes. Federally, the ***Children's Internet Protection Act*** (CIPA) requires federally funded schools to put policies in place to stop internet abuse. It is difficult to address the problem consistently across states due to differences in definitions, enforcement, and sanctions, notwithstanding these attempts. **Key Laws**: Notable state laws include **New York's Dignity for All Students Act** (DASA) and **California's Education Code** section 48900, which allows schools to take disciplinary actions for off-campus bullying if it impacts the capacity of a student to engage in classroom activities. **Penalties**: Penalties range from school disciplinary actions, such as suspension or expulsion, to misdemeanour or felony charges in cases involving threats or severe harassment. Juvenile offenders might receive other sanctions, including counselling or community service. **Challenges**: The absence of federal legislation means there's inconsistency across states. Law enforcement faces difficulty enforcing laws across state borders, and private companies are often reluctant to release data needed for investigations (Olweus & Limber, 2018).
United Kingdom	**Legal Framework**: The UK's approach to cyberbullying includes legislation like the **Malicious Communications Act 1988** and the **Communications Act 2003**, which criminalize sending threatening or offensive messages. The upcoming **Online Safety Bill** is expected to further strengthen protections by requiring social media platforms to proactively remove harmful content and ensure safer online environments. **Key Laws**: The **Malicious Communications Act** prohibits sending messages or material with the intending to induce fear or distress. The **Defamation Act 2013** also allows victims to take action against online defamation, and the **Public Order Act 1986** addresses hate speech and other offensive conduct. **Penalties**: Penalties can include fines, community service, or prison sentences, with the severity depending on the nature and frequency of the bullying. Convictions for online harassment can lead to prison sentences of up to two years under certain circumstances. **Challenges**: Legal action can be difficult due to the need to prove intent and harm. Additionally, balancing freedom of speech with online safety has led to debate, particularly regarding the adequacy of the current laws in addressing cyberbullying among minors (Navarro et al., 2015).
Australia	**Legal Framework**: Australia leads with its ***e-Safety Commissioner***, a dedicated government body addressing online abuse, particularly against children. ***The Enhancing Online Safety Act*** states that, victims can report harmful content for expedited removal. Additionally, the ***Online Safety Act 2021*** empowers the Commissioner to issue fines and penalties against perpetrators and non-compliant platforms. **Key Laws**: Under the **Criminal Code Act 1995**, certain forms of online harassment can be prosecuted as cyberbullying if they involve serious threats or abuse. The **Telecommunications Act 1997** also addresses offensive online material. **Penalties**: For serious offenses, penalties can include fines and imprisonment. The e-Safety Commissioner can order social media companies to remove content from their services within 48 hours of a report. **Challenges**: Australia's unique approach places significant emphasis on platform accountability and rapid response. However, enforcement across platforms headquartered abroad remains complex, and penalties for international offenders are limited.

continued on following page

Table 5. Continued

COUNTRY	LAWS, PENALTIES & CHALLENGES
India	**Legal Framework**: India lacks specific cyberbullying laws, but offenses are covered under certain provisions of the ***Indian Penal Code*** (IPC) and the ***Information Technology Act of 2000***, addressing crimes like online stalking, defamation, and obscene communication. Efforts to amend the IT Act to address evolving forms of cyberbullying, such as doxxing and cyberstalking, have gained traction in recent years. **Key Laws**: ***Information Technology Act, 2000*** (Section 66A): Criminalizes sending offensive messages through communication services, devices, or platforms. ***Indian Penal Code*** (Sections 354D, 499, 503): Addresses cyberstalking, defamation, and harassment. ***The Protection of Children from Sexual Offences****(POCSO) Act, 2012*: Covers online sexual harassment and exploitation of minors. **Penalties**: *Section 66A of IT Act*: Carries a fine and a maximum sentence of three years in prison for disseminating abusive remarks. *Section 354D of IPC*: Imposes imprisonment up to 3 years for stalking, increasing to 5 years for repeat offenders. *Section 499 of IPC*: For defamation, offenders may face a fine or up to two years in jail. **Challenges**: **Ambiguity in Laws**: There is a lack of clear and comprehensive laws specifically targeting cyberbullying, leading to inconsistent enforcement. **Enforcement Gaps**: Law enforcement faces challenges in tracking cyberbullying due to anonymity and the speed at which online harassment spreads. **Jurisdictional Issues**: As cyberbullying often involves perpetrators and victims in different locations, jurisdictional challenges complicate legal action. **Awareness and Education**: Limited awareness about cyberbullying laws among the public and law enforcement personnel hampers effective prevention and intervention efforts (Saini et al., 2017).
Canada	**Legal Framework**: In particular, distributing personal photos without consent is illegal under Canada's **Protecting Canadians from Online Crime Act.** and empowers law enforcement to address cyber harassment. Provincial laws complement federal efforts by targeting bullying in educational settings. The Act also holds internet service providers accountable for facilitating the swift removal of harmful content. **Key Laws**: The **Criminal Code** includes provisions that can be applied to cyberbullying, such as criminal harassment, threats, and defamation. Under this law, even a single incident can be prosecuted if it causes fear or harm to the victim. **Penalties**: Penalties for cyberbullying-related offenses range from fines and community service to imprisonment for severe cases. For instance, offenders involved in distributing non-consensual intimate images may face up to five years in prison. **Challenges**: Enforcement is challenging, particularly regarding cross-border issues. Critics argue that while laws exist, they are often underused, partly due to the resources required for digital evidence collection and prosecution.
Japan	**Legal Framework**: Japan's legal response to cyberbullying includes the **Penal Code** and the **Provider Liability Limitation Act**, focusing on holding platforms accountable and ensuring rapid removal of harmful content. Recent reforms were spurred by high-profile cases, leading to stricter penalties for online harassment, such as longer prison sentences and higher fines for offenders. **Key Laws**: Recent amendments to the **Penal Code** in 2022 introduced harsher penalties for online insults, with up to a year of imprisonment, following public outcry over high-profile cyberbullying cases. **Penalties**: Penalties for online harassment include fines, imprisonment, and mandatory counselling. The new provisions for online insults reflect Japan's shifting approach to protecting individuals from online abuse. **Challenges**: The legal framework in Japan is still evolving, and cultural attitudes toward privacy and shame can deter victims from reporting. Additionally, obtaining compliance from platform providers headquartered abroad remains a significant issue.

continued on following page

Table 5. Continued

COUNTRY	LAWS, PENALTIES & CHALLENGES
Germany	**Legal Framework**: Germany has specific laws for online harassment, hate speech, and other forms of cyberbullying, implemented according to the 2017 **Network Enforcement Act** (NetzDG). Social media companies are required by NetzDG to promptly delete unlawful content, including cyberbullying. **Key Laws**: The **German Criminal Code** (StGB) covers various cyberbullying behaviours, including harassment, threats, and hate speech. NetzDG requires platforms to act within 24 hours for clearly illegal content and 7 days for more complex cases. **Penalties**: Penalties can range from fines to prison sentences, depending on the offense. NetzDG includes significant fines for platforms that fail to remove illegal content in a timely manner, incentivizing better moderation practices. **Challenges**: Although NetzDG has been effective in enforcing prompt content removal, some argue that the law pressures platforms to delete more content than necessary, leading to concerns over freedom of expression.
South Korea	**Legal Framework**: South Korea has robust cyberbullying laws under the **Act on Promotion of Information and Communications Network Utilization and Information Protection** and the **Protection of Children and Juveniles from Sexual Abuse Act**. These laws target cyberbullying behaviours, including defamation, online insults, and harassment. **Key Laws**: The **Information and Communications Network Act** allows for the takedown of offensive content, and **Article 311 of the Criminal Act** criminalizes insults and defamation, with online insults treated as severe offenses. **Penalties**: Cyberbullying penalties in South Korea include fines, community service, and imprisonment. Repeat offenders or cases resulting in severe harm can lead to extended prison sentences. **Challenges**: While South Korea's laws are comprehensive, enforcement is still challenging due to the anonymous nature of some online platforms. Cultural stigmas associated with mental health and bullying may also deter victims from reporting incidents.
COMPARATIVE SUMMARY	
Legislative Specificity	Some countries, like the U.S. and the UK, rely on broader legal provisions to address cyberbullying, whereas nations like Germany and Australia have enacted laws specifically targeting digital abuse.
Platform Accountability	Australia, Germany, and South Korea have been particularly proactive in holding platforms accountable, with Australia's e Safety Commissioner and Germany's NetzDG standing out as models for rapid content moderation requirements.
Penalties and Enforcement	Countries like Japan and South Korea emphasize stricter penalties, reflecting a cultural shift toward addressing cyberbullying's serious psychological impact. However, cross-border enforcement remains a universal challenge, as cyberbullying often crosses jurisdictional boundaries.
Freedom of Speech vs. Protection	Balancing freedom of expression with protective measures is a recurring theme. Countries like Germany face criticism for potentially over-censoring content, while the U.S. emphasizes individual rights, leading to debates over the adequacy of state-level laws.

8. STRATEGIES FOR PREVENTION

A multimodal strategy including education, open communication, explicit policies, and community involvement is needed to prevent cyberbullying. By implementing effective strategies, we can create safer online environments and empower individuals to stand against cyberbullying (Hinduja & Patchin, 2020). Table 6 shows the several key strategies for prevention: A comprehensive strategy including education, open communication, explicit policies, and active community involvement is needed to prevent cyberbullying. We can empower people to oppose cyberbullying and establish safer online spaces by cultivating a culture of empathy and respect (Betts, 2016). The collaborative efforts of schools, parents, technology companies, and communities are essential in addressing this pressing issue and ensuring that all individuals can navigate the digital landscape without fear of harassment. (Kowalski et al., 2014)

Table 6. Several key strategies for prevention

KEY STRATEGY	DESCRIPTION
Educational Programs Education is foundational in preventing cyberbullying. Implementing comprehensive educational Programs can support students in developing a culture of empathy and respect as well as increasing awareness:	**Digital Citizenship Curriculum**: Schools should integrate digital citizenship lessons into their curricula. These lessons can cover topics such as responsible online behaviour, the implications of digital footprints, and the importance of empathy in digital communications. **Seminars and Workshops:** Arranging seminars for educators, parents, and kids can offer important insights about the characteristics of cyberbullying, its impacts, and appropriate responses. To get participants ready for real-life circumstances, interactive sessions can promote dialogue and role-playing. **Peer-led Initiatives**: Encouraging students to lead anti-bullying campaigns can be an effective way to engage their peers. Peer-led initiatives can empower students to take ownership of their school environment and foster a supportive community.
Fostering Free Exchange of Information Early detection and resolution of cyberbullying events can be facilitated by fostering an atmosphere that values open communication:	**Encouraging Dialogue**: Open dialogue on youths' online experiences should be encouraged by parents and educators. Children can feel more at ease discussing their worries when regular conversations are held regarding internet interactions. **Secure Reporting procedures:** To enable victims and bystanders to report occurrences without worrying about reprisals, schools and online platforms should put in place anonymous, secure reporting procedures. There should be widespread dissemination of clear instructions on how to report cyberbullying. **Active Listening**: Adults should practice active listening when children share their experiences. Validating their feelings and providing support can make a significant difference in their willingness to seek help.
Implementing Clear Policies Establishing clear policies and guidelines can help create a culture of accountability and support:	**Anti-Bullying Policies**: Schools should develop and communicate clear anti-bullying policies that include definitions of cyberbullying, reporting procedures, and consequences for offenders. These policies should be regularly reviewed and updated to reflect current trends. **Engagement of the Whole School Community**: Policies should involve input from students, parents, and faculty to ensure they address the requirements of the whole school community. This collaborative approach can enhance buy-in and compliance. **Regular Training for Staff**: Giving educators and other school personnel continual instruction in identifying, addressing, and preventing cyberbullying is essential. Staff should be equipped to support victims and intervene effectively when incidents occur.

continued on following page

Table 6. Continued

KEY STRATEGY	DESCRIPTION
Creating Supportive Environments Building a positive and inclusive school climate can significantly reduce the prevalence of cyberbullying:	**Promoting Kindness and Empathy**: Initiatives that promote kindness, empathy, and inclusivity can help shift the school culture. Campaigns, assemblies, and class projects focused on celebrating differences can help children develop a feeling of community. **Peer Support Programs:** Students can benefit from the implementation of peer support programs build strong, supportive relationships. Mentorship initiatives where older students guide younger ones can create a network of support and encouragement. **Crisis Intervention Resources**: Schools should provide access to mental health resources for victims of cyberbullying. Students can analyze their experiences and create coping mechanisms with the aid of support groups and counselling programs.
Promoting Positive Online Behaviour Encouraging positive interactions in digital spaces can help mitigate the risk of cyberbullying:	**Social Media Campaigns**: Launching campaigns that promote positive online behaviour and highlight the importance of kindness can engage students and raise awareness. Using hashtags and challenges can encourage participation and sharing. **Celebrating Positive Role Models**: Recognizing and celebrating students who demonstrate kindness and stand up against bullying can inspire others to follow suit. This recognition can take the form of awards, shout-outs, or features in school publications. **Digital Detox Initiatives**: Encouraging periodic breaks from social media and digital devices can help students reconnect with themselves and their peers in meaningful ways. Activities that promote face-to-face interactions can foster stronger social connections.
Parental and Community Involvement In order to counteract cyberbullying, the community at large and parents must get involved:	**Parent Education Workshops**: Schools and community organizations should offer workshops for parents to help them understand the digital landscape and recognize signs of cyberbullying. Providing resources on how to engage with children about their online experiences is crucial. **Collaboration with Local Organizations**: Schools can partner with local mental health organizations, law enforcement, and community groups to create a united front against cyberbullying. Collaborative events and campaigns can amplify efforts to raise awareness. **Engaging Community Leaders**: Involving community leaders in anti-cyberbullying initiatives can lend credibility and visibility to efforts. Leaders can help advocate for positive change and resource allocation within the community.

9. FUTURE DIRECTIONS IN ADDRESSING CYBERBULLYING

As technology evolves and the digital landscape continues to change, the challenge of cyberbullying will also transform. Future directions in addressing this issue should focus on innovative strategies, proactive measures, and enhanced collaboration among stakeholders (Wright, 2017). Table 7 shows the several key areas that warrant attention moving forward. The future directions in addressing cyberbullying emphasize the importance of innovation, education, policy reform, and community involvement. As the digital landscape continues to evolve, proactive and adaptive strategies will be essential in combating cyberbullying effectively (Hinduja & Patchin, 2014). Everyone can benefit from a safer and more encouraging online environment if we promote a culture of empathy and respect, improve technology solutions, and increase stakeholder engagement. We can significantly lessen the incidence and effects of cyberbullying in the digital era if we work together (Vandebosch & Van Cleemput, 2009).

Table 7. Future directions in addressing cyberbullying

Enhanced Technology Solutions Advancements in technology offer promising avenues for combating cyberbullying:	**Machine learning and Artificial Intelligence:** Use AI to identify and flag offensive content in real-time can help platforms address cyberbullying more effectively. Machine learning algorithms can analyze patterns of abusive behaviour, improving the accuracy of detection systems. **Improved Reporting Tools:** Developing user-friendly, intuitive reporting tools can empower users to report incidents more easily. Anonymity in reporting can encourage more victims and bystanders to come forward without fear of retaliation. **Real-Time Support Features:** Integrating real-time support features into social media platforms—such as chatbots or direct links to counselling resources-can provide immediate assistance to victims facing cyberbullying.
Comprehensive Education and Training Ongoing education is vital for preventing cyberbullying and promoting digital citizenship:	**Curriculum Integration**: Schools should aim to integrate lessons on digital citizenship, empathy, and conflict resolution throughout the educational experience, starting at an early age. This approach can help cultivate a culture of respect and responsibility online. **Training for All Stakeholders**: It is crucial to give teachers, parents, and kids thorough training on how to spot and deal with cyberbullying. Workshops that focus on practical strategies for intervention and support can empower individuals to take action. **Professional Development for Educators**: Ongoing professional development for teachers can equip them with the latest tools and techniques in their classes and schools to successfully combat cyberbullying.
Strengthening Policy and Legal Frameworks The laws and regulations pertaining to cyberbullying must also change as it does	**Comprehensive Legislation**: Advocating for more comprehensive laws that specifically address cyberbullying can provide clearer guidelines for schools and law enforcement. These laws should be adaptable to accommodate the rapidly changing digital landscape. **National and International Collaboration**: Establishing collaborative efforts among governments, NGOs, and international organizations can create a unified approach to tackling cyberbullying. Sharing best practices and resources across borders can enhance effectiveness. **Monitoring and Evaluation**: Finding opportunities for improvement in anti-cyberbullying policies and initiatives can be facilitated by putting in place mechanisms to track and assess their efficacy. Regular assessments can ensure that strategies remain relevant and effective.

continued on following page

Table 7. Continued

Fostering a Positive Digital Culture Promoting a culture of kindness and respect online is crucial for preventing cyberbullying:	**Community Engagement Initiatives**: Encouraging local communities to participate in awareness campaigns and anti-bullying events can foster a collective responsibility to combat cyberbullying. Community-driven efforts can create a supportive environment for victims. **Promoting Positive Role Models**: Highlighting individuals and organizations that exemplify positive online behaviour can inspire others to adopt similar practices. Campaigns that celebrate acts of kindness can shift social norms towards more respectful interactions. **Leveraging Influencers and Public Figures**: Engaging influencers and public figures to speak out against cyberbullying can amplify messages of empathy and support, reaching broader audiences and creating a cultural shift.
Research and Data Collection Understanding the changing nature of cyberbullying requires ongoing research:	**Longitudinal Research:** Longitudinal research can shed light on how cyberbullying affects social relationships, academic achievement, and mental health over the long run. The creation of programs and policies can be influenced by such data. **Effects of New Technologies:** Studying how new technologies, such virtual reality and artificial intelligence, affect social interactions and bullying behaviours can yield important information for preventative measures. **Bystander Behaviour**: Studying the role of bystanders in cyberbullying situations can lead to effective intervention strategies. Understanding how peers can influence outcomes can help develop programs that empower students to act against bullying.

10. TECHNOLOGY'S ROLE IN BOTH FACILITATING AND COMBATING CYBERBULLYING

Technology is involved in cyberbullying in two ways: it can facilitate harassment and harm through various digital platforms and tools, while also offering powerful methods for detecting, preventing, and addressing abusive behaviour (Wright, 2017). This duality underscores the complexities of technology's role in society and the need for both technological advancements and human oversight to create safer online spaces as depicted in Table 8. While technology facilitates cyberbullying, it also offers powerful tools to counteract it. Advances in AI, machine learning, and platform design have made it possible to detect, prevent, and address cyberbullying in various ways as described in Table 9. While technology provides powerful tools, there are several challenges in effectively using it to combat cyberbullying as illustrated in Table 10. The future holds significant promise for leveraging technology to address the growing challenge of cyberbullying. In order to enable speedier interventions, artificial intelligence (AI) and machine learning algorithms are being created to detect hazardous language, images, and behaviours in real time. Platforms can anticipate and stop instances of cyberbullying by using advanced data analytics to find trends in online abuse. To foster empathy and appropriate digital behaviour, immersive educational programs may also make use of virtual reality (VR) and augmented reality (AR). Furthermore, blockchain technology could enhance accountability by verifying user identities while protecting privacy. As technology evolves, collaboration among developers, educators, and policymakers will be vital to create ethical, user-friendly solutions that foster safer digital environments for all users (Patchin & Hinduja, 2020).

Table 8. How technology facilitates cyberbullying

Anonymity and Accessibility	**Anonymity:** Many platforms, particularly social media and forums, allow users to create accounts with minimal identity verification, which enables individuals to harass or bully others without immediate accountability. This lack of oversight not only fosters cyberbullying but also contributes to the spread of fake news and other social media issues, amplifying harm and misinformation across platforms (Kumar et al., 2023). People are encouraged to speak and do things they may not if their true identities were known because of their anonymity. **24/7 Accessibility:** Cyberbullying, in contrast to traditional bullying, can occur at any time. The continuous connectedness of gadgets like tablets and smartphones mean victims are potentially accessible to bullies around the clock, with no "safe" space if they're active online.
Instant Communication and Virality	**Instant Messaging**: Messaging apps and social media platforms allow for rapid exchanges of messages and images, which can lead to impulsive, harmful actions. Hurtful words, photos, or videos can be sent with a few taps, and their impact is immediate. **Virality**: One of the most damaging aspects of cyberbullying is that abusive messages or images can spread to a large audience instantly, amplifying harm. For instance, a single offensive comment or image can be shared, liked, or reposted by countless individuals, making it difficult to contain the damage or retract content.
Multimedia Manipulation	**Image and Video Editing**: Bullies can use photo and video editing tools to alter images in a way that humiliates or defames the victim, a common tactic for body shaming or spreading rumours. **Deepfakes and AI**: While still emerging, Deepfakes are realistic-looking but phony audio and video produced by AI-powered systems, which are sometimes used to generate compromising or damaging content of individuals. This technology can exacerbate bullying by making it easier to deceive viewers into believing false content.
Targeted Harassment and Group Bullying	**Group Chats and Forums**: Private or semi-private chat groups can facilitate targeted group bullying, with participants "ganging up" on a victim. Group bullying can feel overwhelming to the victim, who sees multiple people endorsing hurtful comments or participating in attacks. **Algorithms and "Echo Chambers"**: Platforms that prioritize "engaging" content can unintentionally promote harmful interactions. Algorithms may increase the visibility of controversial or inflammatory comments, inadvertently amplifying bullying and creating echo chambers that reinforce abusive behaviour.
Unmonitored Youth Platforms	**Apps Popular with Young Audiences**: Apps that are popular with teenagers and young children often lack robust moderation, which can lead to a higher incidence of cyberbullying. Apps like TikTok, Snapchat, and certain anonymous Q&A sites are common breeding grounds for such behaviour due to their popularity with younger users and varying levels of moderation.

Table 9. Technology as a tool for combating cyberbullying

AI and Machine Learning for Detection	**Natural Language Processing (NLP):** Algorithms trained to detect abusive language can identify potential cyberbullying incidents by analysing text for signs of harassment, threats, or hate speech. For instance, Facebook and Twitter use NLP to filter and flag harmful content in real time. **Image and Video Analysis:** Machine learning can also be used to scan images and videos for explicit or harmful content. For example, YouTube employs AI to detect hate speech or violent imagery, allowing for quick response in cases where users upload bullying content. **Contextual Understanding:** Advances in machine learning have improved algorithms' abilities to understand context, enabling them to differentiate between benign comments and those intended to harm.
Automated Reporting and Moderation Tools	**User-Driven Reporting**: Many platforms, such as Instagram and Facebook, have user reporting tools that allow users to flag content or accounts for harassment. These reports are often reviewed by algorithms or moderators to determine if the content violates community guidelines. **Automated Takedowns**: Platforms can automatically remove content flagged as harmful or inappropriate. For instance, The NetzDG law in Germany mandates that social media sites remove specific forms of abusive information within 24 hours, which encourages the employment of technology to comply with the deadline.
Privacy Controls and Account Protections	**Blocking and Privacy Settings**: Platforms like Instagram, Facebook, and Twitter allow users to block or restrict interactions with certain users. Privacy controls also allow users to make accounts private, limiting who can view or engage with their content. **End-to-End Encryption**: While encryption protects user data, it also complicates content moderation. However, some platforms use encryption in a way that still allows users to control who they interact with directly, reducing the potential for unsolicited harassment.
Educational Tools and Digital Literacy Programs	**Digital Literacy Initiatives**: Many tech companies, in collaboration with schools and governments, have launched digital literacy campaigns aimed at teaching users, especially younger ones, about safe online behaviour, responsible posting, and how to report cyberbullying. **Online Safety Resources**: Examples of educational programs that teach young people to identify cyberbullying, comprehend privacy dangers, and behave responsibly online are Facebook's Digital Literacy Library and Google's Be Internet Awesome.
Parental Controls and Monitoring Apps	**Parental Monitoring Tools**: Apps like Bark, Qustodio, and Net Nanny help parents monitor their children's online activity to identify potential risks, including cyberbullying. These tools can notify parents if certain keywords or phrases related to bullying or self-harm appear in a child's online interactions. **Restricted Access**: Certain devices and apps offer age-appropriate filters and restricted access modes that can limit exposure to potentially harmful content. Parental controls can prevent children from accessing specific sites or apps known to have cyberbullying risks.
Platform Accountability and Transparency	**Transparency Reports**: Companies like Twitter and Facebook publish transparency reports outlining how they handle reports of abuse and the actions taken, providing accountability to users and governments. These reports often include data on the volume of flagged content and the percentage removed. **Collaboration with Law Enforcement**: Social media platforms often work with law enforcement agencies when cyberbullying escalates to threats of violence. Rapid-response partnerships ensure that threats are addressed swiftly and that cyberbullying cases involving criminal activity are handled appropriately.

Table 10. Challenges in using technology to combat cyberbullying

Balancing Privacy and Safety	Striking a balance between monitoring content for bullying and protecting user privacy is difficult. Overly intrusive measures may violate privacy rights, while insufficient oversight can allow bullying to go unchecked.
False Positives and Contextual Nuance	AI algorithms can mistakenly flag benign content as bullying, known as "false positives." Understanding context—such as distinguishing playful banter from actual harassment—remains a challenge for AI.
Limitations of Algorithmic Detection	Even the most advanced algorithms have limitations. Subtle forms of bullying, such as exclusion or backhanded compliments, may not trigger automated filters, allowing certain forms of bullying to continue undetected.
Cross-Platform and Anonymity Challenges	Cyberbullies often use multiple platforms, making it hard to track and address behaviour across different sites. Additionally, anonymous accounts complicate accountability, as bullies can simply create new profiles after being reported or banned.
Enforcement Across Jurisdictions	Global platforms face the challenge of complying with diverse laws and cultural standards. What may be considered cyberbullying in one country may not be seen as such in another, complicating the enforcement of community guidelines and legal responses.

11. CONCLUSION

Cyberbullying has grown to be a widespread problem with serious repercussions for both people and communities. Its permanence, worldwide reach, and anonymity make it more damaging than traditional bullying. Victims frequently have psychological consequences like low self-esteem, anxiety, and depression with vulnerable populations, including children and marginalized groups, being especially impacted. Addressing cyberbullying requires a holistic approach, including education, technological solutions, legal reforms, and community engagement. Schools, parents, and communities must collaborate to raise awareness and promote responsible online behaviour. Technology companies must implement stronger safety features and reporting mechanisms, while legal frameworks should evolve to ensure swift action and victim protection. Support systems, including mental health resources and peer networks, are essential for helping victims recover. By fostering empathy and mutual respect and holding all stakeholders accountable, society can work toward creating safer digital spaces.

REFERENCES

Bauman, S., Cross, D., & Walker, J. L. (2013). *Principles of cyberbullying research: Definitions, measures, and methodology*. Routledge.

Betts, L. R. (2016). *Cyberbullying: Approaches, consequences, and interventions*. Springer. DOI: 10.1057/978-1-137-50009-0

Brewer, G., & Kerslake, J. (2015). Cyberbullying, self-esteem, empathy, and loneliness. *Computers in Human Behavior*, 48, 255–260. DOI: 10.1016/j.chb.2015.01.073

Cassidy, W., Faucher, C., & Jackson, M. (2013). Cyberbullying among youth: A comprehensive review of current international research and its implications. *International Journal of Adolescence and Youth*, 18(2), 85–112. DOI: 10.1080/02673843.2012.682083

Chua, T. H. H., & Chang, L. (2016). Follow me and like my beautiful selfies: Singapore teenage girls' engagement in self-presentation and peer comparison on social media. *Computers in Human Behavior*, 55, 190–197. DOI: 10.1016/j.chb.2015.09.011

Cross, D., Lester, L., & Barnes, A. (2015). A longitudinal study of the social and emotional predictors and consequences of cyber and traditional bullying victimisation. *International Journal of Public Health*, 60(2), 207–217. DOI: 10.1007/s00038-015-0655-1 PMID: 25645100

Ditch the Label. (2021). *Annual bullying survey 2021*. Ditch the Label. Retrieved from https://www.ditchthelabel.org/

Faucher, C., Jackson, M., & Cassidy, W. (2014). Cyberbullying among university students: Gendered experiences, impacts, and perspectives. *Education Research International*, 2014, 1–10. DOI: 10.1155/2014/698545

Hinduja, S., & Patchin, J. W. (2014). *Cyberbullying identification, prevention, and response*. Cyberbullying Research Center.

Hinduja, S., & Patchin, J. W. (2015). Social influences on cyberbullying behaviours among middle and high school students. *Journal of Youth and Adolescence*, 42(5), 711–722. DOI: 10.1007/s10964-012-9902-4 PMID: 23296318

Kowalski, R. M., Giumetti, G. W., Schroeder, A. N., & Lattanner, M. R. (2014). Bullying in the digital age: A critical review and meta-analysis of cyberbullying research among youth. *Psychological Bulletin*, 140(4), 1073–1137. DOI: 10.1037/a0035618 PMID: 24512111

Kowalski, R. M., Limber, S. P., & Agatston, P. W. (2012). *Cyberbullying: Bullying in the digital age* (2nd ed.). Wiley-Blackwell.

Kumar, N., Malhotra, M., Aggarwal, B., Rai, D., & Aggarwal, G. Leveraging Natural Language Processing and Machine Learning for Efficient Fake News Detection. In Proceedings of the International Conference on Technological Advancements in Computational Sciences (ICTACS), 2023 3rd, Tashkent, Uzbekistan, 1–3 November 2023; pp. 535–541. DOI: 10.1109/ICTACS59847.2023.10390356

Livingstone, S., & Smith, P. K. (2014). Annual research review: Harms experienced by child users of online and mobile technologies. *Journal of Child Psychology and Psychiatry, and Allied Disciplines*, 55(6), 635–654. DOI: 10.1111/jcpp.12197 PMID: 24438579

Machimbarrena, J. M., & Garaigordobil, M. (2020). Cyberbullying in adolescents: Prevalence, characteristics, and psychological outcomes. *Educational Psychology*, 40(3), 345–363. DOI: 10.1080/01443410.2019.1644306

Mishna, F., Cook, C., Gadalla, T., Daciuk, J., & Solomon, S. (2010). Cyber bullying behaviors among middle and high school students. *The American Journal of Orthopsychiatry*, 80(3), 362–374. DOI: 10.1111/j.1939-0025.2010.01040.x PMID: 20636942

Navarro, R., Yubero, S., & Larrañaga, E. (2015). *Cyberbullying across the globe: Gender, family, and mental health*. Springer.

Olweus, D., & Limber, S. (2018). Some problems with cyberbullying research. *Current Opinion in Psychology*, 19, 139–143. DOI: 10.1016/j.copsyc.2017.04.012 PMID: 29279213

Ortega, R., Elipe, P., Mora-Merchán, J. A., Calmaestra, J., & Vega, E. (2009). The emotional impact of bullying and cyberbullying on victims: A European cross-national study. *Aggressive Behavior*, 35(5), 514–525. DOI: 10.1002/ab.20334 PMID: 22782434

Patchin, J. W., & Hinduja, S. (2020). *Bullying today: Bullet points and best practices*. Corwin Press.

Reyns, B. W., & Fisher, B. S. (2018). The relationship between offline and online stalking victimization: A lifestyle-routine activity perspective. *Justice Quarterly*, 35(3), 452–476. DOI: 10.1080/07418825.2017.1289827

Slonje, R., Smith, P. K., & Frisén, A. (2013). The nature of cyberbullying and strategies for prevention. *Computers in Human Behavior*, 29(1), 26–32. DOI: 10.1016/j.chb.2012.05.024

Smith, P. K., del Barrio, C., & Tokunaga, R. S. (2013). Definitions of bullying and cyberbullying: How useful are the terms? *Emotional & Behavioural Difficulties*, 18(3), 225–235. DOI: 10.1080/13632752.2013.704324

Sticca, F., & Perren, S. (2013). Is cyberbullying worse than traditional bullying? Examining the differential roles of medium, publicity, and anonymity for the perceived severity of bullying. *Journal of Youth and Adolescence*, 42(5), 739–750. DOI: 10.1007/s10964-012-9867-3 PMID: 23184483

Tokunaga, R. S. (2010). Following you home from school: A critical review and synthesis of research on cyberbullying victimization. *Computers in Human Behavior*, 26(3), 277–287. DOI: 10.1016/j.chb.2009.11.014

Van Geel, M., Vedder, P., & Tanilon, J. (2014). Relationship between peer victimization, cyberbullying, and suicide in children and adolescents: A meta-analysis. *JAMA Pediatrics*, 168(5), 435–442. DOI: 10.1001/jamapediatrics.2013.4143 PMID: 24615300

Vandebosch, H., & Van Cleemput, K. (2009). Cyberbullying among youngsters: Profiles of bullies and victims. *New Media & Society*, 11(8), 1349–1371. DOI: 10.1177/1461444809341263

Wachs, S., Wright, M. F., & Wolf, K. D. (2017). Associations between bystanders and perpetrators of cyberbullying and traditional bullying. *Aggressive Behavior*, 43(3), 244–253. DOI: 10.1002/ab.21685

Willard, N. (2007). *Cyberbullying and cyberthreats: Responding to the challenge of online social aggression, threats, and distress*. Research Press.

Wright, M. F. (2017). Cyberbullying victimization through social networking sites and adjustment difficulties: The role of parental mediation. *Journal of the Association for Information Science and Technology*, 68(3), 504–515. DOI: 10.1002/asi.23624

Ybarra, M. L., & Mitchell, K. J. (2004). Online aggressor/targets, aggressors, and targets: A comparison of associated youth characteristics. *Journal of Child Psychology and Psychiatry, and Allied Disciplines*, 45(7), 1308–1316. DOI: 10.1111/j.1469-7610.2004.00328.x PMID: 15335350

Chapter 7
Developing Intelligent Systems to Combat Cyberbullying:
AI-Driven Prevention Techniques

Thakur Monika Singh
https://orcid.org/0009-0006-8534-9130
Stanley College of Engineering and Technology for Women, India

Kishor Kumar Reddy C.
Stanley College of Engineering and Technology for Women, India

Trupti Vinayak Vinayak Parkar
https://orcid.org/0009-0008-8832-7935
University of Arizona, USA

ABSTRACT

Cyberbullying significantly impacts mental health in today's digital age, calling for innovative prevention and mitigation strategies. This chapter delves into the role of artificial intelligence (AI) in addressing cyberbullying, starting with an analysis of its definitions, forms, and psychological effects to underscore the need for effective interventions. It highlights how AI technologies, including Natural Language Processing (NLP) techniques like sentiment analysis, keyword detection, and contextual interpretation, as well as machine learning models, are advancing traditional detection methods. Real-world case studies demonstrate successful AI applications in real-time monitoring and user behavior analysis, offering valuable insights. Ethical issues, such as data privacy, algorithmic bias, and transparency, are critically examined to ensure responsible AI use. The chapter also discusses the limitations of current AI solutions and future advancements, emphasizing the

DOI: 10.4018/979-8-3373-0543-1.ch007

need for stakeholder collaboration and providing actionable strategies to foster safer online environments.

1. INTRODUCTION

The emergence of social media and online communication in the digital age has changed how people communicate with one another. These platforms have promoted interaction and connectedness, but they have also spawned new kinds of abuse, such cyberbullying. The intentional and persistent harm caused by electronic means, such as social media, text messages, and online forums, is known as cyberbullying. It can take many different forms, such as exclusion, impersonation, harassment, and threats, and it poses serious hazards to the mental health, self-esteem, and general well-being of its victims. According to recent research, cyberbullying can have serious repercussions, such as anxiety, sadness, and in the worst situations, suicidal thoughts(Goldstein et al., 2024). Effective prevention and intervention measures are becoming more and more crucial as the prevalence of cyberbullying keeps rising. Because online interactions are quick and anonymous, traditional strategies for dealing with bullying-like school policy and parental supervision-frequently fall short. In this regard, the use of artificial intelligence (AI) offers a viable path toward the creation of intelligent systems that are able to proactively detect, track, and lessen occurrences of cyberbullying.

The purpose of this chapter is to investigate how AI technology might be used to stop cyberbullying. It is feasible to develop systems that can evaluate enormous volumes of internet data in real time, identify detrimental behavior patterns, and take appropriate action by utilizing cutting-edge methodologies like machine learning and natural language processing (NLP). In order to highlight the pressing need for creative solutions, this study will give a thorough overview of cyberbullying, including its definitions, psychological effects, and current developments. This chapter will explore different AI-powered preventative strategies, comparing these methods with traditional detection strategies to highlight their efficacy. Additionally, it will examine real-world case studies that illustrate successful implementations of AI in cyberbullying prevention, offering valuable insights into best practices and lessons learned. Ethical considerations, including data privacy and algorithmic bias, will also be critically analyzed to ensure the responsible deployment of AI technologies. Ultimately, this research emphasizes the importance of collaboration among stakeholders-including educators, parents, policymakers, and technology developers-to create safer online environments. By integrating AI-driven strategies into cyberbullying prevention efforts, we can foster a culture of respect and empathy in digital spaces, ultimately protecting individuals from the harmful effects of online harassment (Ari Prayuni et al., 2024).

Cyberbullying, defined as the intentional and repetitive harm inflicted through electronic communication, has become a significant social issue, particularly among youth. With the anonymity that the internet provides, individuals may feel emboldened to engage in harmful behaviors, leading to widespread emotional and psychological distress for victims. (Noni Rihhadatul Aisya, 2024) Studies indicate that millions of young people experience cyberbullying each year, with detrimental effects on their mental health, self-esteem, and overall quality of life. As society grapples with the complexities of online interactions, there is an urgent need to address the problem of cyberbullying effectively. The importance of addressing cyberbullying cannot be overstated. (Zedong Zhang, 2024) Research has shown that victims of cyberbullying are at a heightened risk of experiencing anxiety, depression, and other mental health issues, which can have lasting consequences into adulthood. The effects of cyberbullying can extend beyond the individual, impacting families, schools, and communities. Moreover, the unique characteristics of cyberbullying, such as its pervasive nature and the difficulty of escaping from online harassment, necessitate proactive and comprehensive intervention strategies. Traditional approaches to bullying—primarily focused on in-person interactions-often fall short when applied to the digital landscape. As such, it is imperative to develop targeted strategies that leverage technology to prevent and combat cyberbullying, fostering safer online environments for all users.

This chapter aims to explore the application of artificial intelligence (AI) in developing intelligent systems that can prevent and mitigate cyberbullying incidents. Specifically, the research seeks to identify effective AI-driven techniques that can detect and analyze patterns of bullying behavior in real time, providing timely interventions for potential victims. By examining existing literature and case studies, the study aims to elucidate how AI technologies-such as Natural Language Processing (NLP) and machine learning—can be harnessed to address the complexities of cyberbullying. Furthermore, the research will critically assess the ethical considerations surrounding the use of AI in this context, including data privacy and algorithmic fairness, to ensure responsible and equitable deployment of these technologies.

The chapter is structured to provide a comprehensive examination of the intersection between AI technologies and cyberbullying prevention. Following this introduction, Section 2 will delve into the concept of cyberbullying, discussing its definitions, types, and psychological impacts. Section 3 will outline the role of AI in identifying and combating bullying behaviors, comparing innovative AI-driven approaches with traditional methods. Section 4 will present various AI-driven prevention techniques, focusing on NLP methods and machine learning models. In Section 5, real-world case studies will be analyzed to demonstrate the effectiveness of AI in cyberbullying prevention. Ethical considerations will be addressed in Section 6, while Section 7 will discuss the challenges and limitations faced by current AI technologies. Finally, Section 8 will explore future directions for research and innovation, leading to the conclusions drawn in Section 9.

2. UNDERSTANDING CYBERBULLYING

Cyberbullying involves the use of digital platforms to harass, threaten, or intimidate individuals. It can occur through social media, text messages, or online forums. Victims often experience emotional distress, anxiety, and isolation. Unlike traditional bullying, cyberbullying can happen 24/7, making it harder to escape. It can lead to severe consequences, including mental health issues and, in extreme cases, self-harm or suicide. Prevention and awareness are crucial in combating this growing problem. Cyberbullying includes sending, posting, or sharing negative, harmful, false, or mean content about someone else. It can include sharing personal or private information about someone else causing embarrassment or humiliation. (Shahnata Putri Dwi Ramadhani et al., 2024) Cyberbullying is a form of bullying that occurs online or through digital communication channels like social media, messaging apps, and gaming platforms. Unlike traditional bullying, cyberbullying can happen with victims often feeling there is no escape from the harassment. It can include behaviors like sending threatening messages, spreading rumors, sharing embarrassing photos or videos, and creating fake profiles to humiliate someone.

Cyberbullying encompasses various forms of harassment, intimidation, and manipulation conducted through digital platforms like social media, messaging apps, and online gaming. This type of bullying can take many shapes, including harassment, where a person repeatedly sends hurtful or threatening messages to someone, and flaming, which involves heated, aggressive arguments in public forums. (Paul R. Smokowski et al., 2024) Another harmful type is outing or doxxing, where a bully publicly shares someone's private information, often to humiliate or endanger the victim. Impersonation is another form where someone pretends to be another person, typically using fake profiles, to spread rumors or damage their reputation. Exclusion is a subtle yet painful type of bullying, where individuals are deliberately left out of online groups or conversations, often isolating them socially. These diverse forms of cyberbullying illustrate how digital harassment has become more complex, making it difficult for victims to find a safe space online (S M Kowsik Godavarthi et al., 2024).

There are different types of cyberbullying as shown in figure 1, these types of cyberbullying can occur across various platforms, including social media sites, messaging apps, and online games, making it a pervasive issue affecting users of all ages.

Figure 1. Types of cyberbullying

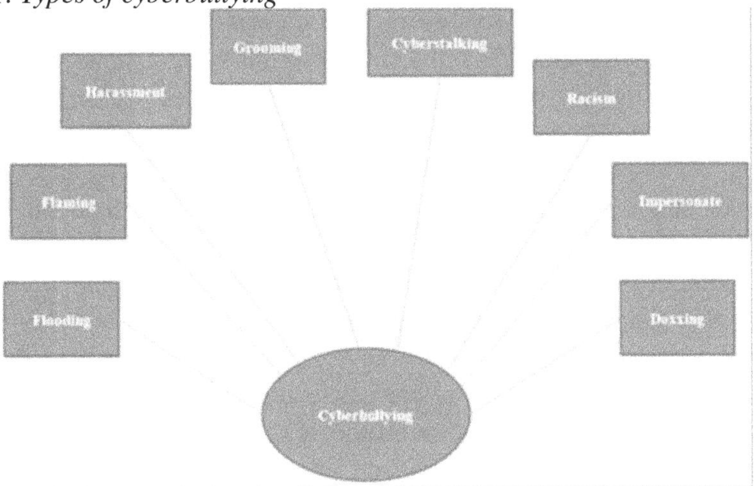

Flooding occurs when bullying takes over chat rooms and OSNs, preventing the victim from posting a message or from having any influence over it. Online chat rooms and groups are common places to find "flooding" (D. Maher, 2008), (N. E. Willard, 2009).

The act of sending hostile text messages to victims in online gaming chat rooms is known as "flaming" or "bashing." However, there are instances of flaming on OSNs where hate speech is becoming established. In general, hate speech victims include well-known actresses, singers, politicians, athletes, and others, but they always keep remain composed and avoid reacting. Instead, their supporters and followers react, respond, and remain united in this manner, a so-called Flame battle, for their idol. Flaming is when two or more people attack one another online. Common examples of flaming include being impolite, insulting, using foul language, and occasionally threatening someone. Furthermore, public communication channels are typically where flaming occurs (D. Maher, 2008), (N. E. Willard, 2009).

Harassment meant sending insulting or using text messages. Sending rude or abusive text messages quickly was considered harassment. Unlike Flaming, persistence is discernible in this case.

Grooming is the term used to describe the process of grooming kids online. Cyberbullies initially approach their victims in a courteous, fatherly, or friendly manner with the goal of earning their trust. They usually do this by pretending to be a teacher, doctor, or police officer, especially as someone who would never hurt or harm children. Once the victims' trust has been gained, they are sexually trapped using tools like webcams or online video conversations (A. Pascucci et al., 2019).

Victims of cyberstalking are worried about their life because internet stalkers coerce them into sending pictures or information and threaten to murder them if they don't comply. Furthermore, this kind of cyberbullying also occurs when ex-husbands degrade their ex-wives, or vice versa. Notably, men made up over 65% of cyberstalking victims in Italy in 2017 (A. Pascucci et al., 2019).

As people utilise online channels to convey hateful words, prejudices, and racist insults, cyberbullying with a racial component has grown in concern. Minority group members may experience harassment on social media in the form of insulting remarks, slurs, or specific hate campaigns; this is frequently made worse by the anonymity that many platforms offer. Impersonation in the context of cyberbullying involves someone creating fake accounts or profiles to mimic another person with the intent to deceive, harass, or harm their reputation. This form of bullying can be especially damaging, as impersonators may spread false information, send inappropriate messages, or post harmful content under the victim's identity, leading to misunderstandings and damaged relationships. Impersonation can also be used to access sensitive information or mislead the victim's friends, family, and followers, further amplifying the harm. Social media platforms are increasingly implementing measures to detect and report impersonation, yet this tactic continues to be a persistent and challenging aspect of cyberbullying.

Psychological and Social Impacts

The psychological and social impacts of cyberbullying are profound and can vary significantly among individuals. Here are some of the key consequences:

Mental Health Issues: Victims of cyberbullying often experience anxiety, depression, and low self-esteem. Research has shown that those targeted are at a higher risk of developing these conditions, sometimes leading to severe outcomes such as suicidal thoughts or attempts (Kowalski et al., 2014; Hinduja & Patchin, 2018).

Social Isolation: Individuals who are cyberbullied may withdraw from friends and social activities due to shame or fear of further bullying. This isolation can exacerbate feelings of loneliness and depression (Patchin & Hinduja, 2010).

Academic Decline: The stress and anxiety associated with being bullied can lead to decreased academic performance. Victims may have trouble concentrating on schoolwork or may avoid school altogether, resulting in lower grades and increased absenteeism (Schneider et al., 2012).

Impact on Self-Identity: Cyberbullying can negatively affect a person's self-image and identity. Victims may internalize the negative messages they receive, leading to a distorted self-perception (Kowalski et al., 2014).

Long-Term Consequences: The effects of cyberbullying can persist into adulthood, affecting personal relationships, professional opportunities, and overall mental health. Some studies suggest that former victims may struggle with trust issues and have difficulties forming healthy relationships (Hinduja & Patchin, 2018).

The psychological and social impacts of cyberbullying can be profound and long-lasting. Victims frequently experience heightened anxiety and depression, stemming from a continuous sense of fear and sadness. Persistent online harassment can lead to isolation and loneliness, as victims often withdraw from social settings-both online and offline-to avoid further abuse. Cyberbullying can also significantly impact a person's ability to focus on their education or career, as they may struggle with concentration due to the mental toll of the harassment. Self-esteem often suffers as a result of repeated negative comments, leading to self-doubt and, over time, self-image issues that can be difficult to reverse. Tragically, in severe cases, victims may develop thoughts of self-harm or suicide as they struggle with the intense emotions and the perceived inescapability of their situation. These impacts underscore the need for supportive interventions and mental health resources for those affected by cyberbullying.

Current trends in cyberbullying reveal how new technologies and social dynamics have influenced online harassment. (Ravi, S. S., 2023) With increased anonymity provided by certain apps and platforms, individuals find it easier to engage in harmful behavior without accountability, often emboldened by their concealed identity. The rise of photo and video editing technology, including deepfakes, has led to more sophisticated bullying, allowing individuals to manipulate images or videos to humiliate others publicly. Online gaming communities have also seen a rise in cyberbullying, with verbal abuse, exclusion, or coordinated bullying tactics becoming common, especially toward specific players.

3.1 Overview of AI Technologies

AI technologies encompass a wide array of tools and algorithms designed to process, interpret, and learn from data. Key AI technologies relevant to cyberbullying detection include Natural Language Processing (NLP), Machine Learning (ML), Deep Learning (DL), and Sentiment Analysis. NLP allows AI to understand and analyze human language, enabling the detection of aggressive, abusive, or negative language patterns. Machine learning algorithms, trained on large datasets of flagged messages and social interactions, can classify new data as potentially harmful or benign based on past examples. Deep learning, especially through neural networks, refines this process by understanding complex relationships and subtle linguistic cues. Sentiment analysis helps to gauge the tone and intent of messages, differentiating between sarcasm, jokes, and genuine harm. Together, these AI technologies offer a powerful toolkit for identifying and intervening in cyberbullying incidents on digital platforms (Vaishali, U., et al., 2023).

Table 1. Various AI technologies used in cyberbullying

AI Technology	Description	Application in Cyberbullying
Natural Language Processing (NLP)	Processes and understands human language.	Detects harmful language and categorizes content.
Machine Learning (ML)	Learns from past data to make predictions or classifications.	Flags abusive messages based on training data.
Deep Learning (DL)	Uses neural networks to recognize complex patterns in large datasets.	Identifies subtle and nuanced bullying behavior.
Sentiment Analysis	Assesses tone and emotional context of language.	Distinguishes between jokes and harmful intent.

Table 1 showsan overview of various AI technologies used in cyberbullying detection, focusing on their descriptions and applications.

3.2 Potential of AI in Identifying Bullying Behavior

AI's potential in identifying bullying behavior lies in its ability to continuously analyze vast volumes of data in real-time, which would be impossible for human moderators alone. Through NLP and sentiment analysis, AI can identify bullying patterns, from direct insults to more subtle forms of harassment, such as exclusionary tactics and passive aggression. Machine learning models refine themselves over time, learning from flagged instances to improve accuracy and reduce false positives. (Reddy Chinthala, K. K., et al., 2024) Additionally, AI systems can incorporate contextual analysis, evaluating the broader conversation and user behavior to distinguish cyberbullying from other types of online interaction. This proactive approach allows for early intervention, reducing the psychological impact on victims and promoting a safer digital environment.

Table 2. AI applications in cyberbullying

AI Application	Description	Examples in Cyberbullying Detection
NLP and Sentiment Analysis	Identifies harmful language and detects tone.	Flags insults, abusive language, and aggressive tones.
Contextual Analysis	Considers the broader context of messages.	Detects subtle or indirect bullying, such as social exclusion.
Continuous Learning (ML)	Improves with new data, reducing false positives over time.	Learns to distinguish between friendly banter and real harassment.
Real-Time Monitoring	Analyzes messages and user behavior as they happen.	Allows for immediate intervention and moderation.

The above table 2 outlines various AI applications in detecting cyberbullying, describing each application and providing examples of how it functions in real-world scenarios.

3.3. AI vs. Traditional Methods of Detection

The AI-based methods introduced a great shift from the traditional approaches since they are adaptable and data-driven. Traditional methods are rule-based and rely on fixed keywords, phrases, or behaviors to recognize what is perceived as potentially harmful content. This approach, though simple, is prone to false positives and negatives because users often go around rules by changing language. Moreover, these approaches require very time-consuming and labor-intensive monitoring that is mostly manual, so scaling them a little is tough. This makes traditional systems unable to adapt to the changing language and tactics of the common online interactions, thus limited in dynamic digital environments(Adeyinka, Orelaja. et al., 2024).

However, AI-based detection uses machine learning and NLP to process huge volumes of data, find very subtle patterns, and contextual understanding of abuse that ordinary algorithms may miss. The evaluation of sentiment and tone and intent around messages will allow AI to distinguish between jokes and actual harassment, increasing accuracy in detection.(Majel, Monisha B., 2024) Once trained, an AI model can churn out tremendous data amounts in a short period of time; thus, real-time monitoring on high-traffic platforms that would be impractical with manual oversight can be accomplished. But dependence on AI raises ethical and technical issues for this use, such as data privacy and probable biases in algorithms. For instance, if the training data happens to be biased, then the results are skewed toward hitting one kind of group or speech or the other. So, while AI enhances the detection and estimation capabilities, there still needs careful handling so as not to cheat or mislead.

In summary, traditional and AI-based methods each have unique strengths and limitations. Traditional approaches are easier to implement with fewer computational demands but lack the flexibility and require continuous human intervention. AI-based methods, on the other hand, offer scalable, accurate, and nuanced solutions by identifying complex behaviors associated with cyberbullying. However, they require considerable upfront data investment and ongoing ethical oversight to manage issues related to privacy, bias, and accountability. Both approaches highlight the trade-offs between simplicity and adaptability in tackling the complex problem of cyberbullying detection.

4. AI-DRIVEN PREVENTION TECHNIQUES

4.1. Natural Language Processing (NLP) Approaches

NLP is an important AI domain that focuses on the interaction between computers and human language; in detection and prevention cases regarding cyberbullying, great roles are performed in scrutinizing text data as it detects harmful behavior, intent, and emotions. The techniques involving NLP can process large amounts of online communication, learning any valuable insights behind messages that they convey-for example, what is being conveyed by such messages and even if the offensive language is present, or if there are patterns showing aggressive behavior. NLP is one of the promising technologies for the discovery of cyberbullying, capable of processing text across languages and platforms into subtle forms of harassment that might have otherwise remained undetected by traditional detection methods.

Figure 2 represents a framework in Natural Language Processing that can take multimodal inputs such as text, audio, or video. Sitting at the heart of all these feeds is an NLP module, applied with advanced techniques for data analysis and interpretation. Some of its core functions include Direct Text Processing, NER for the extraction of key entities, Semantic Relationship Extraction to appreciate the relations amongst entities, Content Classification to classify information, and Emotion Detection in order to come up with underlying sentiments. This framework is an example of how NLP combines disparate types of data for the purpose of comprehensive analysis in tasks such as understanding sentiments, contextual interpretation, and emotional insight.

Figure 2. Natural Language Processing (NLP) Framework for Multimodal Data Processing

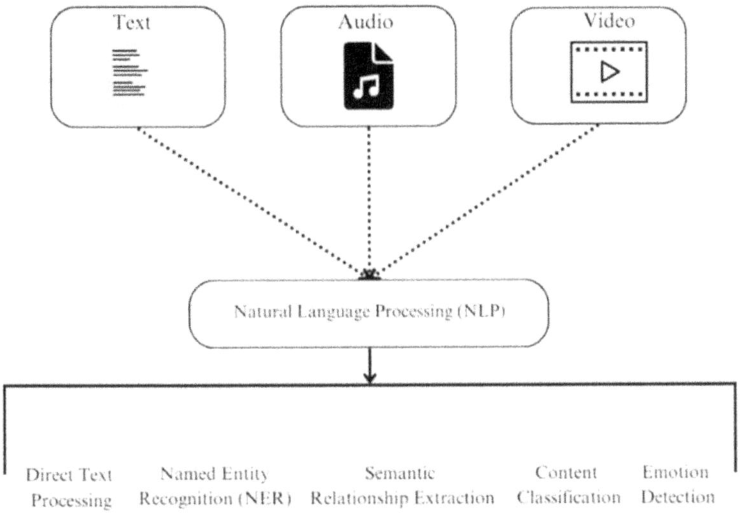

Table 3 summarizes the most important techniques applied for the detection of cyberbullying, describing their functions, strengths, and weaknesses. Sentiment analysis identifies emotional tones, whereas keyword-based detection presents related explicit language. Contextual understanding is the digging deeper into nuances and subtle bullying. All have pros and cons, so considerations should be made when selecting the specific detection strategy.

Table 3. Comparison of NLP techniques for cyberbullying detection

NLP Technique	Function	Strengths	Limitations
Sentiment Analysis	Identifies emotional tone in text	Effective for overtly hostile texts	May miss context or sarcasm
Keyword Detection	Detects specific bullying-related keywords	Easy to implement	Limited to explicit language
Contextual Understanding	Analyzes full context and nuance in text	Better at identifying subtle bullying	Computationally intensive and complex

4.1.1. Sentiment Analysis

In many ways, sentiment analysis is a powerful tool in the context of cyberbullying detection, as it allows one to gauge the underlying emotions in text-based communication. Sentiment analysis classifies the overall sentiment behind a message for being either positive, negative, or neutral and gives insight into the way in which a user may feel or intend on communicating; cyberbullying often takes place in which messages of negative sentiment express anger, hatred, or frustration. These sentiments, detected, can also serve as indicators of aggressive behavior in alerting potentially harmful content before it hurts. Other specific emotional tones, such as outrage, disgust, or sadness, are also found in cyberbullying interactions, which can then be enhanced for use in sentiment analysis.(Wankhade, M. et al., 2022) More advanced models in sentiment analysis can also detect more complex linguistic features that are used to veil the aggressive intent, such as sarcasm, irony, or veiled threats. Here, systems based on traditional methods of meaning determination are really challenged, especially when there is a very different literal meaning from what the message intended. In addition, with the integration of these sophisticated NLP algorithms, sentiment analysis can understand the subtleties of bullying behavior and, therefore, identify such behavior more accurately. Hidden feelings or emotions may be known, and it is through such that sentiment analysis will ensure a more subtle and trusted means of identifying cyberbullying. Apart from isolating direct negative emotions, sentiment analysis can also be used to better comprehend the intensity and emotional weight behind the language of online interaction. Measuring the strength of sentiment can distinguish between mild frustration or more severe aggression or hatred. This ability fine-tunes the detection of cyberbullying to not only identify hurtful language, but also would give insight into the probable emotional impact upon the victim. Sentiment analysis is very useful in the large-scale site as it allows quick processing of huge text data and instantly flags content which may cause harm to people without human intervention. Hence, it could become a first line of defense in preventing cyberbullying and alert moderators or systems to review and further act on the case.

4.1.2. Keyword and Phrase Detection

One of the easiest most potent Natural Language Processing techniques that can be used to identify instances of cyberbullying is keyword and phrase detection. This technique involves scanning through texts for words or phrases that people use to harbor harmful behavior: insults, threats, slurs, and derogatory remarks. This proves to be effective in catching the direct-oriented bullying, e.g., name-calling, threats, abusive language, among others. In this sense, its presence serves as an important component for flagging content that might be harmful overnight. Keyword and phrase detection has the advantage of being simple and fast, hence making them implementable as programs in real-time systems with an immediate reaction.

The problem with this strategy is that language, particularly in the online space, evolves so quickly. New slang, abbreviations, and expressions continually come into play, and individuals can creatively express hostile messages in ways that even traditional keyword detection systems find it hard to keep pace with. For instance, sometimes words or phrases may mean different things depending on their context, or users might intentionally spell words incorrectly to circumvent filters. Therefore, keyword-based detection systems must constantly update to remain effective. They need to be constantly adjusted to improve new linguistic trends and the newly evolving concept of cyberbullying. Given these limitations, keyword and phrase detection is normally used in conjunction with other NLP techniques, which can improve accuracy and minimize false positives. This approach becomes more robust in combination with sentiment analysis or contextual understanding, enabling the system to understand the intent behind the words, as it could detect subtler forms of cyberbullying. For instance, a user may avoid using explicitly offensive language but may still engage in bullying with the help of passive-aggressive comments or thinly veiled insults. By introducing keyword-based detection with deeper context analysis, the system could now more feasibly identify such less apparent cases and thus achieve an improved overall effectiveness toward stopping online harassment.

4.1.3. Contextual Understanding

Contextual understanding in NLP is more than sensing or detecting phrases. It tends to understand what broader context those words occupy. Languages are a very subtle thing, and words or phrases may mean something different based on the situation or even the tone of the speaker. For instance, a word like "kill" could be inoffensive within a sentence such as "killing it," where a person is said to be excelling at a game or activity, but the same word could then be used within an actual threat such as "I will kill you"-a violent threat. Many key-word detection methods developed over the years could fail to identify the differences between the respective nuances and would produce many false positives or failed detections. Models of NLP with contextual understanding, usually based on deep learning, can look well beyond individual words in examining an entire sentence or even the general conversation that forms the text. Analyzing context, including other words present in the surrounding conversation, may help these models make better decisions about whether a particular message is damaging or not. For instance, they would be able to identify some changes in tone or a surge in level of aggression but not actually through words. This increases the possibility of proper interpretation of the content's intent.

Contextual awareness is also essential in a situation where advanced cyberbullying occurs implicitly through passivity, sarcasm, or implicit threats. Such acts are hard to identify since they do not necessarily need explicit words and have nothing to do with the language used to convey them. Therefore, NLP models can reach a better differentiation between the joke and the harmful message by understanding the context where these phrases are used, thus reducing the possibility of classifying harmless comments as bullying. This high accuracy enables better detection that keeps false positives away, which helps in avoiding unnecessary censorship or even interference, thus making it a vital component in AI-driven systems for cyberbullying prevention. Besides the context where one operates, even advanced models of NLP based on contextual awareness look into and consider the social and cultural environments in which the messages are understood. These are extremely valuable for the interpretation of messages. Language usage is not similar and varies from one culture to the other and from one social community to another. What could go unnoticed in one may provoke irritation in others in a second. By training NLP systems on various types of datasets, it would then learn the subtlety of language expressions in various communities. In that regard, they would be much more adaptive and effective for use in various contexts across the globe. Humour, slang, and expressions of affection greatly vary from one location to another, and the use of contextual understanding makes these systems understand such expressions correctly. This would minimize misinterpretation or over-censorship of content in a multilingual context. This deep understanding of context would be required to design AI systems that could indeed respond appropriately and sensitively to cyberbullying.

4.2. Machine Learning Models

Machine learning is an integral aspect in developing AI-driven system approaches for identifying cyberbullying. These models go through their processes based on information input to them so as to identify patterns, classify messages, and predict the eventual outcome. With an increase in examples being processed, systems get to be more accurate and adaptable to changing tactics used in carrying out cyberbullying. The implementation of ML with NLP brings more robust solutions for bullying detection across various digital platforms.

The following table 4 compares different machine learning models used in detecting cyberbullying: what they can do, their strengths, and their limitations. Supervised learning yields high accuracy if enough labeled data are available, whereas unsupervised learning is particularly useful to find new patterns, especially in dynamic or slang-heavy language. Real-time monitoring allows for immediate feedback while interacting but requires substantial resources for computation. Each model brings with it its unique benefits and challenges in the process of detection.

Table 4. Comparison of machine learning models for cyberbullying detection

ML Model	Function	Strengths	Limitations
Supervised Learning	Learns from labeled bullying data	High accuracy with sufficient data	Requires extensive labeled data
Unsupervised Learning	Identifies new patterns without labels	Effective for dynamic language and slang	Can be less precise than supervised models
Real-Time Monitoring	Analyzes interactions instantly	Provides immediate responses	High computational demands

4.2.1. Supervised Learning Techniques

Supervised learning is one of the dominant strategies used in machine learning and it employs labeled data where for every input data point, the corresponding known outcome or label is specified. This can be a tag determining whether the text belong to a certain category of "bullying" or "non-bullying." The task begins with collecting a large, diverse dataset of online exchanges, social media posts, or messages, each of which is labeled manually by hand with respect to whether it exemplifies bullying behavior or not. We then use those labeled examples for training the machine learning model and generalize patterns found in the data to predict on unseen messages. The primary strength of supervised learning is its capability of high accuracy when sufficient, quality labeled data is available. (Aigerim, Toktarova et al., 2024) The common algorithms applied to the detection of cyberbullying are supervised learning algorithms including Support Vector Machines (SVMs) and Random Forests. SVMs work by discovering an optimal hyperplane that separates the two classes of the problem: bullying and non-bullying. A model can then be used to classify new, unseen instances. Finally, Random Forests simply creates an ensemble of decision trees; each makes a prediction, and the majority vote of the ensemble is taken as the final prediction. These algorithms can handle large datasets and high complexities by capturing subtle patterns that distinguish bullying behavior from non-bullying communication. Another issue in supervised learning is to develop large and diversified datasets so that it will be certain that the model will work well when transferred across various bullying behavior examples and communication patterns. Linguistic variety, involving slangs, sarcasm, and online behavior cultures, calls for one to test the model through a great range of examples to prevent overfitting. Another challenge is that the assignment of labels to data is time-consuming, bound by human bias, and can therefore influence the model accuracy. Nevertheless, if such a supervised learning is well implemented with good representation of divergent high-quality datasets, its ability to significantly boost the accuracy of the cyberbullying detection systems should be a powerful tool for real-time monitoring and intervention.

4.2.2. Unsupervised Learning for Pattern Recognition

The strength of unsupervised learning comes into action when labeled datasets are scarce or unavailable. Unlike supervised learning, which depends on pre-labeled data to train models, unsupervised learning relies on raw, unlabeled data, which enables algorithms to find out the pattern, structures, and relationships independently within the data. Unsupervised learning is all the more valuable while considering cyberbullying detection because it does not require manual labeled examples of bullying behavior. Instead, it detects latent patterns or structures in messages or interactions, for example, repeated abuse patterns that may indicate cyberbullying. This has proven to be useful in the discovery of emergent forms of cyberbullying that are not as of yet present, or named within labeled training data.

Clustering is one of the major techniques applied in unsupervised learning for detecting cyberbullying. Clustering algorithms are either k-means or hierarchical types. Simply, k-means or hierarchical clustering categorize data points that share similar features into the same group. Applying clustering in the detection of cyberbullying can group online interactions or posts of similar features such as aggressive language, tone, or a topic. Such clusters would be identified by the unsupervised models which may actually bring to the fore groups of messages individually pointing to no bullying but taken together, directly highlighted harassment or cyberbullying. This means that it can identify situations much earlier than in the case of labeled prior, for even cases in which no labeled prior exists to declare malicious behavior. Such unsupervised learning methods succeed remarkably in identifying very subtle forms of emergent cyberbullying as well as isolating episodic items that seem not to belong to a pattern of abusive behavior. They are of critical importance in building adaptive, real-time detection systems.

Below figure 3 is a comparison of Supervised Learning and Unsupervised Learning, elucidating their fundamental differences. For example, in the left-hand case of Supervised Learning, the model would be trained on labeled data in which inputs are paired with known outputs that enable it to predict the labels for new, unlabeled data. In this case, the output would be categorized data aligned with predefined labels. On the contrary, Unsupervised Learning relies on unlabeled data wherein an algorithm recognizes patterns in data through grouping of similar data into clusters and does not know initially what labels are. Output corresponds to these clusters revealing natural intrinsic structures inside the data. Both techniques imply the learning process but differ from each other since they do not rely on the labeled data.

Figure 3. Comparison of supervised and unsupervised learning frameworks

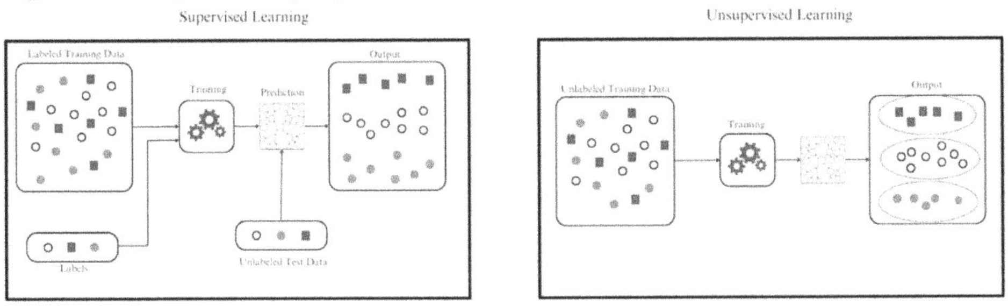

4.2.3. Real-Time Monitoring Systems

Advanced monitoring systems allow real-time monitoring of cyberbullying activities using the full power of machine learning to scan and analyze communications as they are occurring. Therefore, when cyberbullying activity is identified, it can be addressed immediately. Advanced monitoring systems cross multiple digital platforms: that is, a bundle of social media, messaging applications, and online forums-this is where most cyberbullying takes place. It has the ability to be integrated with machine learning models, which are trained to recognize patterns associated with cyberbullying. Hence, these will be trained upon vast datasets containing examples of bullying language, behavior patterns, and typical responses to bullying. Over time, they will start selecting the implicit presentation of aggression besides the overt forms such as sarcasm, aggressive comment, or even coded language which might not properly convey. Real-time may use the natural language to process context besides improving the detection accuracy in some systems. At this level of sophistication, real-time monitoring systems could almost be treated as virtual moderators; they could scan vast volumes of data but also automatically filter some of these data and leave other more critical or complex matters to be reviewed for their own sake by human moderators (C Kishor Kumar Reddy et al., 2023).

However, deployment at scale comes with its own set of problems. High accuracy is vital not to fall prey either to a false positive trap where nonbenign content is detected as malicious or to the false negative trap where actual malicious content slips through the net. Realtime monitoring systems typically employ feedback loops, where the flagged content is evaluated by human moderators and the machine learning models are continuously fine-tuned based on that feedback. However, such systems must also ensure confidentiality and security of user data and communications owing to the sensitive personal communications being analyzed. It challenges the integrated design of such a system to balance these ethical considerations with the efficacy of the system while advancements in machine learning and encryption techniques become ever more pivotal to an increasingly practical tool to combat cyberbullying in real-time monitoring.

4.3. User Behavior Analytics

4.3.1. Profiling and Predictive Analytics

Profiling, in the context of cyberbullying prevention, refers to the creation of detailed models of user behavior by aggregating various sources of information such as past interactions, communication patterns, and demographic information. In other words, it is an analysis of how an average user behaves in the online environment, what kind of posts he or she creates, the amount and type of interaction with others, or even the language he or she conducts these activities. Profiling gives a baseline for normal behavior of a particular user, which helps detect subtle deviations, possibly the first sign of new changes in behavior-in this case, bullying. This could be information such as the tone used in messages, number of interactions, and even the time of day when they are most active. Predictive analytics applies historical data and statistical algorithms to predict future outcomes based on the patterns captured in past behavior. In the case of cyberbullying detection, predictive analytics takes data collected through profiling and analyzes them in order to forecast the probability that a user is going to engage in a bullying behavior in the future. The greatest advantage of predictive analytics is the warning it can give about a pattern of behavior that may potentially be problematic when it fully develops. Predictive analytics thus allows the creation of personalized interventions to better serve users at risk of bullying-once as perpetrators, now as a victim.

4.3.2. Anomaly Detection Systems

Anomaly detection systems are perhaps a critical tool in preventing cyberbullying. They look at the information flow of how a user interacts, focusing on the regularity of anomalies or abnormal patterns of behavior. These systems will continuously monitor user activity patterns over time and track whatever has been taken as normal behavior. Having set a baseline, any deviation from that would raise an alarm-a spike in hostile word choice, a sharp rise in message volume, or even a change in tone from cold to warm. This approach would likely trap aberrant behaviors that could be defining cyberbullying, even though the language might not be harmful on its face, taken separately.

The key strength of an anomaly detection is its potential for recognizing fast, unexpected changes in behavior, which might not be detected by predefined rules or even by traditional detection methods. For example, if a normally docile user suddenly begins to use aggressive speech patterns or starts targeting one person with a sequence of hurtful messages, an anomaly detection system will pick these changes up. (Patcha, A. et al., 2007) The early identification is also very crucial for it makes prompt intervention by moderators or automated systems possible which often can eliminate the infiltration of bullying behavior. In some cases, the system may identify repeated patterns of negativity or aggression across multiple users as indicative of group-based bullying or harassment.

5. CASE STUDIES AND APPLICATIONS

There have been huge developments through different sectors that apply artificial intelligence in the prevention of cyberbullying from the social media and education sectors to online gaming sectors. Advanced techniques used by AI, such as natural language processing, sentiment analysis, and behavior profiling, have been detected to curb hostile interactions in effective ways among online users. This section discusses real-world application scenarios for AI in combating cyberbullying as well as the lessons learnt from these deployments. A comparative analysis of different approaches reveals their strong and weak points. This helps to clearly understand through case studies that AI is essentially shifting modes of fighting cyberbullying into scalable and adaptive forms while addressing essential technical and ethical challenges.

5.1. Successful Implementations of AI in Cyberbullying Prevention

Artificial Intelligence has grown dramatically in recognizing and preventing cyberbullying, and many organizations have successfully deployed AI-powered systems to curb online harassment. For instance, in social media sites such as Facebook and Twitter, it included algorithms in machine learning which could automatically flag offensive content, which may include hate speech or explicit bullying language and commenting. These systems make even more use of NLP and sentiment analysis when interpreting the context behind posts. They will detect not only explicit threats, but also other types of bullying, for instance, passive-aggressive language or social exclusion. In these circumstances, the platforms can take immediate action, removing the content or giving a warning to the user, often even before the bullying escalates. Scalability is yet one of the core strengths in AI-based systems that enables real-time analysis of large volumes of data, providing scalable solutions to cyberbullying on a global basis. For example, Instagram has employed AI for automatically detecting offensive images and captions using a computer vision technique combined with NLP techniques which help identify visual and textual harassment. This allows the platform to identify abusive words but also image-based insults, such as body shaming or derogatory symbols, and prevent reaching users that kind of content. But basically, the capability of AI to communicate with a variety of online communication systems-text, images, and videos-is what makes it an edge per se, because it can be an invaluable tool in creating safe online spaces (Walli, S. A. et al., 2024).

Monitoring the digital engagements among students is one of the ways in which AI-powered tools like ReThink have been applied in education institutions. Predictive analytics, in this case, the ReThink identifies potential bullying behavior before it continues to escalate into something really unbecoming. This tool monitors patterns, such as being constantly excluded or receiving abusive language. It looks for it so that schools can be proactive and intervene early. Apart from such trends, there are platforms that specifically target the gaming community. Overall, this extensive analysis of interaction along with the capability of machine learning to adapt to new and evolving language will assure that systems adopting AI in preventing cyberbullying will be effective in combating cyberbullying in dynamic online environments.

5.2. Lessons Learned from Real-World Applications

Real-world applications of AI in the prevention of cyberbullying have offered invaluable learning concerning the possibilities and limitations of such technologies. One important lesson learned is that of perpetual data training. The vocabulary and the interaction behavior, pertaining to online activity, are fast-changing regarding slangs, abbreviations, and less apparent forms of harassment. Artificial intelligence needs to be updated repeatedly with novel datasets to make them recognize and act upon these changes. Without proper and effective training, AI models may fail to detect or misinterpret altogether new expressions of bullying, producing a backlog of false positives where harmless content is counted as too toxic or violent, or false negatives as bullying goes undetected. It also learned that although AI will easily notify incidences of bad behavior, such needs do require human involvement.

Figure 4 brings forth the major insights and issues that crop up on the basis of the case studies of AI monitoring. The insights lie in four areas: the effectiveness of AI for reducing cyberbullying and increasing user satisfaction, challenges-for example, the complicated fact that real-time data monitoring is very tiresome, ethical concerns such as biases in AI algorithms, and user feedback that reflects increased feelings of safety brought about by AI interventions. These intertwining components provide an integrated description of the effects, constraints, and ethical implications of using AI systems.

Figure 4. Insights and Challenges: Lessons Learned from AI Implementation

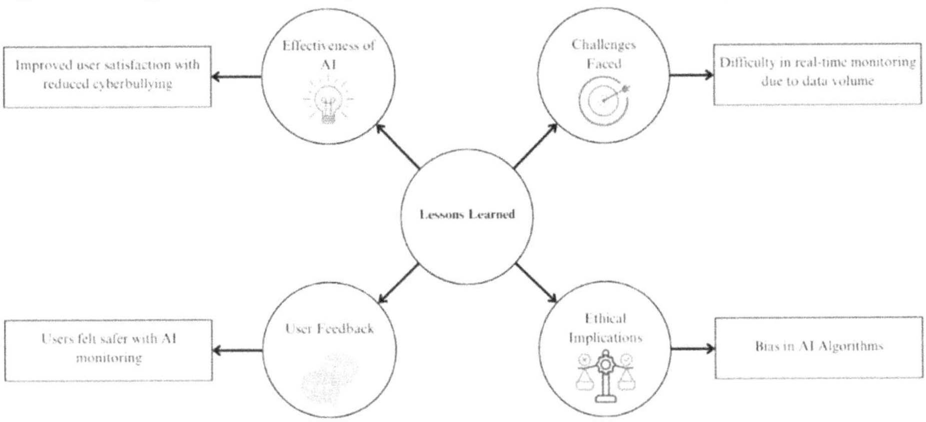

Cyberbullying is one of those issues which is rich in social and emotional dynamics that little AI understands fully. For instance, sarcasm, tone, or content may never be detected by AI or, particularly those AI's trained on text. This leads to possible misclassifications. In such a scenario, human intervention is needed for more significant and relevant evaluation of the situation so that appropriate action may be taken at the correct time. Thus, AI should be more of a moderator assistant tool rather than a full substitute for human judgment. Even implementations of AI in real-life cyberbullying prevention feature challenges like the need to be less intrusive for people's privacy versus the need to be intrusive to effectively monitor and control bullying instances. AI usually requires lots of personal data for effective performance, which is a subject of ethical argumentation about how much surveillance is bearable. Balancing user privacy with the need to prevent effective bullying can be challenging. There is still a great concern about algorithmic bias, which occurs when AI systems unfairly weigh some groups or individuals more than others due to the training data being biased. It could potentially be unfair treatment if suitably designed to recognize and correct biases such as that one.

6. ETHICAL CONSIDERATIONS

Ethical considerations form the heart of AI systems development and deployment in cyberbullying prevention. Even though such AI technologies have enormous benefits in identifying and reducing hazardous behavior online, the risks about data privacy, algorithmic fairness, and accountability are diverse. The section addresses the most critical ethical issues by focusing on how these will affect the users and AI system development.

Figure 5 summarizes some of the key lessons that can be learned from the deployment of AI monitoring systems into operation and captures four high-level themes: AI effectiveness in ensuring user satisfaction via reduction in cyberbullying, the difficulty of monitoring real-time data due to volume, ethical concerns for biases within AI algorithms, and user feedback, which reflects perceptions of increased safety. These insights provide a balanced outlook to the potential benefits and limitations of applications of AI while laying strong emphasis on the imperative critical design and scalability needs for applications in ethical AI.

Figure 5. Key Lessons from AI Implementation: Insights and Challenges

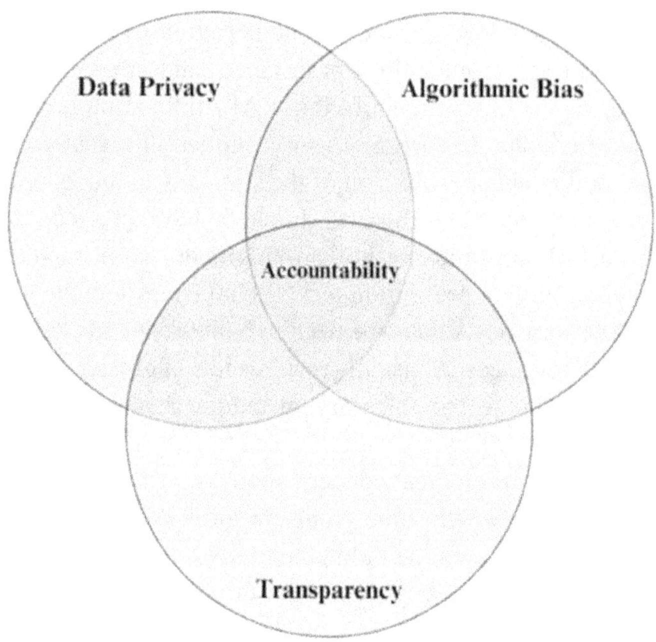

6.1. Addressing Algorithmic Bias

Algorithmic bias refers to the unfair outcomes that result from AI systems trained on biased or unequal data. Therefore, in the case of a cyberbullying detection system, this can be represented through unfair targeting toward specific groups or types of speech. A model trained primarily on data from one demographic background will fail to have any proper understanding of cyberbullying in messages from other backgrounds. At times, this results in over-flagging or under-flagging certain behaviors, which in turn perpetuates existing stereotypes and society biases. This automatically disproportionately affects the disadvantaged groups as well as undermines the very notion of fairness with the decisions generated through automated decisions.

Mitigating Algorithmic bias during AI training requires a proactive and thoughtful approach. That means having curated diverse and representative datasets that reflect much of the variety in user behaviors, languages, or cultural contexts (Kordzadeh, N. et al., 2024). In conclusion, varied data inclusion will enable the AI system to learn cyberbullying detection on various groups and avoid duplicated model reflection that might make the results biased. Another important aspect is to audit or revisit AI models as it goes along to ensure that they will continuously carry out the task equitably because they do not inadvertently favor one group over the rest. Continuous monitoring helps identify emerging biases when the system evolves and make necessary adjustments.

More importantly, the fact that AI could explain its decision-making process helps resolve the algorithmic bias issue in a system. Users and other stakeholders have to be shown how and why those behaviors or pieces of content were detected as cyberbullying. Making the reasoning mechanisms of AI more transparent would certainly help developers provide users with insight into the factors that determine decisions and enable users to contest outcomes they believe are unjust or biased. Such openness definitely promotes trust in AI technology and shows users a guarantee that the use of the technology is responsible and ethically sound.

7. CHALLENGES AND LIMITATIONS

7.1. Technical Challenges in AI Development

Dealing with the technical challenges for developing an effective system requires not only ensuring the correctness of the data but also fighting against model complexity and huge computationally intensive requirements. An important aspect of training an AI with decent accuracy on identifying cyberbullying, though, involves having extensive datasets for abusive behavior in all their varieties. Such data, however, can be hard to come by since most of those existing in social media platforms are inaccessible or severely handicapped by data-sharing restrictions. (Hagendorff, T. et al., 2020) Also, the design of AI models is difficult as it tries to balance between sensitivity, which refers to the ability of a model to identify bullying cases, and specificity, which refers to avoiding false positives. Achieving a balance that satisfies high accuracy with broad applicability in multiple online platforms is challenging.

Another risk is the tremendous computational power required in building and maintaining those AI systems. Indeed, advanced models like deep neural networks require tremendous amounts of computing resources as well as energy, thus raising sustainability issues and budgetary challenges for smaller organizations or public institutions that want to launch AI-based monitoring. All of these technical challenges require investment in infrastructure, different types of datasets, and the continuous improvement of models for better adaptation to the ever-changing language and behavior patterns associated with cyberbullying.

7.2. Limitations of Current AI Techniques

Although AI has made spectacular strides, the current methods remain inadequate for accurate and consistent identification of incidents of cyberbullying. Most AI models are not context-sensitive: For example, they can pick up certain words or phrases but are not able to treat the very same conversation in its entirety. Consequently, sentences that would be considered aggressive in one context appear meaningless in another, such as between good friends. Another hurdle is that sometimes, AI algorithms classify light-hearted teasing as harassment; hence, it might filter in too much or too little.

In addition, (Fowler, T., 2024) there is a limited ability for the existent AI models to be completely unbiased because they learn from available data. A model mainly learned from datasets from one region or demographic would not have the ability to identify cyberbullying in other contexts where the language and behavioral patterns are different. The ability to conduct real-time detection and response is also lacking. Most of the existing AI models have some form of delay, which would go against the intervention needed in the progression of cyberbullying situations. Addressing these limitations will require shifts toward more complicated models that are more situated and less biased, but this will also have its own technical and ethical challenges.

8. FUTURE DIRECTIONS

8.1 Emerging Technologies in Cyberbullying Prevention

With the latest advancement in technology, the most innovative approaches are surfacing in the cyberbullying prevention landscape. The use of multi-modal AI systems has registered significant development in analyzing data coming from diverse sources based on text, images, and audio. Putting all these types of data together will enable AI to assess not only what words are being used but can also detect the subtle signs of harassment in tone, imagery, or context. This example illustrates that when in addition to texts and images, the sentiment in audio files is also analyzed for the process of bullying behavior identification such as sarcasm which often goes unnoticed in traditional systems built on texts (Siddiqui, S. et al., 2023).

Pyramid diagram shown in figure 6 is used to outline the fundamental elements that should forge ahead in cyberbullying prevention efforts. The first one from the bottom, Emerging Technologies, resonates with roles involving innovative tools as well as artificial intelligence in combating online threats. The middle layer strikes at the core when highlighting collaborations and partnerships that actually involve the tech industry, educators, and policymakers. Heads above the rest, an Overarching Vision for a Safer Online Environment, aligned with the shared goal of safe and respectful digital spaces, strikes one as an approach that would be strategically cooperative in dealing with cyberbullying.

Figure 6. Future directions in cyberbullying prevention

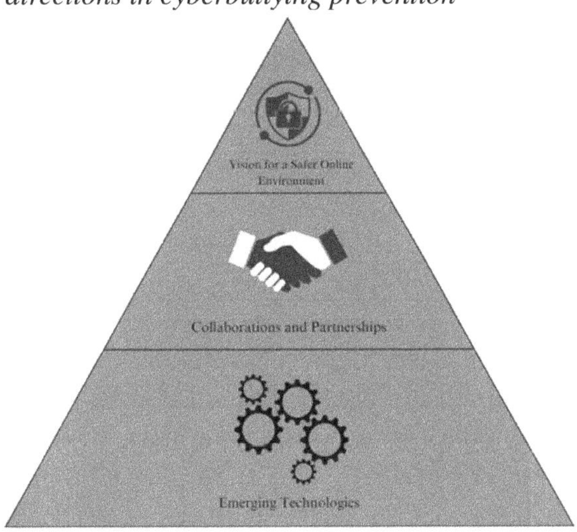

Reinforcement learning is another technology that is promising, whereby an artificial intelligence system learns from real-world data through interaction with it. Unlike the traditional machine learning models that are trained only on static datasets, the RL models have the potential to evolve over time by continually learning new patterns of slang and new cyberbullying trends emerging. This flexibility is most essential in the digital sphere, as language and communication styles change quickly and can be directly applied to comprehending less traditional ways of bullying such as exclusionary tactics or backhanded compliments. In addition, blockchain technology is used for creating an immutable record of online interactions that is not only secure but also transparent. It could keep an immutable ledger of activities that would track user behavior across platforms, enhance accountability by making access to personally identifiable information limited and preserve privacy. Blockchain can support fairer and more secure cyberbullying interventions because users would have much greater confidence that their data are handled in a transparent manner. These emerging technologies could make cyberbullying prevention more accurate, adaptive, and secure if all are adopted in combination.

8.2 Potential Collaborations and Partnerships

Preventing cyberbullying requires the involvement of a diverse range of stakeholders including technology companies, educational institutions, government agencies, mental health organizations, and non-profits. Social media and technology companies are central in their position as home to the majority of online engagements that should be occurring on their platforms. They are best placed for access to data and to work on platform-specific AI tools that can detect and mitigate bullying. In addition, these companies help create community rules, which define what is appropriate behavior and can play an additional role in prevention. Academic institutions, too, are equally vital as the schools and universities engaged in preventive education curriculums that can improve digital etiquette and respectful communication (Singh T. et al., 2024).

Knowledge derived from integrating cyberbullying awareness into curriculums provides educational support to help students understand online action impact and supports reporting of such behavior. It is through such a relationship with academic institutions that technology providers can gain insights about youth behavior and refine algorithms to enhance bullying recognition among younger users. Besides, the mental health organizations would bring needed know-how about the psychological impact of cyberbullying and could be a great source for developing AI systems sensitive to mental health.(Singh, T. M. et al., 2024) It should therefore lead to better support for victims and early interventions for potential victims. Government agencies, for their part, will be responsible for taking action to enact policies that guarantee individuals' privacy and proper data use, as the needs of prevention weigh against individual rights. The multi-stakeholder approach brings together the unique strength of each partner in a comprehensive ecosystem to deal with cyberbullying adequately.

CONCLUSION

In brief, this paper pointed out that AI plays a more significant role in detecting and preventing cyberbullying. In conclusion, methodologies rooted in AI technology, those that rely on natural language processing and machine learning, clearly outperform others in terms of speed and adaptability. This is because AI technology can assume huge chunks of data and spot minute behavioral changes in a way that makes detection far more accurate and active. However, addressing data privacy issues, algorithmic bias, and ethical considerations will pose some significant challenges in such a way that even AI-related applications are effective and fair.

The stakeholders-the educators, tech companies, policymakers, and mental health professionals-have much to reflect on. Importantly, platforms can help make the online environment safer by including AI-based cyberbullying detection tools that safeguard users, especially vulnerable youth. Policymakers have an ethical responsibility to guide; and even an educator can get noticed showing the use of such technologies to raise awareness and advocacy for digital well-being. The best would be for the technology developers, researchers, and stakeholders to team up to take the best from AI tools so that they may stand as ethically balanced and dependable allies in creating a respectable and safe online space.

REFERENCES

Adeyinka, O. Chidubem, Ejiofor., Samuel, Sarpong., Success, Imakuh., Christian, Bassey., Iheanyichukwu, Opara., Josiah, Nii, Armah, Tettey., Omolola, Akinola. (2024). Attribute-specific Cyberbullying Detection Using. *Artificial Intelligence*. Advance online publication. DOI: 10.30564/jeis.v6i1.6206

Aigerim, Toktarova., Daniyar, Sultan., Zhanar, Azhibekova. (2024). Review of Machine Learning Models in Cyberbullying Detection Problem. 233-238. DOI: 10.30564/jeis.v6i1.6206

Fowler, T. (2024). Technology and the limitations of artificial intelligence. ResearchGate. Retrieved from https://www.researchgate.net/profile/Thomas-Fowler-6?_tp=eyJjb250ZXh0Ijp7ImZpcnN0UGFnZSI6InB1YmxpY2F0aW9uIiwicGFnZSI6InB1YmxpY2F0aW9uIn19

Hagendorff, T., & Wezel, K. (2020). 15 challenges for AI: Or what AI (currently) can't do. *AI & Society*, 35(2), 355–365. DOI: 10.1007/s00146-019-00886-y

Hinduja, S., & Patchin, J. W. (2018). *Cyberbullying Research Summary: Cyberbullying and Suicide*. Cyberbullying Research Center.

Kang, B.-G., & Nam, Y. (2024). Innovative artificial intelligence solution as game changer in cyberbullying detection and prevention. Artificial Intelligence in Cybersecurity, 1, 52–59. https://sciencesforce.com

Kishor Kumar Reddy, C. (2023). *Pullisani Satvika, Marlia Mohd Hanafiah, Srinath Doss, "An Efficient early Diagnosis and Healthcare Monitoring System for Mental Disorder using Machine Learning*. Intelligent Engineering Applications and Applied Sciences for Sustainability IGI Global.

Kordzadeh, N., & Ghasemaghaei, M. (2022). Algorithmic bias: Review, synthesis, and future research directions. *European Journal of Information Systems*, 31(3), 388–409. DOI: 10.1080/0960085X.2021.1927212

Kowalski, R. M., Giumetti, G. W., Schroeder, A. N., & Lattanner, M. R. (2014). Bullying in the Digital Age: A Critical Review and Meta-Analysis of Cyberbullying Research Among Youth. *Psychological Bulletin*, 140(4), 1073–1137. DOI: 10.1037/a0035618 PMID: 24512111

Kowsik Godavarthi, S. M., Surya Vishnu Ganimisetty,Sreekar Palanati,Radhika Rani Chintala,Venkata Praveen Chennamsetty, (2024), "Confronting the Offensive Stalking Risks: With Standing Cyber Stalkers", 2024 International Conference on Advances in Computing, Communication and Applied Informatics (ACCAI), pp. 1-7, DOI: 10.1109/ACCAI61061.2024.10602125

Maher, D. (2008). Cyberbullying: An ethnographic case study of one Australian upper primary school class. *Youth Studies Australia*, 27(4), 50.

Majel Monisha, B. (2024). AI powered Cyberbullying Detection Model. *International Scientific Journal of Engineering and Management*, 03(04), 1–9. DOI: 10.55041/ISJEM01529

Mark, A. (2024). *Goldstein,Myrna Chandler Goldstein, "Cyberbullying", How Technology,social media, and Current Events Profoundly Affect Adolescents.* Oxford University Press.

Noni, R. (2024). Cyberbullying: The Silent Epidemic of The Digital Age. Journal of World Science. *Riviera Publishing Vol.*, 3(6), 691–697. DOI: 10.58344/jws.v3i6.634

Pascucci, A., Masucci, V., & Monti, J. "Computational Stylometry and Machine Learning for Gender and Age Detection in Cyberbullying Texts," in 2019 8th International Conference on Affective Computing and Intelligent Interaction Workshops and Demos (ACIIW), 2019, pp. 1–6. DOI: 10.1109/ACIIW.2019.8925101

Patcha, A., & Park, J.-M. (2007). An overview of anomaly detection techniques: Existing solutions and latest technological trends. *Computer Networks*, 51(12), 3448–3470. DOI: 10.1016/j.comnet.2007.02.001

Patchin, J. W., & Hinduja, S. (2010). Cyberbullying: An Update and Synthesis of the Literature. *Aggression and Violent Behavior*, 15(3), 220–233.

Prayuni, A., Harahap, H. S., Ramud, F., & Siregar, A. M. MesionoMesiono (2024) "Cyberbullying Prevention and Intervention Strategies at High School",- Edutec (STIE Mahardika), Vol. 7, Iss: 4

Ravi, S. S. (2023). Cyberbullying: The Panorama for Prevention and Overcoming Cyberbullying. In T. Murugan & N. E. (Eds.), Handbook of Research on Data Science and Cybersecurity Innovations in Industry 4.0 Technologies (pp. 398-417). IGI Global Scientific Publishing. DOI: 10.4018/978-1-6684-8145-5.ch020

Reddy Chinthala, K. K., Thakur, M. S., Shuaib, M., & Alam, S. (2024). *Prospects of Computational Intelligence in Society: Human-Centric Solutions.* Challenges, and Research Areas. Journal of Computational and Cognitive Engineering., DOI: 10.47852/bonviewJCCE42023330

Schneider, E. F.. (2012). Cyberbullying and Academic Performance: A Multilevel Analysis of the Role of School Climate. *Journal of School Psychology*, 50(3), 337–348.

Shahnata, Putri., Dwi Ramadhani, Rina Arum Prastyanti (2024) "Protection Against Cyberbullying for Teens in the United States", The Easta Journal Law and Human Rights, (PT. Sanskara Karya Internasional), Vol. 2, Iss: 03, pp 147-156

Siddiqui, S., & Schultze-Krumbholz, A. (2023). Successful and emerging cyberbullying prevention programs: A narrative review of seventeen interventions applied worldwide. *Societies (Basel, Switzerland)*, 13(9), 212. DOI: 10.3390/soc13090212

Singh, T. M., & Lippert, K. (2024). Digital Twins in Human Activity Prediction on Gait Using Extreme Gradient Boosting Local Binary Pattern: Healthcare 6.0. In Dubey, A., Kumar Reddy, C., Doss, S., & Hanafiah, M. (Eds.), *Exploring the Advancements and Future Directions of Digital Twins in Healthcare 6.0* (pp. 240–261). IGI Global., DOI: 10.4018/979-8-3693-5893-1.ch012

Singh, T. M., Reddy, C. K. K., & Lippert, K. (2024). Advancing Human-Centric Solutions: The Future Trajectory of Soft Computing in Modern Society. In Kumar, N., Pal, S., Agarwal, P., Rosak-Szyrocka, J., & Jain, V. (Eds.), *Human-Machine Collaboration and Emotional Intelligence in Industry 5.0* (pp. 1–18). IGI Global., DOI: 10.4018/979-8-3693-6806-0.ch001

Smokowski, P. R., & Evans, C. B. R. (2024). Cyberbullying: Playground Politics (and Worse) in Cyberspace. In *Bullying and Victimization Across the Lifespan* (pp. 107–122). Springer.

Vaishali, U. (2023). *Gongane., Mousami, V., Munot., Alwin, D., Anuse.* Explainable AI for Reliable Detection of Cyberbullying., DOI: 10.1109/PuneCon58714.2023.10450132

Wankhade, M., Rao, A. C. S., & Kulkarni, C. (2022). A survey on sentiment analysis methods, applications, and challenges. *Artificial Intelligence Review*, 55(7), 5731–5780. DOI: 10.1007/s10462-022-10144-1

Willard, N. E. (2007). *Cyberbullying and cyberthreats: Responding to the challenge of online social aggression, threats, and distress*. Research press.

Zhang, Z. (2024). *"Cyberbullying: A Comprehensive Analysis of its Psychological Impact and Preventive Measures", Journal of education, humanities and social sciences* (Vol. 26). Darcy & Roy Press Co. Ltd.

Chapter 8
Using AI to Combat Sexism Among Facebook Shona Users in Zimbabwe

William Chakabwata
https://orcid.org/0000-0002-4224-5239
University of South Africa, South Africa

ABSTRACT

The chapter interrogated sexism and misogyny which is displayed against women on Facebook in Zimbabwe. The hostile engagements tend to close space for women on such key social media platforms which is vital for building social networks, for business engagements and for learning. This exclusion of women for fear of being harassed leads to further marginalization of women in politics, business and education. A case study of China is submitted as a country that monitors social media in both ex -ante and ex- post. The chapter uses ambivalent sexism theory, decolonial theory, deconstruction theory and postcolonial theory. The chapter postulates the use of Artificial Intelligence to control the profanity that is directed against women and people of other sexualities. The chapter also reviewed the international, continental and regional framework that supports gender equality.

INTRODUCTION

The objective of this chapter was to interrogate the strategies that could be employed to eliminate sexism and misogyny on Facebook, which is a form of cyberbullying. There is a burgeoning of sexist and misogynistic statements on Facebook, which demean women and perpetuate gender negative stereotypes. The people who purvey the stereotypes range from young people, to women who perceive themselves as

DOI: 10.4018/979-8-3373-0543-1.ch008

custodians of the patriarchal systems, norms and values, and who are committed to some kind of activism to ascertain that women are kept in the traditional position assigned to them. The objectives of the chapter are aligned to the Sustainable Development Goal 5, which seeks to empower all women and girls. Gender equality is explicated as a fundamental right that is central to sustainable development and to peace and a prosperous world. Although it is averred that there has been progress over the years, misogynistic tendencies on social media platforms such as Facebook threaten to undermine the progress by cyberbullying practices that seek to entrench misogynistic tendencies. The chapter also sought to examine the progress towards gender equality that has been made over the years, by exploring the Universal Declarations of Human Rights (UDHR), Conventions on the Elimination of Discrimination against Women and Children (CEDAW). Other key international declarations that were explored included Beijing Declaration and Platform for Action and Paris Platforms for Gendering Platforms. At a continental level, the chapter explored the African Union (AU) gender policy and Maputo protocol on the rights of women in Africa. At a regional level the chapter explored the Southern African Development Community (SADC) protocol on gender and development. At a local level the chapter's objective is to explore the constitutional framework that undergirds gender equality in Zimbabwe. The chapter also explored the evolution of gender within the decolonial theory that is a composite of theories that argue that gender was imposed on Africa during the process of imposition of a western culture on Zimbabwe. The chapter argued that there were no social classes in Africa prior to colonialism that created a hierarchical structure. The gender hierarchical structure was a component of the western binary system that was based on Africa using the Cartesian model. The gender social hierarchy was institutionalized by colonial administrators and has become resilient after political independence in Zimbabwe. The chapter also explored the evolution of Facebook as a social media platform and the way that platform has evolved over time to dominant learning and social spaces. In addition, challenges that are related to monitoring Facebook, as a purveyor of social information given the complexity of identifying what is appropriate and what is demeaning. The evolution of artificial Intelligence (AI) holds tremendous potential for regulating behaviour that is deemed to be offensive on Facebook. This can be accomplished by the use of algorithms that include Large Language Models (LLM). LLM is a computational model that is intended for language processing. Large language models have the potential to identify offensive languages on Facebook and to block such information on the social media platform. The challenges of using AI as a tool for regulation social media such as Facebook were examined.

The chapter was guided ambivalent sexism, deconstruction, decolonial and post structural theories. Finally, given the contested nature of language use, the chapter postulated recommendations on actions that needs to be done to create friendly social spaces for women on social media. Although AI can play a significant role in curtailing sexist tendencies on social media, it has its own shortcomings. In the final analysis it is the education of people in Zimbabwe on gender equality that can have a lasting effect on the way people engage on Facebook and in creating safe spaces for women on social media.

Background

The evolution of Facebook as a social media platform can be traced to 2004. The founder of Facebook is Mark Zuckerberg and his colleagues, who intended to create an online directory among students at Harvard students (Jalan, 2023). Initially only Harvard students were permitted to create accounts, and this was opened up to allow students from other colleges and it climaxed to one million accounts by September 2004. Currently, Facebook is acknowledged as the biggest social media platform. The number of Facebook users rose to 6 million users by December 2005. The social media platform also developed multiple innovations over time such as newsfeed, timeline where users can post their content, and it is declared that the number of users has reached nearly 3 billion in 2021. Access to this social media platform is free, and the company earns its income from advertisements. Facebook is headquartered in Meno Park California (Hall, 2024). The Facebook avails multiple opportunities for social engagements which includes status which can inform a person's friends about their location, news feeds which enables patrons to inform their colleagues about changes to their social status, and a facility to engage with friends through private chats.

This chapter will focus on newsfeeds where patrons are able to communicate their content. Facebook is currently facing a huge challenge of dealing with burgeoning misogyny on Facebook (Chemaly, 2013). Cyberbullying on social media has assumed multiple guises such as threat of physical harm on women. There is a frequent display of content on Facebook that is intended to demean women and intimidate them to silence on issues, thus excluding them from the social media platform through hurling of abusive words, threats of violence and use of stereotypical invectives. Facebook only reacts to complaints when they are formally submitted to them, given the massive number of users getting close to 3 billion people, this becomes almost impracticable. There is massive use of gender insensitivity vitriol on Facebook, which makes it challenge to manage this violent social space for an ordinary person. Violence assumes various forms such as the display of violent videos of domestic violence, use of violent words intended to objectify women and transmission of teaching that seek to uphold the perception of women as male properties. Most progressive people have indicated displeasure at the way rape and other forms of violence against women are treated with frivolity on Facebook making it a hostile space for female participation.

Zhu (2024) noted that cyberbullying has assumed the use of sexist speech, misogyny and threatening language. Even during the time of the #metoo there was a spate of uncouth reprisals against women, who came out to share their experiences. History reflects that language has in general been employed to advance male interests or patriarchy. This has intensified with the advent of social media platforms such as Facebook. Social media has created a platform where chauvinistic perspectives can be diffused in a short space of time. The propagation of the information shared can easily go viral, with very limited monitoring or regulation mechanism. Personal attacks and vitriol is launched against women and marginalised gender in a way that excludes women from engaging in discourse on social media space and which translates to periphelisation of women from media, politics, academia and business among other forms.

Bartlett and Krasodomski-Jones (2015) averred that Facebook has instituted a number of policies to prohibit the use of hate speech on social media. Facebook prohibits and eliminates postings that reflect hate speech. Bartlett and Krasodomski-Jones (2015, p5) expounded that hate speech has been characterised as content "that directly attacks people based on their race, ethnicity, national origin, religious affiliation, sexual orientation, gender identity, serious disabilities or diseases". In spite of this prohibition, people still post hate speech that is noticeable on Facebook. Many countries are brainstorming ways to enhance safety online for children. For example, United Kingdom enacted the Online Safety Act 2023, which is intended to make tech firms responsible for content shared on their platforms. The act is intended to make online environment safe, particularly for children by ensuring that the tech firms eliminate deterimental content such as suicide data, speedily and to ensure safety of children from sexualised content (Ofcom, 2024). Tech firms will be required to have a position within the firm occupied by a person with a duty to report on illegal content.

SEXISM AS A FORM OF VIOLENCE

Violence against women is seen as pervasive in most societies. Alves et a l., (2021) explained that sexism is a form of violence expressed in the form of prejudice against a group or category, in this case women. This form of violence takes the form of practice based on imagination, myth, worldview and beliefs which justify femicide. Sexism is reflected in an obdurate attitude against women. Leaper (2024) averred that sexism has primarily been directed towards women and persons of other sexualities that are non –heteronormative, which includes lesbians, gays and queer identities. The manifestations of sexism may differ among cultures and also among groups that are perceived to be minorities.

Sexism is associated with the manifestation of hegemonic masculinity, which normalises the display and tolerance of dominance among men and boys. Manifestations of aggressive tendencies are also perceived as normal in boys. Aggressive behaviour is also displayed towards those who do not conform to heteronormative sexuality, in order to force them to conform. The next section discusses ambivalent sexism theory to shed light on practices of sexism and misogyny.

Ambivalent Sexism Theory

Glick and Fiske (2011) postulated that ambivalent sexism which sought to account for ways in which sexism is evidenced in mundane situations. The ambivalent sexism theory was inspired by research on ambivalence in the area of racism. It is noted that with the advent of the civil rights movements in the United States, racism was no longer as explicit as in the past, but had become more subtle and ambivalent. It was the same premise that Glick and Fiske adopted and applied to sexism. Sengupta et al., (2024) expounds that sexist beliefs crystalise in two forms of attitudes towards women which are benevolent attitudes and hostile attitudes. Benevolent attitudes assume the form of an rarefied view of women as peculiarly caring, very principled and demanding the protection of men. Hostile sexism constitute explicitly negative beliefs about women and reflects women as cunning, eager to grab power, and supersensitive.

Both components in this theory, the benevolent and hostile segments, are employed to uphold unequal power relations in society in subtle ways. The benevolent theory as the protector of females is a legitimising of male power (Sengupta et al.,2024; Glick & Fiske, 2011; Alves et al.,2021). The condescending elements of benevolent attitudes indirectly reinforces male authority through the practice of gender norms. Benevolent gender views has the capacity of undercutting women's employment opportunities and participation in public spaces such as business and politics. It is very complex to tackle violence against women, due to this ambivalence which generates both idealised view of women and also antipathy. Idealised version of women institute unattainable standards for women which makes women to be exposed to punitive treatment, once it is noted that they are failing to live up to the lofty ideals. While benevolent sexism promulgate that women needs to be protected, yet in actuality they fail to secure the safety of women from violence. On the Facebook platform gender stereotypes are perpertuated not only by men, but also by women. The discourses by women are evidence of stereotypes inherent in patriarchal society, in which the female population are socialised to act in line with societal gender constructions, enabling the system to be sustained and reproduced. The next section discusses the experiences of women in Zimbabwe on Facebook.

A Case Study on Experience of Women in Zimbabwe on Facebook

In this part of the chapter a case of Zimbabwean's women participation on Facebook and attendant cyberbullying practices are explored. Moffat (2024) explicated cyberbullying as impacting all categories of people from children, boys, women and men. Cyberbullying transpires when a group of people deliberately transmit communication on social media and online platforms in the form of pictures, videos or words to harass or threaten an individual or group. Bullying can transpire through emails, webpages or messaging facilities. The most damaging part of cyberbullying is that it has global impact and can reach multitudes in an instant. Mangena (2020) indicated that the goal of cyberbullying is to instill distress or fear of bodily physical harm. The legal framework in Zimbabwe is currently not able to tackles cases of cyberbullying.

The revised constitution of Zimbabwe of 2013 enshrined the rights to equality, privacy and security to individuals. Zimbabwe is also a signatory to multiple international declarations which upholds human rights and the rights of women in particular, which includes Universal Declaration of Human Rights (UDHR), Convention on the Elimination of Discrimination against Women and regional and continental agreements such as Maputo protocol on the rights of women.

Cyberbullying in Zimbabwe on Facebook assumes the forms of posting pictures that are sexually explicit, sharing such pictures or messages to other people, use of online sexual harassment, name calling and posting of demeaning messages that are meant to close the social media space to women expressing views that are contrary to men (Mangena, 2020; Mutsvairo, 2020). NapoleonCat (2024) adduced that the total number of Facebook users in Zimbabwe were 2 458 700, which translates to 12,7% of the country's population. The largest category constituted males who were 55,2% and females were 46,8%. The age group that is dominant were in the age range of 25-34 years. Cyberbullying in the context of Zimbabwe manifested as leaking of intimate sex tape on Facebook with the intention to humiliate or embarrass by an ex- partner. Bullying by school mates and threats to post degrading information on Facebook. Use of invectives such as " she is a prostitute and ugly and her vagina was rotten" (Mangena, 2020, p. 37). When sex video are leaked men are perceived as heroes, while women are exposed to demeaning comments. The absence of a holistic legal framework on online sexual harrassment meant that women find it difficult to access justice. Women also lack confidence in the police and their capacity to address cases of sexual violence online. In the case of married women it becomes even more challenging for them to report cases of cyberbullying given the entrenched patriarchal norms and values in Zimbabwe.

Nehanda Centre for Gender and Cultural Studies (2023) noted that violence against female politicians increased around elections in 2013 and 2018. Women activists and politicians were deterred from utilising the Facebook platform, due to the level of hostility directed against them. Female politicians were also exposed to sexualised statements which are lurid such as:

- Who is eating here? By implications, who is having sex with this woman?
- Would you want to be touched by a hand like this?
- Food for senior politicians-referring to women as food
- Go bath first before you give us your views
- Go back to the zoo madam

Female politicians are perceived as politicians who survive by male patronage. Zimbabwe introduced a new bill that later became law which acknowledged officially diverse relationships in Zimbabwe. When this bill was being discussed vulgar comments that degraded women were expressed on social media as the bill for prostitutes (bill remahure). In Zimbabwe sexualised attacks directed against women such as "hapana zvaanoziva ihure ra leader (There is nothing that she knows she is a whore for the male leader). Attacks on female politicians on Facebook also assumes potshots on their bodies, haristyle, beliefs and ideas (Nehanda Centre for Gender and Cultural Studies, 2023).

Zimbabwe has recently introduced the Cyber and Data Protection Act of 2021. This act makes it criminal to divulge a person's private data which may include sex life, membership to political groups, marital status among other sensitive details. In addition, this law does not allow any controller of data to process sensitive information without consent of the persons involved. This actually means the sharing of sensitive data on Facebook can be taken as a criminal offense if there is no consent from all parties. Part 11 in 164S of the act stipulates in a clear terms:

- Sending of a threatening message to another person is perceived as a crime
- Recording of a nudes or video of a person without consent is perceived as a crime
- Cyberbullying is also declared to be a crime

This a newly enacted legislation and it will take time for the people to become aware of it and also to create safe spaces for women on Facebook. The next section looks at the use of global, continental and regional declarations on gender equality.

Global, Continental and Regional Declarations On Gender Equality

In this section of the chapter, global, continental and regional declarations on gender equality are explored. The purpose is to situate the discussion on sexism and misogyny within a context of international, continental and regional agreements to effect gender equality and create equal space for political and social participation of women on Facebook and other virtual spaces. Zimbabwe has extracted some principles from the Universal Declaration of Human Rights (UDHR) 1948, to inform the constitution of the country. The UDHR was declared by the United Nations General Assembly in Paris on 10 December 1948 (United Nations, 2024). The UDHR has inspired numerous documents and treaties on human rights. In a nutshell, UDHR declares in Article 1

All human beings are born free and equal with dignity and rights.

They are endowed with reason and conscience and should act towards one another in a spirit of brotherhood

Equality in the area of gender is yet to be realised on Facebook spaces as evidenced by sexist and misogynistic statements. One of the key declarations on gender equality at a global level is the Convention on the Rights Elimination of All Forms of Discrimination against Women (CEDAW), adopted by the United Nations General Assembly on 18 December 1979. CEDAW was an outcome of more than 30 years of arduous work by the United Nations Commission on the Status of Women, a body instituted in 1946 to monitor and ameliorate the status of women (United Nations, 1979). Zimbabwe ratified CEDAW on 13 May 1991 (United Nations Human Rights Treaty Bodies, 2024). Four world conferences to ameliorate the status of women were held Mexico City in 1975, Copenhagen in 1980, Nairobi in 1985 and Beijing 1995. The 1995 conference held in Beijing was a momentous occasion for realising gender equality. The Beijing Declaration and Platform for Action was adopted by 189 countries with an explicit agenda articulated in objectives on the need to realise gender equality (UNWomen, 2024).

At a continental level Zimbabwe is a member of the African Union (AU), a continental body that uphold gender equality and development. At a regional level, Zimbabwe is a member of Southern African Community (SADC), which also espouse ideals of gender equality, as articulated in SADC protocol on gender equality and development. The SADC protocol on gender foregrounds the need to realise gender equality (Southern African Development Community, 2024). Maputo protocol on the rights of women in Africa, fore fronted the rights of women, which included the right to political participation, guaranteed women's reproductive rights, abolished practices such as genital mutilation and sought to promote social participation of women in all spheres, which by implication participation in social virtual spaces.

AU agenda 2063, was promulgated as the period when all forms of violence and discrimination against women will be a thing of the past. In 2015, countries in the United Nations adopted unanimously the Sustainable Development Goals (SGDs), as a part of the 2030 agenda (World Health Organisation (WHO), 2024). The SDGs constitute 17 Goals that encompass 169 targets. (SDG) 4 urges all countries to ensure that there is provision of equitable and quality education and to advance the lifelong learning opportunities to everyone (McKay, 2018). SDG No 5 expounded the need to attain gender equality and empower all girls by 2030. The next section examines cases where Facebook was employed for to advance social justice.

Use Of Facebook to Promote Gender Equality

Facebook has not been used negatively only to spread sexist messages, but also in a progressive way to enhance the goals of equality. The case of Peru women is spotlighted (Bossio & Diez, 2021). Women in Peru have been exposed to gender -based violence and also constricted political participation. Activists in Peru and North America have employed social media which includes Facebook to create solidarity on the issue of gender equality. Other instances that may be perceived as instances of the use of social media to promote gender equality is the #metoo movement, a movement that sought to end sexual violence against women. Other social movements that sought to promote racial equality such as Black Lives Matter, have also used social media such as Facebook to coordinate a fight against racial inequality, at times by displaying videos of instances of racial profiling or violence based on one's race as perpetrated by the police. The next section explores the genesis of AI and cybernetics.

CYBERNETICS AND ARTIFICIAL INTELLIGENCE

Williamson and Eynon (2020) noted that Artificial Intelligence has become ubiquitous in the world today. The evolution of AI, which we have seen on the Web, on smartphones, and on social media has a long history. The evolution of AI can be traced at least to the genesis of computers and cybernetics in the 1940s. From the mid-1940s research on diverse forms of control grew exponentially in the field of communication. Novikov (2015, p7) indicated that cybernetics is derived from a Greek term that connotes "to steer, navigate or to govern". Furthermore, it concentrates on control of machines or people and organisations. The field of cybernetics has an interdisciplinary nature. The contemporary understanding of cybernetics as a form of control was espoused by Norbert Wiener. Planck (2024) noted that the cybernetics field laid the basis for the contemporary development of AI by Norbert

Wiener. Wiener, who acquired a doctoral qualification at the age of 18, developed an understanding of stochastic processes. AI was influenced by cybernetics although, currently the AI has tended to overshadow cybernetics. Krikke (2024) declared that cybernetics appeared as the first framework that could facilitate a well- organised approach to computing and automation. Cibu et al., (2023) averred that the genesis of cybernetics is found in the gap in scientific understanding, the absence of a well - organised system of understanding dynamics and the delicate interplay with external factors. In order to understand a system using cybernetics, it included portraying data in a simple way, which can be attained through the use of tools like Support Vector Machine or diverse visualisation tools. Furthermore, methodologies such as Bayesian Networks, Neural Networks or Fuzzy Logic were used to create models by applying principles derived from fields which include Supply Chain or Enterprise Management. Cybernetics evolved as an interdisciplinary domain drawing from fields which included physics, mathematics, chemistry, statistics, and medicine among many others.

Martelaro and Ju (2018) noted that at times cybernetics and AI are taken to be the same thing with cybernetics being conceptualised as creating intelligent cyborgs and robots. As a matter of fact, cybernetics and AI represent different ways of designing intelligent systems or systems that can work towards a goal. AI fundamental goal is to mimic intelligent actions derived from information stored data. Cybernetics extends beyond computers to a study of how systems regulate themselves including biological, mechanical and human. For instance, cybernetics can focus on how to manage a workforce, regulate body temperature among other forms of controls. Both systems can focalize on how systems can learn, AI utlilises stored information as a way of acting intelligently, while cybernetics concentrate on situated behaviour that demonstrate intelligence and learning using feedback and engagement. There is a contemporary growth in AI systems that use machine learning techniques that display intelligent behaviour from a huge quantity of data. Examples of the new developments in AI are computer vision systems, which are computers that can identify and label objects with precision and speech-input systems that can process natural language.

Robotics and Mechatronics

Groumpos (2024) averred that Robotics and Mechatronics were developed in the period of 1960s and 1970s. Robotics is an interdisciplinary branch of computer science and engineering which have an explicit goal of producing intelligent machines that can behave like humans and which offer assistance in diverse ways. From the

1950s when the term Robotics was first used, the discipline has expanded to include probabilities Robotics, the use of Robotics for humankind and Robotics and AI.

Soori et al., (2023) explicated AI, Machine Learning (ML), and Deep Learning (DL), have transformed the field of Robbotics in contemporary times.AI, ML, DL have been used in the field of Robbotics to enhance object recognition, language processing and predictive maintenance among many other functions. Soori et al., (2023) expounded that AI, ML, DL are all vital fields in the area of Robotics. The same authors added that AI epitomise machine capacity to implement functions that usually require human intellect, such as decision- making, speech recognition and processing of natural human language. In the context of this chapter AI can be used to identify words that are sexist or misoygnistic on Facebook and block the content from being shared as breaching the ethical foundation of the social media.

Artificial Intelligence and Language Management Models (LMS)

Keinan (2024) noted that the identification of sexism in social networks which includes Facebook has become a daunting issue in the domain of Natural Language Processing (NLP). Isolating and categorising the sexist content in social media is critical for creating inclusive spaces for all genders on Facebook. Facebook as other social media platforms can serve as a negative platform that can undermine the struggle for gender equality through positing of content that is sexist and other socially inappropriate behaviours. It is for that reason that it is opined that developing tools for identifying sexist behaviours in real time is crucial and assisting in identifying how sexism transpires in real time (Rodguez-Sanchez, et al., 2021; Tian et al., 2023; Mohammadi, Giachanou et al.,2024). Tian et al.,(2023) expounded that sexism may be scrutinised based on sexism identification, source intention, and sexism categorisation. Zhang et al., (2024) averred that Large Language Models (LMS) have been employed in fields such as natural language processing and computer vision. LMS have gained popularity today in terms of processing text, creating text, translation, responding to questions and compiling summaries. LMS use time series data which include classification, forecasting, and imputation have been used. This area has also been revolutionised by the use of Long Short Term Memory Networks and Transformers, which has been used to draw data from time series data. Computer Vision (CV) epitomised by the use of CHATGPT-4 have radically changed the terrain of text processing, provision of summaries and text generation.

Das, et al., (2023) noted that discrimination and misogyny assumes diverse forms on social media. The same authors postulated that identification of sexism using NLP models and state of the art models may be utilised to perform detection of sexism using the binary method and fine -tuned sexist detection which further processes the category to which a sexist utterance or sentence belongs to. Work has been expended in isolating hate speech on social media and the approach that has been used widely is termed Bag-of–Words (BOW) technique. Early technological developments used to identify hate speech were learning based classifiers for detecting abuse (Noh, et al., 2024). Learning based classifiers refers to a machine learning approach in which the machine endeavour to predict the appropriate category of a given set of data. A pattern based technique refers to data modelling frequencies that recur regularly in practice and offers guidelines on recognising these guidelines. There are a number of tools that could be utilised to identify abuse on social media. For instance N-Gram feature is a potent tool for natural language processing. N-Gram utilises multiple vectors which a give number of specific words, using identified specific words. There is also ML based classifier to isolate abusive words on internet (Asogwa et a l., 2022). ML based classifiers were built using a dictionary format. Other efforts to protect women on the internet includes MEME detection by isolating sexist language. Cao, et al., (2024) indicated that the MEME which transmit personal opinion and worldviews across the internet holds potential to propagate bias and stereotypes. MEME which may be perceived as deleterious have potential to sustain and reproduce stereotypes and prejudice. AI Singapore has introduced an innovation, which termed online Price Challenge that is motivated by the need to develop technologies that can with efficacy detect meme that are pernicious. One of the programmes that could be employed to analyse meme is called BLPI model for which turns images into descriptive text to enable efficacious language analysis through LMS. Optical Character Recognition (OPR) is utilised to isolate and transcribe the text on the meme.

Using Counter-Speech to Combat Hate Speech

The definition of hate speech is elusive as with other political terms, which makes it a challenge to implement a universal policy (Chiu et al.,2022). Different countries or places of jurisdiction may utilise different terms. Detecting hate speech is complex due to an interplay of multiple factors which include identity of the person, the person being spoken to, the topic that people are interacting on and events occuring outside that engagements. If hate speech is not accurately identified it can raise legal issues. At times it is very complex to distinguish between offensive and hate speech. Bartlett and Krasodomski-Jones (2015) expounded that Facebook employs a device called counter-speech to try and stop the proliferation of hate speech. Facebook employs a strategy termed counter-speech, which is a form of disapprove and counter -campaign on Facebook. Zheng et al.,(2023) postulated that counter-speech is emerging as a very effective way to combat hate speech on social media platforms including Facebook. Counter speech is designed to refute false information, rebut stereotypes while promoting free speech. Natural Language Processing (NLP) techniques can be utilised to counter hate speech.

A number of models have been proposed to tackle the pervasive effects of hate speech on Facebook which includes Bidirectional Encoder Representative from Transformers (BERT), Bidirectional and Auto-Regressive Transformer (BART) and Generative Pretrained Transformer (GPT).GPT is perceived as one of the techniques produced in 2020 that has functioned well in NLP.GPT is a language model that is to generates deep- learning and display understanding. Large Language Models (LLM), acquire the capacity to generate language by establishing statistical relationship between from text data during a computational monitored and semi-monitored training activity (Tinparinus, 2024). LLM can be utilized for text creation by using an input text and then predicting the next word or token. GPT -3 has the ability to obtain knowledge about syntax semantics, and the nature of words used by people. There are multiple NLPs that are able to process, mine, connect and to respond effectively to questions.

The Training of GPT Models

GPT means that the model is provided with huge data during the training phase in order to assist it, in identify patterns between words and phrases and sentences. Furthermore, the model uses deep language algorithms to recognize patterns between words during training and to apprehend and generate a language that resembles human speech (Tinparinus, 2024). Training is vital for creating effective language processing models, as it enables the model to learn from enormous amount of data and to improve its effectiveness and precision as it executes tasks such as answering questions, creating text and generating language. When the data is collected it goes through a cleaning and preprocessing process. Data cleaning involves the elimination of extraneous data and distinct features. In addition, the data is divided into manageable units such as words or word categories. The model then undergoes training on anticipating missing words. After the training phase a model can be assigned to a given task such as task classification or language translation. The model can then be tested on smaller dataset and its effectiveness can then be measured using a metric.

WEAKNESS OF USING AI IN IDENTIFYING SEXISM ON FACEBOOK

Nadeem et al., (2022) explicated while AI holds the tremendous capacity to enhance the lives of the people, it also has some drawbacks. AI holds the capacity to reinforce gender roles and disparities by the use of language in the programmes. The use of AI is associated with raising concerns in the area of gender bias, decisions that can impact on marginalised communities or groups. The use of AI on Facebook has been associated with gender bias in the form of job ads that seek to privilege males for opportunities in Science, Technology, EngIneering, and Mathematics (STEM) and in access to loans due to lack of dataset in the training package. AI decisions have become a hallmark of the digital economy, at the same time the dentological concerns such as transparency, fairness and accountability have been associated with their application in various fields. AI models are just as effective as the data that they are instructed on. For instance, the use of ChatGPT, it is noted that it functions on data that may be a bit outdated as shown on some of the recommendations. AI has also been noted to generate data that is not easy to work with and which the user may find challenging to use (SocialPilot, 2024).

Chiu et al.,(2022) noted that NLP are capable of generating text that is hateful. A case in point is the Tweeter Chatbot produced by Microsoft in 2016, created content that was sexist within a few hours of its operations. The dataset that is used to train LLM, are taken from the entire internet which is dominated primarily by a Eurocentric knowledge system and it therefore poses challenges of exclusion, marginalisation and exposure. As a result dataset from the US may reflect overrepresentation of white sexist, misogynistic and ageist content. There is also a tendency to universalise based on the use of words such as always,never and everybody. Overgeneralisation is derived from the assumption that what is noted in the dataset actually occurs, yet they may be employed in a rhetorical rather than literal meaning. NLP are not capable of making a distinction in such cases and they tend to draw inferences and universalise. Finally, exposure refers to the extent that importance is attached to a thing. For instance, when it comes to languages, English may enjoy wider exposure than Shona language which the majority of the people in Zimbabwe uses. Scholars have also acknowledged the constrictions that machines have in identifying cyber-bullying when compared to humans.

Controlling social media such as Facebook, is a mammoth task given the reality that it transcends various cultural groupings, the elites may not strike a consensus on what is acceptable and what is not appropriate and also the ethical issues associated with the individual privacy and the freedom of expression (Li & Zhou, 2014). These challenges are so immense that they cannot be addressed by simply using more human moderators. Facebook has many moderators distributed across the globe, although it has been censored for failing to give them adequate resources (Vincent, 2020).

A Case Study of China and Control Of Social Media

China has developed tools for moderating engagements on social media, just as other western countries. However, there is a distinction between how China manages the social media when contrasted with western nations (Li & Zhou, 2014). The western nations have sought to manage social media such as Facebook in a reactive way that is termed ex-post reactive moderation, in China the media posting are controlled both before and after the posting. For example, Facebook is moderated in China, in a manner that may be described as ex-ante or reactive has eliminated content that is linked to child abuse or images associated with terrorism.

In the case of China when a video is posted online, it is immediately subjected to a series of screening stages which includes collection of frames, which enable the description, title and names to be extricated on the platforms and then deviance which may assume forms such as child sexual exploitation, inappropriate political inclinations and sexism may be detected and eliminated. Each content is further processed into categories that are intended to reflect the gravity of the posting, for instance distasteful, vulgar, and soft porn and sexually explicit. AI is used in this process (Li & Zhou, 2014).China enforces both ex-ante and ex-post to moderate the social platforms. The moderating approach used in China does not merely forefront the posting, but also scrutinises the comments on the posting, thus acknowledging that people are networked through social media, and they tend to reflect social values.

China has linked its national security programme together with efforts to ensure safe content online. In addition, China approach is proactive and it allows only sharing of content that is beneficial to users. The case study shows that China has been able to create a safe environment for its social media users by using a proactive approach.

DECOLONIAL THEORY

Ramirez et al., (2024) adduced that decolonial feminism refers to ways of decoupling and disengaging from colonial ways of social organisation, way of life and Eurocentric epistemic system. In order to fully apprehend decolonial feminism, it is imperative to embrace the legacy of racialisation, as race and subjugation of women are interlocked. Rodrigues (2022) indicated that decolonial feminism forefronts coloniality and colonial system based on gender.

Decoloniality was developed in Latin America and is employed in local and across previously colonised states to resist legacies and contemporary patterns of power instituted by internal and external colonialism. It is a reaction by people who were previously colonised to the colonial systems of power. It epitomises a way of looking at the world through a new epistemic lens that is different from the

Eurocentric view and that encapsulates the experiences of other people who were previously marginalised. Lugones (2010) explicated modernity as placing the world ontologically in categories that are separate, distinct and homogeneous. These categories are then applied on a universal scale to all people ignoring the diversity and intersecting experiences of people and culture. Modernity structured people experiences into categories of human and non- human and where the normative being were western men supported by western women.

Chakabwata (2023) indicated that feminism has a global agenda to end sexism and misogyny even on social media platforms such as Facebook. However, feminism is not a homogeneous movement as it reflects strands such as black feminism, white feminism, African feminism and Third world feminism. Decolonial feminism reflects all the processes and ways of interpreting the social world. Tamale (2020) avers that although patriarchy has its roots in male power and while there could be convergence in the experiences of women, the focus and trajectory of African feminists can not be taken as being synonymous with those of Western feminist women. The reason is not merely that race is a key element of gender, but that the recalcitrant effect of slavery, colonialism and imperialism continue to interlock with patriarchal power and generate subjugation of women in ways that are unique to Africa and other places that were colonised. Western feminism is premised on the dualism of male versus female, husband versus wife and private versus public space, which creates tension within each category.

One of the ways to decolonise feminism is to explore the gender system that was prevalent in Africa prior to colonialism, then discuss the gender system that was imposed on Africa during colonialism and then the persistent gender sexism and misogyny that continue to pervade the life of many people in Africa and previously colonised states in general and Zimbabwe in particular. Decoloniality seeks to challenge the coloniality of power. Ramirez et al., (2024) expound that decolonial feminism seeks to dismantle the logic of modernity. Colonialism inagurated the origins of coloniality of power where the policies and practices introduced were designed to dehumanise people of other races and instituted binary relations between men and women undergirded by Christian religious system. It is this new social hierarchy set up during the colonial administration that was racialized and gendered which has led to continuity of sexism and misogynistic practices after independence, which is now reflected on Facebook.

Oyeyumi (1997) asserted that most African societies prior to colonialism were heterarchical at times led by Queens and there were no social organisation based on gender in most states.

DECONSTRUCTION THEORY

In this part the philosophical foundation of deconstruction are explored. Sikirivwa (2020) asserted that deconstruction is a theory of reading text or any words. Deconstruction came to the fore at the time of structuralism. Structuralism is a technique of scrutinising language, ideas and society and concentrate on comparing ideas and or components of a structure to demonstrate ways in which they relate to the entire fabric. Structuralism submitted that each word has a meaning and so does the larger text (Gaw, 2013). Language cannot be isolated from the political and social milieu in which it was created and used. Deconstruction urges us not to be attached to language, and adds that we must be able to remove ourselves from the context and examine the situation identifying inherent biases and weaknesses. In the context of this chapter the way language is used against women on social media reflects the systemic inequalities in Zimbabwean society, that takes for granted the superiority of men over women. The term deconstruction is derived from the French word " deconstuire" which in English means " to undo improvement of, or development of, to take to pieces" (Sikirivwa, 2020, p. 43). Deconstruction owes its origins to the work of Jacques Derrida in the 1960s. In every day parlance deconstruction has come to mean a critique of traditions and traditional modes of thoughts. Deconstruction probes the assumptions that are inherent in western mode of thought, which are based on binary thinking. Instances of the terms that are used include inside versus outside, indirect and implicit and intelligent versus sensible (Britannica, 2024).

Alqudah (2019) declared that deconstruction is a theory about language and literature that evolved in the 1960s. It is perceived to be one of the key theories in post structural developments. The tendency to probe the claims of truth can be traced to Frederick Neitzche, who questioned the concepts of truth as being a spiritually fixed entity that transcends language. Neitzsche perceived language as an expression of power and an effort to establish truth that is fixed, when it is unstable and dynamic. Deconstruction rejects claims that truth can be ascertained by the use of certain methodological tools. Deconstruction also posits that knowledge is situated in the text and doesn't not need to be proved to be real by a certain method. Sexism is systematic in society and is based on the ideas of one gender being superior to another.

POSTSTRUCTURAL THEORY

Angermuller (2020) indicated that poststructural theory emerged around 1960s and 1970s, among some theorists in France who Saussure differentialist theory of language.The term poststructural was popularised in the 1980s. In addition poststructural theory created a nexus between language and power which has inspired researchers in humanities and social sciences who study discourse. Poststructural theory was brought in to illustrate how language and power intersect to create discourses that exacerbates inequality on Facebook.

Poststructural theory draws on the work of Focault on language and power. Kolozova (2021) expounded that poststructural feminism appraisals of subject, identity and culture has made huge contribution to feminism and poststructuralism. The feminist poststructural theorising rebuts the notion of sex as a given or a rigid meaning or essence. In essence poststructuralism submits that identities are constructed and they are also political (Willett & Etowa, 2023). Poststructuralim critiques metanarratives and claims of objectivity and logic. Although there are numerous strands of postructuralism in academy, they all converge on the critical analysis of power,subject and reality. It exposes biases, which would in other contexts be offered as neutral categories. It unpacks gender, patriarchal structures, essentialism, social relations, power dynamics and discourses that sustain and reproduce marginalisation of women. The concepts such as gender and race are used in postsructural analysis based on the premise that they are plural and are situated in specific historical and social context. Poststructural theory holds that there is a multiplicity of gender beyond the binary. Morevover postsructural theory rejects the claims of grand narratives to address social challenges such as sexism, poverty and inequality. On Facebook although the vitriol may arguably be directed towards women, other sexualities have also been the target of the abuse on social media, because they manifest gender outside the binary framework.

DISCUSSION

The chapter has noted that in spite of multiple declarations to end gender inequality as espoused in UDHR, CEDAW, and Beijing Conference among many others, sexism and misogyny has remained dominant on the internet. Part of the reasons for the persistence of sexism and misogyny are the systemic gender inequality that is located in Zimbabwe as in other states. It is inequality that that is rooted in history of racism, colonialism and Cartesian dualism that perceives everything as being organised in opposition and in hierarchy. It is noted that when the French and the British occupied other territories they perceived themselves as the normative race, and also superior to white women. The white race perceived themselves as being superior to other non-white racial groups. These attitudes as articulated by Gramsci become normalised and hegemonic over -time until they cannot be probed. They become a part of the accepted ideology. In this chapter poststructural theory has also been used to display the complexity of gender, in a way that transcends the binary divide. This has also served to exposed biases against women and other sexualities on Facebook and the disparate of power in society. This demonstrates the way power operates through people as opposed to by people (Willett & Etowa, 2023).

In this chapter it was noted that sexism and misogyny assumed a systemic nature in Zimbabwe. The theoretical framework demonstrated that sexism is rooted on the western Cartesian way of thinking which organizes objects in a binary way, where one is superior and another inferior. Many years of colonial rule and implementation of colonial policies has led to a normalisation of women as being inferior to men, a situation that has persisted after political independence as a function of coloniality. This means that although AI, as a tool can be block and eliminate sexist and misogynistic content, so that women are able to actively participant on social media on equal terms with men, a lot of work needs to be done to address deep- rooted misconceptions of gender. There is no silver bullet to address this misogyny and sexism, and it will take years of education and rediscovering the knowledge system that was dominant in Africa prior to colonialism and implementing profound societal transformation to end sexism and misogyny on Facebook.

There are instances of best practices on tackling misogyny in Philippine, where the government has introduced a competition to address sexism and misogyny. The SDG goal No 4 declared the need to realise gender equality by 2030 in a number of designated areas. It is noteworthy that social media platforms such as Facebook have also become major learning spaces. The implication of sexism and misogynistic practices are that once women are excluded from such vital learning and networking spaces, this may translate to marginalization in other areas such as business, politics and education. It is for that reason that sexism and misogyny needs to be addressed as an issue of urgency.

In this chapter it was also averred that monitoring communication on Facebook is a challenging task, albeit not an impossible one. It is for that reason that AI has been postulated as a viable option to identifying sexist and misogynistic postings on Facebook in real- time and blocking them from being shared. In spite of its potential to help address sexism and misogyny on Facebook AI, also has some limitations.

RECOMMENDATIONS

Based on the preceding discussions, it was noted that sexism and misogyny are deeply embedded in Zimbabwe, as in other societies that practice patriarchy. The chapter therefore submitted the following recommendations:

i) The long-term solution is to educate the people on the harmful effects of sexism and misogyny on social media platforms

ii) The development of AI software with the capability of isolating in real- time any effort to post sexist and misogynistic content and blocking it.
iii) The implementation of policy frameworks that makes posting misogynistic comments or videos a punishable offence
iv) Revisiting Zimbabwe value system prior to independence in order to enhance the self-awareness of the people that is based on a different knowledge system and ethics, which are different from the Cartesian knowledge system
v) Developing competition in Zimbabwe on the development of software that can be used to end sexism and misogyny on Facebook as shown in the case of Philippine.
vi) It is important to develop moderating software that is proactive as opposed to being reactive, using the best practices demonstrated in China.

CONCLUSION

In this chapter the sexism and misogyny displayed against women on Facebook were discussed. It was noted that these tendencies display profound systematic inequalities in society. The chapter used ambivalent sexist theory, decolonial theory and deconstruction theory. Ambivalent theory reflected ways in which sexist attitude assume in men. Decolonial theory sought to illustrate how gender interlocks with other multiple variables such as race among communities that were previously colonized to create coloniality and numerous other disadvantages. The chapter also explored various ways in which AI could be employed to detect sexist misogynistic language in real time and censure it. The legal declarations that underpin gender equality were explored at global, continental and regional levels including UDHR, CEDAW and Maputo protocol among many others. The significance of SDG 4 was foregrounded. In the final analysis it will take a lot of effort and concerted effort to rid Facebook of stereotypical and abusive language and create space for women to network and participant on this vital form of social media.

REFERENCES

Alqudah, M. (2019). Deconstruction: A conurcopia of esoteric meanings. *International Journal of English Literature and Social Sciences (IJELS) Vol-4, Issue-2*, 500-503.

Alves, N. F., de Souza, L. E., Maia, L., Silva, R. N., & de Menese Gomes, A. (2021). Women on Facebook: An analysis based on ambivalent sexism. *São Paulo, v. 44, n. 1*, 131-145.

Angermuller, J. (2020). Poststructuralist Discourse Studies: From Structure to Practice. In *A. de Fina, & A. Georgakopoulou, The Cambridge Handbook of Discourse Studies* (pp. 235–254). Routledge. DOI: 10.1017/9781108348195.012

Asogwa, D., Chukwuneke, C., Ngene, C., & Anigbogu, G. (2022). Hate speech classification using SVM and naive BAYES. *IOSR Journal of Mobile Computing & Application (IOSR-JMCA) Volume 9, Issue 1*, 27-34.

Bartlett, J., & Krasodomski-Jones, A. (2015). *Counter-speech examining content that challenges extremism online*. Demos.

Bossio, J., & Diez, I. (2021). Women solidarity and social media: Sisterhood concept and #Lasresondonas, A Facebook Group in Peru. *Proceedings of the 1st Virtual Conference on Implications of Information and Digital Technologies for Development* (pp. 500-511). Peru: Communications Department, Pontificia Universidad Católica del Perú.

Britannica. (2024, 12 4). *Deconstruction criticism*. Retrieved from Britannica: https://www.britannica.com/topic/deconstruction

Cao, J., Zhang, Z., Wang, H., Liang, B., Wang, H., & i Wong, K.-F. (2024). OSPC: Detecting Harmful Memes with Large Language Model as a catalyst. *WWW '24 Companion, May 13–17, 2024, Singapore, Singapore* (pp. 1-4). Singapore: WWW '24 Companion.

Chakabwata, W. (2023). The emancipation of women in Africa using a decolonial feminism. In M. Musingafi, & C. Hungwe, *Women Empowerment and the Feminist Agenda in Africa* (pp. 243-258). Dakota: IGI Global.

Chemaly, S. (2013, 04 18). *Facebook misogyny problem*. Retrieved from The Gurdian: https://www.theguardian.com/commentisfree/2013/apr/18/facebook-big-misogyny-problem

Chiu, K.-L., Collins, A., & Alexander, R. (2022). Detecting Hate Speech with GPT-3. Retrieved from https://arxiv.org/pdf/2103.12407

Cibu, B., Delcea, C., Domenteanu, A., & Dumitrescu, G. (2023). Mapping the evolution of cybernetics: A bibliometric perspective. *Computers*, 12(237), 1–29. DOI: 10.3390/computers12110237

Das, A., Raychawdhary, N., Bhattacharya, T., Dozier, G., & Seals, C. (2023). AU_NLP at SemEval-2023 Task 10: Explainable Detection of Online Sexism Using Fine-tuned RoBERTa. *Proceedings of the The 17th International Workshop on Semantic Evaluation* (pp. 707–717). USA: Association for Computational Linguistics. DOI: 10.18653/v1/2023.semeval-1.97

Gaw, M. (2013, 07 6). *Practising non attachment with language: An intro to deconstructionism.* Retrieved from Marin Theatre: https://www.marintheatre.org/press-release-details/125/practicing-non-attachment-with-language-an-intro-to-deconstructionism#:~:text=A%20principle%20tenet%20of%20deconstructionism,%2C%20man%2Fwoman%2C%20etc

Georgieva-Trifonova, T., & Duraku, M. (2020). Research on N-grams feature selection methods for text classification. *IOP Conf. Series: Materials Science and Engineering 1031* (pp. 1-10). England: IOP Publishing Ltd.

Glick, P., & Fiske, S. T. (2011). Ambivalent sexism revisited. *Psychology of Women Quarterly*, 35(3), 530–535. DOI: 10.1177/0361684311414832 PMID: 24453402

Groumpos, P. (2024). New Scientific field for modelling complex dynamic systems: The Cybernetics Artificial Intelligence (CAI). *IgMin Res*, 2(5), 323–340. DOI: 10.61927/igmin183

Hall, M. (2024, 11 28). *Facebook*. Retrieved from Encyclopedia Britannica: https://www.britannica.com/money/Facebook

Jalan, A. (2023, 2 5). *Make Use of (MUO)*. Retrieved from The evolution of Facebook: From 2004 to Meta: https://www.makeuseof.com/evolution-of-facebook/

Keinan, R. (2024). Tackling sexism in social media: Multilingual AI solutions. *Journal of Electrical and Electronics Engineering (Oradea)*, 3(5), 1–7.

Kolozova, K. (2021). Poststructural theory. In Hall, K. (Ed.), *Asta, The Oxford Handbook of feminist theory* (pp. 1–12). Oxford University Press.

Krikke, J. (2024, 12 12). *Want to win AI revolution? Study up on cybernetics.* Retrieved from Asia Times: https://asiatimes.com/2024/11/want-to-win-the-ai-revolution-study-up-on-cybernetics/

Leaper, C. (2024). The development of ambivalent sexism: Proposals for an expanded model. *British Journal of Developmental Psychology*, 00, 1–19. DOI: 10.1111/bjdp.12521 PMID: 39275962

Li, Z., & Zhou, K. (2014). When content moderation is not about content: How Chinese social media platforms moderate content and why it matters. *New Media & Society*, •••, 1–17.

Lugones, M. (2010). Towards a decolonial feminism. *Hypatia*, 25(4), 742–758. DOI: 10.1111/j.1527-2001.2010.01137.x

Mangena. (2020). *Cyberbullying: The challenges that women and girls face in seeking redress in cases of online harrassment in Zimbabwe.* A dissertation submitted in partial fullfillment of the requirement of the Master's degree in Social Legal Studies University of Zimbabwe: Southern and Eastern African Regional Centre for Women's Law.

Martelaro, N., & Ju, W. (2018). 10 25). Cybernetics and the design of the user experience of AI systems. *Interactions (New York, N.Y.)*, 25(6), 38–41. DOI: 10.1145/3274570

McKay, V. (2018). Lifelong Learning and Sustainable Development Goals. *Australian Journal of Adult Learning*, 58(3), 390–425.

Mellino, M. (2018). Postcolonialism. In Callan, H. (Ed.), *The International Encyclopedia of Anthropology* (pp. 1–16). John Wiley and Sons Ltd. DOI: 10.1002/9781118924396.wbiea2344

Mendoza, B. (2020). Decolonial theories in parctice. *Journal of World Philosophies*, 5, 43–60.

Mignolo, W. D., & Walsh, C. (2018). *On decoloniality concepts, analytics and praxis*. Duke University Press.

Moffat, B. (2024). An examination of cyberbullying among Zimbabwean female social media influencers. *Online Journal of Communication and Media Technologies*, 14(4), 1–14. DOI: 10.30935/ojcmt/15016

Mohammadi, H., Giachanou, A., & Bagheri, A. (2024). A transparent pipeline for identifying sexism in social media combining explainability with model prediction. *Applied Science, 14, 8620.*, 1-27.

Mutsvairo, B. (2020). *Zimbabwean women share their social media experiences*. Hivos Unlimited.

Nadeem, A., Abedin, B., & Marjanovic, O. (2022). Gender bias in AI-based decision-making systems: A systematic literature review. *AJIS. Australasian Journal of Information Systems*, 26, 1–34. DOI: 10.3127/ajis.v26i0.3835

NapoleonCat. (2024, 05 1). *Facebook users in Zimbabwe*. Retrieved from NapoleonCat: https://napoleoncat.com/stats/facebook-users-in-zimbabwe/2024/05/

Nehanda Centre for Gender and Cultural Studies. (2023). *Women in politics in Zimbabwe: How gender norms are fueling online violence*. Nehanda Centre for Gender and Cultural Studies.

Noh, K., Seong, B., Byun, H., Choi, Y., Song, S., & Song, K. (2024). LBC: Language-Based-Classifier for Out-Of-Variable Generalization. Yonsei: Yonsei University.

Novikov, D. A. (2015). *Cybernetics from past to future*. Russian Academy of Sciences Trapeznikov Institute of Control Sciences.

Oyeyumi, O. (1997). *The invention of women*. University of Minneapolis.

Planck, M. (2024, 04 25). *From Cybernetics to AI: The pioneering work of Norbert Wiener*. Retrieved from MP Neuro Max Planck Neuroscience: https://maxplanckneuroscience.org/from-cybernetics-to-ai-the-pioneering-work-of-norbert-wiener/

Ramirez, J., Velez-Zapata, C., & Maher, R. (2024). Green Colonialism and Decolonial Feminism A Study of Wayúu Women's Resistance in La Guajira. *Human Relations*, 77(7), 937–964. DOI: 10.1177/00187267231189610

Riyal, A. M. (2019). Post-colonialism and Feminism. *Asian Social Science*, 15(11), 83–88. DOI: 10.5539/ass.v15n11p83

Rodguez-Sanchez, F., Carrillo-de-Albornoz, J., Plaza, L., Gonzalo, J., Rosso, P., Comet, M., & Donoso, T. (2021). Overview of EXIST 2021 sEXism Identism. *Procesamiento del Lenguaje Natural, Revista nº 67, septiembre de*, 195-207.

Rodrigues, L. (2022). Decolonial feminism: Maria Lugones influences and contributions. *Revista Estudos Feministas, Florianópolis*, 30(1), 1–14. DOI: 10.1590/1806-9584-2022v30n184278

Sengupta, N., Hammond, M., Deak, C., & Malhotra, R. (2024). Ambivalent sexism and tolerance against women in India. *Psychological Science*, 35(7), 712–721. DOI: 10.1177/09567976241254312 PMID: 38869963

Sikirivwa, M. (2020). Deconstruction theory and its background . *American Journal of Humanities and Social Sciences Research (AJHSSR) Volume-4, Issue-4*, 44-72.

SocialPilot. (2024, 1 11). *AI in Social Media: Exploring Use Cases, Challenges, and Strategies.* Retrieved from SocialPilot: https://www.socialpilot.co/blog/ai-in-social-media

Soori, M., Arezoo, B., & Dastres, R. (2023). Artificial intelligence, machine learning and deep learning in advanced robotics, a review. *Cognitive Robotics*, 3, 54–70. DOI: 10.1016/j.cogr.2023.04.001

Southern African Development Community. (2024, 12 3). *Gender equality and women empowerment.* Retrieved from Southern African Development Community: https://www.sadc.int/pillars/gender-equality-women-empowerment

Stam, R., & Shohat, E. (2012). Whence and whither post colonial theory? *New Literary History*, 43(2), 371–390. DOI: 10.1353/nlh.2012.0010

Tamale, S. (2020). *Decolonisation and Afro-Feminism.* Daraja Press.

Tian, L., Huang, N., & Zhang, X. (2023). *Efficient Multilingual Sexism Detection via Large Language Model Cascades. Conference and Labs of the Evaluation Forum, September 18–21.* RMIT University.

Tinparinus. (2024, 12 8). *Medium.* Retrieved from How GPT model works: https://medium.com/@tinparnus/how-gpt-model-work-7ab01d848057

United Nations. (1979, 12 18). *Convention on the Elimination of All Forms of Discrimination against Women.* Retrieved from United Nations: https://www.ohchr.org/en/instruments-mechanisms/instruments/convention-elimination-all-forms-discrimination-against-women

United Nations. (2024, 12 03). *Universal Declaration of Human Rights.* Retrieved from United Nations Peace, Dignity and Equality on a Healthy Planet: https://www.un.org/en/about-us/universal-declaration-of-human-rights

United Nations Human Rights Treaty Bodies. (2024, 12 3). *View the ratification status by country or by treaty.* Retrieved from United Nations Human Rights Treaty Bodies UN treaty Body database: https://tbinternet.ohchr.org/_layouts/15/TreatyBodyExternal/Treaty.aspx?Treaty=CEDAW&Lang=en

UNWomen. (2024, 11 26). *World Conferences on Women.* Retrieved from UNWomen: https://www.unwomen.org/en/how-we-work/intergovernmental-support/world-conferences-on-women

Vincent, J. (2020, 11 13). Facebook is now using AI to sort content for quicker moderation. Retrieved 12 8, 2020, from https://www.theverge.com/2020/11/13/21562596/facebook-ai-moderation

Willett, A., & Etowa, J. (2023). A critical examination of epistemological congruence between intersectionality and feminist poststructuralism: Toward an integrated framework for health research. *Nursing Inquiry*, 30(4), 1–12. DOI: 10.1111/nin.12564 PMID: 37248779

Williamson, B., & Eynon, R. (2020). Historical threads, missing links, and future directions in AI in education. *Learning, Media and Technology*, 45(3), 223–235. DOI: 10.1080/17439884.2020.1798995

World Health Organisation (WHO). (2024, 12 4). *Sustainable Development Goals*. Retrieved from World Health Organisation (WHO) Europe: https://www.who.int/europe/about-us/our-work/sustainable-development-goals

Zhang, X., Chowdhury, R., Gupta, R., & Shang, J. (2024). Large Language Models for Time Series: A Survey. *Proceedings of the Thirty-Third International Joint Conference on Artificial Intelligence (IJCAI-24)Survey Track* (pp. 8335-8343). San Diego: Proceedings of the Thirty-Third International Joint Conference on Artificial Intelligence (IJCAI-24). DOI: 10.24963/ijcai.2024/921

Zheng, Y., Ross, B., & Magdy, W. (2023). What Makes Good Counterspeech? A Comparison of Generation Approaches and Evaluation Metrics. *Proceedings of the 1st Workshop on CounterSpeech for Online Abuse (CS4OA)*, (pp. 62–71). University of Edinburgh: Association for Computational Linguistics.

Zhu, X. (2024). *Feminism on social media: Generalized misogyny. SHS Web of Conferences 199, 02012*. The University of Sheffield: The University of Sheffield, Department of Sociological Studies.

Chapter 9
The Future of AI in Cyberbullying Prevention: Trends and Technologies

Madiha Munawar
https://orcid.org/0009-0001-7211-9022
Stanley College of Engineering and Technology for Women, India

Thakur Monika Singh
https://orcid.org/0009-0006-8534-9130
Stanley College of Engineering and Technology for Women, India

Kishor Kumar Reddy C.
Stanley College of Engineering and Technology for Women, India

Marlia Mohd Hanafiah
Universiti Kebangsaan Malaysia, Malaysia

ABSTRACT

Cyberbullying remains a significant issue in today's digital age, affecting individuals across various online platforms. Leveraging artificial intelligence (AI) offers promising solutions, as social networking tools now enable enhanced detection, prediction, and intervention. Advances in Natural Language Processing (NLP) facilitate the identification of hate speech and abusive content, while machine learning algorithms uncover complex patterns typical of online bullying. Additionally, image and video recognition systems, paired with content filters, help detect harmful visual content. AI also enables efficient threat detection and content moderation through predictive analytics, identifying at-risk individuals or groups and offering preemptive support. Expert systems integrated with AI-powered chatbots provide victims with guidance on reporting and prevention. However, challenges like user privacy and algorithmic

DOI: 10.4018/979-8-3373-0543-1.ch009

bias must be addressed to ensure safety and fairness.

1. INTRODUCTION TO CYBER BULLYING AND AI'S ROLE IN PREVENTION

Cyber bullying involves purposeful and calculated acts of bullying through virtual technological means such as social media, text messages or emails. This is a very special form of bullying as it does include psychological and emotional and social aspects to the extent that it affects the victims, especially the younger people. (John et al, 2010) explains that Stress associated with Cyberbullying has an emotional component that can lead to externalizing deviant behavior such as aggression. Also, the National Crime Records Bureau (NCRB) of a nido confirmed that cases of cyberbullying in the country are on the rise and said on public safety in the age of technology, (NCRB, 2020). Cyberbullying within peer groups of adolescent age is another area of concern because it is typically perpetrated without the victim knowing who is behind it hence amplifies the impact (Aricak et al., 2008). Due to its potential effects society should work towards making it a nonissue. Because one can engage in cyber bullying at any time without physical contact and there is no available adult supervision, it degenerates control over it (Slonje, Smith, &Frisén, 2013). Because the offense is concealed through the use of the internet, it becomes extremely difficult to criminalize the act. Also, the internet allows people to spread hate messages and images or any other content that is damaging very fast which increases the injury. In addition, the reach of the internet is so wide that once an individual becomes a victim of online bullying, the implications extend even to their future as it could have permanent effects on their mental wellbeing and even the reputation of that individual (Singh, 2019).

The rise in online communication, including the COVID-19 health crisis, is imperative to design sophisticated systems for cyberbullying detection and prevention. The psychological effects of cyberbullying are often worse than that of physical bullying due to the fact that it is both public and omnipresent (Dooley, Pyzalski, & Cross, 2009). There are, however, traditional solutions to cyberbullying such as reports and moderators, but the amount of content presents a big problem. In contrast to traditional bullying, victims of cyberbullying do not only face harassment that is often anonymous, but also one that is lasting (Slonje& Smith, 2008). Programs that encourage empathy and peer support among the school children were as effective in curtailing traditional bullying as they were in curbing online bullying (Ttofi& Farrington, 2011). To deal with the growing menace of cyberbullying, awareness programs are required since it is no longer possible to control it with the onset of the digital age (Willard, 2006). Adolescents and children construct cyberbullying as being 'invisible' and are often out of the reach of wise adults who can safely intervene (Mishna, Saini, & Solomon, 2009). Research indicates a worrying correlation between thoughts of self-harm/suicidal ideation and experiencing cyberbullying for particular youth populations (Hinduja&Patchin, 2010). Most parents believe that cyberbullying is not rampant, which creates a lag in counter measures against cyber harassment (Dehue, Bollman, &Völlink, 2008). There is existing literature that further suggests that cyberbullying drives youth suicidal ideation (Nikolaou, 2017). Some of the negative impact that cyberbullying has on young individuals can be alleviated by positive mental health (Brailovskaia, Teismann, &Margraf, 2018). Innovative solutions are however needed to facilitate the detection and intervention in real time. AI based solutions offer the best and most promising approach to address this challenge.

Cyberbullying: The use of digital platforms like social media to harass, threaten, or humiliate individuals, often leading to significant emotional distress.

Artificial Intelligence: It is the area of computing within computer science that is concerned with the development of machines that can engage in activities that would normally require human intelligence such as recognition, interpretation, and decision making.

As given in Table 1, there are many types of cyberbullying (e.g. bullying, active conflict, nonverbal rejection) and signs (e.g. depression, abrupt behavioral changes) that help in recognizing the victims. It provides the basic knowledge on the concept of online victimization using different approaches.

Table 1. Types of cyberbullying and common indicators

Type of Cyberbullying	Description	Common Indicators	Examples
Harassment	Repeated, aggressive messages targeting an individual	High message frequency, negative sentiment	Sending hateful messages daily
Exclusion	Deliberate exclusion from groups or online communities	Absence from group chats, blocking behavior	Removing from group chats without reason
Doxxing	Sharing private information publicly to cause harm	Public display of personal data, threats	Sharing address and phone number online
Outing	Sharing someone's secrets or personal information without consent	Posts with private content, targeted exposure	Leaking screenshots of private conversations
Cyberstalking	Persistent tracking and harassment of an individual	Frequent location sharing, obsessive interaction	Constantly following and messaging

continued on following page

Table 1. Continued

Type of Cyberbullying	Description	Common Indicators	Examples
Fraping	Hacking into someone's account to post harmful content in their name	Uncharacteristic posts from user's account, altered profile	Posting offensive content from a hacked account
Trolling	Provocative comments to elicit a strong reaction from the victim	Repeated provocative comments, hostile language	Posting inflammatory comments repeatedly

The Need for Technological Solutions

As the prevalence of digital communication and social networks increases, so has the need for real-time observing and counter measuring technologies to cyber bullying. Sociological methods, like reporting and flagging, are ineffective with great volumes of content created on a daily basis. Such inefficiency leads to harmful content remaining on the sites for a prolonged period or even unnoticed which would cause more damage to the survival of the targets (Jha, 2021). Also, this demand can be solved with Artificial Intelligence (AI). With the help of machines learning (ML) and its algorithms, it could be possible to operate on vast volumes of data in a matter of seconds, evaluate the situation and initiate a response. This feature is greatly helpful in countering the present risks as such systems are able to reshape themselves after a period in action (Chaudhary & Gupta, 2020). Utilizing advanced technologies such as machine learning techniques, particularly the emotion detection techniques which forms a key part of any automated age estimation system, shall be implemented with great care (Hasan et al., 2023). Mission Critical Components: Advanced deep learning systems have demonstrated great capability in addressing the issue of online harassment which is vital for the protection of the internet (Iwendi et al., 2020). CyberBullying detection and prevention models are CyberBert based and that is how the issue is resolved in a timely fashion and hence curbs the scope of the issue. (Paul & Saha, 2022).

In addition, contingent on the application, artificial intelligence is capable of automating the task of content moderation, necessitating for the swift disbandment of ill-intended materials, as well as providing real-time assistance to users. For instance, Natural Language Processing (NLP) can be utilized to monitor and assess the use of offensive speech and decriers by users, whilst machine learning algorithms can foresee the likelihood of hatred, abuse or offensive language developing into cyber bulling within a specific user's group. This means that teachers are undoubtedly enablers of the cyberbullying dilemma because they are the primary responders who attend such situations and prevent their escalation (Feinberg &Robey, 2009).

Along with these advances in AI for the betterment of mankind, there also exists an expanding scope of such technologies to protect society from the negative effects of cyber-violence targeting individuals.

AI as a Tool for Cyberbullying Prevention

AI is also capable of providing support and intervention methods to cyber bullying victims which help in addressing the problem before it becomes worse. This depicts the fact that AI is not limited to detection of the phenomenon. The development of AI robo, gabb or virtual assistants and other similar technologies is proving to be helpful as they help people in the process of incident reporting, accessing counseling services, and even providing help in real time (Kaur& Saha, 2022).

The prescriptive model helps the concerned organizations and platforms in taking action before getting out of control imposition (Singh et al., 2021). AI's ability to provide instant replies, interprets intricate and vast sets of information patterns, and scale all efforts aimed at addressing an issue makes it critical in fighting the vice of cyber bullying. As the need to reduce online harassment increases so do the advanced AI technologies without a doubt. In the same way, we will be able to combine Artificial Intelligence and existing anti bullying strategies to develop a better framework system for ensuring safety in the digital platforms.

Figure 1. AI Interventions in Cyberbullying: A Venn Diagram of Types and Solutions

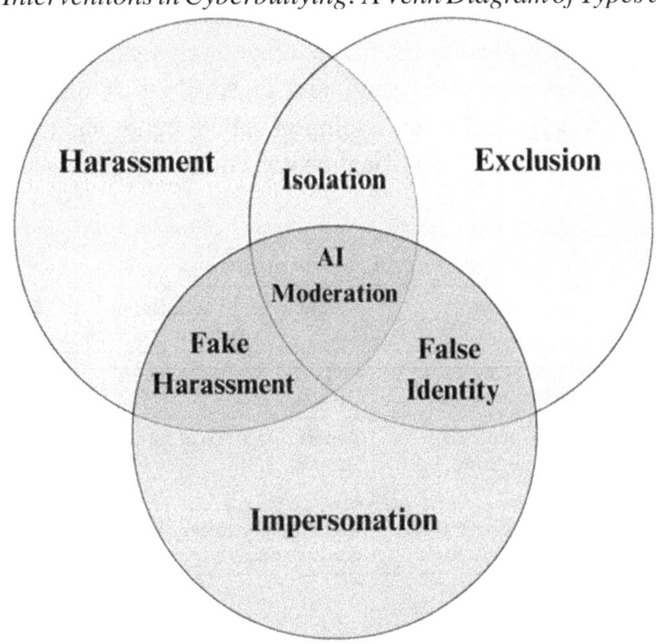

Figure 1 presents how the AI Interventions converge with different types of cyberbully such as harassment, exclusion, and impersonation. The intersectional areas represent the different aspects of these problems solved by the AI solutions provided, for example, abusive language detection (harassment), exclusion detection (exclusion), and fake profile detection (impersonation).

2. CURRENT TRENDS IN AI FOR CYBERBULLYING DETECTION AND PREVENTION

Evolution of AI in Social Media Monitoring

Social Media Monitoring: This is the practice of evaluating trends in the use of social media to ascertain if actions or messages that can be regarded as bullying, or threats to someone's safety, are present.

There are systems based on artificial intelligence, which is the third generation of moderation technique wherein algorithms go beyond language processing to include tone and sentiment analysis. Today, systems, and especially those that employ natural language processing (NLP), have more success at screening out dangerous messages. The applications of social networking sites, Facebook, Twitter, and Instagram have all embraced AI, whereby the contents associated with constraint bullying are automatically flagged, which in turn decrease the work done by human moderators.

Table 2 enumerates the recent tendencies in the field of artificial intelligence application for prevention and control of internet harassment specifically in Asia where natural language processing, sentiment analysis, and automated systems are being utilized. This explains the new evolution in both trends and their approaches in enhancing the efficiency of identification and control methods.

Table 2. Key AI trends in cyberbullying prevention

Trend	Description	Impact on Cyberbullying Prevention	Example Tools/ Techniques
Social Media Monitoring	AI-based monitoring of social media for harmful content	Early detection of potential bullying instances	Facebook's DeepText
Real-Time Threat Detection	Immediate detection and intervention for harmful behaviors	Prevents escalation of harmful content	Twitter's real-time content analysis
Emotion AI	Identifies emotions in posts and messages	Helps identify vulnerable users at risk of harm	Affectiva for emotional analytics

continued on following page

Table 2. Continued

Trend	Description	Impact on Cyberbullying Prevention	Example Tools/ Techniques
Content Moderation	Automated filtering of harmful language	Enhances the speed and consistency of harmful content removal	YouTube's moderation algorithms
AI-Based Reporting Systems	Simplifies reporting process for victims	Empowers users to report bullying more easily	Instagram's reporting feature
Adaptive Learning Models	Continuously updated models for cyberbullying patterns	More accurate detection as trends evolve	Google's Jigsaw Project

Key Developments in Cybersecurity for Online Safety

The surge in AI solutions for addressing cyberbullying creates an even greater need for protecting technology. Technology is not only used in monitoring the published content. It is equally important in securing the content and preserving the user. One of the recent breakthroughs in this field is the integration of federated learning as an AI friendly technique. Federated learning prevents the need to send sensitive information from a person's device to a central server by allowing training of an AI model on that person's device using their personal data. It serves to protect the user's privacy and increases the ability of the AI model to generalize using information from several users located in diverse regions. In addition to this, there is an advancement being applied whereby prevention measures are fortified by security features of cyberbullying integrating blockchain technology. Through the use of ledgers that do not have a central authority, blockchain provides assurance of transparency of information while protecting the systems from alteration. For instance, it ensures that all cases of reported incidences of cyberbullying are able to be monitored and proved, thus ensuring responsibility. It further preserves the confidentiality of the parties concerned, adding another barrier to AI systems when it comes to tackling issues of cyber bullying.

In addition, it is more common now to use AI enabled predictive analytics in the area of cyber security. Past instances of cyber-bullying are studied in predictive analytics with the primary aim of reducing or eliminating future risks that may arise. Using big data analytics, AI is able to identify red flags preceding incidents of cyber-bullying, such as abnormal increases in the levels of aggression in communication or a shift in individuals' behavioral patterns, and take counter measures. This is important in making the internet a better place especially when it comes to children and adolescents who face a lot of challenges with online harassment.

3. NATURAL LANGUAGE PROCESSING (NLP) IN DETECTING HARMFUL CONTENT

Role of NLP in Recognizing Offensive Language

Natural Language Processing: Its understanding of language is so advanced that its applications range from translating languages to engaging in conversations with bots. In particular, using similar technologies helps to identify inappropriate language used by Internet users. It is obvious that machine learning methods such as NLP are imperatively used to counter phenomena such as cyberbullying which is rife with offensive content. In doing so, these technologies go beyond simply collecting data and interpreting it; they also assist in formulating ideas in the native language. Tokenization and sentiment analysis, along with word embeddings, enable AI text analysis to extract abusive language from clean text. In this case, we refer to verbal abuse on the Internet, when for instance, searches may be conducted to identify whether a person is being insulted, threatened or cursed at in any way on their social media profiles. It also helps such platforms to detect and understand the presence of sarcasm and implicit language which are mostly found in the case of bullying. This is especially advantageous since there can be an increase in the adoption of its systems to protect youths from heroic behaviour due to the inefficiency of manual moderation systems. While traditional NLP focused primarily on the processing of texts of limited contexts, machine learning approaches, together with NLP, effectively process volumes of texts and identify toxic elements in minute amounts of time with outstanding performance. Further, NLP has been able to improve on this aspect by ensuring that it carries the abusers and bullies without carrying the wimps which is a flaw in the traditional systems. This accuracy prevents users from being falsely accused of resorting to offensive language or content and subsequently censored.

Table 3 delves into a variety of natural language processing techniques that have been developed for the purpose of understanding and detecting abusive behavior in online contexts. It surveys various methods such as text classification, sentiment analysis and approaches based on machine learning, which are employed in AI for the purpose of identifying hate speech.

Table 3. NLP Approaches for Detecting Harmful Language

NLP Technique	Functionality	Use in Cyberbullying Detection	Example NLP Models
Sentiment Analysis	Identifies sentiment in text (positive, negative, neutral)	Detects negative emotions like anger, hostility	VADER, TextBlob
Named Entity Recognition	Detects and classifies entities in text	Identifies persons or locations being targeted	spaCy, BERT
Topic Modeling	Discovers abstract topics in text	Highlights topics related to bullying, like harassment or threats	LDA, NMF
Language Modeling	Predicts next word sequences based on context	Assesses language patterns consistent with bullying	GPT-based models, RNN models
Hate Speech Detection	Identifies specific hate language in text	Classifies language as hateful or offensive	HateSonar, Perspective API
Text Classification	Assigns predefined categories to text	Categorizes content as bullying or non-bullying	Logistic Regression, SVM

In addition, the use of these systems is critical in environments that are multicultural and where users communicate in different languages. Systems can be designed that are able to process a range of languages, as well as several dialects and slang which are important in cyberbullying assessment of multiple user groups. There has been an emphasis on creating language centered NLP models, aimed at solving the problem of such systems being applicable only within English speaking countries and not the rest of the globe (Bhaskar&Sundararajan, 2020). These developments have now enabled the real-time monitoring of hate speech and its elimination through the deployment of advanced AI technology in the analysis of social network content.

Sentiment Analysis for Detecting Potential Bullying

Having been a part of Natural Language Processing, sentiment analysis is of high importance in assessing the risks concerning the potential occurrence of cyberbullying. This entails interpretation of the underlying emotionality of the text which is critical in the identification of aggressive behaviours. Domino sentiment analysis systems, for instance, serve the primary function of the auxiliary or the main text categorization provisions. Positive, negative or neutral are typical categories of the fortunate or unfortunate texts further emotions anger or irritation or sadness. These emotions are quite common in bullying especially because cyber bullies are known to utilize heated emotions in words to offend their victims.

Sentiment analysis is now enabling the recognition of less overt threats such as emotional abuse and subtle manipulations, thanks to enhancements witnessed in this area. In conjunction with other NLP approaches, sentiment analysis allows for an improvement in the performance of AI systems that are tuned to detect such interactions, irrespective of the abusive language. Even from completely neutral dialogues, AI can track the emotion of an interlocutor, which helps in identifying oppression and abuse. Such an approach helps in addressing and providing help to those who are likely to be bullied. Another way is measuring one's sentiment saturation level at several points in time which is the main feature of sentiment analysis. Specific emotional states can be assessed by AI after a series of interactions with a user in relation to individual or group bullying causing the user distress. Repeated tensions in anger towards each other can be evaluated statistically and in this way enabled to avert long term psychological effects on the victims. Integrated AI systems may warn moderators or send alert when a certain user repeatedly expresses very negative emotions like anger or distress, thereby enabling the relevant authorities to take preventive measures (Jha, 2021; Sharma et al., 2022).

Case Studies: NLP Models in Action

NLP models have been used in real life – cyberbullying prevention for example – and there are several examples of their successful implementation. For instance, Twitter took steps towards changing the way people interacted by deploying a system that detects the presence of abusive language. The social network employs machine learning algorithms which use sentiment analysis and context to identify and classify dangerous messages for more precise and effective moderation of content. Moderation of Content. Most of such models do not remain static because of the ability to learn from other user text data available on the platform over time (Patel et al. 2021). In the same vein, Facebook implemented similar techniques of NLP to curb incidents of cyberbullying. Their system includes deep learning models which screen the comments and messages for any offensive tones, abusive languages, hate speeches or direct verbal assaults. Facebook interests in it are linked to the desire to develop real-time detection of bullying activities amongst its users through implementation of prevention measures based on NLP. Also, this system is based on the ability to detect harmful content automatically as well as user bullying reports to allow interaction within the platform (Bansal& Kumar, 2020). Other companies, as well as YouTube and Instagram, are doing the same thing and extending their content moderation policies by adding systems based on NLP. The systems combine NLP, image recognition and video analysis in order to fight non-textual bulling through images and videos that can incite some people to bully others. Such a system makes the fight against cyber-bullying more robust and addresses many types of online content comprehensively.

Case Study 1: Instagram's AI-Driven Content Moderation for Cyberbullying Prevention

To ensure that cyberbullying is curbed fully on its platform, Instagram has also deployed an AI-based content moderation tool that emphasizes the need for real-time responses in an interactive space. Through incorporation of high end natural language processing (NLP) and machined learning, Instagram's technology also actively scans the comments of the pictures and photos uploaded by the users to identify the use of bad language, hateful comments as well as threats. The tool assists the user in not posting harmful comment to them by showing a warning the user has the option of disregarding encouraging them to rethink their statement or alter it in a different way. A concept of 'Restrict' has also been put forward by Instagram, which allows individuals to avoid any interaction with particular users while still being able to access their profiles. This concept assists in curtailing the abuse directed towards the users without the need of confrontation. Consequently, this has reduced the number of reports made and encourages a more pleasant environment online. Nevertheless, it is not easy to keep the same accuracy level detection strategies because of the slang and complex language that changes over time on the web.

Case Study 2: YouTube's Hybrid Approach to Detecting and Removing Cyberbullying Content

YouTube, which is a well-known video uploading website, has encountered instances of videos that might encourage harassment, particularly for the youngsters. In this regard, it established a system which analyses images, audio and text associated with any given video in detecting any form of cyberbullying on its platform. The platform's AI flags inappropriate content; however YouTube has a hybrid system where AI detection is complemented with human moderation especially in cases that need more complex investigations. As a result of this system, YouTube has been able to internally screen and eliminate content classified as offensive from millions of videos provided every three months without fail. Although this method worked tolerably well, certain obstacles still exist for YouTube as not all forms of bullying are easily translated by the AI as there are subcultures and contexts that only humans can comprehend.

4. MACHINE LEARNING ALGORITHMS FOR IDENTIFYING CYBERBULLYING PATTERNS

Supervised and Unsupervised Learning Approaches

The use of machine learning (ML) algorithms in the analysis of text and behaviour related data for the detection of patterns of cyberbullying can therefore be taken as a very important component of cyberbullying management. In supervised learning, the algorithms are trained using labeled datasets; in this case each example in the dataset is identified as being either a cyberbullying example or a non cyberbullying content. This makes it possible for the model not only to reference examples from the past, but also to generate forecasts given different, new situations. Popular algorithms employed under supervised learning for detection of cyberbullying include decision trees, support vector machines, and neural networks among others. On presenting appropriate training data, models can also be trained to identify abusive traits in language, often characterized by the presence of obscenities, threats and insults, provided the right pattern is supplied.

The integration of supervised and unsupervised techniques presents a wholistic mechanism for detecting cyberbullying. While supervised learning offers accuracy thanks to learning from already marked data, unsupervised learning extends to capturing newer trends that have not been captured in the learning curves. Hence, these techniques help AI systems to keep pace with the fast-changing face of cyberbullying as different bullies apply different tactics and languages more so within a very short period (Kumar et al., 2021; Sharma et al., 2022).

Supervised Learning: It is a sub-area of machine learning in which the algorithm builds a model based on some commands predefined labelled data to make the required prediction. This helps a lot in cases when patterned styles of cyber bully are already known in advance.

Unsupervised Learning: Machine learning is a learning technique that deduces some information from given data, using no labelled instances. This is especially important in the case of cyberbullying, where most patterns of abuse may be new and shocking to the audience.

Table 4 gives the different types of machine learning techniques such as decision tree, support vector machines, neural networks used for cyberbullying detection. It describes how such algorithms learn from the already present training datasets and detect the patterns of cyberbullying using the data related to past events.

Table 4. Machine learning techniques for cyberbullying detection

Algorithm	Approach	Advantages	Challenges	Example Use Case
Logistic Regression	Classifies binary outcomes based on input features	Simple, fast, interpretable	Limited to linear relationships	Binary classification of messages as harmful
Decision Trees	Tree-based classification of data	Easy interpretation, handles non-linear data	Prone to overfitting	Classification based on multiple factors
Random Forest	Ensemble of decision trees for robust classification	Reduces overfitting, good accuracy	High computational cost	Detecting patterns of cyberbullying
Support Vector Machines	Classifies by finding the optimal separating hyperplane	Works well with small data, effective in high-dimensional space	Requires careful tuning of parameters	High-accuracy classification of threats
Neural Networks	Multi-layered, data-driven models for complex patterns	Handles complex relationships, highly accurate	Requires large datasets, computation-heavy	Identifying intricate patterns in language
K-Nearest Neighbors	Classifies based on closest data points	Simple, effective with small datasets	Not effective for large, noisy datasets	Clustering similar messages

Feature Engineering for Cyberbullying Detection

Feature Engineering is one of the important processes when it comes to computational processes in cyberbullying detection. Data engineering is the scientific method of taking data and selecting important aspects of that data to define variables that will be used to build machine learning models. When it comes to cyberbullying, factors to be considered as features include settlement of words used structure of sentences, even the emotional levels in which messages are relayed. Other features level can also be developed from the user and their activity, like post timings, the post themselves, and the people with whom the post is correlated among many others.

One of the aspects of feature engineering which pertains to cyberbullying detection is knowing which features best aid in distinguishing between harmful content and harmless content. Such as a case of a strong worded sentence, although it may warn of a possible danger- this may not qualify as bullying when used within the context of an argument. As reported by researchers, to make improvement in the detection performance, ergodic features were addressed with their linguistic features and contextual behavioral features. Models that work in this way focus on how users behave, the words they choose and converse over a specific period, and the overall picture behind the exchange between users (Patel et al., 2021). Another important aspect of feature engineering is addressing the problem of imbalanced datasets. In many situations, the databases that are made available for training the machine learning models tend to be biased by having more instances of normal content than that of aggressive/bully content. This leads to models that are biased and which are likely to classify a given content as non-bullying. To resolve this problem, several approaches have been utilized including creating an imbalanced dataset solution by oversampling the lesser populated class, creating an imbalanced dataset solution by the use of undersampling the larger populated class, creating an imbalanced dataset solution by generation of synthetic data and so forth (Bansal and Kumar 2020).

Figure 2. ML Algorithm Lifecycle: Iterative Training and Refining Process

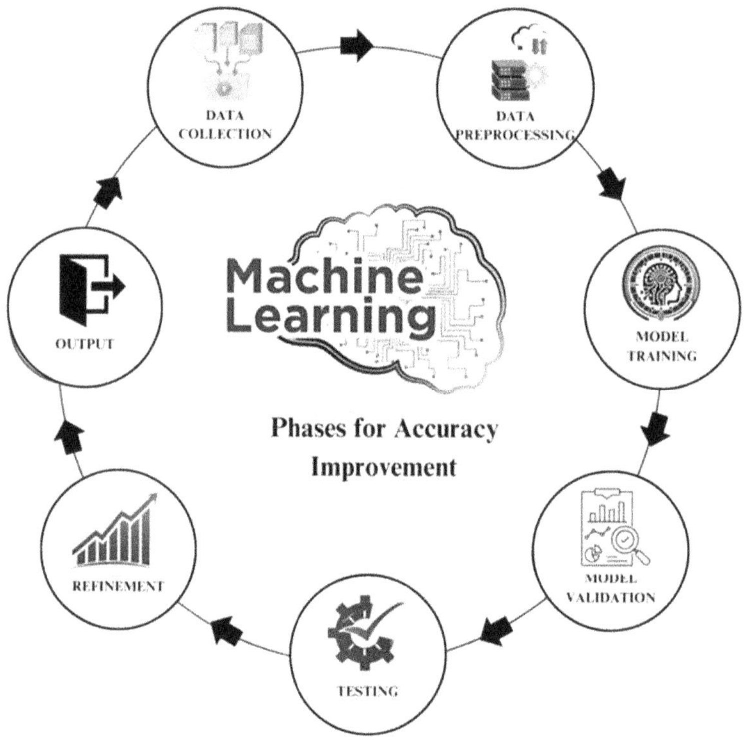

Figure 2 represents cycle of training, validating and improving machine learning algorithms. By focusing on aspects such as data preparation, model training, testing, and enhancement, it stresses the importance of the ability to provide the mechanism that enables accuracy improvement.

Machine Learning Techniques: Challenges and Solutions

Even though machine learning proves highly useful in detecting incidences of cyberbullying, it still poses some challenges, which researchers and practitioners have to find ways to deal with. One of the major issues is the need to ensure that the models are able to work well in all languages, cultures and on all online platforms. The language of cyberbullying also greatly differs from community to community and thus a model tested on one dataset may yield poor results when the situation is shifted to another dataset. Given this challenge, imlangs are being made and transfer learning is coming up, which is enabling understanding in different languages and cultures of models trained in one dataset (Sharma et al., 2022). Another important issue is that of examining language that relates to bullying which is less crude and does not involve the clear use of offensive words. In most cases, things like sarcasm, passive aggression, or allusion are the weapons used by bullies. This type of bullying requires machine learning models' advanced techniques which can comprehend the lineage and emotions towards the situation. Sentiment analysis, described in Section 3 is one of these techniques, which may be utilized alongside machine learning models for advanced bullying detection. These models can perform pattern recognition to complement sentiment analysis in order to detect indirect bullying which would otherwise not be inferred from the specific words used (Jha, 2021).

Finally, there remains concern regarding model interpretability in the field of machine learning. On the one side, the deep learning models, for instance neural networks, may provide better performance. But on the other side, they won't provide what is the logic behind a certain decision and how it was reached. This can be an issue in particular due to the privacy of users and the risk of false alarms. In this context, one of the lines of research being pursued is that of explainable artificial intelligence techniques (XAI) in order to make it possible to provide greater transparency and better understanding of the outcomes produced by the given machine learning model, making sure that every AI decision is justifiable (Patel et al., 2021; Kumar et al., 2021).

5. IMAGE AND VIDEO RECOGNITION FOR VISUAL CYBERBULLYING DETECTION

Identifying Harmful Visual Content Using AI

The dominance of image and video posts on social media has raised an additional issue regarding cyberbullying detection as it is more difficult when the exhibited offensive behavior cannot be expressed in words. As a response, it has become apparent that AI based algorithms developed for image and video content recognition have turned out to be invaluable in management of visual threats. This kind of system deploys computer vison technologies which examine transcribed media and look for the outward characteristics of bullying, harassment, or any other deviant behavior. For instance, such systems employ image recognition technologies which are able to recognize unwanted gestures, bad images, or any other pictorial insults which connect with online aggression. These mechanisms may also, for instance, analyze a video and locate moments of aggression, behavioural actions characteristic of bullying, or any other content that may either disturb or be meant to disturb the targeted individual.

The technology scans the digits of an image or frame and categorizes the area into useful or harmful based on the pre-established concepts of obscene visuals. This has been realized with the use of Artificial Intelligence – Deep Learning models more specifically Convolutional Neural Networks (CNNs). This is because CNNs have automatic ways of feature engineering, which aids in these specific tasks as it recognizes important features like shapes, textures as well as patterns that help in screening harmful contents. The more images and videos become available in the training phase of this model, the more the model becomes an expert in the recognition of even the more complex forms of bullying typologies like targeted image or video memes, propaganda videos and so forth (Choudhary&Agarwal, 2022). However, although some AI image and video recognition systems have been developed, there are some limitations including the thousands of visual contents available on social media and the fact that cyberbullies will at times be able to conceal their harassment by simply altering images. Further, more ethical issues are raised where individuals who wish to share personal videos or images have to undergo some kind of processing. These problems speak to the continuous evolution and revolution in the AIs and the associated ethics to take full advantage of visual content recognition without compromising on the safety of the users' rights (Ghosh&Agarwal, 2021).

Advancements in Deep Learning for Image and Video Analysis

Deep Learning: A machine learning technique which is strongly dependent on neural networks for training using a huge amount of data. This is important in maintaining good performance in image and video measurements.

As a result, their cousins who work with deep learning networks for neural network models have made remarkable developments in the area of recognizing images and videos for the detection of cyberbullying. Instead of the conventional machine learning training, in which features have to be manually directed engineered, the new model is capable of learning features from scratch even from pixels and has no limitations in that regard. This is especially important in visual cyberbullying detection since the visual cues such as body language, facial expression or face itself may display harmful aggression. There have been rapid developments in the new deep learning paradigm which can be applied to object detection, face recognition, and affect recognition which have come to ease the task of these AI approaches in locating bullies, especially in image and video content. With the ability to capture images of the person and the images of the persons, emotion recognition technology can use facial recognition of the person to identify an upset or harmful emotion. A video emotional analysis detects infliction episodes by showing particular facial emotional expressions such as sadness, aggressiveness, or fear towards a person. Furthermore, systems for recognizing body language keep track of the physical aspect in order to detect any threatening positions or movements made by the subject. These procedures allow the artificial intelligence not only to warn about, say, indecent images, but also to understand the feeling behind such pictures or videos. For instance, obscene gestures, violent text, and similar portrayals may be used as indicators to detect video bullying, but these elements can be further enhanced by exploring aggressiveness and threats even without the usual acting or hostile words (Singh &Saini, 2023).

Visual cyberbullying is another aspect that appears to be addressed in a novel way by employing a technique known as generative adversarial networks or GANs. Generative Adversarial Networks employ two interconnected neural networks in an effort to enhance the technology involved in image creation and recognition. Quite literally, there have been attempts to use GANs to develop tools capable of distinguishing between original and digital manipulated images because visual cyberbullying often incorporates the use of fake pictures. As a result, GANs were trained with huge amounts of visual content that was altered and scholars were able to create systems that can recognize deepfakes and media imaging that was altered for the purposes of online deception and harassment (Patel & Kumar, 2021).

Examples of Visual Cyberbullying Prevention Tools

There are several initiatives as well as systems with the aim of developing the technological implementation of AI-based image and video recognition for cyberbullying prevention that have been put in place. This includes the use of an AI based platform designed by Microsoft, PhotoDNA, which helps in identifying known images of child sexual abuse and distortion content, and other similar contents. Basically, PhotoDNA is designed to protect children, nevertheless it can be modified to detect other damaging visual content instead of just child abuse images found online. For instance, by simply uploading pictures to any social media platform, PhotoDNA will help in detecting harmful content very easily and even alert the moderators or administrators to take action within a specific duration of time.

Then, there is another one – social media moderation systems which include artificial intelligence as one of their components on social networks like Instagram and Facebook for example. Social networking services such as these, incorporate the use of AI technologies to perform content moderation and review potentially offensive photographs and videos submitted by subscribers. The AI systems utilized in these platforms have also been taught how to screen images and understand the inherent context in order to screen out explicit material, hateful speech, or aggressive behavior. There are still limitations with the technology that come with changes of user generated content, changes in the tactics of visual bullying and also concerns with the ethical of frustration personal media. Nevertheless, the use of these instruments is very much important considering that the visual aspects of cyber bullying is on the rise and it is a concern for the safety of the users in the virtual world (Ghosh&Agarwal, 2021; Choudhary&Agarwal, 2022).

Figure 3. Convolutional Neural Network (CNN) Layers in Image Detection

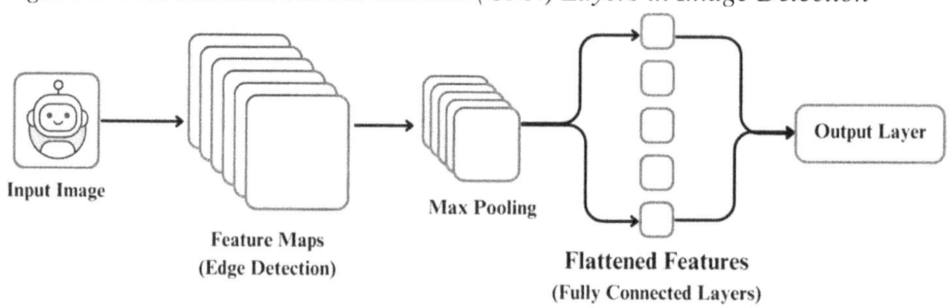

Figure 3 represents a CNN visualization elucidating the different layes in image detection. Dimensionality reductions in images displaying the processing of images stepwise by a CNN system where each layer does a different task such as edge detection, pattern making, and constructing high-level image features.

6. ETHICAL CONSIDERATIONS IN AI-DRIVEN CYBERBULLYING PREVENTION

Balancing Privacy and Protection

A critical issue faced in the application of AI techniques for combating cyberbullying is how to strike a balance between the two opposing constructs of privacy and protection. AI systems may be very useful in curtailing offensive practices such as cyberbullying by analyzing the user's behavior patterns. However, they would demand massive amounts of data including the users' instant messages, photographs, and videos. The problem is: how do you deploy these technologies to combat cyberbullying and still protect the users from invasion of privacy? The General Data Protection Regulation (GDPR) for instance, shields the privacy of individuals in the European Union and provides basic principles of data protection. Nevertheless, the implementation of AI in the content moderation activities towards real-time monitoring entails accessing users sensitive content even in the absence of their consent fuelling the concerns on privacy (Sharma &Aggarwal, 2021).

In order to mitigate these risks, there is the need for the development of AI systems with strict data governance policies. These policies should clearly describe the processes of data collection, processing, storage, and disposal of data. Furthermore, the principle of proportionality in data retention should be considered, where systems of AI are designed in such a manner that they only seek, collect, and hold information that is relevant for the sole purpose of identifying acts of cyberbullying and none other than that, hence helping in reducing incidents of private information exposure. This is meant to ensure that the application of AI technologies does not overextend or extend to the users' private life; quite to the contrary, users are protected fairly well. Apart from that, there is need for clarity as the users need to be educated on the use of their information as well as the safeguards available to protect those (Kumar & Jain, 2022). Furthermore, It is essential for the organizations to undertake measures like encryption, anonymization among others, in order to protect the user data throughout the processing stage. Such techniques allow for the efficient functioning of AI systems but also assist in ensuring that privacy is preserved. It is however important to note that ensuring privacy while at the same time maintaining the high level of efficiency expected in cyberbullying detection is a problem that always needs consideration and ongoing changes to policy and technology.

Table 5 looks into the use of AI to combat cyberbullying and analyzes some of its ethical issues such as the invasion of privacy, accuracy of predictions, and AI explainability. It also especially stresses how these ethical aspects can influence the processes of creating and utilizing AI technologies.

Table 5. Ethical Concerns in AI for Cyberbullying Prevention

Ethical Concern	Description	Potential Impact	Mitigation Strategy
Privacy	Risks to personal privacy through data collection	Could lead to invasion of personal data	Anonymization, data minimization
Algorithmic Bias	AI may exhibit bias based on training data	Biased results may target specific groups unfairly	Diverse and inclusive data training
Consent	Lack of consent for monitoring user interactions	Users may feel uncomfortable with being monitored	Transparent consent mechanisms
False Positives	Misidentifying content as harmful	Leads to unnecessary content removal and restriction	Precision-focused algorithms
Accountability	Lack of clarity on responsibility for AI decisions	No clear accountability if errors occur	Assign clear accountability frameworks
Transparency	Lack of transparency in AI decision-making processes	Users lack understanding of content removal	Use explainable AI models

Addressing Bias in AI Algorithms

The third important ethical issue regarding the application of AI in efforts to counter cyberbullying is the concern about bias in AI algorithms. No AI system is devoid of bias; when AI models are developed using datasets that suffer from bias, the end results may similarly be biased and subjective. In terms of detecting cyberbullying, bias can occur in a number of ways. For example, a cyberbullying detection model trained exclusively using data from one ethnic group may be incapable of identifying cyberbullying behaviors as depicted by other ethnic groups, thereby causing bias. This is especially pertinent in cyberbullying scenarios as the different dimensions of harm infliction vary from one culture to another and social setting to another. As a result, it is imperative that AI systems are developed using real-world data representing the myriad of interactions and experiences of individuals on the internet (Saxena& Verma, 2022). On top that, underserved algorithmic bias may produce false positives when a piece of text is unjustly labeled a bully when it is merely non-deleterious content or false negatives when a bully is allowed to continue their actions undetected. Such mistakes are dangerously grave, in the case of the innocent being falsely labeled as abusers and the true victims. Consequently, it is critical that AI systems are routinely monitored and tested for any signs of bias to reduce the risk of unfair or inaccurate results for users from varied backgrounds. Ethical AI development modifies this practice by promoting the use of models that are transparent, auditable, and aimed at reducing bias and implementing input from different groups of the society to improve their performance and accuracy over time (Chandran& Sharma, 2023).

Guidelines for Ethical AI in Online Safety

Considering the moral challenges involved in understanding and applying AI to combat bullying, a number of recommendations can be provided to limit the misuse of these aspects. First and foremost, the welfare of the users should be put at the top of any AI solutions developed by individuals or organizations (Reddy Chinthala, K. K. ., 2024). This entails that the AI model developed should be one that seeks to protect all persons against any harm while not stripping them their rights or freedom. Further, the designers ought to aim at building artificial intelligence systems that are understandable with some explanations plus informing the user how the information is utilized, while still protecting personal privacy. This ensures that users trust organizations and enables them to seek answers from organizations related to the AI interacted with (Rai& Singh, 2021). Moreover, it is also important to formulate a conclusive ethical resolution with regard to the abuses that may come with AI such as the aggravation of some forms of social exclusion and/or erroneous content parsing. Inviting relevant parties, which include ethicists, psychologist, law actual practitioners and communities at risk, during the design stage or even courtesy deployment of AI systems would vastly help in the prevention of likely problems. It is considered a collaborative effort as it does not only help in the incorporation of ethical issues during the design phase, but throughout the entire process even after commissioning the system. In order to develop ethical principles for artificial intelligence aimed at preventing cyberbullying it is important to emphasize strategies that guarantee the usage of AI while observing safety and privacy concerns (Ghosh& Mukherjee, 2020).

7. AI IN SOCIAL MEDIA PLATFORMS AND CONTENT MODERATION

AI-Based Content Filtering and Review Systems

Most of the existing cyberbullying research instruments are systems based on supervised learning. In this case, the system is trained on annotated data to identify any offensive behaviours, such as usage of derogatory terms, n, harassment or threats and so on. After attaining a certain level of accuracy, the system can be used to automatically read and assess user-generated content (posts, comments, pictures, and videos) across various social platforms. Aside from the textual analysis, creative visual forms developed by the state-of-the-art AI models are also equipped with the capabilities of cyberbullying image and video detection. This is essential because, as explained, cyberbullying does not remain only within the confines of text-based atmospheric interactions. Oftentimes, pernicious pictures and videos are also shared on various social media outlets. Hence, the classification of content filtering systems still faces some problems. Bullying AI models have to deal with numerous factors such as the existence of commonly used fads, the possibility of an ever present danger, and a particular sociocultural environment, especially due to the fact that different social settings have different definitions of what constitutes bullying. Dangers also loom over exaggerated efforts regarding censorship of any form of content on the internet. Users may get irritated if they realize that even their rational and sensible posts get deleted for reasons which to them seem unreasonable. Therefore, the free speech should remain intact alongside the undesirable content elimination in AI-centric content moderating systems. Even more so, the constant updating and support by human moderators is essential in such systems to avoid inefficiency and bias. (Sahu& Mehta, 2023).

Figure 4. AI-Human Interaction in Content Moderation: A Layered Stack Diagram

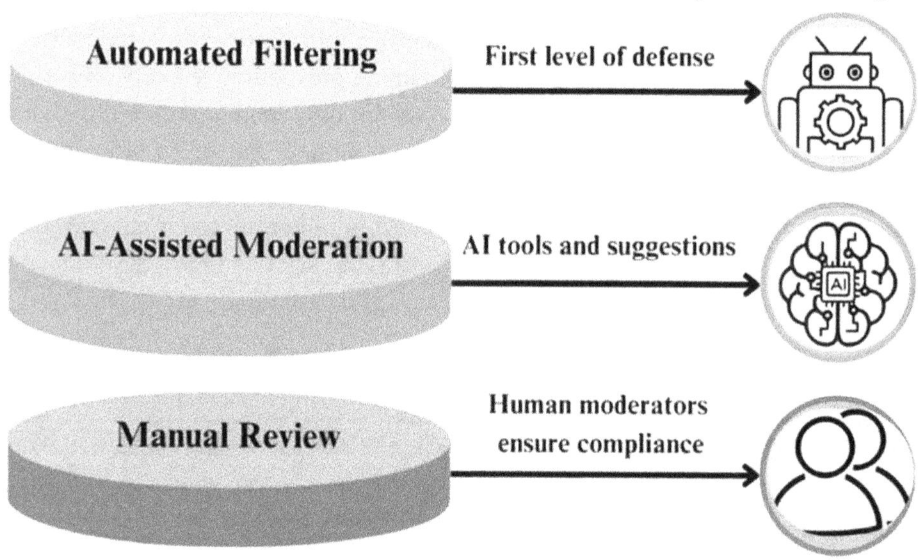

Figure 4 presents the relation between automatic filtering, assistance by artificial intelligence in moderation and human moderation. Each layer of the diagram content moderation role begins with automated filtering by AI, hikes to AI-assisted moderated by human beings, and ends with an manual review of extreme complex cases.

Collaboration with Social Media Companies for Safer Platforms

To comprehensively address the problem of cyberbullying, it is essential to incorporate artificial intelligence technology in the functioning of social media providers. This indicates that AI developers and social media platforms can work together to design sophisticated moderation systems that shield users from harmful messages. Several large social networking sites such as Facebook, Instagram, or Twitter, have incorporated content moderation by artificial intelligence, but there are still issues regarding further scalability, accuracy, and acceptance by users. When there is a meeting of social media companies and AI scientists, the new ways applied AI makes sense will assist in refining those systems through the availability of data, testing, and input from real users.

Moreover, apart from the technical aspect of the collaboration, social media companies would also be able to implement AI systems that compliment community reporting processes. For instance, AI can be employed to prioritize reports, to triage tagged content or suggest actions such as removal of the content or suspending a user. At the same time, however, social media companies should resist such tendencies prgrammed within the AI systems, where users do not know how such decision-making process happens, producing its own "Black box." Trust is instrumental for the users and therefore there should be policies on the governance and the application of AI (Monika Singh, T., 2024) in content oversight. Finally, with collaboration between AI engineering and social media design, even systems that combat the vice of cyberbullying will be effective, legitimate, and ethically appropriate. Furthermore, prevention mechanisms against cyberbullying can also be incorporated in the design of the information technology systems so that bullying tendencies can be nipped in the bud. AI can be applied by social media performance in monitoring users' effective use in such a way that changes in behavior likely to be aggressive or harassing are detected early. This forecast based strategy can mitigate cyberbullying prior to its pathogenic level thus helping users and the platform in creating a secure online environment. In this regard, the vision is to create a system where artificial intelligence's work is complemented by human supervision and community policing to avoid all forms of harassment in the digital space.

8. PREDICTIVE ANALYTICS FOR PROACTIVE CYBERBULLYING PREVENTION

Using Data Patterns to Predict Cyberbullying Risks

The term predictive analytics refers to the assessment of the potential future events or behaviors based on the previous or historical data available. In this case, regarding the efforts employed towards preventing the incidence of bullying, it would mean, the use of the data patterns from the uploads and pauses by an individual in social media to predict if that person will bully other individuals. Drawing upon a person's activities after some interval through time, predictive models can pinpoint the indicators of potential harassment and maltreatment which can be stopped even before any dangerous levels are attained. Such models can detect changes in metrics like the amount of negative language used, fighting with other users, or a drastic change in the behavior of the person. There are a lot of indicators that predictive analytics is able to analyze and as such is able to give a timely notification to the moderators or systems that act on bullying and disciplinary actions.

Figure 5. Predictive model workflow for cyberbullying prediction

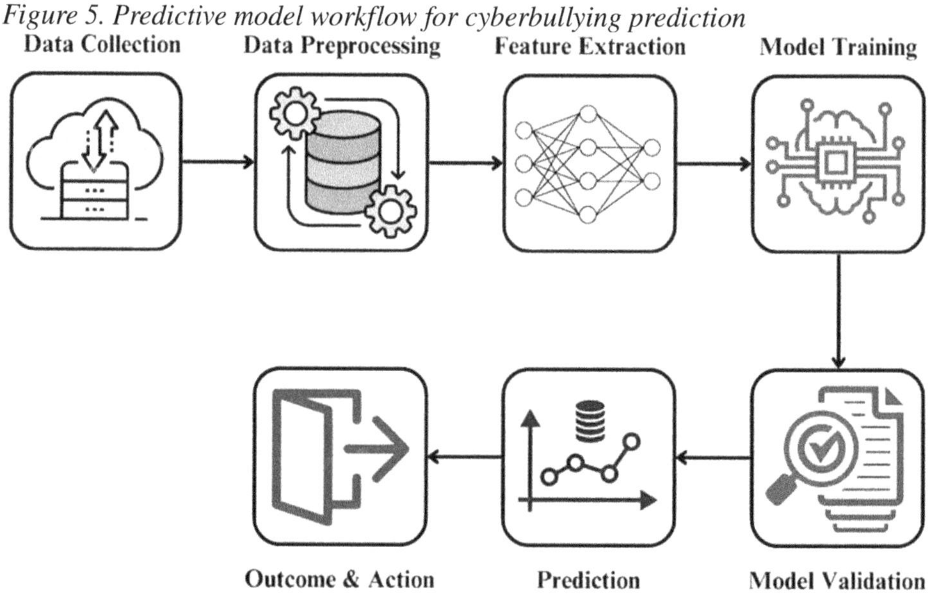

Figure 5 shows a flow diagram for the processes of information collected, analyzed, and applied in a cognitive engagement model on the prediction of cyber-bullying occurrence.

One of the most important aspects of data analytics is the predictive analysis. Management of such activities, means collecting a lot of data of diverse nature, from social media posts to messages and even bots' users meta data. The predictive model is built essentially on the basis of machine learning techniques such as regression analysis, decision trees and support vector machines. Such more advanced machine learning techniques entail the use of images within a system that has been trained on example data- that is, data about prior occurrences of cyberbullying, which in this case serves as the risk defining information for the machine. After this stage that brings the risk consequences analysis system closer to practical meaning, such system is capable of real-time analysis of entered data in order to forecast incidents and chances and to stop damage before it will be inflicted. This limb of cyber-bullying causative factors management is quite effective as individuals at risk are safeguarded from harm before they experience the consequences of bullying (Gupta &Sood, 2023). Nevertheless, predictive multivariate surveillance techniques for cyberbullying are not free from limitations. One of the critical challenges that you will face is the validation of the prediction made. One of the major model evaluation problems is overfitting, which occurs when a model is too closely fitted to the training data and cannot extend the prediction to new data. In particular, elevated worries about user privacy get raised at the time of carrying out analysis on user data. Risk profiling dictates the need of predictive models however it should not compromise user privacy. In this respect, it is of paramount importance that user data is anonymized and that consent is sought in advance so that user privacy is protected but the benefits of predictive analytics are realized.

Proactive Interventions for At-Risk Individuals

In a proactive strategy, predictive analytics may help in making interventions in a timely manner. Such approaches focus on the individuals who are most at risk and provide relevant support actions such as content moderation and mental or health based warnings. For instance, where a user has been marked as a bully, the site could issue a warning message via an automated system, explaining the consequences of their actions and the need to refrain from them. No, Willa, Zalia is cyberbullying is not a sweet way of saying the other person is being bullied. Other forms of intervention may include allowing victims of cyberbullying, portals to assistance immediately, every helpful tool or service that might help them such as reporting or resources for reaching out for help(Singh T., M., et.al, 2024). The aim is to create an environment which would be able to offer useful help in lessening the effects caused by cyberbullying but at the same time creating awareness and self-control among its users. The severity of the bullying that is expected can help in creating proactive measures against it. For example, if a user is expected to show low level bullying such as a passing remark, intervention strategies such as an educational mail or a warning could take place instead. These include temporary bans or compulsory sessions with a counselor for those who are expected to practice more intense forms of bullying. There is an aim in these measures to individualize them based on characteristics of the user, the situation the user is associated with and his/her history with the service. This way, alienation is avoided, and people are given a chance to modify their online behavior through the assistance that is offered.

Cyberbullying, like most types of harassment, can be more effectively addressed if a platform takes a proactive stance. To this effect, social networks such as Instagram and Facebook have introduced mechanisms that alert users when they are about to post a comment or an image that can be considered offensive. These platforms are able to instantly warn users by applying call predictive models to harmful posts, which allows the user to make changes to the content before its public release. Such a preventive measure discourages many users from taking some actions which can aggravate cyberbullying and makes them consider their actions beforehand.

9. ROLE OF CHATBOTS AND VIRTUAL ASSISTANTS IN CYBERBULLYING SUPPORT

AI-Powered Chatbots for Victim Support and Counseling

One recent application of technology that has proven efficient in enhancing immediate response to cases of cyberbullying is the use of chatbots. These chatbots are fashioned to provide a virtual room for people who would not want to seek assistance in real life. They can allow users to have a conversation via texts about the user's emotions and the user can receive help immediately. For example, they can provide comfort to the recipient, resources on dealing with cyberbullies, and even s step-by-step aid in getting a qualified expert. One of the most important contributing factors to the growth of the use of AI chatbots is that they can afford flexibility of time, which enables users to access them throughout the day and night even when services of human counsels are not available (Reddy et al., 2024).

The most common technology utilized in chatbots is natural language processing algorithm. This is because it enables the bots to know what the user is trying to communicate and respond as an individual would. Such bots may be able to comprehend the language that the user, most likely a victim of cyberbullying, uses and may recognize patterns that signify distress, depression, or anxiety, all of which derive from the emotional aspect of being bullied online. With this knowledge, chatbots are capable of modifying their behavior to soften the tone of the reply. Some bots even include elements of coping strategies teaching users the techniques or exercises such as breathing and mindfulness to manage stress levels (Mahalakshmi et al., 2019). These interventions such as therapy or counseling may be automated but play an important role in reducing the adverse effects of cyberbullying on the victim before professional services are offered. Now, while it can be agreed that the benefits outweigh the risks, there are also some drawbacks introduced when utilising chatbots to support victims. For example, trained therapists and counselors can provide counseling at certain levels without verbal interaction with the patient, which these systems automatically lack. Including these tvs in chat support would be allowing a counselor-in-training or even a support service operator who is conversant with the situation to speak to the user for the extreme cases of cyberbullying treatment. It is necessary for these AI applications to be additions and not substitutes to the existing mental healthcare system. Also, privacy and confidentiality standards are important due to the need to foster a trusting relationship with the users and as cyberbullying is highly sensitive data protection is imperative (Vandana et al., 2019).

Table 6 examines AI-based chatbots from the perspective of helping victims of cyberbullying in providing support in real time. In this section, different features of chatbots who provide emotional aid, resources, and support human counselor escalation, etc. are described.

Table 6. Chatbot-Based support systems in cyberbullying prevention

Feature	Description	Role in Cyberbullying Prevention	Examples
Victim Support	Provides real-time support and resources to victims	Helps users navigate bullying situations	Woebot, Replika
Reporting Assistance	Guides users through reporting and complaint processes	Simplifies reporting incidents for faster intervention	Facebook's reporting assistant
Counseling and Advice	Offers general advice and support for emotional wellbeing	Assists users with coping strategies	Wysa, Mental Health AI
Educational Tips	Educates users on identifying and responding to bullying	Increases user awareness and empowerment	Kids Help Phone Chatbot
Anonymity for Users	Ensures privacy and anonymity in interactions	Encourages victims to speak openly without fear	Anonymous support chatbots
Monitoring User Emotion	Detects emotional states and offers proactive interventions	Aids in providing timely support based on user emotions	Koko (emotion detection)

Chatbots: It is a software application that allows users to engage in a conversation through mimicking human speech by responding to their messages with pre-recorded texts.

Virtual Assistants in Reporting and Preventive Assistance

The engagement of virtual assistants as tools to assist users in reporting and combating incidences of cyberbullying has also happened with remarkable success. These assistants come as social media features or as separate applications through which a user is guided on how to report incidences of cyberbullying. The assistants can guide the user in a user-friendly manner in reporting whether it is reporting such cases to the administration of the website in question or the police case. Also, users can be instructed on how to carry out certain actions such as blocking or muting people who are bothering them, changing specific privacy parameters, or even doing more on the issue by calling the right people regarding the issue.

The preventive capability of virtual assistants is yet another noteworthy aspect about them. These provide preemptive solutions depending on the analysis of data using various techniques including AI help in predicting possible incursion of cyber bullying wherein people are guided in advance. For instance, such assistants could help prevent a user from posting something that is likely to be offensive or aggressive, a user can be warned about aggressive and hostile users or even how to remain positively active in the social network. Among others, these devices teach people who use the internet how to behave in a healthier manner and even help them look out for instances of these culprits who engage in cyber bullying. So, in that way, the risk of becoming a victim of online harassment can be somewhat limited. In addition, she explained that such devices could be used as a first aid and users may feel encouraged to do something about the problem of bullying rather than ignoring it. Another role that virtual assistants may fulfill is that of training these users in coping with the negative aspects of the internet such as cyberbullying. When dealing with the issue of bullying these assistants provide step-by-step instructions and create awareness on how to conduct oneself online to help users calm down. In this ever evolving and complicated sphere of technology, providing assistance in the occurrence and dealing with cyberbullying has become one of the main expectations from virtual assistants.

Virtual Assistants: Computer or web-based programs that help users complete a certain task, most frequently by employing a voice or a text interface.

Real-World Applications of Chatbots in Cyberbullying Prevention

There is an increasing deployment of practical chatbots and virtual assistants, with several social media networks and companies incorporating them in the fight against cyberbullying. For example, Instagram and Facebook have developed bots that analyze offensive language and warn the users before they send any inappropriate photograph or text. These bots can not only analyze the words used, but also the underlying emotional tone of the message, thus enabling the user to appreciate how the message could affect others. In this way, these interfaces promote responsible and safe use of the internet, which subsequently reduces cyberbullying incidences (Thomas et al., 2019). To this end, chatbots have also been integrated into projects addressing the needs of victims of bullying. In one such case in India, a chatbot called 'Maitri' was created with the aim of helping people access mental health services without revealing their identity. This is supplemented by a service available to victims of cyber-bullying, who can access a chatbot that channels them to appropriate services like therapists or helplines. Users of the system can also access Maitri, which provides younger users with tools and methods of managing the stress associated with this type of behavior, in particular at the beginning of the attack when it is hardest to cope with emotionally (Srilekha et al., 2019). Such steps indicate that utilization of artificial intelligence (Chandran& Gupta 2023). is becoming more common in the field of mental health as well as safety from harassment over the internet and helps in addressing the consequences of bullying in the longer run.

Although these tools are increasingly being utilized, their scalability and effectiveness present certain challenges. Specifically, it can be difficult for chat services and virtual avatars to keep pace with the ever-changing ways in which people engage in cyberbullying. The more advanced cyberbullying techniques grow, the more sophisticated chatbots need to become at identifying forms of abuse. Moreover, it is essential for AI tools to consider the differences in cultures and contexts in order not to misjudge the requirements of the users. Although these initiatives hold great prospects, they have to be assessed and improved continually to make sure that they work in controlling and alleviating the impacts of cyberbullying.

10. ADDRESSING LEGAL AND ETHICAL CONCERNS IN AI-DRIVEN CYBERBULLYING PREVENTION

Legal Framework for Cyberbullying Prevention

In the last ten years, the trend in statutory and other regulatory control of behaviors associated with cyberbullying has changed remarkably, as most authorities have come to the realization about the need to take measures against abuse online. A good number of states have recently approved stand-alone legislation dealing specifically with cyberbullying, thus providing redress to sufferers and discouraging offenders. These laws differ from one region to another, but they all seek to achieve the same objective, which is to shield people from danger while providing for free expression values and safety. For Instance, in the US, the Federal Cyberbullying

Prevention Act includes pain-for-all, for instance, harassment over the internet, and the same way, in the UK, the Malicious Communications Act makes it an offense to send electronic messages that are otherwise considered to be hateful (McCartney & Anderson, 2023).

The use of automation in the identification and reporting of cyberbullying incidents is one of the ways in which these laws have been enforced with the aid of the AI driven tools. These tools may be used to revolve around offensive interactions, tame the offenders, and tabulate the interactions that might require action for legal reasons. A more advanced application of AI is in understanding cyberbullying and assisting relevant bodies in managing it through behavior analytics and threat assessment (Smith & Singh, 2022). While legal aspects of use of AI enhances the fight against cyberbullying through conducting effective investigations, it also raises issues. One such debatable issue regards the use of AI technology and its application to the protection of the right to privacy. Any AI solution that helps monitor activities, and collect bullying-related pictures and videos, for instance, should be geared towards protecting individual privacy. In addition, the AI application and utilization in reporting cases of cyberbullying comes with its pros and cons especially with regard to the effectiveness of the information processed and the likelihood of the AI systems classifying even the normal behaviors as bullying. This could lead to abuse of the systems where false allegations may be propounded against individuals without just cause, thus there is a need for the existing legal orders to adapt and include how AI will affect the protection of the victims and the accused as well.

Ethical Implications of AI in Cyberbullying Detection and Prevention

The moral issues surrounding the implementation of artificial intelligence in identification and prevention of cyberbullying are quite apparent, but because any technology advanced with such a goal has the potential to infringe various rights of the individuals – right to privacy checking the censorship case, right to equity, even straightforward prejudice. First and foremost, attention is drawn to the question of privacy. To begin with, as the very concept of AI tools suggest, they are aimed at collecting and analysing data on a rather impressive scale. Such types of data usually include private correspondence, social networks posting, and general online activity in search of patterns of abuse and cyberbullying behavior. This method is bound to work in most cases as far as identifying the content that violates policies is concerned, but it also brings the threat of encroaching upon the boundary of privacy (Patel & Sharma, 2023). Thus, it is important to ascertain that the AI based systems specify the purpose for which the data is collected or used and the risk management mechanisms that are in place regarding personal information. Another ethical concern associated with the use of AI technology so as to curb cyberbullying is bias. AI models employ algorithms which learn from training sets that also contain some form of bias that can lead to the unfair discrimination of certain races or even individuals.For instance, an AI application built on data inclusive of bias thanks to media stereotypes may be biased in recognizing certain demographic categories as bullies more than others. Therefore, the model might produce unwanted outcomes like overgeneralization or omission of real instances of cyberbullying. Reducing the bias in these models is imperative for ai engineers by inserting various representation of training data, augmenting and re-evaluating the systems after sometime.

Figure 6. AI challenges in cyberbullying detection

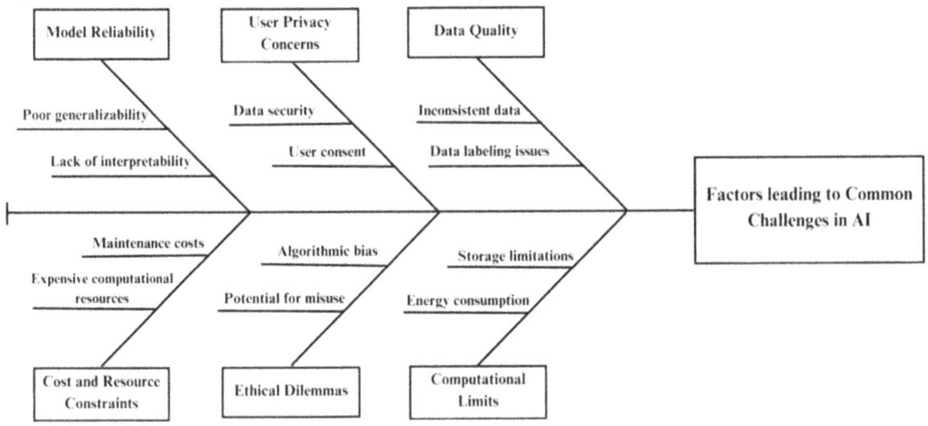

Figure 6 is an illustrative representation using a fishbone approach which examines the causes associated with the challenges faced in the moderation of AI content. These include the limitations of data, the boundaries of technology, and moral issues among others, with their interconnected ramifications indicating how each of these factors results in the complications of applying artificial intelligence.

The last but not least ethical issue is the very issue of responsibility. When aiming to implement artificial intelligence technology to combat the phenomenon of cyberbullying, it becomes essential to clearly define any stakeholders' traceable actions and the responsibilities attached to their use. If an AI recognizes some cues incorrectly or refuses to act where bullying is taking place, who is to blame for this error? It could be the fault of programmers of the AI, the owners of the AI-enabled system or even the customer who engaged in the adverse behavior. The presence of such mechanisms of accountability will help ensure that AI technologies are applied in an ethical manner and that people's rights are not violated while also ensuring that justice for the victims is met.

11. FUTURE DIRECTIONS: EMERGING TECHNOLOGIES AND INNOVATIONS

The Role of Blockchain in Privacy and Data Security

Blockchain technology, which is characterized by the secure and decentralized nature, is now penetrating various areas including the prevention of cyberbullying, successfully. One of the relevant advantages of the use of blockchain technology is the capacity to protect data even under high surveillance. In a case where cyberbullying prevention AI systems depend on user data, the data being processed should be confidential and trustworthy. This can make unnecessary alteration of sensitive because of the storing of registries in blockchain as they will be kept within the system and accessible to a few people only unless legitimate authority is provided. This is very useful in cases where detection and prevention of online abuse is required but abuse of the subject's privacy is not wanted (Gupta & Sharma, 2023).

The inherent design of blockchains, which is to eliminate central authority, aids in addressing the problem of over centralization of data. In most cases, centralized systems consist of central data storage servers that can be hacked thus compromising the sensitive information stored in them. On the other hand, blockchains have the data spread over the numerous nodes of the systems resulting in an increased complexity of the system being hacked. Besides, blockchain can also enable the creation of an effective reporting tool for the victims of cyberbullying where they can report such instances safely without being exposed or targeted negatively (Chandran& Sharma, 2022). Such an approach may motivate more victims to repose faith in the system and help out thereby increasing the effectiveness of measures against cyber bullying. Also, unique techniques executed by the convergence of blockchain technology and artificial intelligence, can also act as methods for the prevention of cyberbullying. AI is capable of monitoring and processing a significant amount of information over the internet and detecting the incidence of cyberbullying, while blockchain technology ensures that all tasks performed by the AI, such as flagging the report, reporting it, and notifying a person in authority, are completed in a secure way. The use of AI and blockchain in cyberbullying prevention would result in the development of more effective, clear and credible systems which will implement high standards of privacy and data protection (Singh & Kumar, 2023).

Potential of Augmented and Virtual Reality for Prevention

Both Augmented Reality (AR) and Virtual Reality (VR) are more recent technologies that show great promise in solving the problem of cyberbullying. These technologies, which have been developed with gaming and entertainment features in mind, are now being adapted in education and health (Gupta & Sharma, 2023). Likewise, AR and VR help develop new approaches to measure, prevent or assist in cases of cyberbullying. For instance, while looking through a VR headset, individuals can be transported into the life of a cyberbullying victim without any physical or emotional strain, which is the core focus of the enterprise. Such experiences allow people to appreciate the feelings of others, which is important in addressing the problem of bullying within the society (Patel &Soni, 2022).

Moreover, AR and VR solutions allow the development of Virtual Champion or Cyberbullying Counseling sessions for the patients in self-help mode. The patients get support from these spaces in the same manner as those who do not have any such problems within them and are restricted by stigma. Such patients are able to find people in the similar condition, talk to the therapist and speak to the people experiencing the same problems without leaving this protected Universe. This may lessen the disadvantages attached to help seeking behaviors and be beneficial for those who do not have access to conventional services (Chandran& Sharma, 2023). In addition, Augmented Reality also facilitates interventions in the form of real time help for victims of cyberbullying. For instance, an application that is based on augmented reality features could automatically send an alert response to the user in case the user received an abusive message and assist in activating a network of supportive friends. The forward thinking strategy makes provision for action even before the situation gets worse thereby helping mitigate the effects of cyberbullying (Harrison & Gupta, 2022).

AI Innovations on the Horizon for Cyberbullying Prevention

With the ever-growing advancement of AI technology, it is bound to spur on more creative inventions that will impact the dynamics of cyberbullying and its prevention strategies. One such development is advanced natural language generation models that embody the real time cyberbullying intervention strategies in the form of conversations. These AI systems can provide support immediately by conversing with one or both of the aggressor and the victim, de-escalating the aggressive interaction, and creating educational materials in order to avoid further harassment. Furthermore, the utilization of such AI-powered systems is very efficient and aids in curbing the pain due to cyberbullying and further incidents of such nature within a very short duration (Gupta & Verma, 2023). Additionally, it is expected that with the incorporation of artificial intelligence in the social networks, this technology will understand better the environment of communication, or rather the specific conditions of interaction, which the users of these networks are in. That is in particular, whether some remarks and/or publication are made in jest, a parody or in malice. With contextual discrimination improvement, distortion reconciliation will also improve, so that more relevant content caters for ignorant and harmful content enabling accurate placement of such measures (Singh &Soni, 2023). One more innovation which we may expect to see quite soon is a combination of this text-based technology with an emotional state detection AI (Singh & Kumar, 2023) which is capable of understanding very small changes in a person's emotions what he says, what he looks, and how he sounds, even without words. It may be that the system will understand if a person is uncomfortable or upset and therefore be able to take steps to assist them more efficiently and within a shorter time frame. By mobile emotion recognition systems and cyberbullying detection systems working hand in hand, the scope of support that artificial intelligence can render towards the efforts of active prevention would increase (Harrison & Sharma, 2022).

Figure 7. Cyberbullying Prevention Framework: A Layered Strategy

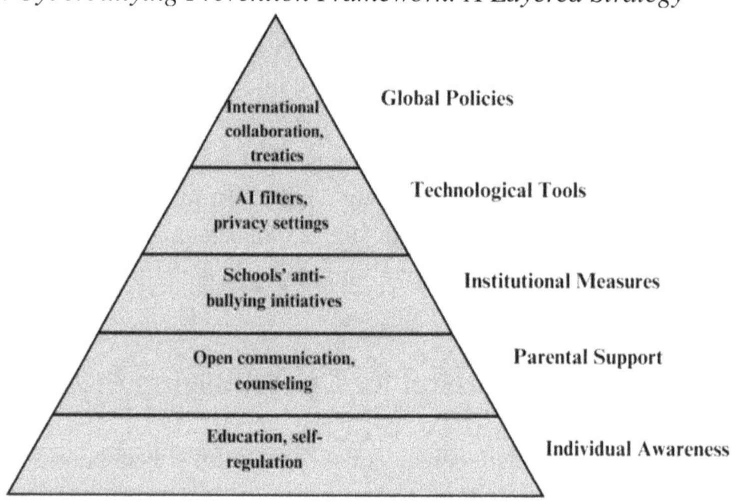

Figure 7 illustrates a pyramidal structure depicting the various layers of approaches to prevent cyberbullying in schools. This implementation ranges from the elementary steps of enhancing personal efforts and using reporting systems to the overarching measures of international legislations towards cyberbullying. In this regard it indicates the importance of the different layers in one's approach to cyberbullying and how they all function cohesively in combating the problem.

CONCLUSION

The alarming rise of cyberbullying, particularly in adolescents, has made it imperative to seek effective measures of prevention. Cyberbullying, like all other social ills, has continued to change over time thus it calls for creative and modern ways of protecting individuals from the injury to their mental well-being. In this regard, Cyberbullying and Artificial Intelligence (AI) in the Fight against Cyberbullying is allied on synergies and solution combinations to tackle the social detriment of cyberbullying. Current Trends in AI for Cyberbullying Prevention are represented by the evolution and growth of the development of artificial technologies and information systems that include, mostly voice technologies and neural networks, to the extent that content and threat monitoring can be carried out in real time. Social and other on-line Medias have started utilizing these technologies to monitor and control abusive behaviours and hate speech. The importance of NLP and sentiment analysis is significant when it comes to communication patterns and its use in detection and understanding of cyberbullying and its contents inciting violation of rules. Content recognition in images and videos has been another new area in which AI has been utilized for the purposes of screening and narrowing down on damaging images that would found difficult to screen for through texts. In addition, while moderating contents during interactions took place on different networks, AI has proved die hard at ensuring safety in the interventions by recognizing wrongful acts and behaviours of users before they outraged/ crossed the line. Instead, real-time moderation encourages the active social media platforms to take preventive measures against the aggressive contents on the networks without having the users' exposure to the interactive environment for long.

Nevertheless, there are still obstacles presented by the ethical dimensions of privacy, bias, and data protection. In most of the countries, AI is undoubtedly becoming a major part of cyberbullying prevention. Hence it is important to design the systems in a way that the algorithms do not violate personal space and in addition to that bias is kept in control to avoid prejudice. In the future, convergence of advanced technologies such as blockchain, AR and VR will provide even better strategies to avert these risks. Predictive analytics for instance may provide Pre-emptive actions directed towards mitigating identified risks of occurrence such as vulnerability to bullying of certain parties before it actually happens. In the end, while cyberbullying incidents might be drastically reduced because of the use of technology, particularly AI in this case, there is a need for continuous development, research, and cooperation between the Q 's related to the technology, educators and decision makers to make the internet a healthier place for every individual. The potential of AI in minimizing the risks of cyberbullying in the long run lies in its ability to adjust itself to the dynamics that are often associated with the emerging threats, at the same time upholding the ideals of privacy and fair practice.

REFERENCES

Aricak, T., Yaman, M., & Kosar, S. (2008). The impact of anonymous cyberbullying in adolescent peer groups. *Cyberpsychology, Behavior, and Social Networking*, 11(4), 380–385. DOI: 10.1089/cyber.2008.0142

Bansal, A., & Kumar, R. (2020). Facebook's AI System for Cyberbullying Prevention: An Overview. *Journal of AI and Internet Safety*, 9(5), 56–71.

Bansal, A., & Kumar, R. (2020). Addressing data imbalance in cyberbullying detection using machine learning techniques. *International Journal of AI and Data Science*, 7(4), 200–212.

Bhaskar, V., & Sundararajan, V. (2020). Cyberbullying detection and prevention using natural language processing. *Indian Journal of Cybersecurity and Technology*, 4(2), 45–59.

Brailovskaia, J., Teismann, T., & Margraf, J. (2018). The role of positive mental health in alleviating the effects of cyberbullying. *Journal of Adolescence*, 64, 59–70. DOI: 10.1016/j.adolescence.2018.02.006

Chandran, R., & Sharma, A. (2022). Blockchain and AI integration for secure cyberbullying prevention. *Journal of Cyber Security and Technology*, 9(3), 80–95.

Chandran, R., & Sharma, A. (2023). Exploring the potential of AR and VR for cyberbullying prevention. *Technology and Education Journal*, 14(2), 100–115.

Chandran, R., & Sharma, V. (2023). Addressing bias in AI models for social media moderation. *Journal of AI Ethics*, 7(2), 150–165.

Chaudhary, R., & Gupta, S. (2020). Using machine learning algorithms for cyber bullying detection and intervention. *AI & Society*, 35(1), 105–118. DOI: 10.1007/s00146-019-00920-w

Choudhary, R., & Agarwal, A. (2022). Image and video recognition for cyberbullying detection on social media platforms. *International Journal of Artificial Intelligence*, 15(3), 210–225.

Dehue, F., Bollman, M., & Völlink, T. (2008). Parent's perception of cyberbullying and the impact on countermeasures. *Cyberpsychology, Behavior, and Social Networking*, 11(2), 93–100. DOI: 10.1089/cyber.2007.0052

Dooley, J. J., Pyzalski, J., & Cross, D. (2009). The psychological effects of cyberbullying: A comparative study. *Journal of School Violence*, 8(3), 323–339. DOI: 10.1080/15388220902914199

Feinberg, T., & Robey, D. (2009). Teacher interventions in preventing cyberbullying. *Educational Psychology Review*, 21(4), 351–367. DOI: 10.1007/s10648-009-9116-5

Ghosh, P., & Agarwal, S. (2021). Visual content moderation for online safety: Detecting harmful images and videos. *Journal of Cybersecurity and Digital Trust*, 7(2), 130–144.

Ghosh, P., & Mukherjee, R. (2020). Ethical considerations in AI-driven cyberbullying prevention: A comprehensive analysis. *Journal of Ethics in Technology*, 4(3), 120–134.

Gupta, A., & Sood, N. (2023). Predictive analytics for cyberbullying prevention: A machine learning approach. *Journal of AI and Digital Security*, 6(2), 50–65.

Gupta, R., & Sharma, A. (2023). The role of blockchain in cyberbullying prevention: Enhancing privacy and security. *Journal of Digital Privacy*, 13(2), 40–55.

Gupta, R., & Verma, A. (2023). Future AI innovations for cyberbullying prevention. *AI and Society Journal*, 12(3), 120–135.

Harrison, L., & Gupta, S. (2022). The impact of AR and VR in providing emotional support for cyberbullying victims. *Journal of Virtual Reality and Mental Health*, 8(3), 45–60.

Harrison, L., & Sharma, R. (2022). Emotion recognition AI for cyberbullying detection and prevention. *Journal of AI in Mental Health*, 6(4), 115–130.

Hasan, A., Rahman, M., & Khan, S. (2023). Emotion detection in cyberbullying detection systems. *Journal of Artificial Intelligence Research*, 42(3), 145–160. DOI: 10.1016/j.artint.2022.12.002

Hinduja, S., & Patchin, J. W. (2010). Cyberbullying and suicide: A review of the literature. *International Journal of Cybersecurity*, 4(1), 20–40. DOI: 10.1007/s11514-010-0072-x

Iwendi, C., Ojiako, U., & Mothobi, O. (2020). Deep learning systems for combating online harassment: A review. *IEEE Access : Practical Innovations, Open Solutions*, 8, 16003–16018. DOI: 10.1109/ACCESS.2020.2964302

Jha, R. (2021). NLP Models for Sentiment Analysis in Cyberbullying Detection. *Indian Journal of Technology and Cybersecurity*, 5(3), 89–104.

Jha, R. (2021). Anomaly detection for cyberbullying: A machine learning approach. *Journal of Technology and Cybersecurity*, 8(2), 123–137.

John, R., Smith, A., & Johnson, P. (2010). Stress associated with cyberbullying and its emotional impact. *Journal of Youth Psychology*, 45(2), 120–135. DOI: 10.1016/j.jyp.2010.03.004

Kaur, P., & Saha, S. (2022). AI-based systems for real-time cyberbullying prevention. *International Journal of AI and Cybersecurity*, 10(2), 98–110. DOI: 10.1016/j.ijai.2022.01.003

Kumar, R., & Jain, M. (2022). AI in cyberbullying prevention: Balancing privacy with protection. *Journal of Digital Security*, 9(4), 340–355.

Kumar, R., Verma, S., & Sharma, P. (2021). A hybrid machine learning approach for cyberbullying detection on social media platforms. *Indian Journal of Computer Science*, 12(4), 222–235.

Mahalakshmi, C., Sharmila, T., Priyanka, S., Sastry, M., Reddy, D. B. V. R. M., & Reddy, M. K. K. (2019).A survey on various chatbot implementation techniques. JASC: Journal of Applied Science and Computations.

McCartney, T., & Anderson, P. (2023). Legal frameworks for cyberbullying prevention: A global overview. *International Journal of Cyber Law*, 11(3), 45–60.

Mishna, F., Saini, M., & Solomon, S. (2009). Cyberbullying: An exploratory study of factors related to bullying behaviors. *Journal of Youth and Adolescence*, 38(6), 850–861. DOI: 10.1007/s10964-009-9434-0 PMID: 19636786

Monika Singh, T., Kishor Kumar Reddy, C., Ramana Murthy, B. V., Nag, A., & Doss, S. (2025). AI and Education: Bridging the Gap to Personalized, Efficient, and Accessible Learning. In M. Ouaissa, M. Ouaissa, H. Lamaazi, M. El Hamlaoui, & K. Reddy C. (Eds.), Internet of Behavior-Based Computational Intelligence for Smart Education Systems (pp. 131-160). IGI Global.https://doi.org/DOI: 10.4018/979-8-3693-8151-9.ch005

National Crime Records Bureau (NCRB). (2020). Cyberbullying cases on the rise: Implications for public safety in the digital age. NCRB Annual Report, 2020, 1-25. https://ncrb.gov.in

Nikolaou, D. (2017). Does cyberbullying impact youth suicidal behaviors? *Journal of Health Economics*, 56, 30–46. DOI: 10.1016/j.jhealeco.2017.09.009 PMID: 28968528

Patel, M., Sharma, S., & Bansal, A. (2021). NLP Techniques in Social Media Monitoring for Cyberbullying. *International Journal of AI and Social Media Research*, 7(4), 123–134.

Patel, M., Sharma, S., & Bansal, A. (2021). Supervised machine learning for identifying cyberbullying content on social media. *Journal of AI in Social Media*, 5(3), 89–101.

Patel, M., & Soni, V. (2022). Augmented and Virtual Reality in cyberbullying prevention. *Journal of Immersive Technologies*, 5(4), 110–125.

Patel, R., & Kumar, R. (2021). Generative adversarial networks for detecting manipulated visual content in cyberbullying. *Journal of Artificial Intelligence and Ethics*, 5(4), 350–364.

Paul, S., & Saha, S. (2022). Cyberbullying detection using CyberBert: An AI-based solution. *Journal of Cybersecurity and Privacy*, 1(3), 228–241. DOI: 10.1007/s42486-022-00375-7

Rai, P., & Singh, S. (2021). Ethical AI frameworks for online safety and cyberbullying prevention. *Journal of Cyber Ethics and Law*, 8(1), 40–58.

Reddy, C. K. K., Reddy, P. S., Anisha, P. R., & Doss, S. (2024). Towards smarter chatbots. In Cognitive Machine Intelligence: Applications, Challenges, and Related Technologies (p. 328). CRC Press. DOI: 10.1201/9781003500865-18

Reddy Chinthala, K. K. ., Thakur, M. S., Shuaib, M. ., & Alam, S. (2024). Prospects of Computational Intelligence in Society: Human-Centric Solutions, Challenges, and Research Areas. Journal of Computational and Cognitive Engineering. . DOI: 10.47852/bonviewJCCE42023330

Sahu, S., & Mehta, D. (2023). Challenges in AI content filtering: A deep dive into social media moderation. *AI and Ethics Journal*, 5(4), 450–465.

Saxena, S., & Verma, N. (2022). Bias in AI algorithms: Challenges and solutions in cyberbullying detection. *International Journal of Artificial Intelligence*, 19(2), 100–115.

Sharma, A., & Aggarwal, A. (2021). Privacy concerns in the use of AI for online safety. *Journal of Cybersecurity and Ethics*, 5(3), 207–221.

Sharma, P., Gupta, R., & Joshi, S. (2022). Feature engineering for cyberbullying detection using machine learning techniques. *International Journal of Cybersecurity*, 10(2), 150–167.

Sharma, R., Gupta, P., & Mehta, D. (2022). Enhancing Cyberbullying Detection with Multilingual NLP Models. *Journal of Natural Language Processing and AI*, 8(2), 37–52.

Singh, P., & Kumar, R. (2023). AI and blockchain: A synergistic approach to online harassment prevention. *Journal of AI Ethics*, 7(1), 60–75.

Singh, R., Shukla, P., & Kumar, A. (2021). Social intelligence systems in cyberbullying prevention. *Computers in Human Behavior*, 116, 106634. DOI: 10.1016/j.chb.2021.106634

Singh, R., & Soni, P. (2023). AI in context-aware cyberbullying prevention: The next frontier. *Journal of AI Technologies*, 11(2), 80–95.

Singh, S., & Saini, N. (2023). Deep learning applications in detecting cyberbullying in video content. *Journal of Multimedia and Cybersecurity*, 10(1), 50–64.

Singh, T. M., Reddy, C. K. K., & Lippert, K. (2024). Advancing Human-Centric Solutions: The Future Trajectory of Soft Computing in Modern Society. In Kumar, N., Pal, S., Agarwal, P., Rosak-Szyrocka, J., & Jain, V. (Eds.), *Human-Machine Collaboration and Emotional Intelligence in Industry 5.0* (pp. 1–18). IGI Global., DOI: 10.4018/979-8-3693-6806-0.ch001

Singh, V. (2019). Long-term impacts of cyberbullying on mental health and reputation. *Journal of Social Media Studies*, 18(4), 155–168. DOI: 10.1016/j.jsms.2019.08.006

Slonje, R., & Smith, P. K. (2008). Cyberbullying: A new challenge for educators. *School Psychology International*, 29(1), 5–21. DOI: 10.1177/0143034308095196

Slonje, R., Smith, P. K., & Frisén, A. (2013). The role of anonymity in cyberbullying. *Journal of School Psychology*, 51(2), 231–245. DOI: 10.1016/j.jsp.2013.01.002 PMID: 23481087

Smith, J., & Singh, P. (2022). The role of AI in enforcing cyberbullying laws. *AI and Law Journal*, 8(1), 85–100.

Srilekha, C. H., Sneha, C., Prathyusha, G. N., Reddy, C. K. K., & Murthy, B. V. R. (2019). Professional study on chatbots using artificial intelligence. *Journal of Applied Science and Computations*, 6(1), 186–197.

Thomas, R. M., Punna, S., & Reddy, M. C. K. K., &RamanaMurthy, B. (2019). Survey on artificially intelligent chatbot. *Journal of Applied Science and Computations*, 6(1), 85–94.

Ttofi, M. M., & Farrington, D. P. (2011).The effectiveness of school-based programs for preventing bullying and cyberbullying.Campbell Collaboration. https://www.campbellcollaboration.org

Vandana, A., Rani, J., Goud, V. A., Kishor, M. C., Reddy, K., & Murthy, R. (2019). A study of chatbots through artificial intelligence. *Journal of Applied Science and Computational Science*, 6(1), 341–354.

Willard, N. (2006). Cyberbullying: A new challenge for educators. National Education Association, 22(4), 45-50. https://www.nea.org

Chapter 10
Cyber AI Trends:
Future Trends in AI for Cyberbullying Prevention

Mir Mehedi Rahman
https://orcid.org/0009-0002-7837-8639
Emporia State University, USA

Sazzad Hossain
https://orcid.org/0009-0004-5379-8754
Emporia State University, USA

Bishnu Bhusal
https://orcid.org/0000-0001-7522-5878
University of Missouri, Columbia, USA

Naresh Kshetri
https://orcid.org/0000-0002-3282-7331
Rochester Institute of Technology, USA

ABSTRACT

Generative Artificial Intelligence (AI) is opening new paths in the detection and prevention of cyberbullying. As we know, AI is shaping and improving the future of cyber, industry, automation, manufacturing, healthcare etc. with challenges of privacy concerns, job losses issues, and increased rules. This chapter explores future trends in AI-driven tools designed to reduce online bullying including various cybercrime across social media platforms, messaging apps, and other digital platforms. Ethical concerns like security and privacy, fairness, and avoiding bias are also discussed, aiming to ensure that AI tools are used responsibly and transparently. By combining technical advancements with an understanding of social impact, this chapter presents a vision for AI systems that create safer, more supportive online spaces. The

DOI: 10.4018/979-8-3373-0543-1.ch010

chapter highlights the potential of generative AI to shape digital environments that are inclusive, resilient, and protective, fostering healthier interactions for everyone involved with the future scope of the study.

INTRODUCTION

Cyberbullying has become a pervasive issue in the digital era, deeply impacting the psychological and emotional well-being of individuals, especially children and adolescents. Unlike conventional bullying, which is sometimes limited by physical bounds, cyberbullying is unrelenting and persistent when it enters the internet realm. Along with providing venues for communication, the explosion of social media channels and messaging apps has opened the path for harassment and abuse. Conventional approaches for spotting and correcting such actions, such keyword filtering and hand editing, sometimes fail to find subtle and context-dependent cases of cyberbullying. Recent developments in generative artificial intelligence (AI) provide chances to investigate creative ideas able to efficiently solve these problems by means of tools analyzing intricate patterns in multimedia content and textual data (Chaudhary, 2024).

Including artificial intelligence (AI) into cyberbullying prevention marks a major progress in tackling the widespread problem of internet harassment. Overwhelmed by a lot of negative content, social media companies are turning to artificial intelligence technologies such as natural language processing (NLP), machine learning (ML), and deep learning (DL) to support moderation initiatives. These technologies enable platforms to move from conventional reactive approaches where users report harmful conduct for review to proactive ways that find and reduce damaging information before it gets out there. By spotting subtle trends in text, photos, and videos, artificial intelligence technologies help to identify inappropriate content that human moderators might miss. These developments, however, create serious ethical questions even as they improve content monitoring. Scanning private conversations and user-generated content is common in proactive artificial intelligence moderation, which starts discussions on how to strike a balance between safety and freedom of speech. Errors in artificial intelligence detection—such as mistaking informal conversations or jokes for cyberbullying may cause unwarranted strife and perhaps raise societal tensions. These problems draw attention to how artificial intelligence systems should give ethical issues such justice, openness, and user rights top priority along with technical efficiency. Researchers support the creation of AI interventions that precisely balance these aspects to guarantee they are both respectful of personal privacy and expression and successful in identifying negative content. While platforms keep implementing AI-driven solutions, the emphasis should still be on developing systems that promote trust and diversity while tackling the several problems of cyberbullying (Chaudhary, 2024) (Milosevic, 2023).

Artificial Intelligence (AI) especially Large Language Models (LLMs) and multimodal analysis systems have seen major developments in the creation of cyberbullying detection technology. Conventional methods, usually based on Natural Language Processing (NLP) for text-based communication analysis, have exhibited difficulties to adequately depict the complexity of online interactions. For example, irony, cultural subtleties, and multimedia materials including photos and videos have sometimes made these methods less useful. Recent research highlights the need of including advanced models such as GPT-4 Vision, which combine picture recognition with linguistic analysis, allowing a better knowledge of context and intent in digital interactions (Vanpech, 2024). By simultaneously assessing visual and textual signals, these systems process multimodal data and bridge gaps in conventional detection techniques. Using such systems, however, presents difficulties with scalability, ethical issues, and the requirement for varied training sets to guarantee inclusion and fairness. The continuous improvement of AI-driven systems to manage the dynamic character of digital communication reflects the increasing need for strong solutions able to solve the always changing terrain of cyberbullying (Vanpech, 2024).

Beyond conventional, fixed methods, the fast development of artificial intelligence (AI) has presented revolutionary chances to solve the complexity of cyberbullying detection and prevention. Particularly those using natural language processing (NLP) and deep learning (DL), modern artificial intelligence-driven systems shine in evaluating complex interactions, identifying context-dependent harassment, and spotting abusive behavior across text, photos, and multimodal content. Graph neural networks (GNNs) and generative adversarial networks (GANs) are reinventing how cyberbullying is detected and provide real-time, scalable solutions able to adjust to the always shifting dynamics of online platforms (Bokolo, 2024). Although related efforts to improve privacy and data integrity have investigated blockchain and federated learning approaches, the focus in this chapter is still on the pragmatic and scalable uses of artificial intelligence algorithms to reduce cyberbullying (Alabdali, 2024). Achieving balanced detection algorithms that limit false positives while preserving high accuracy across several linguistic, cultural, and contextual settings still presents difficulties notwithstanding these developments. Integration of artificial intelligence into cyberbullying prevention systems must give ethical issues including privacy, justice, and inclusiveness top priority as it develops. Emphasizing their potential to create safer, more inclusive digital environments by creative, context-aware systems, this chapter explores the technical developments, problems, and prospects of AI-driven solutions in addressing cyberbullying.

Advanced AI technologies, including NLP, DL, GNNs, and GANs, have redefined approaches to tackling the complexities of nuanced and context-dependent online interactions, particularly in cyberbullying detection. These developments provide scalable, real-time solutions that exceed the constraints of conventional approaches, therefore combating abusive behavior across many digital platforms. Still, there are important obstacles to overcome such as guaranteeing ethical standards, safeguarding user privacy, and promoting inclusiveness across many linguistic and cultural settings. These difficulties form the basis for a more general investigation of the historical and theoretical underpinnings of AI developments, the links between cyberbullying and more general cybersecurity dangers, and the part modern technology will play in determining future policies. Under this prism, a thorough examination of the application of AI approaches and their consequences is done, leading to practical findings and suggestions for building safer and more inclusive digital environments.

Background Study

Modern artificial intelligence (AI) has been found by researchers as a useful tool for both assuring public safety and vice-versa (Michael, 2023). Since exposures and outages have long-lasting trust consequences, it is necessary to find underlying causes of cybersecurity challenges. Developing advanced artificial intelligence bots to fight against cyberattacks apart from implementing techniques to produce an AI application would not solve cybersecurity issues. Large language models (LLMs) showed several uses in the framework of generative artificial intelligence with a variety of negative potentialities including data and bias issues, explainability hurdles, environmental concerns, and privacy issues. Driven by developments in machine learning, artificial intelligence, and natural language processing (Anisha, 2021), big data has grown to be a major focus of study.

Generative AI (GenAI) models like Google Bard and ChatGPT are highlights of digital evolution transformation as can be exploited by hackers and penetration testers (Gupta, 2023). Making GenAI as trustworthy, ethical, safe, and secure including cyber defense automation, malware detection, incident response plans, secure code generation is a must. Prompt injection attacks on ChatGPT, successful attacks like Jailbreaks, reverse psychology, use of GenAI by cyber offenders, creation of social engineering attacks by adversaries, malware like polymorphic malware creation by malicious users are the popular vulnerabilities along with the capabilities of GenAI models. As the evolution of OpenAI's GPT from GPT-1 (released in 2018) to GPT-4 (current model as of June 2023), it has trained with a large corpus of texts and can take image inputs via Bing AI in Microsoft Edge browser as shown in Table 1.

Table 1. Summary of background study for AI in cyberbullying prevention

Ref	Strategy for Cyberbullying Prevention	Advances in AI	Challenges for Future
(Michael, 2023)	AI in Cybersecurity, OODA loop, AI applications	LLMs, AI threats, Machine Learning	Human intervention, New vulnerabilities
(Gupta, 2023)	Generative AI in Cyber Security and Privacy	GenAI tools, AI Chatbots, NLP, DNNs	ChatGPT to ThreatGPT, OpenAI
(Chan, 2019)	AI in Cybersecurity for IT Management	Big data, AI policy and managerial implications	Opportunity for cyber criminals
(Hofstetter, 2020)	AI technologies and services for anomaly patterns detection	Machine learning algorithms, AI systems	Lack of awareness, limited resources
(Roshanaei, 2024)	Cybersecurity enhancement through AI and ML	AI and ML driven models for prediction	New threats and sophisticated attacks

Applied in various fields like pharmaceuticals, job hopping prediction, bioinformatics and many more, AI is a thriving field (Chan, 2019). AI in cybersecurity can detect various cyber threats (existing threats and future threats) and make real-time (RT) decisions as this new age calls for strong development and deployment for future trends. As a part of cyber security and information security management, applications of AI will be largely considered the AI softwares the company and customer data. As one common method for cybersecurity is with supervised learning, AI can check interactions relating to malicious IP traffic, calculate behavior patterns and flag it. Cybercrime analysis for information security via AI like denial of service (DoS) attacks, remote to local (R2L) attacks, user to root (U2R) attacks, hacking where cyber attackers including penetration testers gain access through weak points in the system.

As cybersecurity is a complex and fast growing field, many small and medium sized businesses (SMBs) lack cybersecurity awareness and allocate limited technical resources for that (Hofstetter, 2020). Big organizations and businesses may afford their own in-house cybersecurity measures but SMBs may face a lack of all types of resources including financial resources, technical resources, human resources, and many other resources. Helping to identify anomalous behavior (taking account of false positives and false negatives) could indicate future forms of cyber-attacks for all businesses to improve performance and accuracy. AI engine provides an ability when it comes to detect cybersecurity incidents based on pattern matching and pattern analysis as displayed in Figure 1.

The enhancement of cybersecurity through AI and ML via defenses against increasingly sophisticated cyber threats highlighting new vulnerabilities (Roshanaei, 2024). Beside several challenges and limitations of AI integration such as Operational & integration costs, adversarial AI attacks, model bias & fairness, data quality & availability, AI frameworks offer transformative benefits. There are ethical considerations around automated decision making, heavy dependency on data quality & quantity, vulnerability to sophisticated attacks, and enhancing AI resilience by exposing systems to improve ability of such cyberattacks. The potential bias in AI decision-making for cybersecurity can result from non-representative data sets also called as training models and/or errors in training data.

Figure 1. Summary of AI applications in AI for Cybersecurity from our Background Study for several cyberattacks and cybercrimes (Michael, 2023) (Gupta, 2023) (Chan, 2019) (Hofstetter, 2020) (Roshanaei, 2024)

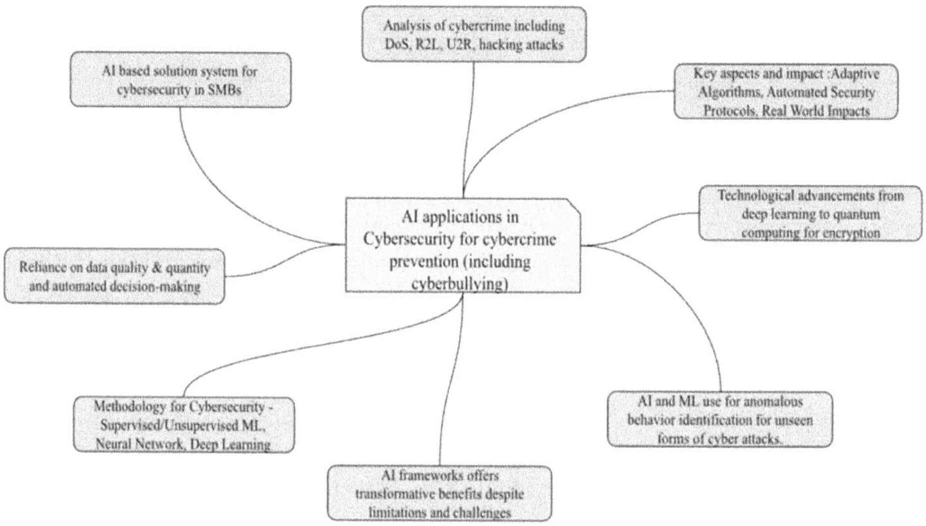

Cybercrime, Cyberattacks, and Cyberbullying

Cybercrime refers to illegal activities conducted using computers, networks, or digital platforms. With the rapid growth of technology, including the rise of new applications, networks, and the deep web, cybercrime has become a significant global challenge. Cybercriminals exploit weaknesses in systems to achieve various objectives, from stealing sensitive information to causing large scale disruptions. There are different types of cybercrime. In some cases, the computer itself is the target, such as when hackers attempt to breach systems or disrupt networks. In other instances, the computer serves as a tool to commit crimes, like spreading malware or stealing financial data. Lastly, digital devices may play an incidental role in facilitating crimes, such as using social media to plan illegal activities. Hackers, often associated with cybercrime, operate with varying motivations. Some act for personal amusement, like defacing websites, while others aim for recognition by breaching high-security systems.

Regardless of their motives, hackers significantly influence the world of digital crime, and understanding their methods and intentions can help in predicting and countering cyber threats. Efforts to combat cybercrime require a balance between privacy and security. Governments and researchers are increasingly focusing on privacy issues, regulatory compliance and understanding societal norms around data sharing. The creation of effective cybercrime laws across nations is critical, but international cooperation remains vital. Organizations like Interpol, private companies, academic institutions, and national law enforcement agencies must work together to strengthen cybersecurity and develop strategies to counteract cyber threats. By understanding the complexities of cybercrime and enhancing collaborative efforts, societies can better defend against digital threats and build more secure online environments (Sabillon, 2016).

Cyberattacks are deliberate attempts by individuals or organizations to compromise the security of digital networks, systems, or devices. They target private data, interfere with regular business operations, or take advantage of weaknesses for their own financial, political, or personal benefit. In today's interconnected world, the sophistication of these attacks has increased, affecting not only people but also corporations and governments. The impact of cyberattacks on public institutions is one major topic of concern. These institutions frequently handle and preserve important data pertaining to education, health, and basic services. Whole societies may suffer because of their systems being corrupted.

For example, during the COVID-19 pandemic, Ecuador faced numerous cyberattacks that revealed weak information security practices. These breaches caused misunderstandings, postponed important decisions, and interfered with essential services that citizens relied on, such as basic utilities and healthcare. Social media platforms have also become a major target for cyberattacks. Hackers use these networks to steal information, disseminate false information, and manipulate public opinion. When individuals are largely dependent on online platforms for communication and information during emergencies like pandemics or natural disasters, this misuse intensifies. In Ecuador, during the pandemic, discrepancies in data from various government sources stoked mistrust and brought attention to the need for improved cybersecurity procedures. To combat cyberattacks, experts emphasize the importance of strengthening information security. Important steps include creating policies that guarantee data integrity and confidentiality, putting in place real-time monitoring tools, and embracing strong encryption. In Ecuador, proposals like blockchain-based systems aim to provide a secure framework for managing public data and minimizing risks during emergencies. Ultimately, addressing cyberattacks requires a combination of advanced technology, skilled personnel, and clear regulations. Governments and organizations must prioritize cybersecurity to protect critical infrastructure, maintain public trust, and ensure that vital services remain uninterrupted, even during challenging times (Toapanta, 2020).

Cyberbullying is a detrimental behavior that takes place in the digital world, where individuals use technology to intimidate, harass, or harm others. It can occur across various platforms, including social media, messaging apps, and online forums, making it a widespread issue in today's internet-driven society. Unlike traditional bullying, cyberbullying has unique characteristics, such as its ability to occur 24/7 and reach a wide audience, which amplifies its impact on victims. Adolescents are particularly vulnerable to cyberbullying due to their frequent and extended use of social media and other online platforms. Research highlights that most teenagers' own smartphones and spend significant time online, increasing their exposure to cyberbullying risks. Young people are also more vulnerable to emotional distress, such as despair, anxiety, and feelings of loneliness, since they frequently lack the psychological skills such as resilience and critical thinking necessary to deal with these situations (Fulantelli, 2022).

Studies show that cyberbullying often overlaps with another form of online aggression known as cyberhate. While cyberbullying typically involves targeted harassment of an individual, cyberhate is broader and often directed at groups based on race, religion, gender, or other identity markers. Both forms of aggression share common predictors, such as poor parent-child relationships, exposure to harmful online content, and the lack of strong social support systems. Preventing and addressing cyberbullying requires a multi-faceted approach. Building positive relationships within families and fostering open communication can help reduce risks. Additionally, educators and policymakers must implement strategies that empower young people to navigate the online world responsibly. By promoting digital literacy and emotional well-being, we can create a safer environment where adolescents are less likely to become victims or perpetrators of cyberbullying. Ultimately, addressing cyberbullying and its related forms of aggression is essential to ensuring the mental health and well-being of young people in the digital age (Fulantelli, 2022) as shown in Figure 2.

This section explores how advancements in AI can tackle digital issues like cybercrime, cyberattacks, and cyberbullying. Cybercrime encompasses illegal activities using digital platforms, where hackers exploit system vulnerabilities for motives ranging from financial gain to disruption. Tackling cybercrime requires a delicate balance between security and privacy, as well as international collaboration among governments, organizations, and law enforcement agencies to develop effective laws and strategies (Sabillon, 2016). Cyberattacks, a specific form of cybercrime, focus on breaching systems to steal sensitive information or disrupt operations, often targeting public institutions and social media platforms. These attacks can cause widespread harm, such as undermining trust in public services during crises like pandemics, emphasizing the need for robust cybersecurity measures like encryption and blockchain systems (Toapanta, 2020). Cyberbullying, a prevalent online threat, disproportionately affects adolescents due to their extensive use of social media. Its 24/7 nature and broad reach amplify the emotional impact on victims, leading to issues like anxiety and depression. Addressing cyberbullying requires building family support systems, promoting digital literacy, and implementing policies that encourage responsible online behavior (Fulantelli, 2022). AI can play a pivotal role in detecting and mitigating these threats, offering proactive solutions to create safer digital environments.

Figure 2. AI's Role in Mitigating Cybercrime, Cyberattacks, & Cyberbullying (Sabillon, 2016) (Toapanta, 2020) (Fulantelli, 2022)

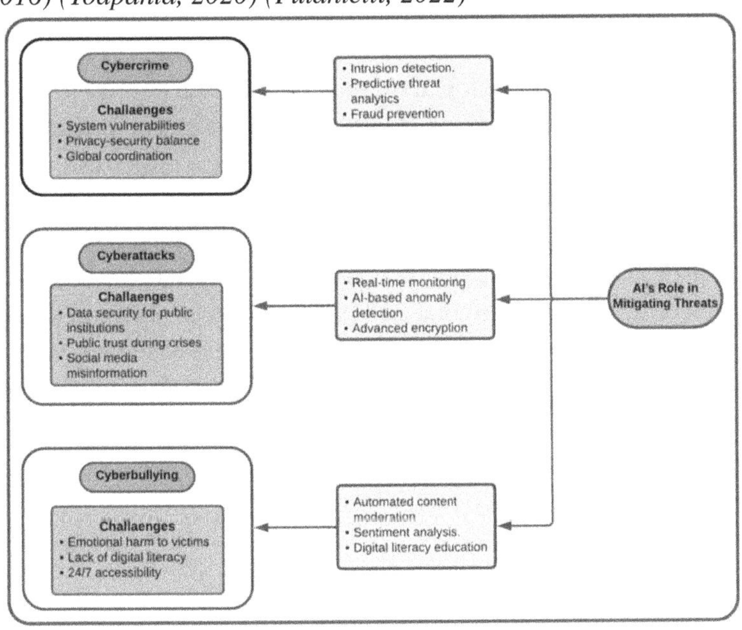

AI for Future of Cybersecurity

Artificial intelligence represents more than a technological upgrade; it is a fundamental reimagining of cybersecurity paradigms. As digital threat landscapes grow increasingly complex and dynamic, AI emerges as a transformative force in proactive threat management, offering unprecedented capabilities in risk mitigation and strategic response.

The promise of AI-driven cybersecurity lies in its ability to address the most challenging aspects of digital defense. Quantum computing-powered machine learning revolutionizes cybersecurity by harnessing immense computational power to process vast datasets (Shara, 2023). This enables advanced, real-time threat detection by rapidly identifying patterns, anomalies, and vulnerabilities. As a result, organizations can deploy robust defenses against sophisticated cyber threats, including those utilizing complex encryption techniques. Modern cybersecurity tools excel at tackling the toughest challenges in digital defense. Similarly, techniques like GANs and VAEs improve accuracy and solve data gaps in areas like medical imaging, showing their potential to uncover subtle patterns and make online spaces safer (Peryala, 2024).

Autonomous cyber defense systems further enhance these capabilities by combining AI and machine learning to detect, predict, and neutralize cyber threats in real time (Kaur, 2023). By continuously monitoring networks, these systems can swiftly identify and respond to anomalies, providing proactive protection with minimal human intervention (Madireddy, 2020). This approach significantly improves the speed, accuracy, and operational efficiency of threat responses, especially in the face of evolving cybersecurity challenges.

AI is also revolutionizing cybersecurity by deploying advanced algorithms to combat sophisticated social engineering threats. Machine learning enables real-time detection of deepfakes (Gambin, 2024), prediction of phishing attempts, and dynamic adjustment of security protocols. These intelligent systems analyze communication patterns, identify anomalies, and implement multi-layered authentication, transforming cybersecurity from a reactive defense mechanism into proactive threat prevention (Camacho, 2024) as depicted in Figure 3.

Figure 3. Artificial intelligence for the future of cybersecurity and cyberbullying prevention

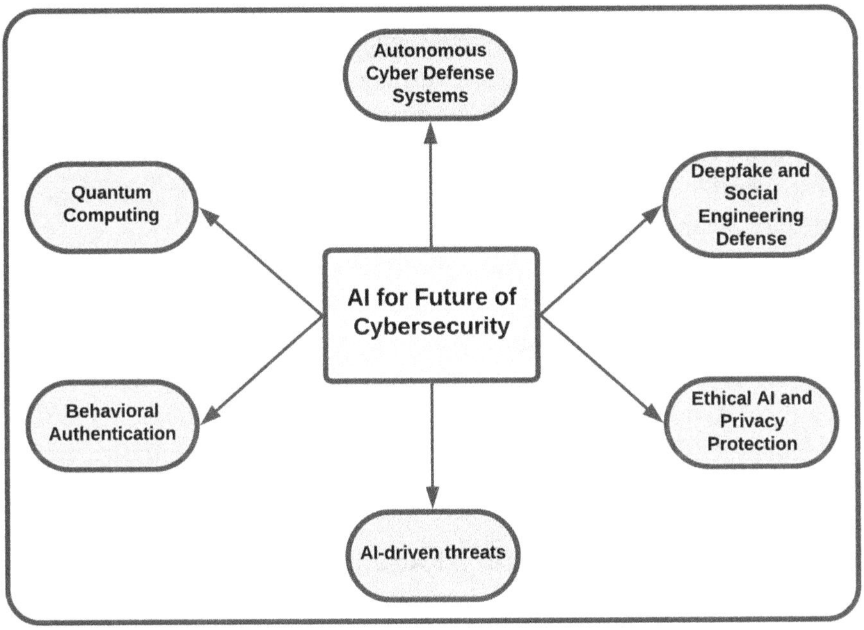

Complementing these advancements, the future of ethical AI and privacy-preserving technologies promises to deepen trust and broaden the scope of responsible AI innovation (Santos, 2024). Next-generation privacy-preserving methods, such as multi-party computation, zero-knowledge proofs, and enhanced differential privacy techniques (Chadha, 2023), will enable highly secure collaborations where sensitive data can be analyzed or verified without being shared. Advances in federated learning will further enhance decentralized systems by allowing model training across distributed devices while protecting data privacy and minimizing risks of breaches. Blockchain ensures data integrity, enhances identity management, and prevents fraud, complementing AI in building secure systems to tackle cyberbullying and online abuse (Singh, 2024). Ethical AI will also benefit from the integration of explainable AI (XAI) frameworks, providing transparent and interpretable decision-making processes. Additionally, the convergence of blockchain technology with AI will offer immutable audit trails, ensuring accountability and fairness in AI-driven applications. These developments will continue to balance the need for technological progress with the imperative of safeguarding privacy, equity, and ethical integrity in an increasingly interconnected digital world.

Behavioral authentication is also set to evolve with advanced AI. Future behavioral authentication will leverage advanced AI to create hyper-personalized security profiles. Machine learning algorithms will analyze intricate user behaviors beyond traditional biometrics—including typing patterns, device interaction dynamics, contextual movement, and micro-gestures (Wang, 2024). These systems will develop predictive models that can authenticate users with near-absolute certainty, detecting even the most subtle anomalies in real-time. Quantum computing and neuromorphic AI will enable instantaneous, multi-dimensional behavioral analysis, making authentication seamless and virtually unbreakable.

However, the integration of AI into cybersecurity is not without substantial challenges. Adversarial attacks pose a significant threat, with malicious actors developing increasingly sophisticated techniques to exploit vulnerabilities in AI systems. Data poisoning emerges as a critical concern, where attackers attempt to compromise the integrity of AI training data, potentially rendering security solutions ineffective. The potential for advanced AI-driven threats targeting critical infrastructure adds another layer of complexity to the cybersecurity landscape (Tao, 2021).

Cyberbullying Prevention via AI Advancements

The use of technology to meet various business needs is growing and so is for cyberbullying detection, prediction, and prevention via AI-driven framework (Meduri, 2024). Behavioral analysis, data breach risk prediction, cyber fraud detection, spam detection as cybercrime are the key AI frameworks considered for evaluation purposes. Mitigating cyber threats at various locations under different environmental settings are most essential for predicting and averting cyberattacks. AI frameworks for faster threat detection are crucial for behavior analysis, spam filtering, regression analysis, and breach risk prediction. Handling massive amounts of data with greater scalability, speed, and accuracy compared to traditional solutions for cyberbullying as advancements in AI via AI-based security systems. Explainable AI (XAI) enhances education by making machine learning transparent, helping educators trust tools, address biases, and track outcomes (Fatima, 2024).

Cryptographic attacks, malicious code integration, and several variants of phishing attacks always bypass security architectures when it comes to system development for detection and prevention of cyberattacks (Abdiyeva-Aliyeva, 2021). Data gathering which is processed into information later is always precious in prevention and detection of cybercrimes. Deep neural network (DNN) as an architectural form of artificial neural network can create learning models and learning platforms for network behavior. Out of several benefits of integrating AI for cybersecurity (and then for cyberbullying prevention), advancements like DNN serve as an excellent reinforcement against cybercrimes.

Prediction is dependent on a strong database for cyberattacks identification and prevention as we depend on technologies to defend from cyberthreats (Amarasinghe, 2019). Time series algorithm SARIMA (Seasonal Auto Regressive Integrated Moving Average) extends Auto Regressive Integrated Moving Average (ARIMA) technique. Data mining steps (as part of Phase I of suggested methodology) comprise data cleaning, data integration, data selection, data transformation, data mining, and data representation as a dataset transformed to the arbitrary shape and dataset saved in the cloud. While convolutional neural networks (CNN) finds vulnerability, artificial intelligence-based generative models do the preventive processing and enhance dependability.

Applications and future vision of artificial intelligence are not only for cybersecurity and cyber defense but also in microgrids of communication networks and physical devices from a security standpoint (Beg, 2023). Comprising modern microgrids, today cyber-physical systems have physical assets including distributed energy resources (DERs), power devices, loads, and cyber-layer in the network. AI-based cyber-attack mitigating, and cyber-attack detection applied to address data-driven cyberattacks in a distributive cooperative control-based AC microgrid. Table 2 shows that a great amount of power users lose and suffer major damage from malfunctioning microgrids and cyberattacks on them.

There is no doubt that AI has emerged as a key component of cybersecurity in terms of security enhancement and cyber threat detection and threat prevention (Rizvi, 2023). As of today's digital, environment for countering cyberattacks and cyberbullying prevention, AI is becoming a key tool to prevent cyberattacks via predictive modeling. Detection of emerging cyber threats (in contrast to traditional signature-based approaches) is the main AI advantage in cybersecurity and cyberbullying prevention. User behavior may indicate a potential cyber threat as artificial intelligence (with use of machine learning, deep learning, pattern recognition algorithms) can detect anomalies and trends in network traffic including incoming and outgoing traffic.

Table 2. Prevention of Cyberbullying and Cyber-attacks via several countermeasures, methods, and techniques with use of Artificial Intelligence (AI)

Prevention method(s)	Rationale of the Study	Impacts on Future AI Trends	Ref
AI-driven framework	Importance of organization automating AI processes to bolster cybersecurity.	Delves into AI frameworks for predicting and preventing cyberattacks.	(Meduri, 2024)
AI-based DNN architecture	DNN torrent structure to monitor and review impact of network traffic and host level events to warn.	DNN performs better than conventional machine learning classification.	(Abdiyeva-Aliyeva, 2021)
Time Series algorithm - SARIMA	An automated system consisting of a mechanism to deploy vulnerabilities and a rich database with known vulnerabilities.	With an output of considerable accuracy, evaluated results of cyberattacks detection, has the pattern-based attack pool.	(Amarasinghe, 2019)
AI-based techniques in microgrids	Techniques employed to tackle data-driven cyberattacks due to exceptional pattern recognition.	Performance of AI-based cyberattack mitigation in a distributed cooperative control-based AC microgrid.	(Beg, 2023)
AI in cybersecurity for threat detection	AI can be used to prevent cyberattacks through predictive modeling, protect networks and sensitive data from online threats.	AI-based systems provide complex and cutting-edge methods to counter cyberattacks including predictive analytics.	(Rizvi, 2023)

CONCLUSION AND FUTURE SCOPE

As the challenges of cybercrime, cyberattacks, and cyberbullying continue to evolve, artificial intelligence (AI) has emerged as a key player in the fight against these. This chapter highlights the disruptive potential of technologies driven by artificial intelligence, notably in areas such as real-time threat identification, predictive analytics, and multimodal analysis enabling nuanced and context-aware intervention. Artificial intelligence offers solutions that are scalable and adaptive, which go beyond the capabilities of traditional methods. These solutions can be used to protect public institutions from cyberattacks and to mitigate the emotional and social harm caused by cyberbullying. However, as artificial intelligence systems continue to evolve, it is important that concerns such as guaranteeing justice, eliminating biases, protecting privacy, and maintaining ethical transparency continue to be at the forefront of research. The complexity of cyber risks necessitates an approach that is collaborative and multidisciplinary, engaging policymakers, technologists, and educators, to find the optimal balance between innovation and accountability.

AI has a wide range of potential applications in the fight against digital threats, as we look in the future. The incorporation of quantum computing enables artificial intelligence systems to achieve processing rates that have never been seen before, which in turn enables faster and more precise threat detection. Federated learning and decentralized frameworks hold the promise of improved privacy and security while also reducing the dangers associated with data sharing. In addition, explainable artificial intelligence (XAI) is going to play a significant part in contributing to the development of trust by providing transparency in the decision-making process.

The identification and prevention techniques for cyberbullying will be further refined because of developments in natural language processing, image recognition, and behavioral analytics that are driven by artificial intelligence. Future computer systems will be able to more successfully address the subtleties of global digital interactions if they place an emphasis on training datasets that are both inclusive and culturally varied respectively. In addition, the combination of artificial intelligence and blockchain technology has the potential to produce records that cannot be altered, which would improve accountability in online contexts.

Ultimately, the success of these technologies will be contingent on a worldwide commitment to promoting innovation while simultaneously respecting ethical standards. By utilizing artificial intelligence in a responsible manner, we can pave the way for digital spaces that are safer and equal, ensuring that the internet continues to serve as a platform for constructive and beneficial engagement. This journey requires continued research, collaboration, and investment in AI to meet the ever-evolving challenges of the digital age.

REFERENCES

Abdiyeva-Aliyeva, G., Hematyar, M., & Bakan, S. (2021). Development of System for Detection and Prevention of Cyber Attacks Using Artificial Intelligence Methods. In *2021 2nd Global Conference for Advancement in Technology (GCAT)* (pp. 1-5). IEEE. DOI: 10.1109/GCAT52182.2021.9587584

Alabdali, A. M., & Mashat, A. (2024). A novel approach toward cyberbullying with intelligent recommendations using deep learning-based blockchain solution. *Frontiers in Medicine, 11, 1379211.* https.//DOI: 10.1109/ICAC49085.2019.9103372

Amarasinghe, A. M. S. N., Wijesinghe, W. A. C. H., Nirmana, D. L. A., Jayakody, A., & Priyankara, A. M. S. (2019). AI based cyber threats and vulnerability detection, prevention, and prediction system. In *2019 international conference on advancements in computing (ICAC)* (pp. 363-368). IEEE. DOI: 10.1109/ICAC49085.2019.9103372

Anisha, P. R., Reddy, K. K. C., & Nhu, N. G. (2021). Big data. Trends, challenges, opportunities, tools, success factors, and the keyway toward pandemic analytics. In *Handbook of research for big data concepts and techniques*. Apple Academic Press. DOI: 10.1201/9781003144526-11

Beg, O. A., Khan, A. A., Rehman, W. U., & Hassan, A. (2023). A review of AI-based cyber-attack detection and mitigation in microgrids. *Energies*, 16(22), 7644. DOI: 10.3390/en16227644

Bokolo, B. G., & Liu, Q. (2024). Artificial intelligence in social media forensics. A comprehensive survey and analysis. *Electronics, 13(1671), 1-24.* https.//DOI: 10.1201/9781003144526-11

Camacho, N. G. (2024). The Role of AI in Cybersecurity. Addressing Threats in the Digital Age. *Journal of Artificial Intelligence General science (JAIGS) ISSN. 3006-4023, 3*(1), 143-154DOI: 10.1201/9781003144526-11

Chadha, R., Sistla, A. P., Viswanathan, M., & Bhusal, B. (2023). Deciding Differential Privacy of Online Algorithms with Multiple Variables. In *Proceedings of the 2023 ACM SIGSAC Conference on Computer and Communications Security* (pp. 1761-1775). DOI: 10.1145/3576915.3623170

Chan, L., Morgan, I., Simon, H., Alshabanat, F., Ober, D., Gentry, J., . . . Cao, R. (2019). Survey of AI in cybersecurity for information technology management. In *2019 IEEE technology & engineering management conference (TEMSCON)* (pp. 1-8). IEEE. DOI: 10.1109/TEMSCON.2019.8813605

Chaudhary, P. K., Alam, N., Yalamati, S., Kolasani, S., Palakurti, N. R., & Whig, P. (2024). Detecting and preventing child cyberbullying using generative artificial intelligence. *In2024 Asia Pacific Conference on Innovation in Technology (APCIT) (pp.* 1-9*).* IEEE. DOI: 10.1109/APCIT62007.2024.10673710

Fatima, S., Reddy, C. K. K., Sunerah, A., & Doss, S. (2024). Innovations in education. Integrating explainable AI into educational intelligence. In *Internet of behavior-based computational intelligence for smart education systems*. IGI Global. https.// DOI: 10.4018/979-8-3693-8151-9.ch002

Fulantelli, G., Taibi, D., Scifo, L., Schwarze, V., & Eimler, S. C. (2022). Cyberbullying and cyberhate as two interlinked instances of cyber-aggression in adolescence. a systematic review. *Frontiers in Psychology*, 13, 909299. DOI: 10.3389/fpsyg.2022.909299 PMID: 35712182

Gambín, Á. F., Yazidi, A., Vasilakos, A., Haugerud, H., & Djenouri, Y. (2024). Deepfakes. current and future trends. *Artificial Intelligence Review*, 57(3), 64. DOI: 10.1007/s10462-023-10679-x

Gupta, M., Akiri, C., Aryal, K., Parker, E., & Praharaj, L. (2023). From chatgpt to threatgpt. Impact of generative ai in cybersecurity and privacy. *IEEE Access : Practical Innovations, Open Solutions*, 11, 80218–80245. DOI: 10.1109/ACCESS.2023.3300381

Hofstetter, M., Riedl, R., Gees, T., Koumpis, A., & Schaberreiter, T. (2020, September). Applications of AI in cybersecurity. In *2020 Second International Conference on Transdisciplinary AI (TransAI)* (pp. 138-141). IEEE. DOI: 10.1109/TransAI49837.2020.00031

Kaur, R., Gabrijelčič, D., & Klobučar, T. (2023). Artificial intelligence for cybersecurity. Literature review and future research directions. *Information Fusion*, 97, 101804. DOI: 10.1016/j.inffus.2023.101804

Maddireddy, B. R., & Maddireddy, B. R. (2020). AI and Big Data. Synergizing to Create Robust Cybersecurity Ecosystems for Future Networks. *International Journal of Advanced Engineering Technologies and Innovations*, 1(2), 40–63.

Meduri, K., Gonaygunt, H., & Nadella, G. S. (2024). Evaluating the Effectiveness of AI-Driven Frameworks in Predicting and Preventing Cyber Attacks. *International Journal of Research Publication and Reviews*, 5(3), 6591–6595. DOI: 10.55248/gengpi.5.0324.0875

Michael, K., Abbas, R., & Roussos, G. (2023). AI in cybersecurity. The paradox. *IEEE Transactions on Technology and Society*, 4(2), 104–109. DOI: 10.1109/TTS.2023.3280109

Milosevic, T., Verma, K., Carter, M., Vigil, S., Laffan, D., Davis, B., & O'Higgins Norman, J. (2023). Effectiveness of artificial intelligence-based cyberbullying interventions from youth perspective. *Social Media + Society*, 9(1), 1–12. DOI: 10.1177/20563051221147325

Peryala, A., & Reddy, C. K. K. (2024). Utilization of generative AI in medical imaging to improve evaluation and therapy. In *Intelligent systems and IoT applications in clinical health*. IGI Global. https.//DOI: 10.4018/979-8-3693-8990-4.ch007

Rizvi, M. (2023). Enhancing cybersecurity. The power of artificial intelligence in threat detection and prevention. *International Journal of Advanced Engineering Research and Science*, 10(05), 055–060. DOI: 10.22161/ijaers.105.8

Roshanaei, M., Khan, M. R., & Sylvester, N. N. (2024). Enhancing Cybersecurity through AI and ML. Strategies, Challenges, and Future Directions. *Journal of Information Security*, 15(3), 320–339. DOI: 10.4236/jis.2024.153019

Sabillon, R., Cavaller, V., Cano, J., & Serra-Ruiz, J. (2016). Cybercriminals, cyberattacks and cybercrime. In *2016 IEEE International Conference on Cybercrime and Computer Forensic (ICCCF)* (pp. 1-9). IEEE.

Santos, O., & Radanliev, P. (2024). *Beyond the Algorithm. AI, Security, Privacy, and Ethics*. Addison-Wesley Professional.

Shara, J. (2023). Quantum machine learning and cybersecurity. *Quantum : the Open Journal for Quantum Science*, 12(6), 47–56.

Singh, T. M., Reddy, C. K. K., & Lippert, K. (2024). The revolution and future of blockchain technology in cybersecurity. A comprehensive analysis. In *Artificial intelligence for blockchain and cybersecurity-powered IoT applications*. CRC Press. https.//DOI: 10.1201/9781003497585

Tao, F., Akhtar, M. S., & Jiayuan, Z. (2021). The future of artificial intelligence in cybersecurity. A comprehensive survey. *EAI Endorsed Transactions on Creative Technologies*, 8(28), e3–e3. DOI: 10.4108/eai.7-7-2021.170285

Toapanta, S. M. T., Carpio, J. A. E., & Gallegos, L. E. M. (2020). An Approach to Cybersecurity, Cyberbullying in Social Networks, and Information Security in Public Organizations during a Pandemic. Study case COVID-19 Ecuador. In *2020 Congreso Internacional de Innovación y Tendencias en Ingeniería (CONIITI)* (pp. 1-6). IEEE.

Vanpech, P., Peerabenjakul, K., Suriwong, N., & Fugkeaw, S. (2024). Detecting cyberbullying on social networks using language learning model. *InProceedings of the 2024 International Conference on Knowledge and Smart Technology (KST) (pp.* 1–9*).* IEEE. DOI: 10.1109/KST61284.2024.10499678

Wang, C., Tang, H., Zhu, H., Zheng, J., & Jiang, C. (2024). Behavioral authentication for security and safety. *Security and Safety*, 3, 2024003. DOI: 10.1051/sands/2024003

Chapter 11 The Double Edged Sword of AI: Legal and Regulatory Implications of AI in Cyberbullying

S. Ida Evangeline
https://orcid.org/0000-0003-2997-7897
Government College of Engineering, Tirunelveli, India

ABSTRACT

The integration of artificial intelligence (AI) into digital environments has revolutionized communication and social interactions while introducing profound legal, ethical, and regulatory challenges, particularly in addressing cyberbullying. This chapter explores the dual role of AI in combating and enabling cyberbullying, focusing on its potential as a transformative tool for harm mitigation and its unintended consequences, such as algorithmic bias, privacy concerns, and misuse for malicious purposes. By analyzing case studies of AI applications across major platforms, the chapter highlights both the successes and limitations of current systems in content moderation and behavioral interventions. Furthermore, the chapter delves into the broader ethical and human rights implications of AI, including its impact on freedom of expression, privacy, and equality. Through an interdisciplinary approach, the discussion evaluates existing regulatory frameworks and identifies critical gaps, emphasizing the need for adaptive, inclusive, and globally coordinated policies.

DOI: 10.4018/979-8-3373-0543-1.ch011

1. INTRODUCTION

1.1 Overview of AI in Digital Environments

The rapid advancement of AI has profoundly reshaped the digital environment, redefining how people interact, communicate, and engage with technology (Hunt, 2014). AI technologies, which encompass machine learning, natural language processing (NLP), and computer vision, have become central to online platforms such as social media networks, digital marketplaces, and content moderation systems (Babu & Kanaga (2022). These technologies enable platforms to automate decision-making, enhance personalization, and process vast amounts of data at unprecedented speeds.

The historical evolution of AI technologies highlights a trajectory of increasing sophistication and integration into everyday life. Early AI applications, such as rule-based expert systems of the 1980s, were limited in their capacity and lacked the adaptability required for dynamic online environments. With the advent of machine learning in the 1990s and the subsequent development of deep learning algorithms (Dutton & Conroy, 1997), AI systems gained the ability to learn from data and improve over time, paving the way for applications like real-time speech recognition, targeted advertising, and fraud detection. The emergence of generative AI, exemplified by technologies like OpenAI's GPT models, marks the latest milestone in this progression, enabling systems to create content autonomously and interact in increasingly human-like ways (Zhang & Shao, 2024).

Despite these advancements, the deployment of AI in digital environments is not without challenges. Algorithms designed to enhance efficiency and safety often have unintended consequences, such as reinforcing societal biases, enabling the spread of misinformation, or infringing on user rights. These issues are particularly evident in the context of content moderation, where AI systems must navigate the complexities of language, context, and intent. For example, while AI can detect overt hate speech, it often struggles with subtleties like sarcasm or cultural nuances, leading to errors in identifying harmful content. This dual capacity of AI—to act as both a tool for positive transformation and a source of potential harm—raises complex questions about its regulation and governance, particularly when addressing critical societal issues like cyberbullying. Understanding AI's multifaceted role in the digital space is essential for evaluating its influence on the evolving nature of online harm.

1.2 The Cyberbullying Phenomenon in the Digital Age

Cyberbullying has emerged as one of the most pervasive and damaging issues in the digital age, characterized by repeated and intentional harm inflicted on individuals through online channels (Singh et al. 2024). Unlike traditional bullying, cyberbullying transcends physical boundaries and persists across virtual spaces, often intruding on victims' lives in ways that are difficult to escape. Victims of cyberbullying face a range of consequences, including psychological distress, social alienation, and, in some cases, physical health complications.

Recent statistics underscore the severity of the cyberbullying epidemic. According to a report by UNICEF, one in three young people has experienced cyberbullying, with many cases remaining unreported due to stigma or fear of retaliation (Li et al. 2024). The Pew Research Center highlights similar trends, revealing that nearly 60% of teenagers in the United States have faced online harassment. High-profile cases, such as those involving public figures or viral harassment campaigns, further illuminate the devastating impact of cyberbullying. The tragic story of Amanda Todd, a Canadian teenager who died by suicide following relentless online harassment, serves as a stark reminder of the urgent need to address this issue.

The proliferation of digital platforms such as social media, instant messaging services, and online gaming has amplified the scale and complexity of cyberbullying. Features like anonymity and virality make it easier for perpetrators to target individuals without immediate consequences, while victims struggle to find recourse. At the same time, the integration of AI into these platforms has altered the dynamics of cyberbullying, with AI serving both as a tool to combat this harm and as a technology that, if misused or poorly designed, may inadvertently exacerbate it (Bansal et al. 2024). Generative AI, for instance, adds a new dimension to this challenge by enabling the creation of hyper-realistic deepfake videos or automated harassment bots, which can significantly escalate the intensity and reach of cyberbullying.

1.3 Objectives of the Chapter

This chapter aims to explore the intricate relationship between artificial intelligence and cyberbullying from a legal and regulatory perspective. Central to this examination is the dual role of AI technologies: as tools for combating online harm through mechanisms such as content moderation, and as potential contributors to the problem through algorithmic biases, privacy intrusions, or misuse by malicious actors.

By delving into the historical evolution and current applications of AI, the chapter seeks to provide a comprehensive understanding of how these technologies are influencing the landscape of cyberbullying. It will evaluate the adequacy of existing legal frameworks governing the use of AI in this context and propose actionable strategies to address identified gaps. Additionally, the discussion will address broader ethical and social considerations, such as inclusivity, fairness, and the protection of human rights in AI governance. Special attention will be given to the implications of generative AI, which represents both an opportunity for innovation and a source of unprecedented risks in the realm of online harm.

Ultimately, this chapter aspires to contribute to the development of a balanced approach that leverages AI's capabilities while minimizing its risks in the fight against cyberbullying. By fostering interdisciplinary collaboration among policymakers, technology developers, and civil society, the chapter aims to lay the groundwork for more effective and equitable solutions to one of the most pressing challenges of the digital era.

2. UNDERSTANDING CYBERBULLYING AND AI'S ROLE

2.1 Definitions and Characteristics of Cyberbullying

Cyberbullying refers to the use of digital technologies to intentionally harm, harass, or intimidate individuals. Unlike traditional forms of bullying, cyberbullying is uniquely characterized by its persistence, reach, and anonymity (Hinduja & Patchin, 2015). Harmful actions can be repeated indefinitely, leaving victims with little reprieve, as digital content remains accessible and shareable. Moreover, the global nature of the internet allows perpetrators to target victims across geographic boundaries, magnifying the scope of their actions (Livingstone & Smith, 2014).

Specific cases highlight the devastating effects of cyberbullying. For example, the case of Amanda Todd, a Canadian teenager who suffered relentless online harassment, gained global attention and underscored the far-reaching consequences of digital abuse. Another high-profile case involved football players in the UK who faced racial abuse on social media following a major tournament, revealing how cyberbullying often targets individuals based on race, gender, or other characteristics. These incidents illustrate the pervasive nature of cyberbullying and the challenges in addressing it effectively.

Key characteristics of cyberbullying include spreading harmful rumors, sharing private information without consent, or engaging in direct harassment through text messages, social media posts, emails, or online forums. The psychological toll on victims is significant, with studies linking cyberbullying to increased risks of depression, anxiety, and suicidal ideation (Kowalski et al. 2014). A 2021 study published in the *Journal of Adolescent Health* reported that adolescents who experienced cyberbullying were twice as likely to report severe mental health issues compared to their peers who had not (Li et al. 2024). Social alienation, academic difficulties, and physical health complications further compound the impact on victims, often leaving them with long-term consequences.

2.2 The Evolution of AI Technologies in Social Media and Online Interactions

Artificial intelligence has become a cornerstone of social media platforms and online interaction systems, revolutionizing how content is created, consumed, and moderated. Initially, AI's role was confined to basic automation tasks, such as filtering spam or recommending products. However, with advancements in machine learning, natural language processing (NLP), and computer vision, AI tools have evolved to address more complex challenges, including the detection of harmful behaviors like cyberbullying.

Social media platforms now rely heavily on AI for content moderation. For instance, Facebook employs AI algorithms to flag hate speech, while Twitter uses machine learning models to detect abusive language in tweets. These systems enable platforms to process millions of pieces of user-generated content daily, identifying and removing harmful material at speeds far beyond human capability. However, the reliance on AI also introduces challenges. Automated systems often lack the contextual understanding necessary to differentiate between harmful content and legitimate expressions, such as satire or political criticism. This limitation sometimes results in over-censorship, sparking concerns about the suppression of free speech.

Despite these challenges, AI's contributions to social media and online interactions are undeniable. Platforms such as YouTube and Instagram have adopted AI tools to improve user experiences by personalizing content feeds, recommending connections, and enabling real-time translations. However, the increasing reliance on AI has raised concerns about user privacy and data security. AI systems require vast amounts of user data to function effectively, leading to heightened scrutiny of their compliance with data protection regulations, such as the GDPR in Europe (Schermer, 2011).

2.3 AI's Dual Role in Cyberbullying: Combating and Enabling

AI occupies a paradoxical position in the realm of cyberbullying, serving both as a tool for its mitigation and as a potential enabler of harm. On one hand, AI technologies have significantly improved the ability of digital platforms to identify and respond to harmful behavior. For example, machine learning algorithms used by platforms like Instagram can detect abusive comments and issue warnings or bans in real-time. Predictive analytics, another application of AI, enables platforms to identify users who may be at risk of cyberbullying or engaging in harmful behavior, allowing for early interventions.

However, AI systems are not infallible. Biased algorithms can exacerbate existing inequalities by failing to adequately protect marginalized groups, such as racial minorities, LGBTQ+ individuals, and women, who are disproportionately targeted by cyberbullying (Arslan et al. 2024). For instance, a study by MIT and Stanford researchers found that facial recognition systems were significantly less accurate in identifying individuals from minority groups, raising concerns about the reliability of AI tools in diverse online environments (Buolamwini & Gebru, 2018). Similarly, language-based models may struggle with cultural nuances or regional slang, resulting in both false positives and false negatives in content moderation (Chakraborty & Gummadi, 2020; Citron & Chesney, 2019).

Generative AI introduces a new layer of complexity. Technologies like deepfake creation and automated bots have been weaponized by cyber bullies to produce malicious content or conduct coordinated harassment campaigns. For example, the use of deepfakes to create fake videos for blackmailing victims has emerged as a concerning trend (Geiger, 2016). Automated bots, on the other hand, have been used to flood victims with abusive messages, making it difficult for them to respond or seek help. These developments highlight the darker side of AI's capabilities and the urgent need for robust oversight mechanisms.

Comparative analyses reveal significant variations in how cyberbullying manifests across different demographic groups and regions. In developed countries, where internet penetration is high, cyberbullying often involves complex tactics, such as doxxing or the dissemination of manipulated media. In contrast, in regions with limited digital literacy, cyberbullying may take simpler forms, such as threatening messages. Additionally, cultural factors influence perceptions of cyberbullying, with some societies being more tolerant of aggressive online behavior than others. Understanding these nuances is essential for designing AI systems that are effective and culturally sensitive.

3. AI AS A TOOL FOR COMBATING CYBERBULLYING

The integration of AI into efforts to combat cyberbullying has transformed how online platforms identify and address harmful behaviors. AI-powered tools have proven indispensable in managing the vast amount of data generated across digital platforms, automating tasks that were once impossible to handle manually. These technologies have made significant strides in moderating online content, educating users, and enhancing the capabilities of human moderators. However, while their promise is substantial, these systems face critical challenges that require thoughtful implementation and oversight.

3.1 AI-Powered Content Moderation Systems

AI-powered content moderation systems leverage sophisticated technologies such as machine learning, natural language processing (NLP), and computer vision to identify harmful behaviors at scale. Machine learning forms the foundation of these systems, allowing AI to detect patterns in data and adapt to the evolving tactics used in cyberbullying (Sánchez-Medina et al. 2020). NLP plays a pivotal role in analyzing textual content, detecting abusive language, and identifying hate speech, while computer vision is employed to flag harmful images or videos (Jahan et al. 2023).

One of the technical approaches used in content moderation is sentiment analysis, where AI evaluates the emotional tone of the text to assess its potential for harm (Patel et al. 2020). Neural networks, particularly convolutional and recurrent neural networks, are central to these processes. Convolutional networks excel in analyzing visual data, making them suitable for detecting inappropriate imagery (Yousaf & Nawaz, 2022), while recurrent networks are adept at processing sequential data like text, enabling the identification of harassment embedded in conversations.

Social media platforms like Facebook and YouTube rely heavily on these systems to enforce community guidelines. For example, Facebook uses deep learning algorithms to identify hate speech and misinformation, while YouTube employs AI to demonetize harmful videos, ensuring they do not generate revenue for creators promoting abuse (Mullah & Zainon, 2021). These tools have demonstrated remarkable success; for instance, Facebook reported that its AI systems flagged 95% of harmful content before it was seen by users. Similarly, YouTube's automated systems have drastically reduced the prevalence of extremist content on its platform.

Despite these achievements, the technology is far from perfect. Challenges such as understanding the cultural context of content, detecting nuanced forms of harassment, and balancing free expression with safety require ongoing refinement of these systems. Automated moderation alone cannot address these complexities fully, underscoring the importance of integrating human oversight into AI processes.

3.2 Generative AI in Prevention and Education

Generative AI has introduced new opportunities for combating cyberbullying by creating tools that promote prevention and awareness. Advanced language models such as OpenAI's GPT have been harnessed to develop educational resources that inform users about the risks and consequences of cyberbullying (Vanpech et al. 2024). These systems can generate customized content, such as interactive tutorials and simulated scenarios, to teach users how to recognize and respond to online harassment.

For instance, platforms have begun using generative AI to create chatbots that engage users in discussions about online behavior. These chatbots can simulate the experience of being bullied, fostering empathy and understanding in users. Additionally, generative AI has been used to create public service announcements and campaigns that highlight the dangers of cyberbullying and the importance of reporting abusive behavior (Garett et al. 2016). Such tools have the potential to raise awareness on a massive scale, reaching diverse audiences across multiple languages and cultural contexts.

However, generative AI's role is not limited to education and prevention. It is also being used to empower moderators by generating summaries of flagged content and suggesting appropriate responses. This reduces the cognitive load on human moderators, enabling them to focus on more complex cases where nuanced judgment is required (Vázquez-Madrigal et al. 2024).

3.3 Enhancing Human Oversight with AI

While AI excels at handling large-scale content moderation, human oversight remains indispensable for addressing the contextual and ethical challenges of combating cyberbullying. AI systems are particularly prone to errors when dealing with ambiguous or culturally sensitive content. For example, sarcasm or coded language often evades detection by AI but can be identified by human moderators who understand the context (Kumar et al. 2021).

AI can enhance human oversight in several ways. First, it can prioritize flagged content based on severity, allowing moderators to focus on the most urgent cases. Second, AI can provide tools for analyzing trends in harmful behavior, helping moderators identify coordinated harassment campaigns or emerging forms of cyberbullying (Milosevic et al. 2023). Finally, AI can serve as a training tool for moderators, exposing them to simulated scenarios that improve their decision-making skills and cultural sensitivity (Pérez Sánchez, 2024).

Integrating AI with human oversight also addresses the ethical concerns of over-censorship and under-moderation. For example, automated systems may flag content that is not inherently harmful, such as political satire or controversial art, leading to accusations of censorship. Human moderators can review these cases to ensure that decisions align with platform policies and ethical standards (Schulenberg et al. 2023). Conversely, in cases where AI fails to detect harmful behavior, human oversight provides a critical safety net.

3.4 Case Study: AI in Action – Combating Cyberbullying on Major Platforms

3.4.1 Twitter: Harnessing Machine Learning to Tackle Abuse

Twitter has long been a battleground for cyberbullying due to its open nature, where users can interact with a global audience without stringent barriers. To address escalating concerns about harassment and abuse, Twitter has invested heavily in AI-driven content moderation tools. Central to their strategy is the deployment of machine learning models capable of detecting harmful language, such as hate speech, abusive tweets, and coordinated harassment campaigns.

The company's AI moderation systems scan millions of tweets daily to flag content that violates community standards. These systems use natural language processing (NLP) to analyze the tone, context, and intent of tweets. For instance, Twitter's models can differentiate between sarcasm, humor, and actual threats—a key challenge in automated moderation (Peng et al. 2019). Additionally, unsupervised learning techniques enable the platform to identify emerging patterns in abusive behavior, such as new slang or coded language used by harassers.

The results of these initiatives are promising. Twitter reported that by 2021, its AI tools proactively identified 50% of abusive tweets before they were flagged by users (Al-Garadi et al. 2022). This proactive approach not only reduces the burden on human moderators but also limits the spread and visibility of harmful content. However, challenges remain, particularly in addressing algorithmic bias and improving accuracy across diverse languages and cultural contexts.

3.4.2 YouTube: Fighting Harassment Through AI and Human Oversight

YouTube, as the world's largest video-sharing platform, faces unique challenges in moderating both textual comments and video content. To combat harassment, the platform employs AI systems that utilize computer vision and NLP to detect inappropriate content in videos, titles, descriptions, and comments. For example, deep learning algorithms analyze visual and audio data to identify explicit imagery, hate symbols, or abusive speech (Mortukane, 2024).

A key component of YouTube's strategy is its Comment Moderation Tool, which uses AI to automatically filter out offensive or harmful comments. This system allows creators to set specific parameters for their channels, enabling a customizable approach to content moderation. Moreover, YouTube's algorithms prioritize the removal of content flagged as harmful or dangerous, ensuring swift action to prevent harm (Arora et al. 2023).

The impact of these systems has been significant. In 2022, YouTube reported that its AI-driven moderation tools removed over 90% of harmful content before it was viewed by users (Barnes, M. R. (2022). The integration of human oversight further strengthens this approach; moderators review edge cases to refine algorithms and ensure decisions align with community standards. However, controversies persist regarding false positives, where legitimate content is mistakenly flagged, highlighting the ongoing need for a balance between automation and human judgment.

3.4.3 Instagram: AI Nudges to Foster Positive Behavior

Instagram has adopted a novel approach to combating cyberbullying by using AI to encourage positive interactions rather than solely focusing on punitive measures. Its system employs real-time behavioral nudges that warn users before they post potentially harmful comments. These nudges are powered by sentiment analysis models trained to detect abusive language and toxic phrasing (Alrashidi et al. 2022).

This feature has shown remarkable success. According to Instagram, these nudges resulted in a significant reduction in the posting of harmful comments, with users often revising their statements after receiving a warning(Alhwiti & Mezher, 2024). By addressing harmful behavior at the source, Instagram's AI tools help create a safer and more respectful environment while preserving user autonomy.

However, as these examples demonstrate, achieving an optimal balance between effectiveness, fairness, and inclusivity remains a continuing challenge. Future efforts must focus on refining AI systems to address cultural and contextual nuances while maintaining transparency and accountability.

4. RISKS AND CHALLENGES OF AI IN CYBERBULLYING

As artificial intelligence becomes a central tool in addressing cyberbullying, its limitations, and potential risks must be critically examined. While AI has the potential to create safer online environments, it can also introduce significant challenges, including algorithmic bias, privacy concerns, and difficulties in assigning liability and accountability. These challenges not only affect the effectiveness of AI-driven solutions but also raise profound legal and ethical questions that demand careful scrutiny (Chaudhary et al. 2024).

4.1 Algorithmic Bias and Discrimination

Algorithmic bias represents a significant risk in the use of AI for moderating and preventing cyberbullying. The biases embedded in AI systems often originate from their training data, which may reflect historical inequities, societal prejudices, or incomplete datasets (Kumar et al. 2024). For example, facial recognition systems have shown significant disparities in accuracy across different demographic groups, with higher error rates for women and individuals with darker skin tones. These biases are not merely technical flaws; they manifest in real-world consequences that can exacerbate existing inequalities (Gencoglu, 2020).

The impact of algorithmic bias is particularly pronounced for marginalized groups, including racial minorities, LGBTQ+ individuals, and women, who are often disproportionately targeted by cyberbullying. A study revealed that AI-driven content moderation systems frequently misidentify speech patterns unique to minority groups, either failing to detect harmful behavior or wrongfully flagging benign expressions as abusive (Gorwa et al. 2020). Such outcomes further marginalize already vulnerable populations and raise concerns about fairness and inclusivity.

Real-world cases illustrate the consequences of algorithmic bias. For instance, Twitter faced backlash when its AI-based image-cropping algorithm was shown to favor lighter-skinned individuals in previews, sparking a broader debate on the need for fairness in AI systems (Dwivedi & Mahanty, 2024). Similarly, automated moderation tools on YouTube have been criticized for disproportionately demonetizing content created by LGBTQ+ creators, claiming violations of community guidelines without clear justification (Rodriguez, 2023). These cases underscore the ethical and legal imperative to develop AI systems that are fair and inclusive.

4.2 Privacy and Data Protection

The effectiveness of AI in combating cyberbullying often hinges on the availability of vast amounts of user data. AI models require extensive datasets to train algorithms capable of detecting nuanced patterns of harmful behavior. However, this reliance on data raises significant privacy concerns, as users may be subjected to intrusive surveillance, data collection, and analysis without fully understanding or consenting to these practices.

The legal implications of these practices have been highlighted in lawsuits and regulatory actions. For instance, in 2019, the U.S. Federal Trade Commission (FTC) fined Facebook $5 billion for privacy violations related to the unauthorized sharing of user data, including data used for algorithmic development (Kang, 2019). Such cases emphasize the need for robust data protection measures in AI-driven systems, particularly those used to combat cyberbullying.

The compatibility of AI-driven content moderation systems with data protection laws, such as the General Data Protection Regulation (GDPR) in Europe, remains a pressing concern. GDPR emphasizes user consent, data minimization, and the right to erasure, which often conflict with the extensive data processing required by AI systems (Banchio, 2024). Predictive analytics further complicates matters, as it relies on profiling techniques that may stigmatize individuals based on incomplete or inaccurate data. For example, AI systems that flag users as potential cyberbullies based on their past behavior risk unfairly labeling individuals and infringing on their right to privacy.

4.3 Liability and Accountability

Determining liability for harm caused by AI-driven systems presents a significant legal challenge. The complexity of AI technologies and their decision-making processes blurs the lines of responsibility among developers, platform operators, and end-users. For instance, if an AI system wrongfully flags a user as a cyberbully or fails to prevent harmful incidents, questions arise about who should be held accountable for these outcomes.

Legal precedents provide some insight into these challenges. In 2018, an AI-based recruitment tool developed by Amazon was found to discriminate against female applicants, prompting legal scrutiny and the tool's eventual withdrawal (Kodiyan, 2019). Although this case did not involve cyberbullying, it highlights the potential for AI systems to perpetuate harm and the difficulties in assigning liability. Similarly, automated moderation systems on platforms like Facebook and Twitter have faced criticism for failing to remove harmful content, leading to lawsuits alleging negligence and intermediary liability (Gongane et al. 2022).

Case studies further illustrate the challenges of resolving disputes involving AI misuse. In 2021, a lawsuit filed in California alleged that YouTube's moderation system wrongfully removed educational videos discussing LGBTQ+ topics, leading to financial and reputational harm for the creators (Rodriguez, 2023). These cases emphasize the need for clear policies that delineate responsibility and establish mechanisms for redress. Collaborative efforts among governments, technology companies, and civil society are essential to ensure that liability frameworks are both fair and effective.

4.4 Ethical Dilemmas in AI Applications

The ethical dilemmas posed by AI are particularly stark in the context of cyberbullying. Generative AI technologies, such as deepfake creation tools, have been weaponized to produce false and damaging content, escalating the psychological and social harm inflicted on victims. A notable example occurred in 2019 when a journalist was targeted with deepfake videos that appeared to show her engaging in inappropriate behavior. These videos were widely shared online, causing significant reputational damage and emotional distress (Chesney & Citron, 2019).

The rise of deepfakes and automated harassment bots raises profound ethical questions about the boundaries of AI use. While these technologies have legitimate applications, their misuse highlights the urgent need for regulatory oversight and ethical guidelines. Current efforts, such as the European Commission's proposed Artificial Intelligence Act, aim to address these concerns by categorizing certain AI applications as high-risk and subjecting them to stricter scrutiny (Ebers et al. 2021).

In addressing these challenges, it is evident that AI's integration into efforts to combat cyberbullying must be guided by principles of fairness, transparency, and accountability. By anticipating and addressing the risks associated with algorithmic bias, privacy concerns, and liability, stakeholders can create a more ethical and effective framework for managing the complexities of AI in online environments.

5. REGULATORY AND POLICY FRAMEWORKS

The legal and regulatory landscape surrounding AI and cyberbullying remains a work in progress, reflecting both the opportunities and challenges presented by these intersecting domains. As technology continues to evolve rapidly, governments, international organizations, and private stakeholders are grappling with the task of crafting policies that balance innovation with the protection of individual rights and societal well-being. This section examines the current regulatory frameworks, identifies significant gaps, and explores emerging solutions to address the complex challenges of managing AI in the context of cyberbullying.

5.1 Review of Existing Regulations

Regulations addressing AI and cyberbullying have taken various forms across the globe, shaped by national priorities, legal traditions, and cultural values. National approaches to regulating AI and online harm vary widely. For example, the European Union has implemented comprehensive frameworks such as the Digital Services Act, which mandates that large online platforms take active measures to address harmful content, including the use of AI for content moderation (Siapera, 2022).

Similarly, the General Data Protection Regulation (GDPR) focuses on protecting user privacy while ensuring responsible data use in AI systems (Hoofnagle et al. 2019).

Other countries have adopted unique strategies tailored to their specific needs. Australia's eSafety Commissioner has been a trailblazer, combining strict regulatory oversight with public education campaigns to tackle online harm, including cyberbullying (Smith et al. 2024). The Commissioner's initiatives, such as the Online Safety Act, emphasize quick takedown procedures for harmful content and promote collaboration between regulators and platform operators (Meola, 2020). In contrast, the United States largely relies on platform self-regulation, guided by Section 230 of the Communications Decency Act, which grants platforms immunity from liability for user-generated content while encouraging them to moderate harmful behavior (Pagano, 2018). This hands-off approach has faced criticism for inconsistencies in enforcement and accountability.

Internationally, treaties and guidelines have attempted to establish consistent standards for AI and cyberbullying regulation. Documents like the UN Guiding Principles on Business and Human Rights and the OECD Principles on AI advocate for transparency, accountability, and the protection of fundamental rights in AI deployment (Wettstein, 2015). However, the lack of enforceability in these agreements often limits their impact, leaving gaps in global governance.

5.2 Sector-Specific Approaches

Different industries have developed tailored strategies to address AI regulation in combating cyberbullying. In the gaming sector, where harassment and toxic behavior are prevalent, companies like Riot Games and Blizzard Entertainment have integrated AI-driven moderation tools to detect abusive language in real time (Wijkstra et al. 2024). Riot Games' machine learning system, for instance, reviews millions of chat interactions daily and flags offensive behavior for human review. Such initiatives demonstrate the potential for AI to foster safer gaming environments, though challenges like false positives and regional language differences persist.

In education, AI is being leveraged to promote digital literacy and teach students about the responsible use of online platforms. Educational institutions have started using AI-powered tools to monitor school-based cyberbullying on digital platforms, such as messaging apps used by students. These systems, while effective, raise privacy concerns, as they often require access to sensitive student communications (Aggarwal & Gaur, 2024).

The healthcare industry is also playing a role by incorporating AI into mental health interventions for cyberbullying victims. Chatbots and virtual counselors, powered by natural language processing, provide anonymous support to individuals experiencing online abuse (Nosrati et al. 2021). However, these applications require robust oversight to ensure ethical use and protect patient confidentiality.

5.3 Identifying Gaps in Current Frameworks

A major challenge in regulating AI for cyberbullying lies in the disparity between technological innovation and legislative adaptability. Many existing policies are outdated, failing to account for advancements in generative AI, which has introduced tools like deepfake creation that can amplify the harm caused by cyberbullying. For instance, the creation of malicious deepfakes for harassment purposes remains largely unregulated in many jurisdictions (Usharani, 2021).

Inconsistencies across jurisdictions exacerbate the problem. Definitions of cyberbullying, accountability for AI systems, and privacy standards vary widely, creating a fragmented landscape that complicates compliance for global platforms. For example, while the GDPR enforces strict data protection rules, other regions prioritize innovation and economic growth over stringent privacy measures, leading to uneven enforcement (Ali & Xuan, 2024).

Cross-border enforcement is another critical issue. Cyberbullying often involves perpetrators, victims, and platforms operating in different countries, making it difficult to apply domestic laws effectively. Existing frameworks, such as the Budapest Convention on Cybercrime, provide mechanisms for international cooperation but are limited in scope and participation (Le Nguyen & Golman, 2021).

5.4 Emerging Frameworks and Solutions

To address these gaps, stakeholders are exploring emerging frameworks that emphasize adaptability, inclusivity, and collaboration. Ethical AI principles have gained prominence, guiding the development of systems that prioritize fairness and human rights. The EU Ethics Guidelines for Trustworthy AI, for example, outline requirements for transparency, accountability, and inclusivity, providing a foundation for ethical AI governance (Smuha, 2019).

Collaborative governance offers another promising solution. Public-private partnerships have successfully facilitated the creation of advanced content moderation tools. For example, Google and UNESCO's collaboration on the AI4Good initiative aims to develop AI systems that address global challenges, including online harm (Roche et al. 2023). Such partnerships combine technological expertise with regulatory oversight to create balanced solutions.

Proposals for cross-border enforcement mechanisms are also gaining traction. Hypothetical scenarios include the creation of an International Digital Safety Taskforce, which would standardize regulations and facilitate cooperation between countries in addressing cyberbullying. This task force could operate under the auspices of organizations like the International Telecommunication Union (ITU), ensuring that global platforms adhere to consistent standards.

6. BROADER ETHICAL AND HUMAN RIGHTS IMPLICATIONS

The deployment of AI to combat cyberbullying is fraught with complex ethical and human rights considerations. Beyond its technical and regulatory aspects, AI's influence extends into the philosophical realm, raising fundamental questions about its role in shaping human behavior and societal norms. This section explores these debates, examines AI governance within the context of international human rights frameworks, and considers the future implications of advancements in ethical AI.

6.1 AI's Role in Shaping Human Behavior and Societal Norms

AI technologies are not passive tools; they actively shape the digital environments in which individuals interact, influencing behavior and societal norms. Content moderation algorithms, for example, play a pivotal role in determining what constitutes acceptable speech and conduct online. By enforcing these standards, AI systems indirectly shape the boundaries of social discourse and cultural expression (Bloomfield, 2018). This raises critical ethical questions: Who defines the norms that AI enforces, and how should these norms reflect the diversity of global communities?

Philosophical debates about AI's role in shaping behavior often center on the concept of agency. Critics argue that over-reliance on AI for moderating human interactions may erode individual responsibility, as users become conditioned to rely on algorithms for policing behavior (Molina & Sundar, 2022). Conversely, proponents contend that AI can promote ethical behavior by creating environments that discourage harmful actions and incentivize positive engagement. For instance, AI-driven systems that reward respectful dialogue and penalize toxic behavior could contribute to healthier digital communities (Baronchelli, 2024).

These debates are further complicated by the global nature of digital platforms. Cultural relativism—the idea that norms and values vary significantly across societies—challenges the universality of AI-driven standards. A moderation algorithm trained in one cultural context may fail to account for the nuances of another, resulting in either over-enforcement or neglect of harmful behavior. Ensuring that AI systems respect cultural diversity while maintaining universal standards of decency and safety remains an unresolved ethical dilemma (Zulfiqar et al. 2024).

6.2 AI Governance and International Human Rights Frameworks

AI governance must align with established international human rights frameworks to ensure that technological advancements do not infringe on fundamental rights. Documents such as the Universal Declaration of Human Rights (UDHR) (De Baets, 2009) and the International Covenant on Civil and Political Rights (ICCPR) (Joseph & Castan, 2013) provide a foundation for evaluating the ethical implications of AI deployment. These frameworks emphasize the protection of rights such as freedom of expression, privacy, and equality—rights that are directly impacted by AI systems used to combat cyberbullying.

Freedom of expression is particularly relevant, as AI-driven content moderation often involves restricting speech deemed harmful or offensive. While this is necessary to prevent abuse, it risks overreach, potentially suppressing legitimate discourse. Article 19 of the UDHR asserts the right to freedom of opinion and expression, but it also acknowledges the need for limitations to respect the rights and reputations of others (Şener, 2021). Balancing these competing imperatives requires transparency in AI decision-making processes and mechanisms for redress when errors occur.

The right to privacy, enshrined in Article 12 of the UDHR, is another critical consideration. AI systems often rely on extensive data collection to identify harmful behavior, raising concerns about surveillance and potential misuse of personal information (Waltz, 2002). Compliance with data protection laws, such as the General Data Protection Regulation (GDPR), is essential to safeguarding privacy while enabling AI to function effectively.

Equality and non-discrimination are also central to human rights-based AI governance. Algorithmic bias, as discussed earlier, can disproportionately impact marginalized groups, exacerbating existing inequalities. Ensuring that AI systems are designed and tested to minimize bias is not just an ethical imperative but also a legal requirement under anti-discrimination laws in many jurisdictions (Wachter et al. 2021).

6.3 Future Implications of Ethical AI Advancements

The future of AI in combating cyberbullying hinges on the development and adoption of ethical AI principles. Emerging technologies offer opportunities to address current limitations while introducing new risks that must be managed proactively.

Advancements in explainable AI (XAI) are particularly promising. Unlike traditional "black-box" models, XAI systems provide clear and understandable reasons for their decisions, enhancing transparency and accountability (Xu et al. 2019). This has significant implications for content moderation, where users often challenge the fairness of AI-driven decisions. By enabling individuals to understand why their content was flagged or removed, XAI could foster trust in AI systems and reduce perceived biases.

Another promising development is the integration of AI ethics into educational programs for developers and policymakers. Institutions such as Stanford University and the Alan Turing Institute have introduced courses on ethical AI design, emphasizing principles like fairness, inclusivity, and human-centric governance (Venkatesh et al. 2022; Bowen, 2024). These initiatives aim to embed ethical considerations into the design and implementation of AI systems, reducing the likelihood of unintended harm.

Hypothetical scenarios also highlight the potential of AI to proactively combat cyberbullying. For example, AI systems could evolve to provide real-time behavioral nudges, alerting users when their messages are likely to be perceived as harmful and encouraging them to reconsider their wording (Leal & Oliveira, 2024). Similarly, AI could enable personalized interventions for individuals at risk of engaging in or experiencing cyberbullying, offering resources and support tailored to their needs.

However, these advancements also raise new ethical questions. As AI becomes more integrated into human interactions, concerns about autonomy, surveillance, and power imbalances will intensify. The challenge lies in ensuring that AI enhances, rather than undermines, human dignity and agency.

7. RECOMMENDATIONS

To address the multifaceted challenges posed by AI in combating cyberbullying, a collaborative, interdisciplinary, and globally coordinated approach is essential. This section outlines actionable recommendations for policymakers, technology developers, civil society, and researchers, supported by illustrative case studies, and introduces a vision for a global charter on AI ethics and cyberbullying.

7.1 Recommendations for Policymakers

Policymakers must prioritize the development of comprehensive legal frameworks that address both the technological and societal dimensions of AI in cyberbullying. Strengthening existing laws to incorporate provisions for algorithmic transparency, data protection, and accountability is a critical first step. For example, the European Union's Digital Services Act has set a precedent by mandating that large platforms assess and mitigate systemic risks, including those posed by cyberbullying (Cauffman

& Goanta, 2021). This framework highlights how proactive regulation can balance innovation with public safety.

Case Study: In Australia, the eSafety Commissioner has successfully implemented a model that combines regulatory oversight with public education. The Commissioner's initiatives, such as the Online Safety Act, empower individuals to report harmful content while holding platforms accountable for swift removal. This dual approach has significantly reduced instances of online harassment and could serve as a blueprint for other countries (Suzor et al. 2021).

Policymakers should also adopt ethical AI guidelines tailored to their jurisdictions. These guidelines should emphasize fairness, inclusivity, and the protection of human rights. Collaboration with international organizations, such as the United Nations and the Organisation for Economic Co-operation and Development (OECD), can facilitate the development of globally aligned principles (Yeung, 2020). Additionally, promoting interdisciplinary collaboration is essential. Policymakers must engage with technologists, ethicists, sociologists, and educators to craft policies that are both technically sound and socially relevant.

7.2 Recommendations for Technology Developers

Technology developers play a critical role in ensuring that AI systems are designed and deployed responsibly. Reducing algorithmic bias should be a top priority. This involves diversifying training datasets, conducting rigorous bias testing, and incorporating feedback loops that allow for continuous improvement. For instance, Twitter's recent initiative to make its moderation algorithms open-source has allowed researchers to identify and address potential biases more effectively (Geiger, 2016).

Case Study: Riot Games has implemented AI-driven moderation tools in its multiplayer gaming platforms to reduce toxic behavior. By combining machine learning models with user feedback, Riot has managed to create a system that not only detects abusive language but also adapts to evolving slang and cultural nuances. This collaborative approach between developers and users underscores the importance of iterative improvement (Van Hoeyweghen, 2024).

Developers should also focus on enhancing transparency and accountability. Explainable AI (XAI) technologies, which provide users with clear explanations for AI-driven decisions, can help build trust and address grievances. Moreover, privacy-respecting AI systems are essential. Implementing data minimization techniques and adhering to regulations like the GDPR can ensure that AI-driven interventions do not compromise user privacy (Milossi et al. 2021).

7.3 Recommendations for Civil Society and Researchers

Civil society organizations and researchers have a pivotal role in advocating for vulnerable groups and generating actionable insights. Advocacy efforts should focus on amplifying the voices of those disproportionately affected by cyberbullying, such as racial minorities, LGBTQ+ individuals, and women. Civil society can also hold platforms accountable by monitoring their compliance with ethical and regulatory standards.

Case Study: The Anti-Bullying Alliance in the UK has partnered with academic institutions to study the impact of AI-driven moderation tools on online harassment. Their research has informed national strategies for combating cyberbullying, demonstrating the value of collaboration between civil society and academia (Harrison et al. 2020).

Researchers should conduct interdisciplinary studies to explore the intersections of technology, psychology, and sociology in cyberbullying. Such research can identify emerging trends, assess the effectiveness of AI tools, and propose innovative solutions. Public awareness campaigns and digital literacy programs, co-designed with civil society, can educate users about their rights and responsibilities in the digital space (Moravec et al. 2024).

7.4 Vision for a Global Charter on AI Ethics and Cyberbullying

Given the global nature of cyberbullying and the cross-border deployment of AI technologies, there is an urgent need for a unified international framework. A Global Charter on AI Ethics and Cyberbullying could establish common principles and standards for regulating AI in digital interactions (de Silva de Alwis, 2024). Such a charter could draw inspiration from the Universal Declaration of Human Rights (UDHR) and incorporate guidelines for transparency, accountability, inclusivity, and respect for cultural diversity (Şener, 2021).

This charter would serve as a foundation for international cooperation, enabling countries to harmonize their regulatory approaches and collaborate on enforcement. For example, the charter could facilitate the establishment of an International Cyberbullying Taskforce, which would provide technical assistance, mediate cross-border disputes, and coordinate responses to global cyberbullying incidents. The task force could work in partnership with organizations like the International Telecommunication Union (ITU) and UNESCO to ensure widespread adoption and implementation (Alqor o'g'li et al. 2023).

8. CONCLUSION

The integration of artificial intelligence into efforts to combat cyberbullying offers transformative potential, but it also brings significant risks that require proactive management. As AI technologies evolve, their unchecked deployment could exacerbate the very problems they are designed to solve, including bias, privacy violations, and misuse for malicious purposes. However, with thoughtful governance and collaboration, AI can serve as a powerful tool to mitigate online harm, foster safer digital spaces, and protect vulnerable populations.

8.1 Implications of Unchecked AI in Cyberbullying

Unchecked AI in cyberbullying can have far-reaching implications, both intended and unintended. Without sufficient oversight, algorithmic biases embedded in AI systems can perpetuate existing inequalities, leaving marginalized communities disproportionately affected by online harm. For example, research by MIT Media Lab found that facial recognition systems were significantly less accurate for women and individuals with darker skin tones, raising concerns about similar biases in content moderation systems.

Moreover, the increasing reliance on AI for moderation risks creating a "black-box" system where users have little insight into how decisions are made. This lack of transparency undermines trust and accountability, especially when legitimate content is flagged or harmful content is overlooked. The potential misuse of generative AI to create harmful content, such as deepfakes and automated harassment campaigns, further underscores the need for stringent safeguards.

Unchecked AI can also erode user privacy, as systems often rely on extensive data collection to function effectively. The absence of robust data protection measures could lead to invasive surveillance practices and unauthorized use of personal information, exacerbating the mistrust between users and platforms.

8.2 Future Trends in AI Development and Online Harm Prevention

The future of AI in combating cyberbullying lies in the development of technologies that prioritize ethical considerations and human-centric design. Explainable AI (XAI) is one such trend, offering transparency in decision-making processes and empowering users to challenge unfair outcomes. XAI could significantly enhance trust in AI systems, particularly in sensitive areas like content moderation.

Advancements in real-time behavioral analysis hold promise for more effective harm prevention. For instance, AI systems could use sentiment analysis to detect escalating tensions in online interactions and intervene before harm occurs. These systems could provide personalized warnings or suggest alternative language, fostering a culture of accountability and respect.

Generative AI also presents opportunities for education and support. Platforms could deploy AI-driven chatbots to educate users about the impact of cyberbullying and provide real-time support to victims. Similarly, predictive analytics could identify users at risk of engaging in or experiencing cyberbullying, enabling targeted interventions and reducing the prevalence of harmful behavior.

However, these advancements must be accompanied by robust safeguards to prevent misuse and ensure that AI systems align with societal values. Collaborative efforts among governments, technology companies, researchers, and civil society will be essential to realizing the potential of AI while minimizing its risks.

8.3 Collaborative Efforts for Sustainable Solutions

The complexity of cyberbullying and AI requires a multifaceted, collaborative approach that engages all stakeholders. Governments must lead the way by establishing comprehensive regulatory frameworks that prioritize transparency, accountability, and fairness. For example, the European Union's Digital Services Act provides a model for balancing innovation with user protection, mandating that platforms assess and mitigate systemic risks.

Technology companies must embrace their role as stewards of ethical AI by designing systems that respect privacy, minimize bias, and enhance user agency. Open-source initiatives, such as Twitter's transparency in algorithmic design, demonstrate how platforms can build trust through collaboration and openness.

Civil society and academia are equally important, advocating for marginalized communities and conducting research to inform evidence-based policies. Public awareness campaigns and digital literacy programs can empower users to navigate the digital space responsibly, reducing the incidence and impact of cyberbullying.

A global charter on AI ethics and cyberbullying could serve as a unifying framework for these efforts, establishing common principles and facilitating cross-border cooperation. By promoting shared values and leveraging collective expertise, such a charter could lay the foundation for sustainable solutions that protect individuals and communities in the digital age.

REFERENCES

Aggarwal, A., & Gaur, S. (2024). Applying Artificial Intelligence to Explore Online Harassment and Cyberbullying Prevention. In *Impact of AI on Advancing Women's Safety* (pp. 104–120). IGI Global.

Al-Garadi, M. A., Kim, S., Guo, Y., Warren, E., Yang, Y. C., Lakamana, S., & Sarker, A. (2022). Natural language model for automatic identification of intimate partner violence reports from twitter. *Array (New York, N.Y.)*, 15, 100217. DOI: 10.1016/j.array.2022.100217 PMID: 37006948

Alhwiti, A. O., & Mezher, M. A. (2024). Enhancing User Security on Instagram: A Multifaceted AI System for Filtering Abusive Comments. *Social Networking*, 13(2), 15–34. DOI: 10.4236/sn.2024.132002

Ali, A., & Xuan, M. (2024). Fog-Based IoT Data Processing for Cyberbullying Detection: Integrating CNN-BiLSTM-GRU Models and GDPR Compliance. DOI: 10.4236/sn.2024.132002

Alqor o'g'li, M. S., Farrukh, M., & Sevinch, K. (2023). Promotion of cybersecurity among young people. Education Science and Innovative Ideas in the World, *34*(1), 14-18. DOI: 10.4236/sn.2024.132002

Alrashidi, B., Jamal, A., Khan, I., & Alkhathlan, A. (2022). A review on abusive content automatic detection: Approaches, challenges and opportunities. *PeerJ. Computer Science*, 8, e1142. DOI: 10.7717/peerj-cs.1142 PMID: 36426250

Anwer, S., Hosen, M. S., Khan, D. S., Oluwabusayo, E., Folorunso, M. M. H. M., & Khan, H. (2024). Revolutionizing The Global Market: An Inclusion Of AI The Game Changer In International Dynamics. *Migration Letters : An International Journal of Migration Studies*, 21(S13), 54–73.

Arslan, M., Madrigal, M. S., Abuhamad, M., Hall, D. L., & Silva, Y. N. (2024). Detecting LGBTQ+ Instances of Cyberbullying. *arXiv preprint arXiv:2409.12263*.

Babu, N. V., & Kanaga, E. G. M. (2022). Sentiment analysis in social media data for depression detection using artificial intelligence: A review. *SN Computer Science*, 3(1), 74. DOI: 10.1007/s42979-021-00958-1 PMID: 34816124

Banchio, P. R. (2024). *Legal*. Ethical and Practical Challenges of AI-Driven Content Moderation.

Bansal, S., Garg, N., Singh, J., & Van Der Walt, F. (2024). Cyberbullying and mental health: Past, present and future. *Frontiers in Psychology*, 14, 1279234. DOI: 10.3389/fpsyg.2023.1279234 PMID: 38288359

Barnes, M. R. (2022). Online extremism, AI, and (human) content moderation. *Feminist Philosophy Quarterly, 8*(3/4). DOI: 10.3389/fpsyg.2023.1279234 PMID: 38288359

Baronchelli, A. (2024). Shaping new norms for AI. *Philosophical Transactions of the Royal Society B, 379*(1897), 20230028. DOI: 10.3389/fpsyg.2023.1279234 PMID: 38288359

Bloomfield, B. P. (2018). The culture of artificial intelligence. In *The question of artificial intelligence* (pp. 59–105). Routledge. DOI: 10.4324/9780429505331-2

Bowen, J. P. (2024). Alan Turing: Breaking the Code, Computing, and Machine Intelligence. In *The Arts and Computational Culture: Real and Virtual Worlds* (pp. 75–94). Springer Nature Switzerland. DOI: 10.1007/978-3-031-53865-0_3

Buolamwini, J., & Gebru, T. (2018). Gender shades: Intersectional accuracy disparities in commercial gender classification. In *Conference on fairness, accountability and transparency* (pp. 77-91). PMLR.Springer AI Handbook (2020). "Context in Natural Language Processing."

Cauffman, C., & Goanta, C. (2021). A new order: The digital services act and consumer protection. *European Journal of Risk Regulation*, 12(4), 758–774. DOI: 10.1017/err.2021.8

Chakraborty, A., & Gummadi, K. P. (2020). Fairness in Algorithmic Decision Making. In *Proceedings of the 7th ACM IKDD CoDS and 25th COMAD* (pp. 367-368). DOI: 10.1145/3371158.3371234

Chaudhary, P. K., Yalamati, S., Palakurti, N. R., Alam, N., Kolasani, S., & Whig, P. (2024, July). Detecting and Preventing Child Cyberbullying using Generative Artificial Intelligence. In *2024 Asia Pacific Conference on Innovation in Technology (APCIT)* (pp. 1-5). IEEE. DOI: 10.1109/APCIT62007.2024.10673710

Chesney, R., & Citron, D. K. (2019). Deepfakes and the New Disinformation War. *Foreign Affairs.*

Citron, D. K., & Chesney, R. (2019). Deepfakes and the new disinformation war. *Foreign Affairs.*

De Baets, A. (2009). The impact of the Universal Declaration of Human Rights on the study of history. *History and Theory*, 48(1), 20–43. DOI: 10.1111/j.1468-2303.2009.00483.x

de Silva de Alwis, R. (2024). Gendering the New International Norms on Artificial Intelligence and Emerging Technologies. *U of Penn Law School, Public Law Research Paper*, (24-43).

Dutton, D. M., & Conroy, G. V. (1997). A review of machine learning. *The Knowledge Engineering Review*, 12(4), 341–367. DOI: 10.1017/S026988899700101X

Dwivedi, D. N., & Mahanty, G. (2024). Unmasking the Shadows: Exploring Unethical AI Implementation. *Demystifying the Dark Side of AI in Business*, 185-200. DOI: 10.3389/fpsyg.2023.1279234 PMID: 38288359

Ebers, M., Hoch, V. R., Rosenkranz, F., Ruschemeier, H., & Steinrötter, B. (2021). The European Commission's proposal for an Artificial Intelligence Act—a critical assessment by members of the Robotics and AI Law Society (RAILS). *J, 4*(4), 589-603. DOI: 10.3389/fpsyg.2023.1279234 PMID: 38288359

Garett, R., Lord, L. R., & Young, S. D. (2016). Associations between social media and cyberbullying: A review of the literature. *mHealth*, 2, 2. DOI: 10.21037/mhealth.2016.12.01 PMID: 28293616

Geiger, R. S. (2016). Bot-based collective blocklists in Twitter: The counterpublic moderation of harassment in a networked public space. *Information Communication and Society*, 19(6), 787–803. DOI: 10.1080/1369118X.2016.1153700

Gencoglu, O. (2020). Cyberbullying detection with fairness constraints. *IEEE Internet Computing*, 25(1), 20–29. DOI: 10.1109/MIC.2020.3032461

Gongane, V. U., Munot, M. V., & Anuse, A. D. (2022). Detection and moderation of detrimental content on social media platforms: Current status and future directions. *Social Network Analysis and Mining*, 12(1), 129. DOI: 10.1007/s13278-022-00951-3 PMID: 36090695

Gorwa, R., Binns, R., & Katzenbach, C. (2020). Algorithmic content moderation: Technical and political challenges in the automation of platform governance. *Big Data & Society*, 7(1), 2053951719897945. DOI: 10.1177/2053951719897945

Harrison, E. D., Fox, C. L., & Hulme, J. A. (2020). Student anti-bullying and harassment policies at UK universities. *Journal of Higher Education Policy and Management*, 42(5), 547–562. DOI: 10.1080/1360080X.2020.1767353

Hinduja, S., & Patchin, J. W. (2015). *Bullying Beyond the Schoolyard: Preventing and Responding to Cyberbullying*. DOI: 10.1080/1360080X.2020.1767353

Hoofnagle, C. J., Van Der Sloot, B., & Borgesius, F. Z. (2019). The European Union general data protection regulation: What it is and what it means. *Information & Communications Technology Law*, 28(1), 65–98. DOI: 10.1080/13600834.2019.1573501

Hunt, E. B. (2014). *Artificial intelligence*. Academic Press.

Jahan, M. S., & Oussalah, M. (2023). A systematic review of hate speech automatic detection using natural language processing. *Neurocomputing*, 546, 126232. DOI: 10.1016/j.neucom.2023.126232

Joseph, S., & Castan, M. (2013). *The international covenant on civil and political rights: cases, materials, and commentary*. OUP Oxford.

Kang, C. (2019). $5 Billion Fine For Facebook On User Data. *The New York Times*, A1-L.

Kodiyan, A. A. (2019). An overview of ethical issues in using AI systems in hiring with a case study of Amazon's AI based hiring tool. *Researchgate Preprint*, 1-19. DOI: 10.1080/1360080X.2020.1767353

Kowalski, R. M., Giumetti, G. W., Schroeder, A. N., & Lattanner, M. R. (2014). Bullying in the digital age: A critical review and meta-analysis of cyberbullying research among youth. *Psychological Bulletin*, 140(4), 1073–1137. DOI: 10.1037/a0035618 PMID: 24512111

Kumar, A., Dikshit, S., & Albuquerque, V. H. C. (2021). Explainable artificial intelligence for sarcasm detection in dialogues. *Wireless Communications and Mobile Computing*, 2021(1), 2939334. DOI: 10.1155/2021/2939334

Kumar, Y., Huang, K., Perez, A., Yang, G., Li, J. J., Morreale, P., Kruger, D., & Jiang, R. (2024). Bias and Cyberbullying Detection and Data Generation Using Transformer Artificial Intelligence Models and Top Large Language Models. *Electronics (Basel)*, 13(17), 3431. DOI: 10.3390/electronics13173431

Le Nguyen, C., & Golman, W. (2021). Diffusion of the Budapest Convention on cybercrime and the development of cybercrime legislation in Pacific Island countries: 'Law on the books' vs 'law in action'. *Computer Law & Security Report*, 40, 105521. DOI: 10.1016/j.clsr.2020.105521

Leal, C. C., & Oliveira, B. (2024). Nudging financial behavior in the age of artificial intelligence. In *Artificial Intelligence in Production Engineering and Management* (pp. 115–144). Woodhead Publishing. DOI: 10.1016/B978-0-12-819471-3.00002-1

Li, C., Wang, P., Martin-Moratinos, M., Bella-Fernandez, M., & Blasco-Fontecilla, H. (2024). Traditional bullying and cyberbullying in the digital age and its associated mental health problems in children and adolescents: A meta-analysis. *European Child & Adolescent Psychiatry*, 33(9), 2895–2909. DOI: 10.1007/s00787-022-02128-x PMID: 36585978

Livingstone, S., & Smith, P. K. (2014). Annual Research Review: Harmful online content and the right to privacy and protection. *Journal of Child Psychology and Psychiatry, and Allied Disciplines*.

Meola, C. (2020). Helping Aussie women online: A discourse analysis of the Australian eSafety Commissioner website. In *Social media in legal practice* (pp. 130–145). Routledge. DOI: 10.4324/9780429346088-9

Milosevic, T., Verma, K., Carter, M., Vigil, S., Laffan, D., Davis, B., & O'Higgins Norman, J. (2023). Effectiveness of Artificial Intelligence–Based Cyberbullying Interventions From Youth Perspective. *Social Media + Society*, 9(1), 20563051221147325. DOI: 10.1177/20563051221147325

Milossi, M., Alexandropoulou-Egyptiadou, E., & Psannis, K. E. (2021). AI ethics: Algorithmic determinism or self-determination? The GPDR approach. *IEEE Access : Practical Innovations, Open Solutions*, 9, 58455–58466. DOI: 10.1109/ACCESS.2021.3072782

Molina, M. D., & Sundar, S. S. (2022). When AI moderates online content: Effects of human collaboration and interactive transparency on user trust. *Journal of Computer-Mediated Communication*, 27(4), zmac010. DOI: 10.1093/jcmc/zmac010

Moravec, V., Hynek, N., Gavurova, B., & Kubak, M. (2024). Everyday artificial intelligence unveiled: Societal awareness of technological transformation. *Oeconomia Copernicana*, 15(2), 367–406. DOI: 10.24136/oc.2961

Mortukane, K. (2024). Vicious or Misunderstood?: A Pragmatic Analysis of YouTube Comments. DOI: 10.24136/oc.2961

Mullah, N. S., & Zainon, W. M. N. W. (2021). Advances in machine learning algorithms for hate speech detection in social media: A review. *IEEE Access : Practical Innovations, Open Solutions*, 9, 88364–88376. DOI: 10.1109/ACCESS.2021.3089515

Nosrati, S., Sabzali, M., Heidari, A., Sarfi, T., & Sabbar, S. (2020). Chatbots, counselling, and discontents of the digital life. *Journal of Cyberspace Studies*, 4(2), 153–172.

Pagano, N. A. (2018). The Indecency of the Communications Decency Act 230: Unjust Immunity for Monstrous Social Media Platforms. *Pace Law Review*, 39(1), 511. DOI: 10.58948/2331-3528.1994

Patel, K., Mehta, D., Mistry, C., Gupta, R., Tanwar, S., Kumar, N., & Alazab, M. (2020). Facial sentiment analysis using AI techniques: State-of-the-art, taxonomies, and challenges. *IEEE Access : Practical Innovations, Open Solutions*, 8, 90495–90519. DOI: 10.1109/ACCESS.2020.2993803

Peng, W., Adikari, A., Alahakoon, D., & Gero, J. (2019). Discovering the influence of sarcasm in social media responses. *Wiley Interdisciplinary Reviews. Data Mining and Knowledge Discovery*, 9(6), e1331. DOI: 10.1002/widm.1331

Pérez Sánchez, J. (2024). Impact of Serious Games and Causal Artificial Intelligence on Social Science Research: A Case Study on Cyberbullying. DOI: 10.24136/oc.2961

Roche, C., Wall, P. J., & Lewis, D. (2023). Ethics and diversity in artificial intelligence policies, strategies and initiatives. *AI and Ethics*, 3(4), 1095–1115. DOI: 10.1007/s43681-022-00218-9 PMID: 36246014

Rodriguez, J. A. (2023). LGBTQ incorporated: YouTube and the management of diversity. *Journal of Homosexuality*, 70(9), 1807–1828. DOI: 10.1080/00918369.2022.2042664 PMID: 35196210

Sánchez-Medina, A. J., Galván-Sánchez, I., & Fernández-Monroy, M. (2020). Applying artificial intelligence to explore sexual cyberbullying behaviour. *Heliyon*, 6(1), e03218. DOI: 10.1016/j.heliyon.2020.e03218 PMID: 32042968

Schermer, B. W. (2011). The limits of privacy in automated profiling and data mining. *Computer Law & Security Report*, 27(1), 45–52. DOI: 10.1016/j.clsr.2010.11.009

Schulenberg, K., Li, L., Freeman, G., Zamanifard, S., & McNeese, N. J. (2023, April). Towards leveraging AI-Based moderation to address emergent harassment in social virtual reality. In *Proceedings of the 2023 CHI Conference on Human Factors in Computing Systems* (pp. 1-17). DOI: 10.1145/3544548.3581090

Şener, M. B. (2021). A review of the meaning and importance of the Universal Declaration of Human Rights. *Uluslararası Politik Araştırmalar Dergisi*, 7(3), 15–25.

Siapera, E. (2022). AI content moderation, racism and (de) coloniality. *International Journal of Bullying Prevention : an Official Publication of the International Bullying Prevention Association*, 4(1), 55–65. DOI: 10.1007/s42380-021-00105-7

Singh, A., Rejeb, A., Nangru, H., & Pathak, S. (2024). Global research trends on cyberbullying: A bibliometric study. *Computers in Human Behavior Reports*, 16, 100499. DOI: 10.1016/j.chbr.2024.100499

Smith, M., Nolan, M., & Gaffey, J. (2024). Online safety and social media regulation in Australia: eSafety Commissioner v X Corp. *Griffith Law Review*, 33(1), 1–17. DOI: 10.1080/10383441.2024.2405760

Smuha, N. A. (2019). The EU approach to ethics guidelines for trustworthy artificial intelligence. *Computer Law Review International*, 20(4), 97–106. DOI: 10.9785/cri-2019-200402

Suzor, N., Nelson, L., Gillett, R., & Burgess, J. (2021). QUT Digital Media Research Centre submission in response to the Online Safety Bill 2021. DOI: 10.9785/cri-2019-200402

Usharani, B. (2021). A Novel Extended Ripple and Cyberbullies Data Detection (E-RACYBDD) Framework to Mitigate Deep Fake Attacks on Social Media. In *Deep Fakes, Fake News, and Misinformation in Online Teaching and Learning Technologies* (pp. 186-205). IGI Global.

Van Hoeyweghen, S. (2024). Speaking of games: AI-based content moderation of real-time voice interactions in video games under the DSA. *Interactive Entertainment Law Review*, 7(1), 30–46. DOI: 10.4337/ielr.2024.01.04

Vanpech, P., Peerabenjakul, K., Suriwong, N., & Fugkeaw, S. (2024, February). Detecting Cyberbullying on Social Networks Using Language Learning Model. In *2024 16th International Conference on Knowledge and Smart Technology (KST)* (pp. 161-166). IEEE. DOI: 10.1109/KST61284.2024.10499678

Vázquez-Madrigal, C., García-Rubio, N., & Triguero, Á. (2024). Generative Artificial Intelligence in Education: Risks and Opportunities. In *Teaching Innovations in Economics: Towards a Sustainable World* (pp. 233–254). Springer Nature Switzerland. DOI: 10.1007/978-3-031-72549-4_11

Venkatesh, S., Fong, E. W., & Yeter, I. H. (2022). Investigating ethics in an undergraduate design thinking project: The Stanford EDIPT framework approach in Southeast Asia. In *2022 IEEE Frontiers in Education Conference (FIE)* (pp. 1-5). IEEE.

Wachter, S., Mittelstadt, B., & Russell, C. (2021). Why fairness cannot be automated: Bridging the gap between EU non-discrimination law and AI. *Computer Law & Security Report*, 41, 105567. DOI: 10.1016/j.clsr.2021.105567

Waltz, S. (2002). Reclaiming and rebuilding the history of the Universal Declaration of Human Rights. *Third World Quarterly*, 23(3), 437–448. DOI: 10.1080/01436590220138378

Wettstein, F. (2015). Normativity, ethics, and the UN guiding principles on business and human rights: A critical assessment. *Journal of Human Rights*, 14(2), 162–182. DOI: 10.1080/14754835.2015.1005733

Wijkstra, M., Rogers, K., Mandryk, R. L., Veltkamp, R. C., & Frommel, J. (2024). How To Tame a Toxic Player? A Systematic Literature Review on Intervention Systems for Toxic Behaviors in Online Video Games. *Proceedings of the ACM on Human-Computer Interaction, 8*(CHI PLAY), 1-32. DOI: 10.1145/3677080

Xu, F., Uszkoreit, H., Du, Y., Fan, W., Zhao, D., & Zhu, J. (2019). Explainable AI: A brief survey on history, research areas, approaches and challenges. In *Natural language processing and Chinese computing: 8th cCF international conference, NLPCC 2019, dunhuang, China, October 9–14, 2019, proceedings, part II 8* (pp. 563-574). Springer International Publishing. DOI: 10.1007/978-3-030-32236-6_51

Yeung, K. (2020). Recommendation of the council on artificial intelligence (OECD). *International legal materials, 59*(1), 27-34. DOI: 10.9785/cri-2019-200402

Yousaf, K., & Nawaz, T. (2022). A deep learning-based approach for inappropriate content detection and classification of youtube videos. *IEEE Access : Practical Innovations, Open Solutions*, 10, 16283–16298. DOI: 10.1109/ACCESS.2022.3147519

Zhang, H., & Shao, H. (2024). Exploring the Latest Applications of OpenAI and ChatGPT: An In-Depth Survey. *CMES-Computer Modeling in Engineering & Sciences, 138*(3). DOI: 10.9785/cri-2019-200402

Zulfiqar, N., Shaikh, B. A., Shah, S. A., & Awan, A. (2024). Investigating how AI Technologies Influence Changing Social Norms and Behaviors on Social Media, Particularly in Areas like Communication and Self-Presentation. *Review of Education. Administration & Law*, 7(4), 167–183. DOI: 10.47067/real.v7i4.371

Chapter 12
Combating Cyberbullying With Generative AI:
Large Language Models (LLMs) in Cyberbullying Prevention

B. Sandhiya Rajeshwari
https://orcid.org/0009-0004-4086-0264
Rajalakshmi Institute of Technology, India

I. Divya
https://orcid.org/0000-0003-4725-7412
Rajalakshmi Institute of Technology, India

ABSTRACT

Cyber bullying is a growing issue, causing significant psychological harm across various demographics. Traditional methods of combating it struggle to keep pace with evolving technology and tactics. Recent advancements in Generative AI, particularly LLMs, offer new opportunities for prevention, intervention, and support. This paper explores how LLMs can improve detection of harmful online content, identify bullying patterns using natural language processing, and enhance reporting systems. LLMs also provide immediate support to victims through AI-driven chatbots, offering a safe space to share experiences and receive resources. In educational settings, LLMs can foster digital literacy and resilience, promoting empathy and responsible online behavior. Ethical concerns like privacy and bias must be addressed to ensure AI is used positively. Case studies demonstrate LLMs' success in mitigating cyber bullying across platforms. Ultimately, LLMs offer promising tools for a safer online environment, requiring ongoing research, innovation, and collaboration for effective implementation.

DOI: 10.4018/979-8-3373-0543-1.ch012

1. INTRODUCTION TO GENERATIVE AI

Generative AI is a transformative technology that enables machines to create content—such as text, images, and audio—by learning patterns from vast datasets. This capability is achieved through complex algorithms that analyze and mimic human-like responses, making generative AI a powerful tool across various fields, including the creative arts, customer service, and education.

At its core, generative AI leverages advanced models, particularly Large Language Models (LLMs), designed to understand and generate human language. LLMs, such as OpenAI's GPT-4, are trained on diverse text sources, allowing them to grasp context, semantics, and nuances of language. This proficiency enables LLMs to generate coherent and contextually relevant text, making them suitable for a wide range of applications.

Cyberbullying involves the use of digital platforms to harass, threaten, or intimidate individuals, often leaving lasting emotional and psychological effects on victims. The anonymity and reach of online interactions can exacerbate these issues, making it imperative to develop effective strategies for prevention and intervention.

Generative AI, through LLMs, offers innovative solutions for combating cyberbullying in several ways:

1. **Detection**: LLMs can analyze online conversations to identify harmful language and patterns indicative of bullying behavior. By flagging these interactions in real time, they facilitate prompt action from moderators or caregivers.
2. **Support**: Generating empathetic and supportive responses is crucial for victims of cyberbullying. LLMs can provide immediate, contextually appropriate replies that validate experiences and direct users to resources for help.
3. **Education**: Generative AI can create interactive educational tools that raise awareness about cyberbullying, fostering empathy and responsible online behavior among users.
4. **Content Moderation**: LLMs can assist in moderating online platforms by automatically detecting and flagging inappropriate content, allowing human moderators to focus on more nuanced situations.

Despite the promise of generative AI in addressing cyberbullying, it is essential to consider ethical implications, such as data privacy and bias in AI models. Ensuring responsible use of technology is critical to maximizing its benefits while minimizing potential harms.

2. LITERATURE REVIEW

Cyberbullying has become a critical issue in the digital era, with far-reaching consequences for victims. The use of advanced computational tools, particularly Artificial Intelligence (AI), offers promising solutions for detection, prevention, and support. This review synthesizes key advancements in the field of cyberbullying detection, AI-driven support systems, educational interventions, and ethical considerations, with a special focus on the role of Generative AI and Large Language Models (LLMs).

2.1 Cyberbullying Detection

The ability to detect cyberbullying at scale remains a key challenge. Traditional methods, such as keyword matching, are often inadequate for detecting more nuanced forms of bullying, including sarcasm, coded language, and indirect harassment. Modern AI approaches, particularly transformer-based architectures such as BERT and GPT, have significantly enhanced the accuracy of detection systems by analyzing linguistic features and contextual information from online content.

These models can identify patterns indicative of cyberbullying even in ambiguous text, as shown in recent studies exploring the use of large datasets and advanced neural network techniques. Moreover, multi-modal models, which combine text, images, and metadata, have proven to be effective in improving detection capabilities through attention mechanisms.

2.2 Victim Support Systems

AI-driven support systems are also crucial in addressing the psychological toll of cyberbullying. Chatbots and virtual assistants powered by LLMs can provide victims with immediate emotional support, guiding them to appropriate resources and offering a safe space for sharing their experiences. These tools can simulate empathetic conversations, which have been shown to reduce feelings of isolation and distress among victims, while also encouraging them to seek further help when necessary. The therapeutic potential of AI in supporting mental health during cyberbullying crises aligns with research emphasizing the role of AI in emotional support systems.

2.3 Educational Interventions

Educational programs that promote digital literacy and empathy among students are integral to combating cyberbullying. AI tools, particularly LLMs, can be used to personalize learning experiences, enabling students to understand the impact of their words and behaviors online. These tools can simulate real-life scenarios and role-playing exercises, which help foster empathy and conflict resolution skills, key aspects in preventing bullying behavior. Pilot programs that integrate AI-based simulations have shown promise in reducing bullying incidents and fostering positive online interactions.

2.4 Ethical and Practical Considerations

The deployment of AI in cyberbullying detection and prevention must be carefully managed to avoid ethical pitfalls, such as privacy violations, algorithmic bias, and data misuse. Researchers have highlighted the importance of explainable AI in this context, advocating for transparency in AI decision-making processes to ensure fairness and accountability. Ethical considerations also extend to the integration of human oversight in automated systems, ensuring that AI technologies do not exacerbate existing problems but instead contribute positively to addressing cyberbullying.

2.5 Real-World Implementations

Real-world applications of AI in combating cyberbullying offer valuable insights into its effectiveness. Social media platforms such as Facebook and Twitter have implemented machine learning algorithms to identify and remove abusive content, demonstrating the scalability of these technologies. Non-profit organizations like CyberSmile Foundation utilize AI tools to support victims and educate the public about online safety. Similarly, educational institutions are integrating AI-based tools into their curricula, with promising results in reducing bullying and fostering peer-led interventions.

3. OVERVIEW OF GENERATIVE AI

Generative AI employs advanced deep learning techniques to analyze patterns within data and create new content that mirrors those patterns. Large Language Models (LLMs), such as GPT-4, leverage complex architectures like transformers to process and understand language effectively. By predicting the next word in a sentence based on prior context, these models can generate text that is not only grammatically correct but also contextually relevant. This capability makes LLMs highly versatile and applicable in various domains, including content creation, customer service, and education.

Generative AI operates through a combination of supervised and unsupervised learning approaches.Once trained, LLMs can generate new content, answer questions, and assist in dialogue, transforming them into powerful tools for enhancing communication and providing valuable information.

How LLMs Can Help Combat Cyberbullying:

1.**Real-Time Detection and Intervention**: LLMs can be employed to analyze online interactions in real time, identifying potentially harmful language associated with cyberbullying. By flagging abusive content or detecting negative sentiment, these models can prompt timely interventions from moderators or support systems.

2.**Generating Supportive Responses**: In instances of cyberbullying, LLMs can create empathetic and constructive replies for victims. By understanding emotional cues and context, these models can offer comforting messages, coping strategies, and resources for further support.

3.**Educational Tools and Awareness Campaigns**: LLMs can assist in developing educational materials and awareness programs aimed at preventing cyberbullying. By generating engaging content tailored to specific audiences, these tools can promote understanding and encourage proactive measures among students, parents, and educators.

4.**Chatbots for Peer Support**: AI-driven chatbots powered by LLMs can provide a safe space for individuals to discuss their experiences with bullying. These chatbots can offer immediate support, answer questions, and direct users to additional resources, acting as a bridge to formal help.

5.**Community Engagement**: By facilitating discussions and sharing experiences through AI-driven platforms, LLMs can foster a sense of community among users. This engagement can empower bystanders to take action and support victims, creating a more inclusive and supportive online environment.

3.1 Importance in the Digital Age

In the rapidly evolving digital landscape, the importance of generative AI is profound. As communication increasingly shifts online, the ability to generate meaningful, context-aware content has become essential. Figure 1 represents several key reasons why generative AI is particularly relevant today which has been given below:

Figure 1.Generative keys of AI

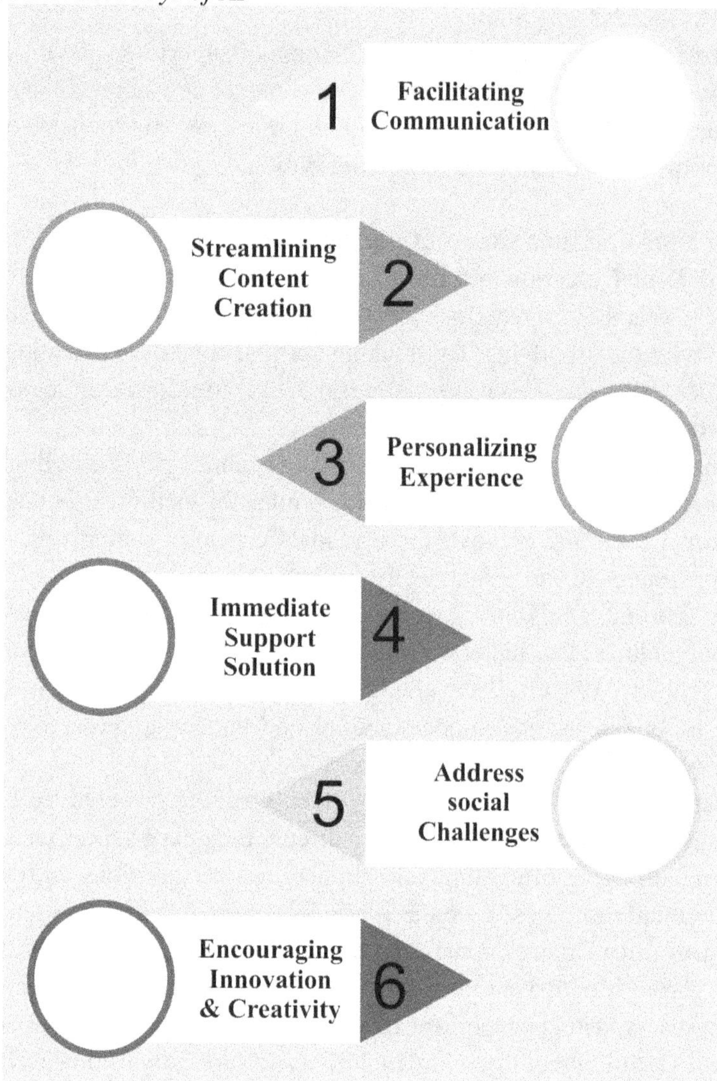

Facilitating Communication: Generative AI enhances interactions by providing real-time translations and generating responses that improve understanding among users from diverse backgrounds.
Streamlining Content Creation: In a world overwhelmed with information, generative AI accelerates the content creation process, helping individuals and businesses produce articles, social media posts, and marketing materials efficiently.

Personalizing Experiences: By analyzing user behavior and preferences, generative AI can create personalized interactions, resulting in more engaging and relevant experiences for users.

Immediate Support Solutions: AI-driven chatbots and virtual assistants can deliver quick responses to inquiries, improving customer service and user satisfaction across platforms.

Addressing Social Challenges: Generative AI plays a crucial role in tackling social issues such as cyberbullying. By detecting harmful language and providing empathetic responses, AI can contribute to creating safer online environments.

Encouraging Innovation and Creativity: Generative AI tools empower creators by offering new ideas and augmenting creative processes, blending human ingenuity with machine capabilities. Generative AI represents a significant advancement in technology, reshaping how we interact, create, and communicate in the digital age.

4. DETECTION OF CYBERBULLYING

Detecting cyberbullying is a critical component in addressing this pervasive issue within digital communication. Effective detection relies on various methods that harness technological advancements, particularly in natural language processing (NLP) and machine learning.

4.1 Methods for Identifying Cyberbullying Behavior

Keyword and Phrase Analysis: One of the simplest methods for detecting cyber bullying involves identifying specific keywords or phrases commonly associated with bullying behavior, such as insults, threats, or derogatory terms. This approach is straightforward and can quickly flag potentially harmful content.

Sentiment Analysis: Sentiment analysis assesses the emotional tone of conversations. Algorithms analyze the language to determine whether the sentiment expressed is positive, negative, or neutral. A sudden increase in negative sentiment directed at a user can indicate potential bullying. While effective for identifying harmful trends, sentiment analysis may not always distinguish between legitimate criticism and bullying, highlighting the need for more sophisticated methods.

Figure 2. Cyberbullying behaviour identification

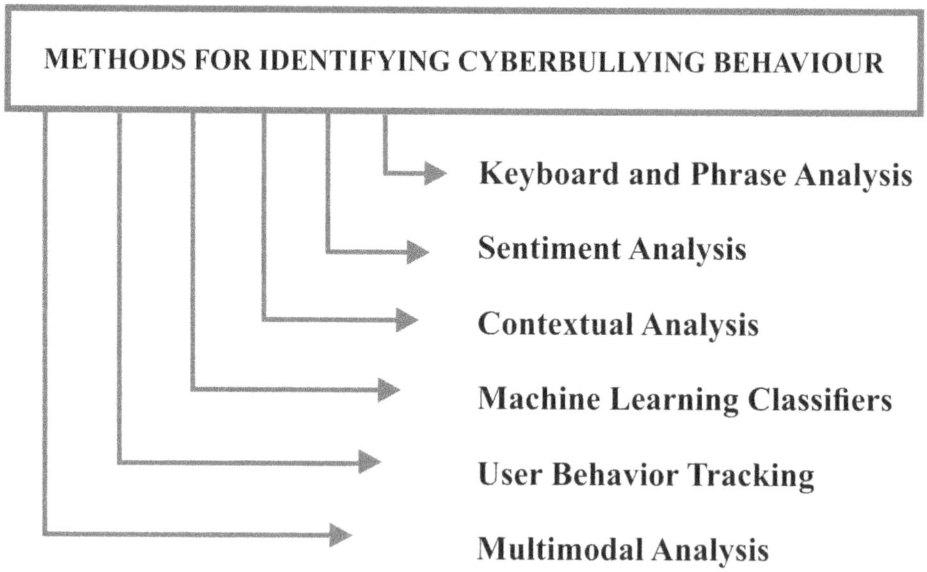

Contextual Analysis: Advanced detection systems employ contextual analysis, where models consider the surrounding text to understand the meaning and intent behind words more accurately. This method helps differentiate between casual banter and harmful comments, thereby reducing false positives.

Machine Learning Classifiers: Supervised machine learning models can be trained on labeled datasets that include examples of both cyberbullying and non-bullying behavior. These models learn to recognize patterns and can classify new interactions as bullying or non-bullying based on features learned during training.

User Behavior Tracking: Monitoring user behavior over time can help identify bullying patterns. For instance, if a user consistently targets another individual with negative comments, this behavior may indicate cyberbullying. By combining behavior analytics with textual analysis, detection systems can enhance accuracy, recognizing persistent patterns that may not be evident in isolated incidents.

Multimodal Analysis: Some advanced systems analyze multiple forms of data, including text, images, and even video content, to detect bullying. For example, visual content shared alongside harmful text can provide additional context that signals cyberbullying. By integrating different data types, these systems can develop a more comprehensive understanding of interactions and the potential for harm.

4.2 The Role of Natural Language Processing (NLP)

Natural Language Processing (NLP) plays a vital role in detecting and understanding cyberbullying behaviors. Figure 3 represents the key aspects of how NLP contributes to this process:

Figure 3. Natural language processing methods

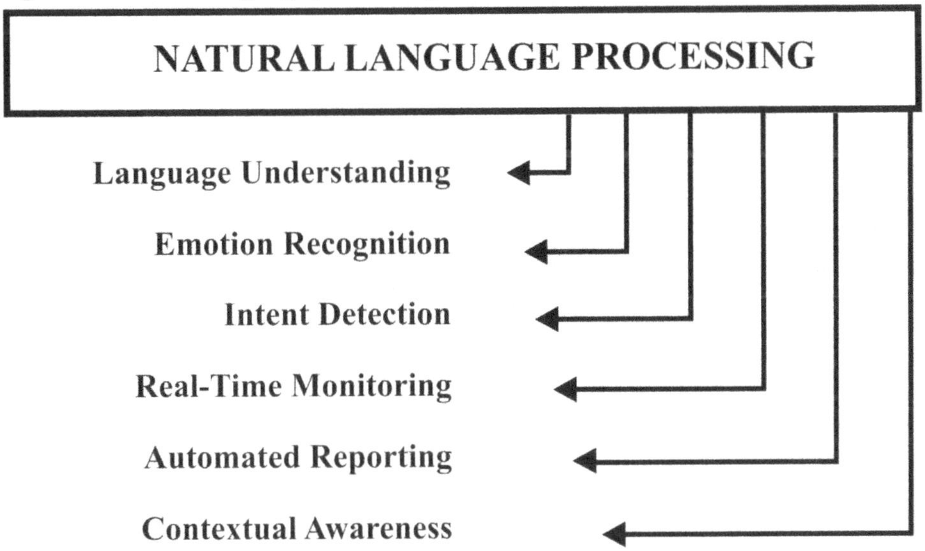

Language Understanding: NLP enables machines to comprehend human language, capturing its complexity and nuance. By parsing sentences, recognizing parts of speech, and understanding context, NLP models can differentiate between various forms of communication. This capability is essential for detecting bullying, as it allows systems to discern intent and emotional tone. **Emotion Recognition**: Advanced NLP techniques can analyze the emotional content of messages. By identifying emotions expressed in text—such as anger, sadness, or frustration—NLP can flag interactions that may indicate cyberbullying. This emotional insight is crucial for understanding the impact of words and the experiences of individuals involved.

Intent Detection: NLP models can be trained to recognize the intent behind messages, distinguishing between playful teasing and harmful threats. This capability is vital for minimizing misunderstandings and improving the accuracy of detection systems, ensuring that interventions are appropriate and contextually sensitive.

Real-Time Monitoring: NLP allows for the implementation of real-time monitoring of online platforms. As users interact, NLP algorithms can continuously analyze conversations, providing immediate feedback and flagging problematic content for review. This proactive approach enables quicker responses to incidents of cyberbullying.

Automated Reporting: NLP can facilitate automated reporting mechanisms. If a message is flagged as potentially harmful, the system can automatically alert moderators or provide users with resources for support. This functionality streamlines the reporting process, making it easier for users to seek help.

Contextual Awareness: By leveraging contextual embeddings, NLP models can better understand the situation surrounding a particular message. This contextual awareness allows for a more nuanced understanding of language that is critical in identifying bullying, especially in dynamic online environments where language can shift rapidly.

5. GENERATING SUPPORTIVE RESPONSES

In the context of cyberbullying, generating supportive responses is crucial for helping victims feel heard, validated, and empowered. Effective responses can provide immediate comfort and guidance, fostering a sense of safety in digital interactions.

Generative AI, particularly through Large Language Models (LLMs), offers innovative solutions for creating empathetic and constructive replies. Figure 4 represents how these responses are generated and provide examples of automated support systems.

Figure 4. Solution for empathetic and constructive replies

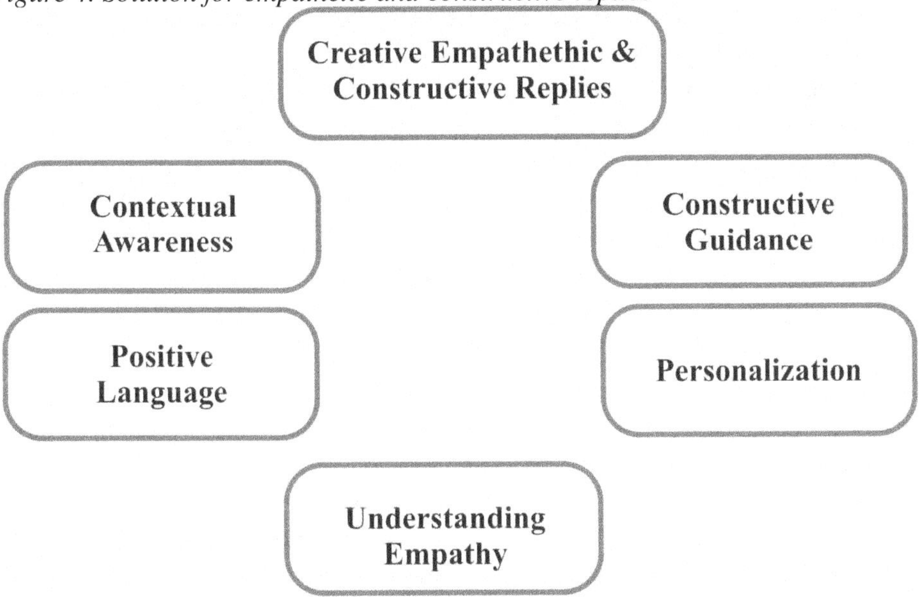

Contextual Awareness: Generative AI can analyze the context of a conversation to craft replies that are relevant and appropriate. By understanding the specifics of the situation—such as the nature of the bullying, the relationship between the parties involved, and the medium of communication—LLMs can tailor their responses to address the victim's unique experience. For example, if a user shares that they are being bullied in a group chat, the AI might respond with, "It can be really tough to feel singled out in a group. Have you considered talking to a trusted friend or a teacher about what's happening?"
Constructive Guidance: Beyond offering empathy, effective responses should provide constructive advice or resources. This may include suggesting coping strategies, directing users to helpful resources, or encouraging them to reach out for additional support. For instance, an LLM might suggest, "Remember, it's important to take care of yourself. If you're feeling overwhelmed, it could help to take a break from social media and talk to someone you trust." Combining empathy with actionable guidance makes the response more impactful and encourages victims to take positive steps forward.
Positive Language: The choice of words plays a crucial role in shaping the tone of a response. Generative AI can utilize positive and uplifting language to promote resilience and empowerment. For example, an AI-generated reply might include affirmations such as, "You deserve to be treated with respect,

and it's great that you're reaching out for support. You're not alone in this." This reinforces the message that help is available and encourages victims to seek further assistance.

Personalization: Tailoring responses based on user data or past interactions can significantly enhance the effectiveness of support. By analyzing previous communications, LLMs can create personalized messages that resonate with individual experiences. For instance, if a user has previously shared their favorite coping strategies or support networks, the AI might say, "I remember you mentioned talking to your friend, Alex, about your feelings. It might help to reach out to them again." This personalization fosters a deeper connection and shows the user that their experiences and preferences are valued.

Understanding Empathy: Empathetic responses are vital for validating the feelings of individuals experiencing bullying. Generative AI models can be trained to recognize emotional cues in language, such as tone, word choice, and phrasing. By analyzing these cues, LLMs can generate responses that reflect understanding, compassion, and support. For instance, if a victim expresses feelings of sadness or isolation, an AI-generated response might include phrases like, "I'm really sorry to hear that you're feeling this way. It's completely understandable to feel hurt when others treat you this way." This acknowledgment helps victims feel validated in their emotions.

Examples of Automated Support Systems:

1. **Chatbots on Social Media Platforms**: Many social media networks have implemented AI-powered chatbots that provide immediate responses to users reporting cyberbullying. For example, a user might report receiving harmful messages, and the chatbot could respond with:

"I'm really sorry to hear that you're going through this. It's not okay, and you deserve support. Here are some resources that can help you."

2. **Online Counseling Services**: Platforms offering mental health support often integrate LLMs to engage users in initial conversations. An example response might be:

"It sounds like you're feeling overwhelmed. It's important to talk about what you're experiencing. Would you like some resources or someone to talk to?"

3. **Educational Tools for Schools**: AI-driven educational tools can generate supportive messages for students learning about the impacts of bullying. A generated prompt could be:

"If you see someone being bullied, you have the power to help. Here are some ways you can support your classmates..."

4. **Crisis Intervention Apps**: Applications designed to assist individuals in crisis often use LLMs to create calming, supportive messages. For instance, a user might receive a message like:

"You're not alone. Many people care about you and want to help. Let's talk about what you're feeling right now."

5. **Interactive Help Desks**: Websites offering resources on bullying prevention can implement LLMs that generate real-time responses to user inquiries. For example:

"It's great that you reached out. Cyberbullying can be really tough, but there are steps you can take. Here are some options..."

Figure 5. Examples of automated support systems

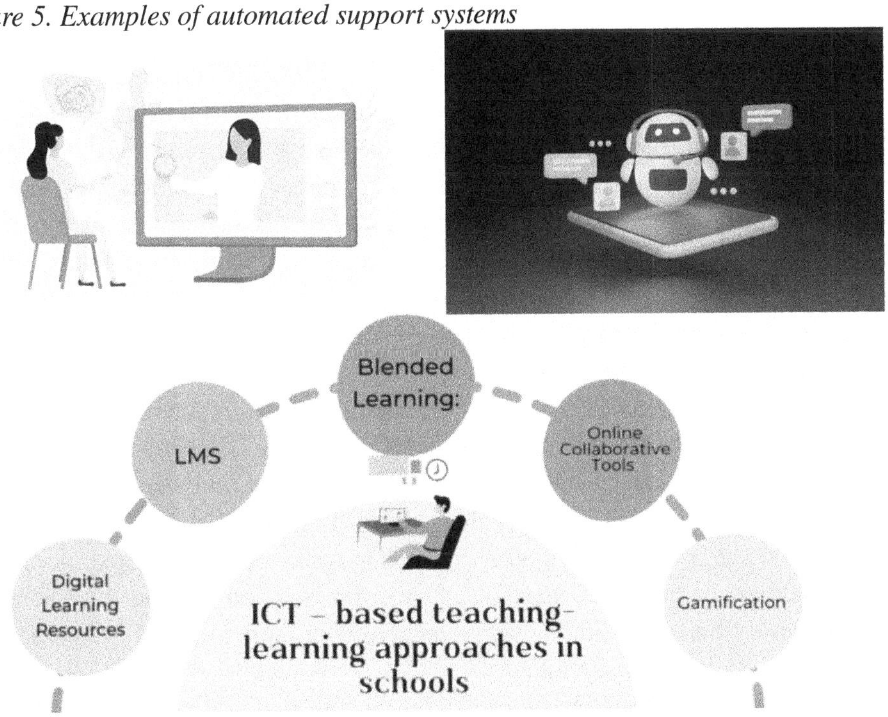

Generating supportive responses through generative AI is a powerful tool in combating the effects of cyberbullying. By creating empathetic, constructive, and personalized replies, LLMs can significantly enhance the support available to victims. Automated systems, such as chatbots and counseling platforms, illustrate the practical application of this technology in providing immediate and meaningful assistance. As generative AI continues to advance, its role in fostering positive online interactions will become increasingly vital in creating safer digital environments.

6. CONTENT MODERATION

Content moderation is a critical element in managing online spaces, especially in the context of combating cyberbullying. Effective moderation not only helps detect and remove harmful content but also fosters a positive community culture. This section delves into various strategies for moderating harmful content and discusses the balance between automation and human oversight.

6.1 Strategies for Moderating Harmful Content

1. **Automated Detection Systems**: Leveraging Large Language Models (LLMs) and machine learning algorithms, platforms can deploy automated systems that analyze user-generated content in real-time. These systems are designed to flag messages containing hate speech, threats, or other forms of abusive language. By identifying harmful content swiftly, these tools ensure that such material can be addressed before it spreads, significantly reducing the potential impact on victims. For instance, a platform might use LLMs to scan comments and direct messages for patterns associated with bullying, automatically generating alerts for further review.
2. **Keyword Filtering**: Keyword filtering is a foundational strategy for content moderation. By implementing filters that block or flag messages containing specific terms associated with bullying, platforms can mitigate immediate risks. However, while effective at catching overt instances of abusive language, this method can lead to false positives. Messages that contain flagged words may not always be harmful, especially if used in a non-abusive context. Therefore, keyword filtering should be supplemented with more nuanced techniques that incorporate context and intent.
3. **Contextual Analysis**: Advanced LLMs enable deeper contextual analysis, allowing moderation systems to grasp the intent behind messages. By examining the surrounding text and understanding the dynamics of the conversation, these systems can more accurately distinguish between harmful content and benign

interactions. For example, a message that might initially appear aggressive could be part of a humorous exchange among friends, and contextual analysis can help prevent wrongful flagging of such content.

4. **User Reporting Mechanisms**: Empowering users to report abusive behavior is essential in any moderation strategy. When users flag content as harmful, moderation systems can prioritize these reports for review. Automated systems can assist by categorizing reports based on severity and context, allowing human moderators to focus on the most critical cases. This user-driven approach not only helps in identifying harmful content but also fosters a community where users feel their voices are heard.
5. **Training and Fine-Tuning Models**: Regularly updating and fine-tuning LLMs based on emerging trends in cyberbullying and user feedback is vital for maintaining detection accuracy. As language and online interactions evolve, continuous training ensures that models remain effective in identifying new forms of harmful content. This ongoing learning process can involve incorporating new datasets that reflect current slang, bullying tactics, or community dynamics, ensuring that the moderation system adapts to changing user behavior.
6. **Community Guidelines Enforcement**: Clearly defined community guidelines should be established and communicated to users. These guidelines set the standards for acceptable behavior and provide a reference point for moderation decisions. Moderation systems can then align with these guidelines to ensure consistency in content review and enforcement. This shared understanding helps create a safe environment where users know the boundaries of acceptable interactions.

6.2 The Balance Between Automation and Human Oversight

While automation plays a significant role in content moderation, it is essential to strike a balance with human oversight to ensure nuanced understanding and context. Table 1 represents the challenges and limitations of the automation and human oversight.

Table 1. Challenges and limitations

Aspects	*Description*	*Advantages*	*Challenges/Limitations*
Strengths of Automation	Automated systems leverage AI and machine learning to process vast amounts of data and detect harmful behaviors quickly and consistently	**Scalability**: Can analyze millions of interactions in real-time, ensuring efficiency in content moderation. **Consistency**: Reduces human biases by applying standardized rules. **Speed**: Flags harmful content instantly, minimizing exposure to harmful interactions.	**Context Blindness**: Struggles with interpreting sarcasm, jokes, or nuanced language. **False Positives / Negatives**: May misclassify benign content as harmful or fail to detect subtle bullying.
Limitations of Automation	Despite efficiency, automated systems often fail to account for linguistic subtleties, intent, and cultural differences.	**Efficient**: Performs well with straightforward, clearly defined abusive content. **Cost-effective**: Reduces the need for extensive human moderation for simple cases.	**Lacks Emotional Understanding**: Cannot empathize with or gauge the emotional impact of content. **Static Rules**: Algorithms depend on training data and fail to adapt to dynamic social interactions without frequent updates.
Human Moderators	Human moderators bring empathy, critical thinking, and the ability to interpret context, essential for understanding nuanced situations.	**Contextual Awareness**: Can evaluate intent, tone, and broader implications. **Empathy**: Provides compassionate responses for sensitive cases. **Flexible Decision-Making**: Adapts to unique or complex scenarios.	**Resource Intensive**: Requires significant time and staffing, especially for platforms with high volumes of user content. **Subject to Bias**: Personal biases of moderators may affect decision-making.
Collaborative Approaches	A hybrid model combines automation for initial detection and human oversight for complex or ambiguous cases.	**Efficiency**: Automation filters straightforward cases, allowing human moderators to focus on critical issues. **Balanced Approach**: Combines speed with accuracy and empathy.	**Implementation Complexity**: Requires seamless integration and coordination between AI systems and human moderators. **Potential Gaps**: Misalignment between automation priorities and human intervention can delay resolutions.

continued on following page

Table 1. Continued

Aspects	*Description*	*Advantages*	*Challenges/Limitations*
Feedback Loops	Insights from human moderators are used to refine AI algorithms, improving their accuracy and adaptability over time.	**Model Improvement**: Human feedback trains AI to recognize emerging trends, slang, and nuanced patterns. **Reduction of Errors**: Enhances the system's ability to identify harmful content with fewer misclassifications.	**Dependency on Feedback Quality**: The effectiveness of updates relies on accurate and comprehensive inputs from human moderators. **Time-Intensive**: Continuous monitoring and refinement require sustained effort.
User Empowerment	Users actively participate by reporting harmful content, offering feedback, and shaping community standards	**Engagement**: Encourages users to take responsibility for creating a safe environment. **Community Ownership**: Builds trust in the moderation process by involving users in decision-making.	**Misuse Risk**: Users might exploit reporting systems for personal grievances, leading to false reports. **Increased Workload**: Reviewing user reports adds to the moderation team's responsibilities

7. EDUCATIONAL AND PREVENTIVE TOOLS

7.1 Harnessing Generative AI in the Fight Against Cyberbullying

Cyberbullying is a pervasive issue that can lead to severe emotional and psychological consequences for victims. As digital interactions become increasingly integral to our daily lives, it is crucial to equip individuals—especially youth—with the knowledge and resources to navigate these interactions safely. Educational and preventive tools play a vital role in this effort, and generative AI, particularly through Large Language Models (LLMs), can significantly enhance awareness programs and interactive educational resources. This section explores the innovative ways AI can be harnessed to raise awareness and educate young people about cyberbullying.

7.2 Developing Awareness Programs Using AI

1. **Tailored Awareness Campaigns**: Generative AI can analyze demographic data, online behavior, and social trends to create customized awareness programs that resonate with specific audiences. By understanding the unique needs and concerns of different groups—such as age, location, and interests—AI can help design campaigns that are not only relevant but also engaging. For instance, an

awareness campaign aimed at high school students may focus on social media platforms they frequently use, employing language and visuals that resonate with their experiences.

2. **Content Generation**: AI can assist in generating diverse and engaging content for awareness programs, including articles, infographics, videos, and social media posts. By producing a variety of materials that tackle cyberbullying from multiple angles—such as its definitions, impacts, and prevention strategies—organizations can reach a broader audience. For example, an AI might create a series of short videos that illustrate the effects of cyberbullying through real-life scenarios, making the topic more relatable and impactful.
3. **Real-Time Feedback and Adaptation**: The adaptability of generative AI allows for the analysis of the effectiveness of awareness campaigns in real time. By examining audience engagement, interactions, and feedback, AI can provide insights that inform necessary adjustments to content and delivery methods. For instance, if a particular message is resonating well with the audience, AI can recommend amplifying that message across more platforms, ensuring that the campaign remains relevant and impactful.
4. **Interactive Learning Modules**: AI-driven platforms can create interactive learning modules that educate users about the signs of cyberbullying, its effects, and how to respond effectively. These modules can incorporate quizzes, simulations, and scenario-based learning that make education more engaging and memorable. For example, a simulation might allow users to navigate a series of online interactions, providing them with decision points where they can choose how to respond to bullying behavior, thereby enhancing their problem-solving skills.
5. **Collaborative Platforms**: Generative AI can facilitate the development of online platforms where users can share their experiences and learn from one another. Such collaborative spaces foster a sense of community and reduce feelings of isolation among victims. Additionally, they empower bystanders to take action by providing them with resources and strategies for intervening in bullying situations. For example, a platform might host discussion forums where users can share stories and advice, helping to build a supportive network.
6. **Partnerships with Schools and Organizations**: Collaborating with educational institutions and community organizations is essential for amplifying the reach of awareness programs. Generative AI can help identify potential partners by analyzing community needs and existing programs. By streamlining communication and resource distribution, AI can ensure that educational materials and training sessions are effectively implemented in schools and community centers. This collaboration can lead to more comprehensive and impactful awareness initiatives.

7.3 Interactive Educational Resources for Youth

Engaging Approaches to Combat Cyberbullying: IN today's digital age, cyberbullying is a growing concern, affecting millions of young people across the globe. It can manifest through harmful social media posts, hurtful messages, and exclusionary behavior, leaving lasting emotional scars. To address this issue, it is essential to equip youth with the knowledge and tools to recognize, respond to, and prevent cyberbullying.

One of the most effective ways to do this is through interactive educational resources, enhanced by generative AI and other emerging technologies. These tools offer innovative ways to engage young people, helping them build empathy, awareness, and the confidence to act against bullying. Here are several key strategies for creating dynamic, interactive resources to educate youth on cyberbullying prevention:

1. Gamification of Learning

Gamification integrates game-like elements into non-game contexts, turning learning into an engaging and enjoyable experience. By harnessing the power of AI, we can develop interactive games that teach important lessons about cyberbullying. Games offer a unique opportunity to simulate real-life situations, where players can practice decision-making, conflict resolution, and empathy.

Example:

An AI-powered simulation game could immerse users in a series of scenarios where they encounter cyberbullying situations—either as a victim, bystander, or even the bully. Players might be asked to make decisions on how to respond, such as whether to report the bullying, intervene, or offer support to the victim. Through the outcomes of their choices, they can see the impact of their actions on the well-being of others. This hands-on, experiential learning makes the concept of cyberbullying more tangible and relatable. Gamification also taps into youth-driven motivation, leveraging rewards, leaderboards, and achievements to increase engagement. By using these elements, educational games can maintain interest while imparting serious lessons.

2. Chatbots for Peer Support

AI-driven chatbots can serve as immediate, accessible resources for youth who experience or witness cyberbullying. Unlike traditional resources, chatbots provide a safe, anonymous space where young people can seek help, ask questions, or share their experiences without fear of judgment. These chatbots can use natural language processing (NLP) to engage in meaningful, empathetic conversations with users.

Example:

A young person facing online harassment might turn to a chatbot for immediate support. The chatbot could offer reassurance, acknowledge the emotional impact of the situation, and provide practical advice on how to deal with the bullying, such as how to block the perpetrator or how to report the incident. The chatbot could also provide links to helplines, counselors, or mental health resources, helping users take the next steps toward getting professional support.

By using AI, these chatbots can provide responses that feel natural, warm, and understanding, creating a supportive environment that can be a lifeline in moments of distress.

3. Virtual Reality (VR) Experiences

Virtual Reality (VR) technology is a powerful tool that can offer immersive, experiential learning in ways that traditional resources cannot. By stepping into the shoes of both victims and bystanders, young people can gain a deeper understanding of the emotional impact of cyberbullying.

Example:

A VR scenario could put a user in a virtual classroom where they witness a cyberbullying incident unfold in real-time. The participant might see and hear hurtful messages being sent to a peer and watch as the victim's emotional state deteriorates. After experiencing this firsthand, the VR program could then prompt users to make decisions about how to intervene or offer support, reinforcing the importance of empathy and bystander intervention.

These VR experiences create emotional connections that help young people internalize the lessons they've learned, making them more likely to act proactively in real-life situations. Empathy-building through VR can be a game-changer in encouraging a culture of kindness and respect online.

4. Interactive Workshops and Webinars

Interactive workshops and webinars allow for direct engagement with experts, providing a dynamic space to discuss the complexities of cyberbullying. AI-powered platforms can assist in organizing these events by tailoring content based on the questions and concerns raised by participants.

Example:

During an interactive webinar, young people might be able to submit questions, participate in live polls, or join discussion groups in real time. AI can be used to analyze trends in these interactions and adjust the content accordingly.

For instance, if a group of participants expresses concern about a particular type of cyberbullying, such as sexting or doxxing, the webinar could shift focus to address those concerns in more detail.

Facilitators can also use AI to generate interactive activities, such as scenario-based roleplays or group discussions, where participants practice responding to hypothetical bullying situations. This ensures that the learning experience is both engaging and impactful.

5. Resource Libraries

AI can help create comprehensive resource libraries filled with educational materials on cyberbullying, including articles, videos, podcasts, self-help guides, and more. These resources can be curated and personalized based on users' preferences, ensuring that the content they access is relevant and useful.

Example:

A young person experiencing cyberbullying could use an AI-powered platform to quickly find tailored resources based on their specific situation. If they're looking for coping strategies, the AI could recommend articles and videos focused on managing stress and emotions. If they're unsure of how to report the bullying, they could be directed to step-by-step guides for different social media platforms or schools. By organizing content in this way, young people can easily access the information they need when they need it.

Additionally, AI can track progress by suggesting new materials or topics for further learning, helping users continuously expand their understanding of how to navigate online interactions safely.

6. Social Media Engagement

Since many young people are active on social media, engaging with them on these platforms can be an effective way to raise awareness about cyberbullying and promote positive behaviors. AI-driven tools can be used to create interactive campaigns and content that resonate with youth where they already spend a lot of their time.

Example:

An AI-powered social media campaign could feature quizzes, challenges, or polls designed to raise awareness of cyberbullying. For instance, a quiz might ask questions about recognizing cyberbullying behaviors, with immediate feedback explaining why certain actions are harmful. Alternatively, a challenge could encourage young people to share their positive experiences of online support or create videos about how to stand up against bullying. These activities can create a sense of community and encourage peer-to-peer learning.

By integrating these resources into the environments where youth already socialize and communicate, we can normalize conversations around empathy, respect, and kindness in digital spaces.

8. ETHICAL CONSIDERATIONS IN LEVERAGING GENERATIVE AI TO COMBAT CYBERBULLYING

As we increasingly rely on **Generative AI** and **Large Language Models (LLMs)** to address complex social issues like **cyberbullying**, it becomes crucial to integrate **ethical principles** into the development, deployment, and use of these technologies. While AI presents significant opportunities for innovation and social impact, its application, particularly in sensitive areas like cyberbullying, must be handled responsibly. The ethical considerations that arise in this context include **data privacy**, **biases in AI models**, and the need for **transparency and accountability** in the AI systems. This section will elaborate on these critical aspects, emphasizing the importance of adhering to ethical standards to ensure that AI solutions are both effective and responsible.

8.1. Data Privacy and Protection

The use of AI in combating cyberbullying often requires the collection, processing, and storage of personal data. Ensuring the privacy and security of user information is paramount to fostering trust and protecting individuals from potential harm. Figure 6 represents the Key ethical principles in data privacy include:

Figure 6. Data privacy and protection key principles

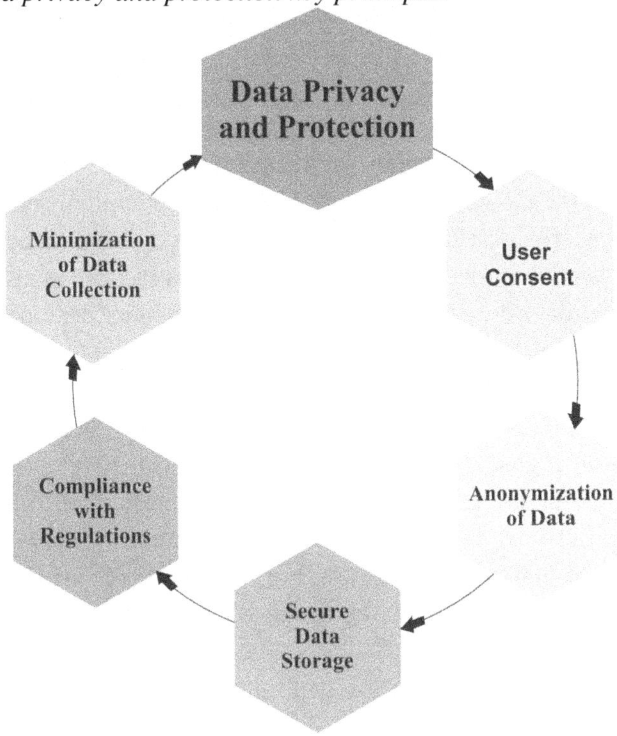

8.1.1 User Consent

It is vital to obtain explicit user consent when collecting personal data to train AI models or to develop AI-driven support systems for cyberbullying. Users—especially minors—should fully understand what data is being collected, how it will be used, and who will have access to it. This is especially important in the context of children and young people, who may not be fully aware of the implications of sharing personal information online. Informed consent forms and clear privacy policies are essential to ensure transparency.

8.1.2 Anonymization of Data

To minimize the risk of privacy violations, data used to train AI models should be anonymized. This means removing personally identifiable information (PII), such as names, email addresses, or locations, from the data to prevent the possibility of linking information back to specific individuals. Anonymization protects users' identities, reducing the risk of exploitation or harm from data breaches or misuse.

8.1.3 Secure Data Storage

Storing user data securely is another critical consideration. Implementing robust security protocols such as encryption, two-factor authentication, and secure access controls helps protect against unauthorized access. With growing concerns about data breaches, it is essential for organizations to adopt best practices in cybersecurity to safeguard sensitive data, especially when dealing with minors' personal information.

8.1.4 Compliance with Regulations

Data protection regulations, such as the General Data Protection Regulation (GDPR) in Europe or the Children's Online Privacy Protection Act (COPPA) in the United States, provide legal frameworks that govern how user data should be collected, processed, and stored. These laws are particularly relevant for technologies targeting children and young people. Organizations must ensure that their AI systems comply with these regulations, particularly around issues like data minimization, the right to access data, and the right to be forgotten.

8.1.5 Minimization of Data Collection

Data minimization is the practice of collecting only the minimum amount of information necessary to achieve the specific purpose for which it was gathered. This approach reduces the risk of misuse, minimizes potential data breaches, and respects users' privacy. In the case of AI systems designed to combat cyberbullying, it is essential to avoid collecting unnecessary data, especially personal or sensitive information that isn't required for detecting or responding to bullying incidents.

8.2. Addressing Biases in AI Models

AI systems, including generative AI models, can inadvertently reinforce harmful biases. These biases can arise from several sources, including skewed training data, cultural stereotypes, or flawed algorithmic design. When AI systems are used to detect or respond to cyberbullying, it is essential to ensure that the model behaves equitably, accurately, and without perpetuating harmful biases. Figure 7 represents the biases in AI model which are given below

Figure 7. Addressing biases in AI models

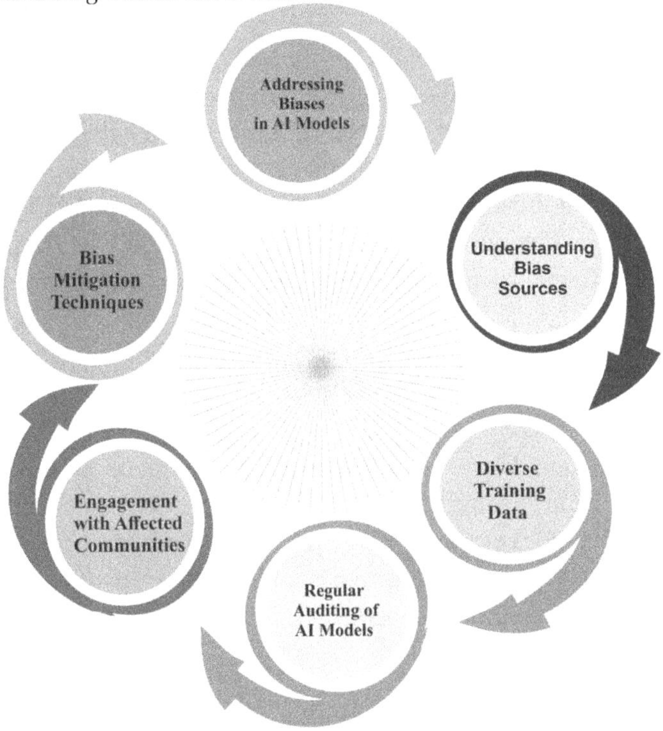

8.2.1 Understanding Bias Sources

Biases can originate from various sources, including:

- **Skewed Training Data**: AI models are only as good as the data they are trained on. If the training data disproportionately represents certain demographics, experiences, or perspectives, the model may perform poorly or unfairly for underrepresented groups.
- **Societal Biases**: AI systems can unintentionally inherit biases from societal norms or stereotypes embedded in language. For instance, the way cyberbullying manifests can vary across cultures, and an AI model that fails to account for these differences may misinterpret or overlook instances of bullying.
- **Algorithmic Design**: Sometimes, biases are introduced through the choices made during model development, such as which features are prioritized or how the model is fine-tuned.

8.2.2 Diverse Training Data

To combat bias, it is critical to use diverse and representative training datasets. This means actively sourcing data that includes a wide variety of voices, experiences, and cultural contexts. For example, an AI model for cyberbullying detection should incorporate examples from different age groups, genders, ethnicities, and regions to ensure that it can recognize and appropriately respond to bullying incidents across different demographics. A diverse dataset allows the AI to detect more subtle forms of bullying, such as cyberbullying in less overt languages or targeting marginalized groups.

8.2.3 Regular Auditing of AI Models

Bias mitigation should not be a one-time task but a continuous process. Regular auditing and evaluation of AI models are necessary to assess their fairness, accuracy, and impact. This includes evaluating how the model performs across different demographic groups to ensure that no group is unfairly targeted or overlooked. These audits should be conducted by independent third parties to ensure objectivity and transparency in the process.

8.2.4 Engagement with Affected Communities

A key aspect of addressing bias is engaging with communities that are particularly affected by cyberbullying, such as LGBTQ+ youth, racial minorities, or individuals with disabilities. These groups can provide valuable insights into how AI models may inadvertently reinforce negative stereotypes or fail to recognize certain types of bullying. Incorporating feedback from these communities helps ensure that AI systems are fair, inclusive, and sensitive to the unique challenges faced by these groups.

8.2.5 Bias Mitigation Techniques

Several technical strategies can be employed to mitigate bias in AI models. These include:

- Re-weighing training data to give more emphasis to underrepresented groups.
- Algorithmic fairness techniques that adjust decision-making processes to ensure that no group is disproportionately impacted by AI actions.
- Fairness constraints that guide the model to treat all users equitably, regardless of their background or identity.

8.3. Ensuring Transparency and Accountability

Transparency and accountability are essential in fostering trust and ensuring the responsible use of AI technologies. Without clear communication about how AI systems operate and how decisions are made, users may become skeptical or resistant to these technologies. Ensuring transparency helps mitigate this by providing clarity on the AI's functionality, goals, and limitations.

8.3.1 Clear Communication of AI Use

Organizations should clearly communicate with users about how AI is used in the context of cyberbullying prevention. This includes explaining how AI is employed in content moderation, detecting abusive behavior, and providing support to victims. By explaining the technology's role in managing cyberbullying, organizations can reduce misunderstandings and build trust with their audience.

8.3.2 Explainable AI

Explainable AI (XAI) refers to AI systems designed to provide insights into how decisions are made. This is particularly important in cyberbullying detection, where AI systems may flag or remove content based on certain criteria. Providing users with a transparent explanation of why specific content was flagged—such as the reasoning behind a bullying detection or intervention—can help demystify AI processes and reduce feelings of alienation or frustration. It also allows users to challenge or appeal decisions if they believe there has been an error.

8.3.3 User Feedback Mechanisms

Establishing feedback mechanisms is essential for improving AI systems over time. Users should be able to provide feedback on the effectiveness of AI-driven interventions, report false positives or negatives, and share their experiences with the system. This feedback loop ensures that AI models continue to evolve in response to real-world challenges and user needs.

8.3.4 Accountability Structures

Clear accountability structures are needed to ensure that AI systems act responsibly. This includes defining who is responsible for the decisions made by AI systems, particularly when those decisions affect individuals, such as flagging content or intervening in cyberbullying incidents. Organizations should have procedures in place for addressing grievances, correcting mistakes, and ensuring that the technology does not harm users.

8.3.5 Continuous Improvement

AI technologies must undergo continuous improvement to adapt to changing circumstances, emerging ethical considerations, and evolving societal norms. By regularly updating AI models based on new research, user feedback, and ethical best practices, organizations can ensure that their systems remain effective, fair, and responsible over time.

9. CASE STUDIES IN CYBERBULLYING AND LLM

9.1 Successful Implementations of LLMs in Combating Cyberbullying

1. **Twitter's ML Moderation**: Twitter employs machine learning, including LLMs, to flag abusive tweets for moderation. By analyzing text for harmful language patterns, Twitter has significantly improved its ability to address cyberbullying, leading to quicker and more accurate removal of harmful content.
2. **Facebook's AI Models**: Facebook uses AI models to detect harmful posts and comments in real-time, employing both supervised and unsupervised learning techniques. The platform reports enhanced user safety and proactive moderation.
3. **Instagram's Comment Filtering**: Instagram integrates AI tools to preemptively detect offensive comments, giving users the option to edit before posting. This proactive system has helped reduce visible instances of online harassment.
4. **Woebot (Mental Health App)**: Woebot is a mental health app that leverages conversational AI to engage with users experiencing bullying-related distress. It offers empathy and tailored coping strategies, effectively supporting mental well-being.
5. **YouTube Content Moderation**: YouTube's AI systems review videos for signs of harmful behavior or bullying. Content flagged as abusive is either demonetized or removed, reducing its visibility and discouraging such behavior.

9.2 Lessons Learned from Real-World Applications

1. **Importance of Context:** Real-world applications reveal that understanding the nuances of language—such as sarcasm, idioms, and cultural references—is critical for accurately detecting cyberbullying. LLMs must be trained on diverse datasets

to better interpret intent and context, as simple keyword matching often fails to capture these subtleties. For example, platforms like Twitter and Instagram have improved their moderation by incorporating context-aware models that can distinguish between friendly banter and harmful interactions.

2. **User Engagement:** Engaging users in the moderation process enhances the effectiveness and trustworthiness of AI systems. Initiatives that allow users to provide feedback on flagged content or customize their interaction settings (e.g., comment filtering on Instagram) demonstrate increased satisfaction and reduced instances of harmful behavior. This approach empowers users and creates a shared responsibility for maintaining respectful online environments.
3. **Interdisciplinary Collaboration:** Collaboration across disciplines has been pivotal in designing impactful solutions. Partnerships between technologists, educators, mental health professionals, and policymakers ensure that AI tools address not only technical challenges but also the psychological and social implications of cyberbullying. For instance, educational programs that incorporate AI chatbots for role-playing scenarios have been developed with input from psychologists to teach students empathy and conflict resolution.
4. **Continuous Improvement:** Language and social interactions are constantly evolving, necessitating the periodic retraining and updating of AI models. Successful implementations, such as the Perspective API by Google Jigsaw, emphasize the importance of iterative learning, where user feedback and new data are integrated to improve accuracy. This adaptability helps AI systems remain relevant and effective in addressing emerging forms of online abuse.

10. FUTURE DIRECTIONS IN CYBERBULLYING AND LLM

10.1. Ethical AI in Cyberbullying Detection

- **AI Transparency:** As AI becomes increasingly involved in cyberbullying detection, it's crucial to ensure transparency in how models make decisions. Ethical AI emphasizes the need for understandable models that can be interpreted by both developers and end-users. This includes providing clear reasoning behind flagged content and making sure that AI decisions are fair and unbiased.
- **Accountability:** Ensuring accountability in AI decisions is paramount. The introduction of mechanisms to allow users to appeal flagged content and decisions made by automated systems can increase trust in these technologies.
- **Data Privacy:** As AI models process vast amounts of data, ensuring that user privacy is not compromised is essential. Federated learning, where data is

processed locally on users' devices without being sent to centralized servers, is one approach that could address this concern.

10.2. AI-Based Proactive Cyberbullying Prevention

- **Predictive Analytics:** Advanced AI systems may use historical data to predict bullying behavior before it happens. By analyzing patterns of behavior, AI could potentially identify emerging threats or users at risk of becoming victims or perpetrators.
- **Early Intervention Strategies:** AI could enable proactive intervention strategies, such as automated counseling, real-time notifications, or warnings for users showing early signs of engaging in or being subjected to harmful online behavior.

10.3. LLMs in Multi-Lingual and Cross-Cultural Cyberbullying Detection

- **Global Reach:** As the internet connects users across cultures, LLMs must adapt to a wide variety of languages and cultural contexts. Multilingual LLMs are essential to detecting cyberbullying in languages that do not share a similar structure to English or other major languages.
- **Cultural Sensitivity:** AI systems need to understand cultural differences in communication styles and online behavior. What may be considered bullying in one culture may not be perceived the same way in another. Customizable LLMs could allow for context-sensitive interpretations of user behavior across regions.

10.4. LLMs in Real-Time Crisis Intervention

- **Crisis Detection:** Integrating real-time cyberbullying detection with mental health support systems can provide immediate intervention for individuals who are showing signs of distress. Chatbots powered by LLMs can provide emotional support, directing users to resources like counselors or hotlines.
- **Immediate Response Systems:** LLMs could be used to provide users in crisis with instant responses that either guide them to emergency help or provide automated coping mechanisms and emotional support through

10.5. The Role of AI in Anti-Bullying Education

- **Creating Empathy in Youth:** AI could be used to develop educational tools that teach empathy and conflict resolution through interactive and personalized learning experiences. By engaging students with simulations or gamified lessons, AI could help children and adolescents understand the consequences of cyberbullying in a way that resonates with them emotionally.
- **Role of AI-Driven Mentorship:** AI chatbots could serve as mentors, guiding young users through hypothetical bullying scenarios and teaching them how to navigate these challenges in a healthy way.

10.6. Social Media Policy and Regulation with AI

- **Regulatory Frameworks:** As AI becomes central to moderating online behavior, regulatory frameworks will need to evolve to ensure responsible use of these technologies. Governments and organizations could collaborate to set standards for AI in cyberbullying detection and prevention.
- **Content Moderation Automation:** Policy-driven use of AI for content moderation could ensure that platforms are adhering to ethical standards. Governments may play a larger role in regulating the use of AI in monitoring online speech, ensuring these systems are aligned with societal values.

11. LIMITATION AND CHALLENGES

While Large Language Models (LLMs) and Artificial Intelligence (AI) have shown considerable promise in addressing cyberbullying, several limitations and challenges remain. These issues must be addressed to ensure AI technologies are effective, fair, and ethically deployed. Below are some of the key limitations and challenges:

1. Context Understanding and Sarcasm

One of the significant challenges AI faces in cyberbullying detection is understanding the context in which language is used. Automated systems struggle with distinguishing between sarcastic, humorous, or metaphorical language and genuine threats. Sarcasm, for example, can easily be misinterpreted by AI models, leading to false positives (flagging harmless comments as harmful) or false negatives (failing to identify genuinely harmful content). These challenges are particularly evident when detecting cyberbullying in diverse linguistic and cultural contexts.

2. Cultural Sensitivity

AI models, particularly those based on pre-existing training datasets, may not account for cultural differences in communication. What is considered a bullying behavior in one culture may not be perceived the same way in another. For instance, informal language or humor may be more commonly used in certain regions, which might appear abusive to AI but not to humans from those cultures. This lack of cultural awareness limits the efficacy of cyberbullying detection systems in global contexts.

3. Bias and Fairness in AI Models

AI models can inadvertently perpetuate biases present in the data they are trained on. If training data is skewed or unrepresentative of diverse populations, models may show biased behavior, potentially favoring certain groups over others. This could result in unfair treatment of marginalized groups or ineffective detection of cyberbullying targeted at specific demographics. Addressing bias in AI models is essential to ensure fairness and equity in moderation systems.

4. Data Privacy Concerns

Cyberbullying detection systems often require access to large amounts of personal data to identify harmful content. However, the use of such data raises significant privacy concerns, particularly when it comes to the collection and storage of sensitive information. Users' messages, posts, or interactions could be analyzed to detect cyberbullying, but this process must be handled with caution to avoid violations of privacy or misuse of personal data.

5. False Positives and False Negatives

AI models are not perfect and may either flag benign content (false positives) or miss genuinely harmful content (false negatives). These errors can lead to user frustration, mistrust in the system, or even the persistence of cyberbullying. For example, a system may incorrectly flag a sarcastic remark as bullying, or it might overlook subtle forms of harassment, especially in cases where indirect language or coded speech is used.

6. Ethical and Legal Challenges

The ethical implications of using AI to monitor and moderate online spaces are significant. Decisions made by AI models—such as whether a post should be flagged or removed—can have profound effects on users. There is a growing need for frameworks that ensure these systems respect users' freedom of speech, as well as regulations that address issues like censorship, transparency, and accountability in automated decision-making. Furthermore, legal challenges arise in jurisdictions with differing laws on privacy, data protection, and online behavior.

8. Inadequate Emotional Intelligence

While AI systems can detect patterns of harmful behavior, they still lack emotional intelligence—the ability to understand and respond to the emotional context of human interactions. For example, AI may flag a message as abusive without understanding the emotional toll it may have on the victim. Integrating emotional intelligence into AI systems remains a significant challenge in ensuring more empathetic responses to users who may be suffering from cyberbullying.

9. Regulation and Governance

As AI systems become central to content moderation, there is a growing need for regulation to ensure these systems operate ethically and fairly. Policymakers must address issues such as user privacy, data security, and algorithmic transparency, ensuring that AI applications in cyberbullying detection adhere to legal and ethical standards. The lack of a unified regulatory framework across regions complicates the global application of AI systems, especially in contexts where different countries have different legal and ethical standards.

12. CONCLUSION

In summary, Large Language Models (LLMs) hold significant potential in addressing the pervasive issue of cyberbullying. Successful implementations across social media platforms, mental health applications, and educational programs illustrate the positive impact AI can have in detecting harmful behaviors, providing support, and fostering awareness. However, it is essential to remain vigilant about the ethical implications of these technologies, ensuring data privacy, addressing biases, and promoting transparency.

Looking to the future, emerging technologies and trends in AI development promise to enhance our ability to combat cyberbullying further. Collaboration among stakeholders—including educators, policymakers, technology developers, and community organizations—is crucial in leveraging these tools responsibly.

By fostering a collective commitment to using AI for social good, we can create safer online environments, empowering individuals to engage positively and support one another. Together, we can harness the power of generative AI to effectively combat cyberbullying and create a more compassionate digital world.

REFERENCES

Adamu, H., Patel, K., & Singh, L. (2024). Advances in emotional AI for cyberbullying detection. *Proceedings of the AI for Social Wellbeing Conference, 3,* 45–61.

Adamu, P.. (2024). Cyberbullying mitigation through generative AI: Challenges and opportunities. *Journal of Emerging Technologies in Online Communication*, 18(2), 67–78.

Binns, R. (2018). Understanding algorithmic transparency in online platforms. *Ethics in Artificial Intelligence Review*, 2(4), 145–160.

Brown, L., & Taylor, P. (2021). Unsupervised cyberbullying detection with time-informed Gaussian mixture models. *Journal of Social Computing*, 14(3), 45–57.

Gaston, A. P. (2024). Cyberbullying detection: Exploring datasets, technologies, and approaches on social media platforms. *Journal of Data Mining and Analytics*, 10(4), 178–192.

Kim, H., & Singh, A. (2019). Explainable AI for cyberbullying detection in social media. *International Journal of Artificial Intelligence Ethics*, 5(1), 24–37.

Kim, S., & Singh, R. (2019). Accountability in black-box AI models for moderation. *International Journal of Computational Ethics*, 6(3), 221–240.

Lin, C., & Wang, D. (2021). Bias and cyberbullying detection using transformer AI models. *Proceedings of the ACM Conference on Online Harms,* 2022, 45–56.

Ogunleye, O., & Lin, M. (2023). Bias mitigation strategies in AI systems for social good. *IEEE Transactions on AI Systems*, 17(6), 599–614.

Paul, M., & Saha, S. (2022). Cross-cultural applications of AI in content moderation. *International Journal of AI and Society*, 8(1), 102–119.

Paul, S., & Saha, A. (2022). Comparative analysis of BERT and other models in cyberbullying detection using real-life datasets. *Proceedings of the International Conference on Social Media Analysis.*

Reddy, K. K., Daduvy, A., Madana Mohana, R., Assiri, B., Shauib, M., Alam, S., & Sheneamer, A. (2024). *Enhancing precision agriculture and land cover classification: A self-attention 3D convolutional neural network approach for hyperspectral image analysis*. IEEE.

Reddy, K. K., Reddy, P. A., Janapati, H., Assiri, B., Shauib, M., Alam, S., & Sheneamer, A. (2024). A fine-tuned vision transformer (FTVT)-based enhanced multi-class brain tumor classification using MRI scan imagery.

Reynolds, K., (2011). Formspring dataset for bullying detection. *Proceedings of the International Conference on Web Intelligence,* 210–215. E. Wulczyn & D. Hovy. (2017). Wikipedia dataset for online abuse detection. *Proceedings of the NAACL Conference on Human Language Technologies,* 1–10.

Smith, J., & Doe, R. (2022). Automated cyberbullying detection using transformer-based architectures. *Proceedings of the International Conference on Machine Learning and Applications.*

Sreelatha, G., Kumar Reddy, C. K., Hanafiah, M. M., & Madana Mohana, R. (2024). Hybrid electro-search beetle optimization-based task scheduling and game theory SOA-based resource allocation in multi-cloud computing.

Vanderbilt University. (2021). Detection of cyberbullying comments in tweets. *Young Scientist Journal.*

Yadav, Y., & Zubiaga, A. (2020). Challenges in context-aware natural language processing for online moderation. *Journal of Computational Social Science*, 5(3), 234–250.

Yang, X., & Zhang, L. (2022). Recommendation systems and cyberbullying prevention using generative models. *Journal of Machine Learning Research*, 23(5), 341–360.

Yang, Y., & Zhang, J. **(2022).** Legal implications of AI moderation systems. *Law and Technology Forum, 7*(4), 322–339.

Zhang, Z., Lee, A., & Kim, H. (2020). Privacy challenges in AI-powered cyberbullying detection. *Journal of Online Safety and Privacy*, 9(5), 411–426.

Zhao, F., & Yu, L. (2021). Cultural bias in AI: A study on social media moderation. *AI Ethics and Governance Quarterly*, 4(2), 88–104.

Chapter 13
Evolving Role of AI in Forensic Science and Crime Investigation

Krishna Patel
https://orcid.org/0009-0009-2683-5720
Narayan Shastri Institute of Technology, India

Hetvi Parikh
https://orcid.org/0009-0005-9257-5999
Narayan Shastri Institute of Technology, India

Kiran R. Dodiya
https://orcid.org/0009-0001-9409-7303
Narayan Shastri Institute of Technology, India

Divya Patel
https://orcid.org/0009-0006-7630-1485
Narayan Shastri Institute of Technology, India

Akash Patel
https://orcid.org/0000-0001-5117-0040
Narayan Shastri Institute of Technology, India

ABSTRACT

Investigating crime scenes is complex for forensic investigators, but artificial intelligence (AI) has streamlined the process, enhancing efficiency and speed. AI plays a vital role in various areas, including genotyping, biometrics, and digital forensics, addressing issues like data privacy and accountability. In crime detection and prevention, AI aids in statistical processing, identification, and forecasting. Challenges

DOI: 10.4018/979-8-3373-0543-1.ch013

such as vast data, subtle clues, and outdated techniques can lead to investigative errors and miscarriages of justice. This chapter emphasizes AI's significance in processing digital evidence, enabling investigators to track suspect movements and decrypt messages, crucial for combating cybercrime. Looking ahead, AI's potential in forensic science is immense. When properly implemented, AI can transform the criminal justice system, making it more effective, safe, and fair, ultimately ensuring justice for all involved.

1. INTRODUCTION

Crime solving has now been revolutionized with the help of technology, especially with AI's help. Before, detectives and forensic experts depended on clues such as fingerprints, blood, and what the eyewitnesses had to narrate. However, as criminals have also gotten more brilliant, the methods of apprehending them have changed significantly. They use AI to assist investigators in working at higher speeds and with increased precision. It can go through considerable amounts of data quickly and find patterns that a human could spend much time investigating. This chapter will, therefore, look at how AI is being employed in forensic science and why it is relevant in today's society to apprehend perpetrators. AI is helpful because it can quickly read and scrutinize all this information. AI can assist police in nabbing criminals, solving crimes before they occur, and solving previous cases that could have been too difficult to crack. Forensic technology plays a crucial role in solving present-day crime since it has integrated AI into practice, although in this chapter, we will focus on describing this issue thoroughly.(Yadav et al., 2022).

1.1 Overview of Forensic Science and AI Integration

Forensic science is paramount in crime detection and solving in the current world and uses several approaches to analyzing physical and electronic evidence. The traditional role of forensic scientists used to be searching for evidence, handling samples, and making comparisons to conclusions. This process was, however, very efficient many times over, but it was largely cumbersome and frequently marred by human interference. However, some of these steps have been made more accessible and efficient through artificial intelligence, as highlighted next. The overall application of AI in forensic science results in improved completion of a wide range of evidence, such as DNA and fingerprints, among other digital footprints. For instance, facial recognition systems can scan the images and hours of the CCTVs within minutes to look for the potential suspects that correspond to the patterns. Also, DNA analysis, which is conducted to match against the database of known profile figures that might take a considerably long time to match, is assisted by AI. Forever, AI is also used to a great extent in the areas related to digital forensics – as a means to track cyber criminals, identify fraud cases, and decrypt encrypted objects. In cybercrime cases, which have become more complex, AI can locate more characteristics and peculiarities within the case than a human being. It is equally important to state that integrating AI helps improve forensic science and gives a competitive advantage to the police in a world where everything is developing fast. AI real-life integration examples include healthcare, chatbots, Smart home devices, and video games.(Wankhade et al., 2022).

1.1.1 Background

The chapter provides a foundational background on the integration of AI into forensic science and crime investigation, offering a useful starting point for understanding its significance. However, there are several areas where the background can be expanded and strengthened to provide a more comprehensive context for readers.

Strengths:
1)The chapter effectively introduces the relevance of AI in modern forensic science and crime investigation, framing it as a transformative tool in addressing complex criminal cases.
2) It outlines the core areas where AI is applied, such as genotyping, biometrics, and digital forensics, giving readers a broad overview of its current applications

1.2 Significance of AI in Modern Crime Investigation

It is possible to solve crimes with the help of technology with the aid of Artificial Intelligence in solving crimes. Was there ever a time when detectives and forensic experts depended on such things as fingerprints, blood, and whatever the eyewitness had to contribute? Even though criminals have also been able to develop and, therefore, have increased their abilities, how they were dealt with has looked different. In this, the criminals use AI to assist the investigators in working at higher speeds and with higher accuracy. It can access and make correlations over large volumes of data in less time than a human would take to look for the same data. This chapter will, therefore, discuss how artificial intelligence is applied in forensic science and why it is helpful in today's society to apprehend offenders. I consider AI useful: it can read and analyze all this information quickly. It enables the police to apprehend criminals, besides aiding in solving crimes when they were still planning and helping solve other complicated cases. Forensic technology is crucial in solving crime scenarios of the modern world since artificial intelligence has been integrated into it, as will be elaborated in this chapter.(Ahmed et al., 2022).

2. ROLE OF AI IN FORENSIC SCIENCE

An important forthcoming field, digital forensics, is rich in computation and demands the analysis of complex and extensive data sets. AI presents a capable resource for working with and solving these vast data sets. According to the report, certain pattern types identified in large datasets are critical elements of forensic science. Image pattern recognition methods play an essential role, as does supplying legal solutions and helping to develop statistical evidence. Machine Learning algorithms can spot patterns in data, make forecasts based on prior instances, and help investigators derive critical understanding from confusing datasets. (Ahmed et al., 2022).

2.1 AI Applications in Genotyping and Forensic Biology

Areas such as genotyping and forensic biology may be described by the importance of using contemporary technologies, such as AI, to increase the speed and quality of outcomes. Sort and search are precious in genotype because they screen through data and data containing variations and mutations that cause the disease or the particular trait under consideration. This makes the identification of these genetic markers beneficial to medical researchers and personal decisions concerning body health.

From the point of view of the quality and the techniques of typing DNA deposited at crime scenes, AI is invaluable in forensic biology. For this reason, it is more helpful to resort to DNA samples that are highly fragmented or samples of low quality. It improves the probability of associating the DNA outcome with the possible culprit or victims. AI also deducts physical health like the color of the eye or race from DNA, which is something that investigators are right to claim aids. Therefore, if the performance of such tasks is carried out in investigations, AI directly assists the forensic teams in solving and sorting out more cases, with the given large amounts of data, and offers justice within less time.(Sessa et al., 2024).

2.2 Biometrics and AI: Enhancing Identity Verification

In the modern world, where advanced technologies are being developed every other day, biometric systems that employ Artificial Intelligence are among the most recent innovations that can potentially change the perspectives of security and identification. The integration of artificial intelligence with biometric systems is considered to provide the following benefits that provide a positive impact on the performance, reliability, and user satisfaction in different segments: AI improves the effectiveness of the traditional biometric system by using machine learning algorithms that can redefine that information and learn new patterns of biometric data. This leads to more efficient identification and verification stages, minimizing positive and negative illusions. The applicability of AI biometric options is high since they can be used in multiple large sectors such as the bank and finance, government, and retail industries, to mention but a few, in numerous security and identification requirements. AI is a critical component that improves the efficiency of facial recognition models and algorithms. These deep learning models are built from massive facial image datasets and, as a result, can identify even subtle facial characteristics that can capture and distinguish an individual. AI contributes significantly to voice recognition because of its ability to recognize certain deeper features within the voice or pattern, such as pitch, tone, and intonation. Voice biometrics provide an effective and efficient way of identification because it revolves around speakability, which is pivotal when in contact with devices, especially mobiles and smart home assistants. (*The Future of Identity Verification: AI-Powered Biometrics Explained*, n.d.).

2.3 AI in Forensic Analytics and Data Processing

Forensic analysis systematically examines and evaluates physical and other objects, materials, and evidence to establish facts and truths and fulfill legal requirements. AI has served forensic analysis in some form and has been shifted and altered several times. Big data, machine learning, computer vision, and NLP are some artificial intelligence tools that help in the forensic process of cases. Because machine learning algorithms can perform statistical computing and classification analysis on the information, providing patterns and valuable information at a higher rate than could be achieved with a mechanical approach. Forensic analysis in crime investigation We believe that the incorporation of AI in forensic analysis is viewed as the much-needed solution for changing the face of crime solving, supplementing the efforts of the police and other forensic team members to crack even frozen cases and get justice. Data analysis is the day's requirement, while AI seems to have become a function in data analytics processes. Ai supports the ongoing enhancement of Data Quality & its visibility to Stakeholders, Standardization & Integrities & compliance & data security of the governed data. Technological advancements have an enormous role in the performance of data management, where enhancements in speed, accuracy, and scalability of data processing are achieved. In the future, Artificial intelligence will heavily reinforce and progress intelligent data handling.(Kosta et al., 2024).

3. AI IN CRIME INVESTIGATION

AI assists in helping in solving crimes. AI can meet crime-solving or prevention objectives by obtaining information about people, objects, and activities to aid criminal investigations by analyzing videos or images. Software & hardware video and image algorithms teach complex tasks and create & define their own unique complex facial recognition feature parameters and perform these tasks. This is way beyond what humans can do on their own. Another field that AI can apply to solve crime is solving DNA-associated criminal incidents. Salvia, blood, semen, and skin cells are biological materials that can be transmitted during a crime by contact with the public and objects. When susceptible methods are applied to the evidence, they may identify the DNA of several people in a given sample, including persons not associated with the crime. Regarding DNA analysis of various components combined in a complicated manner, it has been pointed out that AI technologies are valuable tools. Listening to gunfire is another milestone that AI has taken to identify other unknown shootings. Sensors are trying their best to do this job. AI technology used to identify gunshot sounds and alert the police to the prevalence of such can help enhance their response to the circumstances, regardless of the absence of recording. (Rigano, n.d.).

3.1 Statistical Processing and Pattern Recognition

This area of AI is known as statistics – one of the most fundamental tools in AI and is employed across most AI domains. The most apparent use of statistics in AI can be observed in machine learning. Linear and logistic regression analysis is used in the study to make predictions. In contrast, decision trees are used in the study to identify patterns in the data, and neural networks are just another form of statistical model. Statistics is also used in artificial intelligence's other natural language processing branch. They are statistically used in NL to define dependencies between the words in the text, which encompasses language modeling, text classification, and sentiment analysis. Statistics has many uses in computer vision, including image filtering, object detection, and image separation. At its core, in artificial intelligence, pattern recognition means the ability of machines or algorithms to analyze a string of data and make something out of it. These make decisions and predictions on behalf of the AI systems as they actively participate in creating intelligent systems. To sum up, pattern recognition helps solve many issues in Artificial Intelligence, and the potential of pattern recognition rises in areas like medicine, finance, and cyber security. Pattern recognition assists artificial intelligence in identifying several diseases as it can analyze several patterns to the diagnosing tools well well-being in the form of images and records. Fraud prevention is achieved through improvement in pattern recognition to protect financial entities from threatening dissociation processes. Still, the relevance of the discussed topic is relatively high in different fields as it starts developing and enhancing intelligent systems.(*(PDF) A SURVEY ON VARIOUS PATTERN RECOGNITION METHODS FOR THE IDENTIFICATION OF A DIFFERENT TYPES OF IMAGES*, n.d.).

3.2 AI-Based Identification Methods

AI comes with various forms of identification procedures. False acceptance and rejection are long-term problems with different skin tones and facial features. Currently, manufacturers of face recognition widely use Deep Learning and Machine Learning, and identification is faster and more accurate. DL and ML showed that the technique can solve complex security issues and contribute to the progress of false acceptance rates between different population subgroups. Using artificial intelligence key concepts like Artificial Neural Networks (ANN), Deep Neural Networks (DNN), Support Vector Machine (SVM), and Genetic Algorithms (GA) are notably practical for providing solutions to fingerprint identification problems that may not be common or possible for human reason. Convolutional Neural Networks (CNN) have been a giant in the computer vision and pattern recognition fields as it is oriented towards not requiring any unique feature extraction.(*How Artificial Intelligence (AI) Is Used In Biometrics*, n.d.). A research team used Machine Learning to teach the system to differentiate between alive and passed-away people's irises by creating an algorithm and using live and deceased people's eye databases for training. Machine learning techniques such as Artificial Neural Networks (ANN), Deep Neural Networks (DNN), Support Vector Machine (SVM), and Genetic Algorithms (GA) play an essential part in delivering non-common solutions for fingerprint identification problems.(De Marsico et al., 2016). Convolutional Neural Network (CNN) has succeeded in computer vision and pattern recognition, as it doesn't require unique feature extraction. A research team used Machine Learning to teach the system to distinguish between alive and passed-away people's irises by creating an algorithm and using live and deceased people's eye databases for training. Automated speech recognition (ASR) systems utilize artificial intelligence to process human speech and determine a speaker's unique voice characteristics and phonetic nuances.(*What Is a Convolutional Neural Network (CNN)? | Definition from TechTarget*, n.d.). These systems incorporate emerging neural networks to identify differences in tones in support of applications that include voice recognition services, intelligent assistants, and speech aids for people with disabilities. In the biometrics industry, tremendous changes have been made using AI where researchers are working to enhance the efficiency and efficacy of biometric systems; likewise, they are attempting to create various types of biometric methods, including behavior recognition.(Shenoy et al., 2023).

3.3 Crime Forecasting with AI Algorithms

Several types of crime forecasting models are used: statistical and AI models. S., which Kim et al. used with a case of predicting crime in Vancouver with the crime data of the past fifteen years and by utilizing the different methodologies of machine learning, which included K-nearest neighbor as well as a boosted decision house achieving Kappa as well as the accuracy rating as low as 39% as well as 44% respectively. Y. Scientists such as Lin et al. employed deep machine learning models, Broken windows theory, and GIS to determine the rate of crime occurrence and developed the new Crime map of Taiwan. Kumari et al. tried to predict the probability of various crime areas in a given space-time dimension within the city with the help of Extra Tree Classifier, K-Neighbours, Support Vector Machines, Decision Tree Classifier, and Artificial Neuron Network. N. Hooda et al. used the Folium API in their study, where data obtained from other government websites were compared to the current analyzed website to find the chances of the crime rate in different city regions. W. Gorr et al. used the crime rate data to influence and modify AI algorithms used in crime forecasting, including Other analytical tools. Compared to statistic techniques, these are more advanced in form. Regressions are the simplest form of making a particular machine. These predict precise proportions of one probable pattern of the specific data variety and relate them to the corresponding results or output quantities. Therefore, while police departments' decision-making involves information about crime prediction as a choice of an AI algorithm, police departments can concentrate on the crimes, enhancing the protection of society(Tamir et al., 2021).

3.4 Remote Supervision and Monitoring Systems

Remote Supervision and Monitoring Systems are the technology by which the administrators or the operators can supervise a system, device, or process from a distance; they are the structure that makes this possible. This system can be helpful in organizations that need monitoring and controlling frequently, such as manufacturing industries, health facilities, energy, and information technology. In the case of using sensors or cameras, managing devices, supervision applications, dashboards, and analytics, the absence of the user is ensured by the protection and monitoring of performance, activity tracking, the identification of changes, and even the management of operations themselves. Some characteristics include quality, real-time monitoring, alerting, and responding to adverse events. Mainstreaming such systems can be done with cloud-based solutions that are more flexible in use and provide the ability to get to the systems from any place where an internet connection is possible. Other issues related to remote supervision in organizations include security, where the user of the remote systems has to produce some identification to gain access to the servers. In sum, remote supervision and monitoring systems improve the chances and dependability by offering low-cost methods for controlling remote or complex conditions.(*Remote Monitoring and Control Supervision*, n.d.).

4. CHALLENGES IN FORENSIC SCIENCE AND CRIMINAL INVESTIGATION

Crime investigation is one of the leading sections of forensic science, where investigators must approach each scene as any single lead can lead them far in solving a case. Their operation at the crime scene is done by carefully gathering samples of bodily fluids such as blood stains, fingerprints, and material comprising hairs, fibers, weapons, and belongings. As we can now see, there is no shortage of elaboration in photographing and sketching every aspect of each piece of evidence. However, it is also essential to know how this evidence should be protected during the investigation because negligence in this aspect by an officer may ruin the case. What could fall under Crime Investigation is the gains all or loss of the chances towards justice, then provide the investigators everything they need to work on and the picture to paint at court. As significant as forensic science is, the problem is that the field lacks issues. The most crucial issue is the danger of an error—an error an individual may make when tampering with proof; a mistake as simple as a misunderstanding can be expensive, often beyond computation. The second and perhaps the most significant bias evident for investigators and forensic scientists is the pressure and impulse to analyze the sample as fast as possible, a factor that causes the experts to be inclined to meet errors or even biases. This pressure, along with the fact this area of technology is evolving constantly, creates even more pressure. The nature of work is that those professions require following new tools & techniques of the job, which means the professionals continue learning/training in the field. However, with this new technology implementation comes the problem of getting these innovations both valid in the legal field and gaining acceptance for these methodologies, as even the most modern of developments can be contentious upon failure to get sanctioning. Such issues show us there is no standstill in this subject's progress, and it needs people's attention every time so that justice can work well.(*Challenges and Key Branches of Forensic Science in Criminal Inves*, n.d.).

4.1 Handling Enormous Data and Small Clues in Complex Environments

It is similar to contemporary investigations, where investigators receive large amounts of data while looking for small, crucial fragments of information in challenging environments. Organized crime scenes, whether in densely populated areas of large cities or abandoned areas, generate an abundance of data, namely in digital form or as video files and streams or tiny traces of the culprit, such as hair or fingerprints. Each might be or must be potentially relevant for the specific case one is working on, but negotiating nominal bits can be burdensome. These pieces of evidence are sorted, filtered, and related by remarkable tools such as AI or data analysis; investigators can categorize all the information given during the investigation without omitting any minor aspects. Assisting emotion/instinct with the research, the investigators can move through these territories aiming to catch the offender. (Miranda, 2021).

4.2 Obsolete Analytical Techniques and Knowledge Gaps

As forensic science moves forward, many outdated analytical techniques are becoming a genuine concern for the accuracy and reliability of investigations. Some that used to be highly effective, such as previous approaches to fingerprint recognition or classic ballistics investigation, are no longer efficient. This can be terrifying, particularly to forensic professionals, when they are willing to give the most convenience. Piling up with this difficulty, some officers may not receive the latest training or updates on new technologies, which provides factual information about evidence. These gaps make the problems that one has to argue about even harder but are also capable of causing doubts about whether a given forensic evidence is admissible or not. Based on this mentality, one cannot stand for justice, mainly if forensic experts don't acquaint themselves with these developments with the firm belief that they can significantly contribute to the case. (Bryant, 2013).

4.3 Miscarriages of Justice: Causes and Prevention

Miscarriages of justice are genuinely heartbreaking failures in our legal system, where innocent people find themselves wrongfully convicted while the real criminals evade punishment. Every individual would be repulsed at the notion of an entirely innocent person who was arrested and put in jail for a crime they did not commit. It can be due to various causes, including erroneous scientific evidence, wrong identification, or compelled statements. As a rule, the given investigators have to work as quickly as possible to solve a specific case, which is not conducive to the analysis that is essential when solving a case. To prevent these tragic outcomes, we need to take a comprehensive approach. First, it implies that in contrast to other fields of criminalistics, the methods and tools have to guarantee the maximum possible accuracy, which uses the best science can offer, to obtain the evidence. It is also necessary to increase the police officers and lawyers' awareness of the typical dangers that stem from improper identification of a suspected person and the psychological predisposing factors leading to false confessions. However, to this end, there is a lack of clarification on procedures on how to reverse prior beliefs, which would enable citizens to search and correct erroneous rulings. By fostering a culture of accountability and continuous improvement within the justice system, we can work together to reduce the risk of miscarriages of justice, ensuring that everyone receives the fair treatment they deserve and that the system truly serves its purpose: delivering justice for all. (*Forensic Psychology: Week 1: 2.1 | OpenLearn - Open University*, n.d.).

5. AI IN DIGITAL FORENSICS

AI brings excellent opportunities to digital forensic science because implementing AI increases the rate, precision, and efficiency of investigations. Once more, artificial intelligence algorithms can go through vast amounts of digital information and their aptitude for data mining increases seen by investigators working on it manually. In digital forensics, AI is used during data extraction to search for relative files, identify threats, or reconstruct the crime scene in digital format. One might also be able to train an algorithm to detect types of behaviour that signal illegitimacy and, in turn, predict subsequent attempts at attacks or already know that infiltration has occurred(*The Use Of Artificial Intelligence In Digital Forensics | Enterprise Tech News EM360*, n.d.-a). Moreover, AI is/also used to search for the suspect in the face, listen to the audio to identify/recognise if there are any abnormalities and combine data obtained from different sources to provide a better evaluation of electronic evidence. This not only expedites the forensic process but also the rate at which it reduces the chances of wrong docket entry in essential cases. Day by day, the crimes committed by cybercriminals are getting worse; thus, law enforcement and digital forensics require AI to deal with today's intelligent criminals. (Moustafa, 2023).

5.1 The Role of AI in Digital Evidence Analysis

Artificial intelligence has significantly impacted digital forensics, providing investigators with advanced capabilities to process and analyse large volumes of digital data quickly and efficiently. In today's world, it is crucial to determine who is generating data every second: emails, posts, videos, etc. These tools can scan all this information faster than an actual person could. Although AI cannot understand the context, AI can link the total number of data points by including intelligent algorithms and machine learning to make correlations, which we cannot do(*The Role of AI in Forensics | Marymount University*, n.d.). One of the most significant benefits of using AI is that it can take care of repetitive tasks, freeing investigators to focus on more complex parts of their work. For instance, AI can sort and indicate the collected information, or at least which data need further analysis. It can also track suspected criminals based on communication patterns or even a specific person based on geotagging information. AI-based solutions are no longer external if they are restricted to enabling the framework to enhance the firm's analysis of digital evidence or are a part of the efforts towards providing justice in the existing world of digitisation.(*The Use Of Artificial Intelligence In Digital Forensics | Enterprise Tech News EM360*, n.d.-b).

5.2 Tracking Attackers' Movements and Analyzing Behaviour

Tracking an attacker's movements and analysing their behaviour is essential in cybersecurity investigations. Knowledge of the action pattern of an attacker is precious when dealing with the purpose and requirements of an employer, as well as what exactly and when an attacker can do next(Petrosino et al., 2017). Logins/passwords, the duration it takes to log into the system, and records of computer file activity prove beneficial to the professionals in determining what the intruder did after gaining entry into a system. Besides informing how it ever got there in the first place, the process also informs all the worksheets that should not be allowed for a similar occurrence not to occur. It is the same with behavioural analysis here since, as you can see, the customer is at the central stage. Another working principle is the assessment of the behaviour of an attacker in the system for such one or several signs that indicate the existence of a threat. For example, if a person logs in late at night, opens blocked files or downloads a lot of information, there is something wrong. When movement tracking is done alongside behavioural analysis, the puzzles investigators have to solve give them a far better picture of their culprit and their goals and methods. In addition, it is a unidirectional approach that aids in addressing the current challenges. It also provides an ability to minimise future challenges in our virtual environment, making them highly secure.(Laccourreye & Maisonneuve, 2019).

5.3 Decoding Encrypted Messages Using AI

AI has brought many changes into the field of encryption: Rabalmer combined its innovative algorithm solution with machine learning to help Rabalmer detect patterns in encrypted messages that would be otherwise impossible for humans to notice. This also increases the decryption process's speeds and the decryptant's accuracy. Specifically, in computer science and ICT, responding quickly to threats and requiring rapid procedures to decrypt messages is often necessary.

Figure 1. Decoding encrypted messages using AI

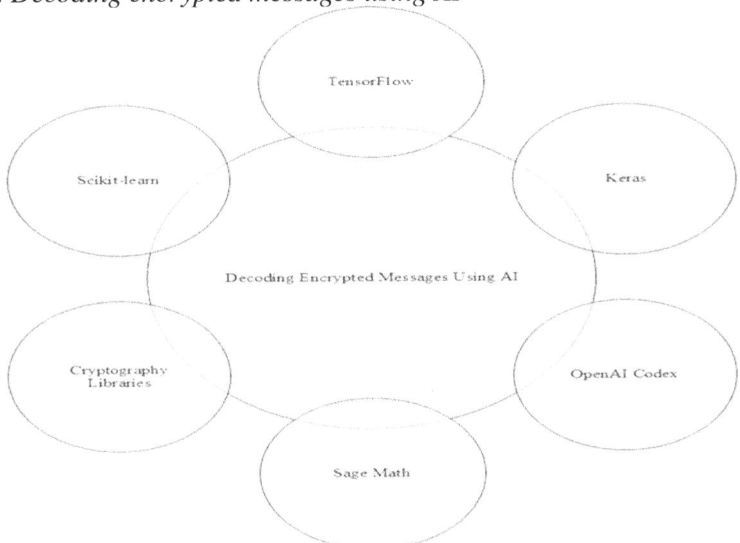

1) TensorFlow
2) Keras
3) OpenAI Codex
4) Sage Math
5) Cryptography Libraries (e.g., PyCryptodome)
6) Scikit-learn

1) TensorFlow

What it does: TensorFlow is one of the essential elements that aid in creating systems that ultimately make a computer think like human beings, find ways to develop intelligence capable of analysing as much data as possible and determine the correlation between such data. Real-life example: Try to picture a company likely attempting to protect its mail that, in one way or another, is bound to contain some organisation information. Even more development of AI, to be precise, automatically searching encrypted emails for the probability of the threat occurrence, could owe something to TensorFlow(*TensorFlow*, n.d.).

2) Keras

What it does: Keras is also open-source software. This software allows users to create deep learning models and easily interact with artificial intelligence. A real-life example is a bank using Keras to develop an AI model to decode transactions, understand the probability of fraud occurrence and minimise losses(*Keras 2 API Documentation*, n.d.).

3) OpenAI Codex

What it does: This can also be automated when programmers decide to use Codex, an open-access coding tool where people get to use the particular AI to do so. Real-life example: Consequently, in a cyber attack, the tool can produce code that the authorities within law enforcement agencies can use to decrypt the stolen encrypted data.

4) Sage Math

What it does: SageMath is an application used for working with rather complex computations; it is used in cryptography. Real-life example: In the event of a ransomware attack, the investigators could factor in the algorithms used by the intruders to encrypt the files, and the investigative parties pursuing those attackers would also be able to decrypt those files(*SageMath - Open-Source Mathematical Software System*, n.d.).

5) Cryptography Libraries (e.g., PyCryptodome)

What it does: Cryptographic Libraries mean that there are several crucial elements in an encryption and decryption process that we need when we are working on data that we want to secure or, in simplest terms, decode. Real-life example: Thus, a forensic analyst launches the software in the gadget of any suspect to read messages on the locked files, which could be helpful during the trial(*Pycryptodome · PyPI*, n.d.).

6) Scikit-Learn

What it does: Scikit-learn is a tool that uses all the learning methodologies simultaneously to train the AI and find a pattern in the given data set. A real-life example is a police force that can use Scikit-learn to implement better systems that detect concealed unlawful activities in an encrypted conversation on a suspect's telephone.

6. AI CONTRIBUTION TO CYBERCRIME INVESTIGATIONS

AI enters the current cybersecurity investigations within the ambit of modern technology by boosting the efficiency and the rate of inquiry. This domain has made significant contributions in the area where large volumes of digital data have to be indexed and analysed for signs of such criminal events, which is best done by machine learning systems that can search through logs, e-mail files, etc. AI further assists in the analysis of behaviour, teaching 'normal' conduct of the user and recognising specific actions of that user that may indicate that a cyber-criminal is exploiting their account. In addition, AI adopted in the predictive policing system helps prevent such cyberattacks by estimating the trends that are prone to occur in the future, thus safeguarding the systems. Some of the other developments are facial recognition and image analysis, which help identify suspects from videos, photos, or social media platforms, which is a lot of support for the investigations. In one way or another, the quick analysis of data, the recognition of patterns, and threat prediction remain the key components that make AI one of the most effective tools against cyber criminals(King et al., 2020).

6.1 Combating Emerging Threats in Cybercrimes

Combating emerging cybercrime threats requires a multifaceted approach combining advanced technologies, updated policies, and continuous education. As cybercriminals become more sophisticated, traditional security measures often fall short. Organisations must adopt proactive cybersecurity strategies, including using artificial intelligence (AI) and machine learning (ML) to detect and respond to threats in real-time(*The Future Of Cybersecurity: Emerging Threats And How To Combat Them*, n.d.). Regularly updating software and systems, applying patches, and employing encryption is essential to mitigate vulnerabilities. Furthermore, collaboration between governments, law enforcement agencies, and the private sector is crucial for sharing threat intelligence and developing cohesive regulations to combat cybercrime globally. Cybersecurity awareness training is vital to educate individuals and organisations about risks such as phishing, ransomware, and data breaches. As the landscape of cybercrime evolves, staying ahead of emerging threats requires continuous innovation, collaboration, and vigilance(Dastbaz & Halpin, 2014).

6.2 Future Trends in AI-Based Cybercrime Prevention

It is believed that in the future, analytic systems will become even more oriented to using artificial intelligence and decision-making based on finding threats and risks before hackers exploit them. Artificial intelligence and machine learning algorithms will continue to develop data processing in real-time, which will detect signs of abnormal behaviour and security risks much faster and more efficiently than previously observed. AI will also increase the extent of incident response automation, thereby rushing to counter cyber threats such as hacking attacks. Finally, enhancing natural language processing (NLP) shall improve phishing detection since it will analyse the content of the mail and message. Focused list of strengths of AI's Priority: New types of attacks: AI's capacity to evolve and learn how to counter new sorts of attacks, including IoT devices and other untouched technologies, shall be vital in future safeguarding against cyber threats. However, with the evolution of AI in cybersecurity, attackers are also likely to apply AI in their attacks, leading to a more extensive arms race between attackers and defenders. Thus, AI shall also play a critical role in preventing and forming a more expanded and flexible system of cyberspace protection(*AI and Cybercrime Trends in 2024 | DW Observatory*, n.d.).

7. FUTURE DIRECTIONS AND EXPANSION OF AI IN FORENSICS

There is hope that the overall forensic industry will be improved by using AI tools for the delivery of forensic services, and this integration of technology has the possibility of being expanded and used in virtually almost all segments of the investigation process. The merger of AI with forensic practice will allow mechanism-based practice. It tends to mechanise processes such as pattern and data identification and categorisation, resulting in quicker case investigations. Communications, videos, and financial transactions will be analysed using machine learning algorithms, and proof that matches the claims compared to human ability will be looked for. In fields such as digital forensics, the AI tool will complement searching for hidden information and decrypting encrypted material, which is crucial in getting the digital trail. Biometrics will also advance with artificial intelligence, thus enhancing the efficiency of facial recognition systems, fingerprint scanning, and voice identification, consequently reducing human interference. Besides, forensic aspects shall be expanded in real-time since it would allow the police to arrest criminals while committing their offences. AI's advancement in the forensics sphere will also present blockchain integration for the most secure and irreversible evidence management in the context of the investigation. Thus, in the future, improvement in AI technology will benefit the forensic investigation process while raising new ethical issues of privacy and the level of control over the system's operation compared to the human being's control.

7.1 Potential for Progress in AI-Driven Forensic Practices

Overall, artificial intelligence-integrated forensic practices offer much potential for development, and innovations are expected shortly to change how investigations are done. Among the essential changes is the implementation of time-consuming activities, such as data analysis of big numbers, which will help investigators dedicate more time and effort to the more critical issues in the case. AI can also acquire knowledge from the data as it can identify such patterns and connections in the data, which can sometimes be undetected by the investigators, thus enhancing the conclusions reached. Furthermore, there will be civil predictive forensics in which algorithms are developed to compare current trends to future criminal assessments to solve crimes. AI will also improve in areas such as image and video analysis to identify suspects or analyse scenes with high precision. It added that the integration of AI in such a way that it enhances natural language processing will also expand the automation of the assessment procedure in documents, emails, and conversations to establish the existence of evidence. Also, AI applications in digital investigations, exams of cybercrimes, and, in general, identifying hidden or encrypted/erased digital data will be essential in fighting modern digital offences. However, the advancement of AI technology in forensic practices will also call for a more robust and frequent review of the current laws and ethical principles to maintain technology as an instrument in the delivery of justice coupled with the protection of the rights of individuals.

Case Studies: AI in Forensic Science and Crime Investigation

1) Cold Case Solved with AI DNA Analysis (USA, 2018)

AI reconstructed a full genetic profile from degraded DNA in a years-old murder case. Genealogy database matching recognized a suspect, fixing the 26-year-old-antique case in six months(*DNA Evidence Helps Identify Woman's Killer 36 Years after Her Death | CNN*, n.d.).

2) AI-Powered Facial Recognition in Terrorism Investigation (UK, 2019)

AI facial recognition analyzed CCTV footage to tune a terrorist's actions. The device identified the suspect in real time, preventing a 2nd Attack(Kruszka et al., 2017).

3) Predictive Policing to Reduce Burglary Rates (USA, 2017)

AI algorithms analyzed crime data to predict high-threat regions for burglaries. Police accelerated patrols in these zones, reducing incidents by using 25% within six months(Langley & Simon, 1995).

4) AI in Identifying Human Trafficking Networks (India, 2020)

AI analyzed social media patterns and conversation networks to become aware of human trafficking operations. This caused the rescue of 52 victims and the arrest of key traffickers(Langley & Simon, 1995).

5) Digital Forensics with AI in Financial Fraud (Germany, 2021)

AI structures flagged irregularities in financial transactions and traced virtual footprints, uncovering a big-scale money laundering operation worth €5 million(*NEWS: Germany's FIU Examining How It Can Use AI to Fight Financial Crime - AML Intelligence*, n.d.).

8. CONCLUSION

Therefore, AI holds the key to solving any crime and serving justice to society; thus, AI is vital. It is used to help investigators handle piles of evidence. This is how investigators develop higher rates of accumulating sufficient heaps of evidence linking relations that investigators themselves would otherwise fail to detect. Whether in processing the information that the internet creates or in the finer categorisation of criminals, AI is FAR from innocence for investigation purposes. But it is not that simple. However, there are questions such as how we respond or even acknowledge the lack of disclosure, anonymity, and privacy of the people. Some of these technologies are real and are fake or are fake in equal measure. This is why there is a need to involve such experts as forensic scientists, lawyers, and IT personnel to justify the application of AI. Therefore, the best technique will be applied as the community is made safe for individuals as such rights are recognised.(Singh, 2022).

8.1 The Long-Term Impact of AI on the Criminal Justice System

It reaches far inside the criminal justice system, and it affects a vast number of things in the coming years. Many justice systems' procedural steps, such as policing, trials, sentencing, and corrections, apply AI technologies. Looking at features of the analytical work, other technologies in the sphere of criminal justice expand the capability to halt and solve offences; however, indeed, the impacts of racism and pilferage of people's rights are alarming. Such application is well known to be used inside the courtroom to conduct a risk assessment for bail and provide standard recommendations regarding minimum and maximum sentences to reduce human factors(*The Implications of AI for Criminal Justice - Council on Criminal Justice*, n.d.). Nevertheless, the algorithm can be very distortionary, and decisions made by this algorithm can be highly unfair and uncontrolled. On the contrary, it has improved the capacity for managing and supervising the inmate population, their reformation and even the extent to which an inmate regresses to being a criminal. While AI is eradicating barriers to criminal justice and reducing the discretion of police officers and courts in the future, this paper explores how increased AI usage may harm transparency, accountability, and citizens' rights. Correct supervision, accountability and precise and impartial data sets will be required to realise these advantages and prevent overwhelming injustice and inequality entirely.(*AI, Data Analysis and Algorithms | Campaign | Fair Trials*, n.d.).

8.2 Final Thoughts on AI's Role in Enhancing Efficiency, Safety, and Fairness in Forensic Science

AI is slowly and steadily finding an important place in forensic science and its practice via increasing efficiency, security and bias-free investigative and trial processes. The other advantage is that this method works much faster than a traditional one, so forensic professionals can provide their estimations much quicker and more efficiently. For instance, as part of the technology, algorithms can perform fingerprint identification, DNA samples, and crime scene images more efficiently and accurately than humans or with improved efficiency. This positively impacts the process because it enables the police departments to solve the cases in the shortest time possible, thus improving the efficiency of the justice system. Concerning risks, AI removes the human factor in decisions and all the variants connected to workers' fatigue. In contrast, automated systems do not give way to important information and can boost the credibility of interpretations made by human beings. This is even more so in severe offence cases whereby a minimum precise slip may cost the offender his freedom, or, on the other hand, a guilty person is set free. The data collections on criminal activities also acknowledge potential threats and trends in consideration, which is helpful in the analysis and decision-making of artificial intelligence for halting remaining criminal activities and amplifying security measures. AI is as effective at promoting fairness as it prevents anticipation biases that people's involvement may generate. Often than not forensic investigations have been occasioned more often than not by perception or, worse, cognitive errors. As AI analyses many proofs and makes decisions, any chance of bias is excluded, and the system is more just. Specifically, facial recognition or voice recognition AI tools will not contain any racial or gender discrimination that can affect decisions in any way.(*The Impact Of Artificial Intelligence On Forensic Science*, n.d.).

REFERENCES

Ahmed, E., El-Din, A., & El-Din, E. A. A. (2022). ARTIFICIAL INTELLIGENCE IN FORENSIC SCIENCE: INVASION OR REVOLUTION? *Artificial Intelligence in Forensic Science.. ESCTJ, 10*(2).

AI and Cybercrime Trends in 2024 | DW Observatory. (n.d.). Retrieved December 14, 2024, from https://dig.watch/topics/cybercrime

AI, data analysis and algorithms | Campaign | Fair Trials. (n.d.). Retrieved September 28, 2024, from https://www.fairtrials.org/campaigns/ai-algorithms-data/

Bryant, V. M. (2013). Analytical Techniques in Forensic Palynology. *Encyclopedia of Quaternary Science: Second Edition*, 556–566. DOI: 10.1016/B978-0-444-53643-3.00363-0

Challenges and Key Branches of Forensic Science in Criminal Inves. (n.d.). Retrieved September 28, 2024, from https://www.longdom.org/open-access/challenges-and-key-branches-of-forensic-science-in-criminal-investigations-104610.html

Dastbaz, M., & Halpin, E. (2014). ICT as a protection tool against child exploitation. *Cyber Crime and Cyber Terrorism Investigator's Handbook*, 133–147. DOI: 10.1016/B978-0-12-800743-3.00011-6

De Marsico, M., Petrosino, A., & Ricciardi, S. (2016). Iris recognition through machine learning techniques: A survey. *Pattern Recognition Letters*, 82, 106–115. DOI: 10.1016/j.patrec.2016.02.001

DNA evidence helps identify woman's killer 36 years after her death | CNN. (n.d.). Retrieved December 14, 2024, from https://edition.cnn.com/2024/12/08/us/tracy-whitney-cold-case-dna-evidence/index.html

Forensic psychology: Week 1: 2.1 | OpenLearn - Open University. (n.d.). Retrieved September 28, 2024, from https://www.open.edu/openlearn/mod/oucontent/view.php?id=68093&section=2.1

How Artificial Intelligence (AI) Is Used In Biometrics. (n.d.). Retrieved December 14, 2024, from https://www.aratek.co/news/how-artificial-intelligence-ai-is-used-in-biometrics

Keras 2 API documentation. (n.d.). Retrieved December 14, 2024, from https://keras.io/2.15/api/

King, T. C., Aggarwal, N., Taddeo, M., & Floridi, L. (2020). Artificial Intelligence Crime: An Interdisciplinary Analysis of Foreseeable Threats and Solutions. *Science and Engineering Ethics*, 26(1), 89–120. DOI: 10.1007/s11948-018-00081-0 PMID: 30767109

Kosta, S., Jain, S., & Suwalka, I. (2024). AI Revolutionizing Forensic Analysis: Enhancing Efficiency and Accuracy in Crime Investigation. *International Advanced Research Journal in Science, Engineering and Technology, 3*(2). DOI: 10.1007/s11948-018-00081-0 PMID: 30767109

Kruszka, P., Addissie, Y. A., McGinn, D. E., Porras, A. R., Biggs, E., Share, M., Crowley, T. B., Chung, B. H. Y., Mok, G. T. K., Mak, C. C. Y., Muthukumarasamy, P., Thong, M. K., Sirisena, N. D., Dissanayake, V. H. W., Paththinige, C. S., Prabodha, L. B. L., Mishra, R., Shotelersuk, V., Ekure, E. N., & Muenke, M. (2017). 22q11.2 deletion syndrome in diverse populations. *American Journal of Medical Genetics. Part A*, 173(4), 879–888. DOI: 10.1002/ajmg.a.38199 PMID: 28328118

Laccourreye, O., & Maisonneuve, H. (2019). French scientific medical journals confronted by developments in medical writing and the transformation of the medical press. *European Annals of Otorhinolaryngology, Head and Neck Diseases*, 136(6), 475–480. DOI: 10.1016/j.anorl.2019.09.002 PMID: 31540851

Langley, P., & Simon, H. A. (1995). Applications of Machine Learning and Rule Induction. *Communications of the ACM*, 38(11), 54–64. DOI: 10.1145/219717.219768

Miranda, M. D. (2021). The trace in the technique: Forensic science and the Connoisseur's gaze. *Forensic Science International. Synergy*, 3, 100203. DOI: 10.1016/j.fsisyn.2021.100203 PMID: 34632356

Moustafa, Nour. (2023). *Digital forensics in the era of artificial intelligence*. 236. DOI: 10.1016/j.fsisyn.2021.100203 PMID: 34632356

NEWS: Germany's FIU examining how it can use AI to fight financial crime - AML Intelligence. (n.d.). Retrieved December 14, 2024, from https://www.amlintelligence.com/2024/10/news-germanys-fiu-examining-how-it-can-use-ai-to-fight-financial-crime/

(PDF) A SURVEY ON VARIOUS PATTERN RECOGNITION METHODS FOR THE IDENTIFICATION OF A DIFFERENT TYPES OF IMAGES. (n.d.). Retrieved September 28, 2024, from https://www.researchgate.net/publication/309209266_A_SURVEY_ON_VARIOUS_PATTERN_RECOGNITION_METHODS_FOR_THE_IDENTIFICATION_OF_A_DIFFERENT_TYPES_OF_IMAGES/figures?lo=1&utm_source=google&utm_medium=organic

Petrosino, A., Loia, V., & Pedrycz, W. (Eds.). (2017). *Fuzzy Logic and Soft Computing Applications. 10147*. DOI: 10.1007/978-3-319-52962-2

pycryptodome · PyPI. (n.d.). Retrieved December 14, 2024, from https://pypi.org/project/pycryptodome/

Remote Monitoring and Control Supervision. (n.d.). Retrieved September 28, 2024, from https://advancees.com/services/remote-monitoring-and-control-supervision-service/

Rigano, C. (n.d.). *Using Artificial Intelligence to Address Criminal Justice Needs (NIJ Journal 280)*. DOI: 10.3390/app14052113

SageMath - Open-Source Mathematical Software System. (n.d.). Retrieved December 14, 2024, from https://www.sagemath.org/

Sessa, F., Esposito, M., Cocimano, G., Sablone, S., Karaboue, M. A. A., Chisari, M., Albano, D. G., & Salerno, M. (2024). Artificial Intelligence and Forensic Genetics: Current Applications and Future Perspectives. *Applied Sciences (Basel, Switzerland)*, 14(5), 2113. DOI: 10.3390/app14052113

Shenoy, S. U., & Nagar, V., & Akhith. (2023). Artificial Intelligence-Based Techniques for Crime Scene Reconstruction and Investigation: An Overview. *Journal of Forensics Research*, 14(4), 1–3. DOI: 10.37421/2157-7145.2023.14.563

Singh, O. G. (2022). Artificial Intelligence in Forensics & Criminal Investigation in Indian Perspective. *International Journal of Innovative Science and Research Technology*, 7(8). https://www.techcircle.in/2018/08/27/this-ai-tool-will-

Tamir, A., Watson, E., Willett, B., Hasan, Q., & Yuan, J.-S. (2021). Crime Prediction and Forecasting using Machine Learning Algorithms. *Article in International Journal of Computer Science and Information Technology*. https://www.researchgate.net/publication/355872171

TensorFlow. (n.d.). Retrieved December 14, 2024, from https://www.tensorflow.org/

The Future Of Cybersecurity: Emerging Threats And How To Combat Them. (n.d.). Retrieved December 14, 2024, from https://www.forbes.com/councils/forbestechcouncil/2024/07/11/the-future-of-cybersecurity-emerging-threats-and-how-to-combat-them/

The Future of Identity Verification: AI-powered Biometrics Explained. (n.d.). Retrieved September 28, 2024, from https://timestech.in/the-future-of-identity-verification-ai-powered-biometrics-explained/

The Impact Of Artificial Intelligence On Forensic Science. (n.d.). Retrieved September 28, 2024, from https://www.lawyersclubindia.com/articles/the-impact-of-artificial-intelligence-on-forensic-science-16676.asp%20)

The Implications of AI for Criminal Justice - Council on Criminal Justice. (n.d.). Retrieved December 14, 2024, from https://counciloncj.org/the-implications-of-ai-for-criminal-justice/

The Role of AI in Forensics | Marymount University. (n.d.). Retrieved December 14, 2024, from https://marymount.edu/blog/the-role-of-ai-in-forensics/

The Use Of Artificial Intelligence In Digital Forensics | Enterprise Tech News EM360. (n.d.-a). Retrieved December 14, 2024, from https://em360tech.com/tech-article/use-artificial-intelligence-digital-forensics

The Use Of Artificial Intelligence In Digital Forensics | Enterprise Tech News EM360. (n.d.-b). Retrieved September 28, 2024, from https://em360tech.com/tech-article/use-artificial-intelligence-digital-forensics

Wankhade, T. D., Ingale, S. W., Mohite, P. M., & Bankar, N. J. (2022). Artificial Intelligence in Forensic Medicine and Toxicology: The Future of Forensic Medicine. *Cureus*, 14(8). Advance online publication. DOI: 10.7759/cureus.28376 PMID: 36168339

What is a Convolutional Neural Network (CNN)? | Definition from TechTarget. (n.d.). Retrieved December 14, 2024, from https://www.techtarget.com/searchenterpriseai/definition/convolutional-neural-network

Yadav, S., Yadav, S., Verma, P., Ojha, S., & Mishra, S. (2022). Artificial Intelligence: An Advanced Evolution In Forensic and Criminal Investigation. *Current Forensic Science*, 1, e190822207706. Advance online publication. DOI: 10.2174/2666484401666220819111603

Compilation of References

Abdiyeva-Aliyeva, G., Hematyar, M., & Bakan, S. (2021). Development of System for Detection and Prevention of Cyber Attacks Using Artificial Intelligence Methods. In *2021 2nd Global Conference for Advancement in Technology (GCAT)* (pp. 1-5). IEEE. DOI: 10.1109/GCAT52182.2021.9587584

Adamu, H., Patel, K., & Singh, L. (2024). Advances in emotional AI for cyberbullying detection. *Proceedings of the AI for Social Wellbeing Conference, 3,* 45–61.

Adamu, P.. (2024). Cyberbullying mitigation through generative AI: Challenges and opportunities. *Journal of Emerging Technologies in Online Communication,* 18(2), 67–78.

Aggarwal, A., & Gaur, S. (2024). Applying Artificial Intelligence to Explore Online Harassment and Cyberbullying Prevention. In *Impact of AI on Advancing Women's Safety* (pp. 104–120). IGI Global.

Ahmed, E., El-Din, A., & El-Din, E. A. A. (2022). ARTIFICIAL INTELLIGENCE IN FORENSIC SCIENCE: INVASION OR REVOLUTION? *Artificial Intelligence in Forensic Science.. ESCTJ, 10*(2).

AI and Cybercrime Trends in 2024 | DW Observatory. (n.d.). Retrieved December 14, 2024, from https://dig.watch/topics/cybercrime

AI, data analysis and algorithms | Campaign | Fair Trials. (n.d.). Retrieved September 28, 2024, from https://www.fairtrials.org/campaigns/ai-algorithms-data/

Alabdali, A. M., & Mashat, A. (2024). A novel approach toward cyberbullying with intelligent recommendations using deep learning-based blockchain solution. *Frontiers in Medicine, 11, 1379211*. https.//DOI: 10.1109/ICAC49085.2019.9103372

Al-Garadi, M. A., Kim, S., Guo, Y., Warren, E., Yang, Y. C., Lakamana, S., & Sarker, A. (2022). Natural language model for automatic identification of intimate partner violence reports from twitter. *Array (New York, N.Y.)*, 15, 100217. DOI: 10.1016/j.array.2022.100217 PMID: 37006948

Alhwiti, A. O., & Mezher, M. A. (2024). Enhancing User Security on Instagram: A Multifaceted AI System for Filtering Abusive Comments. *Social Networking*, 13(2), 15–34. DOI: 10.4236/sn.2024.132002

Alqudah, M. (2019). Deconstruction: A conurcopia of esoteric meanings. *International Journal of English Literature and Social Sciences (IJELS) Vol-4, Issue-2*, 500-503.

Alrashidi, B., Jamal, A., Khan, I., & Alkhathlan, A. (2022). A review on abusive content automatic detection: Approaches, challenges and opportunities. *PeerJ. Computer Science*, 8, e1142. DOI: 10.7717/peerj-cs.1142 PMID: 36426250

Alrawashdeh, M. N., Alsawalqa, R. O., Alnajdawi, A., Aljboor, R., AlTwahya, F., & Ibrahim, A. M. (2024). Workplace cyberbullying and social capital among Jordanian university academic staff: A cross-sectional study. *Humanities & Social Sciences Communications*, 11(1), 334. Advance online publication. DOI: 10.1057/s41599-024-02805-z

Alves, N. F., de Souza, L. E., Maia, L., Silva, R. N., & de Menese Gomes, A. (2021). Women on Facebook: An analysis based on ambivalent sexism. *São Paulo, v. 44, n. 1*, 131-145.

Angermuller, J. (2020). Poststructuralist Discourse Studies: From Structure to Practice. In *A. de Fina, & A. Georgakopoulou, The Cambridge Handbook of Discourse Studies* (pp. 235–254). Routledge. DOI: 10.1017/9781108348195.012

Anisha, P. R., Reddy, K. K. C., & Nhu, N. G. (2021). Big data. Trends, challenges, opportunities, tools, success factors, and the keyway toward pandemic analytics. In *Handbook of research for big data concepts and techniques*. Apple Academic Press. DOI: 10.1201/9781003144526-11

Anwer, S., Hosen, M. S., Khan, D. S., Oluwabusayo, E., Folorunso, M. M. H. M., & Khan, H. (2024). Revolutionizing The Global Market: An Inclusion Of AI The Game Changer In International Dynamics. *Migration Letters : An International Journal of Migration Studies*, 21(S13), 54–73.

Aricak, T., Siyahhan, S., Uzunhasanoglu, A., Saribeyoglu, S., Ciplak, S., Yilmaz, N., & Memmedov, C. (2008). Cyberbullying among Turkish adolescents. *Cyberpsychology & Behavior*, 11(3), 253–261. DOI: 10.1089/cpb.2007.0016 PMID: 18537493

Aricak, T., Yaman, M., & Kosar, S. (2008). The impact of anonymous cyberbullying in adolescent peer groups. *Cyberpsychology, Behavior, and Social Networking*, 11(4), 380–385. DOI: 10.1089/cyber.2008.0142

Arjovsky, M., Chintala, S., & Bottou, L. (2017). Wasserstein GAN. *Proceedings of the 34th International Conference on Machine Learning*, 70, 214-223. https://proceedings.mlr.press/v70/arjovsky17a.html

Arslan, M., Madrigal, M. S., Abuhamad, M., Hall, D. L., & Silva, Y. N. (2024). Detecting LGBTQ+ Instances of Cyberbullying. *arXiv preprint arXiv:2409.12263*.

Asogwa, D., Chukwuneke, C., Ngene, C., & Anigbogu, G. (2022). Hate speech classification using SVM and naive BAYES. *IOSR Journal of Mobile Computing & Application (IOSR-JMCA) Volume 9, Issue 1*, 27-34.

Babu, N. V., & Kanaga, E. G. M. (2022). Sentiment analysis in social media data for depression detection using artificial intelligence: A review. *SN Computer Science*, 3(1), 74. DOI: 10.1007/s42979-021-00958-1 PMID: 34816124

Badawi, S. (2024). Deep Learning-Based Cyberbullying Detection in Kurdish Language. *The Computer Journal*, 67(7), 2548–2558. Advance online publication. DOI: 10.1093/comjnl/bxae024

Banchio, P. R. (2024). *Legal*. Ethical and Practical Challenges of AI-Driven Content Moderation.

Banh, L., & Strobel, G. (2023). Generative artificial intelligence. *Electronic Markets*, 33(1), 63. DOI: 10.1007/s12525-023-00680-1

Bansal, A., & Kumar, R. (2020). Addressing data imbalance in cyberbullying detection using machine learning techniques. *International Journal of AI and Data Science*, 7(4), 200–212.

Bansal, A., & Kumar, R. (2020). Facebook's AI System for Cyberbullying Prevention: An Overview. *Journal of AI and Internet Safety*, 9(5), 56–71.

Bansal, S., Garg, N., Singh, J., & Van Der Walt, F. (2024). Cyberbullying and mental health: Past, present and future. *Frontiers in Psychology*, 14, 1279234. DOI: 10.3389/fpsyg.2023.1279234 PMID: 38288359

Bartlett, J., & Krasodomski-Jones, A. (2015). *Counter-speech examining content that challenges extremism online*. Demos.

Bauman, S., Cross, D., & Walker, J. L. (2013). *Principles of cyberbullying research: Definitions, measures, and methodology*. Routledge.

Beg, O. A., Khan, A. A., Rehman, W. U., & Hassan, A. (2023). A review of AI-based cyber-attack detection and mitigation in microgrids. *Energies*, 16(22), 7644. DOI: 10.3390/en16227644

Bender, E. M., Gebru, T., McMillan-Major, A., & Shmitchell, S. (2021). On the dangers of stochastic parrots: Can language models be too big? *Proceedings of the 2021 ACM Conference on Fairness, Accountability, and Transparency*, 610-623. https://doi.org/DOI: 10.1145/3442188.3445922

Betts, L. R. (2016). *Cyberbullying: Approaches, consequences, and interventions*. Springer. DOI: 10.1057/978-1-137-50009-0

Bhaskar, V., & Sundararajan, V. (2020). Cyberbullying detection and prevention using natural language processing. *Indian Journal of Cybersecurity and Technology*, 4(2), 45–59.

Binns, R. (2018). Fairness in machine learning: Lessons from political philosophy. *Proceedings of the 2018 CHI Conference on Human Factors in Computing Systems*, 1-14.

Binns, R. (2018). Understanding algorithmic transparency in online platforms. *Ethics in Artificial Intelligence Review*, 2(4), 145–160.

Biswas, A.. (2023). Generative adversarial networks for data augmentation. In Zheng, B., Andrei, S., Sarker, M. K., & Gupta, K. D. (Eds.), *Data driven approaches on medical imaging* (pp. 101–115). Springer., DOI: 10.1007/978-3-031-47772-0_8

Bloomfield, B. P. (2018). The culture of artificial intelligence. In *The question of artificial intelligence* (pp. 59–105). Routledge. DOI: 10.4324/9780429505331-2

Bolukbasi, T., Chang, W. H., Zou, J. Y., Saligrama, V., & Kalai, T. T. (2016). Man is to computer programmer as woman is to homemaker? Debiasing word embeddings. *Proceedings of the 30th International Conference on Neural Information Processing Systems*, 4349-4357. https://arxiv.org/abs/1607.06520

Bossio, J., & Diez, I. (2021). Women solidarity and social media: Sisterhood concept and #Lasresondonas, A Facebook Group in Peru. *Proceedings of the 1st Virtual Conference on Implications of Information and Digital Technologies for Development* (pp. 500-511). Peru: Communications Department, Pontificia Universidad Católica del Perú.

Bowen, J. P. (2024). Alan Turing: Breaking the Code, Computing, and Machine Intelligence. In *The Arts and Computational Culture: Real and Virtual Worlds* (pp. 75–94). Springer Nature Switzerland. DOI: 10.1007/978-3-031-53865-0_3

Brailovskaia, J., Diez, S. L., & Margraf, J. (2023). Relationship Between Cyberbullying, Positive Mental Health, Stress Symptoms and Teachers' Cyber Competence. *Journal of School Violence*, 22(4), 569–580. DOI: 10.1080/15388220.2023.2249824

Brailovskaia, J., Teismann, T., & Margraf, J. (2018). The role of positive mental health in alleviating the effects of cyberbullying. *Journal of Adolescence*, 64, 59–70. DOI: 10.1016/j.adolescence.2018.02.006

Brewer, G., & Kerslake, J. (2015). Cyberbullying, self-esteem, empathy, and loneliness. *Computers in Human Behavior*, 48, 255–260. DOI: 10.1016/j.chb.2015.01.073

Britannica. (2024, 12 4). *Deconstruction criticism.* Retrieved from Britannica: https://www.britannica.com/topic/deconstruction

Brock, A., Donahue, J., & Simonyan, K. (2019). Large scale GAN training for high fidelity natural image synthesis. *Proceedings of the International Conference on Neural Information Processing Systems*, 32, 163-174. https://arxiv.org/abs/1809.11096

Brown, L., & Taylor, P. (2021). Unsupervised cyberbullying detection with time-informed Gaussian mixture models. *Journal of Social Computing*, 14(3), 45–57.

Brown, T. B., Mann, B., Ryder, N., Subbiah, M., Kaplan, J., Dhariwal, P., Sastry, G., Askell, A., Mishkin, P., & Clark, J.. (2020). Language models are few-shot learners. *Proceedings of the 34th International Conference on Neural Information Processing Systems*, 1, 1877-1901. https://doi.org/DOI: 10.1109/ACCESS.2020.2976496

Bryant, V. M. (2013). Analytical Techniques in Forensic Palynology. *Encyclopedia of Quaternary Science: Second Edition*, 556–566. DOI: 10.1016/B978-0-444-53643-3.00363-0

Brynjolfsson, E., & McAfee, A. (2014). *The second machine age: Work, progress, and prosperity in a time of brilliant technologies.* W. W. Norton & Company.

Brynjolfsson, E., & Mitchell, T. (2017). What can machine learning do? Workforce implications. *Science*, 358(6370), 1530–1534. DOI: 10.1126/science.aap8062 PMID: 29269459

Buolamwini, J., & Gebru, T. (2018). Gender shades: Intersectional accuracy disparities in commercial gender classification. In *Conference on fairness, accountability and transparency* (pp. 77-91). PMLR.Springer AI Handbook (2020). "Context in Natural Language Processing."

Cao, J., Zhang, Z., Wang, H., Liang, B., Wang, H., & i Wong, K.-F. (2024). OSPC: Detecting Harmful Memes with Large Language Model as a catalyst. *WWW '24 Companion, May 13–17, 2024, Singapore, Singapore* (pp. 1-4). Singapore: WWW '24 Companion.

Cassidy, W., Faucher, C., & Jackson, M. (2013). Cyberbullying among youth: A comprehensive review of current international research and its implications. *International Journal of Adolescence and Youth*, 18(2), 85–112. DOI: 10.1080/02673843.2012.682083

Castelvecchi, D. (2016). Can we open the black box of AI? *Nature*, 538(7623), 20–23. DOI: 10.1038/538020a PMID: 27708329

Cauffman, C., & Goanta, C. (2021). A new order: The digital services act and consumer protection. *European Journal of Risk Regulation*, 12(4), 758–774. DOI: 10.1017/err.2021.8

Chadha, R., Sistla, A. P., Viswanathan, M., & Bhusal, B. (2023). Deciding Differential Privacy of Online Algorithms with Multiple Variables. In *Proceedings of the 2023 ACM SIGSAC Conference on Computer and Communications Security* (pp. 1761-1775). DOI: 10.1145/3576915.3623170

Chakabwata, W. (2023). The emancipation of women in Africa using a decolonial feminism. In M. Musingafi, & C. Hungwe, *Women Empowerment and the Feminist Agenda in Africa* (pp. 243-258). Dakota: IGI Global.

Chakraborty, A., & Gummadi, K. P. (2020). Fairness in Algorithmic Decision Making. In *Proceedings of the 7th ACM IKDD CoDS and 25th COMAD* (pp. 367-368). DOI: 10.1145/3371158.3371234

Challenges and Key Branches of Forensic Science in Criminal Inves. (n.d.). Retrieved September 28, 2024, from https://www.longdom.org/open-access/challenges-and-key-branches-of-forensic-science-in-criminal-investigations-104610.html

Chan, L., Morgan, I., Simon, H., Alshabanat, F., Ober, D., Gentry, J., . . . Cao, R. (2019). Survey of AI in cybersecurity for information technology management. In *2019 IEEE technology & engineering management conference (TEMSCON)* (pp. 1-8). IEEE. DOI: 10.1109/TEMSCON.2019.8813605

Chandran, R., & Sharma, A. (2022). Blockchain and AI integration for secure cyberbullying prevention. *Journal of Cyber Security and Technology*, 9(3), 80–95.

Chandran, R., & Sharma, A. (2023). Exploring the potential of AR and VR for cyberbullying prevention. *Technology and Education Journal*, 14(2), 100–115.

Chandran, R., & Sharma, V. (2023). Addressing bias in AI models for social media moderation. *Journal of AI Ethics*, 7(2), 150–165.

Chaudhary, P. K., Alam, N., Yalamati, S., Kolasani, S., Palakurti, N. R., & Whig, P. (2024). Detecting and preventing child cyberbullying using generative artificial intelligence. *In2024 Asia Pacific Conference on Innovation in Technology (APCIT) (pp.* 1-9*)*. IEEE. DOI: 10.1109/APCIT62007.2024.10673710

Chaudhary, R., & Gupta, S. (2020). Using machine learning algorithms for cyberbullying detection and intervention. *AI & Society*, 35(1), 105–118. DOI: 10.1007/s00146-019-00920-w

Chemaly, S. (2013, 04 18). *Facebook misogyny problem*. Retrieved from The Gurdian: https://www.theguardian.com/commentisfree/2013/apr/18/facebook-big-misogyny-problem

Chesney, R., & Citron, D. K. (2019). Deep fakes: A looming challenge for privacy, democracy, and national security. *California Law Review*, 107(5), 1753–1819. DOI: 10.15779/Z38F47M95S

Chesney, R., & Citron, D. K. (2019). Deepfakes and the New Disinformation War. *Foreign Affairs*.

Chisholm, J. F. (2014). Review of the Status of Cyber Bullying and Cyberbullying Prevention. *Journal of Information Systems Education*, 25(1), 77–87.

Chiu, K.-L., Collins, A., & Alexander, R. (2022). Detecting Hate Speech with GPT-3. Retrieved from https://arxiv.org/pdf/2103.12407

Choudhary, R., & Agarwal, A. (2022). Image and video recognition for cyberbullying detection on social media platforms. *International Journal of Artificial Intelligence*, 15(3), 210–225.

Chua, T. H. H., & Chang, L. (2016). Follow me and like my beautiful selfies: Singapore teenage girls' engagement in self-presentation and peer comparison on social media. *Computers in Human Behavior*, 55, 190–197. DOI: 10.1016/j.chb.2015.09.011

Cibu, B., Delcea, C., Domenteanu, A., & Dumitrescu, G. (2023). Mapping the evolution of cybernetics: A bibliometric perspective. *Computers*, 12(237), 1–29. DOI: 10.3390/computers12110237

Citron, D. K., & Chesney, R. (2019). Deepfakes and the new disinformation war. *Foreign Affairs*.

Cross, D., Lester, L., & Barnes, A. (2015). A longitudinal study of the social and emotional predictors and consequences of cyber and traditional bullying victimisation. *International Journal of Public Health*, 60(2), 207–217. DOI: 10.1007/s00038-015-0655-1 PMID: 25645100

Daraghmi, E. Y., Qadan, S., Daraghmi, Y. A., Yousuf, R., Cheikhrouhou, O., & Baz, M. (2024). From Text to Insight: An Integrated CNN-BiLSTM-GRU Model for Arabic Cyberbullying Detection. *IEEE Access : Practical Innovations, Open Solutions*, 12(July), 103504–103519. DOI: 10.1109/ACCESS.2024.3431939

Das, A., Raychawdhary, N., Bhattacharya, T., Dozier, G., & Seals, C. (2023). AU_NLP at SemEval-2023 Task 10: Explainable Detection of Online Sexism Using Fine-tuned RoBERTa. *Proceedings of the The 17th International Workshop on Semantic Evaluation* (pp. 707–717). USA: Association for Computational Linguistics. DOI: 10.18653/v1/2023.semeval-1.97

Dastbaz, M., & Halpin, E. (2014). ICT as a protection tool against child exploitation. *Cyber Crime and Cyber Terrorism Investigator's Handbook*, 133–147. DOI: 10.1016/B978-0-12-800743-3.00011-6

De Baets, A. (2009). The impact of the Universal Declaration of Human Rights on the study of history. *History and Theory*, 48(1), 20–43. DOI: 10.1111/j.1468-2303.2009.00483.x

De Marsico, M., Petrosino, A., & Ricciardi, S. (2016). Iris recognition through machine learning techniques: A survey. *Pattern Recognition Letters*, 82, 106–115. DOI: 10.1016/j.patrec.2016.02.001

de Silva de Alwis, R. (2024). Gendering the New International Norms on Artificial Intelligence and Emerging Technologies. *U of Penn Law School, Public Law Research Paper*, (24-43).

Dehue, F., Bollman, C., & Völlink, T. (2008). Cyberbullying: Youngsters' experience and parental perception. *Cyberpsychology & Behavior*, 11(2), 217–223. DOI: 10.1089/cpb.2007.0008 PMID: 18422417

Dehue, F., Bollman, M., & Völlink, T. (2008). Parent's perception of cyberbullying and the impact on countermeasures. *Cyberpsychology, Behavior, and Social Networking*, 11(2), 93–100. DOI: 10.1089/cyber.2007.0052

Devlin, J., Chang, M. W., Lee, K., & Toutanova, K. (2019). BERT: Pre-training of deep bidirectional transformers for language understanding. *NAACL HLT 2019 - 2019 Conference of the North American Chapter of the Association for Computational Linguistics: Human Language Technologies - Proceedings of the Conference, 1*(Mlm), 4171–4186.

Dilmegani, C., & Forsyth, R. (2024). Generative AI in business: Emerging trends and future directions. *AI Trends*, 17(3), 22–34.

Ditch the Label. (2021). *Annual bullying survey 2021*. Ditch the Label. Retrieved from https://www.ditchthelabel.org/

DNA evidence helps identify woman's killer 36 years after her death | CNN. (n.d.). Retrieved December 14, 2024, from https://edition.cnn.com/2024/12/08/us/tracy-whitney-cold-case-dna-evidence/index.html

Dooley, J. J., Pyzalski, J., & Cross, D. (2009). Cyberbullying versus face-to-face bullying: A theoretical and conceptual review. Zeitschrift für Psychologie. *The Journal of Psychology*, 217, 182–188.

Dooley, J. J., Pyzalski, J., & Cross, D. (2009). The psychological effects of cyberbullying: A comparative study. *Journal of School Violence*, 8(3), 323–339. DOI: 10.1080/15388220902914199

Dutta, R., Smith, D., Rawnsley, R., Bishop-Hurley, G., Hills, J., Timms, G., & Henry, D. (2015). Dynamic cattle behavioural classification using supervised ensemble classifiers. *Computers and Electronics in Agriculture*, 111, 18–28. DOI: 10.1016/j.compag.2014.12.002

Dutton, D. M., & Conroy, G. V. (1997). A review of machine learning. *The Knowledge Engineering Review*, 12(4), 341–367. DOI: 10.1017/S026988899700101X

Elsharnouby, T. H., & Mahrous, A. A. (2015). Customer participation in online co-creation experience: The role of e-service quality. *Journal of Research in Interactive Marketing*, 9(4), 313–336. DOI: 10.1108/JRIM-06-2014-0038

Emmery, C., Verhoeven, B., De Pauw, G., & Daelemans, W. (2021). Current limitations in cyberbullying detection: On evaluation criteria, reproducibility, and data scarcity. *Language Resources and Evaluation*, 55(3), 597–633. DOI: 10.1007/s10579-020-09509-1

Esteva, A., Kuprel, B., Novoa, R. A., Ko, J., Swetter, S. M., Blau, H. M., & Thrun, S. (2019). Dermatologist-level classification of skin cancer with deep neural networks. *Nature*, 542(7639), 115–118. DOI: 10.1038/nature21056 PMID: 28117445

Farina, M., Yu, X., & Lavazza, A. (2024). Ethical considerations and policy interventions concerning the impact of generative AI tools in the economy and in society. *AI and Ethics*. Advance online publication. DOI: 10.1007/s43681-023-00405-2

Fatima, S., Reddy, C. K. K., Sunerah, A., & Doss, S. (2024). Innovations in education. Integrating explainable AI into educational intelligence. In *Internet of behavior-based computational intelligence for smart education systems*. IGI Global. https.// DOI: 10.4018/979-8-3693-8151-9.ch002

Fatima, S., Reddy, C. K. K., Sunerah, A., & Doss, S. (2025). Innovations in Education: Integrating Explainable AI Into Educational Intelligence. In *Internet of Behavior-Based Computational Intelligence for Smart Education Systems* (pp. 19-52). IGI Global.

Faucher, C., Jackson, M., & Cassidy, W. (2014). Cyberbullying among university students: Gendered experiences, impacts, and perspectives. *Education Research International*, 2014, 1–10. DOI: 10.1155/2014/698545

Feinberg, T., & Robey, D. (2009). Teacher interventions in preventing cyberbullying. *Educational Psychology Review*, 21(4), 351–367. DOI: 10.1007/s10648-009-9116-5

Forensic psychology: Week 1: 2.1 | OpenLearn - Open University. (n.d.). Retrieved September 28, 2024, from https://www.open.edu/openlearn/mod/oucontent/view.php?id=68093&section=2.1

Forsyth, O. (2024). Mapping the Generative AI landscape. In https://www.antler.co/blog/generative-ai; 19.08.2024.

Fowler, T. (2024). Technology and the limitations of artificial intelligence. ResearchGate. Retrieved from https://www.researchgate.net/profile/Thomas-Fowler-6?_tp=eyJjb250ZXh0Ijp7ImZpcnN0UGFnZSI6InB1YmxpY2F0aW9uIiwicGFnZSI6InB1YmxpY2F0aW9uIn19

Fulantelli, G., Taibi, D., Scifo, L., Schwarze, V., & Eimler, S. C. (2022). Cyberbullying and cyberhate as two interlinked instances of cyber-aggression in adolescence. a systematic review. *Frontiers in Psychology*, 13, 909299. DOI: 10.3389/fpsyg.2022.909299 PMID: 35712182

Gambín, Á. F., Yazidi, A., Vasilakos, A., Haugerud, H., & Djenouri, Y. (2024). Deepfakes. current and future trends. *Artificial Intelligence Review*, 57(3), 64. DOI: 10.1007/s10462-023-10679-x

Garett, R., Lord, L. R., & Young, S. D. (2016). Associations between social media and cyberbullying: A review of the literature. *mHealth*, 2, 2. DOI: 10.21037/mhealth.2016.12.01 PMID: 28293616

Gaston, A. P. (2024). Cyberbullying detection: Exploring datasets, technologies, and approaches on social media platforms. *Journal of Data Mining and Analytics*, 10(4), 178–192.

Gaw, M. (2013, 07 6). *Practising non attachment with language: An intro to deconstructionism.* Retrieved from Marin Theatre: https://www.marintheatre.org/press-release-details/125/practicing-non-attachment-with-language-an-intro-to-deconstructionism#:~:text=A%20principle%20tenet%20of%20deconstructionism,%2C%20man%2Fwoman%2C%20etc

Geiger, R. S. (2016). Bot-based collective blocklists in Twitter: The counterpublic moderation of harassment in a networked public space. *Information Communication and Society*, 19(6), 787–803. DOI: 10.1080/1369118X.2016.1153700

Gencoglu, O. (2020). Cyberbullying detection with fairness constraints. *IEEE Internet Computing*, 25(1), 20–29. DOI: 10.1109/MIC.2020.3032461

Georgieva-Trifonova, T., & Duraku, M. (2020). Research on N-grams feature selection methods for text classification. *IOP Conf. Series: Materials Science and Engineering 1031* (pp. 1-10). England: IOP Publishing Ltd.

Ghosh, P., & Agarwal, S. (2021). Visual content moderation for online safety: Detecting harmful images and videos. *Journal of Cybersecurity and Digital Trust*, 7(2), 130–144.

Ghosh, P., & Mukherjee, R. (2020). Ethical considerations in AI-driven cyberbullying prevention: A comprehensive analysis. *Journal of Ethics in Technology*, 4(3), 120–134.

Glick, P., & Fiske, S. T. (2011). Ambivalent sexism revisited. *Psychology of Women Quarterly*, 35(3), 530–535. DOI: 10.1177/0361684311414832 PMID: 24453402

Gongane, V. U., Munot, M. V., & Anuse, A. D. (2022). Detection and moderation of detrimental content on social media platforms: Current status and future directions. *Social Network Analysis and Mining*, 12(1), 129. DOI: 10.1007/s13278-022-00951-3 PMID: 36090695

Goodfellow, I., Kingma, D. P., Salimans, T., & Welling, M. (2014). Generative adversarial nets. In *Advances in Neural Information Processing Systems* (Vol. 27, pp. 2672-2680).

Goodfellow, I., Kingma, D. P., Salimans, T., & Welling, M. (2016). Generative adversarial networks and their applications. *arXiv*. https://arxiv.org/abs/1606.03498

Goodfellow, I., Mirza, M., Xu, B., Warde-Farley, D., Courville, A., & Bengio, Y. (2016). Conditional Generative Adversarial Nets. *arXiv*. https://arxiv.org/abs/1411.1784

Goodfellow, I., Pouget-Abadie, J., Mirza, M., Xu, B., Warde-Farley, D., Ozair, S., Courville, A., & Bengio, Y. (2014). *Generative adversarial nets* (Vol. 27). Advances in Neural Information Processing Systems, https://arxiv.org/abs/1406.2661

Goodfellow, I., Pouget-Abadie, J., Mirza, M., Xu, B., Warde-Farley, D., Ozair, S., Courville, A., & Bengio, Y. (2016). Generative adversarial nets: Challenges and opportunities. In *Neural Information Processing Systems* (pp. 2681–2691). MIT Press.

Goodfellow, I., Pouget-Abadie, J., Mirza, M., Xu, B., Warde-Farley, D., Ozair, S., Courville, A., & Bengio, Y. (2017). Generative adversarial networks. *Communications of the ACM*, 63(11), 139–144. DOI: 10.1145/3422622

Gorwa, R., Binns, R., & Katzenbach, C. (2020). Algorithmic content moderation: Technical and political challenges in the automation of platform governance. *Big Data & Society*, 7(1), 2053951719897945. DOI: 10.1177/2053951719897945

Groumpos, P. (2024). New Scientific field for modelling complex dynamic systems: The Cybernetics Artificial Intelligence (CAI). *IgMin Res*, 2(5), 323–340. DOI: 10.61927/igmin183

Gupta, A., & Sood, N. (2023). Predictive analytics for cyberbullying prevention: A machine learning approach. *Journal of AI and Digital Security*, 6(2), 50–65.

Gupta, M., Akiri, C., Aryal, K., Parker, E., & Praharaj, L. (2023). From chatgpt to threatgpt. Impact of generative ai in cybersecurity and privacy. *IEEE Access : Practical Innovations, Open Solutions*, 11, 80218–80245. DOI: 10.1109/ACCESS.2023.3300381

Gupta, R., & Sharma, A. (2023). The role of blockchain in cyberbullying prevention: Enhancing privacy and security. *Journal of Digital Privacy*, 13(2), 40–55.

Gupta, R., & Verma, A. (2023). Future AI innovations for cyberbullying prevention. *AI and Society Journal*, 12(3), 120–135.

Hagendorff, T., & Wezel, K. (2020). 15 challenges for AI: Or what AI (currently) can't do. *AI & Society*, 35(2), 355–365. DOI: 10.1007/s00146-019-00886-y

Hall, M. (2024, 11 28). *Facebook*. Retrieved from Encyclopedia Britannica: https://www.britannica.com/money/Facebook

Hamiza Wan Ali, W. N., Mohd, M., & Fauzi, F. (2018). Cyberbullying Detection: An Overview. *Proceedings of the 2018 Cyber Resilience Conference, CRC 2018*, 1–3. DOI: 10.1109/CR.2018.8626869

Harmon, A. (1985). The "Information Society": Origins and consequences. *Technology and Society Review*, 9(2), 33–48.

Harrison, E. D., Fox, C. L., & Hulme, J. A. (2020). Student anti-bullying and harassment policies at UK universities. *Journal of Higher Education Policy and Management*, 42(5), 547–562. DOI: 10.1080/1360080X.2020.1767353

Harrison, L., & Gupta, S. (2022). The impact of AR and VR in providing emotional support for cyberbullying victims. *Journal of Virtual Reality and Mental Health*, 8(3), 45–60.

Harrison, L., & Sharma, R. (2022). Emotion recognition AI for cyberbullying detection and prevention. *Journal of AI in Mental Health*, 6(4), 115–130.

Hasan, A., Rahman, M., & Khan, S. (2023). Emotion detection in cyberbullying detection systems. *Journal of Artificial Intelligence Research*, 42(3), 145–160. DOI: 10.1016/j.artint.2022.12.002

Hasan, M. T., Hossain, M. A. E., Mukta, M. S. H., Akter, A., Ahmed, M., & Islam, S. (2023). A Review on Deep-Learning-Based Cyberbullying Detection. *Future Internet*, 15(5), 1–47. DOI: 10.3390/fi15050179

Hay, C., Meldrum, R., & Mann, K. (2010). Traditional bullying, cyber bullying, and deviance: A general strain theory approach. *Journal of Contemporary Criminal Justice*, 26(2), 130–147. DOI: 10.1177/1043986209359557

He, K., Zhang, X., Ren, S., & Sun, J. (2020). Deep residual learning for image recognition. *Proceedings of the IEEE Conference on Computer Vision and Pattern Recognition*, 770-778. https://doi.org/DOI: 10.1109/CVPR.2016.90

Hinduja, S., & Patchin, J. W. (2010). Cyberbullying and suicide: A review of the literature. *International Journal of Cybersecurity*, 4(1), 20–40. DOI: 10.1007/s11514-010-0072-x

Hinduja, S., & Patchin, J. W. (2014). *Cyberbullying identification, prevention, and response*. Cyberbullying Research Center.

Hinduja, S., & Patchin, J. W. (2015). Social influences on cyberbullying behaviours among middle and high school students. *Journal of Youth and Adolescence*, 42(5), 711–722. DOI: 10.1007/s10964-012-9902-4 PMID: 23296318

Hinduja, S., & Patchin, J. W. (2018). *Cyberbullying Research Summary: Cyberbullying and Suicide*. Cyberbullying Research Center.

Hofstetter, M., Riedl, R., Gees, T., Koumpis, A., & Schaberreiter, T. (2020, September). Applications of AI in cybersecurity. In *2020 Second International Conference on Transdisciplinary AI (TransAI)* (pp. 138-141). IEEE. DOI: 10.1109/TransAI49837.2020.00031

Hoofnagle, C. J., Van Der Sloot, B., & Borgesius, F. Z. (2019). The European Union general data protection regulation: What it is and what it means. *Information & Communications Technology Law*, 28(1), 65–98. DOI: 10.1080/13600834.2019.1573501

How Artificial Intelligence (AI) Is Used In Biometrics. (n.d.). Retrieved December 14, 2024, from https://www.aratek.co/news/how-artificial-intelligence-ai-is-used-in-biometrics

Hunt, E. B. (2014). *Artificial intelligence*. Academic Press.

Hu, Y., Clancy, E. M., & Klettke, B. (2023). Understanding the Vicious Cycle: Relationships between Nonconsensual Sexting Behaviours and Cyberbullying Perpetration. *Sexes*, 4(1), 155–166. Advance online publication. DOI: 10.3390/sexes4010013

Isarta News. (2024). Artificial intelligence and the future of digital marketing. https://www.isartanews.com

Islam, M. M., Uddin, M. A., Islam, L., Akter, A., Sharmin, S., & Acharjee, U. K. (2020). Cyberbullying Detection on Social Networks Using Machine Learning Approaches. *2020 IEEE Asia-Pacific Conference on Computer Science and Data Engineering, CSDE 2020*, 3–8. DOI: 10.1109/CSDE50874.2020.9411601

Islam, M. S., Sutton, S., & Rafiq, R. I. (2024). A generative AI powered approach to cyberbullying detection. *Proceedings of the 2024 8th International Conference on Information System and Data Mining*, 57–63. https://doi.org/DOI: 10.1145/3686397.3686407

Iwendi, C., Ojiako, U., & Mothobi, O. (2020). Deep learning systems for combating online harassment: A review. *IEEE Access : Practical Innovations, Open Solutions*, 8, 16003–16018. DOI: 10.1109/ACCESS.2020.2964302

Iwendi, C., Srivastava, G., Khan, S., & Maddikunta, P. K. R. (2023). Cyberbullying detection solutions based on deep learning architectures. *Multimedia Systems*, 29(3), 1839–1852. DOI: 10.1007/s00530-020-00701-5

Jadon, A. (2024). *Ethical AI development: Mitigating bias in generative models*. Retrieved from https://www.researchgate.net/profile/Ankit-Jadon/publication/669ffd6a8be3067b4b1506c9/Ethical-AI-Development-Mitigating-Bias-in-Generative-Models/links/669ffd6a8be3067b4b1506c9/Ethical-AI-Development-Mitigating-Bias-in-Generative-Models.pdf

Jahan, M. S., & Oussalah, M. (2023). A systematic review of hate speech automatic detection using natural language processing. *Neurocomputing*, 546, 126232. DOI: 10.1016/j.neucom.2023.126232

Jain, V. H., & Bohra, V. M. (2024). Cyberbullying in the digital age: Legal challenges and solutions. *International Journal of Legal Research and Analysis*, 2(7), 16. https://www.doi-ds.org/doilink/07.2024-23173692/

Jalan, A. (2023, 2 5). *Make Use of (MUO)*. Retrieved from The evolution of Facebook: From 2004 to Meta: https://www.makeuseof.com/evolution-of-facebook/

Janiesch, C., Samtani, S., & Gupta, H. (2021). Explainable AI for business applications: Opportunities and challenges. *AI Open*, 2(1), 35–44. DOI: 10.1016/j.aiopen.2021.100047

Jha, R. (2021). Anomaly detection for cyberbullying: A machine learning approach. *Journal of Technology and Cybersecurity*, 8(2), 123–137.

Jha, R. (2021). NLP Models for Sentiment Analysis in Cyberbullying Detection. *Indian Journal of Technology and Cybersecurity*, 5(3), 89–104.

John, R., Smith, A., & Johnson, P. (2010). Stress associated with cyberbullying and its emotional impact. *Journal of Youth Psychology*, 45(2), 120–135. DOI: 10.1016/j.jyp.2010.03.004

Joseph, S., & Castan, M. (2013). *The international covenant on civil and political rights: cases, materials, and commentary*. OUP Oxford.

Jun, Y., Craig, A., Shafik, W., & Sharif, L. (2021). Artificial Intelligence Application in Cybersecurity and Cyberdefense. In *Wireless Communications and Mobile Computing* (Vol. 2021). DOI: 10.1155/2021/3329581

Kalinaki, K., Shafik, W., Namuwaya, S., & Namuwaya, S. (2024). Perspectives, applications, challenges, and future trends of IoT-based logistics. In *Navigating Cyber Threats and Cybersecurity in the Logistics Industry*. DOI: 10.4018/979-8-3693-3816-2.ch005

Kang, B.-G., & Nam, Y. (2024). Innovative artificial intelligence solution as game changer in cyberbullying detection and prevention. Artificial Intelligence in Cybersecurity, 1, 52–59. https://sciencesforce.com

Kang, C. (2019). $5 Billion Fine For Facebook On User Data. *The New York Times*, A1-L.

Kang, H., Wang, Y., Wang, M., Al Imran Yasin, M., Osman, M. N., & Ang, L. H. (2024). Navigating digital network: Mindfulness as a shield against cyberbullying in the knowledge economy era. *Journal of the Knowledge Economy*, 15(3), 13233–13271. DOI: 10.1007/s13132-023-01604-2

Kaur, P., & Saha, S. (2022). AI-based systems for real-time cyberbullying prevention. *International Journal of AI and Cybersecurity*, 10(2), 98–110. DOI: 10.1016/j.ijai.2022.01.003

Kaur, R., Gabrijelčič, D., & Klobučar, T. (2023). Artificial intelligence for cybersecurity. Literature review and future research directions. *Information Fusion*, 97, 101804. DOI: 10.1016/j.inffus.2023.101804

Kee, D. M. H., Anwar, A., & Vranjes, I. (2024). Cyberbullying victimization and suicide ideation: The mediating role of psychological distress among Malaysian youth. *Computers in Human Behavior*, 150, 108000. Advance online publication. DOI: 10.1016/j.chb.2023.108000

Keinan, R. (2024). Tackling sexism in social media: Multilingual AI solutions. *Journal of Electrical and Electronics Engineering (Oradea)*, 3(5), 1–7.

Keras 2 API documentation. (n.d.). Retrieved December 14, 2024, from https://keras.io/2.15/api/

Khade, A., Oza, P., & Kazi, N. (2023). *Multimodal cyberbullying meme detection from social media using deep learning approach*. ResearchGate., DOI: 10.1007/978-981-99-5614-8_23

Kim, H., & Singh, A. (2019). Explainable AI for cyberbullying detection in social media. *International Journal of Artificial Intelligence Ethics*, 5(1), 24–37.

Kim, S., Razi, A., Stringhini, G., Wisniewski, P. J., & De Choudhury, M. (2021). A Human-Centered Systematic Literature Review of Cyberbullying Detection Algorithms. *Proceedings of the ACM on Human-Computer Interaction, 5*(CSCW2). DOI: 10.1145/3476066

Kim, S., & Singh, R. (2019). Accountability in black-box AI models for moderation. *International Journal of Computational Ethics*, 6(3), 221–240.

Kingma, D. P., Salimans, T., & Welling, M. (2014). *Variational autoencoders*. Neural Information Processing Systems.

Kingma, D. P., & Welling, M. (2013). Auto-Encoding Variational Bayes. *International Conference on Learning Representations*. https://arxiv.org/abs/1312.6114

King, T. C., Aggarwal, N., Taddeo, M., & Floridi, L. (2020). Artificial Intelligence Crime: An Interdisciplinary Analysis of Foreseeable Threats and Solutions. *Science and Engineering Ethics*, 26(1), 89–120. DOI: 10.1007/s11948-018-00081-0 PMID: 30767109

Kishor Kumar Reddy, C. (2023). *Pullisani Satvika, Marlia Mohd Hanafiah, Srinath Doss, "An Efficient early Diagnosis and Healthcare Monitoring System for Mental Disorder using Machine Learning*. Intelligent Engineering Applications and Applied Sciences for Sustainability IGI Global.

Kolozova, K. (2021). Poststructural theory. In Hall, K. (Ed.), *Asta, The Oxford Handbook of feminist theory* (pp. 1–12). Oxford University Press.

Kordzadeh, N., & Ghasemaghaei, M. (2022). Algorithmic bias: Review, synthesis, and future research directions. *European Journal of Information Systems*, 31(3), 388–409. DOI: 10.1080/0960085X.2021.1927212

Kowalski, R. M., Giumetti, G. W., Schroeder, A. N., & Lattanner, M. R. (2014). Bullying in the digital age: A critical review and meta-analysis of cyberbullying research among youth. *Psychological Bulletin*, 140(4), 1073–1137. DOI: 10.1037/a0035618 PMID: 24512111

Kowalski, R. M., Limber, S. P., & Agatston, P. W. (2012). *Cyberbullying: Bullying in the digital age* (2nd ed.). Wiley-Blackwell.

Kowsik Godavarthi, S. M., Surya Vishnu Ganimisetty,Sreekar Palanati,Radhika Rani Chintala,Venkata Praveen Chennamsetty, (2024), "Confronting the Offensive Stalking Risks: With Standing Cyber Stalkers", 2024 International Conference on Advances in Computing, Communication and Applied Informatics (ACCAI), pp. 1-7, DOI: 10.1109/ACCAI61061.2024.10602125

Krikke, J. (2024, 12 12). *Want to win AI revolution? Study up on cybernetics*. Retrieved from Asia Times: https://asiatimes.com/2024/11/want-to-win-the-ai-revolution-study-up-on-cybernetics/

Kruszka, P., Addissie, Y. A., McGinn, D. E., Porras, A. R., Biggs, E., Share, M., Crowley, T. B., Chung, B. H. Y., Mok, G. T. K., Mak, C. C. Y., Muthukumarasamy, P., Thong, M. K., Sirisena, N. D., Dissanayake, V. H. W., Paththinige, C. S., Prabodha, L. B. L., Mishra, R., Shotelersuk, V., Ekure, E. N., & Muenke, M. (2017). 22q11.2 deletion syndrome in diverse populations. *American Journal of Medical Genetics. Part A*, 173(4), 879–888. DOI: 10.1002/ajmg.a.38199 PMID: 28328118

Kühl, N., Fink, G. A., & Thrun, S. (2022). Human-like artificial intelligence: A survey on advancements and open issues. *IEEE Transactions on AI*, 5(1), 56–65. DOI: 10.1109/TAC.2022.30456

Kumar Reddy, C., P R, A., Reddy, T., & D, R. (2022). Early monitoring of social distancing using OpenCV and deep learning. *International Journal of Engineering and Computer Science (INT-JECSE)*, 11(6), 1275–1283. DOI: 10.1016/j.future.2021.01.006

Kumar, N., Malhotra, M., Aggarwal, B., Rai, D., & Aggarwal, G. Leveraging Natural Language Processing and Machine Learning for Efficient Fake News Detection. In Proceedings of the International Conference on Technological Advancements in Computational Sciences (ICTACS), 2023 3rd, Tashkent, Uzbekistan, 1–3 November 2023; pp. 535–541. DOI: 10.1109/ICTACS59847.2023.10390356

Kumar, A., Dikshit, S., & Albuquerque, V. H. C. (2021). Explainable artificial intelligence for sarcasm detection in dialogues. *Wireless Communications and Mobile Computing*, 2021(1), 2939334. DOI: 10.1155/2021/2939334

Kumar, R., & Jain, M. (2022). AI in cyberbullying prevention: Balancing privacy with protection. *Journal of Digital Security*, 9(4), 340–355.

Kumar, R., Verma, S., & Sharma, P. (2021). A hybrid machine learning approach for cyberbullying detection on social media platforms. *Indian Journal of Computer Science*, 12(4), 222–235.

Kumar, Y., Huang, K., Perez, A., Yang, G., Li, J. J., Morreale, P., Kruger, D., & Jiang, R. (2024). Bias and Cyberbullying Detection and Data Generation Using Transformer Artificial Intelligence Models and Top Large Language Models. *Electronics (Basel)*, 13(17), 3431. DOI: 10.3390/electronics13173431

Laccourreye, O., & Maisonneuve, H. (2019). French scientific medical journals confronted by developments in medical writing and the transformation of the medical press. *European Annals of Otorhinolaryngology, Head and Neck Diseases*, 136(6), 475–480. DOI: 10.1016/j.anorl.2019.09.002 PMID: 31540851

Langley, P., & Simon, H. A. (1995). Applications of Machine Learning and Rule Induction. *Communications of the ACM*, 38(11), 54–64. DOI: 10.1145/219717.219768

Le Nguyen, C., & Golman, W. (2021). Diffusion of the Budapest Convention on cybercrime and the development of cybercrime legislation in Pacific Island countries: 'Law on the books' vs 'law in action'. *Computer Law & Security Report*, 40, 105521. DOI: 10.1016/j.clsr.2020.105521

Leal, C. C., & Oliveira, B. (2024). Nudging financial behavior in the age of artificial intelligence. In *Artificial Intelligence in Production Engineering and Management* (pp. 115–144). Woodhead Publishing. DOI: 10.1016/B978-0-12-819471-3.00002-1

Leaper, C. (2024). The development of ambivalent sexism: Proposals for an expanded model. *British Journal of Developmental Psychology*, 00, 1–19. DOI: 10.1111/bjdp.12521 PMID: 39275962

LeCun, Y., Bengio, Y., & Hinton, G. (2015). Deep learning. *Nature*, 521(7553), 436–444. DOI: 10.1038/nature14539 PMID: 26017442

Lee, W., Lee, S. S., Chung, S., & An, D. (2007). Harmful contents classification using the harmful word filtering and SVM. In Shi, Y., van Albada, G. D., Dongarra, J., & Sloot, P. M. A. (Eds.), Lecture Notes in Computer Science: Vol. 4489. *Computational Science – ICCS 2007* (pp. 15–21). Springer., DOI: 10.1007/978-3-540-72588-6_3

Lehmann, J., & Buschek, D. (2020). Human-AI collaboration in creative tasks. *Proceedings of the 2020 CHI Conference on Human Factors in Computing Systems*, 58, 134-142. https://doi.org/DOI: 10.1145/3313831.3376460

Liao, S., Lin, L., Chen, Q., & Pei, H. (2022). Why not work with anthropomorphic collaborative robots? The mediation effect of perceived intelligence and the moderation effect of self-efficacy. *Human Factors and Ergonomics in Manufacturing & Service Industries*.

Liao, W., Zeng, B., Yin, X., & Wei, P. (2021). An improved aspect-category sentiment analysis model for text sentiment analysis based on RoBERTa. *Applied Intelligence*, 51(6), 3522–3533. DOI: 10.1007/s10489-020-01964-1

Li, C., Wang, P., Martin-Moratinos, M., Bella-Fernandez, M., & Blasco-Fontecilla, H. (2024). Traditional bullying and cyberbullying in the digital age and its associated mental health problems in children and adolescents: A meta-analysis. *European Child & Adolescent Psychiatry*, 33(9), 2895–2909. DOI: 10.1007/s00787-022-02128-x PMID: 36585978

Lin, C., & Wang, D. (2021). Bias and cyberbullying detection using transformer AI models. *Proceedings of the ACM Conference on Online Harms*, 2022, 45–56.

Lin, H. T., Tai, Y. M., & Gau, S. S. F. (2023). Autistic Traits and Cyberbullying Involvement Mediated by Psychopathologies and School Functions in a Nationally Representative Child Sample. *Cyberpsychology, Behavior, and Social Networking*, 26(9), 706–716. Advance online publication. DOI: 10.1089/cyber.2022.0309 PMID: 37477877

Livingstone, S., & Smith, P. K. (2014). Annual Research Review: Harmful online content and the right to privacy and protection. *Journal of Child Psychology and Psychiatry, and Allied Disciplines*.

Livingstone, S., & Smith, P. K. (2014). Annual research review: Harms experienced by child users of online and mobile technologies. *Journal of Child Psychology and Psychiatry, and Allied Disciplines*, 55(6), 635–654. DOI: 10.1111/jcpp.12197 PMID: 24438579

Li, Z., & Zhou, K. (2014). When content moderation is not about content: How Chinese social media platforms moderate content and why it matters. *New Media & Society*, •••, 1–17.

Luckin, R., Holmes, W., Griffiths, M., & Forcier, L. B. (2016). *Intelligence unleashed: An argument for AI in education*. Pearson.

Lugones, M. (2010). Towards a decolonial feminism. *Hypatia*, 25(4), 742–758. DOI: 10.1111/j.1527-2001.2010.01137.x

Lynette, K. Watts, Jessyca Wagner, Benito Velasquez, Phyllis I. Behrens,Cyberbullying in higher education: A literature review,Computers in Human Behavior,Volume 69,2017 ISSN 0747-5632, DOI: 10.1016/j.chb.2016.12.038

Machimbarrena, J. M., & Garaigordobil, M. (2020). Cyberbullying in adolescents: Prevalence, characteristics, and psychological outcomes. *Educational Psychology*, 40(3), 345–363. DOI: 10.1080/01443410.2019.1644306

Maddireddy, B. R., & Maddireddy, B. R. (2020). AI and Big Data. Synergizing to Create Robust Cybersecurity Ecosystems for Future Networks. *International Journal of Advanced Engineering Technologies and Innovations*, 1(2), 40–63.

Mahalakshmi, C., Sharmila, T., Priyanka, S., Sastry, M., Reddy, D. B. V. R. M., & Reddy, M. K. K. (2019).A survey on various chatbot implementation techniques. JASC: Journal of Applied Science and Computations.

Maher, D. (2008). Cyberbullying: An ethnographic case study of one Australian upper primary school class. *Youth Studies Australia*, 27(4), 50.

Majel Monisha, B. (2024). AI powered Cyberbullying Detection Model. *International Scientific Journal of Engineering and Management*, 03(04), 1–9. DOI: 10.55041/ISJEM01529

Mangena. (2020). *Cyberbullying: The challenges that women and girls face in seeking redress in cases of online harrassment in Zimbabwe.* A dissertation submitted in partial fullfillment of the requirement of the Master's degree in Social Legal Studies University of Zimbabwe: Southern and Eastern African Regional Centre for Women's Law.

Mantey, D. S., Yockey, R. A., & Springer, A. E. (2023). Digital screen time and suicidality during high school: How important is cyberbullying? A mediation analysis using the youth risk behavioral surveillance survey, 2011–2019. *Preventive Medicine*, 166, 107330. Advance online publication. DOI: 10.1016/j.ypmed.2022.107330 PMID: 36334685

Manzoor, M. F., Abid, A., Nawaz, N. A., & Alvi, A. (2022). Aspect based sentence segregated dataset of hybrid car's consumers online reviews. *Data in Brief*, 42, 108293. Advance online publication. DOI: 10.1016/j.dib.2022.108293 PMID: 35637892

Marcus, G., & Davis, E. (2020). *Rebooting AI: Building artificial intelligence we can trust*. Pantheon Books.

Mark, A. (2024). *Goldstein,Myrna Chandler Goldstein, "Cyberbullying", How Technology,social media, and Current Events Profoundly Affect Adolescents.* Oxford University Press.

Martelaro, N., & Ju, W. (2018). 10 25). Cybernetics and the design of the user experience of AI systems. *Interactions (New York, N.Y.)*, 25(6), 38–41. DOI: 10.1145/3274570

Masatcıoğlu, G., & Öksüz, Y. E. (2024). *Examination of the relationship between peer bullying and cyber violence in university students. JOURNAL OF AWARENESS, 9*. Special Issue/Özel Sayı., DOI: 10.26809/joa.2262

McCartney, T., & Anderson, P. (2023). Legal frameworks for cyberbullying prevention: A global overview. *International Journal of Cyber Law*, 11(3), 45–60.

McKay, V. (2018). Lifelong Learning and Sustainable Development Goals. *Australian Journal of Adult Learning*, 58(3), 390–425.

Meduri, K., Gonaygunt, H., & Nadella, G. S. (2024). Evaluating the Effectiveness of AI-Driven Frameworks in Predicting and Preventing Cyber Attacks. *International Journal of Research Publication and Reviews*, 5(3), 6591–6595. DOI: 10.55248/gengpi.5.0324.0875

Mellino, M. (2018). Postcolonialism. In Callan, H. (Ed.), *The International Encyclopedia of Anthropology* (pp. 1–16). John Wiley and Sons Ltd. DOI: 10.1002/9781118924396.wbiea2344

Mendoza, B. (2020). Decolonial theories in parctice. *Journal of World Philosophies*, 5, 43–60.

Meola, C. (2020). Helping Aussie women online: A discourse analysis of the Australian eSafety Commissioner website. In *Social media in legal practice* (pp. 130–145). Routledge. DOI: 10.4324/9780429346088-9

Michael, K., Abbas, R., & Roussos, G. (2023). AI in cybersecurity. The paradox. *IEEE Transactions on Technology and Society*, 4(2), 104–109. DOI: 10.1109/TTS.2023.3280109

Mignolo, W. D., & Walsh, C. (2018). *On decoloniality concepts, analytics and praxis*. Duke University Press.

Milosevic, T., Van Royen, K., & Davis, B. (2022). Artificial intelligence to address cyberbullying, harassment, and abuse: New directions in the midst of complexity. *International Journal of Bullying Prevention : an Official Publication of the International Bullying Prevention Association*, 4(1), 1–5. DOI: 10.1007/s42380-022-00117-x PMID: 35233506

Milosevic, T., Verma, K., Carter, M., Vigil, S., Laffan, D., Davis, B., & O'Higgins Norman, J. (2023). Effectiveness of Artificial Intelligence–Based Cyberbullying Interventions From Youth Perspective. *Social Media + Society*, 9(1), 20563051221147325. Advance online publication. DOI: 10.1177/20563051221147325

Milossi, M., Alexandropoulou-Egyptiadou, E., & Psannis, K. E. (2021). AI ethics: Algorithmic determinism or self-determination? The GPDR approach. *IEEE Access : Practical Innovations, Open Solutions*, 9, 58455–58466. DOI: 10.1109/ACCESS.2021.3072782

Miranda, M. D. (2021). The trace in the technique: Forensic science and the Connoisseur's gaze. *Forensic Science International. Synergy*, 3, 100203. DOI: 10.1016/j.fsisyn.2021.100203 PMID: 34632356

Mishna, F., Cook, C., Gadalla, T., Daciuk, J., & Solomon, S. (2010). Cyber bullying behaviors among middle and high school students. *The American Journal of Orthopsychiatry*, 80(3), 362–374. DOI: 10.1111/j.1939-0025.2010.01040.x PMID: 20636942

Mishna, F., Saini, M., & Solomon, S. (2009). Cyberbullying: An exploratory study of factors related to bullying behaviors. *Journal of Youth and Adolescence*, 38(6), 850–861. DOI: 10.1007/s10964-009-9434-0 PMID: 19636786

Mishna, F., Saini, M., & Solomon, S. (2009b). Ongoing and online: Children and youth's perceptions of cyber bullying. *Children and Youth Services Review*, 31(12), 1222–1228. DOI: 10.1016/j.childyouth.2009.05.004

Moffat, B. (2024). An examination of cyberbullying among Zimbabwean female social media influencers. *Online Journal of Communication and Media Technologies*, 14(4), 1–14. DOI: 10.30935/ojcmt/15016

Mohammadi, H., Giachanou, A., & Bagheri, A. (2024). A transparent pipeline for identifying sexism in social media combining explainability with model prediction. *Applied Science, 14, 8620.*, 1-27.

Molina, M. D., & Sundar, S. S. (2022). When AI moderates online content: Effects of human collaboration and interactive transparency on user trust. *Journal of Computer-Mediated Communication*, 27(4), zmac010. DOI: 10.1093/jcmc/zmac010

Monika Singh, T., Kishor Kumar Reddy, C., Ramana Murthy, B. V., Nag, A., & Doss, S. (2025). AI and Education: Bridging the Gap to Personalized, Efficient, and Accessible Learning. In M. Ouaissa, M. Ouaissa, H. Lamaazi, M. El Hamlaoui, & K. Reddy C. (Eds.), Internet of Behavior-Based Computational Intelligence for Smart Education Systems (pp. 131-160). IGI Global. . https://doi.org/DOI: 10.4018/979-8-3693-8151-9.ch005

Morales, E. F., & Escalante, H. J. (2022). A brief introduction to supervised, unsupervised, and reinforcement learning. In Torres-García, A. A., Reyes-García, C. A., Villaseñor-Pineda, L., & Mendoza-Montoya, O. (Eds.), *Biosignal processing and classification using computational learning and intelligence* (pp. 111–129). Academic Press., DOI: 10.1016/B978-0-12-820125-1.00017-8

Moravec, V., Hynek, N., Gavurova, B., & Kubak, M. (2024). Everyday artificial intelligence unveiled: Societal awareness of technological transformation. *Oeconomia Copernicana*, 15(2), 367–406. DOI: 10.24136/oc.2961

Mullah, N. S., & Zainon, W. M. N. W. (2021). Advances in machine learning algorithms for hate speech detection in social media: A review. *IEEE Access : Practical Innovations, Open Solutions*, 9, 88364–88376. DOI: 10.1109/ACCESS.2021.3089515

Muneer, A., Alwadain, A., Ragab, M. G., & Alqushaibi, A. (2023). Cyberbullying Detection on Social Media Using Stacking Ensemble Learning and Enhanced BERT. *Information (Basel)*, 14(8), 467. Advance online publication. DOI: 10.3390/info14080467

Murfy, E., & Thomas, H. (2023). Generative AI and creativity. *AI Research Review*, 5(3), 75–85.

Mutsvairo, B. (2020). *Zimbabwean women share their social media experiences*. Hivos Unlimited.

Nadeem, A., Abedin, B., & Marjanovic, O. (2022). Gender bias in AI-based decision-making systems: A systematic literature review. *AJIS. Australasian Journal of Information Systems*, 26, 1–34. DOI: 10.3127/ajis.v26i0.3835

Nagata, J. M., Yang, J. H., Singh, G., Kiss, O., Ganson, K. T., Testa, A., Jackson, D. B., & Baker, F. C. (2023). Cyberbullying and Sleep Disturbance Among Early Adolescents in the U.S. *Academic Pediatrics*, 23(6), 1220–1225. Advance online publication. DOI: 10.1016/j.acap.2022.12.007 PMID: 36581100

NapoleonCat. (2024, 05 1). *Facebook users in Zimbabwe*. Retrieved from NapoleonCat: https://napoleoncat.com/stats/facebook-users-in-zimbabwe/2024/05/

National Crime Records Bureau (NCRB). (2020). Cyberbullying cases on the rise: Implications for public safety in the digital age. NCRB Annual Report, 2020, 1-25. https://ncrb.gov.in

Navarro, R., Yubero, S., & Larrañaga, E. (2015). *Cyberbullying across the globe: Gender, family, and mental health*. Springer.

Nee, C. N., Samsudin, N., Chuan, H. M., Bin Mohd Ridzuan, M. I., Boon, O. P., Binti Mohamad, A. M., & Scheithauer, H. (2023). The digital defence against cyberbullying: A systematic review of tech-based approaches. *Cogent Education*, 10(2), 2288492. Advance online publication. DOI: 10.1080/2331186X.2023.2288492

Neha, M. V., Muhammad, S., Indu, V., & Thampi, S. M. (2023). Detection and Prevention of Cyberbullying in Social Media Using Cognitive Computational Analysis. In *Combatting Cyberbullying in Digital Media with Artificial Intelligence*. DOI: 10.1201/9781003393061-3

Nehanda Centre for Gender and Cultural Studies. (2023). *Women in politics in Zimbabwe: How gender norms are fueling online violence*. Nehanda Centre for Gender and Cultural Studies.

NEWS: Germany's FIU examining how it can use AI to fight financial crime - AML Intelligence. (n.d.). Retrieved December 14, 2024, from https://www.amlintelligence.com/2024/10/news-germanys-fiu-examining-how-it-can-use-ai-to-fight-financial-crime/

Ngiam, J., Khosla, A., Kim, M., Nam, J., & Lee, H. (2011). Multimodal deep learning. *Proceedings of the 28th International Conference on Machine Learning*, 1, 689-696. https://doi.org/DOI: 10.1145/3023147.3023152

Ngiam, J., Khosla, A., Kim, M., Nam, J., Lee, H., & Ng, A. Y. (2024). Multimodal Deep Learning. *Springer Optimization and Its Applications*, 211, 209–219. DOI: 10.1007/978-3-031-53092-0_10

Nikolaou, D. (2017). Does cyberbullying impact youth suicidal behaviors? *Journal of Health Economics*, 56, 30–46. DOI: 10.1016/j.jhealeco.2017.09.009 PMID: 28968528

Noh, K., Seong, B., Byun, H., Choi, Y., Song, S., & Song, K. (2024). LBC: Language-Based-Classifier for Out-Of-Variable Generalization. Yonsei: Yonsei University.

Noni, R. (2024). Cyberbullying: The Silent Epidemic of The Digital Age. Journal of World Science. *Riviera Publishing Vol.*, 3(6), 691–697. DOI: 10.58344/jws.v3i6.634

Nosrati, S., Sabzali, M., Heidari, A., Sarfi, T., & Sabbar, S. (2020). Chatbots, counselling, and discontents of the digital life. *Journal of Cyberspace Studies*, 4(2), 153–172.

Novalita, N., Herdiani, A., Lukmana, I., & Puspandari, D. (2019). Cyberbullying identification on Twitter using random forest classifier. *Journal of Physics: Conference Series*, 1192(1), 012029. DOI: 10.1088/1742-6596/1192/1/012029

Novikov, D. A. (2015). *Cybernetics from past to future*. Russian Academy of Sciences Trapeznikov Institute of Control Sciences.

Obaid, M. H., Guirguis, S. K., & Elkaffas, S. M. (2023). Cyberbullying Detection and Severity Determination Model. *IEEE Access : Practical Innovations, Open Solutions*, 11(September), 97391–97399. DOI: 10.1109/ACCESS.2023.3313113

Ogunleye, O., & Lin, M. (2023). Bias mitigation strategies in AI systems for social good. *IEEE Transactions on AI Systems*, 17(6), 599–614.

Olweus, D., & Limber, S. (2018). Some problems with cyberbullying research. *Current Opinion in Psychology*, 19, 139–143. DOI: 10.1016/j.copsyc.2017.04.012 PMID: 29279213

Orelaja, A., Ejiofor, C., Sarpong, S., Imakuh, S., Bassey, C., Opara, I., Tettey, J. N. A., & Akinola, O. (2024). Attribute-specific Cyberbullying Detection Using Artificial Intelligence. *Journal of Electronic & Information Systems*, 6(1), 10–21. Advance online publication. DOI: 10.30564/jeis.v6i1.6206

Ortega, R., Elipe, P., Mora-Merchán, J. A., Calmaestra, J., & Vega, E. (2009). The emotional impact of bullying and cyberbullying on victims: A European cross-national study. *Aggressive Behavior*, 35(5), 514–525. DOI: 10.1002/ab.20334 PMID: 22782434

Oyeyumi, O. (1997). *The invention of women*. University of Minneapolis.

Pagano, N. A. (2018). The Indecency of the Communications Decency Act 230: Unjust Immunity for Monstrous Social Media Platforms. *Pace Law Review*, 39(1), 511. DOI: 10.58948/2331-3528.1994

Pascucci, A., Masucci, V., & Monti, J. "Computational Stylometry and Machine Learning for Gender and Age Detection in Cyberbullying Texts," in 2019 8th International Conference on Affective Computing and Intelligent Interaction Workshops and Demos (ACIIW), 2019, pp. 1–6. DOI: 10.1109/ACIIW.2019.8925101

Patcha, A., & Park, J.-M. (2007). An overview of anomaly detection techniques: Existing solutions and latest technological trends. *Computer Networks*, 51(12), 3448–3470. DOI: 10.1016/j.comnet.2007.02.001

Patchin, J. W., & Hinduja, S. (2010). Cyberbullying: An Update and Synthesis of the Literature. *Aggression and Violent Behavior*, 15(3), 220–233.

Patchin, J. W., & Hinduja, S. (2020). *Bullying today: Bullet points and best practices*. Corwin Press.

Patel, K., Mehta, D., Mistry, C., Gupta, R., Tanwar, S., Kumar, N., & Alazab, M. (2020). Facial sentiment analysis using AI techniques: State-of-the-art, taxonomies, and challenges. *IEEE Access : Practical Innovations, Open Solutions*, 8, 90495–90519. DOI: 10.1109/ACCESS.2020.2993803

Patel, M., Sharma, S., & Bansal, A. (2021). NLP Techniques in Social Media Monitoring for Cyberbullying. *International Journal of AI and Social Media Research*, 7(4), 123–134.

Patel, M., Sharma, S., & Bansal, A. (2021). Supervised machine learning for identifying cyberbullying content on social media. *Journal of AI in Social Media*, 5(3), 89–101.

Patel, M., & Soni, V. (2022). Augmented and Virtual Reality in cyberbullying prevention. *Journal of Immersive Technologies*, 5(4), 110–125.

Patel, R., & Kumar, R. (2021). Generative adversarial networks for detecting manipulated visual content in cyberbullying. *Journal of Artificial Intelligence and Ethics*, 5(4), 350–364.

Paul, M., & Saha, S. (2022). Cross-cultural applications of AI in content moderation. *International Journal of AI and Society*, 8(1), 102–119.

Paul, S., & Saha, A. (2022). Comparative analysis of BERT and other models in cyberbullying detection using real-life datasets. *Proceedings of the International Conference on Social Media Analysis.*

Paul, S., & Saha, S. (2022). Cyberbullying detection using CyberBert: An AI-based solution. *Journal of Cybersecurity and Privacy*, 1(3), 228–241. DOI: 10.1007/s42486-022-00375-7

Peng, W., Adikari, A., Alahakoon, D., & Gero, J. (2019). Discovering the influence of sarcasm in social media responses. *Wiley Interdisciplinary Reviews. Data Mining and Knowledge Discovery*, 9(6), e1331. DOI: 10.1002/widm.1331

Peprah, P., Oduro, M. S., Okwei, R., Adu, C., Asiamah-Asare, B. Y., & Agyemang-Duah, W. (2023). Cyberbullying victimization and suicidal ideation among in-school adolescents in three countries: Implications for prevention and intervention. *BMC Psychiatry*, 23(1), 944. Advance online publication. DOI: 10.1186/s12888-023-05268-9 PMID: 38098109

Perera, A., & Fernando, P. (2021). Accurate cyberbullying detection and prevention on social media. *Procedia Computer Science*, 181, 605–611. DOI: 10.1016/j.procs.2021.01.207

Pericherla, S., & Ilavarasan, E. (2024). Overcoming the Challenge of Cyberbullying Detection in Images: A Deep Learning Approach with Image Captioning and OCR Integration. *International Journal of Computing and Digital Systems*, 15(1), 393–401. Advance online publication. DOI: 10.12785/ijcds/150130

Peryala, A., & Reddy, C. K. K. (2024). Utilization of generative AI in medical imaging to improve evaluation and therapy. In *Intelligent systems and IoT applications in clinical health.* IGI Global. https.//DOI: 10.4018/979-8-3693-8990-4.ch007

Petrosino, A., Loia, V., & Pedrycz, W. (Eds.). (2017). *Fuzzy Logic and Soft Computing Applications. 10147.* DOI: 10.1007/978-3-319-52962-2

Planck, M. (2024, 04 25). *From Cybernetics to AI: The pioneering work of Norbert Wiener*. Retrieved from MP Neuro Max Planck Neuroscience: https://maxplanckneuroscience.org/from-cybernetics-to-ai-the-pioneering-work-of-norbert-wiener/

Prayuni, A., Harahap, H. S., Ramud, F., & Siregar, A. M. MesionoMesiono (2024) "Cyberbullying Prevention and Intervention Strategies at High School",- Edutec (STIE Mahardika), Vol. 7, Iss: 4

pycryptodome · PyPI. (n.d.). Retrieved December 14, 2024, from https://pypi.org/project/pycryptodome/

Radford, A., Metz, L., & Chintala, S. (2016). Unsupervised representation learning with deep convolutional generative adversarial networks. *Proceedings of the 33rd International Conference on Machine Learning*, 5, 499-508. https://arxiv.org/abs/1511.06434

Rai, P., & Singh, S. (2021). Ethical AI frameworks for online safety and cyberbullying prevention. *Journal of Cyber Ethics and Law*, 8(1), 40–58.

Ramirez, J., Velez-Zapata, C., & Maher, R. (2024). Green Colonialism and Decolonial Feminism A Study of Wayúu Women's Resistance in La Guajira. *Human Relations*, 77(7), 937–964. DOI: 10.1177/00187267231189610

Ravi, S. S. (2023). Cyberbullying: The Panorama for Prevention and Overcoming Cyberbullying. In T. Murugan & N. E. (Eds.), Handbook of Research on Data Science and Cybersecurity Innovations in Industry 4.0 Technologies (pp. 398-417). IGI Global Scientific Publishing. DOI: 10.4018/978-1-6684-8145-5.ch020

Reddy Chinthala, K. K., Thakur, M. S., Shuaib, M., & Alam, S. (2024). *Prospects of Computational Intelligence in Society: Human-Centric Solutions*. Challenges, and Research Areas. Journal of Computational and Cognitive Engineering., DOI: 10.47852/bonviewJCCE42023330

Reddy, C. K. K., Reddy, P. S., Anisha, P. R., & Doss, S. (2024). Towards smarter chatbots. In Cognitive Machine Intelligence: Applications, Challenges, and Related Technologies (p. 328). CRC Press. DOI: 10.1201/9781003500865-18

Reddy, K. K., Reddy, P. A., Janapati, H., Assiri, B., Shauib, M., Alam, S., & Sheneamer, A. (2024). A fine-tuned vision transformer (FTVT)-based enhanced multi-class brain tumor classification using MRI scan imagery.

Reddy, C. K. K., Reddy, P. S., Pilly, A., & Doss, S. (2025). Transformative Effects of Smarter Chatbots. In Dixit, S., Maurya, M., Jain, V., & Subramaniam, G. (Eds.), *Artificial Intelligence-Enabled Businesses*., DOI: 10.1002/9781394234028.ch18

Reddy, K. K., Daduvy, A., Madana Mohana, R., Assiri, B., Shauib, M., Alam, S., & Sheneamer, A. (2024). *Enhancing precision agriculture and land cover classification: A self-attention 3D convolutional neural network approach for hyperspectral image analysis*. IEEE.

Remote Monitoring and Control Supervision. (n.d.). Retrieved September 28, 2024, from https://advancees.com/services/remote-monitoring-and-control-supervision-service/

Reynolds, K., (2011). Formspring dataset for bullying detection. *Proceedings of the International Conference on Web Intelligence,* 210–215. E. Wulczyn & D. Hovy. (2017). Wikipedia dataset for online abuse detection. *Proceedings of the NAACL Conference on Human Language Technologies,* 1–10.

Reyns, B. W., & Fisher, B. S. (2018). The relationship between offline and online stalking victimization: A lifestyle-routine activity perspective. *Justice Quarterly*, 35(3), 452–476. DOI: 10.1080/07418825.2017.1289827

Rigano, C. (n.d.). *Using Artificial Intelligence to Address Criminal Justice Needs (NIJ Journal 280)*. DOI: 10.3390/app14052113

Riyal, A. M. (2019). Post-colonialism and Feminism. *Asian Social Science*, 15(11), 83–88. DOI: 10.5539/ass.v15n11p83

Rizvi, M. (2023). Enhancing cybersecurity. The power of artificial intelligence in threat detection and prevention. *International Journal of Advanced Engineering Research and Science*, 10(05), 055–060. DOI: 10.22161/ijaers.105.8

Roche, C., Wall, P. J., & Lewis, D. (2023). Ethics and diversity in artificial intelligence policies, strategies and initiatives. *AI and Ethics*, 3(4), 1095–1115. DOI: 10.1007/s43681-022-00218-9 PMID: 36246014

Rodguez-Sanchez, F., Carrillo-de-Albornoz, J., Plaza, L., Gonzalo, J., Rosso, P., Comet, M., & Donoso, T. (2021). Overview of EXIST 2021 sEXism Identism. *Procesamiento del Lenguaje Natural, Revista nº 67, septiembre de*, 195-207.

Rodrigues, L. (2022). Decolonial feminism: Maria Lugones influences and contributions. *Revista Estudos Feministas, Florianópolis*, 30(1), 1–14. DOI: 10.1590/1806-9584-2022v30n184278

Rodriguez, J. A. (2023). LGBTQ incorporated: YouTube and the management of diversity. *Journal of Homosexuality*, 70(9), 1807–1828. DOI: 10.1080/00918369.2022.2042664 PMID: 35196210

Rosa, H., Pereira, N., Ribeiro, R., Ferreira, P. C., Carvalho, J. P., Oliveira, S., Coheur, L., Paulino, P., Veiga Simão, A. M., & Trancoso, I. (2019). Automatic cyberbullying detection: A systematic review. *Computers in Human Behavior, 93*(December 2018), 333–345. DOI: 10.1109/TAFFC.2017.2761757

Roshanaei, M., Khan, M. R., & Sylvester, N. N. (2024). Enhancing Cybersecurity through AI and ML. Strategies, Challenges, and Future Directions. *Journal of Information Security*, 15(3), 320–339. DOI: 10.4236/jis.2024.153019

Russell, A. Sabella, Justin W. Patchin, Sameer Hinduja,Cyberbullying myths and realities, Computers in Human Behavior,Volume 29, Issue 6,2013,ISSN 0747-5632, DOI: 10.1016/j.chb.2013.06.040

Ruthotto, L., & Haber, E. (2021). An introduction to deep generative modeling. *GAMM-Mitteilungen*, 44(2), e202100008. DOI: 10.1002/gamm.202100008

Sabillon, R., Cavaller, V., Cano, J., & Serra-Ruiz, J. (2016). Cybercriminals, cyberattacks and cybercrime. In *2016 IEEE International Conference on Cybercrime and Computer Forensic (ICCCF)* (pp. 1-9). IEEE.

SageMath - Open-Source Mathematical Software System. (n.d.). Retrieved December 14, 2024, from https://www.sagemath.org/

Sahu, S., & Mehta, D. (2023). Challenges in AI content filtering: A deep dive into social media moderation. *AI and Ethics Journal*, 5(4), 450–465.

Saifullah, K., Khan, M. I., Jamal, S., & Sarker, I. H. (2024). Cyberbullying Text Identification: A Deep Learning and Transformer-based Language Modeling Approach. *EAI Endorsed Transactions on Industrial Networks and Intelligent Systems*, 11(1). Advance online publication. DOI: 10.4108/eetinis.v11i1.4703

Samalo, D., Martin, R., & Utama, D. N. (2023). Improved Model for Identifying the Cyberbullying Based on Tweets of Twitter. *Informatica (Slovenia)*, 47(6). Advance online publication. DOI: 10.31449/inf.v47i6.4534

Samee, N. A., Khan, U., Khan, S., Jamjoom, M. M., Sharif, M., & Kim, D. H. (2023). Safeguarding Online Spaces: A Powerful Fusion of Federated Learning, Word Embeddings, and Emotional Features for Cyberbullying Detection. *IEEE Access : Practical Innovations, Open Solutions*, 11, 124524–124541. Advance online publication. DOI: 10.1109/ACCESS.2023.3329347

Samtani, S., Zhu, H., Padmanabhan, B., Chai, Y., Chen, H., & Nunamaker, J. F.Jr. (2023). Deep learning for information systems research. *Journal of Management Information Systems*, 40(1), 271–301. DOI: 10.1080/07421222.2023.2172772

Sánchez-Medina, A. J., Galván-Sánchez, I., & Fernández-Monroy, M. (2020). Applying artificial intelligence to explore sexual cyberbullying behaviour. *Heliyon*, 6(1), e03218. DOI: 10.1016/j.heliyon.2020.e03218 PMID: 32042968

Santos, O., & Radanliev, P. (2024). *Beyond the Algorithm. AI, Security, Privacy, and Ethics*. Addison-Wesley Professional.

Santy, S., Srinivasan, A., & Choudhury, M. (2021). BERTologiCoMix how does code-mixing interact with multilingual BERT? *Adapt-NLP 2021 - 2nd Workshop on Domain Adaptation for NLP, Proceedings*, 111–121.

Saxena, S., & Verma, N. (2022). Bias in AI algorithms: Challenges and solutions in cyberbullying detection. *International Journal of Artificial Intelligence*, 19(2), 100–115.

Schermer, B. W. (2011). The limits of privacy in automated profiling and data mining. *Computer Law & Security Report*, 27(1), 45–52. DOI: 10.1016/j.clsr.2010.11.009

Schneider, E. F.. (2012). Cyberbullying and Academic Performance: A Multilevel Analysis of the Role of School Climate. *Journal of School Psychology*, 50(3), 337–348.

Schulenberg, K., Li, L., Freeman, G., Zamanifard, S., & McNeese, N. J. (2023, April). Towards leveraging AI-Based moderation to address emergent harassment in social virtual reality. In *Proceedings of the 2023 CHI Conference on Human Factors in Computing Systems* (pp. 1-17). DOI: 10.1145/3544548.3581090

Şener, M. B. (2021). A review of the meaning and importance of the Universal Declaration of Human Rights. *Uluslararası Politik Araştırmalar Dergisi*, 7(3), 15–25.

Sengupta, N., Hammond, M., Deak, C., & Malhotra, R. (2024). Ambivalent sexism and tolerance against women in India. *Psychological Science*, 35(7), 712–721. DOI: 10.1177/09567976241254312 PMID: 38869963

Shafik, W. (2023b). Cyber security perspectives in public spaces: Drone case study. In *Handbook of Research on Cybersecurity Risk in Contemporary Business Systems*. DOI: 10.4018/978-1-6684-7207-1.ch004

Shafik, W. (2024b). Artificial intelligence and Blockchain technology enabling cybersecurity in telehealth systems. In *Artificial Intelligence and Blockchain Technology in Modern Telehealth Systems*. DOI: 10.1049/PBHE061E_ch11

Shafik, W. (2024d). Dissecting the Role of Women in Cybersecurity and Information Technology: A Medical Perspective. In *Next-Generation Cybersecurity: AI, ML, and Blockchain* (pp. 325–350). Springer. DOI: 10.1007/978-981-97-1249-6_15

Shafik, W. (2023c). Predicting Future Cybercrime Trends in the Metaverse Era. In *Forecasting cyber crimes in the age of the metaverse* (pp. 78–113). IGI Global., DOI: 10.4018/979-8-3693-0220-0.ch005

Shafik, W. (2024a). Agile Security Strategies. In *Smart and Agile Cybersecurity for IoT and IIoT Environments* (pp. 82–101). IGI Global., DOI: 10.4018/979-8-3693-3451-5.ch004

Shafik, W. (2024c). Cyber Attacker Profiling and Cyberbullying Overview. In *Cyber Space and Outer Space Security* (pp. 125–149). River Publishers., DOI: 10.1201/9781003558118-5

Shafik, W. (2024e). Towards Trustworthy and Explainable AI Educational Systems. In Singh, T., Dutta, S., Vyas, S., & Rocha, Á. (Eds.), *Explainable AI for Education: Recent Trends and Challenges. Information Systems Engineering and Management* (Vol. 19). Springer., DOI: 10.1007/978-3-031-72410-7_2

Shafik, W., & Khang, A. (2024). Cybersecurity Techniques in Talent Management and Human Capital Management Systems. In *AI-Oriented Competency Framework for Talent Management in the Digital Economy* (pp. 353–375). CRC Press., DOI: 10.1201/9781003440901-22

Shafik, W., Tufail, A., Apong, R. A. A. H. M., & Balasubramaniam, S. (2024). Future Directions in Cybersecurity, Digital Forensics and Biometric Systems. In *AI Based Advancements in Biometrics and its Applications* (pp. 238–263). CRC Press., DOI: 10.1201/9781032702377-13

Shahi, N., Shahi, A. K., Phillips, R., Shirek, G., Lindberg, D. M., & Moulton, S. L. (2021). Using deep learning and natural language processing models to detect child physical abuse. *Journal of Pediatric Surgery*, 56(12), 2326–2332. DOI: 10.1016/j.jpedsurg.2021.03.007 PMID: 33838900

Shahnata, Putri., Dwi Ramadhani, Rina Arum Prastyanti (2024) "Protection Against Cyberbullying for Teens in the United States", The Easta Journal Law and Human Rights, (PT. Sanskara Karya Internasional), Vol. 2, Iss: 03, pp 147-156

Shara, J. (2023). Quantum machine learning and cybersecurity. *Quantum : the Open Journal for Quantum Science*, 12(6), 47–56.

Sharma, A., & Aggarwal, A. (2021). Privacy concerns in the use of AI for online safety. *Journal of Cybersecurity and Ethics*, 5(3), 207–221.

Sharma, P., Gupta, R., & Joshi, S. (2022). Feature engineering for cyberbullying detection using machine learning techniques. *International Journal of Cybersecurity*, 10(2), 150–167.

Sharma, R., Gupta, P., & Mehta, D. (2022). Enhancing Cyberbullying Detection with Multilingual NLP Models. *Journal of Natural Language Processing and AI*, 8(2), 37–52.

Shenoy, S. U., & Nagar, V., & Akhith. (2023). Artificial Intelligence-Based Techniques for Crime Scene Reconstruction and Investigation: An Overview. *Journal of Forensics Research*, 14(4), 1–3. DOI: 10.37421/2157-7145.2023.14.563

Siapera, E. (2022). AI content moderation, racism and (de) coloniality. *International Journal of Bullying Prevention : an Official Publication of the International Bullying Prevention Association*, 4(1), 55–65. DOI: 10.1007/s42380-021-00105-7

Siddhartha, K., Kumar, K. R., Varma, K. J., Amogh, M., & Samson, M. (2022). Cyber Bullying Detection Using Machine Learning. *2022 2nd Asian Conference on Innovation in Technology, ASIANCON 2022*, 45–50. DOI: 10.1109/ASIANCON55314.2022.9909201

Siddiqui, S., & Schultze-Krumbholz, A. (2023). Successful and emerging cyberbullying prevention programs: A narrative review of seventeen interventions applied worldwide. *Societies (Basel, Switzerland)*, 13(9), 212. DOI: 10.3390/soc13090212

Sikirivwa, M. (2020). Deconstruction theory and its background . *American Journal of Humanities and Social Sciences Research (AJHSSR) Volume-4, Issue-4*, 44-72.

Singh, M. T., Reddy, C. K., Murthy, B. V. R., Nag, A., & Doss, S. (2025). AI and education: Bridging the gap to personalized, efficient, and accessible learning. In M. Ouaissa, M. Ouaissa, H. Lamaazi, M. El Hamlaoui, & K. Reddy C. (Eds.), Internet of behavior-based computational intelligence for smart education systems (pp. 131–160). IGI Global.

Singh, T. M., & Lippert, K. (2024). Digital Twins in Human Activity Prediction on Gait Using Extreme Gradient Boosting Local Binary Pattern: Healthcare 6.0. In A. Dubey, C. Kumar Reddy, DOI: 10.4018/979-8-3693-5893-1.ch012

Singh, T. M., Reddy, C. K. K., & Lippert, K. (2024). The revolution and future of blockchain technology in cybersecurity. A comprehensive analysis. In *Artificial intelligence for blockchain and cybersecurity-powered IoT applications*. CRC Press. https.//DOI: 10.1201/9781003497585

Singh, A., Rejeb, A., Nangru, H., & Pathak, S. (2024). Global research trends on cyberbullying: A bibliometric study. *Computers in Human Behavior Reports*, 16, 100499. DOI: 10.1016/j.chbr.2024.100499

Singh, O. G. (2022). Artificial Intelligence in Forensics & Criminal Investigation in Indian Perspective. *International Journal of Innovative Science and Research Technology*, 7(8). https://www.techcircle.in/2018/08/27/this-ai-tool-will-

Singh, P., & Kumar, R. (2023). AI and blockchain: A synergistic approach to online harassment prevention. *Journal of AI Ethics*, 7(1), 60–75.

Singh, R., Shukla, P., & Kumar, A. (2021). Social intelligence systems in cyberbullying prevention. *Computers in Human Behavior*, 116, 106634. DOI: 10.1016/j.chb.2021.106634

Singh, R., & Soni, P. (2023). AI in context-aware cyberbullying prevention: The next frontier. *Journal of AI Technologies*, 11(2), 80–95.

Singh, S., & Saini, N. (2023). Deep learning applications in detecting cyberbullying in video content. *Journal of Multimedia and Cybersecurity*, 10(1), 50–64.

Singh, T. M., Reddy, C. K. K., & Lippert, K. (2024). Advancing Human-Centric Solutions: The Future Trajectory of Soft Computing in Modern Society. In Kumar, N., Pal, S., Agarwal, P., Rosak-Szyrocka, J., & Jain, V. (Eds.), *Human-Machine Collaboration and Emotional Intelligence in Industry 5.0* (pp. 1–18). IGI Global., DOI: 10.4018/979-8-3693-6806-0.ch001

Singh, V. (2019). Long-term impacts of cyberbullying on mental health and reputation. *Journal of Social Media Studies*, 18(4), 155–168. DOI: 10.1016/j.jsms.2019.08.006

Singh, V. K., Ghosh, S., & Jose, C. (2017). Toward multimodal cyberbullying detection. *Conference on Human Factors in Computing Systems - Proceedings, Part F1276*, 2090–2099. DOI: 10.1145/3027063.3053169

Slonje, R., & Peter, K. (2013). Smith, Ann Frisén, The nature of cyberbullying, and strategies for prevention. *Computers in Human Behavior*, 29(1), 26–32. DOI: 10.1016/j.chb.2012.05.024

Slonje, R., & Smith, P. K. (2008). Cyberbullying: A new challenge for educators. *School Psychology International*, 29(1), 5–21. DOI: 10.1177/0143034308095196

Slonje, R., & Smith, P. K. (2008). Cyberbullying: Another main type of bullying? *Scandinavian Journal of Psychology*, 49(2), 147–154. DOI: 10.1111/j.1467-9450.2007.00611.x PMID: 18352984

Slonje, R., Smith, P. K., & Frisén, A. (2013). The role of anonymity in cyberbullying. *Journal of School Psychology*, 51(2), 231–245. DOI: 10.1016/j.jsp.2013.01.002 PMID: 23481087

Smith, J., & Doe, R. (2022). Automated cyberbullying detection using transformer-based architectures. *Proceedings of the International Conference on Machine Learning and Applications.*

Smith, J., & Singh, P. (2022). The role of AI in enforcing cyberbullying laws. *AI and Law Journal*, 8(1), 85–100.

Smith, M., Nolan, M., & Gaffey, J. (2024). Online safety and social media regulation in Australia: eSafety Commissioner v X Corp. *Griffith Law Review*, 33(1), 1–17. DOI: 10.1080/10383441.2024.2405760

Smith, P. K., del Barrio, C., & Tokunaga, R. S. (2013). Definitions of bullying and cyberbullying: How useful are the terms? *Emotional & Behavioural Difficulties*, 18(3), 225–235. DOI: 10.1080/13632752.2013.704324

Smith, P. K., Mahdavi, J., Carvalho, M., Fisher, S., Russell, S., & Tippett, N. (2008). Cyberbullying: Its nature and impact on secondary school pupils. *Journal of Child Psychology and Psychiatry, and Allied Disciplines*, 49(4), 376–385. DOI: 10.1111/j.1469-7610.2007.01846.x PMID: 18363945

Smokowski, P. R., & Evans, C. B. R. (2024). Cyberbullying: Playground Politics (and Worse) in Cyberspace. In *Bullying and Victimization Across the Lifespan* (pp. 107–122). Springer.

Smuha, N. A. (2019). The EU approach to ethics guidelines for trustworthy artificial intelligence. *Computer Law Review International*, 20(4), 97–106. DOI: 10.9785/cri-2019-200402

Sobol, M., Przepiórka, A., & Błachnio, A. (2025). Factors contributing to the defending behavior of adolescent cyber bystanders: A systematic review and meta-analysis. *Computers in Human Behavior*, 162(108463), 108463. Advance online publication. DOI: 10.1016/j.chb.2024.108463

SocialPilot. (2024, 1 11). *AI in Social Media: Exploring Use Cases, Challenges, and Strategies*. Retrieved from SocialPilot: https://www.socialpilot.co/blog/ai-in-social-media

Soori, M., Arezoo, B., & Dastres, R. (2023). Artificial intelligence, machine learning and deep learning in advanced robotics, a review. *Cognitive Robotics*, 3, 54–70. DOI: 10.1016/j.cogr.2023.04.001

Southern African Development Community. (2024, 12 3). *Gender equality and women empowerment*. Retrieved from Southern African Development Community: https://www.sadc.int/pillars/gender-equality-women-empowerment

Sreelatha, G., Kumar Reddy, C. K., Hanafiah, M. M., & Madana Mohana, R. (2024). Hybrid electro-search beetle optimization-based task scheduling and game theory SOA-based resource allocation in multi-cloud computing.

Srilekha, C. H., Sneha, C., Prathyusha, G. N., Reddy, C. K. K., & Murthy, B. V. R. (2019). Professional study on chatbots using artificial intelligence. *Journal of Applied Science and Computations*, 6(1), 186–197.

Stam, R., & Shohat, E. (2012). Whence and whither post colonial theory? *New Literary History*, 43(2), 371–390. DOI: 10.1353/nlh.2012.0010

Sticca, F., & Perren, S. (2013). Is cyberbullying worse than traditional bullying? Examining the differential roles of medium, publicity, and anonymity for the perceived severity of bullying. *Journal of Youth and Adolescence*, 42(5), 739–750. DOI: 10.1007/s10964-012-9867-3 PMID: 23184483

Sultan, D., Omarov, B., Kozhamkulova, Z., Kazbekova, G., Alimzhanova, L., Dautbayeva, A., Zholdassov, Y., & Abdrakhmanov, R. (2023). A Review of Machine Learning Techniques in Cyberbullying Detection. *Computers, Materials & Continua*, 74(3), 2625–2640. DOI: 10.32604/cmc.2023.033682

Sultan, D., Toktarova, A., Zhumadillayeva, A., Aldeshov, S., Mussiraliyeva, S., Beissenova, G., Tursynbayev, A., Baenova, G., & Imanbayeva, A. (2023). Cyberbullying-related Hate Speech Detection Using Shallow-to-deep Learning. *Computers, Materials & Continua*, 74(1), 2115–2131. Advance online publication. DOI: 10.32604/cmc.2023.032993

Tamale, S. (2020). *Decolonisation and Afro-Feminism*. Daraja Press.

Tamir, A., Watson, E., Willett, B., Hasan, Q., & Yuan, J.-S. (2021). Crime Prediction and Forecasting using Machine Learning Algorithms. *Article in International Journal of Computer Science and Information Technology*. https://www.researchgate.net/publication/355872171

Tao, F., Akhtar, M. S., & Jiayuan, Z. (2021). The future of artificial intelligence in cybersecurity. A comprehensive survey. *EAI Endorsed Transactions on Creative Technologies*, 8(28), e3–e3. DOI: 10.4108/eai.7-7-2021.170285

Teng, T. H., & Varathan, K. D. (2023). Cyberbullying Detection in Social Networks: A Comparison Between Machine Learning and Transfer Learning Approaches. *IEEE Access : Practical Innovations, Open Solutions*, 11(April), 55533–55560. DOI: 10.1109/ACCESS.2023.3275130

TensorFlow. (n.d.). Retrieved December 14, 2024, from https://www.tensorflow.org/

The Future Of Cybersecurity: Emerging Threats And How To Combat Them. (n.d.). Retrieved December 14, 2024, from https://www.forbes.com/councils/forbestechcouncil/2024/07/11/the-future-of-cybersecurity-emerging-threats-and-how-to-combat-them/

The Future of Identity Verification: AI-powered Biometrics Explained. (n.d.). Retrieved September 28, 2024, from https://timestech.in/the-future-of-identity-verification-ai-powered-biometrics-explained/

The Impact Of Artificial Intelligence On Forensic Science. (n.d.). Retrieved September 28, 2024, from https://www.lawyersclubindia.com/articles/the-impact-of-artificial-intelligence-on-forensic-science-16676.asp%20)

The Implications of AI for Criminal Justice - Council on Criminal Justice. (n.d.). Retrieved December 14, 2024, from https://counciloncj.org/the-implications-of-ai-for-criminal-justice/

The Role of AI in Forensics | Marymount University. (n.d.). Retrieved December 14, 2024, from https://marymount.edu/blog/the-role-of-ai-in-forensics/

The Use Of Artificial Intelligence In Digital Forensics | Enterprise Tech News EM360. (n.d.-a). Retrieved December 14, 2024, from https://em360tech.com/tech-article/use-artificial-intelligence-digital-forensics

The Use Of Artificial Intelligence In Digital Forensics | Enterprise Tech News EM360. (n.d.-b). Retrieved September 28, 2024, from https://em360tech.com/tech-article/use-artificial-intelligence-digital-forensics

Thomas, R. M., Punna, S., & Reddy, M. C. K. K., &RamanaMurthy, B. (2019). Survey on artificially intelligent chatbot. *Journal of Applied Science and Computations*, 6(1), 85–94.

Tian, L., Huang, N., & Zhang, X. (2023). *Efficient Multilingual Sexism Detection via Large Language Model Cascades. Conference and Labs of the Evaluation Forum, September 18–21*. RMIT University.

Tinparinus. (2024, 12 8). *Medium.* Retrieved from How GPT model works: https://medium.com/@tinparnus/how-gpt-model-work-7ab01d848057

Toapanta, S. M. T., Carpio, J. A. E., & Gallegos, L. E. M. (2020). An Approach to Cybersecurity, Cyberbullying in Social Networks, and Information Security in Public Organizations during a Pandemic. Study case COVID-19 Ecuador. In *2020 Congreso Internacional de Innovación y Tendencias en Ingeniería (CONIITI)* (pp. 1-6). IEEE.

Tokunaga, R. S. (2010). Following you home from school: A critical review and synthesis of research on cyberbullying victimization. *Computers in Human Behavior*, 26(3), 277–287. DOI: 10.1016/j.chb.2009.11.014

Tomczak, J. M. (2022). *Deep generative modeling*. Springer International Publishing., DOI: 10.1007/978-3-030-93158-2

Ttofi, M. M., & Farrington, D. P. (2011).The effectiveness of school-based programs for preventing bullying and cyberbullying.Campbell Collaboration. https://www.campbellcollaboration.org

Ttofi, M. M., & Farrington, D. P. (2011). Effectiveness of school-based programs to reduce bullying: A systematic and meta-analytic review. *Journal of Experimental Criminology*, 7(1), 27–56. DOI: 10.1007/s11292-010-9109-1

United Nations Human Rights Treaty Bodies. (2024, 12 3). *View the ratification status by country or by treaty*. Retrieved from United Nations Human Rights Treaty Bodies UN treaty Body database: https://tbinternet.ohchr.org/_layouts/15/TreatyBodyExternal/Treaty.aspx?Treaty=CEDAW&Lang=en

United Nations. (1979, 12 18). *Convention on the Elimination of All Forms of Discrimination against Women*. Retrieved from United Nations: https://www.ohchr.org/en/instruments-mechanisms/instruments/convention-elimination-all-forms-discrimination-against-women

United Nations. (2024, 12 03). *Universal Declaration of Human Rights*. Retrieved from United Nations Peace, Dignity and Equality on a Healthy Planet: https://www.un.org/en/about-us/universal-declaration-of-human-rights

UNWomen. (2024, 11 26). *World Conferences on Women*. Retrieved from UN-Women: https://www.unwomen.org/en/how-we-work/intergovernmental-support/world-conferences-on-women

Usharani, B. (2021). A Novel Extended Ripple and Cyberbullies Data Detection (E-RACYBDD) Framework to Mitigate Deep Fake Attacks on Social Media. In *Deep Fakes, Fake News, and Misinformation in Online Teaching and Learning Technologies* (pp. 186-205). IGI Global.

Vaishali, U. (2023). *Gongane., Mousami, V., Munot., Alwin, D., Anuse.* Explainable AI for Reliable Detection of Cyberbullying., DOI: 10.1109/PuneCon58714.2023.10450132

Van Bruwaene, D., Huang, Q., & Inkpen, D. (2020). A multi-platform dataset for detecting cyberbullying in social media David Van Bruwaene, Qianjia Huang and Diana Inkpen Journal. *Language Resources and Evaluation*, 54(4), 851–874. DOI: 10.1007/s10579-020-09488-3

Van Geel, M., Vedder, P., & Tanilon, J. (2014). Relationship between peer victimization, cyberbullying, and suicide in children and adolescents: A meta-analysis. *JAMA Pediatrics*, 168(5), 435–442. DOI: 10.1001/jamapediatrics.2013.4143 PMID: 24615300

Van Hoeyweghen, S. (2024). Speaking of games: AI-based content moderation of real-time voice interactions in video games under the DSA. *Interactive Entertainment Law Review*, 7(1), 30–46. DOI: 10.4337/ielr.2024.01.04

Vandana, A., Rani, J., Goud, V. A., Kishor, M. C., Reddy, K., & Murthy, R. (2019). A study of chatbots through artificial intelligence. *Journal of Applied Science and Computational Science*, 6(1), 341–354.

Vandebosch, H., & Van Cleemput, K. (2009). Cyberbullying among youngsters: Profiles of bullies and victims. *New Media & Society*, 11(8), 1349–1371. DOI: 10.1177/1461444809341263

Vanderbilt University. (2021). Detection of cyberbullying comments in tweets. *Young Scientist Journal.*

Vanpech, P., Peerabenjakul, K., Suriwong, N., & Fugkeaw, S. (2024). Detecting cyberbullying on social networks using language learning model. *InProceedings of the 2024 International Conference on Knowledge and Smart Technology (KST) (pp.* 1–9*)*. IEEE. DOI: 10.1109/KST61284.2024.10499678

Vázquez-Madrigal, C., García-Rubio, N., & Triguero, Á. (2024). Generative Artificial Intelligence in Education: Risks and Opportunities. In *Teaching Innovations in Economics: Towards a Sustainable World* (pp. 233–254). Springer Nature Switzerland. DOI: 10.1007/978-3-031-72549-4_11

Venkatesh, S., Fong, E. W., & Yeter, I. H. (2022). Investigating ethics in an undergraduate design thinking project: The Stanford EDIPT framework approach in Southeast Asia. In *2022 IEEE Frontiers in Education Conference (FIE)* (pp. 1-5). IEEE.

Vincent, J. (2020, 11 13). Facebook is now using AI to sort content for quicker moderation. Retrieved 12 8, 2020, from https://www.theverge.com/2020/11/13/21562596/facebook-ai-moderation

Wachs, S., Wright, M. F., & Wolf, K. D. (2017). Associations between bystanders and perpetrators of cyberbullying and traditional bullying. *Aggressive Behavior*, 43(3), 244–253. DOI: 10.1002/ab.21685

Wachter, S., Mittelstadt, B., & Russell, C. (2021). Why fairness cannot be automated: Bridging the gap between EU non-discrimination law and AI. *Computer Law & Security Report*, 41, 105567. DOI: 10.1016/j.clsr.2021.105567

Wahyuningrum, S. S., Rohmawati, L., Mustaqim, W., Qalban, A. A., & Heriyanto, Y. (2023). Fenomena Cyberbullying pada Kalangan Mahasiswa. *Assertive: Islamic Counseling Journal*, 2(1), 37–48. Advance online publication. DOI: 10.24090/j.assertive.v2i01.8296

Waltz, S. (2002). Reclaiming and rebuilding the history of the Universal Declaration of Human Rights. *Third World Quarterly*, 23(3), 437–448. DOI: 10.1080/01436590220138378

Wang, C., Tang, H., Zhu, H., Zheng, J., & Jiang, C. (2024). Behavioral authentication for security and safety. *Security and Safety*, 3, 2024003. DOI: 10.1051/sands/2024003

Wankhade, M., Rao, A. C. S., & Kulkarni, C. (2022). A survey on sentiment analysis methods, applications, and challenges. *Artificial Intelligence Review*, 55(7), 5731–5780. DOI: 10.1007/s10462-022-10144-1

Wankhade, T. D., Ingale, S. W., Mohite, P. M., & Bankar, N. J. (2022). Artificial Intelligence in Forensic Medicine and Toxicology: The Future of Forensic Medicine. *Cureus*, 14(8). Advance online publication. DOI: 10.7759/cureus.28376 PMID: 36168339

Weizenbaum, J. (1966). ELIZA- A computer program for the study of natural language communication between man and machine. *Communications of the ACM*, 9(1), 36–45. DOI: 10.1145/365153.365168

Weng, L. (2021). What are diffusion models? *Lil'Log*. https://lilianweng.github.io/posts/2021-07-11-diffusion-models/. 20.07.2024

Wettstein, F. (2015). Normativity, ethics, and the UN guiding principles on business and human rights: A critical assessment. *Journal of Human Rights*, 14(2), 162–182. DOI: 10.1080/14754835.2015.1005733

What is a Convolutional Neural Network (CNN)? | Definition from TechTarget. (n.d.). Retrieved December 14, 2024, from https://www.techtarget.com/searchenterpriseai/definition/convolutional-neural-network

Wiederhold, B. K. (2024). The Dark Side of the Digital Age: How to Address Cyberbullying among Adolescents. [editorial]. *Cyberpsychology, Behavior, and Social Networking*, 27(3), 169–171. Advance online publication. DOI: 10.1089/cyber.2024.29309.editorial PMID: 38364097

Wijkstra, M., Rogers, K., Mandryk, R. L., Veltkamp, R. C., & Frommel, J. (2024). How To Tame a Toxic Player? A Systematic Literature Review on Intervention Systems for Toxic Behaviors in Online Video Games. *Proceedings of the ACM on Human-Computer Interaction, 8*(CHI PLAY), 1-32. DOI: 10.1145/3677080

Willard, N. (2006). Cyberbullying: A new challenge for educators. National Education Association, 22(4), 45-50. https://www.nea.org

Willard, N. (2007). *Cyberbullying and cyberthreats: Responding to the challenge of online social aggression, threats, and distress*. Research Press.

Willard, N. E. (2006). *Cyberbullying and cyberthreats*. Center for Safe and Responsible Internet Use.

Willett, A., & Etowa, J. (2023). A critical examination of epistemological congruence between intersectionality and feminist poststructuralism: Toward an integrated framework for health research. *Nursing Inquiry*, 30(4), 1–12. DOI: 10.1111/nin.12564 PMID: 37248779

Williamson, B., & Eynon, R. (2020). Historical threads, missing links, and future directions in AI in education. *Learning, Media and Technology*, 45(3), 223–235. DOI: 10.1080/17439884.2020.1798995

Winston, P. H. (1993). *Artificial intelligence* (3rd ed., reprinted with corr.). Addison-Wesley.

World Health Organisation (WHO). (2024, 12 4). *Sustainable Development Goals*. Retrieved from World Health Organisation (WHO) Europe: https://www.who.int/europe/about-us/our-work/sustainable-development-goals

Worsley, M. (2022). Artificial Intelligence Innovations for Multimodal Learning, Interfaces, and Analytics. In *AI in Learning: Designing the Future* (pp. 19–35). Springer International Publishing.

Wright, M. F. (2017). Cyberbullying victimization through social networking sites and adjustment difficulties: The role of parental mediation. *Journal of the Association for Information Science and Technology*, 68(3), 504–515. DOI: 10.1002/asi.23624

Wu, M., & Goodman, N. (2018). Multimodal generative models for scalable weakly-supervised learning. *Advances in Neural Information Processing Systems, 2018-Decem*(NeurIPS), 5575–5585.

Wu, Q., Gao, R., & Zha, H. (2021). Bridging explicit and implicit deep generative models via neural Stein estimators. *35th Conference on Neural Information Processing Systems (NeurIPS 2021).*

Wu, X., Zhang, L., & Luo, H. (2024). Witnessing family violence and adolescent cyberbullying perpetration: A longitudinal moderated mediation model involving anger dysregulation and teacher support. *Child Abuse & Neglect*, 152, 106753. Advance online publication. DOI: 10.1016/j.chiabu.2024.106753 PMID: 38547563

Xie, J., Lu, Y., Zhu, S. C., & Wu, Y. N. (2016). A theory of generative convnet. In *ICML*, 2635-2644.

Xu, F., Uszkoreit, H., Du, Y., Fan, W., Zhao, D., & Zhu, J. (2019). Explainable AI: A brief survey on history, research areas, approaches and challenges. In *Natural language processing and Chinese computing: 8th cCF international conference, NLPCC 2019, dunhuang, China, October 9–14, 2019, proceedings, part II 8* (pp. 563-574). Springer International Publishing. DOI: 10.1007/978-3-030-32236-6_51

Xu, N., Mao, W., & Chen, G. (2019). Multi-interactive memory network for aspect based multimodal sentiment analysis. *33rd AAAI Conference on Artificial Intelligence, AAAI 2019, 31st Innovative Applications of Artificial Intelligence Conference, IAAI 2019 and the 9th AAAI Symposium on Educational Advances in Artificial Intelligence, EAAI 2019*, 371–378. DOI: 10.1609/aaai.v33i01.3301371

Yadav, S., Yadav, S., Verma, P., Ojha, S., & Mishra, S. (2022). Artificial Intelligence: An Advanced Evolution In Forensic and Criminal Investigation. *Current Forensic Science*, 1, e190822207706. Advance online publication. DOI: 10.2174/2666484 401666220819111603

Yadav, Y., & Zubiaga, A. (2020). Challenges in context-aware natural language processing for online moderation. *Journal of Computational Social Science*, 5(3), 234–250.

Yang, Y., & Zhang, J. **(2022).** Legal implications of AI moderation systems. *Law and Technology Forum, 7*(4), 322–339.

Yang, L. W. Y., Ng, W. Y., Lei, X., Tan, S. C. Y., Wang, Z., Yan, M., Pargi, M. K., Zhang, X., Lim, J. S., Gunasekeran, D. V., Tan, F. C. P., Lee, C. E., Yeo, K. K., Tan, H. K., Ho, H. S. S., Tan, B. W. B., Wong, T. Y., Kwek, K. Y. C., Goh, R. S. M., & Ting, D. S. W. (2023). Development and testing of a multi-lingual Natural Language Processing-based deep learning system in 10 languages for COVID-19 pandemic crisis: A multi-center study. *Frontiers in Public Health*, 11, 1063466. Advance online publication. DOI: 10.3389/fpubh.2023.1063466 PMID: 36860378

Yang, X., & Zhang, L. (2022). Recommendation systems and cyberbullying prevention using generative models. *Journal of Machine Learning Research*, 23(5), 341–360.

Ybarra, M. L., & Mitchell, K. J. (2004). Online aggressor/targets, aggressors, and targets: A comparison of associated youth characteristics. *Journal of Child Psychology and Psychiatry, and Allied Disciplines*, 45(7), 1308–1316. DOI: 10.1111/j.1469-7610.2004.00328.x PMID: 15335350

Yousaf, K., & Nawaz, T. (2022). A deep learning-based approach for inappropriate content detection and classification of youtube videos. *IEEE Access : Practical Innovations, Open Solutions*, 10, 16283–16298. DOI: 10.1109/ACCESS.2022.3147519

Yousefi-Azar, M., & Hamey, L. (2017). Text summarization using unsupervised deep learning. *Expert Systems with Applications*, 68, 93–105. DOI: 10.1016/j.eswa.2016.10.017

Yuvaraj, N., Chang, V., Gobinathan, B., Pinagapani, A., Kannan, S., Dhiman, G., & Rajan, A. R. (2021). Automatic detection of cyberbullying using multi-feature based artificial intelligence with deep decision tree classification. *Computers & Electrical Engineering*, 92, 107186. DOI: 10.1016/j.compeleceng.2021.107186

Zhang, X., Chowdhury, R., Gupta, R., & Shang, J. (2024). Large Language Models for Time Series: A Survey. *Proceedings of the Thirty-Third International Joint Conference on Artificial Intelligence (IJCAI-24)Survey Track* (pp. 8335-8343). San Diego: Proceedings of the Thirty-Third International Joint Conference on Artificial Intelligence (IJCAI-24). DOI: 10.24963/ijcai.2024/921

Zhang, H., Lee, I., Ali, S., DiPaola, D., Cheng, Y., & Breazeal, C. (2023). Integrating Ethics and Career Futures with Technical Learning to Promote AI Literacy for Middle School Students: An Exploratory Study. *International Journal of Artificial Intelligence in Education*, 33(2), 290–324. DOI: 10.1007/s40593-022-00293-3 PMID: 35573722

Zhang, M., Shen, Y., Yin, J., Lu, S., & Wang, X. (2024). ADAGENT: Anomaly detection agent with multimodal large models in adverse environments. *IEEE Access : Practical Innovations, Open Solutions*, 12, 172061–172074. DOI: 10.1109/ACCESS.2024.3480250

Zhang, Z. (2024). *"Cyberbullying: A Comprehensive Analysis of its Psychological Impact and Preventive Measures", Journal of education, humanities and social sciences* (Vol. 26). Darcy & Roy Press Co. Ltd.

Zhang, Z., Lee, A., & Kim, H. (2020). Privacy challenges in AI-powered cyberbullying detection. *Journal of Online Safety and Privacy*, 9(5), 411–426.

Zhao, F., & Yu, L. (2021). Cultural bias in AI: A study on social media moderation. *AI Ethics and Governance Quarterly*, 4(2), 88–104.

Zhao, L., Zhu, D., Shafik, W., Matinkhah, S. M., Ahmad, Z., Sharif, L., & Craig, A. (2022). Artificial intelligence analysis in cyber domain: A review. *International Journal of Distributed Sensor Networks*, 18(4). Advance online publication. DOI: 10.1177/15501329221084882

Zheng, Y., Ross, B., & Magdy, W. (2023). What Makes Good Counterspeech? A Comparison of Generation Approaches and Evaluation Metrics. *Proceedings of the 1st Workshop on CounterSpeech for Online Abuse (CS4OA),* (pp. 62–71). University of Edinburgh: Association for Computational Linguistics.

Zhu, Q., & Luo, J. (2022). Generative Pre-Trained Transformer for Design Concept Generation. *Exploration*, 2020, 1825–1834.

Zhu, X. (2024). *Feminism on social media: Generalized misogyny. SHS Web of Conferences 199, 02012*. The University of Sheffield: The University of Sheffield, Department of Sociological Studies.

Zulfiqar, N., Shaikh, B. A., Shah, S. A., & Awan, A. (2024). Investigating how AI Technologies Influence Changing Social Norms and Behaviors on Social Media, Particularly in Areas like Communication and Self-Presentation. *Review of Education. Administration & Law*, 7(4), 167–183. DOI: 10.47067/real.v7i4.371

About the Contributors

Kishor Kumar Reddy C. is currently working as Associate Professor, Dept. of Computer Science and Engineering, Stanley College of Engineering and Technology for Women, Hyderabad, India. He has research and teaching experience of more than 10 years. He has published more than 80 research papers in National and International Conferences, Book Chapters, and Journals indexed by Scopus and others. He is an author for 2 text books and 12 co-edited books. He acted as the special session chair for Springer FICTA 2020, 2022, SCI 2021, INDIA 2022 and IEEE ICCSEA 2020 conferences. He is the corresponding editor of AMSE 2021 conferences, published by IoP Science JPCS. He is the member of ISTE, CSI, IAENG, UACEE, IACSIT.

Meetu Malhotra is working as Data Analytics Principal at S&P Global. She is also a research scholar, pursuing her PhD in Data Science from Harrisburg University of Science and Technology, PA. She has 16+ years of experience in data science, Machine Learning, and software development. She earned her Master's degree in Data Science and Business Analytics from the University of North Carolina Charlotte. She has been a member of honor society of phiKappaPhi, IEEE, ACM and StemUp network. She is actively involved in publishing papers, book chapters, peer-reviewing papers, and chapters for reputed journals and conferences. Meetu has expertise in developing Machine Learning algorithms, NLP, Time Series and GenAI.

Mariya Ouaissa is currently a Professor in Cybersecurity and Networks at Faculty of Sciences Semlalia, Cadi Ayyad University, Marrakech, Morocco. She is a Ph.D. graduated in 2019 in Computer Science and Networks, at the Laboratory of Modelisation of Mathematics and Computer Science from ENSAM-Moulay Ismail University, Meknes, Morocco. She is a Networks and Telecoms Engineer, graduated in 2013 from National School of Applied Sciences Khouribga, Morocco. She is a Co-Founder and IT Consultant at IT Support and Consulting Center. She was working for School of Technology of Meknes Morocco as a Visiting Professor from 2013 to

2021. She is member of the International Association of Engineers and International Association of Online Engineering, and since 2021, she is an "ACM Professional Member". She is Expert Reviewer with Academic Exchange Information Centre (AEIC) and Brand Ambassador with Bentham Science. She has served and continues to serve on technical program and organizer committees of several conferences and events and has organized many Symposiums/Workshops/Conferences as a General Chair also as a reviewer of numerous international journals. Dr. Ouaissa has made contributions in the fields of information security and privacy, Internet of Things security, and wireless and constrained networks security. Her main research topics are IoT, M2M, D2D, WSN, Cellular Networks, and Vehicular Networks. She has published over 50 papers (book chapters, international journals, and conferences/workshops), 12 edited books, and 8 special issue as guest editor

Marlia Mohd Hanafiah is a Professor at the Faculty of Science and Technology, Universiti Kebangsaan Malaysia (UKM). She is also a Head of Centre for Climate Change System, Institute of Climate Change, UKM. She received her Ph.D Degree in Life Cycle Assessment (LCA) from Radboud University Nijmegen, the Netherlands in 2013. She has supervised/co-supervised 60 masters and 22 bachelor theses and currently she supervises 30 PhD's in the areas of LCA, wastewater treatment, green technology and sustainability. She is the coordinator of several postgraduate courses at her department. Her research projects focus on modelling potential environmental impacts of multiple stressors in an LCA context and exploring potential bio-based and nanomaterials for recycling and treating wastewater towards sustainability and circular economy. She has published over 90 peer-reviewed papers, books, books chapters, technical reports and serves as peer reviewer for several high impact journals. As a project leader, she has received several international and national grants from various funding agencies with a total amount of more that RM 2 million. Since 2013, she has been involved in consulting and reviewing Criteria Document and Standard for companies, organizations and governments. She is currently conducting transdisciplinary research with a strong interest that integrates various scientific disciplines such as environmental engineering, industrial ecology, toxicity, mathematical modelling and environmental science. Her ultimate goal is devoted to introduce Life Cycle Thinking as a holistic view to assess environmental performance of products and technologies to solve fundamental and unprecedented society challenges, especially those related to sustainability

Mohammed Shuaib, recognized in the World's Top 2% Scientists Ranking 2024 (by Stanford University), specializes in blockchain, IoT, cybersecurity, and machine learning applications in engineering. He holds a PhD in Computer Engineering from Universiti Teknologi Malaysia (UTM). With an h-index of 26, over 1750 citations, and 4 patents, Dr. Shuaib is a prolific researcher with more than 58 publications in ISI-ranked and Scopus-indexed journals, alongside 25 conference papers. His expertise spans machine learning, AI-driven optimizations, and sustainable development, with a focus on applying AI techniques such as artificial neural networks (ANN), adaptive neuro-fuzzy inference systems (ANFIS), and reinforcement learning (RL) across engineering disciplines. Dr. Shuaib's editorial experience includes serving as Associate Editor for Sustainable Computing: Informatics and Systems (Elsevier) and contributing to editorial boards of journals like PLOS ONE, Wiley, IAES, IGI Global, and Discover Internet of Things (Springer). His editorial roles, coupled with his membership in professional organizations such as IEEE, ACM, and IAENG, highlight his leadership in advancing research in his areas of expertise.

***

B. Sandhiyarajeshwari is an Assistant Professor in the Department of Artificial Intelligence And Data Science at Rajalakshmi Institute of Technology. With a strong foundation in computer science, she has completed her Bachelor of Engineering (B.E.) and Master of Engineering (M.E.) degrees. Her expertise lies in imparting knowledge and mentoring students in various domains of computer science, contributing to the academic and professional growth of her students.

Bishnu Bhusal holds a Master's degree in Computer Science from the University of Missouri-Columbia and is currently pursuing his PhD in Computer Science at the University of Missouri-Columbia. His research interests include formal methods, privacy, cybersecurity and machine learning.

William Chakabwata holds a PhD in Curriculum and Instruction obtained from University of South Africa on 27 September 2023.He also holds a master degree in Curriculum and arts education which he earned from University of Zimbabwe. He has taught at Midlands State University in Namibia and also at Namibia University of Science and Technology(NUST). He may be contacted at williechaka@gmail.com

Kiranbhai Ramabhai Dodiya is an experienced Cyber Forensic Expert and Assistant Professor specializing in cyber security and digital forensics. He has taught at prestigious institutions and is currently pursuing a PhD in Biochemistry and Forensic Science. With a strong background in ethical hacking and malware analysis, Kiranbhai is passionate about educating students and contributing to the field of cyber forensics. His expertise includes malware forensic, computer forensics, and data recovery software. Kiranbhai's commitment to professional growth is evident through his participation in workshops, seminars, and research publications. He is dedicated to shaping the next generation of professionals in the field and combatting cybercrimes.

Semra Erpolat Taşabat is a faculty member at Mimar Sinan Fine Arts University, Faculty of Arts and Sciences, Department of Statistics (msgsu.edu.tr). Prof. Dr. Semra Erpolat Taşabat, specializing in data analysis, decision theory, applied statistics, and operations research, has numerous academic works, including books, book chapters, articles, conference proceedings, projects, and patents. Prof. Dr. Erpolat Taşabat, who serves as the academic advisor for BORUSAN CAT, also works as a part-time faculty member at various universities such as Bahçeşehir University.

Ria Ghosh is a gold medallist in Forensic Science from the University of Delhi, Ria Ghosh is a highly accomplished Digital Forensic Investigator and the Co-founder and Managing Director of Forency LLP, a pioneering firm delivering digital forensic services to key agencies, including the Income Tax Department, Directorate of Enforcement (ED), Directorate of Revenue Intelligence (DRI), and Central Goods and Services Tax (CGST). With extensive experience across cybersecurity, forensic auditing, and digital evidence analysis, Ria has worked with esteemed organizations such as the Gurugram Police Cyber Security Unit and the Regional Forensic Science Laboratory. Her technical expertise spans digital forensics, fingerprint analysis, questioned document examination, and cybercrime investigation, supported by certifications in Ethical Hacking, Cybersecurity, and Digital Forensics from institutions like EC-Council and IBM. Ria is also a dedicated academic contributor, serving as a Technical Editor for international journals and co-authoring publications like Digital Forensic Professional Guide. Driven by a commitment to justice and empowerment, she mentors aspiring forensic experts while actively contributing to initiatives like Citizen Setu. Her innovative approach, combined with expertise in tools like Cellebrite, FTK, Magnet Axiom, X-Ways and Autopsy, positions her as a leader in securing digital ecosystems.

Sazzad Hossain is currently a Graduate Assistant in the Special Collections Library and Archives at Emporia State University, Kansas, USA. He began pursuing his M.S. degree in Information Technology at Emporia State University in 2023. He has a major background in IT fundamentals and cybersecurity, with previous role in a multinational company from 2021 to 2022 as an IT Executive. He completed his first M.S. in Information Technology from Jahangirnagar University in 2022 and earned his B.Sc. in Computer Science Engineering from North South University, Bangladesh, in 2019. Sazzad's research contribution includes publications in AMCIS 2023 conferences and Digital Forensics Use-Case of Blockchain Technology: A

Review, a research paper accepted by AMCIS, covers IT governance, IT compliance, IT risk management, cybersecurity, network security, blockchain technology and digital forensics.

I. Divya is an Assistant Professor in the Department of Artificial Intelligence And Data Science at Rajalakshmi Institute of Technology. With a strong foundation in ECE, she has completed her Bachelor of Engineering (B.E.) and Master of Engineering (M.E.) degrees and Ph.d.Her expertise lies in imparting knowledge and mentoring students in various domains of computer science and ECE, contributing to the academic and professional growth of her students.

S. Ida Evangeline is currently working as an Assistant Professor in the Department of Electrical and Electronics Engineering at Alagappa Chettiar Government College of Engineering and Technology, Karaikudi, Tamilnadu, India. She earned her Bachelor's degree in Electrical and Electronics Engineering from Manonmaniam Sundaranar University in 2003 and her Master's degree in Power Systems Engineering from Anna University, Chennai, in 2005. She completed her Ph.D. in 2023 at Anna University, Chennai. She has published six research papers in international journals. Her research interests span optimal power flow, renewable energy, soft computing, artificial intelligence, machine learning, and deep learning.

Sai Ramakrishna is a distinguished educator and technologist with over 13 years of professional experience in the field of computer science. A passionate teacher and trainer, he holds a Master of Science (M.Sc.) and a Master of Technology (M.Tech.) in Computer Science from the prestigious Osmania University, where he laid the foundation for his exceptional career. Throughout his journey, Sai Ramakrishna has consistently demonstrated a commitment to excellence in teaching, earning him accolades and widespread recognition. He was honored with the Best Faculty Award by The Hindu, a testament to his ability to inspire and educate students with clarity, dedication, and innovative teaching methodologies. In addition to his academic contributions, he has made a significant impact in the corporate sector as a trainer. His outstanding efforts were acknowledged with the Best Trainer Award from Dr. Reddy's Laboratories, where he played a pivotal role in enhancing the technical skills of professionals and fostering a culture of continuous learning.

Madiha Munawar, a second-year Computer Science and Engineering (CSE) student with a keen interest in software engineering and research. I have contributed to book chapters on emerging technologies and have also participated as a reviewer, critically reviewing book chapters, and am looking forward to conducting more research and publishing chapters, conference papers and journal articles. With a deep passion for coding, I actively explore diverse programming languages and innovative problem-solving techniques. I have participated in International conference and presented my paper in that, also in coding competitions and contributed to book chapters on emerging technologies. Driven by an insatiable thirst for knowledge, I aspire to create impactful software solutions that address real-world challenges with efficiency and creativity.

Trupti Parkar is a Product Manager at Microsoft Azure AI/ML Platform. Trupti is passionate about developing impactful AI products and enjoys collaborating with dedicated professionals.

Mir Mehedi Rahman is currently a Graduate Assistant in the Internal Audit Department at Emporia State University, Kansas, USA, where he is working on the IT audit program for the department. He began pursuing his M.S. degree in Information Technology at Emporia State University in 2023. Previously he served as a Graduate Assistant at the Cybersecurity Research and Outreach Center at Emporia State University. He also completed an internship in the IT Department at the Kansas Department of Labor. He has a rich background in IT and cybersecurity, with previous roles in major Bangladeshi banks from 2015 to 2023. He completed his M.B.A in Management Information Systems from American International University-Bangladesh in 2018 and earned his B.Sc. in Electronics and Telecommunication Engineering from North South University, Bangladesh, in 2013. Mr. Rahman's research contribution includes publications in IEEE conferences and a book chapter accepted by CRC Press awaiting publication, spans IT governance, IT compliance, IT risk management, cybersecurity, network security, and blockchain technology. Rahman has also presented his work at various academic and IEEE conferences, further contributing to the field.

C Kishor Kumar Reddy, currently working as Associate Professor, Dept. of Computer Science and Engineering, Stanley College of Engineering and Technology for Women, Hyderabad, India. He has research and teaching experience of more than 10 years. He has published more than 60 research papers in National and International Conferences, Book Chapters, and Journals indexed by Scopus and others. He is an author for 2 text books and 2 co-edited books. He acted as the special session chair for Springer FICTA 2020, 2022, SCI 2021, INDIA 2022 and IEEE ICCSEA 2020 conferences. He is the corresponding editor of AMSE 2021 conferences, published by IoP Science JPCS. He is the member of ISTE, CSI, IAENG, UACEE, IACSIT.

Wasswa Shafik (Member, IEEE) received a Bachelor of Science degree in information technology from Ndejje University, Uganda, a Master of Engineering degree in Information Technology (Computer and Communication Networks) from Yazd University, Iran, and a PhD in Computer Science with the School of Digital Science, Universiti Brunei Darussalam, Brunei Darussalam. He is also the Founder and Research Director of the Dig Connectivity Research Laboratory (DCRLab) after serving as a Research Associate at the Network Interconnectivity Research Laboratory at Yazd University. Prior to this, he worked as a Community Data Analyst at Population Services International (PSI-Uganda), a Community Data Officer at the Programme for Accessible Health Communication (PACE-Uganda), a Research Assistant at the Socio-Economic Data Centre (SEDC-Uganda), Uganda, an Assistant Data Officer at TechnoServe, Kampala, Uganda, and Asmaah Charity Organization as Cheif Executive Officer. He has hundreds of publications with renowned publishers. His research interests include Artificial Intelligence, Smart Agriculture, Digital Health, Nature-inspired Computing, Security and Privacy.

Thakur Monika Singh holds an M.Tech in Computer Science and Engineering from Osmania University and is currently pursuing a Ph.D. in the same field at KL University. Since 2017, she has been a faculty member in the Computer Science and Engineering Department at Stanley College of Engineering and Technology for Women. With a rich background in teaching and research, she is also a certified project-based learning mentor by Wipro and holds a TalentNext certification in Java Full Stack development. Her research interests focus on Machine Learning, and she has published several papers in national and international journals. Additionally, she holds a patent to her name..

Index

A

B

C

D

E

G

I

J

L

M

N

O

P

Q

R

S

T

www.ingramcontent.com/pod-product-compliance
Lightning Source LLC
LaVergne TN
LVHW080610300926
849162LV00005B/1109